AN OUTSIDER IN
THE WHITE HOUSE

AN OUTSIDER IN THE WHITE HOUSE

Jimmy Carter, His Advisors, and the Making of American Foreign Policy

Betty Glad

CORNELL UNIVERSITY PRESS   **ITHACA AND LONDON**

First published 2009 by Cornell University Press
Printed in the United States of America

Library of Congress Cataloging-in-Publication Data

Glad, Betty.
  An outsider in the White House : Jimmy Carter, his advisors, and the making of American foreign policy / Betty Glad.
       p. cm.
  Includes bibliographical references and index.
  ISBN 978-0-8014-4815-7 (cloth : alk. paper)
  1. United States—Foreign relations—1977–1981.   2. Carter, Jimmy, 1924–
3. Presidents—United States—Staff.   I. Title.

  E872. G534   2009
  973.926092—dc22

                                        2009027812

Cloth printing   10   9   8   7   6   5   4   3   2   1

Contents

Tables

Acknowledgments

This book is the result of ten years, off and on, of research, writing, and Carter watching. Along the way the University of South Carolina provided me with several research assistants. One of the first of these individuals, Daniel Crabtree, accompanied me to the Jimmy Carter Library and Museum and prepared detailed summaries of the materials relevant to Carter's opening of relations with China. Later, Samuel Lucas McMillan worked with me on the last chapter of the book and filled in some of the blanks as the book neared completion. Stoyan S. Stoyanov, Fahrettin Sumer, and Chenwei Zhang worked on specific sections of this work.

From funds provided by my endowed professorship I was able to secure the assistance of several brilliant undergraduate students. They checked endnotes, ferreted out articles and books of relevance, composed chronologies dealing with specific topics, and occasionally provided digests of these materials. These students include Beth Ewoldsen, Joseph Ferguson, Elizabeth Jenkins, Ralph Lawson, Josiah Moody, Jonathan Slager, Jonathan Tillotson, and Jeremiah Wolfe. Shorter-term assistance was provided by Marcielly Assuncao, Sarah Charles, Tara Farrell, and Sarah Higgs. Dennis Litoshick, my exchange student "son" from Minsk, Belarus, provided me with a chronology of Carter's major undertakings during his years in the presidency.

Donna Lynn Hedgepeth worked with me for several months locating and filing source material, creating chronologies, and keeping my notes in order. Sameer Popat located the intelligence reports from the National Archives that are referred to in chapter 22, "Shadowing the Soviets."

When I was felled by an automobile accident as this book neared completion, five very active USC students took over the mechanics of preparing the manuscript for final publication by editing, word processing, securing permissions, and performing a myriad of other onerous tasks. I am deeply indebted to Joseph Chen, Grant Hamilton, Alana Lewis, Michael Masters, and Daniel Robinson. Helen Knight came on board in the autumn of 2008 to deal with permissions for photographs from the Carter Library and Museum and to aid in putting the final copy in order.

Several friends and colleagues—Fred Greenstein, Robert Dallek, Don Lamm (former editor at W. W. Norton), and John White—provided moral support during this long process and suggested revisions that clearly improved the manuscript. Two professional editors—David Condon and Mary Beth Crawford—made valuable suggestions as to how to clarify the narrative. My editor at Cornell University Press, Michael McGandy, suggested title changes and chapter consolidations that improved the readability of the manuscript.

I am also grateful to the many people who answered queries or gave interviews regarding certain aspects of the Carter administration: Robert Bergland, Harold Brown, Warren Christopher, Hermann Eilts, Stuart Eizenstat, Fritz Ermarth, Leslie Gelb, Richard Holbrooke, Henry Kissinger, Robert Lipshutz, Donald McHenry, David Newsom, Robert Pastor, Richard Pipes, Jody Powell, William Quandt, Harold Saunders, and Leon Sloss all helped me keep certain facts straight. David Ryan gave me useful background information on liberation theology. Above all, I am indebted to Zbigniew Brzezinski, who expeditiously answered my e-mails and was very open about his interactions with Carter in both his memoir and Weekly Reports to the President as well as the other papers he donated to the Carter Library and Museum.

Above all, I want to thank James Yancey and Albert Nason at the Carter Library and Museum. They filed my Freedom of Information Act requests and kept me informed about items recently declassified, cheerfully processed my Xeroxed materials and gave me leads on photos and other items of relevance to my research. Jay Hake, the Director of the Carter Library, discussed his work on Senator Henry Jackson, giving insight into some of the reasons Carter was so concerned about winning Jackson's support for the Strategic Arms Limitation Treaty. I cannot imagine a more hospitable research environment than the one I encountered at the Jimmy Carter Library.

A Note on Sources

Most of the material in this work is from the Jimmy Carter Library in Atlanta, Georgia. Particularly useful was the library's Plains File, which contains material Carter had taken home to Plains, Georgia, from the White House as background for his own memoir; he transferred these papers to the library in December 1982. Carter's daily diary and his correspondence with Leonid Brezhnev are in this collection. An equally rich source was the material Zbigniew Brzezinski donated to the library. His Weekly Reports, in particular, provide a running commentary on his views of policy and his own role relative to that of the president. Reports and minutes of Special Coordinating Committee (SCC) meetings were also very useful. Another collection in the Carter Library, the White House Staff Office Files, contains memos to Carter from top aides including Robert Beckel, Landon Butler, Robert Cutler, Hamilton Jordan, Robert Lipshutz, Frank Moore, Jody Powell, and Gerald Rafshoon. These memos show both the nature of the aides' work and their relationships with Carter.

Fortunately for this author, several documents regarding U.S.-Soviet relations underwent an early declassification for a 1995 conference in Ft. Lauderdale, Florida, titled "Global Competition and the Deterioration of U.S.-Soviet Relations, 1977–1980." In a transcript of that conference, the perspective of the Soviet side of policy-making during the Cold War is provided. Several participants retrospectively evaluate their roles. These materials are found in the White House Central Files.

Two major oral histories within the Carter Library collection also proved invaluable to this work. In the 1980s, the White Burkett Miller Center of Public Affairs at the University of Virginia conducted interviews with twenty-six of the Carter administration's top players. A second set of exit interviews were conducted by representatives from the National Archives between 1977 and 1981 in the Eisenhower Executive Office building adjacent to the White House. My own contact with Carter advisors via interviews, questionnaires, and letters was oriented to particular issues I encountered in the early research process. A complete list of these three sets of contacts can be found in the bibliography.

The second manuscript collection, the Cyrus R. Vance and Grace Sloane Vance Papers, is housed at the Yale University Library and was compiled by Mark Bailey and the Yale Library's staff of Manuscripts and Archives. These papers provide Vance's itinerary and relevant documents for his Beijing trip; the advice Henry Kissinger, Walter Slocombe, Brown, and others gave Carter during the 1976 election and transition period; and the letters to Vance upon his resignation as secretary of state. Henry Kissinger has consented to the extensive use of a transcript of advice he gave Carter in

Plains during the transition. (Kissinger, Henry. October 21, 2008. Permission granted to quote and cite his comments in conversation in Plains, Georgia, November 20, 1976, Cyrus Vance Papers, Manuscripts and Archives, Box 8, F: 6, Yale University and Library.) A letter from Ambassador Thomas Watson about Vance's resignation is partially reproduced here, courtesy of the IBM Corporate Archives. (Watson, Tom Jr. Letter to Cyrus Vance, February 20, 1980, Cyrus Vance Papers, Manuscripts and Archives, Box 54/78, Yale University Library. Permission to cite letter granted by International Business Machines Corporation.)

At a third collection, the National Archives in College Park, Maryland, the National Intelligence Estimates for the period Carter was in office are available. Some of the minutes or reports of SCC meetings are also available online from that source. The Central Intelligence Agency has itself published some retrospective analyses, as noted in chapter 22, "Shadowing the Soviets."

The major published sources consulted are as follows. Carter's speeches can be found in *Public Papers of the Presidents of the United States, 1977–81*, published by the National Archives. Vance's speeches and those of other foreign policymakers are often reproduced in the *U.S. Department of State Bulletin*. Presidential directives can be found at the Jimmy Carter Library and are also available online at http://www.jimmycarter library.org/documents/pres_directive.phtml. Congressional hearings and investigatory reports cited are noted in the bibliography.

The full citations for all U.S. government documents, PhD dissertations, exit interviews, and the many memoirs and books by and about the actors referred to in this work are listed in the bibliographies. For the original source materials, as well as contemporary journal and newspaper articles and specialized materials from the United Nations and from other digital collections, full citations are made in the end-notes of each relevant chapter. Abbreviations used throughout the work are noted in endnotes.

The photographs in this book are provided courtesy of the Jimmy Carter Library and Museum. The cartoons on the Strategic Arms Limitation Treaty process were provided courtesy of Tony Auth of the *Philadelphia Inquirer*.

Abbreviations

Agencies, Offices, Institutions, and Committees

ACDA	Arms Control and Disarmament Agency
CIA	Central Intelligence Agency
DIA	Defense Intelligence Agency
DCI	Director of Central Intelligence
IOC	International Olympic Committee
NSC	National Security Council
NORAD	North American Air Defense Command
NATO	North Atlantic Treaty Organization
OMB	Office of Management and Budget
OAU	Organization of African Unity
OAS	Organization of American States
PLO	Palestinian Liberation Organization
PRC	People's Republic of China
PRC	Policy Review Committee of the NSC
SAC	Strategic Air Command, US Air Force
SCC	Special Coordinating Committee of the NSC
USOC	U.S. Olympic Committee

AN OUTSIDER IN
THE WHITE HOUSE

INTRODUCTION

What happens when an outsider with lofty moral and political goals and little experience or education in foreign policy takes over the U.S. presidency? Clearly, he is going to be very dependent on his staff. But how does he use them?

Jimmy Carter made some choices along these lines that put him in a place where he did not want to be. As president he started out with the view that East–West conflicts should be less determinative of U.S. foreign relations and pledged himself to drastic cuts in nuclear arms. He wound up with a world in which the Strategic Arms Limitation Treaty (SALT) was in limbo, and a nuclear counterforce doctrine had been adopted. Both sides bristled with thousands of land-, sea-, and air-based nuclear-tipped launchers pointed at each other with the threat that they might actually be used to settle political differences. And more weapons were on the way. He also began his presidency with the vow that human rights would be a "fundamental tenet" of U.S. policy. He ended up soliciting the help of the Vatican to oppose the human rights efforts of Archbishop Oscar Arnulfo Romero y Galdámez of El Salvador, politically isolating the archbishop in the process.

Carter's dependence on his national security advisor, Zbigniew Brzezinski, played a key role in these outcomes. His secretary of state, Cyrus Vance, an able and experienced diplomat, was dedicated to the task of fulfilling Carter's more idealistic goals. But Cyrus Vance found his way blocked by a national security advisor who employed all the tactics noted in the management literature to move Carter in an anti-Soviet direction. A hard-line Cold Warrior at heart, Brzezinski used his superior access and ability to frame issues, control agendas, and find allies to move Carter in the direction Brzezinski desired. Initially he supported Carter's asymmetric arms-control proposals to the Soviet Union, then won control over the administration's China policy and tilted it in an anti-Soviet direction. Throughout he supported a U.S. military buildup that ended in Carter's embrace of a nuclear war fighting strategy.

In part, Carter was vulnerable because he did not have a well-developed strategic vision. Embracing the traditional ideal that the United States had a special moral mission to perform in the world, he failed to appreciate the subtle play between power and the ability to attain what is good. In attributing the opposition of adversaries to bad motives, he failed to see that adversaries also have interests and that a successful diplomacy must be based on an appreciation of the relative power of the contenders and an accommodation of competing interests in terms of that power balance. Indeed, as his dealings with the Soviet Union suggest, Carter failed to see that his moral abstractions were actually complicating relations with that state and thus inhibiting his ability to secure the national security goals he sought.

In these circumstances Brzezinski was able to provide Carter with something he needed in the foreign policy arena—an overall strategic concept. These formulations were usually stated in one- to two-page memos that the president could easily digest. Vance attempted no such formulations in his reports to the president. Brzezinski's hand was strengthened by Carter's strong distrust of the Soviet Union from the beginning of his campaign for the presidency and his subsequent irritations at the USSR when it responded negatively to what it saw as his entry into their domestic policies and relationships to allies on its border.

Could Carter's problems in the foreign policy realm be understood in terms of the more complex domestic and international environments in which he operated? The Cold War consensus had fragmented as a result of the Vietnam War, and at home Carter faced a divided foreign policy elite. Some of the old Cold War internationalists now saw armed conflict with the USSR as almost inevitable, and therefore the United States should use its superiority to confront the Soviet Union now rather than later. In the mid-1970s they were mobilizing into the Committee on the Present Danger and other organizations in order to have an impact on policy. A more moderate group of post–Cold War internationalists was also concerned about Soviet advances, but placed a higher priority on global North–South relations. A third group, the neoisolationists, considered internal (economic, social, and environmental) issues to be the primary problems facing the United States.[1] Almost anything Carter did would lead to criticism at home from one source or the other. But when Carter took steps to come to terms with the Soviet Union, he would be excoriated by those old Cold Warriors who saw a showdown with the USSR as inevitable. They were the ones that aroused in him the greatest concerns.

Actually, divisions within the foreign policy elite over how to deal with the Soviet Union were evident in the earlier days of the Cold War, albeit along sometime different lines. Within the military itself, as Morris Janowitz argues in his classic work *The Professional Soldier*, there were conflicts over how to deal with the Soviet Union.[2] The absolutists, focused around General Douglas McArthur, saw "victory" in its wars with the Soviet Union or its satellites as a means by which to achieve political goals. The pragmatists, organized around General George Marshall, saw nuclear weapons as changing the very meaning of "winning." Within the U.S. Congress and the broader foreign policy elite, those who identified with the absolutist positions saw the imposition of communism on the Eastern European countries as the result of the Yalta Agreement. Some even coalesced around Senator Joseph McCarthy, attributing the victory of the Communist Party in China in 1949 to communists in the U.S. State Department.

But these early presidents were all pragmatists. For them, the problem was to confront the Soviet Union without triggering a World War III. To this end they confronted or outmaneuvered the absolutists in their midst. Harry S. Truman dealt with the first major conflict in Berlin with an airlift rather than a head-on confrontation on the ground, as recommended by General Lucius Clay and other advisors. Truman's decision not to take the Korean War to China in 1951 and to fire General MacArthur led to a massive outcry around the country and calls for his impeachment. In the fall of 1956, Dwight D. Eisenhower backed off from the rollback theories of many in his own party and administration, taking the Hungarian uprising off the National Security Council agenda and deciding, on his own, not to send in U.S. troops.[3] To resolve the Cuban Missile Crisis peaceably, John F. Kennedy countered the Joint Chiefs of Staff and others within the Executive Committee of the National Security Council who wished to begin a massive air strike against Cuba by cutting a secret deal with Nikita Khrushchev. In the arrangement, which was kept secret for several years, U.S. missiles in Turkey would be traded off against Soviet missiles in Cuba. Lyndon Baines Johnson had to resist the entreaties of hawkish joint chiefs to take the war in Vietnam to the north, risking the direct entry of the People's Republic of China or the Soviet Union into the conflict.

Only Richard Nixon, known as a tough anticommunist fighter since he first emerged on the national political scene, was able to negotiate agreements that would hopefully constrain the arms race between the United States and the Soviet Union while publicly embracing a policy of détente. His goal was to dampen down the level of mutual hostility between the two nations.[4]

Actually, Carter had some advantages over his predecessors. President Richard Nixon and Secretary of State Henry Kissinger had lain the groundwork for an early SALT II agreement with the Soviet Union. Kissinger even provided President-Elect Carter, in a document revealed here for the first time, with an overall view of how to deal with Soviet and Chinese leaders. In addition, Carter dealt with Leonid Brezhnev, not Joseph Stalin, and Deng Xiaoping, not Mao Zedong. At home, the Democrats controlled both Houses of Congress throughout Carter's term and the leaders of both Houses (Robert Byrd and Thomas O'Neill) were loyal Democrats who assisted Carter in his major foreign policy projects.

Carter, too, was a man with considerable talents. The very qualities that had won him the presidency—a willingness to take risks, tenacity, and mastery of the relevant details—were manifest in his very real successes in the negotiations over the Panama Canal and Middle Eastern issues at Camp David. In both these efforts he was aided by the professionalism and dedication of clearly unified negotiating and advisory teams. In these cases he had one clear goal, and his national security advisor played a minor role.

Perhaps a word should be said here about this author's observations of how Carter changed over time. Though he remains the same proud man I delineated in my earlier biography, *Jimmy Carter: In Search of the Great White House*, he turned out, while in office, to be more open to the negative feedback of members of his inner circle than I had previously thought. Over time he came to understand complex nuclear strategies better than he had at the beginning of his term. In the postpresidency years, he has shown an ability to walk in the shoes of an adversary—something that was quite lacking in his early dealings with the Soviet Union. Indeed, from his experience at Camp David, he learned a lot about how to negotiate, and would write a primer on it after leaving the White House.[5] These themes will be explored in this book's final chapter, "Jimmy Carter and the American Mission."

Part 1
THE PLAYERS

HIGH EXPECTATIONS

Jimmy Carter was going to be different as president. Running against what he some-times called the "big shots," he publicly cast himself as an outsider. As Carter said in a commercial, "There is one major and fundamental issue. And that is the issue be-tween the insiders and the outsiders. I have been accused of being an outsider and I plead guilty."[1] Certainly, he had pulled off a miracle in his campaign for the presidency. In an October 1975 Gallup poll, he had been the first choice of less than 3 percent of Democrats polled.[2] Thirteen months and 297 electoral votes later, he would be president.

In his campaign Carter had contrasted his decision-making style with that of Richard Nixon. He would have no "all powerful palace guard" in the White House; the cabinet system would be restored to prominence in the government; and his staff would have free access to him and would be encouraged to tell him when he was wrong.[3] There would be "no anonymous aides—unelected, unknown to the public, and unconfirmed by the Senate—wielding vast power from the White House base-ment."[4] His main campaign strategist, Hamilton Jordan, even stated on CBS's *Face the Nation* that "the concept of a chief of staff is alien to Governor Carter and those of us around him."[5] Carter's appointments, moreover, would be distributed on the basis of merit, not as political rewards. Indeed, in an operation called Talent Bank 77, thou-sands of mimeographed letters were sent to African Americans and other minorities, women, and middle-level professionals, suggesting that the recipient was qualified for an executive-level government job should Carter win.[6]

Once in Washington, D.C., Carter acted to distinguish his administration from those that preceded it. At the inauguration he wore a two-piece business suit (pur-chased in Americus, Georgia, for $175) and walked over a mile down the parade route to the White House. At the swearing in of eight cabinet officers and four other cabinet-level officials, he announced that the U.S. Marine Band would no longer precede him with the traditional "Ruffles and Flourishes" and "Hail to the Chief." The next day, at his first cabinet meeting, Carter informed new department heads that he was eliminat-ing chauffeur services for his White House aides and suggested they do the same with their own staffs. Foreign dignitaries, too, would be greeted without the usual military and other ceremonial display. A short time later, he vowed that 5 to 10 percent of the guests at state dinners would be "average" Americans.[7]

More important, Carter set up his advisory staff so that it would differ from the hierarchically organized system of the Nixon administration. "The idea," Jody Powell explained in a follow-up interview, "is to make sure that no one or two people will be able to cut him off from dissenting opinions." Powell used the metaphor of a wheel with Carter at the hub to characterize the White House organization; the staff would have access to him through lines similar to spokes.[8]

Organizational and Political Realities

Carter would soon find that he could not live up to several of these promises. "Hail to the Chief" would be restored to announce his entry into a hall. Lavish ceremonies would be undertaken at the conclusions of the Panama Canal and Camp David negotiations to celebrate some well-deserved accomplishments. The Middle East peace talks at Camp David would be secret, the conferees closed off from access even to many of their own political advisors. Talk of inviting average people to state dinners fell by the wayside as cartoonist Gary Trudeau and others had a little fun at his expense. In one *Doonesbury* comic strip a woman was insulted when a "Secretary of Symbols" looking for "average people" offered her an invitation to a White House Affair.[9] Even the Talent Bank 77 questionnaires returned by thousands of political hopefuls were never processed. Rather, they were packed away in crates and stored in the Executive Office Building across the street from the White House.[10]

To find the politically experienced cabinet department heads he needed, Jimmy Carter—the outsider—called upon many old Washington insiders. As journalist Hugh Sidey commented, the Washingtonians might feel that the past years were some kind of dream, and that what they had eight years ago would resume as Carter took over the White House.[11] Like every other politician, Carter also found governmental offices for his political supporters.[12] The White House Office would be largely staffed with younger people who had served on Carter's earlier political or campaign staffs, differing from some previous presidential staffs in both age and experience.[13] Three of the top advisors—Hamilton Jordan, Jody Powell, and Frank Moore—were under age 35 and had worked only for Carter. Stuart Eizenstat, who would head the Domestic Policy Council, was the sole advisor with prior Washington, D.C., experience. Margaret Costanza, liaison for special interest groups, was the only one not from Georgia.[14]

Even Carter's attempts to reform the way in which he made decisions would fall victim to certain organizational and political imperatives. The foreign policy organization would come to resemble, in many respects, the Nixon administration, with a powerful national security advisor. The cabinet proved too unwieldy a body for policymaking, which meant that most decision making would not be that different from previous administrations. Eventually, the entire cabinet met in closed sessions and then only to keep the various department heads of Carter's administration informed of what was going on.

This White House staff, too, was so large that most aides lacked the kind of access Carter had originally envisaged for them. The relatively small White House Office had grown from the nine professionals counseling Franklin D. Roosevelt to around five hundred people who would serve Carter.[15] This system, in short, would require a

Table 1.   The Carter Cabinet

POSITION	NAME
Secretary of State	Cyrus R. Vance, 1977–80
	Edmund S. Muskie, 1980–81
Secretary of the Treasury	W. Michael Blumenthal, 1977–79
	G. William Miller, 1977–81
Secretary of Defense	Harold Brown
Attorney General	Griffin B. Bell, 1977–79
	Benjamin R. Civiletti, 1979–81
Secretary of the Interior	Cecil D. Andrus
Secretary of Agriculture	Robert S. Bergland
Secretary of Commerce	Juanita M. Kreps, 1977–79
	Philip M. Klutznick, 1979–81
Secretary of Labor	F. Ray Marshall
Secretary of Health, Education and Welfare	Joseph A. Califano Jr., 1977–79
(Health and Human Services, after 1979)	Patricia R. Harris, 1979–81
Secretary of Housing and Urban Development	Patricia R. Harris, 1977–79
	Maurice E. "Moon" Landrieu, 1979–81
Secretary of Transportation	Brock Adams, 1977–79
	Neil E. Goldschmidt, 1979–81
Secretary of Energy	James R. Schlesinger, 1977–79
	Charles W. Duncan, 1979–81
Secretary of Education (post established 1979)	Shirley Hufstedler, 1979–81
Director of Central Intelligence	Stansfield Turner
Assistant to the President for National Security Affairs	Zbigniew Brzezinski

Note: Range of years provided for cabinet members who did not serve for the full Carter term.

greater percentage of the president's time and resources to manage if the presidency were to function properly.[16]

For three years Carter did avoid appointing a chief of staff. Hamilton Jordan, the logical person to perform that role, did not want the job;[17] moreover, Jordan lacked the organizational talent requisite to overseeing a large group. Carter may also have resisted because he wanted to keep control over his administration by being his own chief of staff. "From Carter's point of view," his friend and Office of Management and Budget director Bert Lance would later argue, "he wanted those surrounding him to have only partial knowledge."[18]

Eventually Carter would reorganize to meet some of the management imperatives all contemporary presidents face. Hamilton Jordan would have a brief and not-too-successful stint as chief of staff. Jack Watson, who succeeded him, helped to bring greater order to the whole White House operation. In the foreign policy arena, Zbigniew Brzezinski would become preeminent in managing foreign relations. The

Table 2.   White House Office Staff: Relevant Actors

POSITION	NAME
Deputy Assistant for National Security Affairs	David L. Aaron
Special Assistant to Congressional Liaison (House)	Robert G. Beckel
Special Assistant to the President for Health Issues	Peter G. Bourne
Assistant to the President for National Security Affairs	Zbigniew Brzezinski
Deputy Assistant to the President	Landon Butler
Deputy Assistant for Congressional Liaison (House)	William H. Cable
Deputy Director, Domestic Council, 1977–79	Bertram W. Carp
Special Assistant to the President for Administration	Hugh A. Carter Jr.
Personal Assistant/Secretary to the President	Susan S. Clough
Assistant to the President for Public Liaison	Margaret Constanza
Counsel to the President	Lloyd Cutler
Senior Advisor to the President	Hedley Donovan
Assistant to the President for Domestic Affairs and Policy	Stuart E. Eizenstat
Chief Speechwriter	James M. Fallows
Deputy Press Secretary	Rex. L. Granum
Assistant to the President	Hamilton Jordan
Chief of Staff of the White House	
Counsel to the President	Robert J. Lipshutz
Assistant to the President for Congressional Liaison	Frank B. Moore
Press Secretary to the President	Joseph L. Powell
Assistant to the President for Communications	Gerald M. Rafshoon
Deputy Assistant for Domestic Affairs and Policy Director	David M. Rubenstein
Assistant Press Secretary	Jerrold Schecter
Assistant to the President	James R. Schlesinger
White House Projects	Gregory S. Schneiders
Secretary to the Cabinet and Assistant to the President for Intergovernmental Affairs	Jack H. Watson Jr.
Assistant to the President	Sarah Weddington
Deputy Assistant for Domestic Affairs and Policy, 1979–81	
Assistant to the President	Anne Wexler

Source: United States Government Manual, 1977/78–1980/81. Published by the Office of Federal Register, National Archives and Records Service, and General Services Administration, Washington, D.C.

problem with placing too much power in the persons at the top of the White House hierarchy, as the Nixon presidency demonstrated, is the potential overfiltering of information that reaches the president. An overly zealous chief of staff may go beyond simply limiting a president's schedule for purposes of efficiency to barring top political actors from presidential access. In the Eisenhower and Nixon presidencies, Sherman Adams and H. R. Halderman, to various degrees, had been accused of such conduct. In the Carter administration, Brzezinski controlled access to the president on matters of concern to him. Would this gatekeeper turn out to be a strategic actor?

Inner/Outer Circles

Before Jordan actually became chief of staff, an inner circle revolving around Carter emerged. The foreign policy inner circle, to be discussed in the next three chapters, was composed of National Security Advisor Zbigniew Brzezinski, Secretary of State Cyrus Vance, Secretary of Defense Harold Brown, and Vice President Walter Mondale. The domestic policy inner circle was composed of Stuart Eizenstat, Hamilton Jordan, Jody Powell, and, to a lesser extent, Frank Moore. Bert Lance, a personal friend and former head of the Georgia Department of Transportation, was also a key member of this circle early in the administration. Robert Lipshutz, the president's legal counsel, and Jack Watson, secretary to the cabinet and assistant to the president for intergovernmental affairs, were also influential members of Carter's domestic policy circle.[19] Farther down the totem pole were the members of the economic inner circle. They had the least access to President Carter.[20]

Others within the president's inner circle were from outside of the formal governmental chain of command. Carter talked to his wife Rosalynn "about absolutely everything."[21] During her years at the White House, Mrs. Carter would make many trips and served as the president's personal representative in holding substantive meetings with Central and South American policy leaders on matters such as human rights, arms reduction, and drug trafficking.[22] Charles Kirbo, an attorney in the same firm with Attorney General Griffin Bell, sometimes met with Carter and sent him advice. He had worked with Carter since Carter's first race for the Georgia Senate, and brought many of his highly placed friends to Carter's presidential campaign in 1976.[23] Robert Strauss, former chair of the Democratic National Committee and an old-time political pro from Texas, was a major political consultant throughout the Carter administration. Indeed, as Secretary of Agriculture Robert Bergland later noted, Strauss was "probably the single most important political advisor." Over time, as the president saw the need to be more political, Strauss's influence increased, for he was a man who had "absolutely superb contacts on Capitol Hill and other places around the country."[24] Patrick Caddell, the administration's pollster, was very influential via the memos he sent to Carter, suggesting how Carter should present himself to maximize his public support.[25]

Outside of the foreign policy "inner circle" members was a second ring of people who had frequent access to the president, but mainly in the presence of their superiors, among them were Deputy Secretary of State Warren Christopher and Brzezinski aides William Odom and Michel Oksenberg.

Issue-specific advisors had limited contact with the president when their particular expertise was needed. In foreign policy areas Ambassadors Sol Linowitz and Ellsworth Bunker, for example, had access to the president during the negotiations of the Panama Canal treaties. On occasion, junior staff had a significant impact on policy via the service they provided the president in drafting measures and winning supports for policies the president favored. Notable along these lines was the work Mary Schuman did on the deregulation of the airlines and trucking industries.[26] Rachel Starr, an aide in the office of Alfred Moses, the president's special assistant for Jewish affairs, also played a role in bringing the concerns of Soviet dissidents to the president.

FIGURE 1. A breakfast meeting. Left to right: Walter Mondale, Cyrus Vance, Jimmy Carter, and Zbigniew Brzezinski. Photograph courtesy of the Jimmy Carter Library.

FIGURE 2. Press aide Jody Powell (left) and political aide Hamilton Jordan (right). Photograph courtesy of the Jimmy Carter Library.

Table 3. Major Players: The Inner Circle

INNER CIRCLE

POSITION	NAME
President	Jimmy Carter
Assistant to the President for National Security Affairs	Zbigniew Brzezinski
Secretary of State, 1977–80	Cyrus Vance
Secretary of Defense	Harold Brown
Vice President	Walter Mondale
Assistant to the President, 1977–79 White House Chief of Staff, 1979–80	Hamilton Jordan
Press Secretary	Jody Powell
Director of Central Intelligence	Stansfield (Stan) Turner
Assistant to the President for Congressional Liaison	Frank Moore
Assistant to the President for Domestic Affairs and Policy	Stuart Eizenstat
Director of the Office of Management and Budget, Sept. 1977–81	James McIntyre
Secretary of the Treasury, 1977–79	Michael Blumenthal

Note: Inner Circle members are determined from *The Presidential Kaleidoscope: Advisory Networks in the Nixon and Carter Administrations* by Michael William Link (Ph.D. dissertation, University of South Carolina, 1996). Using multidimensional scaling of interaction data, Link calculated the members of Carter's inner circle each year. The listing here reflects persons included in two or more years of the inner circle. However, Jack Watson (Secretary to the Cabinet and Assistant to the President for Intergovernmental Affairs) and Charles Schultz (Chairman of the Council of Economic Affairs) are not included because searches through the Carter manuscript collection reveal they were not major foreign policy players.

INFORMAL ADVISORS

POSITION	NAME
First Lady	Rosalynn Carter
Atlanta attorney	Charles Kirbo
Former DNC Chairman; U.S. Trade Representative, 1977–79	Robert (Bob) Strauss
Jimmy Carter's Pollster	Patrick Caddell

PERIPHERAL ADVISORS

POSITION	NAME
Deputy Secretary of State	Warren Christopher
Military Assistant to the National Security Advisor and NSC Crisis Coordinator	William (Bill) Odom
Chairman of the Joint Chiefs of Staff, 1974–78	George Brown
Deputy Assistant to the President for National Security Affairs	David Aaron

Note: Range of years provided only for cabinet members who did not serve for the full Carter term.

Relationships

For Carter, as for other presidents, members of the inner circle served in a variety of ways. At the instrumental level, advisors shaped the policy alternatives sent to him, winnowed out the amount of information and number of subordinates going into the Oval Office, and followed through on his decisions to make sure that the relevant government agencies did as he wished.[27] Lance oversaw departmental budget negotiations and kept in touch with key businessmen and congressional members. Powell and Jordan advised Carter on every aspect of his presidency, ranging from how he presented himself in public to the timing of items on his agenda. During the early phase of the Strategic Arms Limitation Treaty (SALT II) talks for example, Jordan argued that it would be counterproductive to go for the Comprehensive Test Ban treaty before SALT II. Moore gave him similar advice.[28] White House Communications Director Gerald Rafshoon suggested it would be best to present SALT II as a measure curtailing a potentially costly arms race rather than an agreement that would allow a military buildup by the United States.[29]

A few close aides also met the emotional needs of the president. At the Camp David meetings on the Middle East, Secretary of State Vance and first lady Rosalynn Carter reassured the president that he should adhere to his mission, even when matters looked bleak. Pollster Patrick Caddell played a similar, if less constructive, role in prompting Carter's "malaise" speech.[30] Regarding the USSR and China, as we shall see, Brzezinski both bolstered the president when he was engaged in difficult talks and encouraged him to be "tough."

At times advisors even compensated for the president's vulnerabilities, employing their own personal and political talents on his behalf.[31] Carter, who had difficulties in politicking for himself one-on-one, sometimes depended on others to do it for him. Earlier in his career Bert Lance, as head of the Georgia Department of Transportation, tied road-building opportunities to votes in the Georgia legislature. In the few months he served in the presidency, Lance performed similar services. When Carter and his congressional liaison staff were at odds with many members of that august body, he tried to smooth things over. Lance also wooed the business community to pave the way for Carter's programs.[32] Jordan, too, reminded the president of the need for political work, mapped out his various campaigns, and sometimes did the campaigning for him.[33]

On occasion, aides acted as proxies for the president, filling in where Carter did not want to be personally associated. Carter did not engage in the kind of dark operations that had been evident in the Nixon administration, but Jordan would sometimes play the "bad cop" in overseeing certain department heads.[34] As Jordan wrote Secretary of Health, Education, and Welfare Joseph Califano in early 1977, Carter should not have to read about appointments from the newspaper: "The President asked that you clear them with me. You have been completely insensitive to our modest requests."[35] Related to this function, an aide might serve as a "lightning rod" for the president, attracting the political flack that could otherwise diminish the president's prestige. Brzezinski, Carter claims, performed that kind of role for him.

Group Dynamics

The Carter White House was not exempt from the problems endemic to presidential staffs. Key members of the White House Office or the National Security Council created extra hurdles for departmental heads to jump over before reaching the president.[36] Department heads would complain that they could not even get Jordan to return their telephone calls. Agriculture Secretary Bergland came to clearly dislike Jordan on these grounds.[37] Attorney General Bell was upset with Brzezinski, stating that the national security advisor would schedule National Security Council (NSC) meetings to which Bell, despite his wishes, was not invited.[38] Even Lance came to actively dislike Brzezinski. The national security advisor, he charged, tried to keep him out of the NSC meetings during the first weeks of the administration by scheduling them at times when Lance could not be there.[39]

"Court politics" was also a sometime occurrence for Carter's staff.[40] Lance saw more competition than teamwork among Jordan, Powell, and Brzezinski.[41] Nor did advisors always speak frankly to Carter. Jordan, as early as the spring of 1977, was concerned that few staff members spoke frankly to Carter partly due to the nature of the office. "The institution of the presidency," Jordan wrote, "is still a powerful and awesome thing."[42] In May 1977, Appointments Secretary Greg Schneider wrote Powell that cabinet members were afraid to speak out on issues, forcing Carter to be identified as the "lead person" on too many topics and thereby paying the "political price when they pop."[43] Indeed, as President Lyndon Johnson's former press secretary George Reedy puts it, the White House pecking order is not necessarily determined by the "individual strength and forcefulness of the chicken" but "depends upon his relationship to the barnyard keeper. To maintain a privileged relationship with the President, advisors may hesitate to directly contradict him."[44] Flattery and support are often proffered rather than serious critiques that could enhance the president's ability to test reality.[45]

Carter inadvertently contributed to this lack of critical feedback. As Lance warned him, he was alienating department heads "because you're showing how smart you are, you're losing the input of people who do know what's going on."[46] Carter's desire for grand accomplishments, moreover, would sometimes be expressed in ways that cut off discussion. In the early SALT II talks he made it so clear that he wanted drastic cuts in land-based nuclear missiles that even those who had doubts about the approach went along with the proposals. Later, at the April 11, 1980, meeting when the decision to undertake a hostage rescue operation in Iran was made, Carter opened with a statement indicating that he was leaning toward the rescue operation. When he called upon others at the meeting for comment, they assured him that the rescue plan he had in mind was feasible. Secretary of State Vance, who would have questioned the whole operation, was away in Florida for a much-needed vacation and had not been told that an important decision was to be made at that meeting.[47]

Still, Carter generally liked it when aides stood up to him—as long as they remained clearly loyal to him. Lance had discovered this in his earlier relationship with Carter. As Georgia Department of Transportation head, Lance scolded then governor Carter for keeping him waiting on one occasion, noting that Carter then became more respectful of his time.[48] Carter's aides could be remarkably critical of his style, at least in writing. Powell admonished Carter in a February 2, 1977, letter, telling him to curb a proclivity for speaking in superlatives: "For example, had you expressed a desire for the most rapid possible progress toward a cessation of nuclear testing instead of calling for 'eliminating the testing of all nuclear devices, instantly and completely' your statement would have been viewed as much more reasonable." By January 16, 1978, Powell was urging early morning staff meetings to better coordinate White House operations.[49] As Eizenstat told Carter, "your remarks in some instance are so harsh and biting that they do not appear Presidential."[50] In preparation for the 1980 campaign, Rafshoon even told him, "Mr. President, you smile too damn much."[51]

The Need for Strategic Oversight

Whatever controversies his aides might engage in, Jimmy Carter saw himself as the man who made the final call on all policy matters.[52] In this expression, Carter embraced an idea often reiterated by students of the American presidency. As Ted Sorensen, former speechwriter to President John F. Kennedy, has noted, "in the White House, unlike the Congress, only one man's vote is decisive, and thorough and thoughtful debate before he has made up his mind can assist him in that task."[53] Presidential scholar Stephen Hess says that he has observed "no Svengali on the White House staff." Even under the "most pyramidal arrangements, those of Dwight Eisenhower and Richard Nixon, the men at the top served the purposes of the President."[54]

The present volume provides another perspective: the president is not just one man with agents who follow his directions, for better or worse; rather, he is at the center of a complex web of men and women, with common and conflicting goals, in which big and small decisions are made at several points. Advisors shape the policy options the president receives, screen the information that crosses his desk, advise him on appropriate courses to take, and implement his policies with greater or lesser vigor.

At times, especially when a president is inexperienced in policymaking and the ways of Washington, advisors may actually put their own goals ahead of the president. Brzezinski, as we shall see, subtly undermined Carter's SALT II policy and maneuvered the president into dealing with China as a counterpoise to the Soviet Union. In this respect an advisor acts as a "motivated tactician."[55] To curtail such possibilities, presidency expert Alexander George has suggested that chiefs of staff and other advisors who manage the access of others to the president should be wary of the risks of their becoming policy advocates. Whatever their own policy predisposition, aides who control key access points are obliged to prevent "impediments to information processing and ensuring balanced and dispassionate appraisal of options."[56]

Each president, as Fred Greenstein has suggested, will bring a particular set of political, rhetorical, and personal skills to the office. But as this work suggests, the president can only bring coherence to his organization and the web in which he is embedded if he has a clear strategic vision. He must be able to articulate goals and develop techniques to maintain a measure of organizational discipline. What this means, as presidential scholar Paul Quirk has suggested, is that a strategically competent president in today's setting may not be able to follow the Franklin D. Roosevelt model in which the president depends on himself for coordination and overseeing all basic aspects of his administration.[57] But neither should he follow the "chairman of the board" model, delineated by Ronald Reagan, in which the president delegates all but the most abstract policy guidelines to administrative aides and policy wonks. That policy allows too much free play to staff members. Minimally, a strategically smart chief executive will choose aides who share his basic policy commitments, keep him informed about the obstacles he faces, give him notice of disagreements over how to obtain his goals, and avoid premature closure on their debates. He will delegate or exercise hands-on control over matters according to their importance and the character of the aides upon whom he relies.[58]

For Carter, then, as for other presidents, the qualities of the staff he chose and how he used it is crucial to understanding his presidency. The particular makeup of his foreign policy team suggests some of the problems he would have in an arena where he spent most of his energy and time.

THE FOREIGN POLICY TEAM

Jimmy Carter started off his first day in office with the choice of a desk, "the Resolute," for the Oval Office. Last used by John F. Kennedy, it had been named after a British vessel and presented to Rutherford B. Hayes in 1880 by Queen Victoria.[1] In subsequent days, Carter would show that the name of the desk underscored his tough management style. In the foreign and domestic arenas he could call cabinet ministers as well as junior staffers to account from time to time.[2] Once he had confidence in a person, he later testified, he didn't mind "loading them up" with as much as they could bear and then proceeding to forget about it.

In time he also won a reputation for being detail-oriented. He corrected the grammar—usually for the better—of some of the memos that crossed his desk. He asked for reports on the academic curricula at service academies. He decided who would have access to the White House tennis courts; and when he invited someone to join him in a game, he played to win. But he did not like backbiting: "When any of my subordinates are criticized, I defend them. They know it....The worst thing they can do in my eyes is to criticize one another. I don't even let Rosalynn criticize my staff."[3]

President Harry Truman and Admiral Hyman G. Rickover, the very exacting first head of the U.S. nuclear submarine fleet, were Carter's role models.[4] The impact Rickover's stringent standards had on Carter is evident in Carter's campaign autobiography, *Why Not the Best?* His admiration for Truman had to do with Truman's ability to make difficult decisions easily. Like him, Carter suggested, "I don't anguish over things." Moreover, Carter said he could delegate authority. "I don't look over somebody's shoulder."[5]

In the domestic arena Carter promoted good government, and tackled long-term issues such as energy conservation and development, the protection of the environment, the deregulation of the airline and trucking industries, and a staggered increase in the Social Security payroll tax. Most of these goals should have provided him with a relatively easy ride through the legislature: the Democrats controlled both houses of the U.S. Congress, and Robert Byrd (D-WV), the majority leader in the Senate, and Tip O'Neil (D-MA), the Speaker of the U.S. House of Representatives, were committed party leaders who would provide loyal service for him. At the White House, moreover, Stuart Eizenstat, an experienced aide who worked with a relatively harmonious support team, sustained him. But Carter's propensity to go it alone and his inattention to the political interests of the very congressional leaders he would depend on made his modest accomplishments in these areas somewhat more difficult than they might have been.[6]

In the foreign policy arena he set himself an even more ambitious agenda—drastic reductions in the number of nuclear weapons and the protection of human rights around the world. As former secretary of defense Clark Clifford noted, Carter "wanted to solve every problem the nation faced, and at first set out a bold agenda to do so."[7] As it turned out, Carter spent most of his time on international rather than domestic affairs. That was where the president could have more influence, he later explained.[8] But in this arena, Carter had the least experience, and the most conflict-ridden set of advisors.

Carter's experience with foreign policy had been limited to a few trips abroad and efforts to sell Georgia business to foreign investors. Even his education at Georgia Tech and the U.S. Naval Academy in Annapolis, Maryland (the latter on a wartime three-year accelerated program) had been primarily technical. His only liberal arts courses at Annapolis consisted of Spanish, literature, American government, modern European history, and U.S. foreign policy. His final year was dedicated solely to naval engineering: naval correspondence, navigation, strategy and tactics, gunnery, military law, ballistics, thermodynamics, and alternating current.[9]

But Carter had always embraced the idea that self-help is a valuable aspect of learning, and as president he prepared for issues he would face by spending long hours at his desk, poring over papers, reading books, and discussing foreign policy in depth. Over time he developed a reputation for immersing himself in details of weapons systems, the budget, and other such matters.[10] Carter would discuss broader philosophical matters with National Security Advisor Zbigniew Brzezinksi who would drop over on a Saturday morning, and when the time permitted, provide him with mini-seminars on the Russian nationalities problem or other issues.[11] Carter even made time for Spanish lessons and a speed-reading class at the beginning of his administration. But the president was no workaholic; he had time for frequent swims, sometimes with daughter Amy, in the White House pool. And he and Rosalynn saw movies at the White House and Camp David, sometimes three times a week. They also attended concerts and plays in Washington, D.C.[12]

Would his religious commitments influence his foreign policymaking? Carter was clearly a devout Christian in his private life. He attended church regularly, knew his Bible well, had taught Sunday school, and helped others. He even did missionary work at times. During his presidential campaign, he noted that he was a born-again Christian, talked of his religion while the cameras were rolling, and invited members of the press to the Sunday school class in Plains, Georgia, where he sometimes conducted the meetings.[13]

Yet his religious views were mainstream. During the campaign, Carter came out of a Plains Bible class with a lesson plan in which he had underlined a core tenet of the Baptist tradition: the separation of church and state. Even his *Playboy* interview, which did considerable damage to his campaign when it was published in fall 1976, was designed to show that he understood temptation and could distance himself from self-righteousness. Not only that, Carter enjoyed an occasional scotch, talked of "kicking ass" when referring to his political opponents, and used the spoils of office to forward his personal positions and agendas. Indeed, any tendency he might have had to over-play his religious hand was checked by the good advice of Press Secretary Jody Powell. In a handwritten letter, Powell urged Carter to avoid phrasing "positions on specific issues in religious terms." His views on the Bible should not infuse "the formulation of American foreign policy," because "whether or not you think fornication or homo-sexuality is a sin should have nothing to do with legality. Nor should your views on the validity of Biblical prophecies play a role in the formulation of American foreign policy."[14]

Carter's religion did have a subtle impact on his policies, however. His faith under-girded his perception that he had a political mission to perform, providing him with the tenacity that was requisite to his success in the Panama Canal and Middle East ne-gotiations. But his moral enthusiasm led him to infuse U.S. policies toward the USSR with a sense of mission that was at times counterproductive.

To aid him in the policy process, Carter chose an experienced person for secretary of state. Cyrus Vance was a lawyer with a prestigious New York firm and several years of dedicated government service. He arrived at Carter's home in Plains on November 26, 1976, to confer with the soon to be president in a session that was clearly a job inter-view. Over soup and sandwiches prepared in the kitchen by Carter himself, the two men talked for over five hours. The only breaks occurred when they washed the dishes and when Carter put Amy to bed.[15] Both men agreed on the need to improve relations with the Soviet Union and conclude a Strategic Arms Limitation Treaty (SALT) while maintaining an "unquestioned military balance." Relations with China, they concurred, should be normalized, but only after careful study of the internal properties of the Chinese government while considering the future of the U.S. relationship with Taiwan. The "tour d'horizon" concluded at midnight. They had agreed on a set of principles that suggested that the president and his secretary of state could form a harmonious foreign policy team. Vance even welcomed the possible appointment of Brzezinski as national security advisor, saying that the infusion of new ideas would help the administration. When the two were preparing to exit to their respective rooms, Carter asked Vance if he would be his secretary of state; Vance accepted with "gratitude and a sense of optimism."[16]

Several days later, on the evening of December 7, at a meeting at the governor's man-sion in Atlanta, Carter formally offered Brzezinski the role of national security advisor.[17] Brzezinski had been Carter's chief advisor and mentor on foreign policy issues during the campaign, as well as a consultant on the makeup of an overall foreign policy team. Embracing Carter's desire for a "team approach" to foreign policy, Brzezinski had earlier suggested that Carter might embrace the Kennedy model, which had combined a "strong President" with a "relatively secure and strong" secretary of state (Dean Rusk) and "an equally confident and energetic" White House through McGeorge Bundy, Kennedy's national security advisor.[18] For secretary of state, Brzezinski recommended Cyrus Vance over George Ball, the other major contender for the office. Vance would be a team player compared to Ball, who would be would be a "dominant" secretary of state.[19]

Both men brought relevant experience and expertise to their positions. Vance had served as the general counsel for the Department of Defense under Kennedy, and as secretary of the Army and deputy defense secretary under Lyndon Johnson. He also had experience as a negotiator, dealing with Fidel Castro in the negotiations to release prisoners taken during the Bay of Pigs invasion and as Johnson's special envoy to mediate the conflict between Greece and Turkey over Cyprus in 1967. In 1968, Vance dealt with the South Koreans at the time of the USS *Pueblo* crisis and served as the deputy chief of the U.S. Army delegation to the Paris Peace Conference on Vietnam. His attention to detail and his ability to understand or empathize with an adversary had served him well in these endeavors.[20] Employing a bottom-up processing of information, Vance approached issues on a case-by-case basis. Walter Mondale notes that Vance avoided disputes and backbiting more than any other member of the cabinet, yet maintained his matter of principle. Even Hamilton Jordan admitted that Vance ran the State Department as well as it could be run.[21] Above all, he was a "survivor," a man who did not leave "any tracks."[22] Vance was the first or second choice of all the people Carter consulted about this position.[23]

Brzezinski, a Columbia University professor with a PhD from Harvard University, brought to the Carter foreign policy table the intellectual skills that potentially suited him to the role of a foreign policy broker. A naturalized American, he was the son of a Polish diplomat who had been based in Canada shortly before the Germans occupied Poland in 1939. At Columbia University, Brzezinski founded and directed the Research Institute on Communist Affairs (subsequently the Research Institute of International Change). By 1970 he had authored eight books dealing with the USSR and its satellite states in Europe. Though his role in government was more limited than that of Vance, he had served during the Johnson administration on the Policy Planning Staff in the State Department (1966–68). He had also advised Presidents Kennedy, Johnson, and Nixon on foreign policy matters.[24] As director of Vice President Hubert Humphrey's foreign policy task force in 1968, he incorporated the Asia factor in the European problem, and he wrote a book on Japan's world role.[25] Like his Harvard classmate Henry Kissinger, Brzezinski made his way up the policy ladder by working for a Rockefeller. With David Rockefeller, chairman of Chase Manhattan Bank, he put together the prestigious Trilateral Commission, a group of influential businessmen, academics, and lawyers who came together to promote cooperation among the United States, Japan, and Europe. As executive director of the organization, Brzezinski let several Democratic candidates know that he was available as a foreign policy advisor. Jimmy Carter was the only one who took him up on this offer.[26]

Two other men would play major roles in Carter's foreign policymaking. Harold Brown, president of Cal Tech when Carter named him as his choice for secretary of defense, was a brilliant nuclear scientist and a whiz kid who had earned his PhD from Columbia in 1949 when he was twenty-one years old. An expert on various weapons systems, he had served as a director on weapons research in the Pentagon and as secretary of the Air Force. He referred to himself, shortly before becoming secretary of defense, as a "pragmatist with a world view." Those who commented on Carter's appointment of Brown noted his skills as a manager, his political orientation as a moderate, and his reputation as a man awesome in debate. Over time he would be rated by the Washington media as one of Carter's best cabinet officers.[27] Carter had chosen Brown because he saw the Pentagon as needing "some discipline"; he wanted "both a scientist with a thorough knowledge of the most advanced technology and a competent business manager, strong-willed enough to prevail in the internecine struggles among the different military services."[28]

Vice President Mondale, a protégé of Hubert Humphrey and a U.S. senator since 1964, brought to the table political skills that would enable him to give advice and assistance to Carter in selling policies to Congress and the American public. Educated in Minnesota, he had begun his political career with the anticommunist, but liberal, political organization Americans for Democratic Action. After a stint in the U.S. Army and a period as Minnesota's attorney general, Mondale went to the Senate as a replacement for Humphrey, who was running for vice president in 1964.[29] His long experience in Washington, Carter noted, "was a compensating factor for the ignorance among the Georgia group concerning Washington."[30]

Though Mondale came to an office that humorist Mr. Dooley referred to as a "kind of a disgrace...like writing anonymous letters," Mondale would play a significant role in the Carter administration.[31] He not only aided Carter in the selection of his cabinet members but worked closely with him to decide on the agenda that the president would pursue during his first year in office.[32] With an office in the White House, a sizable staff, weekly luncheon meetings with the president, and access to all meetings and presidential papers, Mondale was in a position to play a significant role in foreign policy matters. Indeed, next to Brzezinski, Mondale spent more time with the president in 1977 than any other advisor or staff aide did.[33] Though Mondale would devote some of his time to ceremonial occasions, Carter encouraged him to weigh in on a wide variety of substantive issues "of short duration." As Mondale saw it, he would be a general advisor on almost any issue—as a troubleshooter, a representative of the president on some foreign affairs matters, and as a political advocate of the administration. Eventually, Mondale had a staff of fifty-five people. Several of his assistants worked out of the Senate offices, where he also had an office. But most were housed in the grey rococo building across the street from the White House, the Old Executive Office Building. His former foreign policy advisor, David Aaron, would become one of Brzezinski's most influential aides.[34]

Other significant appointees included Warren Christopher as deputy secretary of state. A senior partner in a prominent California law firm, he had served as deputy attorney general in the Johnson administration. Stansfield Turner, Carter's choice for director of the Central Intelligence Agency (CIA), had been voted "most likely to succeed" in Carter's class at Annapolis, was a Rhodes Scholar, and had served as commander of the U.S. Navy's Second Fleet and as commander in chief of the North Atlantic Treaty Organization's Southern flank.[35] Andrew Young, an early African American supporter of Carter, rather reluctantly gave up a safe seat in Georgia's Fifth Congressional District to become Carter's first United Nations ambassador.[36] Paul Warnke, who would become the head of the Arms Control and Disarmament Agency and chief arms negotiator, had served as assistant secretary of defense in the Johnson administration, the third-ranking position in the Pentagon. George Brown, former Air Force chief of staff, would continue in his role as chairman of the Joint Chiefs of Staff.[37]

On the surface, at least, it seemed that Carter had assembled a team that would work in harmony on the foreign policy front. Vance and Brzezinski had both embraced Carter's idea that he wanted a collegial approach to the policymaking process. All four inner circle players (Vance, Brzezinski, Brown, and Mondale) were members of the Trilateral Commission, an elite roster of foreign policy influentials that advocated strengthening U.S. ties with its allies in Japan and Western Europe through consultation and cooperation on international projects.

The diplomatic arm of the government was well staffed, too, as Vance had chosen mostly foreign policy professionals for top positions in the Department of State. Anthony Lake, a career Foreign Service officer, was named director of policy planning in state. Earlier, he had served Nixon as special assistant to the president for national security affairs. Richard Holbrooke, assistant secretary of state for East Asian and Pacific affairs, had served as staff assistant to Ambassadors Maxwell Taylor and Henry Cabot Lodge. At the time of his appointment, Holbrooke was managing editor of the new quarterly magazine *Foreign Policy*. Only two people at the assistant secretary level lacked previous experience in foreign affairs. Patricia Derian, who was to become assistant secretary of state for human rights and humanitarian affairs, had been active in the civil rights movement in Mississippi. But she told Warren Christopher, "'If you want a magnolia to decorate foreign policy, I'm the wrong person. I expect to get things done.'" Carter's presence at her swearing-in ceremony suggested that he would give Derian his full support. Lucy Benson, former president of the League of Women Voters, was named undersecretary of state for security assistance.[38]

On the crucial issues relevant to U.S.-Soviet relations and arms limitation, there were portents of difficulties ahead. Several officials had taken diverse stances on the Vietnam War, a defining experience for some of them. As governor of Georgia, Carter had led the "Anyone but McGovern" movement at the Democratic Convention in 1972. He had even hedged on the issue of Lieutenant William Calley's conviction for killing the innocent civilians in a Vietnamese village during the infamous My Lai Massacre, in violation of the Army Rules of Land Warfare. At an April 4, 1971 press conference, he suggested that Calley had been made a scapegoat and that his conviction put every young man sent to Vietnam in a very doubtful position.[39] Brzezinski had given the Vietnam War his full support and saw some people as so burned by that experience that they distanced themselves from the more muscular approach to foreign policy that he embraced.[40] The new secretary of defense, Harold Brown, had also supported the war from beginning to end. General David Brown as chief of staff had even urged U.S. air and naval deployment to South Vietnam following the U.S. pullout in 1975.[41]

Other key players in the administration had questioned or opposed U.S. involvement in Vietnam. An early supporter of the war, Vance was, by 1968, convinced that the bombing of that country had become counterproductive. Out of this experience he developed a disdain for "concept driven thinking" seeing it as "a flaw in our foreign policy—too narrowly rooted in the concept of an overarching US–Soviet geopolitical struggle."[42] Mondale also came to oppose U.S. involvement in Vietnam and raised questions about CIA and Federal Bureau of Investigation operations during

Table 4. Foreign Policy Department Heads and Staff

POSITION	NAME	DATES SERVED
U.S. DEPARTMENT OF DEFENSE		
Secretary of Defense	Harold Brown	1977–81
Chairman of the Joint Chiefs of Staff	George S. Brown	1974–78
	David C. Jones	1978–82
Secretary of the Army	Clifford L. Alexander Jr.	1977–81
U.S. DEPARTMENT OF STATE		
Secretary of State	Cyrus R. Vance	1977–80
	Edmund S. Muskie	1980–81
Deputy Secretary of State	Warren Christopher	1977–81
Under Secretary for Political Affairs	David D. Newsom	1978–81
Under Secretary for Security Assistance	Lucy W. Benson	1977–80
Assistant Secretary for Human Rights and Humanitarian Affairs	Patricia M. Derian	1977–81
Assistant Secretary for Politico-Military Affairs	Leslie H. Gelb	1977–79
Assistant Secretary for East Asian and Pacific Affairs	Richard C. Holbrooke	1977–79
Assistant Secretary for African Affairs	Richard Moose	1977–81
Assistant Secretary for the Near East and South Asia Affairs	Harold (Hal) Saunders	1978–81
Deputy Assistant Secretary of State	Robert Beckel	1979–81
Director, Arms Control and Disarmament Agency	Paul Warnke	1977–78
Director of Policy Planning	Anthony M. Lake	1977–81
Special Advisor to the Secretary for Soviet Affairs	Marshall Shulman	1978–81
NATIONAL SECURITY COUNCIL		
Assistant to the President for National Security Affairs	Zbigniew Brzezinski	1977–81
Deputy Assistant for National Security Affairs	David L. Aaron	1977–81
Military Assistant and National Security Council Crisis Coordinator	William E. Odom	1977–81
Special Assistant to the Assistant to the President for National Security Affairs	Karl F. Inderfurth	1977–79
	Robert M. Gates	1979
	Leslie G. Denend	1979–81
Coordinator for National Security Planning	Samuel P. Huntington	1977–78
Press Officer and Associate Press Secretary	Jerry Schecter	1977–80
Congressional Relations Officer	Madeleine Albright	1978–81
Director of the Office of Global Issues	Jessica Tuchman	1977–79
Middle East and North Africa	William Quandt	1977–79
	Gary Sick	1977–81
USSR and Eastern Europe	Marshall Brement	1979–81
East Asia and China	Michel Oksenberg	1977–80
Latin America and the Caribbean	Robert Pastor	1977–81

the war.[43] Paul Warnke, as assistant secretary of defense in the Johnson administration, had publicly questioned U.S. involvement in the Vietnam War, the highest-ranking member of the administration to do so. Tony Lake at the State Department had quit Kissinger's National Security Council (NSC) staff in the spring of 1970, purportedly concerned about the U.S. intervention in Cambodia. Two years later, on May 12, 1972, Lake was joined by eight other former Kissinger aides, denouncing the mining of North Vietnam's harbors as "an ill conceived effort to preserve the present concept of American presidential prestige."[44] Several months later, Lake and Leslie Gelb, who also joined the Carter administration, would pen an article condemning the Christmas bombing of North Vietnam. Carrying the "wounds" of the Vietnam experience, one observer has noted, some of these men would be "extremely wary of sucking the United States into other quagmires."[45]

The presence of so many Vietnam War critics in policymaking positions became an issue behind the scenes. Concerned at what he saw as too many doves being placed in key foreign policy positions, Brzezinski moved to create a counterbalance to them at the NSC and the Department of Defense.[46] Several weeks later, Eugene Rostow, the Yale University law professor and an organizer of the hawkish Committee on the Present Danger, wrote Brzezinski, "I hope the hobbley-hoy period ends soon. The confusion, Andy Young, conflicting signals, the prevalence of Tony Lake, is causing deep concern."[47]

Most directly relevant to later conflicts, however, were Brzezinski's and Vance's divergent beliefs on the nature of the Soviet Union and the use of force in foreign policy situations. Vance, as we shall see, viewed the Soviet Union as a state that the United States could deal with on the basis of their complementary interests in matters such as the limitation on the arms race, and he plainly saw the limitations of U.S. military power in the world order of the late 1970s. As secretary of state he stressed "the use of diplomacy as a foreign policy instrument...in his public pronouncements."[48]

In contrast, Brzezinski saw the Soviet Union as a megalomaniac state bent on world domination, and he viewed U.S. military power and the threat that it might actually be utilized as the most important factors in shaping Soviet policies. These views were sometimes buried in more complex statements Brzezinski made in various books and public speeches. But as Steven Campbell shows in his survey of thirty-nine national security Weekly Reports that Brzezinski submitted to Carter throughout 1977 (of which twenty-five were relevant), Brzezinski was tough on the Soviet Union from the very beginning. Of his service to Carter, in February 1977, for example, he wrote the president, "The primary task of the U.S." was "to inhibit disruptive Soviet acts....Our policies in every region must be related to an overarching coherent strategy for gradually transforming the nature of the Soviet challenge." In May, he wrote that the "dominant position of the Soviet military industrial faction has been underestimated in the West."[49]

Related to these ideological stances were profound differences in personal styles. Both men, it is true, had aristocratic backgrounds: Vance's father, who died when Vance was five years old, was from a well-established West Virginia family. His mother was from the upper-crust Philadelphia Main Line. And his uncle, John W. Davis, was the Democratic presidential candidate in 1924 and later head of the American Bar Association. Vance's wife, Gay (Grace) Sloane, was an heiress of the Sloane family of New York, the founders of the largest furniture manufacturing company at the time; he had met her while a student at Yale.[50] Brzezinski's father was the son of a diplomat with roots in the Polish nobility. His wife, Emilie Anna (Muska) Benes, was the grandniece of Eduard Benes, the former Czech president deposed by the Communists in 1948.[51]

Otherwise these two men were quite different. Vance was not only from a socially well-connected family, but he also had the qualities that facilitated an easy rise up the corporate ladder. He had a pleasing personality and was a very hard worker. He was noted for his integrity, his dedication to detail, and his cooperative spirit. "We never had to struggle," Vance's attorney brother noted shortly after his appointment was announced.[52] His strengths, as Henry Kissinger noted, were that he was a fair, prudent, patient man. If he had any weakness, it was that he was not sufficiently assertive.[53]

Brzezinski, on the other hand, had to fight to recover an earlier status. His father had been the Polish consul general in Montreal when Adolph Hitler and Russia divvied up Poland in 1939, and the family decided to make Canada their permanent home. In Montreal he had attended a Catholic grade school, and later received a BA and an MS from McGill University. At Harvard, Brzezinski secured a PhD and a teaching assignment. But unlike his classmate Henry Kissinger, he did not receive a tenured appointment at Harvard. Still, while there, Brzezinski did study with Merle Fainsod, the premier Soviet specialist in the country, as well as Carl Friedrich, a specialist on Nazi totalitarianism, whom he helped with his interviews of Russian refugees. He also co-taught a course with Friedrich in which they extended the totalitarian concept to include not only German fascism but the Soviet experience as well.[54]

It was through this gamut of life experiences that Brzezinski's anti-Soviet stance solidified and his proclivities for political combat developed. As Robert Gates, the CIA representative on the NSC staff, noted of Brzezinski, "He relished verbal dueling and gave no quarter to the professional staff or others in the government. He debated like he played tennis—to win and to win all the time. The intellectually weak or deficient or slow merited no sympathy."[55]

It was the very qualities of these two men that led some observers to express their concerns that Brzezinski would "overwhelm" Vance.[56] Former secretary of defense Clark Clifford advised president-elect Carter against the appointment of Brzezinski along these lines:

> [Brzezinski was] too much of an advocate and not enough of an honest broker to fill this post in the way I believed appropriate. Also, I was certain he would clash with the gentle and collegial Vance. This I stated frankly to the President-elect, who was not pleased…Even after Carter told me Vance had said he could work with Brzezinski, I persisted in my objections. Finally, he said, "Well, if we don't put Zbig there, what should I do with him?" With deliberately exaggerated seriousness, I replied, "Make him the first American

Ambassador to the Bermuda Triangle." The President-elect laughed, and our conversation was over.[57]

The organizational philosophy Brzezinski pressed on the president would also provide a milieu in which their competition would flourish. The initial commitment to the team approach made it clear that the secretary of state would not be the dominant one in the foreign policy process. But Brzezinski went beyond that, envisaging himself as the architect of foreign policy. Vance would be consigned to the role of the "builder" of foreign policy—the one who implemented the policies that were made.[58] Contrary to early denials that he sought such a role for himself, Brzezinski would model himself after Kissinger as national security advisor. He would be the advisor who led an overall policy direction.

Still, conflicts between Vance and Brzezinski were muted for some time. Carter disliked backbiting, and at the beginning he had good relationships with both men. In tune with the president's desires, in 1977 Vance and Brzezinski developed a collaborative relationship at work and became good personal friends. Brzezinski actually had a signed picture of Vance hanging on his wall.[59] At first, Defense Secretary Brown and Vice President Mondale mediated the policy differences that arose between the two men.[60] Furthermore, Vance and his wife Gay were also close personal friends of Jimmy and Rosalynn Carter. As Carter noted, "He and I were to spend many good times together—talking, fishing, skiing, playing tennis—as well as less enjoyable hours negotiating a Middle East settlement and working and praying for the hostages."[61]

Some of the organizational arrangements reflected the commitment to the collegial system originally envisaged by Carter. The president, as he later confided to Brzezinski, found the Friday morning foreign policy breakfasts "one of the best times of the week for me."[62] The initial members of this breakfast club were Vance, Brown, Brzezinski, and Mondale. At these meetings they would discuss the relationship between foreign policy decisions and domestic matters.[63] In addition, Vance, Brzezinski, and Brown had their own luncheon meetings once a week (referred to as the "VBB meetings"). Working without a formal agenda, they engaged in free-ranging discussions. No note takers or aides were present. Over time, the meetings became somewhat more routine, with an agenda negotiated in advance by staff. When these men could agree on a recommendation, it would be directly sent to the president for his approval, or to the Policy Review Committee or Special Coordinating Committee, where it would usually sail through without much trouble.[64]

On two of Carter's major foreign policy undertakings—the Panama Canal treaties and the Camp David agreements—the Carter foreign policy team would act as a harmonious, collegial whole. But over time, as policy differences over SALT II, the Soviet Union, and China became manifest, personal and turf battles bubbled to the surface. As Brzezinski later suggested, their policy differences had some kind of a domino effect. "I think once policy disagreements surfaced, then all of the institutional rivalries and resentments which always are there, particularly when a small elite and staff dominates a department, also intensified, and that became sharper and sharper," he later commented. "The press got onto it, and I think the press pumped it up a great deal.

Then gradually things began to get more competitive, and in a way, one was almost driven to keeping score to see who wins and who loses, and that's probably never too good in a power setting, especially if you feel strongly that you are right."[65]

By early 1978 it became clear that Brzezinski, as he would later admit, had become—in fact, if not law—a chief of staff for American foreign policy.[66] On Soviet and related strategic issues, the national security advisor carried the policy debate, relegating the secretary of state to a marginal role in the process. By late 1979, the press was reporting that Brzezinski and Vance could not stand one another, a fact that they had tried to cover up for some time.[67] Hamilton Jordan had commented, even before this time, that he'd "seen them at the Friday morning breakfasts argue like cats and dogs."[68] Though Jordan probably overstated the overt conflicts between them, he did sense the underlying tensions that came to characterize their relationship.

How do we account for this shift from the original model of collegial teamwork? This transformation was partly due to the worsening of relations with the Soviet Union, an apparent substantiation of Brzezinski's more hard-line views about the administration's overarching goals. And it was partly due to the movement over time of Secretary of Defense Brown and Vice President Mondale toward a harder line on foreign policy, making a subtle but important change in the balance of the key foreign policy decision-making bodies. But the shift was also due to two other factors, to be discussed in detail in the next chapter. Organizational arrangements gave Brzezinski several advantages in any competition for influence. Moreover, Carter came to like, trust, and depend on Brzezinski. Over time, he so identified with Brzezinski that he came to see attacks on his national security advisor as attacks on his own policies, and maybe even on himself.

THE BRZEZINSKI ADVANTAGE

Unlike earlier national security advisors, Zbigniew Brzezinski was a member of the president's cabinet. He also had a large office assigned to him in the West Wing of the White House and a limousine for his ride to work each morning. With these assets Brzezinski could travel with ease around official Washington, D.C., sit in on major policy meetings at the White House, and drop in on the president several times a day. He eventually met with the president so often that the in-house record keepers gave up trying to keep track of his drop-ins. No other member of the Carter administration had such opportunities for "amphibious" (insider-outsider) operations.[1]

Brzezinski also accompanied the president on his foreign trips, providing him an opportunity to cement their relationship. Sometimes he even joined Carter in his early morning runs. Though Brzezinski was not always enthusiastic about this latter activity, he had the kind of sense of humor that Carter relished. On the president's trip to Korea in the summer of 1979, for example, Brzezinski tried to dodge Carter's invitation to jog by stating he had neither his running shoes nor his shorts with him. Provided with shoes and shorts by the president, Brzezinski, at 5:30 the following morning, had no choice but to join Carter, a company of Marines, a general, and a camera crew on a ten-mile jog. Ever energetic, Carter made a point of running ahead of the entire company, leaving Brzezinski and his press secretary in the rear. With good humor, Brzezinski made the best of the situation by raising his hand as he ran by the camera, announcing that he and his press secretary "had done an extra lap."[2]

The Organizational Arrangements

Before he became president, Carter made it clear to Brzezinski "that he [Carter] wanted to make foreign policy...and the Secretary of State would execute his orders." From this pronouncement, Brzezinski concluded that the national security advisor would be an "initiator" as well as a "coordinator" of policy, not simply an honest broker.[3] What this meant, Brzezinski assured the president, was that the implementation would be relatively simple and responsive to his personal control, with the National Security Council (NSC) playing a central role in that process.[4] "He needed someone like me to do what I was doing," Brzezinski would later state. "Of course he could have found somebody else to do it for him, but until he had somebody else to do what I was doing, he needed someone like me."[5] Brzezinski's rationale, in effect, was that his power as national security advisor was the president's power.

Building on this idea, Brzezinski laid down the groundwork for what would become his domination over the foreign policy process. At the prepresidential planning session at Sea Island, Georgia, he had suggested seven NSC committees, three of which he would chair as national security advisor. When Carter said he wanted something simpler, Brzezinski came back with a plan for only two NSC committees. The Special Coordinating Committee (SCC), to be chaired by Brzezinski, was to concern itself with the Strategic Arms Limitation Treaty (SALT II) talks, intelligence policy issues, and crisis management. The Policy Review Committee (PRC), to be chaired by the State Department, and occasionally by the Department of Defense, would deal with broader foreign policy, defense, and international economic issues. What this meant was that the national security advisor should be in charge of the "hot" issues on the foreign policy agenda. Lower-level interdepartmental groups would deal with matters not requiring the attention of the higher officials of the government.[6] Presidential Directive 2 (PD 2), authorized by Carter on the eve of the inauguration, codified these new arrangements.[7]

Not only was Brzezinski the first national security advisor to chair an NSC subcommittee, the SCC, but he was also given the authority to control most of the paper flow coming in and out of all NSC meetings. Thus he prepared the Presidential Review Memos (PRMs) that directed the NSC to look into certain matters. When no conclusions were reached at a meeting, he would prepare the summary report for the president. If recommendations for policy actions were reached, Brzezinski would submit a presidential directive (PD) to Carter for signature. Moreover, the summaries or PDs were not to be circulated to the SCC or PRC participants for review before they went to the president. Thus, the national security advisor had the power to influence which reviews were undertaken and to make his own interpretation of SCC and PRC committee discussions and recommendations.[8]

Concerned that Brzezinski's voice would dominate these reports, Secretary of State Cyrus Vance on one occasion called Carter and Brzezinski to protest that the national security advisor had submitted summaries without prior consultation and to argue that SALT and crisis management should be the domain of the State Department.[9] The president told Vance that he was free to review Brzezinski's summaries in their draft stages at the White House. But for a busy secretary of state working in an office across town, this was not a realistic option.[10] Indeed, Brzezinski's rationale for handling these matters was that his physical proximity to the president meant that on issues for which Carter needed to be highly attentive—SALT II and international crises, for example—Brzezinski should take the lead. Essential communications, he added, were located in the situation room in the White House and thus were the domain of the national security advisor.[11]

Later, Vance would admit that he made a grave error in not pushing the president to require the draft memoranda be sent to the principals before they went on to the president. "The summaries quite often did not reflect adequately the complexity of the discussion or the full range of participants' views," he noted. "The reports were too terse to convey the dimensions and interrelationship of issues. Sometimes, when the summaries or PDs—with the President's marginal notes, or his initials or signature—arrived back at the State Department by White House courier....I found discrepancies, occasionally serious ones, from my own recollection of what had been said, agreed, or recommended."[12]

As national security advisor, Brzezinski also sidelined Admiral Stansfield Turner, Director of the Central Intelligence Agency. Though Turner had been a classmate of Carter at Annapolis, they were not good friends, as some observers surmised. Turner, not Carter, had been at the top of the class, and he was the one who had secured a Rhodes Scholarship. Indeed, Carter's disappointment that he never secured the Rhodes Scholarship for which he had applied suggests a competitive motivation rather than an accurate reading of his own relative position. Carter's academic ranking at the time of his graduation from The U.S. Naval Academy at Annapolis, Maryland, was 60 in a class of 877; his leadership aptitude grade, assigned by the faculty and the company commander, was 99 out of 822.[13]

Whatever the reason might have been, Brzezinski was able to edge Turner out of the traditional role in the morning intelligence briefing by simply changing the name of the meeting to "national security briefing." Nor was Turner a regular member of the Friday morning foreign policy breakfasts. When the president saw Turner—at first once a week, later only twice a month—Brzezinski was always in attendance. All major NSC decisions regarding the CIA would be vetted by the SCC or in private one-on-one meetings between Brzezinski and Turner. The CIA, in short, would be supervised by the National Security Council, a relationship Brzezinski saw as in keeping with the National Security Act of 1947.[14]

As for the content of the morning intelligence briefings, Brzezinski had a relatively free hand: "I had a half of an hour allotted to me...and I would therefore prepare myself before coming in...to tell him what line I intended to take or what I would push. Or I would take the opportunity to say, 'here is the policy dilemma, you have to really think about it, and this is the way I would perceive it and approach it.'"[15]

Brzezinski also monitored what others told the president on foreign policy matters. He was practically always at the president's side when foreign policy was being discussed.[16] A distinguished visitor wishing to see the president alone might find Brzezinski attending their meetings. Even W. Averell Harriman, a senior political influential and former ambassador to the Soviet Union, was unable to see the president alone at one point, despite expressing his wishes along these lines.[17]

Brzezinski also had the power to decide whether to send papers through the routine White House system or to give them to the president directly. One NSC aide estimated that Brzezinski reviewed "approximately three to four hundred pages a day and the President saw some fraction of that—something like a hundred or less than a hundred pages."[18] Brzezinski also forwarded many papers directly to the president without anyone else seeing them. Most matters he "felt strongly about" would be sent this way. Brzezinski sent Carter Weekly Reports on the state of the world, the administration's foreign policy, and the president's performance. These papers were "very candid personal papers, which just went from me to him and came straight back to me," notes Brzezinski. Broken down into three sections—opinion, alerts, and analyses—they were short, articulate pieces heavily laden with political advice as well as Brzezinski's particular views of the world.[19] Carter found these reports very valuable.[20]

By way of contrast, Vance had the opportunity to talk to the president during the weekly foreign policy breakfasts, but with Brzezinski, Walter Mondale, and Harold Brown present. Later, Deputy Secretary of State Warren Christopher, Press Secretary Jody Powell, Assistant to the President Hamilton Jordan, Senior Advisor Hedley Donovan, and Legal Counsel Lloyd Cutler attended the breakfast meetings.[21] Vance's nightly reports to the president, between two and five pages in length, summarized major events around the world, but very rarely contained policy advice.[22] Brown spent even less time with the president—about two-thirds as much time as Vance, plus a few telephone calls. His letters usually dealt with specific issues concerning weapons developments and related items.[23]

Eventually, Brzezinski would occasionally inform the president in writing about decisions enacted on his behalf. The president often asked for too many details. His solution to the problem, Brzezinski admits, was to make decisions without informing the president. "He'll discover it was done," Brzezinski would conclude.[24]

Over time, Brzezinski added to his own power base by becoming a chief policy spokesman for the administration. Vance had insisted during the transitional period that the secretary of state be the chief spokesman for the administration, and the president agreed with him at the time.[25] But by early 1978 Brzezinski was taking on that role. Though he was never formally charged with that task, the president did not object when he went out in front. As Brzezinski recalls, "There certainly was [conflict] between our [NSC and State Department] staffs....On the one hand I was made a spokesman; on the other hand, I was never designated as a spokesman and I was therefore attacked for speaking up....The problem was that we never clarified that we didn't have that system [president holding back; secretary of state as principal officer], to the degree it was necessary."[26]

Brzezinski was the first national security advisor to have his own press secretary. Jerry Schecter, formerly a *Time* magazine correspondent, filled the spot with the new title of associate press secretary. Brzezinski claimed that he did not employ Schecter to build up his personal image; instead, Schecter was hired to "make certain that the president's line on foreign policy was properly articulated," since Jody Powell "did not know much about foreign affairs."[27]

Brzezinski's role as policy spokesman, as both Carter and Vance would later note, was enhanced in part by Vance's vulnerabilities in this area.[28] Carter, Brzezinski claims, "wasn't satisfied with Vance's ability to articulate and present the case." He adds, "I think, though he never said it, that there was also some feeling that the nuances weren't quite right."[29] Carter has explained it this way:

> Now, Cy was not a shrinking violet or anything, but when we had a controversial policy to be presented to the public, Cy didn't want to do it…And if I wanted Cy to sit down with four or five of the top columnists, Scotty Reston, Joseph Kraft, and others, he wouldn't do it. I'm not saying this in criticism of Cy, it was just the way he was. Brzezinski on the other hand was always

eager to be the spokesman and he liked to be on *Meet the Press*, or brief the White House press corps on a non-attributable basis. So there were many times when I told Zbig to go ahead and do it.[30]

A further way in which Brzezinski enhanced his power was to expand the responsibilities of the National Security Council into the area of international economics. At first, NSC staffer Leslie Denend, whom William Odom describes as the "best economist…probably the only trained economist on the staff," largely worked alone, coordinating economic issues on an ad hoc basis.[31] But in 1978, with the president preparing for an international economic summit, Brzezinski suggested to the president that he formally appoint a person to be special representative for economic summit preparations and White House staff coordinator of international economic affairs. His nominee for this position was Henry Owen, who had joined the administration as a temporary consultant on economic summit planning.[32] Other government officers involved with international economic affairs, Brzezinski noted, welcomed Owen coming on board.[33]

But Stuart Eizenstat, the president's domestic policy advisor, did not like it. He wrote to Carter his strong objection to such an arrangement, noting, "Zbig and I wrote you a memo last summer in which we proposed to *share* the responsibility for the White House co-ordination of international economic issues, with the lead determined by the nature of the issue involved. You approved that memo."[34] Carter, however, sided with Brzezinski. Owen was appointed as special representative for economic summit preparations and follow-up.[35] Though he was not placed on the National Security Council staff payroll, Owen's influence would expand after Michael Blumenthal's departure from the Department of the Treasury. The coordinating, as Brzezinski noted, could then be exercised from the White House.[36]

Summarizing his own domination over the policy process, Brzezinski noted that secretaries of state Cyrus Vance and Edmund Muskie attempted to alter the system because of Brzezinski's control over most summaries going to the president. "Muskie eventually succeeded," he noted, "only to the extent that he was able to see the minutes of the meetings he chaired before we sent them to the President, and could make changes in them. He still couldn't see my cover note, and when he sometimes made changes in them, I wrote in a covering note saying, 'Mr. President, the Secretary of State has amended the minutes to read as follows….' He [Muskie] gained nothing from it."[37]

Brzezinski was also an efficient and effective chair of meetings. Odom, one of his top aides, noted that "he would come in and structure the discussion, pick out the two or three key points with lightning-like speed, drive the meeting to a conclusion, get some actionable recommendations, and get them to the President."[38] Typically, Brzezinski came in with a "slim memo" on the morning of the meeting. The other two cabinet secretaries brought "huge binders" with them.[39]

The NSC staff, too, did not manifest the kind of open rivalries that plagued Carter at the broader level. Given a free hand in the hiring of his own National Security Council staff, Brzezinski brought in top political aides, many of them former colleagues or students. Specialists dealing with matters of greatest concern to him—Soviet relations, Chinese relations, and arms limitation issues—shared his views and thus could work together with him as a harmonious team. In a bow to the concerns of the Trilateral Commission, Brzezinski created a new Office of Global Issues, headed by Jessica Tuchman, who had a PhD in molecular biology from the Massachusetts Institute of Technology.[40]

Yet whatever their own political views might have been, the staff, Leslie Denend said, "was remarkably substantive and did not make overtly political arguments."[41] Moreover, few NSC staff members had direct access to the president. Brzezinski's deputy William Odom saw Carter "a lot" in the first year of the administration, but "it became less often later." Leslie Denend and Madeleine Albright, who were "to some extent exceptions," saw Carter at meetings with members of the U.S. Congress, but Albright acknowledged, "Domestic policy staff members saw the President more."[42] It was Brzezinski who gave the political advice. In his role as advisor to the president, he was "markedly more pointed" than any of his staff members.[43]

Still, Brzezinski resisted outside review of his staff and its operations. When such a study was proposed, he wrote Carter on June 12, 1978, that it was unnecessary because the system was "working quite well."[44] Carter decided that the study should go ahead, but showed his faith in Brzezinski by indicating Brzezinski should be a part of the reorganization study.[45]

Backstopping Brzezinski

Carter gave Brzezinski his complete and absolute support. "Zbig...didn't have to protect his turf," Carter later testified, "I don't think he ever felt that Vance or Brown was coming between me and Zbig. Zbig and I had a relationship not nearly as close as Jody and I, but we joked with each other, we argued about issues, we were together four or five times every day. I started off my days meeting with Zbig." Even when Brzezinski pestered Carter about going to Taiwan or China or Germany, which he did a couple of times a week, their relationship did not suffer. Carter often said "hell no, you're not going, you're going to stay here." Their relationship seems never to have been impaired by these requests.[46]

Certainly Brzezinski was one of the few people Carter never reprimanded. Jody Powell and Hamilton Jordan were subordinates, Brzezinski noted, like sons to him. They could say things to Carter—"four letter words and things like that"—that Brzezinski never would utter, and Carter at times got mad at them. But Carter "never once was nasty" with his national security advisor. In four years, the president never once "raised his voice" or "growled" at Brzezinski.[47] Carter's memos to Brzezinski substantiate this view, indicating that Carter very seldom, if ever, was sharp with him.

And Carter dismissed all criticisms of Brzezinski that might come his way. When Vance complained to him on behalf of the State Department, Carter found the reports "in most instances" were "inaccurate or exaggerated; they had been precipitated by an honest difference of opinion, a leak from a subordinate officer in the State Department, or a speech or interview by Zbig concerning diplomatic philosophy or a particular item of public interest. Almost without exception, Zbig had been speaking with my approval and in consonance with my established and known policy. The underlying State Department objection was that Brzezinski had spoken at all."[48]

Instructive is Carter's handling of Vance's concern—after a surprise announcement that recognition of the People's Republic of China would soon take place—that the NSC was circumventing the State Department inappropriately. Rather than the private meeting Vance requested, Carter staged a confrontation between Vance and Brzezinski, with Vice President Walter Mondale and cabinet members Warren Christopher, David Aaron, and Hamilton Jordan as an audience.

Vance's charges were several—that Brzezinski had sent cables to Vance's ambassadors without his knowledge; that Warren Christopher and Richard Holbrooke, assistant secretary for the East Asian and Pacific Affairs, had been only belatedly brought into the negotiations with the Chinese; and that Brzezinski negotiated with the Chinese on normalization without informing the State Department.[49] Brzezinski was given a chance to respond. He claimed that Chinese relations had been assigned to him that "for the last twenty months there had been a fairly sustained press campaign directed at me, with much of it openly derived from State Department officials, and that I would like to be shown a single personal attack on Vance which clearly emanated from the NSC."[50]

Carter backed up Brzezinski. He had divided up responsibility for parts of the world between his two major advisors, he declared. Furthermore, the State Department was the source of personal leaks against Brzezinski. His national security advisor, he continued, "had been attacked more than any member of his administration, in part as a surrogate for attacks on himself." Brzezinski, he was suggesting, was a lightning rod—absorbing criticisms for the tough policies that the president embraced.[51] With regard to China, he wanted Brzezinski to get out in front, since the Chinese trusted him. Vance, he noted, bore major responsibility for SALT and the Middle East. The persons involved in the normalization process, were limited and chosen by Carter. Overall, the NSC system, Carter affirmed, was doing satisfactory work and he desired no changes to it.

On another occasion, Carter resisted suggestions that leaks might also originate in Brzezinski's organization. On August 9, 1978, Congressmen Bob Carr and Tom Downey wrote Carter that the details of his decision to seek a depressed-trajectory flight test ban at SALT II had been leaked to Clarence Robinson of *Aviation Weekly* magazine by a member of the National Security staff: "As we know, seeing a U.S. negotiating proposal in the press before they hear it from us has traditionally had an unfavorable influence on prospects of Soviet acceptance.…Even worse, the leaker has described the proposal as 'liable to set SALT back two years'—an extreme version of Dr. Brzezinski's reaction during our meeting."[52] Carter responded to the letter with a tough query: "What is the basis for your statement concerning a deliberate leak from NSC to *Aviation Week*? I doubt that this happened."[53]

Why the Carter–Brzezinski Tie?

When Carter awarded Brzezinski the Medal of Freedom near the end of his term in office, he noted, "I don't know of a single time in the last four years when he has ever made a public statement of any kind, privately or publicly, which was not compatible with my own policies."[54]

Beyond mere agreement, Jimmy Carter developed over time what in some respects was a symbiotic relationship with Brzezinski. Often the president "would repeat" something Brzezinski had told him one day "in the same words the next day."[55] Madeleine Albright, Brzezinski's legislative liaison at this time, confirms that: "Brzezinski really did have Carter's mind." If there was to be a "shoot-out" between new secretary of state Edmund Muskie and Brzezinski in a second term, Albright comments, "I would have picked Brzezinski as the winner." Indeed, the president relied "tremendously" on the ways in which Brzezinski presented information to him.[56]

Why did the president allow Brzezinski to exert this kind of influence? So great a chemistry between any two persons is bound to be a mystery to outside observers. But a closer look at the relationship between the two men may provide some insight.

Partly, Carter was dependent on Brzezinski for his foreign policy education. Brzezinski had been the first member of the foreign policy establishment to befriend Carter and was his chief foreign policy advisor and speechwriter in the 1976 presidential campaign.[57]

In office, Brzezinski not only controlled access to the president; his Weekly Reports gave the president feedback on the political responses to his messages, advice on framing issues, giving opinions about the impact of a particular policy on Carter's reputation.[58] Informal Saturday afternoon meetings with Carter often turned into mini-seminars, with Brzezinski telling a fascinated president about the internal workings of the USSR and other such matters. Occasionally Brzezinski misinformed Carter about an important historical event or drew a controversial conclusion.[59] But the president, who had little education in the field of foreign affairs, was in no position to reject those lessons. In his own words, Carter was "an eager student and took full advantage of what Brzezinski had to offer. As a college professor and author, he was able to express complicated ideas simply."[60] His specialty was Soviet and European affairs, Carter later noted, but he was interested in China, the Middle East, and Africa as well.[61]

Furthermore, Brzezinski rarely opposed the president directly on issues over which Carter had dug in his heels. Notable was Brzezinski's failure to speak out when the president stubbornly stuck to his campaign promise to withdraw U.S. troops from South Korea.[62] Prior to Carter's visit to Korea in July 1979, the CIA had come up with a reassessment of North Korean troop strength, suggesting that earlier assessments were about 30 percent low and the North Koreans were capable of attacking with almost no warning. Despite this information, Carter was not prepared to discuss the issue with Park Chung Hee in their meetings in Seoul. When the South Korean president, in their very first meeting, gave a long speech on the dangers of U.S. troop withdrawal to the security of his country, Carter was irritated but made no retort at the time. To avoid a possible rupture, Vance and others on the presidential team scurried around that afternoon to reach North Korean diplomats. They insisted Park should not raise the issue again that evening. A pleasant dinner ensued, with Carter drawing Park aside afterward to discuss certain Korean human rights issues. Later Carter "unburdened himself" in the presidential limousine. According to Vance, he indicated that he "felt isolated, opposed by all his advisers except Zbig."[63]

Other factors brought the two men together. Carter and Brzezinski were near the same age, had a similar sense of humor, appreciated good-looking women, liked the same foreign statesmen (Anwar Sadat of Egypt, Valéry Giscard d'Estaing of France, Deng Xiaoping of China), and shared a distaste for others (Helmut Schmidt of Germany and José Lopez Portillo of Mexico). They also enjoyed each other's company. Carter once said that if he were on a plane trip, the person he would most like to be beside him, other than Rosalynn, was Brzezinski. As for Brzezinski, he felt he could relate to the president easily: "I like him as a person. I like the way he thinks."[64]

The two men also may have identified with each other as outsiders. "I think we were both kind of strange birds," Brzezinski notes. "He was a Georgian and very conscious of the fact that he was a Georgian, and he was the first Southern president in a long time, and very conscious of the real or sensed hostility of others toward him as a Southerner and a Georgian. And maybe my sort of strange origins and mixture was kind of curious and interesting to him."[65]

More important, Carter needed and admired the strategic skills and the toughness in dealing with others that Brzezinski offered. Carter's hero had been the very exacting Admiral Hyman Rickover, and in his past he had always had a few individuals around him—Bert Lance, David Rabhan, even the younger Hamilton Jordan and Jody Powell—who performed some of the political services he needed to raise and sustain him in the political world. Brzezinski offered similar services in dealing with the Russians and the foreign policy establishment.[66]

Typical was advice Brzezinski offered Carter on February 24, 1978; echoing a theme found in Niccolò Machiavelli's The Prince, Brzezinski wrote that a president "must not only be loved and respected; he must also be feared." An impression has been formed, he went on to note, that this administration—especially Carter himself—operated cerebrally and quite unemotionally. To counter those who might wish to take advantage of them, the administration should at some point act "with a degree of anger and even roughness, designed to have a shock effect.... The central point is to demonstrate clearly that at some point obstructing the United States means picking a fight with the United States in which the president is prepared, and willing, to hit the opponent squarely on the head and to knock him down decisively."[67] The need to be tough was a recurrent theme in Brzezinsi's Weekly Reports, appearing at least nine times in those sent to Carter in 1977 and 1978 alone.[68]

More than that, Brzezinski made the kind of historical analogies that make "presidents feel they are doing big things."[69] In a memo he wrote to the president in the summer of 1978, Brzezinski claimed that success in normalizing relations with the Chinese would prove to be "a very major and historical accomplishment" for Carter.[70] In a remarkable memo written on December 28, 1978, Brzezinski explained the president's own Soviet policies, stating that the nation had a "historic chance to start shaping

FIGURE 3. Zbigniew Brzezinski and Jimmy Carter on *Air Force One*. Photograph courtesy of the Jimmy Carter Library.

a new global system, with the United States as its predominant coordinator if no longer the paramount power." Carter's policies, he suggested, could be categorized as "reciprocal accommodation." What that meant, he explained, was that the United States was following a policy of "containment," plus ideological competition, resistance to indirect expansion, and the creation of a framework within which the Soviet Union would accommodate the United States or face the prospect of global isolation.[71]

Brzezinski's presentations were congenial to the president's taste in another way. Brzezinski did not take much time to put across a point, and he did it clearly and simply. Brzezinski himself recalls that during the presidential campaign he "could communicate to him, crisply, to the point, and quickly. . . . I'd get in the car and say, 'Look, four things you need to know, the things you need to do, the things you need to say'—like that, bang, bang, bang—that's it, finish, okay, bye—that's it."[72]

The national security advisor's ability to simplify things is evident in the memo he provided Carter shortly after the Soviet intervention in Afghanistan. In five short bullet points he summarized Soviet objectives over several decades. The 1940s was marked by postwar disarmament and "Soviet probes for Western weakness." The 1950s hallmarks were the Iron Curtain and Korean Conflict. The 1960s were a period of "premature Soviet global challenge and increasing competition in other areas"— namely, space, economics, Vietnam, and Cuba. "Détente and the continued buildup of Soviet strength" were the earmarks of the 1970s. The 1980s, Brzezinski predicted, would be known for "the danger of conflict in the context of wider global turbulence."[73] Brzezinski, in short, had a quick tongue and a sharp mind.[74]

Indeed, Brzezinski's ability to articulate a broad historical perspective, outline strategies, come up with quick and attractive solutions to difficult questions, and maintain control over his staff were no doubt the basis for Carter's views that the National Security Council was capable of more creative and decisive action than were Vance and the Department of State. As Carter came to see it, the national security advisor put together an efficient, creative, and harmonious staff: "They were particularly adept at incisive analyses of strategic concepts, and were prolific in the production of new ideas, which were unrestrained in their proposals, and consequently had to reject a lot of them. And, in the resulting discussions, we often found a better path worth following. Zbigniew was a first-rate thinker, very competent in his choice of staff members and able to work harmoniously with them. I do not remember any dissension at all."[75]

The State Department, by way of contrast, served to restrain action. Vance, Carter noted in many ways, was much like the organization he headed. Experienced, smart, honorable, as well as sound in his judgments, Vance was inquisitive, loyal, and protective of the State Department and its status and heritage. But the department, Carter concluded, seldom came up with innovative foreign policy solutions.[76]

Brzezinski and his staff, in short, appealed to Carter's desire to do new big things and act quickly. The nature of this appeal as delineated by Gary Sick, was that "Brzezinski was the very antithesis of Cyrus Vance.... This restless energy and persistent pursuit of fresh approaches made Brzezinski a natural alter ego to Jimmy Carter's activism. Brzezinski sparked new ideas at a dazzling rate and refused to be constrained by the status quo in devising his strategies. Although Carter probably rejected more of Brzezinski's ideas than he accepted, he obviously valued the irreverent inventiveness that Brzezinski brought to any subject."[77]

Brzezinski reflected only one side of Carter, as we shall see in more detail later. Like Brzezinski, Carter wanted to be seen as tough. But he also wanted to secure peace and achieve other great and idealistic goals. What this meant, as Leslie Gelb, later to become the president of the Council on Foreign Relations, explains, was that Carter's instinct was one of cooperation. But if that did not work he would then be "firm with the Soviets," purportedly to raise the "odds of a cooperative solution."[78]

A somewhat different proposition is offered in the present work. Vance, it seems, appealed to one side of Carter's brain, Brzezinski to the other. When Carter was clear as to his goals and the diplomacy needed for their accomplishment, Vance and his colleagues in the State Department would have an open field. But in "big power" relationships, where Carter simultaneously desired to cooperate and compete, he would be subjected to a tug of war between his two top advisors and the allies each gathered along the way. In these battles, Brzezinski had the advantage. The collegial system that Carter had favored at the beginning of his presidency evolved into a system in which Brzezinski was the first among equals. A master at bureaucratic politics, Brzezinski knew how to use his organizational position, as well as his personal relationship to the president, to get the better of policy battles.

The bottom line is that Brzezinski had this advantage because the president wanted to control foreign policy. He had become convinced that the key to this control was relying on a national security advisor he trusted. What we can note at this time is that Carter, an inexperienced president, placed in Brzezinski's hands the formal position and control over access he sought. This allowed the national security advisor to lead the president in the direction he thought best. Whether or not Brzezinski actually served the president well is one of the concerns of this book. The nature of Brzezinski's influence and his conflicts with Vance is particularly salient in the battle over SALT II—an item Carter had placed at the top of his foreign policy agenda.

Part 2
EARLY COMMITMENTS

EARLY FUMBLES

Two months after Jimmy Carter took office as president, Secretary of State Cyrus Vance and Arms Control and Disarmament Agency (ACDA) head Paul Warnke, accompanied by an entourage of advisors and media people, arrived at Moscow's Vnukovo Airport with arms limitation proposals in hand. On Sunday, March 27, the weather was mild, with an unusually light scattering of snow on the ground. The greeting from Soviet Foreign Minister Andrei Gromyko was warm, and Secretary Vance was given the traditional bouquet of red carnations. During the ride into Moscow, General Secretary Leonid Brezhnev extended his own welcome to the secretary of state via car phone. That night Vance and Gromyko attended the Bolshoi Ballet for a delightful performance of *Anna Karenina*.[1]

Vance had two proposals to deliver. The preferred deep cuts proposal would require a substantial reduction in land-based intercontinental ballistic missiles (ICBMs) and impose stringent limits on qualitative improvements in weapons. A second proposal—the deferral option—was built on previous exchanges among President Gerald Ford, Secretary of State Henry Kissinger, and Brezhnev at the 1974 summit at Vladivostok.[2] These proposals were of major importance to the new president. Carter had pledged to work toward the elimination of nuclear weapons from the world both in his campaign autobiography *Why Not the Best?* and in his inaugural address.[3] And in his first letter to Brezhnev, Carter had written that an armaments race could be avoided given perseverance and wisdom.[4]

But when the conference opened on the morning of Monday, March 28, the Soviet moves were far from positive. Brezhnev brushed aside Vance's attempt to present these proposals to him. "Such technical matters should be dealt with by others," he said. Later, over a luncheon of caviar and white salmon, Gromyko picked up on a theme that Brezhnev had introduced in the first meeting; the Soviet Foreign Minister warned that the U.S. human rights push was a serious mistake.[5] The White House had vetoed another fallback option for which Vance had earlier sought approval.

Not until the third day did Brezhnev return to the conference. Entering the meeting room, Vladimir Lenin's old study in the Kremlin, he seemed out of sorts. When he spoke, he blasted both U.S. proposals by calling them "inequitable." The U.S. deep cuts proposal, as he saw it, would cut in half the Soviet land-based heavy missiles, while the United States would only defer certain technological innovations. Moreover, he suggested that raising new issues such as these would lead the Soviet Union to insist that the issue of European-based nuclear missiles should be revisited. As the proposal stood, Brezhnev charged, thousands of missiles could be dropped on the Soviet Union from Europe. Except for a proposal to meet again in May to consider more

Table 5. Weapons Systems: Abbreviations and Definitions

ABM	Antiballistic Missiles
ALCM	Air Launched Cruise Missile
Backfire Bomber	Soviet long-range, supersonic strategic bomber cruise missiles with the capacity for aerial refueling; Backfire A (1971/72); Backfire B (1972); Backfire C (1976)
B-1 Bomber	U.S. intercontinental range bomber; B1-A (1970); B1-B (1980) developed high speed and radar navigation
B-2 Bomber	U.S. stealth bomber; top speed below speed of sound; travels 6,900 miles (11,102 km) without refueling; refuels in flight; low observability by hiding from radar and infrared sensors; developed in the late 1970s
Cruise Missile	Unmanned self-propelled guided vehicle that flies close to the ground and is equipped with a built-in navigational system that allows it to deliver its single bomb
GLCM	Ground Launched Cruise Missile
ICBM	Inter-Continental Ballistic Missile; range greater than 3,418 miles (5,500 km)
INF	Intermediate-range Nuclear Forces; nuclear-armed ballistic and cruise missiles with a range between 311 and 3,418 miles (500 and 5,500 km)
IRBM	Intermediate-Range Ballistic Missile; range between 1,664 and 3,418 miles (3,000 and 5,500 km)
Launcher	Complex consisting of related facilities used for firing missiles, usually including a launch pad, liquid propellant storage tanks, site instrumentation
Mark 12A	Re-entry system for missiles, consisting of a payload mounting platform, penetration aids, three reentry vehicles, and an aerodynamic shroud
Minuteman Missiles	U.S. land-based ICBMs; Minuteman I (1962); Minuteman II (1965); Minuteman III (1970); Minuteman III was the first MIRV-ed ICBM—capable of carrying multiple (2 or 3) warheads and directing each to a separate target; its guidance system also referred to as NS 20 guidance system
MIRV	Multiple Independently Targeted Re-Entry Vehicles; increased the number of warheads/missiles (whether land or sea-based) with greater accuracy and less collateral damage
MX	U.S. "Missile Experimental" ICBM under development since 1971; designed to replace the Minuteman III by carrying 10 warheads and having a range of 6,835 miles (11,000 km); entered service in 1986
Neutron Bomb	Enhanced Radiation Weapon (ERW); considered an anti-missile designed to protect U.S. missile silos; produces neutron radiation that harms biological tissues and electrical systems otherwise protected from the heat blast without causing nuclear fallout; tactically intended to kill soldiers protected by armor
Pershing II Missile	U.S. IRBM with a terminally guided reentry vehicle; effective in covering longer ranges with reduced collateral damage over the Pershing Ia; first fired in 1977
Polaris	SLCMs first successfully tested in 1960 by the Navy; on submarines
SLCM	Sea (or Submarine) Launched Cruise Missile

(continued)

Table 5. *(continued)*

Soviet Heavy Missiles	Soviet ICBMs (SS-16, -18, and -19) that could carry several MIRVs or warheads and had ranges over 6,214 miles (10,000 km); SS-18 was most feared because of its alleged threat to U.S. ICBM silos
Strategic weapons	Intercontinental weapons designed to attack targets to debilitate an enemy's capacity to wage war, i.e., urban, industrial, and military centers
Throw-weight	The size of the nuclear warhead or set of warheads that a missile can carry
TRIAD	Air, Ground (Land), and Sea Launched Cruise Missiles
Trident Missiles	Trident I and II missiles were SLBMs; Trident II had a range of 4,000 nautical miles (7,360 km); Trident Submarine was a ballistic missile submarine class in the U.S. Navy
Warhead	The part of the missile that contains the nuclear explosive; the size may vary and is used to count in determining limits as applied to deployed ICBMs, SLBMs, and heavy bombers

limited options and resolve some of issues leftover from Vladivostok, no other alternatives were explored. The meeting, which had lasted only fifty minutes, broke up. The Americans gloomily stuffed papers into their briefcases and headed back to the U.S. embassy to inform Carter of the impasse.[6] Tass, the Soviet news agency, said Carter was using "propaganda tactics" to shape U.S. disarmament views.[7]

At a press conference in Moscow, Vance attempted a recovery, suggesting that the United States had presented two new but fair and equitable proposals—one for major cuts, the other based on Vladivostok. Not only did the Soviets reject both of them outright, they did not even propose any alternatives of their own.[8] In a rare move, Gromyko countered with his own press conference. Giving the figures in the American proposal that Vance had refused to reveal, Gromyko accused Carter of "seeking a public victory, and proposing a deliberately unacceptable set of proposals." His motives, Gromyko explained, were to counter what he saw as an American propaganda effort.[9] After the meeting in Moscow, Warnke remembers Gromyko saying, "Just as fast as a snake you were in press conferences trying to make us look bad."[10]

Back in Washington, word of the breakdown cast a pall over the White House. Administration officials had not expected an immediate acceptance of the basic proposal, but they had not expected such a crude rejection. "Appointments were being canceled left and right," said one aide.[11]

In a hastily called press conference, Carter tried to put a good face on the recent occurrence. "Hi everybody," he said as he strode to the podium. He was not discouraged, he insisted. But as one news reporter noted, he seemed shaken by the turn of events.[12] Negotiations would proceed but he warned that if the Soviets did not bargain in "good faith" in the future he would have to "consider a much more deep commitment to the development and deployment of additional weapons."[13]

On April 1, Brzezinski added fuel to the fire, charging that the Soviets had rejected a reasonable and equitable proposal. Deep cuts in land-based missiles, he offered, would have promoted stability in the nuclear balance.[14] Paul Warnke, however, would not join in this chorus, rejecting Brzezinski's suggestion that he appear on NBC's *Meet the Press* to defend the administration's position. Any effort to publicly defend the proposal, he thought, would amount to the United States painting itself in a corner from which it would be hard to escape.[15]

The response of the mainline U.S. press to this setback was almost universally negative. Brezhnev, *Newsweek* noted, had "handed Jimmy Carter his first major foreign policy setback and left Soviet-American relations at their chilliest state in years."[16] Hedrick Smith of the *New York Times* reported that Soviet specialists saw this impasse in negotiation with the Kremlin as the "worst public turn in Soviet-American relations in five years of détente" and held the Carter administration responsible for the debacle.[17]

Even Henry Kissinger, Richard Nixon's and Gerald Ford's secretary of state, seemed to take wry "satisfaction at the setback for the Carter administration." The Soviet Ambassador Anatoly Dobrynin remembers Kissinger telling him that Carter, "for all his sincere desires for disarmament…tried to be different from all other administrations in every respect. In fact, he was so bent on doing things his own way that he would not even repeat the good moves made by his predecessors."[18] Carter's entry on the world political scene, in short, was marked by a fumble.

What Might Have Been

If Carter had started with a more modest proposal, the United States and the USSR might have quickly capped a process initiated by the Ford/Kissinger team. The two countries had already agreed on a major limitation of nuclear weapons at the 1974 summit in Vladivostok. Going beyond the first round of Strategic Arms Limitation Treaty talks (SALT I), the Soviets had accepted the American demand for numerical equality in all launchers. The numbers were set sufficiently high so that the Soviets would not have to dismantle a large number of their existing launchers and could still expand their smaller force of multiple independently targeted reentry vehicle (MIRV) launchers. The Soviets had also agreed to drop any count of American nuclear weapons in Europe, and, in exchange, the United States had agreed to drop their demand for a reduction in the number of heavy Soviet launchers. Finally, the United States had agreed to include its strategic bombers in the total of 2,400.

The stumbling block to any further progress revolved around the issue of what to do with the Soviet Backfire bomber and the U.S. cruise missiles. Until those matters were resolved, forward motion could not be expected. The deferral option Vance offered in Moscow did not address those issues. Still, "SALT could have been terminated very quickly, in time for a summit at the beginning of 1977," notes Dobrynin. Instead, U.S.-USSR tensions rose, especially in Africa with the "irritant [issue] of human rights."[19]

Indeed, Kissinger, who flew down to Carter's hometown of Plains, Georgia, shortly after the 1976 elections, had advised the president-elect that Vladivostok created no special problems in terms of the overall balance between the two countries. The Soviets, he admitted, were ahead on "throw weight [and] number of strategic delivery vehicles," and were "catching up in MIRVs." But the United States had decided "not to have as many strategic systems as the Soviet Union." In the area of cruise missiles, the United States was ahead of the Soviets by three to five years. Moreover, the United States had the option to build up its launchers, thereby meeting attacks from the political right that the U.S. government had agreed upon unequal numbers.[20]

One could deal with the Soviet leaders, Kissinger assured Carter. They ordinarily did not make false offers, "though their interpretation of what they mean may vary from ours." Brezhnev, Kissinger continued, would never directly lie about an issue, though he might become vague when it was to the Soviet advantage.[21]

Kissinger also suggested a possible course of action. The Soviets were prepared to yield on their insistence that cruise missiles be counted in the total ceiling of 2,400 delivery systems and Brezhnev might be induced to write a letter to President Carter on how many Backfires would be deployed by 1985, the year the agreement would be coming to an end. If they decided in the main agreement to prohibit aircraft upgrade, that—along with some reductions—would "make a deal possible and desirable."[22]

The U.S. military establishment, Kissinger warned, could become an obstacle to further deals. Kissinger had expected a "rapid conclusion of the SALT II agreement" after the Vladivostok Accords. But the issues of the Backfire bombers and MIRVs intervened, Kissinger explained. Initially introduced in the SALT talks as bargaining chips, they had developed sanctity of their own. The Soviets took the view that a tradeoff had been made. They had given up insisting that U.S. forward-based systems be included in an agreement (i.e., weapons in Europe), in exchange for an understanding that their middle-range system (the Backfire bomber) would not be included in the agreement.[23]

But Carter was not content to just build on the work of his predecessors. In the 1976 election campaign he had run against the Ford-Kissinger Soviet policies. The reference to the Soviet Union as a "warlike power" in the draft of his speech announcing his run for president was only dropped when an aide told him it sounded too "Jacksonian."[24] In his television commercials that aired in the South, he piggybacked on Ronald Reagan's critiques of the Ford/Kissinger détente policies, claiming that he "had no illusions about Russia's intentions."[25] In his foreign policy debate with President Ford on October 6, 1976, Carter charged, "the Soviet Union knows what they want in détente....We have not known what we wanted, and we've been out traded in almost every instance."[26] Somewhat paradoxically, he also criticized Ford for abandoning the term *détente*.[27]

As president, however, he did follow a routine similar to that of the Nixon/Kissinger team. The confidential channels from Moscow to Dobrynin's office and between the secretary of state and the U.S. president would be maintained. Most of Carter's correspondence with Brezhnev traveled through these channels, and a number of high-level diplomatic meetings took place with Dobrynin at the White House and the Soviet embassy in Washington, as well as at the State Department.[28] The result was that Ambassador Malcolm Toon in Moscow, a Soviet expert fluent in Russian, was largely ignored in the president's dealings with the Soviet government. So was Tom Watson Jr., who replaced him in late 1979.[29]

But unlike the Nixon–Kissinger team, Carter wanted a radical reduction of ICBMs. As president-elect, he suggested that their numbers be cut to 200. Alarmed, the Joint Chiefs of Staff informed him that cuts of this order could undermine nuclear deterrence. The United States had to possess a sufficient number of weapons so that it could survive a first strike from the Soviet Union and respond in kind. Deep cuts could give an advantage to an adversary who might choose to strike first. They went on to suggest that no major concession should be made concerning cruise missiles. Their very mobility made it almost impossible for them to be located by an adversary and taken out in a first strike. Observing these discussions, Brzezinski later wrote, it was "unclear to me at the time whether the Joint Chiefs of Staff were more astonished by this notion [of deep cuts] or more tempted to exploit it."[30]

The Road to Moscow

Backing off from his more radical proposals, Carter, in one of his first interviews as president, said it might be best to work first from the Vladivostok Accords, postponing the two major issues on which contention remained—the Backfire bomber and cruise missiles. Following that, a SALT III agreement could bring about additional reductions in long-range missiles and for the first time apply stringent limits on the short- and intermediate-range weapons being heavily deployed in Eastern and Western Europe. Similar views were expressed in Carter's press conferences of February 8 and March 9, 1977. In his first communications with Brezhnev, noted above, he urged the Soviet leader to support "a SALT agreement without delay," and suggested that they meet personally to discuss the remaining issues.[31]

Still, Carter at this time had not made a clear strategic choice on whether he should go slow or seek drastic reductions from the very beginning.[32] To complicate matters further, his top four advisors on arms control held different opinions on the matter. Vance and Warnke, the latter of whom headed the ACDA, favored a gradualist approach on arms limitation. Brzezinski saw the Soviets as being on the move politically and suggested using the deep cuts as a test. Their refusal, he implied, would reveal their true motivation. If they chose to work with the U.S. SALT II proposals, the momentum of the Soviet military buildup would be stopped or slowed down.[33] On the other hand, a Soviet rejection might also be advantageous, providing a propaganda victory for the United States, enabling the administration to establish its own record on arms control.[34] Secretary of Defense Harold Brown favored cuts, but at a more realistic level than Carter proposed. Back in May 1976, as an advisor to the presidential candidate, Brown had noted that the U.S. goal should be to enhance "stable deterrence at a lower level of force than now exists." The figure of 2,000, he noted, "Would send a welcome signal to the world…a goal of 1000 strategic weapons should be sought by 1986."[35]

A variety of proposals would be on the table in the Special Coordinating Committee (SCC) and National Security Council (NSC) meetings that followed. These ranged from the Vladivostok formula or some minor modification thereof, to "deep cuts" of the sort envisaged by Brown, to Carter's desire for even deeper cuts. Brzezinski's role, as he later noted, was to keep these alternatives on the table throughout the talks.[36] The available documentary records suggest, however, that it was Carter himself who put the deep cuts option on the docket and played a role in its staying there.

Brzezinski placed himself at the center of the process. At the SCC meeting on February 3, for example, Brzezinski asked Carter to preside for a short time, and when he left, to turn the meeting back over to Brzezinski. National security advisors in the past had not chaired cabinet-level meetings, and by this move the president would legitimate Brzezinski's occupation of an unprecedented position.[37]

At the meeting, Carter called for an analysis of the impact of "profound mutual reductions" on overall nuclear capability. To reassure the Joint Chiefs, he stated that he would not forward any arms reduction proposals without their adequate prior consultation. Moreover, he could make tough choices. He would hate to order nuclear strikes, but had no intention of forgoing their use to defend the United States or its European allies. "We need to let our allies know what we are doing," he continued, but "not allow their nervousness to drive our negotiations."[38] After Carter left, the participants agreed that two packages would be prepared: one would be based on the 1976 Vladivostok agreements and variations thereof; the other would envision significant reductions.

The quick solution of opting for what Kissinger and Ford had done (i.e., accepting Vladivostok numbers and deferring on the Backfire bomber and cruse missiles) was seen as a negotiating alternative. But Brzezinski advised the president against adopting the quick solution of simply opting for the Ford–Kissinger compromise—that is, accepting the Vladivostok numbers and deferring the still unresolved issues of the Backfire bomber and cruise missiles. Rather, he suggested it might not be "politically desirable" to defer these two issues since doing so would generate "criticism" that the agreement was "too narrow in scope."[39]

Deep cuts were kept on the agenda at subsequent meetings, many of which the president was too busy to attend. On February 25, for example, three approaches were outlined. The first alternative was designed to maintain Vladivostok levels, though it would reduce the number of permitted launchers from 2,400 to 2,300. The second alternative countenanced "significant reductions" to about 2,000. The third proposed "major reductions" to about 1,500. All proposals dealt with MIRV subceilings, varying treatments of Backfire and cruise missiles, and various ways of dealing with mobile ICBMs.[40] On March 10, the SCC considered four options—three of which Brzezinski characterized as Vladivostok-based proposals, and the fourth of which he described as the "deep cuts" option. The proposal, an overall aggregate of 2,000 launchers, matched Brown's preelection recommendation and was a compromise between the original Vladivostok numbers of 2,400 and the deep cuts option of 1,500 at the February 25 meeting.[41]

At a "principals only" meeting on March 12, Carter personally expressed his desire for "real" arms control and his impatience with the Vladivostok formula. Vice President Walter Mondale also stated his support for the new proposal, as did Secretary Brown, who attended the meeting at Brzezinski's request. Though the invitation of Brown, Brzezinski later explained, was to achieve "greater balance," it tilted the meeting toward the preliminary adoption of the deep cuts option. With the president, vice president, and secretary of defense behind the deep cuts option, Vance fell in line. As an incentive, he was told that he could take two fall back positions with him to Moscow.[42]

A few days later, Vance and Warnke wrote Carter that the deep cuts proposal was a long shot. But "it might be that the Soviets, confronting a new President and the prospect of having to deal with him for at least four or perhaps eight years, would be willing to take a bold step. We would not know unless we tried."[43] At no point did either man voice his concern about this option with any vigor. Warnke later admitted he and Vance had "[not] fought that hard to try and get a Vladivostok proposal as contrasted to the deep cuts option" because they thought that "politically it might not be a bad play." Vance rationalized his compromise by shifting to the hope that the proposals would provide a foundation on which further negotiations and relationships could flourish.[44] As Deputy Under Secretary of Defense Walter Slocombe later explained, nobody opposed deep cuts.[45]

On March 17, Carter unveiled his deep cuts proposal, albeit in broad strokes, in a speech before the United Nations General Assembly. Soviet suspicions that the sensation was part of an anti-Soviet propaganda campaign were reinforced when he later announced his intention to increase funds for Radio Free Europe and Radio Liberty shortly before the Moscow conference.[46]

That evening Carter sought to bring Kissinger on board. At a White House dinner, as Carter remembers it, Kissinger told him that there was a strong possibility that the Soviets, if they were sincere, would accept the SALT deep cuts proposal.[47] Carter never even considered the possibility that Kissinger might not wish to level with a naïf from Plains, Georgia, who during the presidential campaign had undertaken a running attack on his détente policies, critiqued his "lone ranger" decision-making style, ignored the advice he had given in Plains, and was now trying to outdo him. Kissinger would later tell journalist Strobe Talbott that he did not recall the exchange.[48]

Carter was still not satisfied. On March 19, two days after his talk with Kissinger and presentation to the UN, Carter was back with recommendations for even greater cuts than Brown or anyone else had ever proposed. The caps on ICBMs, he suggested, should be reduced from 2,000 to 1,800. The MIRVed ICBMs cuts should be reduced from 1,200 to 1,100.[49]

The deep cuts proposal to be taken to Moscow, it turns out, was not as low as the president suggested on March 19. The March 23 PD/NSC 7 negotiating guidelines envisaged two "acceptable" outcomes. The preferred alternative would be the "reductions to a level of about 2000"—a figure to include the cruise missiles and the Backfire bomber. It was clearly a compromise between something close to the Vladivostok Accords favored by the State Department and the ACDA, and the president's more extreme proposals. The second alternative, a fallback position Vance had no chance to present at Moscow, would accept the Vladivostok Accords as a base, deferring the Backfire bomber and cruise missile controversy to a SALT III treaty.[50]

Carter had placed a very deep cuts option on the table at the first NSC meeting dealing with the matter and it remained there with the help of Brown and Brzezinski until its final adoption, albeit in a more moderate form. It appears then that Talbott was wrong when he suggested that it was Brown who prepared and delivered "like a beautifully tied, juicy fly dropped right in front of a hungry trout's nose" the deep cuts alternative that the president bit and swallowed.[51]

Still, as Talbott suggested, the deep cuts plan was never vetted like the more moderate options as they worked their way up to the agenda. In any event, several arms professionals in the State Department and the Central Intelligence Agency (CIA) were stunned when they realized what the official proposal contained. The possible response of the USSR to the proposal, and the consequence of a potential outright rejection, never seemed to be explored.[52]

Throughout this whole process Carter pursued his human rights campaign vis-à-vis the Soviets with vigor. The campaign was undertaken despite warnings from several disparate sources. Kissinger had cautioned Vance in their first meeting that a public confrontation over human rights should be avoided.[53] The State Department alerted Carter to the possible negative consequences of his direct correspondence with the dissident Soviet physicist Andrei Sakharov.[54] Dobrynin warned the administration that the human rights campaign would impede negotiations.[55] By mid-February, Vance, who at first embraced the human rights campaign, was a bit concerned that the focus on dissidents could be counterproductive both in terms of U.S.-Soviet relations and SALT II negotiations.[56] Even the tough U.S. ambassador to the Soviet Union, Malcolm Toon, tried to distance himself from the Carter campaign. Ducking his first assignment—to deliver Carter's letter to Sakharov—he sent a junior officer in his place. Warned by Soviet officials that another meeting with Sakharov would finish him in Moscow, Toon generally tried to distance the embassy from Carter's human rights concerns. His fear was that any incident might slow down the SALT II process.[57]

The Soviet leaders saw the human rights enterprise as an attempt to delegitimize their regime in both the USSR and Eastern Europe.[58] They might have been even more concerned if they had learned that sometime in March 1977 Carter had authorized Brzezinski's proposal to consider undertaking human-rights-related covert operations in Eastern Europe. Though the most ambitious proposals would be whittled down by the State Department and CIA analysts, the Carter administration would eventually obtain materials from behind the Iron Curtain and circulate them via radio and the clandestine CIA distribution network in a propaganda campaign that in its "determination and intensity" differed "from its predecessors."[59]

SALT II: What Happened

The Soviet leaders wanted to deal. The arms race was putting a strain on the Soviet economy, and Brezhnev, recalling the devastation of Soviet society during World War II, made the avoidance of World War III one of his major goals. Indeed, W. Averell Harriman, a former ambassador to the Soviet Union, told Carter on a trip to Plains that the Soviets were "quite insistent on making him understand that his business of testing U.S. presidents was nonsense and that in any case they certainly planned no such unpleasant surprises for the Carter presidency."[60]

Then why did the Soviets so bluntly reject the U.S. deep cuts proposals presented to them? Clearly the proposals were an attempt to secure an advantage through diplomacy. They cut deeply into land-based missiles, in which the Soviets were particularly strong, and would have curtailed modernization programs in which the Soviets were already engaged. The United States, as Talbott has pointed out, was "seeking substantial reductions in existing Soviet systems in exchange for marginal cuts in future American ones."[61]

Brezhnev's credibility in the USSR was also on the line. He had made it clear the Soviet Union would not approve of any major departures from the Vladivostok Accords, and the principle of equality they saw recognized therein. In a speech in Tula, Russia, on January 18, 1977, Brezhnev stated that the Soviet Union did not seek military superiority or any capacity beyond what is sufficient for deterrence. "Détente," he said, "is above all an overcoming of the 'cold war,' a transition to normal, equal relations between states…and it takes into account the legitimate interests of one another."[62] In his February 4 letter to Carter, Brezhnev insisted that any deliberations must be completely equitable and that the tradition of "noninterference in the internal affairs of the other side" remained paramount. He stressed that personal meetings between the two leaders should be of special importance "if progress towards arms reduction were to be made."[63] Dobrynin, too, had clearly warned Vance that the proposals the United States was taking to Moscow would provide no basis for discussion.[64]

In making these commitments at Vladivostok, Brezhnev had put himself out ahead of many of his military leaders. Dobrynin recalls that the Soviet minister of defense at the time, Andrei Grechko, protested some of the concessions Brezhnev had made in these negotiations. The conversation proceeded as follows:

> GRECHKO: "You are conceding too much to the Americans. I, as a minister, disagree with you, Mr. Secretary General…and many people in the Politburo agree with me."
>
> BREZHNEV: "I think the deal we are making with the Americans in Vladivostok is a good one. If I will listen what you say, we will destroy this treaty, and for how many years will we have no treaty at all?"
>
> GRECHKO: "No, no, Leonid Ilych; do not take it as an affront. If you feel this way, go ahead."[65]

This was the first time Brezhnev was challenged openly. But the Americans compounded his political problems at home. When President Ford, in the heat of the 1976 presidential campaign, abandoned the term "détente," the United States seemed to be abandoning the very foundation of the agreement Brezhnev had worked so hard to achieve.

When Carter as president went a step beyond Ford by personally leading the human rights campaign and rendering up a SALT II proposal that went beyond Vladivostok, the Politburo met in a special session to consider how they should counter the "subversive" policies of the new U.S. administration. Brezhnev's letter of February 25, which one Russian saw as relatively "polite," reflected their concerns. Carter was informed that the proposal for deep cuts was "deliberately unacceptable" and a direct violation of specific terms agreed upon earlier in Vladivostok. Brezhnev also took a shot at Carter's human rights stance, charging that he was intervening in Soviet internal affairs under the guise of "pseudo-humanitarian slogans."[66]

Carter felt personally insulted by some of the "frank" language in the letter. And Brzezinski reinforced Carter's indignation, saying that he found Brezhnev's letter "brutal, cynical, sneering and even patronizing."[67] As he wrote the president on March 5, "the Brezhnev response to you might be a foretaste of some very hard bargaining, and it is quite conceivable that our first report to the American people on SALT II negotiations will have to emphasize not areas of agreement but the reasons why we have been unable to agree."[68] Only one American in the inner circle, Cyrus Vance, took Brezhnev's tough letter seriously. As he told Dobrynin, he personally welcomed plain language by a Soviet general secretary who "does not beat around the bush."[69]

In his reply to Brezhnev, Carter sternly noted that "no final agreement was ever reached at Vladivostok or in subsequent negotiations regarding cruise missiles or the Backfire bomber," and he asked Brezhnev to cease "erroneous assumptions" about the sincerity and integrity of the American government.[70] It was at this time that Carter thought about playing another political card. He might take new initiatives toward China.[71]

This was not the end of the exchange. The Politburo also had a card to play. At a meeting held shortly before the U.S. mission was to arrive in Moscow, the decision to reject the two American proposals outright was made. "Around the table," the Politburo members demanded that Brezhnev "show the Americans how we are strong and they are not serious."[72] Carter had forgotten, in a phrase that the Soviets often used, that "it takes two to tango."

As for the American leaders, they carried away a variety of lessons from this setback. Perhaps not too surprisingly, Brzezinski was not particularly upset at the Soviet response. He had always seen U.S. policy as putting pressure on the Soviet Union. He wrote in his diary on March 30, the eve of the conference, "We have developed an approach, which is very forthcoming; on the one hand, we are urging reductions, with the other hand we are urging a freeze, and at the same time we are urging for more recognition for human rights.... However, all of that could begin to collapse if any of our colleagues begins to act weak-kneed and starts urging that we start making concessions to the Soviets."[73] He even saw the failure in Moscow as a sort of success. As he wrote Carter on April 1, "By committing ourselves to reductions, we have made the Soviets seem opposed to arms limitations. In the past, they have often made the United States look as if it was opposed to arms limitations. The tables have now been turned." He even found some foreign newspapers that welcomed Carter's stance as a positive indicator that the United States was at last getting tough with the Soviet Union.[74]

Vance admitted that the Americans made some serious substantive miscalculations. The Soviets, he said, may have had legitimate concerns about the comprehensive proposal. It would cut into the land-based missiles, which constituted the bulk of their strategic political cost in the past. Or, it might have been viewed as an attempt at a propaganda victory.[75] Warnke would later note that the Soviets took Vladivostok as a deal and viewed the later U.S. proposals as reneging on that deal.[76] Brown, in his retrospective on the Moscow meeting, admitted that going public was a mistake that made it more difficult for Vance to say, "Look, we can go this way, or we can go that way, which I understood to be the intention of proposing it."[77] Walter Slocombe also admitted that by proposing a limit on Soviet heavy missiles, the United States was reopening an issue "which the Russians could legitimately claim had been negotiated with Ford and Kissinger at Vladivostok."[78]

Carter would later note quite accurately all his missteps. But this admission was made with an interesting qualifier:

> The only mistake that I made was in underestimating the Soviets' displeasure in three things. One was our human rights policy. Second was the somewhat radical change from the Vladivostok proposal. And the third one was my inclination to make public the American position on the SALT discussions....I was inclined as an incoming President to make some of these issues public so the American people could understand what was going on. I think the Soviets looked upon my making these issues public as a propaganda effort which was contrary to sincere negotiating efforts. They misjudged me.

Still, even in hindsight, Carter would not have done anything substantially different. Only if he had known what he later learned about the Soviets, he would have approached it differently, in a little bit slower fashion and with more preparation before Vance's mission was publicized.[79]

Whatever the difficulties Carter may have had in accepting full responsibility for this early reversal in SALT II talks, he really wanted an agreement. To accomplish that he would give Vance a more central role in negotiations, and though he sometimes wobbled in his approach to the Soviet Union, he would proceed with efforts to get back and stay on track.

RECOVERY

Shortly after the Moscow fiasco, President Jimmy Carter invited Soviet Ambassador Anatoly Dobrynin to the White House "to discuss ways of getting a SALT agreement back on track." The following conversation (slightly paraphrased) ensued:

> CARTER: Why did [Leonid] Brezhnev and [Andrei] Gromyko reject the American proposals without so much as even discussing them?
>
> DOBRYNIN: The Soviet leadership is profoundly convinced that the American proposals could not provide any basis whatsoever for agreement because they had been prepared without reckoning on the Vladivostok accord and carried a definite advantage to the United States.
>
> CARTER: You should assure Brezhnev I have not tried to cheat in order to obtain advantages for the United States. My sole idea was to start an exchange of views on a broad range of problems—first on really deep cuts in nuclear arsenals, which was...[my] sincere aspiration.[1]

The sincerity and honor of the president, however, was not the issue. A real clash of interests revolved around the new role of the USSR in the world and the U.S. response to it. The Soviet goal at the time was to secure recognition of its equality with the United States and a mutual understanding "that each superpower not only controlled its own sphere of international life, but also consulted the other on major international issues." To back their claims along these lines, the Soviets were engaged in the steady buildup of their military power.[2] By 1979, according to one of their top military officials, they had gained military parity—nuclear and conventional—with the United States.[3]

The new technology, however, was beginning "to outrun the frameworks and context in which SALT and other arms control proposals had been framed and presented."[4] A drawn-out negotiation process would confront Carter and other SALT II conferees with a host of concerns. The modernization and introduction of new weapons on both sides of the divide, as well as changes in surveillance and verification modalities, would tax the minds and energies of many individuals.

To compound Carter's problems, there were profound differences within his inner circle in how to respond to these events. Cyrus Vance and some others in the State Department favored moving ahead on SALT II in terms of the principle of equality and diplomatic negotiations to mediate conflicts in other parts of the world. But many other advisors would have real difficulty in conceding that the Soviets had legitimate regional concerns in territories near their own borders. And if U.S. weapons were inferior or smaller than those of the Soviets, they wanted the same "without much regard for the more basic question of whether we needed more throw-weight, or more numbers."[5]

Foremost in this latter group was national security advisor Zbigniew Brzezinski. Even Carter's decision to proceed with the negotiations with the Soviets concerned him. As Brzezinski wrote in his diary on April 3, 1977, "I do feel that neither they nor the president really appreciates the extent to which the Soviets are hostile to our proposal and the degree to which they wish to put us under pressure."[6] After a meeting on April 25, Brzezinski noted in his diary, "there is a tendency on our side to want an agreement so badly that we begin changing our proposals until the point is reached that the Russians are prepared to consider it."[7]

To win support for his concerns, Brzezinski sought help from within the White House. Hamilton Jordan "became an increasingly valued ally" in his attempts to maintain a tough position. "He [Jordan] agreed that no further changes should be made, for this would weaken the president politically," wrote Brzezinski later on. "I hoped that he would tell the president this directly and thereby make the president more resistant to Vance and [Paul] Warnke's entreaties for a more conciliatory approach."[8] At the Department of Defense, Secretary Harold Brown was a natural ally, reflecting the push within the defense establishment to develop new and better weapons to counter the Soviet threat.

Carter, torn internally between dealing with and being tough toward the Soviets, would respond to these varying external pressures by blowing hot and cold, confusing members of his own team and the public. His indecisiveness even left members of the National Security Council (NSC) staff puzzled about what Carter really wanted.[9]

Still, in the late spring of 1977, with the president backing him, Vance was able to move forward on many of these issues. At the close of the Geneva talks on May 21, 1977, the two parties agreed upon a basic framework for the SALT II negotiations. They would work on a treaty, a protocol, and a statement of general principles to be followed in later SALT III negotiations. The SALT II treaty would run until 1985; the protocol would be for a three-year period, and negotiation principles would guide the new set of SALT talks. The parts were interdependent and, while substantive differences remained, the two countries would talk at three different levels. Technical meetings would be held in Geneva, ambassadorial talks at the two capitals, and Vance and Gromyko would meet to provide basic direction for the whole process.[10]

Encouraged, Carter began pursuing the possibility of a meeting with Brezhnev. Ignoring Henry Kissinger's earlier advice that summit meetings were useless unless they were tied to concrete accomplishments, Carter was impatient in his desire to meet the Soviet leader.[11] In his first letter to Brezhnev, Carter had suggested that he looked forward to meeting with him to discuss "our differences as well as our common interests."[12] On June 3, 1977, Vance sounded out Dobrynin about a meeting between the two heads of state as a key to improving negotiations. On June 18, the president expressed his belief that the sooner the meeting with Brezhnev took place the better it would be for Soviet-American relations. In July he sought a meeting once again. This time, at Brzezinski's insistence, the proposal was redrafted as a statement from

W. Averell Harriman rather than the president so that it would be a less personal request and the president wouldn't appear to be begging.[13]

It might have been a good idea for the two heads of state to meet. Carter would have been able to directly assess Soviet attitudes for himself, and he might have better understood some of their concerns. Indeed, the Soviets had sent out signals shortly before Carter took office that they would be open to such a meeting.[14] But Brezhnev was in declining health, and on June 18 the Politburo decided to stick to a post–SALT II meeting summit. As Gromyko explained to Dobrynin, without a guarantee in the form of a SALT II agreement ready to be signed, it would be difficult for Brezhnev to go through a long, complicated discussion with Carter on a broad range of topics. Brezhnev put an end to these pleas with a letter on June 30. Reiterating the Soviet position on SALT, he ended with the comment, "Now about our meeting. We have already brought to your attention our considerations on the subject. Therefore, there seems to be no need of repeating them here."[15] It was a nasty response, given earlier Soviet suggestions that the two men might stage a meeting.[16]

Shortly thereafter, on July 6 and 7, the broad overview of Soviet goals and capabilities, originally commissioned by the president back on February 18, 1977, as Presidential Review Memoranda 10, came before Special Coordinating Committee (SCC) meetings chaired by Brzezinski. His aide William Odom and project director Sam Huntington, who carried major responsibilities for the study, had produced a document that envisaged some "realities" requiring a tougher anti-Soviet stance. Odom and Huntington had "a rather clearly defined program" contrary to the policies that Kissinger had designed.[17]

The end product was Presidential Directive 18, issued on August 24. In that document Carter called for a basic reformulation of U.S. foreign policy along the lines favored by Brzezinski. Though the U.S.-Soviet military balance was portrayed in this document as one of "essential equivalence," the directive envisaged policies in which the United States would use its political, economic, and technological edge over the Soviets to compete with them. The Soviet military buildup would be countered with increased U.S. support for the North Atlantic Treaty Organization (NATO). The U.S. triad of strategic forces—intercontinental ballistic missiles (ICBMs), submarine-launched ballistic missiles, and manned bombers—were seen as providing reinforcing and partially overlapping capabilities for the achievement of its goals. Beyond that, it directed that a secure and mobile reserve force be developed, enabling the United States to move globally.[18] The document, as Brzezinski noted, provided the conceptual underpinnings for the kind of "assertive, and historically optimistic policy of détente" he favored. It assumed that detente would have to be based on a decision to enhance U.S. military capabilities, reversing the trend of the previous decade.[19]

Despite this new policy orientation and the holding operation on SALT II, Vance and Gromyko resolved several technical issues at meetings in Geneva in July 1977. There was also a thaw in U.S.-Soviet relations. The USSR permitted a stream of emigrants to leave their country, and the Carter administration responded to the improved human rights situation in the USSR by approving some oil-drilling equipment it had initially denied the Soviets.[20]

Then, on September 23 and 27, 1977, Carter met with Soviet foreign minister Gromyko, its ambassador Dobrynin, and its deputy foreign minister Georgi Markovich Kornienko in Washington, D.C.

At the September 23 meeting, a surprisingly innocent Carter decided on the spur of the moment to give Gromyko a going-away present. It was a small wooden display that he kept on his desk showing all of the American and Soviet missiles known to exist. Apparently a prop that Defense Department officials often used in their public relations, it was clearly an inappropriate gift. Gromyko, Carter recalls, "was taken aback that I would do such a thing, because the set of models showed the gigantic size and many types of their missiles, contrasted with the few and relatively compact American ICBMs."[21]

Gromyko, who saw Carter as a man "not overburdened with foreign policy expertise," gave another interpretation of Carter's action. The president had pointed to "two Soviet missiles that were clearly much bigger than the U.S. ones, saying, 'These are the ones we are most afraid of.' He seemed satisfied, and evidently thought his demonstration a proper substitute for real debate."[22] Later Gromyko handed the set to Dobrynin, saying he did not "play with toys." Dobrynin reported in his memoirs that Carter's souvenir "is still in my apartment."[23]

Still, as Carter recalls, a basic framework was accepted at this time, setting forth overall limits of 2,250 total missile launchers, of which 1,250 could contain multiple warheads, provided no more than 820 were land-based in silos instead of in submarines and on long-range bombers.[24]

Impasse

Twenty-three months would pass before the summit would take place.[25] Indeed, in spring 1978, the United States and the Soviet Union seemed to be rekindling the Cold War. The Soviets punished their dissidents at home, and the United States responded with economic sanctions. Carter saw a de facto link between the success of SALT II talks and the Soviets' deep involvement in the Horn of Africa and elsewhere. Caustic exchanges between the two leaders heated up the political climate. In SALT II meetings there would be ups and downs as issues were visited and revisited. The United States would periodically return to proposals for deep cuts on heavy missiles and restrictions on the Backfire bombers. The Soviets would always insist that these items were nonnegotiable.[26]

W. Averell Harriman, ambassador to the Soviet Union during World War II and a go-between for the Carter camp and Soviet leaders during the transition, became concerned at the heightening tension between the United States and the USSR and inserted himself into the process.[27] In a meeting with Carter on March 8, 1978, he told the president that Brezhnev was very emotional about the deterioration in the U.S.-Soviet relationship, seeing it as the worst it had been in ten years. To counter this downturn, Harriman suggested that Carter open direct correspondence with Brezhnev. Part of the problem, Harriman ventured in an aside directed at Brzezinski, resided in aides who talked about the Horn of Africa too much in public. Anticipating problems the treaty would face in the U.S. Senate, he suggested that the president establish a committee of scientists to combat Paul Nitze's arguments that the Soviets were working on a nuclear first strike.[28]

Harriman may not have been as candid in this talk as he would have liked. Though he had requested a meeting alone with the president, Brzezinski sat in on the discussion. Hamilton Jordan, who had arranged the meeting, was "upset" when he learned from Harriman that Brzezinski had not honored Harriman's request and had been in the Oval Office with him.[29] Certainly Harriman remained sufficiently concerned throughout 1978 and early 1979 that he continued this conversation with similar meetings with Brezhnev, Vance, Warnke, Brzezinski, and Dobrynin.[30]

The public posture of the administration at this time was that SALT was a long-term process requiring patient efforts. In their demands on each other, both sides made certain that the process would be a long one. The United States would propose that a range limit of 2,500 kilometers be passed on all cruise missiles, and the Soviet Union would object that the limits should be shorter. The Soviets would propose that the United States take their word on the Backfire bomber, and the United States would reject the proposal. They went around and around, each repeatedly conveying concerns to the other side while continuing to push objectives that the other side would not accept.

To complicate matters further for the U.S. negotiators, Brzezinski insisted at an SCC meeting on September 1, 1978, that all decisions going to the president be unanimous. "I was determined to secure a consensus and I chaired [the meeting] in a very tight fashion, insisting that we reach decisions unanimously so that the following day, at the NSC, the President could approve a series of recommendations."[31] The process, in effect, gave Brzezinski a veto over all items going to the president.

At the NSC meeting the next day, Brzezinski urged the president, by then vacillating on the issue, not to "leave the Backfire for the summit." The administration, he argued, could "get more leverage by settling it beforehand, exploiting the Soviet desire for a SALT II summit." Given the Soviet insistence throughout the negotiations that the Backfire bomber was off limits, this assertion could have stalled the agreement again, and the issue was not resolved at this meeting.[32]

In late September, with the Camp David talks behind him, Carter turned his attention again to SALT II and the negotiations took on a new life. In a meeting with Gromyko on September 30, the two men dealt with the status of cruise missiles with no nuclear warheads and discussed whether or not the range of a weapon should be defined as a straight line or the less clear path of a cruise missile seeking out its target. The meeting, Carter recalled, was "one of the best meetings" he ever had with any foreign leader. "Gromyko genuinely seemed to want my opinion where we should go from here." Pleased that the SALT negotiations had nearly ended, he gave Vance permission to discuss a possible summit meeting.[33]

Still, Carter, buttressed by advice from Brzezinski, continued to take tough stances. Vance was only given permission to make a trip to Moscow after he assured Carter that the meeting was explicitly for the purpose of arranging a summit meeting with

Brezhnev and not for further negotiations.[34] Remaining issues could be handled between Brezhnev and Carter at the summit, "after our subordinates had hammered out acceptable compromises ahead of time."[35]

Later, at a meeting in the Oval Office on October 13, Carter pushed Vance hard on his view that the Backfire bomber issues could be resolved via a U.S. statement of understanding. According to Brzezinski, "The President looked rather startled, fixed him [Vance] with a rather icy stare, and said 'Cy, are you saying that this is good for our country, or is it something that you think the Soviets will simply accept?' Both Cy and Paul looked rather startled and then made the case that if the U.S. simply asserts that they are producing thirty a year and they do not reject that when they receive our letter, it is in effect a confirmation." Carter later insisted on written statements from the Soviets.[36]

As the diplomats and technicians whittled away at the remaining differences, some administration spokesmen began publicly suggesting that the SALT negotiations were nearing an end. Concerned about these reports, Brzezinski wrote Carter that when making public statements he should note that while the number of differences had been narrowed, the remaining issues were difficult and complex. This way, Brzezinski suggested, expectations of a successful outcome would not mount and the Soviets would be held responsible for any failure to come to terms.[37]

Throughout this whole negotiating process, Brzezinski's Weekly Reports to the president suggest that he would not have been at all unhappy had there been no early agreement on SALT II. He never spelled out the mutual interests the United States and the Soviet Union might have had in a constructive agreement. Rather, Brzezinski wrote on June 24, 1977, that he saw "that the West in general and the United States in particular has the power to greatly aggravate the Soviet dilemma. And it is this consciousness that, in the end, will bring Brezhnev back to a foreign policy of moderation."[38] On July 8, 1977, he suggested, "The Soviets have misinterpreted our willingness to compromise last May on a three-part SALT agreement....They may have felt that the rough treatment they gave us at the time paid off," and the United States was buckling.[39] Negotiations, he suggested in October 1977, should be drawn out so as to give the Soviets a continuing incentive to moderate their behavior.[40] Brzezinski suggested on April 7, 1978 that the Soviets had no genuine commitment to détente; for them, it was a way to prevent a U.S. military buildup, generate a more passive U.S. attitude on other issues, and induce the "Finlandization" attitudes on the part of many Europeans.[41] More than that, as he warned the president on May 5, 1978, "The Soviet appetite for aggrandizement had increased each decade since the end of World War II.... At the present they are engaged in an attempt to undermine U.S. influence in the Middle East."[42] In June 1978, he wondered, should it be made it clear to the Soviets that the United States was done making concessions and that further proposals should come from them, or should they "sit tight until September when perhaps [the Soviets] will decide it is better to make a concession?"[43]

On December 2, 1978, Brzezinski provided the president with a view of the negotiating process so tough that even the president had to make some wry remarks in the margins of the memo:

BRZEZINSKI: In negotiation there often comes the time to force the issue to a head by making the other side take stock of the consequences of failures. One should even be willing to deliberately create such circumstances, as [Anwar] Sadat had done from time to time. Of course, before one does so one should carefully marshal ones resources and calculate timing very carefully.

We have been dribbling our concessions, and asserting from time to time that we would go no further. Yet time after time we would then make additional concessions.

CARTER NOTE: The Soviet Union does the same.

BRZEZINSKI [ON AIR-LAUNCHED CRUISE MISSILES]: As a major concession we told the Soviets that we would accept the limit of 35 as an average. The Soviets countered with 25. We immediately offered 30 as a compromise. The Soviets are now talking of a figure of between 25 and 30 as the outcome, despite our accommodation on the definition issue.

CARTER NOTE: Only symbolically important.

BRZEZINSKI: I am convinced the Soviets want a SALT agreement and I think there is a good probability that we could have obtained one some months ago had we been prepared to establish credibly the position that we are no longer able to make further adjustments and that we can wait.

CARTER NOTE: We've waited 2 years.

Brzezinski then went on in this report to articulate his famous "arc of crisis" theory. The United States, he claimed, was confronting "the beginning of a major crisis in some ways similar to the one in Europe in the late 40's." Fragile social and political institutions in an area of vital interest to the United States were creating a vacuum in which elements sympathetic to the Soviet Union could take advantage of the situation: "This is especially likely since there is a pervasive feeling in the area that the U.S. is no longer in a position to offer effective political and military protection."[44]

Shortly thereafter, Carter played the China card. On December 15, two weeks before the scheduled announcement date of January 1, 1979, the president announced the normalization of relations with China in a dramatic presentation on national television.[45] The final communiqué suggested that the two powers would cooperate in opposition to "hegemonic powers," a phrase the Chinese often used to talk about the Soviet Union.

The Soviet leaders interpreted these events as a deliberate slap in the face. The ever-proud Brezhnev would not be squeezed into Carter's schedule shortly before or after a meeting with Chinese vice premier Deng Xiaoping. And the final communiqué pledging cooperation against hegemonic powers deeply offended them. Vance would later argue that the Soviets had suddenly stiffened their positions at Geneva and that this was primarily due to developments in regard to China.[46]

In spite of this, at the Geneva meetings a few days later, Vance, Gromyko, and other members of their delegations were able to work out a possible deal on the issue of encryption. On December 22, Vance sent the text of the proposed compromise back to

Washington and asked for authorization to resolve the issue. Gromyko, according to Dobrynin, had instructions from the Soviet government to announce that they were prepared to sign SALT if the telemetry issues could be compromised.[47] Indeed, State Department Soviet specialist Marshall Shulman and Paul Warnke, on a final mission as consultant after his resignation as head of the ACDA, stayed up late into the night and "killed several bottles of Scotch, celebrating the fact that we had finally managed to do it."[48]

This was not to be. On December 23, after a nightlong meeting in the White House, Brzezinski relayed to Vance on an open telephone line that "telemetry encryption as practiced in certain recent Soviet missile tests would violate the ban on deliberate concealment." Moreover, because any explanation would reveal too much about U.S. intelligence capabilities, Vance was not able to tell Gromyko specifically what U.S. objections were. Gromyko did not respond to the statement, announcing instead that there "were still too many issues to resolve to set a conference date."[49]

A few days later, Brezhnev wrote Carter, warning that unless the United States prevented its European allies from selling weapons to China there might not be any further progress on arms control.[50]

Brzezinski was not concerned. Rather, he advised the president on December 28 that he may have made a "mistake in putting so many deadlines on SALT and on Brezhnev's visit here; that simply conveys over-anxiousness; the Soviets exploit that against us." What he needed to do at the forthcoming meetings with European leaders at Guadalupe, Brzezinski counseled, was to counter the impression that the United States was no longer prepared "to impose its will on the flow of history." Brzezinski felt that Carter had a chance to shape a new global system, depending on how he handled the USSR, China, and Indian Ocean situations.[51]

Brzezinski even defined Carter's policy for him, describing it along the following lines: The goal of Carter's policy, he stated after a modest caveat ("if he understood it"), should be one of "Reciprocal Accommodation." This meant containment, resistance to indirect expansion, ideological competition, and creation of a framework within which the USSR could work with the United States or risk global isolation. It meant that the U.S. government should be prepared to cooperate but ready to assert its interests if there was no reciprocity. In particular, reciprocal accommodation required giving the Soviets no guarantees on China and a U.S. military posture adequate to balance the USSR, which meant carrying out Presidential Directive 18, with or without SALT. It also meant acting collectively along the "arc of instability" bordering the Indian Ocean. This policy, he suggested, was both distinctive and historically more relevant than those propounded by Ronald Reagan (confrontation), Richard Nixon and Henry Kissinger (condominium), or George McGovern (partnership).[52]

SALT II: Breakthrough

In January and early February 1979, U.S.-Soviet relations remained in limbo as world events roiled the diplomatic waters. The Soviets were angry about the timing of the

FIGURE 4. Zbigniew Brzezinski with David Aaron and General Jones. Photograph courtesy of the Jimmy Carter Library.

FIGURE 5. Helmut Schmidt, Jimmy Carter, James Callaghan, Valéry Giscard de'Estaing, and their wives in Guadeloupe, 1979. Photograph courtesy of the Jimmy Carter Library.

normalization announcement and stalled the talks with new technical issues. Chinese vice premier Deng Xiaoping's triumphal visit to the United States in late January must have "lived up to [the Soviets'] worst nightmares."[53] The Chinese invasion of Vietnam, a Soviet ally, shortly after Deng's return to China put another damper on the Soviet desire to talk. With the overthrow of the shah of Iran in early February, Carter and his aides also had other significant national security issues to confront.

By late February 1979, "There was a new note of despair at the State Department. Officials who had previously confined their worries to the danger that the Senate might reject the treaty, now, for the first time, began to talk about the possibility that there would be no treaty for the Senate to consider."[54]

At this nadir in U.S.-Soviet relations, Brzezinski made an extraordinary suggestion to the president. To counter the impression that he was being buffeted about by his two major foreign policy advisors, Carter should try another tactic. Franklin Delano Roosevelt had purposefully chosen advisors who would present different views to him, showing his strength by orchestrating their differences. Carter, Brzezinski suggested, could show a similar mastery over his advisors by sending Brzezinski to Moscow and Vance to China. He wrote, "For example, when the crisis in Indochina is over, it would be useful for Cy and some of his top assistants to go to Peking [Beijing] at your direction to engage in high-level discussions. Similarly, it might be useful, and domestically even appealing, to have me spend a couple of days in Moscow in consultation with the Soviets on issues of common concern, perhaps with my counterpart who works for Brezhnev. This could be in preparation for the Summit."[55] But Carter had high hopes for SALT II, and he was not prepared at this point to keep Vance from capping his months of effort. In February, Carter met with Soviet Ambassador Dobrynin and made it clear that he wanted a SALT II agreement. Dobrynin left the White House with the impression that Carter was beginning to show real interest in a shift in U.S.-Soviet relations. Remarkably, Dobrynin noted, it was the first time that he did not touch on his favorite subject of human rights.[56]

Carter also resumed his correspondence with Brezhnev. While their exchange may not have resolved any specific issues in the SALT II agreement, it kept the two leaders aware of the positions and opinions of the other. Brezhnev mostly complained that the United States liked to revisit issues like telemetric information after they had already been resolved. The United States, he charged, "is creating ever new problems at the negotiations." Throughout this and his other letters, Brezhnev asked Carter to consider how American actions would look if they were coming *from* the USSR rather than directed toward the Soviets.[57] Carter responded to each letter by reassuring Brezhnev how committed he and the American people were to the SALT treaty. He also kept pushing for a date for the two to meet.[58]

With the renewed interest of the players at the top, Dobrynin and Vance were able to tie up several loose ends. Even through the diplomatic storms in January and February of 1979, they had not given up, meeting over twenty-five times.[59] Then, in early March, they came to a deal on encryption, a resolution close to the one marked out earlier by Vance and Gromyko in Geneva.[60] They also marked out permissible changes that could be made in modernizing existing ICBMs (later agreeing to modifications of only 5 percent) and agreed to a final set of limitations and definitions relating to cruise missiles. The United States gave up the right to test multiple warheads on long-range air-launched cruise missiles and on ground- and sea-launched cruise missiles during the term of the protocol. As regarded Backfire bombers, the United States would announce that they understood that the Soviets would limit the number to thirty, and the Soviets wouldn't contradict them. In early April, Vance told Carter that the Soviets had accepted the SALT II proposals.[61]

Even after these hurdles had been cleared, new problems arose. In early April, when the United States planned a war exercise that explicitly simulated a nuclear exchange with the USSR, Brezhnev wrote Carter a letter of protest.[62] Even more significant, SALT opponents on Capitol Hill leaked classified testimony of Central Intelligence Agency Director Stansfield Turner stating that it would take four to five years to recoup the monitoring capabilities of Soviet weapons and actions that had been lost in Iran. On April 17, Defense Secretary Brown announced that it would only take a year, but fears had already been stimulated.[63] As Robert Gates—the CIA's representative at the NSC—later pointed out, the CIA hurt the treaty's chances of ratification by making the telemetry issue so critical and public.[64]

Brzezinski once again warned the president about possible Soviet double-dealing. On May 12, 1979, he wrote that Soviets might try to get a crucial technical concession that would permit them to build two new ICBMs. They were developing a lighter missile, not because they were offloading fuel as the United States had expected, but "to test a missile with a payload and launch weight significantly lighter than the existing missiles."[65]

A major issue that had to be resolved at this time was choice of venue for the summit. Carter suggested that it was Washington's turn, since the last summit had been held with President Gerald Ford on Soviet soil at Vladivostok. Brezhnev, however, had serious health problems and suggested Moscow on doctor's orders. Carter replied that he could not go to Moscow because some in the U.S. Congress might accuse him of yielding another point to the Soviets, which could affect ratification. At long last the two parties agreed on Vienna.[66]

The agenda itself was limited at the insistence of the Soviets. They wanted a friendly and constructive summit: no new ground, no surprises on SALT II or SALT III. On June 5, 1979, a memo prepared for the Department of State by Marshall Shulman and Robert Barry reflected this concern and was ready to go to the president.[67]

Carter, however, was annoyed when he got this memorandum. Failing to see the limitations under which his own advisors were working, he confided in his diary on May 25 that he was encountering "the same degree of timidity that was apparent before we went to Camp David for the Middle-East talks....I told them to set maximum goals and work toward them; if we didn't reach those goals, at least we would have done our best—that I wasn't just interested in going to Vienna to the opera."[68] He also instructed Brzezinski to cut back the U.S. delegation to the size of the Soviet team.[69]

To prepare himself for the meeting with Brezhnev, Carter met with Harriman again on June 6, with Brzezinski, as usual, in attendance. Noting that he had dealt with Soviet leaders for over fifty years, Harriman told the president that Brezhnev's major concern was to "work for the rest of his life to prevent war on Soviet soil, particularly nuclear war." Additionally, in his talk with Brezhnev the previous December, Harriman had found him less energetic than in the past, but his "mind clear, alert and the discussion completely coherent." Harriman warned the president that Brezhnev did not make decisions completely on his own. The Soviets, like the Americans, had a spectrum of policy specialists running from "hardliners to reasonable people."[70]

The day before the president and his party left for Geneva, Harriman gave Brzezinski further advice via a telephone conversation on dealing with the Soviet leadership. The Soviet Defense Department reports directly to the Politburo, he said, and frequently Brezhnev "parrots what he hears." Should Brezhnev make any statements about military matters that were of concern to the Americans, the president should suggest that the two ministers of defense get together rather than have an "acrimonious argument which would be profitless."[71] Cyrus Vance gave the president similar advice, adding that Brezhnev had his own domestic constituency to deal with. "[Brezhnev] has had to mold elite opinion in the USSR to accept something more complex that the black-and-white-stereotype of Marxism-Leninism versus U.S. imperialism."[72]

Vienna

Finally, from June 15 to June 17, 1979, the meeting between Carter and Brezhnev took place. Experts worked on a few details that still had to be resolved. The Backfire bomber issue was handled at the highest level. Brezhnev at first refused even to make a statement on that issue, but when Carter informed him that the whole SALT deal would fall through if no statement were made, he finally blurted out that only thirty Backfire bombers would be produced each year. A Soviet statement to that effect would be attached as an addendum to the treaty.[73]

Brezhnev and Carter also made long presentations reflecting their differing interpretations of each other and the world. Brezhnev began the exchange. Alluding to U.S. reversals in the early SALT II negotiations, Brezhnev warned that there should be continuity of policy and that once reached, agreements should not be undone. Carter gave Brezhnev his wish list for future arms limitations, and argued that the United States had vital interests in the Persian Gulf and the Arabian Peninsula that the Soviet Union must recognize. Brezhnev retorted that the Soviet Union was not the source of instability in Northern Africa or the Persian Gulf. The Soviet leaders, he said, have been "surprised and disturbed at the lackadaisical way the United States refers to quite remote regions of the world as being of vital interest" to it. In a regular tour de horizon the two officials roamed the world, discussing the U.S.-Soviet relationship, human rights, military expenditures, and other basic foreign policy differences.[74]

The Soviets even engaged in a little dinner table rivalry. The elegance of the Russian offerings at their embassy, as Carter observed, outdid the American offerings at the U.S. embassy the previous night. As Brezhnev noted, the American dinner only had menus available in English, while the Russian menus were printed with both languages.[75]

On June 18 came the grand finale. "The lawyers," as Gromyko noted, tongue in cheek, "checked every comma and full stop for the umpteenth time, in case one of them

FIGURE 6.   Jimmy Carter and Leonid Brezhnev in Vienna at the signing of the Strategic Arms Limitation Treaty (SALT). Photograph courtesy of the Jimmy Carter Library.

had come out of place and changed the treaty's whole meaning." Then in the sparkling Redoubt Hall of the Hofburg Palace, Carter and Brezhnev placed their signatures on the SALT II Treaty. Afterward, according to Gromyko, Carter took the initiative, "sealing the treaty with a formal embrace and a kiss, to the loud applause of everyone present."[76] At their final conference session on June 18, 1979, Carter and Brezhnev expressed hopes that they would meet more often.[77] That same day, Carter sent Brezhnev a handwritten letter in which he hoped for future cooperation between the United States and the USSR.[78]

Twenty-seven months and thousands of work hours after the Moscow meeting, the deal they put their hands to that day provided for modest cuts in major weapons delivery systems. It also attempted to resolve the issues remaining after Vladivostok as well as the weapons issues that had developed as the months went by. The limits of all missiles were set at 2,400, though the number would be slightly reduced by January 1, 1981. Either side could develop and deploy one new missile system. For the United States, this meant it could move ahead on its MX missile plans. Submarine and land-based multiple independently targetable reentry vehicle (MIRV) missiles would be counted in the subtotal of 1,320 on MIRV launchers; no missiles could have more than ten warheads. In a concession to the Soviets, no limits were placed on Soviet heavy missiles or the Backfire bomber.[79] Heavy bombers were counted against the total number of launchers permitted and against the subtotal for MIRV launchers. Other provisions concerned verification and weapon types. Both sides signed communiqués saying they would proceed with future negotiations.

The new arrangement fell far short of Carter's initial dream that the nuclear arms race would be substantially minimized by the talks. During the months of the negotiations and after, the United States and the Soviet Union continued to compete with each other. The USSR deployed new and better intercontinental and intermediate range heavy missiles; the United States moved ahead on its air-based cruise missile, and the administration announced it was pursuing the development of the new MX missile and the Trident submarine after the treaty had been signed. Not covered by the treaty were Pershing 2 intermediate range missiles. Carter pushed these Pershing missiles on the Europeans, later to be deployed by the Reagan administration in Germany.[80]

The new technology was in some cases outrunning "the frameworks and context in which SALT and other arms control proposals had been framed and presented." Both parties were moving toward a greater reliance on "offensive" strategies and weapons as the best defense.[81]

SALT II, however, was an accomplishment in a less than perfect world. It provided for regulated competition and prompted ongoing negotiations to limit other weapons. The very fact that a deal had been reached also promised to cool the ever-growing political tension building between the United States and the Soviet Union.

On June 22, the Politburo, the Council of Ministers, and the Presidium of the Supreme Soviet published a joint resolution approving the results of the summit as "an important stride ahead toward normalizing Soviet-American relations and the international climate on the whole."[82]

Carter would have more problems in securing support for the treaty in the U.S. Senate. Kissinger had warned him about the opposition he might meet on the home front. A coalition of civilians in the Pentagon, the Joint Chiefs of Staff, and groups in Congress would make progress difficult. Indeed, Kissinger suggested, congressional staff members would show considerable skills in such battles, sometimes being better informed on SALT than many in the top echelon of the executive branch.[83] Even as the SALT talks were underway, this opposition had been forming.

HUMAN RIGHTS AND
THE SOVIET TARGET

The negotiations with the USSR were complicated by Jimmy Carter's insistence on confrontations over the Soviet human rights record. The president, in his first meeting with Soviet ambassador Anatoly Dobrynin, stated that he would have a new policy regarding Soviet dissidents. Unlike previous presidents, he might receive Russian novelist Aleksandr Solzhenitsyn in the White House or issue a statement of support for an individual such as Soviet physicist and Nobel Peace Prize winner Andrei Sakharov. Carter would not abuse the right to make such declarations; he realized that to do so might complicate relations. But he would honor dissidents from time to time according to his convictions.

Dobrynin reminded Carter of Leonid Brezhnev's promise not "to test the new American president.... You, Mr. President, have reacted to it favorably. Now let us not test Moscow, either. That will certainly benefit Soviet-American relations."[1]

Four days later, the president wrote Sakharov that the United States would use its "good office" to seek the release of prisoners of conscience in the Soviet Union. It was the first direct communication between a Western leader and a Soviet dissident.[2] Shortly thereafter, on March 1, Carter met the exiled Soviet dissident Vladimir Bukovsky, telling him that the United States had a "permanent" commitment to human rights.[3]

At this time, several new forces were blowing across the political waters, suggesting that morality, not power alone, should provide navigational guides in international relations. Thirty-five nations had signed the Helsinki Accords, in which the parties agreed to recognize certain fundamental rights of their citizens. Some scholars were arguing that the new provisions went beyond mere statements of moral aspiration to legal commitments.[4] Dissidents within Russia and Eastern Europe were finding their voices and broadcasting their concerns to a world audience. The Charter 77 movement was formed in January 1977 when Czech intellectuals accused their government of violating the Helsinki Accords. Human Rights Watch was established the next year to monitor Soviet Bloc countries' compliance with the accords. Earlier, in 1961, Amnesty International had been formed by British lawyer Peter Benenson, and it set up a model that the United States would adopt. The organization published annual reports on human rights records as a means of bringing moral suasion against those who recklessly violated the rights of their subjects. In addition, the awards of the Nobel Prize in Literature to Alexander Solzhenitsyn in 1970 and the Nobel Peace Prize to Andrei Sakharov in 1975 generated worldwide attention for Soviet dissidents.[5]

The Carter administration's policy toward the Soviet Union, however, as one State Department official has noted, had "grown like topsy and seemed to be feeding on itself."[6] Other officials noted that the administration did not have a "comprehensive and consistent policy on human rights." In May 1977, State Department official Jane Pisano wrote David Aaron, a member of National Security Advisor Zbigniew Brzezinski's staff, that the Interagency Group on Human Rights was deciding the U.S. position on individual loans in the absence of country studies and explicit criteria for assessing human rights performance.[7]

The president's first attempt to define his human rights policies suggested that his concerns transcended Soviet practices. In his commencement address at Notre Dame University in May 1977, Carter saw "human rights as a fundamental tenet of our foreign policy." He than noted, "For too many years, we've been willing to adopt the flawed and erroneous principles and tactics of our adversaries, sometimes abandoning our own values for theirs. We've fought fire with fire, never thinking that fire is better quenched with water. We know better now. Democracy's great recent successes—in India, Portugal, Spain, Greece—show that our confidence in this system is not misplaced. Being confident of our own future, we are now free of that inordinate fear of communism which once led us to embrace any dictator who joined us in that fear." In a passing allusion to the policies of President Richard Nixon and his secretary of state, Henry Kissinger, he declared that, "Our policy must shape an international system that will last longer than secret deals" and "policy by manipulation."

Even in this address he did not completely ignore Soviet sins. The USSR, he noted, had to realize "that one country cannot impose its system of society upon another, either through direct military intervention or through the use of a client state's military force, as was the case with Cuban intervention in Angola. He finished with an upbeat note, affirming, "Our policy is rooted in our moral values, which never change....And it is a policy that I hope will make you proud to be Americans."[8]

These last lines were delivered with a fervor that impressed several observers. One person in the audience saw it as "either a very important speech or a prayer"; International observers cynically noted "piety strikes again."[9] Some State Department officials saw his human rights pronouncements as reflecting Carter's missionary impulse.[10] What the president was saying was that the administration could address human rights violations in other nations, not just those of the Soviet Union. Fear of that adversary had diminished to the point that the United States could counter the practices of right-wing regimes with which it had allied itself in the early years of the Cold War.[11]

Not until February 1978, however, were specific guidelines concluded. Just before boarding *Air Force One* to begin a weekend trip in New England, Carter signed Presidential Directive (PD) 30. The memo began, "It shall be a major objective of U.S. foreign policy to apply the human rights objective globally—but with due consideration to the cultural, political and historical characteristics of each nation, and to other fundamental U.S. interest[s]."[12]

PD 30 was certainly a sophisticated document, one in which the kinds of rights the United States might pursue as well as the tools it might employ were delineated:

> It shall be the objective of the U.S. human rights policy to reduce worldwide governmental violations of the integrity of the person (e.g., torture; cruel, inhuman or degrading treatment; arbitrary arrest or imprisonment)…and, to enhance civil and political liberties (e.g., freedom of speech, of religion, of assembly, of movement and of the press; and the right to basic judicial protections). It will also be a continuing US objective to promote basic economic and social rights (e.g. adequate food, education, shelter and health).

To promote these objectives, the United States should use its "full range of diplomatic tools," rely more on "positive inducements," and note human rights conditions when considering the allocation of U.S. foreign aid. Compromises were evident in the provisions for interagency reviews and the exemption of international monetary institutions from policies that might undermine their functions.[13]

The new initiative, Brzezinski argued, gave the United States the moral initiative around the globe. Strobe Talbott noted that PD 30 was one of the more important papers to come out of the White House. National Security Council (NSC) aide Jessica Tuchman said PD 30 would salvage human rights from between the push of two extremes—that is, those who thought human rights had to be a major concern in all issues versus those who in the interest of more realistic foreign policy would jettison it all together.[14]

At this time most of the new institutional forms to apply these policies were in place. At the State Department the position of coordinator for human rights and humanitarian affairs had been upgraded to assistant secretary of the bureau of human rights and humanitarian affairs. Pat Derian, Carter's deputy campaign manager and a civil rights leader from Mississippi, headed the new section on human rights. To integrate human rights with national security concerns, an Interagency Group on Human Rights and Foreign Assistance, chaired by Deputy Secretary of State Warren Christopher, was formed. At the NSC, Brzezinski put Jessica Tuchman in charge of an umbrella group for global issues with the responsibility of coordinating various human rights efforts. Also at the White House, the Office of Jewish Affairs relayed the human rights concerns of American Jewish leaders and organizations to relevant policymaking officials.[15]

Beginning in 1977, the State Department also issued annual country reports on the human rights record of other states. Each embassy had a human rights officer who aided in the construction of these studies. The content of these reports led to the rejection of American military aid by five Latin American nations in 1977. Though Pat Derian and others at the State Department would come to find the compilation of these reports to be a particularly onerous task, they would over time be accepted as an almost routine exercise, while remaining a moral weapon in the hands of the U.S. government. As Representative Don Fraser, a leading proponent of early human rights legislation, noted, "the most useful provision in section 502(B) [governing human rights and military aid] was the requirement that the State Department report on human rights in each of the countries."[16]

The president's commitments were also evident in his support of several international agreements that would govern the actions of his own country in the human rights arena. In 1978 he urged the U.S. Senate to pass five international human rights conventions—the International Covenant on Civil and Political Rights; the International Covenant on Economic, Social, and Cultural Rights; the Convention on Elimination of all Forms of Racial Discrimination; the American Convention on Human Rights (drafted by the Organization of American States in 1969); and the International Genocide Convention (originally drafted in 1925 and adopted by the United Nations at its founding).[17]

Nonetheless, throughout the Carter administration, battles continued behind the scenes over the very definition of such rights, their ordering, and the kind of countries that should be targeted and how. Purists clashed with pragmatists while others fought over whether the Soviet Union or other dictatorial regimes should be targeted.[18]

Central to these conflicts were major differences within the administration over the objectives sought relative to the Soviet Union. Brzezinski aide William Odom envisaged the human rights commitment as a propaganda tool to be used against the Soviet Union: "I saw human rights as a brilliant policy. I saw it as the obverse to the Soviet's support of the international class struggle…a very pragmatic tactic…a way to really beat up morally on the Soviets…It offered some basis of a new domestic U.S. foreign policy consensus."[19] Brzezinski too, saw the advantages of putting the Soviets on the spot. Secretary of State Cyrus Vance, though committed to the advancement of human rights at the world level, had concerns that Carter's policy, as it evolved, would sabotage the second series of Strategic Arms Limitation Treaty (SALT II) talks. As early as April 1977, the secretary had embraced a nuanced version of the various kinds of human rights that one government could pursue relative to another. These views were spelled out in more detail in his Georgia Law Day speech.[20]

As for Carter, he had embraced human rights as a policy during the presidential campaign as a means of welding together various components of the Democratic base. As Stuart Eizenstat told him, it was one of the few elements upon which most of the Democratic factions could agree. "To groups like the Poles, Ukrainians…and others, human rights is the single most important political issue in the field of foreign policy.…The issue is of major importance to groups like the Coalition for a Democratic Majority in the Jackson-Moynihan wing of the party." Another aide added, "the human rights issue helps him with the Jews if he has to bring pressure on Israel; it helps him with the right; it helps him in the south; it helps him with the Baptists. And he also happens to believe in it. And he won't be deterred."[21]

Carter's choices were not rooted in earlier stances he had taken during the civil rights movements in Georgia. As civil rights marches and confrontations took place in Americus and Albany, towns not far from his home in Plains, Carter kept himself politically neutral—viable for future Georgia political runs.[22] Indeed, as chairman of the Sumter County School Board in the late 1950s and early 1960s, Carter followed the practices of his time and place, providing leftover blinds and typewriters to black schools within his district.[23] Although he was depressed that he ran behind Lester Maddox in the 1966 primaries for the governorship of Georgia, Carter nevertheless refrained from backing the progressive Ellis Arnold in the runoff race.[24] In his own contest for the governorship in 1970, he won the endorsement of segregationist governors, publicly met with the head of the States Right Citizens, criticized then governor Carl Sanders for praising Martin Luther King Jr., and ran a radio ad stating that that unlike the liberal Governor Sanders, he would never seek the "block" vote, blurring the word *block* to the point it sounded almost like *black*.[25]

Later he hedged on the issue of how to deal with Lieutenant William Calley, who was convicted in a court martial of killing unarmed Vietnamese civilians in the infamous My Lai Massacre. When enraged Georgians suggested he proclaim a Lieutenant Calley Day, Carter instead opted for a suggestion that people turn on their lights to show they cared for the U.S. servicemen then serving in Vietnam.[26]

Though Carter admitted that he had not been active in the civil rights movement in Georgia, he claimed to have elevated the issue to a higher plane. Indeed, at his inauguration as governor, he declared that the day for racial discrimination was over. But that statement also served his political interests, putting him on the cover of *Time* magazine as an exemplar of the new breed of liberal governors coming out of the South. It was a choice that opened up the road to possible national office in the future.[27]

To the Russians, Carter's human rights stances were perceived as an anti-Soviet bludgeon. Certainly his statement at Notre Dame—that the "inordinate fear" of communism was over—seemed premature. Months after that statement, Carter took up the defense of the dissident Anatoly Shcharansky, who had recently been arrested along with Alexander Ginzburg for treason and anti-Soviet agitation. A conversation with Soviet foreign minister Gromyko went nowhere at first:

> GROMYKO: "Who is Shcharansky?"
> CARTER: "Haven't you heard about Shcharansky?"
> GROMYKO: "No."

As Gromyko later reported, "I asked the President straight out: 'Isn't it time to drop such ploys as utterly unproductive?' On that note, the discussion came to a close."[28] As for Carter, he "was surprised at how uncooperative Gromyko was" and "hoped that his inflexibility was a temporary tactic."[29]

At first, Dobrynin thought that Gromyko "had shown great diplomatic skill in handling such a sensitive subject by feigning ignorance over who Shcharansky might be.... But on their return to the Soviet embassy Gromyko asked him, 'Who really is Shcharansky? Tell me more about him.' Gromyko, it seems, had instructed his subordinates in Moscow not to bother him with what he called such 'absurd' matters."[30]

PD 30 had not signaled a turn in Carter's policies relative to the Soviet Union. Carter met Soviet activities in the Horn of Africa in the spring of 1978 with blistering attacks on the very legitimacy of the Soviet regime. Later that summer, when the USSR was preparing to place Soviet dissidents Shcharansky and Ginzburg on trial, Carter personally warned foreign minister Gromyko that he was concerned that these two men not automatically be given maximum sentences. "Trade and scientific and cultural exchanges" might suffer as a result of these trials, he warned.[31]

Ignoring these warnings, the Soviets scheduled the trials for mid-July 1978—at the very time Vance was to meet Gromyko in Geneva. In response to this action, U.S. Ambassador Toon cabled Washington, D.C., from Moscow that the Vance-Gromyko meeting should be cancelled. In a debate over the matter at the White House, most of those present supported Toon; only Vance and Paul Warnke were in opposition. In this situation, Carter decided to let the Vance-Gromyko meeting proceed. But some punitive action had to be taken. On July 9, Marshall Shulman, Vance's Soviet specialist, told Dobrynin that presidential science advisor Frank Press's planned visit to the Soviet Union would be canceled.[32]

On July 13, Ginzburg was sentenced to eight years in a labor camp for "anti-Soviet agitation and propaganda." Shcharansky received thirteen years in prison and labor camps for "treason, espionage, and anti-Soviet agitation."[33]

Shortly thereafter, NSC staffer Jessica Tuchman warned Brzezinski that a Jackson amendment was in the works and if enacted would politically weaken the president. She recommended that the president issue an executive order suspending all trade, government-sponsored exchanges, and technology transfers with the Soviet Union for ninety days while the administration "reevaluate these measures of cooperation in light of the recent events."[34]

At this point Carter denied Moscow an export license for a Sperry Univac computer for purchase by the Soviet news agency Tass, imposed new licensing requirements for the export of equipment for oil and gas exploration, and decided that all sales of U.S. oil technology would be placed under the administration's review. Brzezinski, Secretary of Defense Harold Brown, and Secretary of Energy James Schlesinger backed these and other measures. In opposition were Secretary of the Treasury Michael Blumenthal and Secretary of Commerce Juanita Kreps.[35]

Only when the USSR loosened its limits on the emigration of Soviet Jews did Carter reconsider his policies. In early December 1978, Kreps and Blumenthal made a trip to Moscow. There they announced the approval of sales of some of the oil drilling equipment originally denied to the Soviet Union that summer.[36]

But Carter had not given up on the issue of the Soviet dissidents. After the United States and the USSR came to terms on SALT II, Carter again put the Soviets on edge. At their meeting in Vienna where SALT was finalized, Carter reminded Brezhnev that the Helsinki Accords provided the basis for the United States to protest how the Soviets were treating their dissidents.[37]

More significant, the president decided at a 1979 breakfast meeting on July 27 that he would move ahead only on most favored nation (MFN) status for the People's Republic of China. This was a strange move, given the history of the whole issue. MFN status had originally been withheld from the Soviet Union on the grounds that they should free up emigration from their country. By 1979, some 50,000 Soviet Jews had been allowed to emigrate, nearly triple the average that had been released during the administration of President Gerald Ford.[38] Why not reward them for their new policies?

Doubling the impact of the blow was the fact that Romania, led by one of the worst despots in the communist world, had been granted MFN status back in 1975.

Then, in late August in the midst of the phony Cuban Soviet Brigade crisis, the United States detained an Aeroflot airliner for three days before it determined that Bolshoi Ballet dancer Ludmilla Vlasova on board was leaving the United States of her own free will. The dancer's husband, ballet star Alexander Godunov, had defected a week earlier, and U.S. officials wanted to make sure that she was not being intimidated by Soviet officials on board the plane. This delay enraged both the Soviet officials and the ballerina on board. Upon her return to Russia, she denounced the United States for forbidding her to leave.[39]

Impact

What impact did Carter's tough human rights stance have on Soviet behavior? Brezhnev and Henry Kissinger had warned Carter that his human rights policies might complicate matters regarding SALT II. And Vance wrote Carter on May 29, 1978, that some U.S. policies could lead to tough Soviet actions, even causing them to "to crack down harder on...dissidents."[40]

Certainly, Soviet leaders let their irritation be known on many occasions. At his first meeting with Vance, Brezhnev objected to continuing American "interference" in Soviet internal affairs over human rights policies.[41] Brezhnev, in his letter to Carter on February 25, 1977, wrote that he would not "allow interference in our internal affairs, whatever pseudo-humanitarian slogans are used to present it."[42] On March 28, 1977, Dobrynin delivered an oral note on the basis of a Politburo text angrily protesting State Department interference in the case of Alexander Ginzburg. The presentation was made to Arthur Hartman, who was acting as secretary of state during Vance's absence from Washington. Hartman said to Dobrynin that "he had nothing to add to Carter's official position" but remarked privately that "as a professional diplomat, he anticipated major difficulties in [U.S.-Soviet] relations on account of the new, activist administration policy supporting Soviet dissidents."[43]

But Carter remained impervious to all these warnings. On March 22, 1977, he told a congressional group that criticisms of human rights practices would not impair U.S.-Soviet relations. He said that there was no need to worry "every time Brezhnev sneezes." He saw Soviet protests about his policies as either based on misunderstanding or their own propaganda campaign. He was not singling out the Soviet Union for special treatment, he insisted. Carter argued that despite many Soviet protests to the contrary, there really was "[no] connection between the two in the minds of the Soviets." He was surprised, he admitted, by "the degree of disturbance by the Soviets" about what he considered to be "a routine and normal commitment to human rights." But he proposed that the Soviet response might be motivated by their desire to exaggerate the disagreements between the two countries "for political reasons."[44]

Carter attributed the soured atmosphere between Washington and Moscow to the mistaken Soviet belief "that our concern for human rights is aimed specifically at them or is an attack on their vital interests." U.S. policy, he explained, was directed at "all countries equally, including our own." To the extent that the Soviet criticisms of his policy were based on a misconception of American motives, he vowed to redouble U.S. efforts to make them clear. But to the extent that they were merely "designed as propaganda to put pressure on us, let no one doubt that we will persevere."[45]

The Carter human rights campaign relative to the Soviet Union had mixed results. The Soviet government began to exile its dissidents rather than put them in prison. For a time the number of people permitted to emigrate increased.[46] But Carter's emphasis on the issue complicated negotiations with the Soviet Union on SALT II and the overall impact of U.S. pressures on Soviet treatment of its dissidents was not significant. The first Soviet response to the Jackson-Vanik Amendment to the 1974 Trade Act, designed to promoted emigration of dissidents from the USSR, had just the opposite effect. Nor did the pressure on behalf of Shcharansky lead to a fair trial. At the session of the Politburo chaired by Brezhnev on June 22, 1978, Yuri Andropov noted that the USSR could not satisfy Carter's request against prosecution and that no correspondents would be allowed into the trial.[47] Andropov even knew the results of the trial before it happened: Shcharansky's sentence would be fifteen years, he said. According to one source, President Carter also asked Ambassador Dobrynin to insure that Shcharansky's purported connections with the Central Intelligence Agency were not mentioned during the trial. Andropov said this would be up to the court and to how the defendant behaved himself.[48]

What Carter did not seem to realize was that there are problems in applying political sanctions to powerful adversaries. Shaming may work as a social whip in interpersonal relations, or even bring about compliance in interstate relations from those who are weak, dependent, or desirous of more cooperative relations. But are powerful adversaries apt to reform themselves in response to such condemnations?

The Soviets found ways to retaliate. On June 11, 1977, the Soviet Union arrested and expelled *Los Angeles Times* reporter Robert Toth on bogus charges of receiving state secrets; a dissident scientist had given Toth a copy of a paper on parapsychology.[49] On July 18, 1978, journalists Craig Whitney and Hal Piper were convicted of libel and ordered to pay a fine and to print a retraction within five days. They paid their fines in absentia on August 4.[50]

The Soviets also waged their own propaganda campaign against the United States. The directives to the USSR delegation to the thirty-fifth session of the UN Commission on Human Rights on January 5, 1979, noted that the Soviet delegation should emphasize its commitment to human rights and liberties part and parcel of socialist structures; expose the negative consequences for fruitful international collaboration of the hostile propaganda campaign that had been unleashed in all countries by Western countries and, above all, by the United States; and oppose the creation within the framework of the UN of organs whose activity would be directed toward interfering in the internal affairs of governments. Specifically, the Soviet team should condemn massive human rights violations by the fascist junta in Chile, the South African government, and the Arab countries occupied by Israel, and offer a resolution "condemning plans for the production of the neutron bomb as a malicious encroachment on human rights."[51]

Carter's emphasis on human rights contributed to an increasingly tense relationship with the USSR. Perhaps even more important, his responses to Soviet political and economic forays in the Horn of Africa led to conflicts within his own foreign policy team and an increasingly negative public opinion at home that would eventually cool the reception of SALT when he presented it to the U.S. Senate.

COMPETITION IN THE HORN OF AFRICA

"There is an overwhelming cooperation and compatibility between Secretary Vance, Dr. Brzezinski, Harold Brown…and others who help me shape foreign policy," Jimmy Carter declared at a Texas civic luncheon in Fort Worth on June 23, 1978.[1] Three days later Carter underscored this message in a meeting at the National Press Club: "I think it's easy for someone who disagrees with a decision that I make to single out Dr. Brzezinski as a target, insinuating that I'm either ineffective or incompetent or ignorant, that I don't actually make the decision….And it gives an easy target for them without attacking the President of the United States….But I've noticed that President Brezhnev, Mr. Castro and others always single out Dr. Brzezinski as their target. It's not fair to him."[2]

Carter was responding to charges of conflicts between his advisors—not from Moscow or Havana but from Washington, D.C. On June 8, fourteen members of the U.S. House of Representatives Foreign Relations Committee had sent Secretary of State Cyrus Vance a letter, asking him to clear up "confusion and doubt" as to U.S. policies with respect to several crucial areas "such as Soviet-American relations and Africa."[3]

At issue was the American response to Soviet involvement in Somalia and Ethiopia, two Marxist regimes strategically placed in the shipping lanes for Middle East oil. Somalia bordered the Red Sea, the Gulf of Aden, and the Indian Ocean. Its neighbor Ethiopia, a landlocked kingdom throughout much of its history, had gained geopolitical significance because of the ports on the Red Sea it had acquired in 1962 when Eritrea was made an integral part of the country. In Somalia, Mohammed Siad Barre, who had been in control of the government since 1969, joined the Arab League and forged strong ties with the Soviet Union. In Ethiopia, Colonel Mengistu Halle Mariam took over the government in 1977, cut back that country's ties to the United States, and sought Soviet support.

For a while the Soviet Union tried to support both these leftist governments. But in late summer 1977, Somalia sent troops into the Ogaden region, recognized by most other African nations as a part of Ethiopia. Making claims to an area largely populated by Somali people, Somalia solicited the support of the United States. When the Soviet Union countered by sending arms and money to Ethiopia to help that country regain the lost territory in the Ogaden, the Somalis denounced their treaty arrangements with the Soviet Union and expelled its military forces from the country. At the same time, Ethiopia was confronted with the continuing rebel movement in Eritrea, which was supported by neighboring Arab nations.[4]

At first, administration officials tried a low-key approach to address these matters in the Horn of Africa. The Policy Review Committee, for example, on April 11, 1977, chose to rely on a memorandum that provided a nuanced analysis of the interests of the various parties in the area and suggested a primarily diplomatic approach for the United States.[5] Later that summer the United States called on other nations to refrain from supplying arms to either party in the area, to strengthen their ties to the neighboring countries of Sudan and Kenya, to keep up a dialogue with the Somalis, and to maintain some influence relative to Ethiopia. The United States even backed two small aid projects to Ethiopia to show its concern for their people.[6]

But the following fall, as Cuban troops and Soviet war materiel poured into Ethiopia to back its war with Somalia over the Ogaden, the Carter administration began to express its concerns. In the United Nations, U.S. Ambassador Andrew Young spoke out against the Soviet-Cuban presence in Africa.[7] National Security Advisor Zbigniew Brzezinski briefed the press on "the growing Soviet-Cuban military presence." By mid-November 1977, newspaper articles on this threat to the United States began to appear in the U.S. press.[8]

In addition, both Brzezinski and Vance voiced their concerns to Soviet ambassador Anatoly Dobrynin. At a private dinner on December 14, 1977, Brzezinski flatly asserted that the continued influx of Cubans and Soviet war materials to Ethiopia would alter the U.S. position from that of restraint to a more active involvement in the Horn of Africa.[9] At a later meeting Brzezinski suggested that the Cuban military presence in Ethiopia was a threat to the West, endangering "the safety of the transport links for oil between the Middle East and the United States and Western Europe."[10] Vance had at least two private conversations with Soviet ambassador Anatoly Dobrynin on the subject in January 1978. At the second meeting he warned Dobrynin that the Soviet combat and landing ships concentrated in the Red Sea were undermining his own arguments for maintaining good relations with Moscow. Vance said, "Let me tell you straight that there are people close to the President telling him that the latest Soviet actions are a direct personal challenge to the president, a test of his firmness, and he should show the Russians he is not to be trifled with."[11]

Still, members of Carter's inner circle would differ over the actual interests at stake in the area and how the United States should respond. For Vance, the Soviet actions in Africa were not part of "a grand Soviet plan, but rather attempts to exploit targets of opportunity." Realism dictated that the United States deal with each problem in terms of the local situation "in which they had their roots." The heart of U.S. strategy, as Vance saw it, was to "combine diplomacy, negotiations, concerted Western actions, and the powerful forces of African nationalism to resolve local disputes and to remove ostensible justification for Soviet involvement."[12]

Brzezinski thought more was at stake than a "deserted piece of desert." Ethiopia and South Yemen as "Soviet associates" could threaten access to the Suez oil pipelines from Saudi Arabia and Iran. The credibility of the United States was also on the line. As Brzezinski noted, "Skeptical allies in a region strategically important to us" could falter "if Soviet-sponsored Cubans determined the outcome of an Ethiopian-Somali conflict." There could be "wider regional uncertainty and less confidence in the United

States." Even if the Soviet Union was acting out of some "sort of strange territorial legalism, their presence so close to Saudi Arabia was bound to have strategic consequences, whatever the Soviet intent may have been."[13]

With these differing diagnoses of the problem, the two men engaged in something bordering on open warfare in the spring and early summer of 1978. Vance was determined that U.S. involvement in the area would be limited, and these issues should be kept separate from Strategic Arms Limitation Treaty (SALT II) talks. Brzezinski was equally committed to putting the Soviets on notice that their involvement in Africa would be costly to them in terms of domestic support for SALT. Additionally, verbal protests should be backed up by a display of force. Early in 1978 he pushed for the dispatch of a U.S. aircraft carrier task force to the area to back U.S. verbal messages.[14] Secretary of Defense Harold Brown and Vice President Walter Mondale, as will be shown later, moved back and forth between the positions staked out by Vance and Brzezinski.

The Debate over Responses: Show of Force, Linkage?

At a Special Coordinating Committee (SCC) meeting on February 10, 1978, Brzezinski proposed that the United States send a naval task force to the Red Sea. The other powers in the region, he argued, had to see that the United States was not "passive in the face of Soviet and Cuban intervention in the Horn and in the potential invasion of Somalia." His assistant David Aaron, who had just returned from a special mission to Ethiopia, supported him.[15]

But Vance countered, "We are getting sucked in....The Somalis brought this on themselves. They are no great friends of ours, and they are reaping the fruits of their actions." His voice rose, his face got red. Joining Vance in opposition to the proposals was Assistant Secretary for African Affairs Richard Moose and Defense Secretary Brown.[16]

Days later, at the February 22 SCC meeting, the debate over the task force continued. Concerned about U.S. "passivity" toward Egypt, Israel, and Saudi Arabia, Brzezinski argued that the United States needed to show countries in the region that it stood with them. At one point he suggested that the U.S. government would "protect the flow of arms (into the area), and will provide protection from the Russians."[17]

Sending a special task force into the Indian Ocean without specific purpose, Brown countered, would have negative consequences, outweighing any possible positive effect. A mere bluff would not be reassuring. An unfavorable outcome would lessen the credibility such a task force would supposedly provide. Neither did he recommend the use of force against the Ethiopians should they cross the border into Somalia. What if it encouraged Iran, Saudi Arabia, or Egypt to enter Somalia to deter Ethiopia? What if Ethiopia, with Soviet assistance, would "kick the shit out of those forces"? Authorizing the use of U.S. equipment would require the permission of the U.S. Congress. As long as the Somalis were in the Ogaden there would be no support for any of these actions.

Brown also noted that no one in the Defense Department supported fighting Cubans or Ethiopians. The Soviet Union, which Brzezinski wanted to deter, did not need to be deterred.[18]

In the course of the discussion, Vance suggested that a political settlement would make it easier for Siad Barre of Somalia to withdraw from the Ogaden. But he was wary of any attempts to characterize Somalia as a friend. If the United States encouraged the Iranians, Saudis, and Egyptians to provide military support for Somalia, Vance suggested the United States might be worse off, unable to answer hard questions about its involvement in such operations.[19]

At this meeting, Brzezinski felt that everyone was against him. He later noted, "The Defense Department speaking through Harold [Brown], the JCS speaking through General Jones, and [Department of] State speaking through Cy [Vance]—all of them seem to me to be badly bitten by the Vietnam bug and as a consequence are fearful of taking the kind of action which is necessary to convey our determination and to reassure the concerned countries in the region."[20]

Unable to secure support for a show of force in the Red Sea, Brzezinski began making public statements indicating the SALT negotiation process was linked to Soviet behavior. At first, he formulated the connections in ways that were palatable to the president. Bad Soviet behavior could so disturb the political process in the United States that it would make U.S. Senate approval of the treaty less likely.[21] But on March 1, he skated close to a formal linkage policy, telling reporters that Soviet involvement in the Horn of Africa might also have an adverse effect on "the negotiating process of SALT."[22]

The next day, March 2, in an address at the National Press Club, Carter picked up on Brzezinski's theme. The American public would turn against SALT II if the Soviet Union appeared unwilling to cooperate on other issues, he suggested. "The Soviets' violation of these principles would be a cause of concern to me, would lessen the confidence of the American people in the word and peaceful intentions of the Soviet Union, would make it more difficult to ratify a SALT agreement or comprehensive test ban agreement if concluded, and therefore the two are linked because of actions by the Soviets."[23]

Distressed by this speech, Vance confronted Brzezinski in the SCC meeting on that same day. The following exchange took place:

> VANCE: I think it is wrong to say that this [Soviet involvement in the Horn of Africa] is going to produce linkage, and it is of fundamental importance.
> BRZEZINSKI: It [the Soviet involvement in the Horn] is going to poison the atmosphere.
> VANCE: We will end up losing SALT and that will be the worst thing that could happen. If we do not get a SALT treaty in the President's first four years, that will be a blemish on his record forever.
> BRZEZINSKI: It will be a blemish on his record also if the Senate rejects the treaty.

VANCE: Zbig, you yesterday and the President today said it may create linkage, and I think it is wrong to say that.

BROWN: There is going to be linkage—but we should not encourage it.

BRZEZINSKI: What we are saying is that if there is an aggravation of tensions because of what the Soviets are doing in the Horn, there is going to be linkage. That is a statement of fact.

BROWN: Not all statements of fact should be made.[24]

Other issues were addressed at this meeting in a free-ranging discussion. Should those nations in the area that were friendly to Somalia be asked to urge Siad Barre to get out of the Ogaden? Should they be encouraged to provide support to Somalia as a counter to possible Ethiopian, Cuban, and Soviet actions against that country? How should the United States respond to intelligence reports indicating that arms sent to the Saudis and possibly others were being shipped to Somalia? If the Ethiopians were to attack Somalia proper, what should the military role of the United States be? Perhaps the Somalis could handle Ethiopia, while the United States issued deterrent threats to keep the Soviets and the Cubans from further action. In the meantime, who would mediate the conflict in the Horn—the Organization of African Unity (OAU), the United Nations, or some combination of both? What other leverage might the United States have relative to the Soviet Union?[25]

Vance provided a note of realism in several of these exchanges. The nations in the area, he pointed out, would not be very helpful in providing assistance. The Iranians were supportive of the U.S. warnings to the Somalis "to get out of the Ogaden," but under no circumstances would they send their troops or airplanes into Somalia. The Sudanese had made their peace with the Ethiopians and were "no longer in the picture. The Egyptians were blowing hot and cold." The Saudis were a problem. Suspicious of Ethiopia as a Christian nation, they looked at this as a kind of holy war. That very morning, Central Intelligence Director Stansfield Turner interjected that the CIA had a report of a Saudi shipment of ammunition to Somalia. Moreover, some of the arms provided were of U.S. origin, which presented legal problems.[26]

At one point, Brown suggested a joint statement of concern with the Chinese about the Horn of Africa. Vance retorted that this would "get their attention." But he went on, "We are on the brink of ending up with a real souring of relations...that it may take a long while to change and may not be changed for years."[27]

The next day, March 3, Brzezinski supported what the president had stated at the National Press Club. He wrote Carter, "The Soviets must be made to realize that détente, to be enduring, has to be both comprehensive and reciprocal. If the Soviets are allowed to feel that they can use military force in one part of the world—and yet maintain cooperative relations in other areas—then they have no incentives to exercise any restraint."[28] In his subsequent Weekly Report to the president, Brzezinski was "troubled by the potential Soviet success in the African Horn: first, because it would demonstrate to all concerned that the Soviet Union has the will and capacity to assert itself in the Third World; second, because it would encourage Libya, Algeria, and Cuba to act even more aggressively."[29]

In the next three months, Carter continued to speak against a litany of Soviet misdeeds. In an address at Wake Forest University on March 17, 1978, he spoke of the "projection of Soviet or proxy forces into other lands and continents."[30] At a town meeting in Spokane, Washington on May 5, Carter saw "innate racism toward black people in the Soviet Union." Placing his own distinctive interpretation on the nature of the conflict in the Horn of Africa, he saw it as a battle between atheism and religion. Thus Carter noted "a strong sense of religious commitment throughout northern and black Africa. They may be Arabs, they may be Moslems [sic], they may be Christians or others, but they worship God. And that creates a feeling of 'brotherhood and sisterhood.' They recognize that the Soviet Union is a Communist and atheistic nation."[31]

In remarks at the opening ceremonies of the North Atlantic Treaty Organization (NATO) Summit in Washington on May 10, Carter stated, "Soviet power has increasingly penetrated beyond the North Atlantic area. As I speak today, the activities of the Soviet Union and Cuba in Africa are preventing individual nations from determining their own future."[32] The Soviets, he said on another occasion, do not "impose upon themselves the same constraints that we do." Because the trade interests of the United States in the area had been minimal, countries turned to Marxist or Eastern European countries for support. But they would have rather had a democratic friend than to have a totalitarian friend, "and I want to make sure they have that option." Then he suggested that the Soviets' lack of respect for basic human rights and their behavior in the Horn would "have a strong adverse effect on our country and make it much more difficult to sell to the American people and to have ratification in Congress of a SALT agreement."[33]

By this time Carter had come to believe that when "violence occurred in almost any place on earth, the Soviets or their proxies were most likely to be at the center of it."[34] As for Cuba, the president saw it as "a surrogate for the Soviet Union."[35]

In late May, upon his return from China, Brzezinski ratcheted up the rhetoric another notch. "One of the goals of Soviet Union," he charged in an interview on NBC's *Meet the Press*, was to "encircle and penetrate the Middle East" and stir up racial difficulties in Africa.[36]

Two days later the Communist Party newspaper *Pravda* published a statement from the Politburo naming Brzezinski "one of the enemies of détente." It also claimed that there were no Soviet armed forces in Angola or Zaire; the U.S. president was engaging in disinformation.[37]

Then the following transcontinental exchange took place:

> [SOVIET FOREIGN MINISTER ANDREI] GROMYKO: We have no intention of grabbing the whole of Africa, or any of its parts. We don't need it.
> [PRESS SECRETARY JODY] POWELL: The President wishes to make it completely clear that there is no doubt in his mind about the accuracy of the information which the President received on that matter.
> GROMYKO: Sometimes conclusions are drawn from incorrect and inexact information. And that is bad.[38]

Troubled by the deteriorating state of U.S.-Soviet relations, Vance sent Carter a letter outside "the regular bureaucratic channels." His goal was to "dispel" current perceptions about the linkage policy toward the Soviet Union. A coherent strategy, he suggested, might "undertake a prudent increase in our defense spending and continue our efforts to strengthen NATO." SALT should be completed in order to stabilize strategic competition. The human rights initiative with regard to the Soviet Union should be rethought. Furthermore, the United States should not link SALT with third world issues and be careful in trying to use China as a bargaining tool.[39] Most important, Vance argued for "consistency" when the administration spoke about such matters.[40]

Carter paid little heed to Vance's concerns in his subsequent speech at the U.S. Naval Academy in Annapolis, Maryland, on June 7, 1978. After a tour of the academy grounds and Bancroft Hall, where he had lived as a midshipman, Carter stood before the midshipmen to make the commencement address. Secretary of Defense Brown, National Security Advisor Brzezinski, and several high-ranking naval officials and other influentials lined up behind him.[41]

The speech began in a low-key manner. "Détente between our two countries is central to world peace," Carter said. He went on to note, "To be stable, to be supported by the American people, and to be a basis for widening the scope of cooperation, then détente must be broadly defined and truly reciprocal." That admonition was followed by a list of his many peacemaking initiatives. These included work on the SALT II agreement and the Comprehensive Nuclear Test Ban Treaty, reductions in conventional arms transfers between countries, prohibition of weapons in space, the stabilization of force deployment in the Indian Ocean, and increased trade and scientific and cultural exchange. "We must be willing to explore such avenues of cooperation despite the basic issues which divide us. The risks of nuclear war alone propel us in this direction," he noted.[42]

Carter then made a radical shift in tone and message. For the Soviet Union, détente seemed to mean "a continuing aggressive struggle for political advantage and increased influence." In Korea, Angola, and Ethiopia, the Soviets preferred "to use proxy forces to achieve their purposes." He even disparaged their economy and foreign policies suggesting that this aggressive power was a feeble giant. Economic growth in the USSR was slowing down, and the Soviet standard of living does "not compare favorably with that of other nations at equivalent stages of economic development." Soviet attempts to "export a totalitarian and repressive form of government" had led to its increasing isolation abroad. Even Marxist-Leninist groups no longer looked on the Soviet Union as a model to be imitated.[43]

Carter's aide Greg Schneider, who had read an advance copy of Carter's speech, thought it "conflicted and vacillating," suggesting that the "gratuitous insults to the Soviets on pages 10 through 14 be cut. Need to emphasize our strength rather than stridently pointing out their weaknesses."[44]

The speech did not assure many observers that the United States was on a balanced course. The *Washington Post* would call Carter's words "two different speeches."[45] Senator Frank Church scoffed that this was the same old cry that the Russians are coming. Tass, the Soviet news agency, observed that his speech was in some ways strange.[46]

Dobrynin, in a meeting the day after the address, "bluntly" told Vance, "in my personal opinion the speech could be described as anything but balanced."[47] Vance tried to explain the president's speech as a response to domestic political concerns. Carter was increasingly being viewed at home, he said, as "an irresolute and vacillating politician." This image, he continued, was largely created through the failure to persuade Congress to pass a number of his important bills, his acceptance of much lower reductions in the strategic arms ceilings, and his waffling about whether to deploy the neutron bomb. He also believed, according to Vance, that "the image of a weak and ill-starred President was the reason behind Moscow's tough challenges."[48]

Vance would later suggest that the speech was a pastiche of ideas he and Brzezinski had formulated in the drafts they prepared for him.[49] But Brzezinski would later claim that many of the toughly worded statements were Carter's own. The president was the one who inserted unfavorable comparisons between the United States and the Soviet Union and who posed the stark choice of "cooperation or confrontation."[50]

Whatever the mechanics of the speechmaking process, it is clear that the president was attempting to meld together Vance and Brzezinski's views. With Vance, he made the commitment to proceed with SALT whatever the climate. The two superpowers had a common interest in preventing nuclear war and containing the nuclear arms race. But with Brzezinski, Carter saw the Soviet ambitions in Africa as grounded in a grand strategic design, and he had to be tough to check their imperial ambitions.[51]

The Presidential Disadvantage

During the "crisis" in the Horn of Africa, Carter was also dealing with the ongoing SALT talks and the conflicts between Israeli and Egypt in the Middle East. With little time to attend NSC meetings, he depended on Brzezinski for two- to three-page summaries of those discussions. Most of these briefs suggested a consensus that the longer minutes of the meeting do not reveal. Differences were noted in passing and few briefs provided arguments of the various alternatives considered. The president could respond by checking off "I agree," or "I disagree," or he could write a short note in the margin.

For example, in Brzezinski's summary of the March 2 SCC meeting, "disagreements" about the deployment of a U.S. carrier to the region were noted. But he did not mention the extent of the opposition. Cooperation with the Chinese should be studied, he suggested, not noting that Brown had only mentioned this possibility in passing. He closed as follows: "The Saudis, along with Iranians and Pakistanis, should be told that the transfer of arms of U.S. origin to Somalia could have a serious impact on future U.S. arms sales." Then he added they did not object to their providing non-U.S.-origin equipment to the Somalis. Despite Brzezinski's report, there is no evidence in the minutes of the meetings that this last alternative was discussed.[52]

Brzezinski, in short, brought more clarity to the discussions than was warranted by a reading of the transcripts. He provided closure on those items that he usually favored; for example, nations in the area should be informed that they were not to ship U.S.

arms into the area, although they could send other items at their discretion. But he kept open other matters where he did not approve of the drift of the conversation, such as sending a task force to the Indian Ocean, or tilting toward China.[53]

By way of contrast, the various summaries the State Department sent to the president's advisors were usually highly sophisticated and complex. Many anticipated future developments and offered a variety of possible solutions. For example, Presidential Review Memorandum 21, approved at the NSC meeting on April 11, 1977, noted that the Soviets had no major military strategic advantage in Ethiopia, that their decision to give Ethiopia substantial military equipment probably reflected their attempts to shore up their position in Ethiopia while hopefully not alienating Somalia. It was anticipated that Cuba would play a role in Somalia to keep Eritrea from defecting.[54]

A background paper on Eritrea in the spring of 1978 delineated other complexities in the Horn. By the end of 1977, the report suggested, insurgents controlled most of Eritrea except for some cities. But the Ethiopians, aided by a Soviet sealift and the Cuban air force, were able to stabilize the situation. Still, the Ethiopians and the Soviets had different expectations for the next part of the plan. Ethiopia's Mengistu Haile Mariam envisaged a military solution to the Eritrean problem, while the Soviets and the Cubans preferred a negotiated settlement. The Ethiopian government, they predicted, would reestablish effective control over major urban areas in the next few months, as well as all of the sea coast.[55]

The ultimate pacification of the area would take years. Various Arab nations, too, were involved in the conflict. Muslim nations supported Eritrea against the Ethiopian Christians. The Saudis were backing independence for Eritrea. Supplies were being shipped to Eritrea through Sudan and Iraq; Iran, Egypt, Kuwait, North Yemen, and the Palestine Liberation Organization were also involved in some ways. The OAU, committed to the postcolonial territorial boundaries in Africa, did not recognize the Eritrean liberation movement. Cuba, moreover, was no mere surrogate of the Soviet Union, but an autonomous nation acting in concert with them in the Horn.[56]

A careful reading of SCC discussions and some key State Department memos would have informed the president that not all conflicts in the Horn were Soviet-inspired, that the Cubans were not simply the proxies of the Soviet Union, and that religion could be a divisive rather than a uniting force in the region. Instead, Carter relied on Brzezinski's short summaries, including his Weekly Reports. They provided the bold, clear, and apparently broad perspectives that Carter favored.

Retrospectives

At the SCC meeting on March 2, 1978, Vance had suggested that the crisis in the Horn was made in the United States: "A year ago the Soviets were in Somalia and in Ethiopia as well—now it has become a daily crisis. We are stirring it up ourselves." Even Mondale wondered if the United States had not hyped the issue too much. He stated that he had "not heard any remedies which I think will change Russian policy one bit. By trying to press on these issues we underline our impotence on the Horn." Mondale even suggested, "Pumping up the press on the Russians and the Cubans might be giving Siad some hope that we will come to his aid."[57]

Vance later gave U.S. policies mixed reviews. The Department of State's policy toward Africa, he suggested, was sound in terms of what was realistically attainable. U.S. interests lay in preventing the resumption of Soviet influence in Somalia with the limited diplomatic means at its disposal. In casting events in the Horn as an East–West struggle, the United States placed power into the hands of the Somali leader, Mohamed Said Barre, who was "perfectly willing to treat the Horn crisis as an East–West confrontation in order to gain American political and military support." By "setting impossible objectives in U.S. policy…we were creating a perception that we were defeated when, in fact we were achieving a successful outcome," Vance noted later. The inflated rhetoric got the nation "into kind of a shooting match in which the United States was shooting itself in the foot."[58]

Brzezinski, on the other hand, later argued that "had we conveyed our determination sooner, perhaps the Soviets would have resisted, and we might have avoided the later chain of events which ended with the Soviet invasion of Afghanistan and the suspension of SALT.…I was convinced for political reasons that SALT would be damaged if we did not react strongly, for the American public was prepared to support détente only in the context of genuine reciprocity in the American-Soviet relationship."[59] The problem, he wrote, went back to the day he "advocated that we send in a carrier task force in reaction to the Soviet deployment of the Cubans in Ethiopia. At that meeting not only was I opposed by Vance, but Harold Brown asked for what reason would we deploy our cannon to the area, not taking into account that that is a question that should perplex the Soviets rather than us.…'In brief, under-reaction then bred over-reaction.' That is why I have used occasionally the phrase 'SALT lies buried in the sands of the Ogaden.'"

For Brzezinski, however, there was one "beneficial outcome" from these troublesome months. "We started reviewing more systematically the advisability of developing strategic consultations with the Chinese in order to balance the Soviets."[60]

Carter does not mention the Horn in his memoirs. If he had, he might have recognized that his own tough talk contributed to the kind of de facto linkage that could sink all the programs that he favored in the first half of his Annapolis speech. Rather than treating the competition between the United States and the Soviet Union as a rivalry between two major powers, as Vance preferred, Carter fell back onto rhetoric that saw the Soviet Union and its "surrogates" as not only the source of most evil in the world but also as weak and despicable. If he had paid more attention to the State Department reports on the Horn, Carter would have learned that the battles in that part of the world were much more complex than those between good and evil or those between people with religious commitments and atheists. He might have understood that most conflicts in Africa had little to do with the Soviet Union, but were based on conflicting tribal identification and histories.

Soviet motives in the Horn were also more complex than either Carter or Brzezinski suggested. As Dobrynin notes, for some members of the Politburo, there were ideological motivations: "Each of these situations [in Africa], of course, had its own local peculiarities," he wrote. "But underlying them all was a simple but primitive idea of international solidarity, which meant doing our duty in the anti-imperialist struggle. It made no difference that often it had nothing to do with genuine national liberation movements but amounted to interference on an ideological basis into the internal affairs of countries where domestic factions were struggling for power."[61]

Others in the Kremlin, Dobrynin continues, "were flattered at our country's involvement in far away conflicts because they believed it put the Soviet Union on an equal footing with the United States as a superpower." Defense ministers Andrei Grechko and Dimitri Ustinov "were emotionally pleased by the defiance of America, implied by our showing the flag in remote areas. I also suspect that they privately played on Brezhnev's vanity on the theory that all this somehow demonstrated that the Soviet Union was already a world power to be reckoned with." They had no understanding of what had caused agitation for the United States.[62]

Whatever its objectives, subsequent developments suggest that the USSR's entry into the Horn gave the Soviets no real strategic advantages. In the short term, Soviet support of Ethiopia was in some way stabilizing. With the aid of Russian money and arms and Cuban military personnel, Ethiopia was able to drive Somalia out of the Ogaden. But this was not followed by an Ethiopian incursion into Angola proper. U.S. support for Siad Barre may have curtailed any possible Soviet moves along those lines.[63]

In the long run, the Horn proved to be a morass. Guerilla warfare in the Ogaden continued for several years. The leaders in power in Somalia and Ethiopia were deposed. Eventually the countries themselves disintegrated as a result of ethnic and religious conflicts. Eritrea became an independent nation, cutting off Ethiopia's access to the sea. A border war between Ethiopia and Eritrea followed when Eritrean forces occupied disputed territory. Only by the end of 2000 was Ethiopia able to secure the disputed territory and sign a peace treaty with Eritrea.[64]

And the United States never did secure any real benefit from the millions it poured into the Siad Barre regime from 1980 on, though it did have the use of former Soviet military bases for a time.[65] After his overthrow in 1992, massive drought led to a famine that resulted in the deaths of over 300,000 Somalis. In 1992 President George H. W. Bush sent in 30,000 troops on an ill-fated humanitarian mission to Mogadishu. It ended in an ignominious U.S. retreat under President Bill Clinton in 1993.[66]

Karen Brutents, a Soviet scholar, later argued that both the United States and the Soviets were driven into these and other conflicts by a "fighting spirit," a kind of "ideological gambling motive," and not by a desire to understand the other side.[67] But perhaps Dobrynin had the last word on the significance of the whole controversy. Soviet-American relations during this period, he suggested, "resembled a complicated game of chess, with only one essential difference: in reality it ended with both rivals losing the game and the policy of détente in ruins."[68]

Ironically, Carter's support for Soviet dissidents and the harsh rhetoric he employed in response to their forays in the Horn of Africa may have slowed down any momentum for a deal on SALT he might have been able to sign and deliver upon early in his administration. Certainly some of his actions along these lines contributed to the hardening of anti-Soviet opinion in the United States to the point that there was no real groundswell for SALT II when he brought it to the Senate.

NEGOTIATIONS WITH PANAMA

In a second set of negotiations begun at the beginning of his term in office, Jimmy Carter expeditiously came to terms with a foreign adversary. In early September 1977, Jimmy Carter and Panama's General Omar Torrijos Herrera put their signatures to treaties that would transfer control of the Panama Canal to Panama by 2000. The representatives of twenty-six other Western Hemisphere nations witnessed the ceremony, including several heads of state.

A bit of history was introduced into the proceedings with Carter's presentation of former president Gerald Ford, Lady Bird Johnson (widow of former president Lyndon Johnson), and former secretaries of state William P. Rogers and Henry Kissinger to the crowd. The president observed that three previous U.S. administrations had been involved with the issue.

General Torrijos noted in his remarks that the original treaty had been signed not by Panama but by a French citizen and that the new accords created some potential problems for the Panama Canal. But Panamanians, he said, "hold no feelings of rancor" for the people of the United States and that President Carter, by raising "morality as a banner in our relations," was representing the 'true spirit of the American people.'"[1]

In accordance with the wishes of presidential aide Hamilton Jordan, the Pan-American aspects of the treaty were noted by the press, not just Torrijos. But CBS's Walter Cronkite did not cover the story as Jordan envisaged; NBC provided live coverage of the event.[2]

At a White House dinner after the ceremony, foreign ministers and U.S. senators mingled with Ford and Kissinger as well as Coretta Scott King, Muhammad Ali, Ted Turner, and other notables. Sol Linowitz, one of the chief negotiators, sat next to General Augusto Pinochet of Chile. Afterward, Isaac Stern and André Previn entertained their distinguished audience, performing sonatas on the violin and piano. At the State Department, Cyrus Vance held a separate reception for ministers and their guests.[3]

Carter, it appeared, had many good reasons to celebrate. He had in hand what appeared to be a major diplomatic triumph. The administration had taken on an important task and, against considerable odds, had finally carried it off. Diplomatic professionals primarily conducted the negotiations, but Carter's commitment to their efforts was essential to their success. Later, the Carter administration, like many others before it, faced impediments in the home base beyond any it experienced in the foreign field. This was an old American story.

The Commitment

Jimmy Carter had placed Panama near the top of his foreign policy agenda for several reasons. Confronting rising nationalist sentiments in Latin American and the threats of revolutionaries disrupting traffic on the canal, the Linowitz Commission on U.S.–Latin American Relations had called the matter "the most urgent issue to be faced in the hemisphere."[4] Moreover, there was Republican support for taking on the matter. The Ford administration had been working on the project and Kissinger told Carter in a private session shortly after his election that in the canal matter U.S. relations with Latin America were at stake. All Latin American governments supporting Panama believed that the United States should give up some sovereignty; even Barry Goldwater (R-AZ) might be a supporter. The Mexican government, it seems, had told the senator that they would "send a division to help the Panamanians in the event of conflict with the U.S." Though Kissinger "didn't know whether or not the Mexicans were bluffing, they had impressed Goldwater."[5]

The president's advisors were all in accord. Carter saw the controversy as "sapping away our nation's influence in the Southern hemisphere." Vance thought that Torrijos, the strong man governing Panama, might be "forced to yield to ultra nationalist pressures and to acquiesce to violent disruption of the canal operations" should the canal not be returned. "Such an outcome could easily have expanded into an international confrontation, with world opinion solidly against the United States."[6] Brzezinski thought the administration should take advantage of the president's honeymoon period to secure support for a Panama Canal treaty. Possible electoral damage would be minimized with swift legislation, "leaving them aside and trying to get them ratified in the third and fourth year would have been impossible."[7] A possible side benefit to the whole enterprise was noted by Hamilton Jordan. The Panama Canal treaties would serve as a dry run for the Strategic Arms Limitation Treaty talks (SALT II). "[I]f you looked at the basic groups that were going to be opposed to any SALT treaty," noted Jordan, "you were fighting a lot of the same people."[8]

What neither Carter nor any of his advisors anticipated was the intensity of the political opposition they would encounter at home. The traditional leadership of the Republican Party supported Carter's efforts. But that party was in a state of flux. Right-wing conservatives who were becoming increasingly influential in the party would vehemently oppose the return of the canal to Panama and the whole undertaking raised negative feelings in a majority of the American people.

The Negotiations

To lead the negotiating team, Carter selected two widely respected professionals with notable careers in business and diplomacy. Special Representative Sol Linowitz was a former ambassador to the Organization of American States (OAS) and head of the

Commission on U.S.–Latin American Relations. Joining him as chief negotiator was Ellsworth Bunker, U.S. ambassador to Vietnam from 1967 to 1973, and Linowitz's predecessor as U.S. ambassador to the OAS. Over eighty years old at the time, Bunker was known for his hawkish views on Vietnam. Bunker also had a career in the sugar business and Linowitz was board chairman of a company that would become Xerox.[9] Appointed in February, their terms were to run for six months.[10]

The two men were given a wide berth. The exact timing of their operations was up to them, and they were given "as much latitude as possible to explore various formulations without being constrained by detailed instructions." As Linowitz noted, "My mission was to get the job done, and how Bunker and I did it was our problem."[11]

The United States faced three major issues during the course of the negotiations. First, they had to determine whether or not Torrijos really wanted a treaty on terms that the United States could accept; he might prefer to agitate Panamanians against the U.S. presence as a means of consolidating his domestic political supporters. Second, when and under what conditions should the canal be returned to the Panamanians? The U.S. Army administered the canal, and U.S. citizens in the Panama Canal Zone wanted to maintain as many of the bases and privileges there as possible. The Panamanians, however, saw American presence in the Canal Zone as cutting a swathe across their country, dividing it in two and undermining their sovereignty. Third, what would be the U.S. role in preserving the neutrality of the canal after its return to Panama? The United States would require as a bottom line the permanent right to intervene to keep the canal open. The Panamanians were concerned that the United States might use such a guarantee to intervene in their domestic affairs. They wanted a joint guarantee and an elimination of the words "in perpetuity," a phrase in the original treaty that, for them, emphasized U.S. dominance in the area.[12]

At the opening of the negotiations on Panama's Contadora Island in February 1977, it seemed that Torrijos might simply use the issue to insult the American negotiators. The talks did not really begin until the third night of their stay, and when they started the Americans heard tirades on how the United States exploited the developing world and engaged in other perfidious practices. Accusations were followed by demands so extreme that they could not be taken seriously. Convinced that the Panamanians were simply testing them, Bunker and Linowitz rode out this first meeting.[13]

The experience convinced them that a U.S. setting would be more conducive to businesslike negotiations. To satisfy the Panamanians, several of these talks would be held in Panama's embassy in Washington, D.C.—"a bit of Panama in the United States," as one of Panama's negotiators would say. Alternating with this site would be the conference room of the Under Secretary of State at the State Department. At one point Linowitz insisted that the talks remain in Washington, saying he had eye trouble and had to remain near his doctor.[14] Another decision made after the Contadora meetings was to hold the meetings in secret.[15]

Supplementing these meetings were those of William Jorden, U.S. Ambassador to Panama, and Panama's Ambassador to the United States, Gabriel Lewis. They agreed to talk frankly about issues and never lie to each other, opting for silence if they could not speak openly. Both men were complete professionals and devoted to understanding the issues dividing them.[16]

On March 13, the U.S. team made a proposal that would move the talks forward. Meeting in the residence of the Panamanian ambassador, which was vacant at the time and bitterly cold, the American diplomats suggested that the conferees work on two separate canal treaties. Bundled up in an overcoat, Bunker suggested that one treaty would provide the time and the terms of transfer of the canal to Panama. The other, indefinite in duration, would give the United States the right to act to maintain the canal's neutrality even after Panama assumed full control of it.[17]

Suggesting the two treaties was a "brilliant stroke" according to Vance. The neutrality treaty would deal with the concerns of those in the United States who felt that the turnover of the canal would threaten U.S. security. Seeing the "political importance" of this suggestion, Carter immediately authorized Bunker and Linowitz to follow this course.[18] The U.S. team also stated its intention to bring forward the expiration date of the treaty to the year 2000. The Ford administration had previously talked in terms of at least forty years—2017 at the earliest.

Before they could agree on a neutrality treaty, however, the Americans had to deal with the lands and waters held by the United States in the Canal Zone. On May 10, Ellsworth Bunker started the discussion with a modest concession—the United States would transfer the railroad running parallel to the canal from Balboa to Colon—as well as the top of Ancon Hill to the Panamanians. It was a limited transfer of territory, hedged with many reservations. The Panamanians were not at all pleased.[19]

Ambassador Jorden broke what could have been an impasse with the suggestion that the United States "give Panama what it feels it needs for pride, first, and for economic development." When the other members of the team did not take him seriously, he spoke up at length and with "vehemence." The railroad should be given back to Panama without any reservations. Panama should be allowed to run the ports. Moreover, all of Ancon Hill, he insisted, should be returned to the Panamanians. Handing over only the top of that hill, as he saw it, was akin to giving the Greeks the Parthenon without the Acropolis.[20]

The U.S. Army, protective of its rights in Panama, had been at first rigid on these land and water issues. But Linowitz called an old acquaintance, Secretary of the Army Cliff Alexander. The next morning, he and Bunker went to the Pentagon with their proposals. At the next negotiating session, Bunker was able to make some serious concessions. The ports would pass to Panama on entry into force of the agreement. Panama would have control over all shoreside activities, and a joint port authority would be established to run the canal and handle traffic along the waterway. The railroad would be returned to Panama, without reservations, and civilian housing would be jointly managed and turned over to Panama at five-year intervals. Other significant transfers of property included the whole of Ancon Hill, not just the top; the entire city of Cristobel; and the Albrook airstrip bordering downtown Panama City.

The Panamanians were stunned.[21]

The neutrality issue still had to be resolved, and here the president's involvement was crucial. On May 16, Carter handed the Panamanian Ambassador, Gabriel Lewis, a written statement for Torrijos. As he wrote, "a new treaty must protect the interests of both countries…for our part, we need an agreement that grants us the necessary rights to operate, maintain and defend the canal during the treaty period. In addition, we need an arrangement that provides reasonable assurance that the Canal will remain permanently open to world shipping on a secure and non-discriminatory basis." He added that any "unnecessary delay" would complicate chances for a treaty's success in the U.S. Congress. Torrijos responded that he understood the need for a neutrality treaty.[22] A few days later, on May 26, the U.S. and Panamanian negotiators agreed on its terms.[23]

One other major issue remained—the Panamanian claims that payments should be paid for previous injustices. In the past, tolls for transit through the canal had been set at a low level, a subsidy to the United States and other shipping that Panama had in effect been forced to pay. Nor had Canal Zone residents paid taxes to Panama. Furthermore, Panamanians had not been permitted to open shops and hotels in the Canal Zone. But the Panamanians were putting a politically unrealistic dollar amount on their claims. On May 30, they called for a $1 billion lump sum payment by the United States, to be followed by $300 million annually until 2000. Linowitz retorted that it was "wholly unrealistic to think that Congress would appropriate American taxpayers' money for the purpose of persuading the Panamanians to take away 'our' canal."[24]

Carter, by now quite intimately involved in the negotiations, responded furiously that this was a "ridiculous request" and "great news for the treaty's opponents."[25]

Eventually a compromise package containing loan concessions and guarantees worth about $350 million over five years were worked out, the funds to be taken from a variety of sources including the Export Import Bank and the Overseas Private Investment Corporation. Other payments to the Panamanians would be made only out of the revenues from the canal itself. On July 29, 1977, Carter warned Torrijos that this was the last offer from the United States. A few days later, on August 5, Torrijos announced his acceptance of the U.S. proposal.[26]

Still, at a wrap-up meeting at the Holiday Inn in Panama City on August 7, the Americans were handed a Spanish version of the treaty that resurrected issues the Americans thought they had already resolved. Disappointed, Linowitz put in a call to Jordan that night to warn him that the negotiations might be on the verge of collapse.[27] But then, on August 10, Linowitz's last day as ambassador, Panamanian Foreign Minister Rómulo Escobar Bethancourt began the meetings saying, "We will try to conclude agreement today as a present to Sol."[28]

The outcome should never have been in doubt. As Linowitz later noted, "This was a negotiation between a superpower and a tiny principality on the Isthmus. His [Torrijos's] only real weapon was the threat that by civil disturbance and sabotage he could block the operation of the canal." But though "the canal was important to the [United States]," Linowitz continued, it was "Panama's lifeblood. The failure of the negotiations…would have been catastrophic for him [Torrijos]."[29]

The Deal

That evening the heads of the U.S. and Panamanian negotiating teams reached an agreement on the principles of two new canal treaties.[30] Later that night, Carter called Linowitz and Bunker to congratulate them on their accomplishment.[31] Though Carter would later say that he would not approve the treaties without reading them line by line, he did approve these early texts solely on the bases of Linowitz and Bunker's judgment.[32]

The proposed deal was explained to the press at a meeting in the White House Briefing Room on August 1. The Panama Canal treaty proper provided that at the end of 1999, Panama would assume full control over the operation of the canal as well territorial jurisdiction of the Canal Zone. In the neutrality treaty, the U.S. retained the permanent right to defend the canal from any threat that might interfere with its continued neutral service to the ships of all nations. U.S. warships would have a permanent right to transit the canal expeditiously. All canal employees would continue in employment of the U.S. government until retirement. An economic package had been negotiated that would not involve any congressional appropriations. Panama would receive a share of the canal tolls, and the United States would pledge its best efforts outside of the treaty to arrange for a program of loans, guarantees, and credits.[33]

For all the skills of the U.S. negotiation and professional support teams, the treaty's conclusion could not have been accomplished without Carter's personal commitment to the effort. As Linowitz notes, the United States had a president "who was truly insistent on getting a treaty, and was prepared to pay a political price for it."[34]

Still, Carter's foibles created some difficulties during the course of the negotiations. As the talks drew to a close, the president met with Linowitz and sometimes Bunker several times a week. He could not restrain himself from clutching for details in a way that Linowitz thought could bog down the talks. In one meeting at which Carter asked the tonnage of U.S. ships that had cleared the canal the year before, Linowitz simply retorted that he did not know, thereby avoiding a long path of follow-up queries.[35]

Near the end of negotiations, the president also put a new and somewhat distracting issue on the table. Inspired by a visit from Senator Mike Gravel (D-AK), Carter told people at a town meeting in Yazoo City, Mississippi, that the treaty would give the United States an exclusive right to any new sea-level canal in the isthmus.[36] By bringing up this measure, Carter was clearly trying to tie down the votes of Alaskan senators to the Panama Canal treaties. Carter may have thought that the idea of an alternative route would reassure other senators worried about the United States losing the existing canal. It was a stance recommended to him by his congressional liaison, Frank Moore.[37]

An exclusive right to build a sea-level canal, however, did not reflect any substantial national security concerns.[38] Years before, President Lyndon Johnson had been interested in such a possibility, thinking that nuclear explosions could be used to build a waterway large enough that nuclear-powered supercarriers could pass through it. But when engineering studies suggested that it would be too expensive to consider, the matter ceased to be of interest to most U.S. officials. Moreover, as Stuart Eizenstat wrote Carter in October 1977, a feasibility study would require major environmental impact studies and put new, potentially controversial issues on the table.[39]

As Linowitz later noted, he attempted to dissuade Carter from raising this sea-level canal issue. The Panamanians had decided that the United States should not have an exclusive right to build such a canal. Most important, there was no need for it, given that there was no other Central American site offering a real alternative route and it would simply distract from the important issues. Carter did secure a face-saving out— the United States in effect retained a veto power over the possible construction of any such canal by other parties.[40]

Now came the hard part. The negotiations with Torrijos had been relatively easy, but getting the treaty through the U.S. Senate would be much more difficult, and a president busy with the SALT talks, human rights, Soviet involvement in the Horn of Africa, and other matters would have to eke out time to deal with a Congress more reluctant to confront the issue than anyone had anticipated it might be.

DEALING WITH CONGRESS

There were harbingers of difficulties ahead as early as the summer of 1977. Driving up to the Pan-American Union building in Washington, D.C., for the original signing ceremony, Special Negotiator Sol Linowitz and his wife, Toni, saw a crowd of people gathered at a corner on Constitution Avenue. Under a huge banner, an effigy of Linowitz was hung. The crowd shouted, "Linowitz! LINOWITZ!"[1] Earlier, the Associated Press had published a story noting that Panama's General Omar Torrijos Herrera had studied at the School of the Americas and led a 1968 coup against Arnulfo Arias, the democratically elected president.[2] Jimmy Carter was the first president not invited to a national convention of the Veterans of Foreign Wars in twenty-seven years. The organization's concern, according to one of its officers, was Carter's policies regarding the Panama Canal Treaty, among several other matters.[3]

The Republican Party, too, was divided in the mid-1970s over the possible return of the canal to Panama. Ronald Reagan had tapped into a deep reservoir of resistance to such a policy in the North Carolina Republican primaries of 1976. When the treaties were signed, Reagan exclaimed that "the campaign was intended to convince Americans 'that somehow keeping the canal represents colonialism, imperialism on our part.'…Nothing could be farther from the truth."[4] Former presidential candidate Barry Goldwater, who had earlier implied he might go along with the treaty, moved into open opposition to it. As he told Frank Moore in early September 1977, he had received 8,000 letters from constituents opposing the treaty.[5] U.S. Congressman Robert Bauman, a former head of Young Americans for Freedom and a leader of anti–Panama Canal treaties efforts in the U.S. House of Representatives, exclaimed of the canal, "We bought it. We built it. We paid for it. It's ours."[6] Even John Wayne, the actor and hero of conservatives in the United States, received hate mail after he announced that he supported the treaty; it was the first such mail he had received in his life.[7]

The Campaign Begins

To deal with the opposition, the White House undertook a major effort to win over the opinion of relevant elites. In August 1977, shortly after the original agreement with Panama had been reached, Ambassador Linowitz, Chairman of the Joint Chiefs of Staff George Brown, and former president Gerald Ford's national security advisor Brent Scowcroft made a trek to Vail, Colorado, where they met with Ford at his vacation residence. After a ninety-minute briefing, Ford called Carter at Camp David to say he would give the treaty his full support. He was "absolutely convinced it's in the national interest of the United States that the treaty be approved."[8] Henry Kissinger, who had met with Carter a couple of days earlier, followed Ford's commitment, saying that it was his "'strong view' that [the treaty] would be in 'the national interest of the United States.'"[9] Both men also agreed to brief Republican senators on the values of the Panama Canal treaties.

Shortly thereafter, other political conservatives fell in line. Journalist William Buckley changed his mind on the treaties after a visit to Panama.[10] SALT critic and anti-Soviet hardliner Paul Nitze wrote the president that he would support the treaty, subject to a more detailed study of its provisions.[11] John Wayne composed a three-page summary of his views on the treaties and mailed it to each member of the U.S. Senate.[12] The administration was also successful in recruiting top military leaders to the cause. In late August the Joint Chiefs endorsed the treaties.[13] Later, the former Chief of Naval Operations Admiral Elmo Zumwalt and prior members of the Joint Chiefs Lyman Lemnitzer and Maxwell Taylor announced their support for the treaties.[14]

Even before the United States had come to its initial terms with Panama, a Citizens Committee had been set up. Henry Kissinger, Dean Rusk, David Rockefeller, William Buckley, and Admiral Zumwalt were early members.[15] Eventually the committee was headed by W. Averell Harriman, and membership expanded to include such notables as former Defense Secretary Clark Clifford, Coca-Cola Chairman J. Paul Austin, Douglas Dillon of Dillon Read and Company, AFL-CIO Secretary-Treasurer Lane Kirkland and giants in the communications industry such as Gardener Cowles, William Randolph Hearst Jr., and Jack and Eleanor Howard of Scripps Howard Publications.[16]

Other business, labor, and religious leaders were invited to briefing sessions at the White House. The Carter staff aide in charge of women's affairs, Margaret Constanza, organized sessions for various leaders of women's organizations.[17]

The Carters hosted many of these sessions.[18] As First Lady Rosalynn Carter noted, "So successful was this 'guest policy' with the Panama Canal issues that it became a pattern over the next years to garner support for all important legislation."[19] Her husband later observed that people "would go back home…and tell the folks in their home state that the Panama Canal treaties were needed. So this was an indirect, but a very effective way, to change public opinion, at least adequately, in a state, to let the members of the Congress do what they knew ought to be done to begin with."[20]

In support of these efforts Linowitz, in the late summer and fall of 1977, was a virtual perpetual motion machine. After the signing of the original agreements, he briefed the U.S. cabinet, members of the Organization of American States in town for the ceremony, leaders of the business community, and present and former members of the Joint Chiefs of Staff. He also spoke at a dinner of the Economic Club of New York, the Commonwealth Club in San Francisco, the World Affairs Council, and the Pan American Society; he appeared on NBC's *Meet the Press* and other television and radio shows.[21] Secretary Vance and Vice President Walter Mondale undertook similar tours.

The Senate Campaign: The Players

In the Senate the battle for the Panama Canal treaties was conducted as a major political campaign. At the top, the heads of state called the basic shots. Jimmy Carter worked out differences with Torrijos, oversaw his White House staff, and talked to and sometimes made promises to senators to win their support. Torrijos met with many U.S. senators during the ratification process, usually kept a low profile, and remained in close touch with his Foreign Minister, Rómulo Escobar, and with Panama's Ambassador to the United States, Gabriel Lewis, as they relayed messages to and from Carter at crucial points in the debate.[22]

Neither Vance nor Zbigniew Brzezinski played major roles in this process. Vance was expending most of his energies on the negotiation of the Strategic Arms Limitation Treaty and on U.S. relations with the Soviet Union and China. Brzezinski, preoccupied with Soviet forays into the Horn of Africa, paid little attention to the Panama Canal effort, coming in on the debate only when some "real hardliners" needed to be countered. As Bob Beckel, of Congressional liaison staff, pointed out, Brzezinski was involved in "consolidating his power on matters of greater interest to him."[23] Secretary of Defense Harold Brown and Joint Chiefs of Staff Chairman General George Brown provided assistance when it was needed and deemed proper on the Panama Canal issue.[24]

Many others, however, provided assistance in what became a major campaign. In October 1977, Linowitz drafted a joint statement for Carter and Torrijos that clarified disputed phrasing in the treaty.[25] U.S. Ambassador to Panama William Jorden arranged the visits of congressmen and staffers to Panama, soothed Panamanian tempers, and warned the White House about amendments that would be unacceptable to the Panamanians.[26] In the later phases of the ratification process, William Rogers, a prominent attorney with ties to Senate Minority Leader Howard Baker(R-TN), acted as Torrijos's emissary, negotiating with Senate leaders and the White House.[27]

On the Senate floor, Deputy Secretary of State Warren Christopher led the administration's efforts. He was aided by a resource group from the Department of State—the so-called Gang of Four (Ambler Moss, Mike Kozak, Larry Jackley, and Betsy Frawley). Working out of a small office in Vice President Mondale's suite at the Capitol, they provided treaty details, legal arguments, and historical data to those who needed them. Jorden notes that they worked "excruciating hours" in providing "an uncommonly high quality of technical detail, legal precision, and solid historical background." Though "their names were never mentioned in the *Congressional Record*, their ideas and even their words filled many of its pages."[28]

At the White House, the brunt of the campaign fell upon the shoulders of Hamilton Jordan. Beginning in August 1977, he mapped out plans for informing key players of the terms of the treaty, came up with ideas for the signing ceremony, and made suggestions for winning over the Senate. Advice was forwarded to the president regarding the speech he might make at the signing ceremony.[29] At times Jordan even served as the president's special emissary to Torrijos.

White House legislative aides Frank Moore and Robert Beckel worked directly with Deputy Secretary Christopher. They provided materials that could be placed in the *Congressional Record*, did background work for markup sessions in the Senate, and anticipated possible misunderstandings or reservations. They also orchestrated, with the help of others on the staff, a series of telephone calls to undecided senators. Lists were made that noted how the legislators were lining up, complete with specifications about their concerns and possible side interests.[30] The president would sometimes personally call, while Vice President Mondale and others aided in these solicitation efforts if they had closer personal contacts with particular senators.[31] Even former president Ford made some calls.[32] At times, Carter and his staff would make side deals with undecided Senators in exchange for their support. Secretary of Defense Harold Brown and General George Brown, the chairman of the Joint Chiefs of Staff, provided assistance as needed and proper on the Panama Canal issue.[33]

Opening Moves

Secretary of State Vance opened the battle in the Senate. On September 26, 1977, he warned the members of the Senate Foreign Relations Committee that "if thirteen years of effort were lost, and these treaties rejected, our relations with Panama would be shattered, our standing in Latin America damaged immeasurably, and the security of the Canal itself endangered."[34] The next day, the secretary of defense and the chairman of the Joint Chiefs of Staff stressed the importance of the treaties in providing for the security of the canal, stating that the most important threats to the canal were sabotage and terrorist actions.[35]

Yet the action had barely begun when there was a crisis to be faced. Foreign Minister Escobar suggested in speeches in Panama that the United States had not been granted any right to intervene in his country. That was not the understanding of the Americans, and on October 11, Carter promised concerned senators that he and Torrijos would work out a joint statement on the matter. Eventually, a reluctant Torrijos accepted a statement drafted by Linowitz and Escobar and cleared by members of the Senate Foreign Relations Committee. Both countries, Torrijos and Carter proclaimed, understood that the United States could defend the canal against threats against its neutrality, but did not have the right to interfere with Panama's internal affairs.[36] In addition to that statement, the U.S. team was able to secure an even clearer statement that both U.S. and Panamanian warships and auxiliary vessels would receive expedited passage through the canal and would have the right "in case of need or emergency, to go to the head of the line of vessels in order to transit the Canal rapidly."[37]

Following the resolution of this issue, several senators visited Panama. On November 9, 1977, Senator Byrd led a delegation there. In the middle of January 1978, Senate Foreign Relations Committee members traveled to Contadora and later that month, Senator Alan Cranston (D-CA) led a group of ten other senators. The U.S. embassy in Panama, as Ambassador Jorden wryly noted, had become a kind of travel office. Other observers noted that Jorden began to look fatigued and had conflicts with some members of the Torrijos regime over who should manage these trips.[38]

Sensitive to the fact that Torrijos had come to power through a coup nine years earlier and was no real democrat, the administration downplayed the human rights issue. White House staffers Landon Butler and Joseph Aragon had earlier suggested that a briefing be held in the White House for the leaders of human rights groups, "provided that adequate explanations can be given beforehand to the alleged human rights violations in Panama."[39] Following Senator Byrd's trip to Panama, Brzezinski cautioned the president not to couple human rights issues with the approval of the treaties; in a memo to the president he wrote:

> If Torrijos does not make the concessions regarding democracy that several believe he promised, they could use that as an excuse to vote against the treaties. Therefore, I think it is in our interest not to couple the democracy-in-Panama issue with the Canal treaties. I think we are more likely to lose votes if Torrijos does not make good on his supposed concessions than win them if he does.[40]

Then, in early December 1977, White House aide Hamilton Jordan went to Panama to quell some of Torrijos's concerns about the treaties. Upon his arrival, Jordan praised Torrijos for his handling of Byrd's Senate delegation, expressed confidence in Torrijos's ability to cope with visitors, and begged the general to maintain the same confidence in Carter's U.S. ratification efforts. Pleased that Carter had sent his top assistant to see him, Torrijos was temporarily mollified. As Jordan would later note, "You have never seen two different men than Cy Vance, who I love, and Omar Torrijos, who I also loved." As Brzezinski noted, Jordan and Torrijos developed a "buddy-buddy" relationship that was extremely useful to us."[41]

The Senate Foreign Relations Committee began its markup sessions on the treaties in late January, 1978. At this point, Senate Majority Leader Byrd publicly vowed to support the treaties, subject to the condition that the Carter-Torrijos interpretation of the U.S. right to intervene be incorporated in the official agreement as a separate article to the treaty. When Torrijos vehemently objected to a new article along these lines, saying it would require a new referendum in Panama, Robert Byrd and Howard Baker (the Republican leader in the Senate) rewrote the provision to incorporate it in an article dealing with a related matter. Finally, on January 30, the Committee voted 14–1 to recommend approval of the treaties.[42] Other hearings in the Armed Services Committee provided a forum for the antitreaty forces, but these meetings received little attention at the time.[43]

The Floor Debates

On February 8, the floor debates began. Opponents of the treaties questioned the integrity and patriotism of treaty supporters and issued scathing critiques of the Panamanians. Senator Paul Laxalt (R-NV) charged that the Panamanians did not have the skilled personnel needed to run the canal. Senator Jesse Helms (R-NC) spoke

FIGURE 7.   Frank Moore, Senator Robert Byrd, and Jimmy Carter meet in the Oval Office. Photograph courtesy of the Jimmy Carter Library.

of the brutality of the "guardia and Panamanian justice." Senator Orrin Hatch (R-UT) suggested that Panama might simply shut down the canal to harass the United States.[44] Linowitz was attacked as a supporter of Salvador Allende's Chile and a tool of the New York banks. Senator Barry Goldwater (R-AZ) now saw a larger plot, noting that the negotiators of the treaties, almost the entire Carter administration, and even the members of the Senate Foreign Relations Committee were part of the Trilateral Commission. Others focused on Panamanian leader Torrijos, calling him a tinhorn dictator and a drug dealer. Senator Robert Dole (R-KS) alleged that Panamanians were involved in the heroin trade.[45]

Responding to some of these critiques, Senator Thomas J. McIntyre (D-NH) questioned the "moral arrogance" of some of the treaty opponents, who were claiming a "corner on patriotism, morality, and God's own truth."[46]

Invectives, however, were not the major problem. Scores of amendments, reservations, and understandings concerning the treaty were offered. The leadership group saw some offerings as relatively harmless and included them as reservations in one way or another. Stipulations that would have killed the treaty were either rejected outright or reframed into more innocuous statements.

But Senator Dennis DeConcini's (D-AZ) proposed amendments to the Neutrality Treaty caused a legislative mini-crisis. On February 9, 1978, the day after the floor debate began, he filed an amendment to the treaty that would have given the United States a broad right to intervene in Panama. His concern was "the possibility that internal Panamanian activities might also be a threat to the waterway. Labor unrest and strikes; the actions of an unfriendly government; political riots or upheavals—each of these alone or in combination might cause a closure of the Canal."[47]

At first, DeConcini's proposed amendment won little attention. But by mid-February, the administration's head count of senators supporting the treaty was stalled at sixty, seven short of the required two-thirds majority. Emboldened by the leverage he now had, DeConcini met with Warren Christopher on March 7, 1978, and demanded that the neutrality treaty be altered in two respects. First, there would have to be an amendment giving the United States the right to keep at least three military bases in Panama for five years after the treaty expired. The second change DeConcini insisted on was "a specific guarantee that the obstruction of the Canal arising out of internal Panamanian activities can be swiftly and adequately dealt with."[48]

Rather than quietly dealing with DeConcini's concern, Christopher gave the young senator maximum exposure by arranging a one-on-one meeting for him with the president. And Carter, assured by Christopher that these revisions could be "handled," accepted the proposed changes. The amendment to the neutrality treaty gave the United States the authority to intervene in Panama against any action that impeded the operations of the canal. The Neutrality Treaty then passed the Senate on March 16 by a vote of 75–23.[49]

Torrijos was considerably upset at this development. Only after delicate maneuvering by a member of his own team did he hold his tongue.[50] Ambassador Jorden had foreseen this reaction and warned Washington that the administration should not go along with DeConcini's amendment.[51]

When the United States made no real concessions to his concerns, Torrijos penned a letter to the heads of state of almost every country in the world, noting the U.S. Senate's approval of the Neutrality Treaty on March 16 and quoting the two leadership amendments, which were the basis of his understanding with Carter. The principles in those amendments flowed from "generally accepted norms of international law, which are effectively consecrated in multilateral international agreements." On March 28, Jorge Illueca, Panama's Ambassador to the United Nations, wrote a letter to UN Secretary General Kurt Waldheim. He enclosed a note paraphrasing Torrijos's letter, and four attachments. The letter was distributed to all UN members.[52] Newspapers in Washington interpreted the Panamanian response as a rejection of the treaties.[53]

Meanwhile, in the Senate, DeConcini was determined to add similar provisions to the second agreement. This treaty would hand over operation of the canal to Panama, and DeConcini was determined to preserve in relatively broad terms the U.S. rights to intervene in the Canal Zone. Upset about the problems DeConcini was posing, Hamilton Jordan wrote Brzezinski that the DeConcini amendment could determine the fate of the treaty and that the administration had to talk to him.[54]

To deal with this problem, treaty supporters in the Senate rewrote DeConcini's proposed amendment, specifying that protection of the canal would never be used to intervene in Panama's internal affairs.

When DeConcini found this unacceptable, Carter canceled a meeting he had scheduled with the Arizona senator.[55]

DeConcini then appeared on CBS, National Public Radio, and several other television and radio broadcasts. His amendments, he claimed, would serve to "toughen" and "clarify" the treaty. Asked about Panama's negative reaction, he blithely replied, "It's not my problem what Panama thinks."[56]

The senator had overplayed his hand. The backlash against him began with a *Washington Post* article criticizing the president's handling of the senator and referring to DeConcini as a "lightweight whom serious senators should regard as an institutional embarrassment."[57] Indeed, as White House aides Frank Moore, Robert Beckel, and Bob Thomson wrote Carter on March 20, 1978, DeConcini had hurt himself badly in regard to his colleagues: "Many see his amendment as pure political opportunism on an issue where the stakes are dangerously high."[58]

For a moment, Carter considered appearing on television himself to counter the DeConcini media blitz.[59] But Senate leaders convinced him that he should not further inflate DeConcini's importance by responding with a speech. Feeling that the White House had mismanaged DeConcini badly on the neutrality treaty, they decided to deal with him from now on. The State Department also came to a conclusion that the administration should cease to woo the recalcitrant senator.[60]

From that point on, Senators Byrd and Church worked on an alternative "leadership reservation" to the second treaty. Their strategy, initially suggested by Mike Kozak of the Gang of Four and Byrd's top aide Hoyt Purvis, was to come up with a "clarifying" statement for the Panamanians that would limit the scope of the DeConcini amendment. Consulting with all interested parties, including Ambassador Lewis and President Torrijos, they arrived at a compromise just before the scheduled vote on the treaty was to begin. It proclaimed that "nothing in the treaties should have as its purpose or be interpreted as a right of intervention in the internal affairs of the Republic of Panama or interference with its political independence or sovereign integrity."[61] Byrd then informed a group of Democratic senators of what had passed and secured the support of Minority Leader Baker.[62]

DeConcini was brought in line shortly thereafter. At a meeting with the Senate leaders, the junior senator was stopped when Byrd turned to him, his eyes "as cold and barren as a West Virginia mineshaft." Said Byrd, grimly, "It has to be like this, Dennis. I will not accept any changes." Looking at the stern faces of the others assembled and knowing how the leadership group could still affect the career of any young senator, DeConcini concluded that the new wording was acceptable and agreed to cosponsor it.[63] On April 16 the Senate passed the leadership reservation forged by Byrd and others by a vote of 73–27.

Two days later, on April 18, the roll call for the treaty on joint operations proceeded at the scheduled time. Only an hour before the final countdown did the Senate leadership know that DeConcini and three other holdouts—Senators Howard Cannon (D-NV), James Abourezk (D-SD), and S. I. Hayakawa (R-CA)—would vote for the treaty.[64]

Sitting in the gallery, Jorden and Linowitz were not at all certain about the outcome. The final vote on the second treaty was 68–32, the same as it had been for the first treaty.[65] At the White House, Carter joined Brzezinski and Jordan in his secretary's

FIGURE 8.   Jimmy Carter and Omar Torrijos at the signing of the Panama Canal Treaty. Photograph courtesy of the Jimmy Carter Library.

office to catch the event on radio. When it was over, a much-relieved president called Senator Byrd to congratulate him. "You're a great man. It was a beautiful vote."[66] That night he announced that Torrijos had agreed to accept the series of treaties complete with the reservations that had been attached to them.[67]

Three months later, on June 16, 1978, the ceremony marking the exchange of ratifications took place in Panama. To prepare for the event, scores of operatives from the White House converged on the meeting site with demands on how the backdrop should be handled, the people seated, and even the color of the lights changed. Private citizens and persons who had aided the administration in one way or the other were in the audience as guests of President and Mrs. Carter.[68]

Photos showed Carter and Torrijos signing the documents with Zbigniew Brzezinski, Senator John Sparkman (D-AL), and UN Ambassador Andrew Young in the background. Behind them, one could see Panamanians in T-shirts blazoned with a likeness of Carter.[69]

But Senators Byrd and Baker, who had played such crucial roles in securing the consent of the Senate, were not even in Panama. Three other key actors, Warren Christopher and Senators Frank Church and Paul Sarbanes (D-MD), were seated in the VIP section rather than on the stage. Jordan noted, "The list was drawn up by protocol, not by common sense."[70] Afterward Carter spoke at a rally, saying in Spanish that a new era "of inter-American understanding and cooperation is at hand."[71] Shortly thereafter General Torrijos introduced a sour note in the whole affair, suggesting that Panama would have taken the canal had the United States not met its concerns.[72]

The celebration in Panama was not the end of the story. The narrow victory for the Panama Canal treaties in the Senate was a reflection of the fears that the senators would have political problems at home if they voted for what the opposition was successfully painting as a giveaway. In this political climate, implementing legislation still had to be passed in the House; the administration would have new hurdles to contend with for months to come.

Problems in the House

The debate over measures to implement the canal treaties raged in the House for sixteen months, coming to an end shortly before the transfer of control over the canal to Panama would begin. Carter would later recall that the whole effort was a "horrible experience."[73]

Four committees provided multiple forums for opponents to voice their concerns. These panels "revised, rewrote, and altered the legislation in ways that were unprecedented." Proposals were made that no money or territory could be turned over to Panama without approval from the House, that no land could be returned to Panama without implementing legislation from the House, that the members of the new commission operating the canal would have to be approved by the Senate, and that no money would go to Panama to improve education and health care in rural areas. This attempt to restrict disposal of territory was in clear violation of an earlier U.S. Supreme Court ruling that disposal of land through treaties was lawful. The proposed requirement that commission members would have to be approved by the Senate was in clear opposition to treaty provisions that Panama could choose its own members on that commission.[74]

The opposition came from two major sources. Congressman John Murphy (D-NY), chair of the House Merchant Marine and Fisheries Committee, wanted to retain as much U.S. power over the operation of the canal as possible, albeit within the framework of new obligations undertaken in the treaties.

Another group, led by conservative Congressman Robert Bauman (R-MD), undertook what could only be described as a wrecking operation. The young congressman and some like-minded colleagues introduced restrictions that contradicted the obligations undertaken in the treaties. Ignoring the traditional House norms of courtesy in their debates, they also suggested that their "friends in the State Department" were leading the supporters of the treaty, or that they should be given the "Cy Vance Award." The power of this group, as Ambassador Jorden has pointed out, came from their connections to a moneyed political network, mobilized to defeat many of the treaty supporters in forthcoming elections.[75]

In these circumstances, Carter finally opted for Congressman Murphy's resolution. The bill first passed the House in June 1979 and was followed up in July by a more moderate Senate version. On September 20, the report of the first conference committee was voted down in the House. Finally, on September 26, a second conference committee report was approved by a vote of 224–202.

On September 27, 1979, a mere three days before the transfer of authority to Panama was to begin under the treaties, Carter finally was able to sign the implementation bill. Long and arduous negotiations that stretched back to the administration of President Lyndon Johnson and had absorbed the efforts of Carter and his staff for almost three years were finally brought to a close. Carter was not far from the mark when he noted, "Members of my Administration and many other American leaders had risen to meet successfully one of the greatest legislative challenges of all time."[76]

Outcomes

From a national interest point of view, there is much to be said for settling the canal issue at that time. As Carter pointed out, the treaties not only protected U.S. interests in the canal but also showed that "a great democracy will practice what it preaches."[77] Vance noted that it was "difficult to imagine how the United States could hope to deal in any affirmative way with the turbulence in Central America and the Caribbean today if, in addition to problems in Nicaragua and El Salvador, we also confronted Panamanian nationalism directed against the canal and the Canal Zone."[78] Brzezinski suggested that "a crisis in U.S.–Latin American relations was averted."[79] Beyond that, the United States set a new tone for its dealings with Latin America. As Hamilton Jordan pointed out, "When a large and powerful country like the United States treats a small nation like Panama with dignity and respect, it pays off in the long run."[80] Madeleine Albright, a member of Brzezinski's staff, saw the Panama Canal treaties as a "great victory," a successful conclusion to complex negotiations she had foreseen would eventually "come out that way."[81]

Still, as Carter would later admit, if he had known how difficult dealing with the Panama Canal would be, he might not have taken it on when he did.[82] Brzezinski also came to think that in retrospect maybe the administration "had paid too high a political price for it."[83]

Certainly the administration had underestimated the political difficulties of this task. Though there was bipartisan support for the measure at the leadership level, there was also the strong opposition of many in the American public.[84]

Responding to these events, an aroused public mobilized to defeat members of Congress inclined to "give away" the canal—enabling people like Congressman Bauman and his ultraconservative allies in the House to eviscerate and hold up for over a year the implementation of legislation.[85] The loss of seventeen pro-treaty senators in the elections of 1978 and 1980 and the ensuing changes in the makeup of the Senate also raises the question of whether the effort was worth the political cost.

The drawn-out ratification battle, moreover, did little to boost the administration's political stock. Determined, tough, and dedicated as Carter and his aides were, they lacked the political finesse that would win them credit within the Washington establishment. Carter had never forged strong links with individual congressmen. Deputy Secretary of State Warren Christopher, an accomplished diplomat, proved to be less skilled politically in dealing with the Senate. Even after the debate closed and the treaties were pushed through the Senate, the administration did not sufficiently acknowledge the substantial roles of Senators Byrd and Baker in securing the final success of the treaties.[86] As Ambassador Jorden suggests, the administration made mistakes in dealing with the House. Carter first relied on his own staff, and then Congressman Murphy, rather than finding strong congressional leadership to shepherd the legislation through the House.[87] As Hamilton Jordan noted, the result was that "we got no political momentum whatsoever from the Panama Canal."[88]

Perhaps most important, Carter and his advisors overestimated the value of the exercise as a test run for the SALT II treaty. The final approval of the implementation measures by both houses of Congress would not be forthcoming until three months after the SALT agreements with the Soviet Union had been concluded. In the Senate, Howard Baker and other Republicans had harmed themselves politically within their own party and were not willing to do battle for the Democratic administration on the SALT treaty. In undertaking what the political right saw as a giveaway, Carter contributed to the image that he was weak in defining U.S. interests. This perception intensified demand from the political right to show that he was tough on the SALT II treaty.

Reflecting this latter perspective, the conservative columnist William Safire wrote at the time that had he been a senator he would have offered Carter his support for the Panama Canal treaties conditioned on demonstrations that the president would be tough on SALT II. "A President strong enough to act weakly is better than a President unable to act at all," wrote Safire, adding, "if I were a senator I would remain undecided until Mr. Carter offered specific assurances that any SALT treaty would insure veritable security, that the Senate's lawful right to approve arms sales would not be subverted by a doctrine of executive package deals, and that Cuban mercenaries in Africa would be no longer considered a 'force for stability' as voiced by the ideologue who misrepresents us at the United Nations."[89]

SALT AND THE SENATE

Jimmy Carter's plane from the Geneva Strategic Arms Limitation Treaty (SALT) talks landed on June 18, 1979, at Andrews Air Base. Two hours later the president was addressing a joint session of the U.S. Congress, urging support of the treaty he had just brought back with him from Vienna. The SALT II Treaty, he explained, was not a favor the United States was doing for the Soviet Union. It was a move to serve U.S. goals of security and survival. Militarily, he noted, "Our power is second to none." Economically, diplomatically, and politically, he said, the United States was so strong that "we need fear no other country." A nuclear war would bring "horror and destruction and massive death that would dwarf all the combined wars of man's long and bloody history."[1]

Even with powder to hide the fatigue under his eyes, and dressed in a fresh suit, Carter appeared tired and the assembled audience greeted his speech halfheartedly. Only when he condemned the war and urged Congress to keep U.S. defenses strong and to counter Soviet expansionism was there any applause.[2]

The outlook for favorable action on the treaty was not positive at this time. U.S. Senate Majority Whip Alan Cranston (D-CA) said he had only fifty-eight votes, nine short of the necessary two-thirds majority. Partisans on the right were suggesting that they would amend the treaty to death—a possible rerun of the tactics used to deflect Woodrow Wilson's Treaty of Versailles. Partisans on the left suggested that the new agreements had not accomplished much in the way of arms reduction.[3] Polls, moreover, revealed no strong public sentiment for SALT that the president could build upon to win over senators on the borderline. Anti-Soviet feelings in the country had increased in 1978 and early 1979. After the Vienna conference, opposition to the treaty increased. Eighty-two percent of the public had heard about the treaty, but only 39 percent of these supported it, while 22 percent were against it and 21 percent had no opinion.[4]

The administration had contributed to the tepid political climate. Carter's decision not to deploy the neutron bomb and his cancellation of the B-1 bomber were widely viewed by hawkish critics as indicators that he was too "soft" in countering the Soviet military threat.[5] And his characterization of the USSR in the Horn of Africa as an atheistic nation and a strategic threat to the United States reinforced this anti-Soviet sentiment in the public.

Indeed, as Senator Frank Church told Anatoly Dobrynin in 1978, the White House had come to depend on a primitive anticommunism, a tactic that hurt the administration's aims to get a SALT II agreement through the Senate.[6] In one of his letters to Moscow, Dobrynin explained quite clearly what was going on:

Flirting with the conservative moods in the country (the strength of which he at times clearly overestimates), Carter frequently resorts to anti-Soviet rhetoric in order to, as they say, win cheap applause. The danger is found in the fact that such rhetoric is picked up and amplified by the means of mass communication, in Congress, and so forth. Ultimately, as often happens in the USA, the rhetoric is transformed, influences policy, and sometimes itself becomes policy.[7]

Carter had also deferred to Senator Henry "Scoop" Jackson (D-WA), enhancing his considerable influence in Washington political circles. Carter needed Jackson for his energy program, but the president's consultations with Jackson on Soviet foreign policy had been counterproductive. He would never win Jackson over to a SALT II agreement that the Soviets would sign. Indeed, Carter's initial SALT proposals were close to a long memo of Jackson's, providing public markers that opponents of SALT II could portray as appeasement.[8] Even then, in November 1977, Brzezinski had to tell the president that he should not personally meet with Jackson.[9]

There were other reasons for this lack of public support. The administration had been slow in its attempt to counter the growing anti-SALT efforts of organizations such as the Committee on the Present Danger. In the spring of 1977, Hamilton Jordan's deputy, Landon Butler, had pushed for the establishment of a General Advisory Committee on SALT and suggested possible contacts with both hard-line and progressive leaders.[10] But, as the administration focused its efforts on the Panama Canal issue, months went by without anything being done. Movement on this front occurred only after the Director of Arms Control and Disarmament Agency Paul Warnke wrote Butler on December 20, 1977, urging that the nominations for committee membership be submitted by January.[11]

Finally, in 1978, the administration moved ahead on its SALT II campaign. The General Advisory Committee on SALT was appointed, and the Department of State created the SALT Working Group within the Bureau of European Affairs. Headed by Matt Nimitz, the number three man in the department, the Salt Working Group noted the leanings of various Senate groups and the bad news in the polls, and also warned that congressional amendments or modifications could be used to defeat the treaty. Supplementing these efforts, the Department of State's Bureau of Public Affairs tracked public opinion on SALT II and forwarded these summaries to Secretary of State Cyrus Vance and others within the foreign policy bureaucracy. President Carter had greater faith in the polls of Patrick Caddell, a public opinion specialist with whom Carter had a long working history.[12] At the National Security Counsel, Roger Molander was given the responsibility of dealing with technical concerns arising out of the treaty and answering questions from both the staff and the Senate. At the Department of Defense, Walter Slocombe headed another task force. Within the White House Office, Communications Director Gerald Rafshoon came up with an overall strategic plan. In a letter to the president in December, he suggested the administration should employ "simple and easily understood" themes that would "strike a responsive chord" and appeal to the public's "common sense."[13]

In the Congressional Liaison Office, Frank Moore and Robert Beckel set up the SALT Working Group, discussed strategy, and arranged briefings for individual senators. Over a period of time they realized they had little support from the central Senate leadership and would "have to create their own leadership corps." To this end they advised that the administration should try to insure that the Senate Foreign Relations Committee be the first to hold hearings. The American people should get their first impressions of SALT with Frank Church as committee chair; Scoop Jackson was not to be given the opportunity of "tearing us apart in Armed Services Committee hearings." As for the Armed Services hearings, Chairman John Stennis should be persuaded to take charge, rather than turning the matter over to Jackson's subcommittee.[14] By May 1979, seventy-five senators had been briefed individually by Vance, Secretary of Defense Harold Brown, National Security Advisor Zbigniew Brzezinski, Assistant Secretary for Military Affairs-Political Affairs Leslie Gelb, or members of the Office of Congressional Relations. As the Vienna summit approached, the White House Office of Congressional Relations sent each senator lengthy briefing books on SALT II.[15]

Anne Wexler's Public Liaison Office provided outreach service, mobilizing labor, environmental, religious, and other groups to support the ratification efforts. By the fall of 1979, her office had secured endorsements from "four constituencies whose support for SALT should be more widely advertised." These included a group of about thirty pro-SALT retired military personnel; all seven former national science advisors; evangelicals, of whom Billy Graham was the most prominent SALT supporter; and labor leaders. She suggested short photo opportunities with the president or with Vice President Walter Mondale as a way to focus press attention and to orient these groups toward Senate activity. Her work with several major church groups, including the National Council of Churches, the U.S. Catholic Conference, and the Southern Baptist Convention, was of significant importance. Materials on SALT were sent to over a thousand members of the clergy nationwide in the hope that they would preach sermons related to SALT.[16]

To coordinate all these efforts a task force had been formed in February 5, 1979, and Hamilton Jordan took over its leadership for a few months. In late July, after the Senate Foreign Relations hearing had begun, Jordan was named White House Chief of Staff and his deputy Landon Butler took over for the SALT Task Force. Finally, in late August, Lloyd Cutler headed up that group. Cutler had the political clout in Washington that Carter's earlier aides lacked, but he started late in the game. Even after his appointment Cutler delayed his service to carry through on his plans for a vacation on the French canals.[17]

In addition to the difficulties caused by organizational delays, there were serious differences within the administration over how to navigate the domestic political terrain. Should the emphasis be on winning over hard-line senators? Butler peppered Jordan with suggestions that Senators Jackson, Sam Nunn (D-GA), and John Culver (D-IA) were the real players in the battle, and that consultations should be carried out with them to discuss possible increases in the levels of defense spending for such items as the MX missile, the cruise missile program, and research and development.

He even suggested that the administration attempt to win over hardliner Paul Nitze by consulting him on Minuteman missile questions and giving him credit for alerting the administration on this matter.[18] Moore and Beckel argued that an endeavor along these lines was necessary to win the support of Robert Byrd (D-WV) and other undecided senators.[19]

Others argued that the emphasis should be on the importance of the treaty for promoting nuclear stability and a stable relationship with the USSR. Back on March 2, pro-SALT senators George McGovern (D-SD), Mark Hatfield (R-OR), and William Proxmire (D-WI) had warned Carter that the emphasis on a military buildup was obscuring the whole purpose behind the SALT II agreements.[20] And Carter's communications director Rafshoon warned the president that any attempt to sell SALT II in "terms of strengthening our national defense…mean[t] he would be playing the game on the opponents' turf and the debate would revolve around numbers, striates and weapons systems that the public will never understand."[21]

To sell the treaty, the administration settled on both arguments. Emphasizing the vulnerabilities in the Soviet system, Mondale, in an address before the Greater Minneapolis Chamber of Commerce on February 22, 1979, noted that the United States had easy access to the seas and friendly neighbors on its borders, whereas the Soviet Union had narrow straits to the high seas, a severe winter, and longer and more vulnerable borders with an adversary at each side.[22]

That same day, Carter stated, "The United States continues to be the most powerful nation on Earth.…I am committed to preserving and even enhancing that power."[23] In a major speech on April 25, 1979, he noted that the United States and the Soviet Union "have a common interest in survival" so that the "possibility of mutual annihilation makes a strategy of peace the only rational choice for both sides." But he went on to note that the combined economies of the United States and its allies were more than "three times as productive" as those of the Soviet Union and its allies. The United States was "equipping its submarines with the new, more powerful, and longer-range Trident I missiles. Next year we are working on even more powerful and accurate Trident II missiles for these submarines. In addition, the U.S. cruise missile program will greatly enhance the effectiveness of our long-range bomber force. These missiles will be able to penetrate air defense systems which the Soviet Union could build in the foreseeable future." In short, the United States, with its upcoming cruise missiles and bomber capabilities, could pierce the Soviet air defenses with relative impunity.[24]

Other administration spokespeople repeated these refrains. Brzezinski noted on April 4, 1979, that the treaty would not signal "the end of East-West competition. The Soviets in the past two decades had expanded and modernized their armed forces in all areas."[25] The next day Secretary Brown, in an address before the Council on Foreign Relations and the Foreign Policy Association in New York, saw a "troubling trend in both strategic and tactical nuclear areas." SALT II, overall, would be advantageous in that it would limit Soviet warheads and launchers and thus help resolve the U.S. "vulnerability" problem. Nor would the agreement, he assured his audience, limit the U.S. ability to modernize its weapons system or to work with its allies on "the important issues of modernization of NATO tactical nuclear forces."[26]

The decision to go for new military commitments created difficulties for Carter in his pro–SALT II base. Senators McGovern, Hatfield, and Proxmire had warned the president back on March 2, 1979, that the emphasis on a military buildup was obscuring the whole purpose behind the SALT II agreements.[27] On June 11, Hatfield argued that the administration's decisions regarding the MX missile would move the United States from a deterrent nuclear policy to a counterforce strategy that would place a "hair trigger" on nuclear war.[28] In August, twelve senators, led by Democrats McGovern, Howard Metzenbaum (OH), Adlai Stevenson III (IL), and Republican Lowell Weicker (CT), wrote the president, urging him to resist demands for an increase in the arms budget as a condition for approval of the pact. The military budget, they declared, should be debated separately from the treaty issue.[29] To deal with this strongly pro–SALT II group, the administration promised to introduce new measures for limiting weapons in the projected SALT III talks.[30]

Warnings by the SALT Task Force that the administration would receive little help from Senate leadership also proved to be accurate. Of the leadership group, only Minority Whip Alan Cranston was on board from the beginning.[31] Minority Leader Howard Baker (R-TN), who at first pronounced himself "undecided," announced in June that he would oppose the treaty. Sam Nunn (D-GA) had the prestige and expertise on defense matters that would have allowed him to effectively counter Jackson, but he had earlier criticized Carter's cancellation of the B-1 bomber and refusal to deploy the neutron bomb.[32] On August 2, 1979, he joined Senators Jackson and John Tower (R-TX) in a letter to Carter stating that the treaty was not worthy of ratification without real increases in the military budget of at least 4 to 5 percent.[33] Majority Leader Byrd did not finally commit himself until late October 1979. Henry Jackson was clearly a lost cause. Shortly before Carter signed the SALT II Treaty, Jackson had compared the agreement to the appeasement of Germany at Munich, an image that caused Carter to order members of his delegation to never carry umbrellas.[34]

The Committee Hearings

Finally, on Monday July 9, 1979, the Senate Foreign Relations Committee began its hearings in room 318 of the Russell Senate Office Building. Frank Church, who had made some of the most articulate arguments for the SALT process in the debate over Warnke's nomination, replaced John Sparkman as committee chair, but he was running for reelection in Idaho, where a dovish record would be a negative for many voters. At the opening, Church noted that the committee problem was to "find the right balance between arms control and armaments."[35] Before the process was over he would for a moment join the "Russians are coming" crowd he had earlier deplored (see chapter 24). In addition, three new conservative Republicans—Jesse Helms (NC), Richard Lugar (IN), and S. I. Hayakawa (CA)—were sitting on the committee, the result of the 1978 midterm congressional elections. Senator John Glenn (D-OH) would also create problems for the administration with his critiques of the treaty and the amendments he proposed that would have required new negotiations with the USSR.[36]

Secretary of State Vance, the first witness before the committee, argued that the treaty served both the cause of peace and the military interests of the United States: "Nuclear war would be a catastrophe beyond our imagination—for the aggressor as much as the victim." He went on to note that SALT II would permit the "necessary modernization of each of these three legs of the U.S. triad of delivery systems—land-based missiles, submarine-based missiles, and long range bombers."[37] The follow-up witnesses, Secretary of Defense Brown and General David Jones, chair of the Joint Chiefs of Staff, testified that the United States had essential equivalence with the Soviet Union, though it would have to undertake important strategic modernization programs to maintain that parity. Indeed, General Jones testified that the treaty would not constrain U.S. efforts to attend to concerns expressed by the Committee of the Present Danger published in an article in *Foreign Affairs*.[38]

Paul Nitze, who had led the attack on the appointment of Paul Warnke as the chief SALT negotiator, was back as one of the leading opposition witnesses to the treaty. On July 12 he focused on what he saw as the U.S. "vulnerability" to a Soviet first nuclear strike. "Strategic parity," he warned, was "slipping away from the United States." He was particularly concerned that the treaty allowed the Soviet Union to keep the SS-18 heavy ICBMs while prohibiting the United States from developing similar missiles.[39] Senator Jackson's ally, General Edward Rowney, who had earlier resigned from the SALT II negotiating team with a public denouncement of its efforts, now told the committee in a long presentation that the "Treaty does not meet minimally acceptable standards." When pushed, he claimed that he had remained on the Carter negotiating team as long as he had because "hope springs external." But now he suggested they could go back to the bargaining table and achieve a better deal. Republican Senator Lugar found Rowney's views "astonishing"—given the fact that Carter, Soviet foreign minister Andrei Gromyko, and purportedly even the USSR's general secretary, Leonid Brezhnev, had made it clear that they saw no possibility for changes along these lines: "Who are you, General Rowney, to come before us today, given this august testimony by the leadership of this great nation, and indicate as a matter of fact that the Soviets do want to get back to the table, as opposed to having no Treaty at all?"[40]

An unanticipated event—discovery of an alleged Soviet "combat" brigade in Cuba—led to a thirty-day moratorium on the hearings.

Finally, on October 15, the markup sessions began. By that time, as Senator Church indicated, the hearings had been the most extensive in the Senate Foreign Relations Committee's history. Thirty public hearings had been conducted, over one hundred expert witnesses had testified, and a record of 4,000 pages had been compiled. Moreover, the Senate Select Intelligence Committee had summarized for the Foreign Relations Committee the results of a two-year inquiry into the verification problem, complete with eleven volumes of documentation.[41]

The discussions in the markup sessions focused on possible Soviet advantages in heavy missiles, the U.S. ability to monitor the agreements, and the possibility of a U.S. nuclear buildup in MX and cruise missiles in accord with the treaty. Those senators who were concerned about the Backfire bomber argued that it could be used as an intercontinental weapons carrier should the Soviets be able to fuel it in flight or utilize it in one-way missions. Defenders of the treaty pointed out that the Soviets had other uses for the Backfire in mid-range missions and that their bombers could not make the trip without in-flight refueling capabilities. Opponents of the treaty wondered about the Soviet advantage in heavy missiles. The supporters noted that the Joint Chiefs did not even want to develop heavy missiles. Moreover, these concessions to the Soviets had been made on the basis of an understanding with them that U.S. missiles, and other missiles in Europe, would not be placed in the equation.

On November 9, the Senate Foreign Relations Committee voted to recommend ratification of the treaty to the full Senate. Seven Democrats and two Republicans voted in favor,[42] and those in support of the report gave a variety of reasons for their decisions. Church noted in his closing comments that the United States and the Soviet Union were "in a way, like two gladiators locked in some sort of death dance, and finding a way to separate those two gladiators is going to be not only difficult, as indeed this SALT Treaty, in the seven years that were required, makes plain, but it will take time." Senator Edmund Muskie (D-ME) argued that the United States had defense needs that differed from those of the Soviets and that those who opposed the treaty did not take the related asymmetries in weapons deployments into account. Senator Edward Zorinsky (D-NE) saw the treaty as providing for the first time a database for calculating the weapons of the two countries. Senator McGovern noted that his backing of the treaty was on the condition that no new deals should be brought back to the Senate unless they pledged "significant and substantial reductions of arms on both sides."[43] Two Republican moderates, Jacob Javits (NY) and Charles Percy (IL), simply supported the treaty on the grounds that it would serve the national interest of the United States and reduce the risk of a nuclear war.[44]

Six senators voted against the treaty, including two Democrats. John Glenn said he would not vote for it because he did not think its terms were verifiable.[45] Richard Stone (FL) simply claimed that the treaty would "result in a strategic imbalance that favors the Soviet Union." Even two moderate Republicans on the committee voted against it: Howard Baker and Richard Lugar expressed their concerns that the provisions regarding Soviet heavy missiles and the Backfire bomber gave the Russians an advantage. Conservative Senator Helms argued that the treaty would allow the Soviets to build up to an overkill campaign that could destroy the United States three and a half times over rather than two and a half times. Senator Hayakawa argued that the treaty had codified Soviet strategic superiority for the 1980s.[46]

The major battle in the committee revolved around the conditions that it would attach to its recommendations for approval. Opponents of the treaty did not have the votes to stop a favorable recommendation to the Senate, but they could weigh it down with conditions that would cause the Soviet Union to reject it. Gromyko had warned on June 25, 1979, that any amendments to SALT II "would be the end of negotiations."[47] To achieve their ends, opponents introduced proposals to require on-site inspection of missiles in both countries, to count the Backfire bomber as a strategic weapon, and to enable the United States to deploy heavy missiles.[48] General Rowney, who in an unprecedented move had been made a member of the staff as a consultant, backed these and other "killer" amendments, claiming that the Soviets would back down and accept these conditions.[49]

Supporters of the treaty countered these efforts by creating three classes of understandings. Category 1 consisted of Senate interpretations of the treaty agreements. Category 2 would require the U.S. President to communicate certain items to the USSR at the exchange of ratification. Understandings placed in Category 3 would require Soviet recognition of these conditions.[50] The strategic goal of the supporters was to either defeat the possible "killer" Category Three conditions, or revise and transform them to Category One or Two. Senator Glenn's Category Three proposal that would have prohibited increases in the range, payload, or production rate of Soviet Backfire bombers was dealt with in this way. By a vote of 7–8 it was rephrased and transferred into a Category Two amendment.[51] Senator Church finessed some rash statements that he made in the fall of 1979 in this manner. A Soviet "combat brigade" camp in Cuba, he charged, would have to be removed before SALT would be approved. A Category One understanding, adopted on Friday, November 2, specified that the president would affirm "that Soviet forces in Cuba were not engaged in a combat role, and that they will not become a threat to any country in the Western Hemisphere."[52]

At the end of the hearings, only two conditions were placed in Category Three: one stipulated that the various provisions contained in the SALT protocol would have the same legal status as the treaty itself; the other required that the letter Brezhnev would write to Carter concerning the limits on the Backfire bomber would be legally binding for the Soviet Union. Both were relatively innocuous demands that would require no new negotiations with the Soviets.[53]

Even as these hurdles in the Senate Foreign Relations Committee were cleared, new problems were encountered. On December 17, Senator Nunn and nineteen other undecided senators (eight Democrats and eleven Republicans) sent Carter a letter suggesting that the Senate vote be deferred. They were concerned over the protocol terms and what they saw as "the ongoing slippage in America's comparative military position, awareness of which has been accentuated by the Senate's deliberations on SALT and by recent international events."[54]

To compound problems, the Armed Services Committee released a report on December 20 authored by Senator Jackson and his hawkish aide, Richard Perle, concluding that the treaty was not in the national security interests of the United States. Ten senators voted for the report, and seven voted "present" to express their opposition to its release. Senator John Stennis (D-MS), chair of the Armed Services Committee and one of the seven who opposed, explained that only the Senate Foreign Relations Committee was entitled to report on foreign treaties. Byrd dealt with the questionable exercise of jurisdiction of the committee by not filing the report with the clerk of the Senate for several months.[55]

Richard Perle later remarked, that the "treaty was dead after the hearings."[56] Certainly administration leaders saw the vote as a setback, but we will never know for certain how devastating this vote was, for several other events intruded on the whole process.[57]

On December 26, 1979, the Soviet Union invaded Afghanistan, and on January 3, 1980, Carter withdrew the treaty from Senate consideration.

Post Mortem

Winning Senate approval of a new SALT II agreement would have been difficult for almost any president. But Carter contributed to his problems by failing to build on the earlier Vladivostok Accords at the very beginning of his term. The Soviets were prepared to bargain using those accords as a framework, and in all probability a deal would have been arrived at earlier had Carter been a little less ambitious. Clearly there would have been the opportunity to present the agreement to the Senate as a bipartisan measure. After all, it had its origins in the earlier negotiations by President Gerald Ford and his secretary of state, Henry Kissinger. Instead, Carter adopted policies that prolonged the negotiation process, and in the meantime, other difficulties with the Soviets—combined with his own heated rhetoric—had undermined support for coming to terms with the USSR. By the fall of 1979, when the hearings commenced, there was not the bipartisan network of support that Carter might have had earlier.

The decision to present SALT as an agreement that would permit U.S. military buildup while limiting the Soviet Union also served to diminish the importance of the treaty. The need to win over a few undecided Senators might have made that buildup a political imperative, as White House aides Moore and Beckel had advised Carter.[58] But the result of these choices was that SALT II would be seen as not making much of a difference. "There has been very little clear-cut positive publicity about the Treaty," one Carter aide noted. "Editorials, articles and testimony—including that by supporters— have been largely hedged with warnings that our national security is threatened and that the Treaty won't correct the problem." There should be little surprise that the public attitude might thus have been, "Why take a chance on this Treaty when the opposition is so vehement and the support so half-hearted?"[59]

To fully understand Carter's SALT II policies one has to look at several other items on his agenda. Carter and his key advisors had envisaged the negotiations with Panama in 1977–78 over the return of the Panama Canal as a test run for SALT II. The slow start on the campaign to sell SALT II was the direct result of the heavy burden the staff carried on behalf of the Panama Canal Treaties. Of even greater importance, Carter had to rely on Republican moderates to eke out a narrow victory in the Senate on Panama. Exhausted by this battle, several of these moderates were not inclined to make political sacrifices for Carter's SALT II when the measure came to the floor. As George Moffett III has pointed out, the Carter administration in its successes over the Panama Canal Treaties had secured a Pyrrhic victory.[60]

Equally important, Carter's response to Soviet treatments of its dissidents and their forays into the Horn of Africa contributed to the decline for public support of arms limitations.[61] Although he won over a few hawks in the Senate, it undermined the public support he might have used to move those in the center. The doves stuck with the administration in the Senate Foreign Relations Committee. But Senate moderates such as Glenn, Lugar, and Baker made it clear they saw no political benefit in supporting a treaty that had such lukewarm support.

Carter would later say that his failure to secure support for SALT was his greatest disappointment as president. But at midterm, before he faced the loss of SALT II, he was able take pleasure in two major foreign policy successes. The opening of U.S. relations with China and the Camp David Accords were his most substantial foreign policy accomplishments as president. Both came to term in very different ways. In China, Brzezinski led the way, while at the Camp David talks, Carter and Vance paired up from the very beginning in a very hands-on enterprise.

Part 3
MIDTERM ACHIEVEMENTS

THE TILT TOWARD CHINA

On Friday, December 15, 1978, National Security Advisor Zbigniew Brzezinski invited Anatoly Dobrynin, Soviet Ambassador to the United States, to the White House for a visit. He had Press Secretary Jody Powell alert the media so they would be outside photographing him. Brzezinski chatted amiably with a cheery Dobrynin for a while, then "out of the blue" informed him that the United States would announce that evening the full-scale resumption of diplomatic relations with the People's Republic of China (PRC). Dobrynin looked absolutely stunned. His face turned "kind of gray."[1] It was a very short meeting, and at the time of his departure reporters quizzed Dobrynin about what he and Brzezinski had discussed. "Christmas," he said. When pressed for a better answer, he replied, "Chess."[2]

Seated at his desk in the Oval Office at 9:00 p.m., President Jimmy Carter announced that the United States and the People's Republic of China would establish normal diplomatic relations on January 1, 1979, and exchange ambassadors on March 1. Reading from a joint communiqué, he noted that both countries agreed that there was but one China, and Taiwan was part of China. Notable in that communiqué was the pledge that neither nation "should seek hegemony in the Asia-Pacific region or in any other region of the world and each is opposed to efforts by any other country or group of countries to establish such hegemony." The agreement, Carter went on to note, would "not jeopardize the well-being of the people of Taiwan. The people of our country will maintain our current commercial, cultural, trade and other relation with Taiwan through nongovernmental [channels]." He concluded his speech by noting that Chinese Vice Premier Deng Xiaoping had accepted his invitation to visit Washington, D.C., in late January, that normalization was the result of a bipartisan U.S. effort and that its goal was "the advancement of peace."

Simultaneously, Chinese premier and Communist Party chairman Hua Guofeng read the same joint communiqué statement in Beijing and offered his own side statements. It was the first press conference ever held by the chairman.[3]

After finishing his brief speech Carter reclined in his chair and, unaware that the microphone remained on, remarked, "Massive applause…throughout the nation." *Time* lauded this foreign policy statement the most significant announcement of Jimmy Carter's presidency and one of the most important in recent U.S. history. Former Presidents Gerald Ford and Richard Nixon supported him, as did most of the Democratic leaders in the U.S. Congress.[4]

Still, the president overestimated the positive public response to his "breakthrough." Senator Barry Goldwater (R-AZ) dismissed the Carter administration's actions as "cowardly," and said that it stabbed Taiwan in the back. Even New York's moderate

Republican Senator Jacob Javits refused to endorse the idea fully.[5] In New York's Chinatown, police mediated between two thousand Beijing supporters and about six thousand Taiwanese sympathizers. One placard read, "Carter Sells Peanuts and Friends." The American public, too, failed to fully approve the result. Pieces of mail to the president's office ran four to one against the normalization process. Taiwan was cited as the main reason for opposition.[6]

Secretary of State Cyrus Vance had barely made it to the White House in time for the presidential speech. Assured that the announcement would not be made before January 1, he had been in Jerusalem at Carter's behest, attempting to keep the Middle East peace talks on track. Only forty-eight hours before the announcement was to be made, the president called him about the new date. Concerned that an announcement at this time would make it more difficult for him to tie up loose ends in the Strategic Arms Limitation Treaty (SALT II) negotiations scheduled for late December, Vance tried to talk the president out of such an early announcement. But Carter, thinking that the agreement with the PRC might unravel, resisted Vance's plea to keep the statement as originally scheduled.[7] Upon his return Vance put the best possible face on the event, telling a reporter from *Time* that the goal was to treat the Soviet Union and China equally, not create a competition between them.[8]

But using China as a counter to the USSR was exactly what Brzezinski had in mind. The normalization process he was working on would go beyond Nixon's goal of restoring diplomatic relationships. New economic and security ties with China would be fashioned. There was a foreshadowing of this tilt toward China in the final communiqué, which condemned any state seeking hegemony over another—with *hegemony* being a Chinese code word pointedly used to refer to Soviet expansionism. The timing of the normalization agreement complicated Vance's SALT II negotiations with the Soviet Union. Brzezinski himself noted at the time that the United States had an interest in a multicentered political world. He went on to note that the normalization of relationship with China should have been done regardless of the U.S. relationship with the Soviet Union—for better or worse.[9]

Brzezinski had clearly prevailed over Vance in their battles over how and when to recognize the PRC. Brzezinski's brilliance at bureaucratic politics and some of the reasons Carter came to give him such a wide berth will be delineated in this chapter and the two that follow. He could not have led the way, however, without some real opening for action. Let us first look at the situation confronting the administration in the late 1970s.

Policy Conflicts and Resolutions

During Carter's years in the presidency, new geopolitical facts would facilitate a U.S. tilt toward China. Chinese Communist Party (CCP) Chairman Mao Zedong died in September 1976, and a coalition of political and military leaders deposed and imprisoned the awful Gang of Four that had led the Chinese Cultural Revolution. Shortly thereafter, the more pragmatic Deng Xiaoping was restored to power. Like other

Asian revolutionaries, Deng had been educated in France and worked in factories where he discovered Marxism-Leninism. He became a leader in the Youth League in Europe and slowly rose to power upon his return to China in 1927. As deputy chair of the Communist Party, he was nominally second in line to Hua Guofeng, Mao's successor. But it soon became clear that Deng would be the major force in Chinese politics. In his first foreign policy trip, Deng indicated that the new Chinese leaders had two major goals—to build up China economically and to end China's isolation from the rest of the world.[10]

Events in Cambodia and Vietnam created additional incentives for a possible tilt toward China. The Khmer Rouge's conquest of Phnom Penh in 1975 signaled the final defeat of the Lon Nol government supported by the United States. When the newly installed Kampuchean People's Republic engaged in genocidal policies designed to obliterate the well-educated and those of the upper classes, people around the world were outraged. As for Vietnam, Assistant Secretary of State for Far Eastern Affairs Richard Holbrooke and Vietnamese diplomat Nguyen Co Thach agreed in late September 1978 to the normalization of relations between the two countries.[11] Then, in late 1978, Vietnam invaded Cambodia, installing a moderate communist regime that brought the worst outrages to an end. But when the Vietnamese also signed a friendship treaty with the Soviet Union on November 3, 1978, the Chinese rallied around Cambodia's Prince Norodom Sihanouk, providing him refuge in China. There he proceeded to set up a government in exile—a coalition that included representatives of the Khmer Rouge regime.[12]

Carter's top two foreign policy advisors embraced differing views on how to deal with these events in the Far East. Brzezinski had barely reached his desk in the White House when he wrote to Carter that developments in China provided "a genuine strategic opportunity...to offset the Soviet military buildup and to prompt the Soviet Union into a greater recognition of its stake in a reasonable accommodation with the United States." China, much weaker than the Soviet Union, he continued, posed no immediate threat to the United States. Generally, he felt, "Normalization should be followed by extension of economic, and gradually, security ties."[13] Soviet activities in the Horn of Africa reinforced his conviction that the United States should not be "excessively deferential" to Soviet sensitivities.[14] His opposition to the administration's move toward normalization of relations with Vietnam was based on concerns that the move would be seen as anti-Chinese.[15] When the Vietnamese entered Cambodia, Brzezinski argued that they were simply acting as "proxies" for the Soviet Union.[16]

Vance was concerned that too steep a tilt in the Chinese direction would harm U.S. relations with the USSR. In the spring of 1977, he argued that the normalization of relations with China should proceed cautiously and that any significant military relationship between the United States and the Chinese would be a mistake. As he wrote the president on April 15, 1977, the links established with the People's Republic of China should consist of diplomatic rather than security arrangements in order to "maintain the fragile equilibrium." Furthermore, the well being and security of the Taiwanese people must not be jeopardized.[17] Later, as the president increasingly favored a tilt toward China, Vance warned him to act with restraint. The U.S. understanding with

China, he suggested, had been a factor in deterring Soviet adventurism. Developing it further with military technology would be "less likely to produce moderation in Soviet behavior than strategic claustrophobia and irrationality."[18]

Initial Moves

Preoccupied with SALT II and the Panama Canal Treaties, Carter provided little direction to Chinese policies in early 1977. Mainly, Carter signaled that he desired friendly relations with the PRC while putting normalization behind other issues. On March 7, three weeks into his administration, Carter first met with Chinese diplomat Huang Chen. At this time, the U.S. State Department and the national security advisor were in relative accord on what the president should tell him—namely, that while mutually beneficial agreements with the Soviets would be sought, the United States would not act in concert against China. To this advice Brzezinski added that Carter might also assure the Chinese government—then in the midst of a significant leadership transition—of the continued frankness of the United States in regard to the "the triangular relationship between the U.S.-USSR-China."[19] In April, staff aides were put to work on Presidential Review Memorandum (PRM) 24, flushing out the pros and cons of various alternative policies toward China and the Far East.[20] In his speech at Notre Dame University on May 22, Carter simply noted in passing that the United States had an interest in good relations with the People's Republic of China and would address at some time the issue of normalization of relations with the regime.[21]

Later that year, when Vance's instructions for his official trip to Beijing were first being worked out, the president made it clear he wanted to move slowly. A resolution of the Panama Canal issue was his first priority. For Carter, normalization with China should be deferred, and his advisors at this time concurred with this approach.[22] Even Brzezinski, who favored the exploration of common political and security interests with China, wanted to go slowly on the issue of Taiwan. When the president asked him to prepare a draft communiqué on U.S. policy should the Chinese respond positively to the United States during Vance's forthcoming trip, Brzezinski demurred. He was "pleased but worried" about the president's desire to speed up the process of normalization, but before that occurred, other areas of cooperation should be explored. A "contingency plan" should be developed to "put more stress on political and economic actions short of normalization."[23]

In line with these recommendations, the president's directive to Vance made any movement toward Chinese demands regarding Taiwan difficult. Carter acknowledged that existing policies regarding both the People's Republic of China and the Republic of China (Taiwan) would be subject to modification. But he also insisted that American actions must "in no way jeopardize the confidence of the people of Taiwan." He demanded flexibility from the mainland in regard to the treatment of Taiwan, and said that Taiwan's access to defensive arms should remain intact.[24]

Vance's trip to Beijing in August 1977, it seems, was destined to be exploratory, and the Chinese seemed to know it. No dancing girls greeted the arrival of Vance's party as they had the Nixon delegation back in 1972. The welcoming dinner that night was held in a small banquet hall at the Great Hall of the People. The food was not quite comparable to the menu at banquets given for former secretary of state Henry Kissinger. But contrary to some accounts Vance was not diplomatically slighted. The Chinese foreign minister met him at the airport and attended the first sessions in the Great Hall, and Vance also met with Chairman Hua Guofeng.[25]

Several issues were explored in the subsequent sessions, including cultural exchanges, trade, and the problem of old U.S. claims to property in China. The Chinese were even shown PRM 10, a highly secret, only recently declassified document delineating the need for a new study of U.S. policies toward the USSR. But there was no breakthrough on the crucial issue of the status of Taiwan. Indeed, at the August 24 session, China characterized the U.S. stance relative to Taiwan as a step backward from the original Nixon/Kissinger Shanghai communiqué. By refusing to make a clear statement on the possible removal of diplomatic and military personnel from Taiwan, Vance was forced to "reproduce in a new form the formula already rejected by the Chinese side." Vance saw these sessions as the "beginning of a long and undoubtedly difficult road." Still, at the conclusion of the talks, Foreign Minister Huang Hua called the meeting with Vance "significant" and stated that the Chinese were very pleased with the visits.[26]

Vance's instructions, in short, made it impossible for him to move forward on the normalization of relations with the PRC. On Vance's trip home, moreover, Vice Chairman Deng Xiaoping introduced a sour postlude to the Beijing talks. He suggested in an interview with an Associated Press delegation that included Katherine Graham, publisher of the *Washington Post*, that the normalization process had actually suffered a setback as a result of Vance's visit. Responding to a leak from the National Security Council (NSC) staff that there had been progress in Beijing, the Chinese leader wanted to make clear that they had not been flexible on such a serious matter of principal.[27] As Richard Solomon, an NSC staff member under Kissinger, later noted, the Chinese response was a way of increasing their leverage in the normalization talks. It also provided an opening for Brzezinski.[28]

Brzezinski Takes the Lead

Cyrus Vance, Brzezinski suggests, was "a gentleman in the tradition of the old WASP elite that had controlled U.S. foreign policy." Decent though these men were, they lacked the vigor for a new style of politics in which ideology and power had become increasingly important. "Vance played according to their rules. But those values and rules," Brzezinski continues, "were of declining relevance" to American domestic and world politics.[29]

Certainly, Brzezinski had some advantages over this traditional gentleman in the coming struggle for control over China policy. As the president's gatekeeper and personal advisor, he had extraordinary access to the president and the Oval Office.[30] But access alone did not determine his influence. Brzezinski was a motivated tactician and on China, in particular, he carried a message that the president was inclined to hear. In addition, he employed a series of salami-slicing tactics, restricted others' access to Carter, wooed and won over allies in the administration, all the while amassing support for his own goals. He framed issues and presented himself in a way that made his objectives attractive to the president.

One of Brzezinski's first moves was to ensure that Leonard Woodcock, the head of the U.S. liaison office in Beijing, would work through him. Brzezinski wrote the president in early 1977 that he should feel out Woodcock's position on several issues: "Given Woodcock's negotiating experience in intractable situations, how would he approach the Chinese? What does he think our minimum demands ought to be in regard to the Taiwan issue?" These were all questions the Chinese expert on the NSC staff, Michel Oksenberg, had prepared for Brzezinski.[31]

Beyond that, Brzezinski wrote that the president should make it clear that the White House would be the key communications link in the negotiation process. He should tell Woodcock, "[The president] will be engaged in the negotiating process. Vance will not be commuting to Peking [Beijing], as Kissinger did. Woodcock's role will thereby be augmented." Woodcock should also be told, "When appropriate, other Administration officials may be sent to Peking [Beijing] as well."[32] In this way Brzezinski kept himself in the loop, monitoring all correspondence with Woodcock. Indeed, in the final phase of the normalization agreements with China, Brzezinski and Vance sent cables to Beijing jointly. The result, Brzezinski said, was that Woodcock "knew that the President [thus Brzezinski] was engaged."[33]

In the fall of 1977, through a series of incremental moves, Brzezinski would place himself at the center of foreign policy toward China and convince the president that the United States should attempt to build a security relationship with the PRC as it moved toward diplomatic normalization.[34] First, he assembled a cluster of senior officials in his office, including his China advisor Michel Oksenberg.[35] In September, Brzezinski urged Carter to send friendly messages to the Chinese and to meet with Foreign Minister Huang the following month in Ottawa.

Brzezinski then went to work on setting himself up as an envoy to China. On October 21, 1977, Oksenberg casually suggested at a luncheon with two Chinese liaison officers that a trip by Brzezinski to China would be "productive." Brzezinski was "considering a trip to East Asia, possibly sometime in the spring" he said, but "would not wish to visit China unless he had been formally invited to do so." Oksenberg noted that Brzezinski would probably be "most interested" in discussing "global strategic issues," but would be keen to talk about diplomatic, economic, and cultural topics as well. Oksenberg notes that he concluded the conversation with "the ball is now in your court." When informed of the result of this meeting, Brzezinski wrote, "Good."[36]

The move paid off. At the Iranian embassy on November 1, 1977, the Chinese diplomat Han Hsu bounded over toward Oksenberg, a big smile on his face. The Chinese would be happy for Brzezinski to visit China. Reporting the news to Brzezinski, Oksenberg suggested that "the next step...should be a social invitation from you to Han Hsu and several of his aides....I also recommend that when you see Han Hsu during [Vice President Walter] Mondale's lunch, you limit your remarks to an indication that I communicated his message to you, that you are pleased with the prospect, and that we will be in contact with them on several substantive and procedural matters which concern you in order to make the trip successful."[37]

But Brzezinski knew the political value of acting boldly. At a Mondale luncheon honoring a departing Chinese diplomat, he not only accepted the invitation to visit China but acknowledged the invitation in front of the press. An upset Vance called Brzezinski to inform him that his own negotiations with the Chinese would be undercut. But Brzezinski tried to reassure Vance by downplaying the importance of the invitation. It would only be polite to respond that he would go to China at some indeterminate date. The two men finally agreed to a wording indicating that Brzezinski would be delighted to come at some point.[38]

With invitation in hand, Brzezinski began pressing the president to send him to Beijing. On November 22, he wrote that Woodcock had received an invitation for him to visit China.[39] On February 16, 1978, he wrote Carter, "The Chinese have gone out of their way on several occasions to make clear that they would welcome a visit by me."[40] To overcome the president's reluctance to send him to Beijing, rather than Vance or Mondale, Brzezinski wrote Carter that he would "not expect to be drawn into negotiations on the terms of normalization."[41] In March, as Carter leaned toward sending Mondale to China, Brzezinski once again contacted the president and told him that his visit would be a less visible and a lower-key consultation than Mondale's visit could be.[42] State opposition to his trip, he stated, was based on turf considerations. Brzezinski wrote the president that the State Department "is probably more 'turf conscious' than any other agency in Washington; and the Secretary of State was, I imagine, concerned about the political symbolism of a mission to China undertaken by the president's assistant for national security affairs."[43]

Finally, on March 16, 1978, Carter relented, sending a handwritten note to Mondale and Vance, informing them that he had "decided it would be best for Zbig to go to China."[44]

In March, Brzezinski's staff informed him that Vance was telling some senators that the administration's intention was to normalize relations with the People's Republic of China after the fall elections. Oksenberg argued that Vance was making a "mistake," since the timing could not be decided upon by the United States alone, and he ought to be cautioned because such statements could leak.[45]

Brzezinski, however, was not going to wait until after the fall elections. With the president committed to his trip, he proceeded to gradually upgrade his mission. One of his first steps was to tell Han Hsu, Acting Chief to the PRC's Liaison Office, that he wanted "to have authoritative consultation with Chinese leaders on international issues of mutual concern." At this time it was still a "low-key" visit.[46] But on April 8, Brzezinski secured an agreement from Carter that the United States undertake more sustained initiatives with the Chinese, and that Brzezinski should be the one to start these talks.[47] In late April, Brzezinski told Hsu that he would be speaking for the president on the trip, and that he would be seeking authoritative consultations at the "highest levels." Brzezinski expected Deng Xiaoping and other top Chinese leaders to be in Beijing during his visit.[48]

In early May, Brzezinski enlisted Democratic senators Henry Jackson (WA) and Ted Kennedy (MA) as allies in his attempts to add normalization to his agenda. He wrote the president on May 4 that Jackson expressed concern that the Chinese had been slighted by the administration and that Ambassador Woodcock had developed a reputation of being too soft on the Soviets. The administration, he suggested, should move boldly on normalization in the fall.[49] Senator Kennedy's concern, he wrote the next day, was that the "trip to China will be counterproductive if I do not focus in some fashion on normalization."[50]

When Carter's instructions for the trip to China were finalized several days later, it was clear that Brzezinski would have a kind of latitude in the talks relative to Taiwan that Vance had never had. The first pages were mostly filled with the need for Brzezinski to explore a common front to counter Soviet "hegemony" in the Far East. The instructions pointed to the Soviet potential to "exploit local turbulence and to intimidate our friends in order to seek political advantage and even political preponderance." An "assertive response" to the Soviet military buildup would include the strengthening of the North Atlantic Treaty Organization and encouragement of Chinese aid to Somalia. Underlying these specifics was a common interest. "This is why your visit," Carter's instructions stated, "is an expression of our strategic interest in a co-operative relationship with China, an interest that is both fundamental and enduring."[51]

The normalization of relations between the United States and the PRC was only mentioned at the bottom of the next to last page of the instructions. The United States would meet the Chinese conditions: the termination of diplomatic and official military relations with Taiwan, and the withdrawal of all U.S. personnel, as well as understanding that any attempt at reunification be peaceful. The United States reserved the right to export defensive arms to Taiwan.

As the wording suggests, Brzezinski clearly played a key role in drafting the very rules under which he would operate in Beijing.

The national security advisor's trip had been transformed from a consultative, low-key mission into a genuinely major undertaking in which the possibility of resolving issues concerning the status of Taiwan as well as a new kind of common security arrangement with China could be worked out. As Brzezinski noted, the president had given him a broad and important mandate to negotiate with the Chinese.[52]

When Brzezinski landed in Beijing in May, the Chinese gave him the red carpet treatment usually reserved for a Secretary of State. Included was an official dinner in his honor given by the Foreign Minister Huang Hua. The real negotiations followed in his subsequent talks with Vice Premier Deng Xiaoping and CCP Chairman Hua Guofeng.[53] Holbrooke accompanied Brzezinski, along with Brzezinski's own China specialist, Oksenberg.[54]

Unlike Vance before him, Brzezinski was able to suggest in these meetings that some compromise might be made on Taiwan. Official U.S. diplomatic and military ties with Taiwan could be cut. The United States would retain the right to ship arms to Taiwan for defensive purposes. And it hoped for a pledge from Beijing that it would not contradict any U.S. statements that efforts to unify Taiwan with the People's Republic of China would consist only of peaceful means. These latter two points would become the subject of much controversy in the following months.[55]

The anti-Soviet tilt, as contrasted to the earlier Vance visit, was evident throughout the meeting. At the opening banquet, Foreign Minister Huang delivered an impassioned critique of détente, characterizing it as a "cover" for Soviet imperialism; and calling for the people of all countries to unite and "adopt a tit-for-tat policy to upset the hegemonies' strategic deployments."[56] In his trip to the Great Wall, Brzezinski challenged the Chinese to a contest—the one who ascended the wall first would "go in and oppose the Russians in Ethiopia." Chinese naval cadets, accompanying Brzezinski on his trip, tagged him the "polar bear hunter." At the farewell banquet given in his honor in the Great Hall of the People, Brzezinski claimed that the Soviet Union was a mutual adversary of the United States and China, and that the two nations had a mutual interest in countering Soviet influence in Africa. Neither the United States nor China dispatches "international marauders...to advance big power ambitions in Africa....neither of us seeks to enforce the political obedience of our neighbors through military force."[57] Brzezinski was with Hua and Deng, who at this time and later made anti-Soviet statements that were at least as strong as those voiced by Brzezinski.

On the trip home Brzezinski stopped over in Tokyo, where he encouraged Prime Minister Takeo Fukuda to end Japanese resistance to an antihegemonic clause in the China-Japan friendship treaty then being negotiated. Acting on his own, Brzezinski only informed Carter of what he had done after the fact.

Brzezinski's aide Oksenberg also had one on-board confrontation with Holbrooke, who had been excluded from some of the high-level talks between Brzezinski and the Chinese. When Holbrooke asked to see the transcript of those meetings, Oksenberg, on Brzezinski's orders, refused. It led to a minor scuffle between the two men. Debate over this episode would later reach the pages of *Foreign Affairs*.[58]

Upon his return to the United States, Brzezinski was scathing in his attacks on the Soviet Union. In a *Meet the Press* interview on May 28, he denounced Soviet activities as violating "the code of détente." He criticized "the shortsighted Soviet conduct in the course of the last two or so years" in building up Soviet forces in Eastern Europe and on the Chinese border. He claimed that the Soviets were waging a worldwide propaganda movement against the United States to control the Middle East and to elicit racial tensions in Africa.[59] Afterward, Carter castigated Brzezinski by remarking, "'You're not just a professor; you speak for me. And I think you went too far in your statements. You put all of this responsibility on the Soviets. You said they were conducting a worldwide vitriolic campaign, encircling and penetrating the Middle East, placing troops on the Chinese frontier. All this simply went too far.'" But Carter did nothing further to restrict Brzezinski's speech making.[60]

Shortly after the meetings in Beijing, the administration took further steps to further amicable relations with China. The sale of 60 U.S. F-4 warplanes to Taiwan was canceled. The president's science advisor, Frank Press, and energy secretary, James Schlesinger, made trips to China. Both trips were successful events in the eyes of the Chinese and the visiting Americans.[61]

Following Through

In the fall of 1978, two sets of talks were undertaken to tie up the deal. In Washington, Brzezinski settled into several sessions with Chai Zemin, the new head of the Chinese liaison office in Washington. In Beijing, Woodcock conducted talks that paralleled the Carter-Brzezinski negotiations. Contrary to Brzezinski's early suspicions that he might be an independent player, Woodcock had become one of the strongest advocates of coming to terms with the PRC, and a Brzezinski ally.[62] He would perform yeoman service at the Beijing end of the negotiations.

On September 19, President Carter set out two conditions for U.S. approval of the final agreement. In talks with Chai Zemin, Carter stressed that the United States would continue its nonoffensive arms sales to Taiwan. Moreover, it would expect the PRC not to contradict a U.S. statement that any attempt to unite Taiwan to the mainland would be accomplished via peaceful means.[63]

Then, on October 11, in a meeting with Brzezinski and Woodcock, Carter decided to drop the normalization talks with Vietnam that under Holbrooke's direction had been drawing near a successful conclusion. The Vietnamese had met all U.S. conditions, but the Americans stalled.[64] Brzezinski had been telling the president for some time that the movement toward the normalization of relations with Vietnam would impede the progress they were making in their talks with the Chinese.[65] He even questioned the motives of those eager to bring the normalization talks with Vietnam to a close—namely, Vance and Holbrooke. They may have been motivated by a post–Vietnam War guilt, Brzezinski suggested. Carter wryly rejected this argument with a handwritten note stating he backed normalization and he had no such guilt.[66]

The president decided to demonstrate his seriousness in concluding a deal with China by preparing a draft for a normalization agreement. He also set a January 1, 1979, deadline for the announcement of the projected deal. The draft was drawn up and, in a series of meetings in Beijing, Ambassador Woodcock relayed the U.S. proposals to the Chinese leaders. The last presentation occurred on December 4, 1978.[67]

When several days went by without a Chinese response, Brzezinski called Ambassador Chai into his office. Acting on an idea he had tentatively forwarded earlier, on December 11 Brzezinski offered either Deng or Hua an invitation to visit Washington. The Chinese leader could come before the Soviets could make it. Not knowing for sure who would come out on top in a power struggle going on in Beijing, Brzezinski left it up to the Chinese to determine who would accept his invitation. The next day, December 12, Deng met with Woodcock, and the following morning Woodcock cabled Washington that the Chinese had accepted the U.S. normalization proposals and that Deng would visit the United States. To solidify the commitment, the president and Brzezinski decided to make the deal public. On December 13, Brzezinski called Chai to suggest that an announcement be made.[68]

Even then, the whole deal was on the verge of unraveling. In Beijing, on December 14, Deng told Woodcock that the Chinese expected the United States to cease all arms shipments upon signing the normalization agreement. But Carter held to his bottom line, maintaining that the United States would insist on its right to sell arms to Taiwan under the appropriate conditions. Deng, too, refused to budge from his position.[69]

In Washington, Brzezinski discovered an out. The two parties, he told Ambassador Chai Zemin, could deal with the issue of arms shipments later. The administration had agreed to a one-year moratorium, after which sales of defensive arms would be resumed. Reluctantly, Deng gave his consent to this formulation of the problem and communiqués were exchanged as scheduled on December 15.[70] Clearly the decision to go public on that early date was prompted, as Vance later suggested, by a fear that if it were not announced the deal could fall through at any moment.[71]

The fear of leaks provided a rationale for keeping the State Department out of all the discussions in the final four hours. Brzezinski had been arguing that normalization talks should be tightly held, that the involvement of people from the State Department would inevitably result in leaks that would undermine the process.[72] Only after Deputy Secretary of State Warren Christopher got suspicious that something was going on at the White House was he admitted to the deliberations and Holbrooke given access to copies of cables from Woodcock and drafts of the final American counterproposals.[73] Carter would later argue that as president, he had directed all these final moves, and he "was leery of channeling his proposal through the State Department, because he did not feel that he had full support there....It was because of my orders to hold information closely so our efforts would not be observed."[74]

There was a downside in this neglect. Experts from the State Department often see things that others overlook. When Holbrooke saw the final U.S. statement on normalization in mid-December 1978, he pointed out an ambiguity in the wording on the U.S. right to sell arms to Taiwan that would contribute to final conflicts with congressional supporters of Taiwan.[75] Officials in the State Department were demoralized by the White House policies of cutting them out of deliberations when it served no clear foreign policy purpose. The concern over State Department leaks ignored the fact that the NSC staff could also offer inside information to the press when it suited their purposes.[76] One State Department official would later remark, "Zbig may be proud of this little game, but it served no purpose."[77]

Whatever the rationale, the timing of Sino-American normalization and the blacking out of State Department participants in the final hours of discussion undermined Vance's authority as Secretary of State and put a damper on his subsequent talks with the Soviets at Geneva. The agreement also prepared the way for a security relationship that Brzezinski had long worked for and which the president now embraced. The first substantive step along these lines was taken during Deng's eight-day visit to the United States in early 1979.

BUILDING THE SECURITY RELATIONSHIP

Everyone, it seemed, wanted to meet the diminutive but charismatic Chinese vice premier. But the first dinner, at Zbigniew Brzezinski's home on Sunday, January 28, 1979, was a private affair. Using good Soviet vodka (a gift from Anatoly Dobrynin), Brzezinski toasted Deng Xiaoping with Leonid Brezhnev's favorite drink. Cyrus Vance—along with Richard Holbrooke, Leonard Woodcock, and Mike Oksenberg—was merely an invited guest. Washingtonians with sensitive political antennae would note that a shift in power had taken place within President Jimmy Carter's foreign policy inner circle.[1]

At the formal White House affair, Deng dined with former Secretary of State Kissinger and former President Richard Nixon and many others. At a lunch with eighty-five senators, several anxiously awaited their turn to catch Deng's ear and get his autograph. Even Senator Henry Jackson, who created so many problems for the administration on the SALT II talks, was captivated by Deng, saying, "He is determined to find a peaceful solution, but strong leaders never throw away their last option." At a special gala given at the Kennedy Center for the Arts, Deng met the Harlem Globetrotters, showing—as some newspapers would note—that he had the skills of an American politician.[2] Deng ended his stay in Washington with a question-and-answer luncheon on January 31 at Blair House and an interview later that afternoon with noted newsmen Walter Cronkite, Jim Lehrer, Frank Reynolds, and David Brinkley.[3]

At one of the events, National Security Council (NSC) aide Michel Oksenberg passed a note to political advisor Hamilton Jordan that said, "This is a historic meeting—you're witnessing the takeoff of Sino-American relations." Carter himself called the visit "one of the most historic in our nation's history."[4]

Escorted by Ambassador Woodcock and Richard Holbrooke, Deng then visited three other U.S. cities. In Atlanta, Deng received a standing ovation from businessmen at a chamber of commerce dinner. The following day, he stopped by Martin Luther King Jr.'s grave and toured a Ford Motor Company plant with Henry Ford II and Woodcock. In Houston, Deng inspected some of the U.S. technology he admired, played on a space shuttle simulator, and donned a "ten-gallon" cowboy hat. In Seattle, Deng courted the public by kissing babies and shaking hands. Deng's appearance in the United States, *Newsweek* noted, "seemed to tap deep into a long hidden wellspring of American goodwill toward China."[5]

Deng also had a political mission. The Chinese had come to terms with the United States partly out of a desire to solicit support in their battles vis-à-vis the Soviet Union. Deng warned administration officials that the Soviet Union could lead the world into another war and advocated an "alliance of the United States, China, Japan, Western

FIGURE 9. Zbigniew Brzezinski and Deng Xiaoping in a toast at Brzezinski's home, with Cyrus Vance and others looking on. Photograph courtesy of the Jimmy Carter Library.

Europe and the Third World against Moscow."[6] At the lunch at Blair House he addressed the issues of hegemony in depth, called the Vietnamese "the Cubans of the Orient," and acknowledged that the Chinese had shipped weapons to the Pol Pot regime in Cambodia. Behind the scenes, a highly secret plan for permanently sharing intelligence regarding Soviet capabilities in western China was finalized. The objective was to replace the monitoring capabilities that the United States had lost in Iran with the overthrow of the shah. Stations would be staffed by Central Intelligence Agency (CIA) officials with help from the National Security Agency and the Chinese. Deng and Carter also signed other agreements for cooperation in "science, technology, space and cultural exchanges."[7]

The final communiqué of the United States and the People's Republic of China also included, at Brzezinski's urging, a reference to the threat of "hegemony"—a phrase clearly directed against the Soviet Union.[8] Vance had objected to the inclusion of that term in the communiqué, but had settled for a compromise offered by Brzezinski—the addition of another phrase "or domination over others." An additional statement Vance proffered, which would note the continued importance of Soviet-U.S. cooperation, was rejected out of hand. At the foreign affairs breakfast on February 2, Carter handed the proposed statement back to Vance without even seriously reading it. He muttered, "Is it another apology?"[9]

At a more immediate level, Deng's goal was to keep the United States neutral in the attack China was planning against Vietnam. Shortly after the opening of the conference in Washington, on January 30 Deng warned Carter, Vice President Walter Mondale, and Brzezinski of Chinese plans to invade Vietnam.[10] At that moment in the Oval Office, Carter simply noted that this was a serious matter he wanted to talk over with his advisors. He later wrote that he thought the Chinese invasion might produce sympathy for the Vietnamese; after their invasion of Cambodia, he noted, they had been cut off from the world community. The next day he wrote Deng that the Chinese should exercise restraint in the matter, noting the adverse international consequences of war.[11] Still, Brzezinski thought he had the room to tell Deng at the helicopter pad upon his departure from the United States that he had presidential support.[12]

On February 16, 1979, less than two weeks after Deng's return to Beijing, the Chinese sent the United States a cable stating that their attack on Vietnam would take place on February 17.

Forewarned, Brzezinski had a contingency plan ready. Members of the National Security Council agreed at a meeting on February 16 that the United States would demand that China and Vietnam both pull their forces out of Cambodia. Such a proposal, Brzezinski knew, "would be totally unacceptable to the Vietnamese and to the Soviets, and hence would provide a partial diplomatic umbrella for the Chinese action without associating the United States with it."[13]

Carter, however, was not willing to be drawn into a broader conflict with the USSR. This was apparent at the NSC meeting on February 17, 1979. To sense the tone of the session, a summary of the meeting is useful:

> CIA DIRECTOR [STANSFIELD] TURNER: The Chinese have 14 divisions in North Vietnam, totaling about 170,000 men, and the Vietnamese are at the moment responding in ways that suggested the defense of Hanoi was their chief concern.
>
> VANCE: The Soviets should be sent a demarche "to dispel any notions we are involved; and to provide the framework which will guide our policy. We wish to avoid any miscalculation on their part."

The president, Brzezinski, Vance, Richard Holbrooke, and David Aaron, Brzezinski's deputy and Mondale's former aide, then worked on the language of the demarche, concerned that it neither suggest too many limits on U.S. action nor be too provocative. Eventually, Brzezinski proposed a compromise message they all agreed upon. Then the following exchange occurred:

> VANCE: Should this go as a President to Brezhnev message?
>
> CARTER: That is my wish.... The dispatch shows we have not colluded with the Chinese. We were condemning Chinese actions and are acting separately from them.... My honor is at stake, and I wished to ally any Soviet fear with a direct communication.

The discussion turned to how to deal with possible questions about advance U.S. knowledge of the operation. The consensus was that if asked, U.S. officials would say that Deng had alluded to the operation, that he had not been specific as to Chinese intentions, and that the United States had informed him of its position:

> CARTER: Ever since the first Kampuchean Vietnam clash, our position has been to deplore violence. We should say publicly that even during the last few hours, we have made our position clear to all the parties concerned. Our degree of knowledge should be minimized. And we should not emphasize we have been discussing the issues. We do not wish to appear to be deeply involved in this conflict, though we recognize its dangers.[14]

That same day, Carter sent Brezhnev the demarche he and his aides had worked on in the NSC meeting. The United States had "just learned," he wrote, of Chinese forces crossing into Vietnam. He discouraged any USSR behavior that would exacerbate the situation, including Soviet naval visits to Vietnamese ports.[15]

President Leonid Brezhnev responded to Carter, saying, "The Soviet Union cannot remain a non-participant."[16] The following day Moscow Radio charged that "a number of facts prove that the aggression against Vietnam was planned as early as when Brzezinski...visited China. Details were finalized when Deng Xiaoping visited Washington....As the Chinese troops were beginning to invade Vietnam, the Chinese NPC Standing Committee was meeting in Beijing to endorse the results of Deng Xiaoping's visit to the United States, his collusion with the U.S. militarists and their decisions on the invasion of Vietnam."[17]

Shortly thereafter, Soviet Ambassador Anatoly Dobrynin told Vance that many in Moscow believed the "anti-Soviet, pro-China attitude" of the United States had encouraged Beijing to attack.[18] On February 27, 1979, Gromyko warned China to leave Vietnam "before it is too late."[19] The following day, *Pravda* echoed this warning to withdraw "'quickly' from Vietnam or risk the spread of warfare."[20]

Whatever Carter's worries about what the Soviet response might have been, he rejected Vance's suggestion that Treasury Secretary Michael Blumenthal's scheduled visit to China that month should be postponed as a sign of protest against Chinese actions in Vietnam. Thus, on February 24, one week after the Chinese invasion of Vietnam, Blumenthal arrived in Beijing. He engaged in discussions with the Chinese on what would be a new trade treaty. But Blumenthal did issue a warning to Chinese leaders to withdraw their troops from Vietnam "'as quickly as possible' because the invasion 'ran risks that were unwarranted,'" and it received front-page coverage in the *New York Times*.[21] Concerned that Blumenthal might make statements too critical of the PRC, Brzezinski wrote the secretary that his public comments related to the Chinese should focus on trade issues and nothing else.

A possible crisis in Southeast Asia was avoided when China pulled out of Vietnam after seventeen days. The Chinese claimed to have resolved their border issues. But they had met an unexpectedly harsh resistance.[22] The United States, though it acquiesced in the PRC's operation, was urging the PRC behind the scenes to make the intervention a short one. At one point in the tense atmosphere that ensued, unnamed

U.S. officials in the White House claimed there was a Soviet buildup on the Chinese border, but, as Vance insisted, there was in fact no evidence of this.[23]

After the Chinese pulled out of Vietnam, Brzezinski resumed what he called his "trip diplomacy." Brzezinski was in the process of soliciting invitations for as many members of the administration as possible to visit Beijing. The goal, as he later admitted, was to win a wider constituency for the policies he favored.[24]

In August 1979, it was Mondale's turn to visit China. Though the vice president had earlier opposed the development of a security arrangement with the Chinese, he now agreed to visit China.[25] Brzezinski suggests that he may have been motivated by his desire to polish his foreign policy credentials for a future run for the presidency.[26] Certainly Mondale desired to contribute to what now seemed to be one of the administration's major foreign policy successes. Holbrooke, who at this time was solidly behind the administration's policies, would accompany him to Beijing. David Aaron, who helped the vice president prepare for the trip, no doubt reinforced that new mind-set.[27]

Perhaps more important, Mondale had some gifts to bring to the Chinese. At the August 3, 1979, foreign policy breakfast, the president decided to extend Most Favored Nation (MFN) to the PRC, reversing an earlier determination to simultaneously offer MFN treatment to the USSR and the PRC. Once this decision was made, Brzezinski immediately informed the Chinese ambassador of the decision, an action that would make any backpedaling highly improbable. Vance reluctantly went along, promising to propose MFN status for China before the end of the year. China would be declared a friendly nation and thus exempt from the restrictions on trade applied to some of the other communist countries. But, he added, "I will hold my nose and do it for you."[28] On November 30, 1979, as the SALT II agreement languished in committee, Brzezinski asked Mondale to persuade Senate leader Robert Byrd (D-WV) to put it into effect in 1980. In short, Carter had abandoned his earlier policies of pushing for simultaneous approval of MFN status for both China and Russia.[29]

In late August 1979, Mondale's plane set down at the airport in Beijing, where he was met by Vice Premier Deng Xiaoping and Foreign Minister Huang Hua. An honor guard of the Chinese Army, Navy, and Air Force performed for him. Foreign Minister Huang was host for a dinner at the elegant Summer Palace.[30] The lavish welcome was an appropriate response for one who came bearing gifts; at his address at Peking University, Mondale announced a new agreement for U.S. exports to help with several Chinese dam projects, and in a speech broadcast to the Chinese people—the first one ever made by an American political figure to the nation—Mondale asserted "any nation which seeks to weaken or isolate you" runs "counter to American interests." He also announced that Washington was prepared to extend up to two billion dollars in Export-Import Bank credits to the Chinese over five years, and perhaps more if needed. Administration officials agreed that to allow the effort China had been designated a friendly nation under the Foreign Assistance Act. China was the only communist nation other than Yugoslavia to be so designated.[31]

In the meantime staff aides were working on a possible trip by former president Richard Nixon. Hamilton Jordan had initiated the approach to the former president several months earlier. Nixon's support would "make it difficult for the Republicans to make [China] a partisan issue," he argued.[32] But Nixon suggested that President Carter ought to visit the country before he did, and Rick Inderfurth, an NSC staffer, agreed with Nixon. Carter himself rejected Brzezinski's suggestion that he support the Nixon visit.[33] But then in early August 1979, when informed that White House staff aide Hugh Carter had put together a memorandum to President Carter regarding Nixon's visit, Brzezinski did not risk another presidential rejection. "You tell Hugh," he wrote, "no need to bother the President."[34]

With Mondale's trip out of the way, Nixon, in mid September 1979, proceeded to Beijing. Two banquets were given in his honor, and he had a private meeting with Deng. At one point one of the Chinese hosts noted in his toast that the Chinese, when drinking the water, don't "forget those who dug the well. We don't forget our friends." When Deng lifted his glass to honor Nixon, he noted once again how the new relationship between China and the United States contributed to world peace and countered hegemonism. Nixon did not talk to journalists about his discussion with Deng.[35]

In early January 1980, Harold Brown had his turn. The defense secretary had carte blanche to discuss the exportation of nonlethal military sales to China, including technology not available to the Soviet Union. Vance fought one more rearguard action to keep the meeting from taking place. But Brzezinski argued that Richard Holbrooke of the State Department had been with Mondale in Beijing when the matter was discussed. It would be "silly" to back down on it at this late date, Brzezinski claimed. As he wrote to the president, "Change in our posture now would look like a zigzag, and it is likely to have a negative impact on some sensitive negotiations which I am now about to initiate."[36]

Later that year William Perry, Under Secretary of Defense for Research and Engineering, led a trip to China to assess the country's overall defense needs. In December 1980, Stansfield Turner was the first, but not the last, CIA director to make such a trip.[37]

Most of the players in Carter's inner circle and his Asia team, in short, saw where the president was going and had rallied around the Brzezinski approach. Woodcock, as we have seen, assisted Brzezinski in his negotiations with the PRC. Vice president Mondale, too, had interests that Brzezinski was able to use to his own advantage.[38] Defense Secretary Brown was a natural supporter from the very beginning. His desire for a tilt toward China was evident in the NSC meeting about the Horn of Africa in early 1978. By early 1979, Brown and other key people in the Defense Department and the intelligence agencies were interested in securing new observation posts and were willing to trade military equipment for that opportunity.[39] Holbrooke had joined in that small coterie who discussed foreign policy in Brzezinski's office in the fall of 1977, gave up on the Vietnamese normalization process in the fall of 1978, and backed Brzezinski rather than Vance on the issue of Blumenthal's visit to China. Holbrooke also squared off against those in the administration who had qualms about keeping the Pol Pot representative in the UN as Cambodia's representative.[40]

Brzezinski also benefited from his relationships with the three people who were closest to Carter. Political advisor Hamilton Jordan and Press Secretary Jody Powell grew "increasingly very close" to Brzezinski. Initially puzzled by what they saw as

Carter's "softness" in his dealings with the Soviet Union, both men supported Brzezinski whenever he wanted the president to take a tougher line. First Lady Rosalynn Carter's attitude toward him was perhaps an even more important factor in his gaining influence with the president. She liked Brzezinski, and when she left the White House, she remarked to him that he was her "special person." As Brzezinski later noted, this backing gave him his sense of confidence that "if we ever had a fight with Mondale or [Secretary of State Edmund] Muskie, I felt pretty confident that I would win."[41]

Brzezinski's own staff also kept him informed of the moves of possible competitors. NSC aide Michel Oksenberg and Brzezinski aide William Odom had warned Brzezinski that Vance "would make an effort to delay the [Secretary of the Treasury] Michael Blumenthal trip. Your goal should be that it [the delay] never takes place.... If Blumenthal can visit Moscow while the Soviets ferry their Cubans to Ethiopia and Yemen and back a Vietnamese invasion of Cambodia, he ought to be able to visit Peking [Beijing]." They suggested that Brzezinski should "make sure that Cy is not in charge" of the U.S. response to China in the United Nations. "We want to make sure that our UN position is exactly in line with our first policy objective of obtaining the withdrawal of both Chinese and Vietnamese forces."[42]

On one issue though, Brzezinski went too far, even for one of his most loyal aides. His deputy David Aaron argued that Brzezinski's proposal that China be treated as a developing country in the World Bank and that it be added to the countries aided by its International Bank for Reconstruction and Development "could do serious—perhaps fatal—damage to that institution. Its future hangs by a thread in the Congress; adding China to the countries the IBRD has to aid would powerfully multiply its enemies. I'm not sure how this affects the issue you're grappling with, but I wanted to be sure you had it clearly in mind."[43]

THE IMPACT OF A MOTIVATED TACTICIAN

On the opening to China Zbigniew Brzezinski employed all the tactics of a motivated tactician delineated in the management literature.[1] We have seen how he employed salami tactics to get to Beijing. Then he set the agenda, introduced decision rules, and controlled access to the decision making process in ways that furthered his objectives. To bolster the desired option, he sought allies on the presidential staff and elsewhere, and in all probability he permitted NSC leaks in an effort to influence public responses. But he did more than that. Brzezinski also framed issues in ways that would have the most impact on his president and the public—providing historical and other material arguments to bolster the perceived value of the desired option. Along the way he was careful to maintain a good relationship with Carter, publicly extolling his policies, complimenting the president on the choices he made.[2]

As early as the spring of 1978, for example, Brzezinski had argued that the Soviet involvement in the Horn of Africa could best be countered by playing the China card. Typical was his statement on March 3, 1978:

> If the Soviets do not conclude that we are prepared to stand up to them, you can only anticipate worsening difficulties in the years ahead.... [Their] greatest area of sensitivity is China.... The development of cooperation with the Chinese in science and technology and the encouragement of west European arms sales to China would give the U.S. needed leverage.
>
> The Chinese are worried about the Middle East and the African Horn, and they could even help us more directly. In any case, the Soviets are willing to operate on several levels in their dealings with us; we should not be unduly sensitive to Soviet concerns and similarly operate on several levels towards them.[3]

Any moves he might make to fashion a new relationship to China Brzezinski assured the president was not so much the result of the United States playing the China card as a response to Soviet actions. They had "so frightened the Chinese that they [the Chinese] turned to us."[4]

The shift away from equal to preferential treatment was also introduced gradually. As Oksenberg warned Brzezinski on January 26, 1979, "A sudden move toward the word 'balance' from our previous and less adequate 'evenhandedness' formulation would attract immediate press attention, would be taken as an indication of a change in policy, and would be the lead story." He added that Brzezinski should, in the "transition period," employ both phrases, saying, "We intend to pursue an evenhanded, or balanced, policy toward China and the Soviet Union."[5]

Brzezinski himself, in a letter to Carter on December 25, 1958, even framed the Vietnamese invasion of Cambodia as a Soviet threat. This was the "third time a country which has concluded a friendship and cooperation treaty with the Soviet Union has shortly thereafter engaged in a recourse to arms." Earlier, the Indians had done this to Pakistan; and the Ethiopians had done it to Somalia and Eritrea.[6] But the Chinese invasion of Vietnam on February 17, 1979, was due to the situation in Southeast Asia, a situation in which Vietnam and its supporters shared responsibility. "Present circumstances require wisdom and restraint by our governments to prevent any widening of this conflict and to restore peace in Indochina," noted Brzezinski. "To achieve this most important and urgent goal, it is essential that all foreign forces withdraw from both Kampuchea and Vietnam."[7]

Brzezinski also complimented Carter on his intellectual skills, comparing him on one occasion to Secretary of State Cyrus Vance. "Your statement on the Shanghai Communiqué [showed U.S. commitment]," he wrote the president, "as Vance tried to do in his Asia speech."[8] Opposition to his policies could be dismissed as reflections of turf and personal consideration.[9]

Brzezinski also suggested that sharing information and policy debates with the Department of State could lead to leaks. Even consultation with the State Department on technical matters, such as the handling of the treaty with Taiwan, should be limited. The danger in this case was evident in the fact that journalist Strobe Talbott knew about Secretary Vance's meetings with former Attorney General Herbert Brownell on that matter. Brzezinski suggested that the leak was due to the inclusion of the Far East desk, over his protest, in the recent talks with Chinese Foreign Minister Han Hsu.[10]

Carter not only let Brzezinski lead the way on China policy, he gave him the leeway, at times, to act on his own. Brzezinski was allowed considerable discretion in writing his own instructions for his trip to Beijing. In his stopover in Tokyo to deal with Japanese concerns over the antihegemony clause in their proposed treaty with China, he acted on his own. Brzezinski's controversial hard-line performance on NBC's *Meet the Press* in May 1978 was another.[11] The management of former president Richard Nixon's trip to China seems to have been one more such event.

The confidence that Carter had in Brzezinski's ability and the nature of their close relationship has been discussed elsewhere. Suffice it to say, at this point, that Brzezinski's influence was due not only to institutional and political considerations but to psychological factors as well. Brzezinski explained foreign policy in the kind of broad strokes the president seemed to appreciate and which, according to Brzezinski, Carter could not articulate himself. A doer, Brzezinski was proud of his ability to confront, to bring issues to a head, and to cut through the "Gordian knots" even if this assertive style increased the risk of confrontations with the Soviets.[12] This quality appealed to the president. In one revealing moment, Carter identified himself and Brzezinski as agents for change, contrasting the two of them to the more reserved Vance.[13] At the most basic level, Brzezinski played the role of strategist for Carter in the foreign policy area, much as Jody Powell and Hamilton Jordan did in the realm of domestic politics.

All these moves by Brzezinski worked because Carter took pleasure in being regarded as tough. But as Carter's various aides noted, it was a posture from which he could stray.[14] Brzezinski helped keep him in line. To this end, he reminded the president on a variety of occasions that if he were not tough, he would face more difficulties in the years ahead. To the same end, he also persuaded Carter to pick up Deng Xiaoping's words in a summary statement at the end of their meeting in Washington in 1979. He noted that though the two countries did not have a formal alliance, they had joint interests in Africa, the Middle East, and the nonaligned movements of Korea.[15]

Perhaps most important, Brzezinski had used his influence to give President Carter one of his most important foreign policy successes. Brzezinski later noted that the president told him the China dealings "impressed him a great deal and he several times referred to it—that he got me to do something and it got done."[16]

Charmed by the Chinese?

For all his tough-mindedness about the Soviets, Brzezinski was somewhat naive about the People's Republic of China (PRC). After his return from China, Carter noted that Brzezinski seemed to have been seduced by the Chinese.[17] At the time of Deng's visit to Washington in early 1979, Brzezinski himself enthused over the "deliberate and resolute tone" of Deng's resolve to teach Vietnam a lesson.[18] When the PRC's incursion proved that it was not efficient in dealing with its neighbor to the south, Brzezinski remained unusually quiet. Another time, when Ambassador Chai Zemin turned up in conventional Western dress for a meeting with Brzezinski, the National Security Advisor turned rhapsodic. "A total sartorial transformation, symptomatic of the ideological transformation of contemporary China," Brzezinski noted in his journal.[19]

Carter initially did not want to "brownnose" the Chinese as he saw the Nixon-Kissinger team doing. But he did rely on former secretary of state Henry Kissinger's suggestion, shortly after his election victory, that negotiations with China's representatives could be productive. They were shrewd but patient negotiators, Kissinger told him, and they would honor the letter and the spirit of any agreements they made.[20]

In his own dealings with the Chinese, Carter saw these qualities displayed. They approached their negotiations with "patience and stubbornness." His early 1977 meeting with Huang Chen, liaison chief of the PRC, in Washington convinced Carter that the Chinese, without being "condescending" about it, "still considered themselves members of the Middle Kingdom—at the center of the civilized world—prepared simply to wait until others accepted their position on 'matters of principle.'"[21]

Still, the Chinese ultimately won over Carter. Contrasted with the Russian leaders, he would later note, they were gracious and friendly. American delegations going to the Soviet Union would often come back with negative attitudes regarding their experiences; everyone who came back from China had positive experiences to relate.[22]

After his first meetings with Deng, Carter noted that the Chinese vice premier was a "pleasure to negotiate with....He's small, tough, intelligent, frank, courageous, personable, self-assured, friendly." Carter would find the whole experience with the Chinese more "pleasant and gratifying" than he had expected.[23] As he wrote,

> Both before and after normalization, the Chinese exhibited a fine sensitivity about my other duties, and also about our domestic political realities. They were helpful in their statements about SALT II, the resolution of the Taiwan issue, the stabilizing influence in the western Pacific of our new diplomatic ties, the need for strong cooperation between us and Japan—and refrained through all of this from casting our new relationship with them in an anti-Soviet tone. In the process, I learned why the Chinese are the most civilized people in the world.[24]

The Chinese may have been sensitive to American officials because the United States met their interests and, for the most part, did so in a way that showed a concern for their sensibilities. They could be quite rough in their talks about the Soviet Union, often using stronger language about the USSR than would Brzezinski. On occasion, they showed little finesse in dealing with the United States. Even back in the fall of 1978, Diplomat Tom Thornton questioned their lack of concern for the appropriate diplomatic etiquette when dealing with President Carter. When Han Hsu, the Chinese Foreign Minister, said he could not change his schedule when visiting the United Nations in New York City to see Carter because he could not take a later flight to Canada, was he slighting the United States? Imagine, Thornton said, if Vance were in Beijing and the Chinese head of state asked to see him; would he not adjust his schedule?[25] The Chinese orientation toward Vance, too, was unusually arrogant, if Brzezinski's recollection of one episode is accurate. Departing from one affair in the United States, Han muttered in an aside that perhaps he should also pay his respects to the U.S. secretary of state—"What is his name?"[26]

Policy Results

Acknowledging the existence of China, one of the most powerful nations in the world, was certainly an accomplishment for the Carter administration. The deal, however, was settled with the whole issue of Taiwan's status remaining unresolved. The Chinese had rejected any statement saying that Taiwan would be only united with the People's Republic of China only via peaceful means. Instead they issued a side statement saying that the means of unifying Taiwan with mainland China was their domestic concern.[27] Eventually, large majorities in the U.S. Congress rallied around a measure that would guarantee the sale of American arms to Taiwan sufficient to maintain its self-defense capabilities. In March the measure passed both houses of Congress with veto-proof majorities.[28]

But standing tough relative to the Soviet Union had few of the strategic payoffs that Brzezinski had forecast. When Hamilton Jordan informed Domestic Affairs Advisor

Stuart Eizenstat on December 15, 1978, that Carter was going to announce a normal-ization agreement with China, a stunned Eizenstat retorted, "Why the hell is he going to do that?" Jordan replied, "Well you know that it's an important initiative and some-thing we ought to do." Eizenstat responded that it would drive the Soviets up a tree and that the whole thing would further hinder a SALT treaty."[29] Certainly the stance did not win Carter the support of Senate hawks for the Strategic Arms Limitation Treaty (SALT II) talks. Ignoring Chinese human rights violations, too, raised ques-tions about Carter's claim that his commitments to human rights were universalistic, a matter to be dealt with in depth in chapter 26.

In addition to the opening to China, Carter, at midterm, had one other major for-eign policy success. While Brzezinski pushed through the tilt toward China, with Carter coming on to the negotiations as they neared conclusion, Carter placed his reputation and his person on the line throughout the Mideast Talks. In this operation, perhaps his most significant as president, Carter would play a major role, with Vance aiding him in the negotiations.

MAESTRO OF THE CAMP DAVID TALKS

On Monday, September 18, 1978, Israeli Prime Minister Menachem Begin, Egyptian President Anwar el-Sadat, and First Lady Rosalynn Carter arrived at the U.S. House of Representatives, taking their seats in the front row balcony. When President Jimmy Carter entered the crowded chamber, he was greeted by wild applause. During his twenty-five-minute address, he was interrupted by applause twenty-five different times. Noting that it had been two thousand years since "there was peace between Egypt and a free Jewish nation," Carter said that such a peace might be secured "this year." At one point he turned toward Begin and Sadat, saying, "Blessed are the peace makers, for they shall be called the children of God."[1]

The agreements Carter presented in the U.S. House of Representatives, however, were not final but frameworks in which some issues were provisionally settled while others were left open. The most conclusive arrangement, a framework for a peace treaty between Israel and Egypt, would have Israel return the Sinai Peninsula to Egypt. In return, Israeli ships would be allowed passage through the Suez Canal, and limitations would be imposed on the armed forces that Egypt could station east of the Suez Canal. The two countries would formally recognize each other and the opening of the boundaries to tourism and trade would follow. The second agreement provided a framework for a comprehensive peace in the Middle East, to be concluded somewhat further down the road. It set as goals Palestinian autonomy and the withdrawal of Israeli armed forces from the West Bank and Gaza. Jordanian and Palestinian representatives would participate in the talks to determine the status of the occupied territories. No mention was made as to the status of Jerusalem.[2]

The reception Carter received in Washington that night was partly due to his success in reversing, against considerable odds, a downward cycle in Middle East negotiations. Earlier, Carter had backed off from the U.S.-Soviet statement of October 1, 1977, that called for a joint approach to Middle East peace. Domestic affairs advisors in his administration had warned him that members of the American Jewish community, as well as Soviet hard-liners, were opposed to joint action.[3] By the late summer of 1978, the positive impact of Sadat's bold trip to Jerusalem in the preceding November had evaporated. The Mideast peace talks at Leeds Castle in mid-July 1978 had not been followed by the expected conference at the U.S. monitoring station in the Sinai, and Begin and Sadat were exchanging hostile remarks.[4] Saudi Arabia was pressuring Sadat to reconcile his differences with Syria's Hafez Assad, a hard-liner in the Middle East conflict. Such reconciliation could bring Sadat back into the radical Arab bloc, thereby increasing the likelihood of another round of Middle East wars, a resurgence of Soviet influence in the area, and a possible oil embargo against the United States.[5] A bad situation was getting worse.

This particular foreign policy venture tapped into Jimmy Carter's values. His study of the Bible and a visit to the Holy Land in Israel while governor had deepened his personal commitment to peace in the region. His personal strengths—his willingness to take risks, his tenacity, and his ability to master detail evident in his early climb to power—would contribute to his success at Camp David. As one of his Middle East advisors, William Quandt, later remembered,

> In many ways the thirteen days at Camp David showed Carter at his best. He was sincere in his desire for peace in the Middle East, and he was prepared to work long hours to reach that goal. His optimism and belief in the good qualities of both Sadat and Begin were reflections of a deep faith that kept him going against all odds. His mastery of detail was often impressive. And he was stubborn. He did not want to fail. These were precisely the qualities that he had brought to his electoral campaign in 1976 and that the American people had apparently admired.[6]

The Israeli defense minister Ezer Weizman would later note that he was

> full of admiration for the American president....He earned my respect with his bulldog like persistence and his ability to deal with the tiniest details. He attended numerous discussions, listening in and making notes in his neat engineer's handwriting on a yellow letter pad. He led his talks with great authority, alternatively growing angry or flashing his teeth in a brilliant smile as the need arose. His swift grasp was a clear advantage; he could understand immediately what was being discussed.[7]

Foreign Minister Moshe Dayan testified, at a press conference upon his return to Israel on September 19, that "all of us, to a man, are full of admiration for him [Jimmy Carter]....Were it not for him...I do not see that there would have been a possibility of arriving at this agreement within those 12 days."[8]

Why was it that Jimmy Carter's particular talents paid off at Camp David? Perhaps it was the clear vision Carter had for his goals, and the overlapping interests of the parties in conflict, that made agreement a possibility. To turn this possibility into an actual accomplishment, Carter would need the determination of Sadat to achieve a deal and the willingness of several members of the Israeli team to cut around Begin. Carter was also flexible and collegial in managing his own delegation at Camp David. The result was a team effort that contributed to the success of the conference. The explanation of Camp David's success, as in almost all turning point events, resides in a confluence of factors working in the same direction.

Preparations

Carter's decision to hold a summit meeting at Camp David was clearly a high-risk strategy. It would involve a departure from his previous policy of trying to work with the Soviet Union on Middle East issues, and a successful outcome was by no means certain. Failure would irreparably impair Carter's political reputation and the chance at a second term in office. The president's vulnerability on the domestic front was quite evident: he had a 61 percent negative rating in the Harris Polls, and his "strong" approval rating in the Gallup Polls was only 11 percent.[9] The press coverage of the White House was so harsh that Press Secretary Jody Powell's "despondency" was "damned close" to clinical.[10] With these considerations in mind, many members of the president's inner circle suggested that he not call the conference or were pessimistic about its possible results.[11] These hardly seemed like the best circumstances for untying the "Gordian knot" of Middle East peace.

Yet on July 20, 1978, Carter informed his advisors that he was considering a summit meeting with Sadat and Begin.[12] Several days later, on August 5, Secretary of State Cyrus Vance left for the Middle East to propose a high-level meeting at Camp David. Begin and Sadat agreed to participate.

Upon his return to the United States, Vance met with the U.S. Ambassador at Large for Middle East Negotiations Roy Atherton, Assistant Secretary of State for Near East Affairs Harold Saunders, and National Security Council (NSC) Middle Eastern expert William Quandt at former New York governor and U.S. ambassador (to both the USSR and the United Kingdom) W. Averell Harriman's estate to prepare for the talks. Building on earlier work done by Saunders at Leeds Castle, they drafted a background report for Carter, *The Pivotal Issue: The Sinai/West Bank Relationship*, in which they argued for a relatively modest agenda at Camp David. Begin and Sadat both had an interest in the return of the Sinai to Egypt, and the problem of Israeli settlements in the Sinai was not considered insurmountable. But it was felt that these issues should be kept somewhat open to secure leverage in dealing with the more intractable problem of the Israeli settlements in the West Bank and the Gaza Strip; after Begin was out of office, peace could be traded for land. The specific goal at Camp David was to secure an Egyptian-Israeli agreement on a framework of principles for future negotiations on the status of the inhabitants of the West Bank and Gaza.[13]

Others joined in the preparations for the conference. Hamilton Jordan, Press Secretary Jody Powell, Vice President Walter Mondale, and National Security Advisor Zbigniew Brzezinski acquainted themselves with the paper drafted at Harriman's estate. Jerrold Post's office at the Central Intelligence Agency worked up psychological profiles of Sadat and Begin. The White House historical office examined precedence for Camp David. They determined that this was the first type of negotiations of their kind; Theodore Roosevelt had helped Japan and Russia in their negotiations after the war of 1905, but had not participated directly in the talks.[14]

Carter himself had studied the briefing books on a short fishing trip to Jackson Lake in Wyoming. The psychological profiles of Begin and Sadat were of particular value to him. He wanted to know the backgrounds of these men, how they operated, and what they valued.[15]

Back in Washington, he called his aides together. "You are not aiming high enough," he said. At a minimum, he insisted, the talks should be directed toward the conclusion of an agreement on the framework for an Egyptian-Israeli peace treaty. The linkage of the issue of Palestinian autonomy and the governing of the West Bank and Gaza Strip to the return of the Sinai would provide an unnecessary obstacle to achieving any substantive agreement at Camp David.[16]

In taking this stance, Carter was not committed to a fool's mission. True, there was real risk involved. Sadat's absolute bottom line was the return of the Sinai to Egypt, unencumbered with any sort of Israeli presence there, plus a framework of principles for dealing with the West Bank, the Gaza Strip, and Jerusalem. For Begin, the status quo was preferable to any serious compromise of Israeli control of Judea and Samaria, the names he used to refer to the Israeli-administered territories on the West Bank, as well as East Jerusalem, and the Gaza Strip. But a peace treaty with Egypt could cut into the phalanx of Arab states that denied the very legitimacy of an Israeli state. Dependent as it was on U.S. support for its security interests and advanced weapons systems, Israel could not afford to alienate the United States.[17] An agreement at Camp David was a possibility, though by no means a high-probability outcome.

The main obstacle to this more limited agreement, as Carter saw it, was the distrust between Begin and Sadat. As Carter told his advisors shortly before the conference,

> Let me tell you what's going to happen at Camp David. I've invited Sadat and Begin here to help overcome a real problem, and that is the fact they don't trust one another, and they don't see the good point in each other's position. And by getting them to Camp David, away from the press and out of the glare of publicity and away from their own political constituencies, I think I can bring them to understand each other's positions better. My intention is to meet with them for a couple of days, try to work through the misunderstanding, and within a very few days—two or three at the most, we will reach agreement on broad principles. Then we can give instructions to the foreign ministers, and they can go off and negotiate an agreement. That's what we're going to do at Camp David.

"Oh my goodness," William Quandt said to himself upon hearing this. "We're here for group therapy. What are we doing?" Yet, as Quandt later admitted, Carter's search for a narrower but more complete agreement was what made a success at Camp David possible.[18]

Camp David offered some advantages along these lines. The conferees could be isolated from outside pressures that produced "political posturing or defense of transient stands or beliefs." A double security fence surrounded the 125 acres of forest and rocky land, which made it possible to limit contact with the outside world. A central switchboard staffed by the U.S. Army Signal Corps enabled the Americans to control all telephone calls coming into or going out of the compound. Press Secretary Powell would be responsible for any press briefings made; he would meet the journalists, stationed six miles away in Thurmont, Maryland, at the Camp David gate once a day, list the meetings that took place, and provide a little color—and that was it. These details, limited though they might be, would be cleared with Dan Pattir and Osama el-Baz, the Israeli and Egyptian press spokesmen, respectively.[19]

The arrangement of physical facilities within the camp also provided other advantages for the talks. The limited cabin space provided a rationale for limiting the size of each delegation.[20] The arrangement of the cabins provided the necessary separation between the three major negotiating teams, plus a facility for coming together to break down barriers. Holly, the site chosen for the actual talks, had a small cozy reading room. A movie projector in a side room would run about twenty-four hours a day except when the room was to be used as a chapel, a synagogue, or a mosque. At Laurel, members of the delegations would be served in a central dining hall in the hope that the delegates would mingle. For purposes of relaxation, tennis courts, bicycles, and a bowling alley were available to the delegates.[21] In addition, two social events—a performance of the U.S. Marine Corps Silent Drill Team on the first Thursday evening of the talks and a trip to Gettysburg, Pennsylvania, the following Sunday morning—would provide relief from any possible tension in the talks.

Most important, as it turned out, the camp arrangements enabled President Carter to stroll over to the cabins of Sadat or Begin, as the situation required, and make threats, more or less tacit, that the intransigence of their delegation would harm their relationship with the United States or shift the blame for the failure of the conference to their country. To have delivered those messages via formal challenges would have risked a substantial backlash.

Carter and his aides came to deal primarily with Sadat in the Egyptian delegation and with Aharon Barak, Ezer Weizman, and Moshe Dayan in the Israeli delegation. From the Israeli delegates they would informally secure advice on how to deal with Begin and send messages to him through those who exerted the most influence over him.[22]

An Inauspicious Beginning

The Camp David Conference opened on Tuesday, September 5, 1978. Jimmy Carter, aided by Cyrus Vance, headed the American delegation. The American delegation also included Vice President Mondale, National Security Advisor Brzezinski, Press Secretary Powell, political advisor Jordan, Assistant Secretary of State for Near East and South Asian Affairs Harold Saunders, National Security Council staff member William Quandt, and three diplomats: Alfred Atherton, ambassador at large; Hermann Eilts, ambassador to Egypt; and Samuel Lewis, ambassador to Israel. A second expert group would provide yeoman service throughout the talks. Vance orchestrated the roles of the various members and chaired meetings. As Israeli Defense Minister Ezer Weizman later noted, Vance had a "quiet determination that left no doubt who was the boss."[23]

Israeli Prime Minister Begin was accompanied by Foreign Minister Dayan; Defense Minister Weizman; Aharon Barak, Israel's attorney general and member-designate of its supreme court; General Avraham Tamir, director of the planning branch of the Israeli Army; Dan Pattir, public affairs advisor to the prime minister; and Simcha Dinitz, Israel's ambassador to the United States. In addition to President Anwar el-Sadat, the Egyptian team included Minister of Foreign Affairs Mohamed Kamel, Minister of State for Foreign Affairs Boutros Ghali, and Under Secretary of Foreign Affairs Osama el-Baz.[24]

At Rosalynn Carter's suggestion, the conference started with a joint prayer for success. Israeli Foreign Minister Dayan met the proposal with a grin and wry side remark: "You will have to take off your hat for the Christians and your shoes for the Muslims—and then you'll end up putting on a yarmulke for the Jews." Begin, in a gesture that would characterize many of his responses throughout the conference, took out a pen and made some minor modifications to the wording of the prayer's text.[25]

When it came to substantive issues, Carter took the lead. His expectation that the Camp David woods would promote a spirit of amity between Sadat and Begin was quickly dashed. When Begin, Sadat, and Carter began the first round of the "Big Three" talks on Wednesday, September 6, Sadat produced a document outlining several tough demands. The Egyptians insisted on the language of United Nations Resolution 242, which noted the "inadmissibility of acquisition of territory by war," a measure that would require the Israelis to admit that all their claims to the West Bank and the Gaza Strip, as well as the Sinai Peninsula, were illegitimate. Israeli settlements in the Sinai would thus have to withdraw along with the Israeli troops. A complete surprise to the Israelis was the Egyptian demand for compensation for the oil Israel was pumping from the Sinai and the damages inflicted on Egypt during the October War.[26]

As the Egyptian proposal was read, Begin had a hard time controlling himself. But when Sadat finished his presentation, Carter joked, "Well, Mr. Begin, it would save us all a lot of time if you would just accept these terms?" Everyone laughed and Begin joined in the frivolity, saying, "Mr. President, would you advise me to do so?"[27]

At the end of the presentation, Carter asked Begin not to respond immediately and invited him for a stroll. "The document is extremist," he told Begin, and it had probably been "designed to make an impression on the Arab world."[28] Later that same day, Carter assured Israeli Defense Minister Weizman that the Egyptian plan was unacceptable to the United States.[29] Carter was not risking much in this assurance. Sadat, in their first private meeting at Camp David, had provided Carter with a memo noting concessions that the Americans might propose at the appropriate times. His goal, he told Carter, was to discover where Begin actually stood.[30]

At the second meeting of the conference, on Thursday morning, Begin responded orally with a "brutally frank" assessment of each issue raised in Sadat's paper.[31] At one point, the two men began arguing about who had conquered whom, and only Carter's intercession stopped the battle. According to Carter, "It was mean. They were brutal with each other, personal."[32] Later that afternoon, Begin and Sadat got into another round of heated exchanges and seemed at a deadlock on the Sinai settlements.[33]

At one point, Sadat announced that there was no reason for the discussion to continue. As the two men walked toward the door, Carter jumped in front of them, urging them to give him "another chance to use my influence and analysis, to have confidence in me." Begin agreed. Sadat relented with a reluctant nod. As Carter later noted, "we had accomplished little so far except to name the difficult issues. There was no compatibility between the two men."[34] The first three trilateral meetings thus ended with more, not less, animosity between Sadat and Begin.[35]

Thursday night, at the concert performed by the Marine Corps Silent Drill Team, gloom settled over the assembled crowd. Word had spread like wildfire through Camp David that the talks had broken down.[36] Sadat, according to Rosalynn Carter, seemed particularly forlorn.[37]

Shifting Gears

At this impasse, President Carter decided to change the structure of the talks. The United States would put its own proposal for agreements on the table, and become an active participant in the substance of the discussions.

Taking advantage of the lull in the talks due to the Jewish Sabbath, Carter and the U.S. team went to work. On Friday afternoon, Harold Saunders, building on his earlier drafts, produced a third paper that envisaged a comprehensive solution to the problems faced. Palestinian autonomy was linked with matters pertaining to the conclusion of peace between Egypt and Israel. Vance and Brzezinski had insisted on this linkage.[38]

When Carter got the draft, he took out the linkage of Palestinian autonomy issues from the withdrawal of Israel from the Sinai. It was a crucial decision, permitting the two issues to progress independently.[39] The president then went to work on his own draft for the Sinai portion of the agreement. He would shepherd it, albeit with numerous changes, through the remaining session of the meetings at Camp David.[40]

On Sunday, September 10, after an excursion to the Gettysburg National Military Cemetery, Carter read the seventeen-page document to the assembled Israeli delegation. The American proposal would set a three-month deadline for the conclusion of a peace treaty between Israel and Egypt, provide for the restoration of Egyptian sovereignty over the Sinai, commit both countries to peaceful resolution of conflicts, and provide for the free passage of Israeli vessels through all international waterways. The particularly sensitive issues of Israeli settlements in the Sinai and timetables for withdrawal of Israeli forces were left for later discussions.

With regard to the broader Middle East negotiations, the proposals called for Palestinian participation in the negotiations over the West Bank and Gaza, the establishment of Palestinian autonomy as well as the withdrawal of most Israeli forces from the West Bank and Gaza, and the relocation of the remaining troops to specified security points. There was no mention of the thorny issue of Israeli settlements in the region, or the exact meaning of Palestinian "autonomy."[41] Begin was clearly quite distressed as the American proposals were read, and he insisted that the Israeli delegation could not respond until they had time to consider them.[42]

In subsequent discussions, U.S. negotiators would deal with the two delegations separately. Begin and Sadat would not meet again until Sunday, September 17, the thirteenth and final day of the conference.[43]

Carter would lead the talks over the reestablishment of Israeli-Egyptian political ties and the disposition of the Sinai. Vance took major responsibility over the negotiations of Palestinian rights and issues dealing with the West Bank and Jerusalem. Brown handled military issues, and Turner brought the relevant intelligence information to the table. Brzezinski operated as a troubleshooter, going between the Israeli and Egyptian teams from time to time. Hamilton Jordan began thinking of what would happen in the event that the talks failed.[44]

In the week that followed, Carter held marathon talks, dealing with Begin first, obtaining the exact wording he insisted upon. He then would consult with Sadat on important matters of policy. Working drafts, based on these general principles, would be negotiated with relatively flexible members of the two delegations—el-Baz for Egypt and Aharon Barak for Israel. The sticking points, according to Weizman, were the legitimate rights of the Palestinian people, the possibility of an Arab flag over Jerusalem's Temple Mount, a freeze on new settlements while the negotiations were in process, and the return of the Sinai airfields and settlements.[45]

On Monday, September 11, the Israelis presented their reactions to the first U.S. proposal. They had crossed out all the language in the preamble dealing with the inadmissibility of the acquisition of territory by war and deleted references to the Palestinian people, substituting instead the phrase Palestinian Arabs. The words "administrative councils" replaced references to a "self-governing authority." They flatly refused to discuss either a freeze on settlements in Judea, Samaria, or Gaza or a withdrawal of settlements from the Sinai.[46]

On Tuesday, September 12, a division within the Israeli delegation surfaced in their private meetings. Defense Minister Weizman noted that Israel had a clear choice in front of them—the Israeli settlements in the Sinai, or peace. "I heard you," Begin barked angrily. But he did not seem moved. Israeli Foreign Minister Dayan, reporting to the Israeli delegation on a conversation with Sadat earlier that day, proclaimed that the Israelis had come to the "end of the road"; Sadat, he said, was clearly not movable. Dayan went to his room, where he began packing his suitcase. Weizman who had followed Dayan, tried to persuade him not to leave.[47]

General Abraham Tamir of the Israel delegation saved the day. He suggested that Weizman call his friend, Agricultural Minister and future Prime Minister Ariel Sharon, to get his view on the matter. Weizman agreed there was no harm in making the call, though he thought Sharon, as the father of Israeli settlement policies, would have a negative response. To Weizman's surprise Sharon agreed to call Begin back to say that if these settlements were the only block to a deal, that he would favor making some concessions. Some time later a deeply moved Begin told the members of the Israeli delegation that he had received a call and that General Sharon favored the evacuation of the settlements if they were the only obstacles to a peace agreement.[48]

On Wednesday, September 13, tension within the Egyptian delegation was even sharper than that within the Israeli group. Sadat was at one point seen arguing with his men on the porch of the cabin. Osama el-Baz had made a demand that Carter discovered had not been cleared with Sadat. And when Carter tried to talk to Sadat at 10:00 p.m. that night, he was told the president had retired for the evening. Normally,

Sadat kept long hours and the light was still on in his cabin. Concerned with Sadat's safety, an apprehensive Carter ordered, at 4:00 a.m. on Thursday, tighter security controls over access to Sadat's cabin. Carter breathed with relief only when Sadat appeared for his morning walk.[49]

By Thursday, September 14, Carter had a draft agreement in hand. He told Dayan, Weizman, and Barak that Sadat supported his proposals. But the Israeli settlements would have to be removed from the Sinai if a peace were to be secured. In a subtle shift of position Dayan now stated that Israel could not agree on the matter of the Sinai settlements without the consent of the Israeli cabinet and the Knesset. This latter phrase suggested a compromise that members of the Israeli delegation would eventually sell to Begin.[50] Carter suggested to Vance that he take Brzezinski with him to deliver a tough and direct statement to Begin. To Brzezinski, "It was clear that he wanted someone to be with Cy so that Cy would be quite tough."[51]

That same day Weizman took the initiative regarding another stumbling block—the dismantling of Israeli airfields in the Sinai. "Could the U.S. build us substitute airfields?" he asked Defense Secretary Brown, who responded in the affirmative. On Friday, Weizman moved to firm up the deal, making an explicit offer along these lines to Brown and Brzezinski at lunch. When briefed on the matter, Carter agreed that U.S. support would be forthcoming for the building of airfields outside the Sinai. But the Israelis would have to agree to withdraw all their settlements in the Sinai and meet the other points still outstanding in the U.S. package.[52]

Unaware of this movement on the Israeli and U.S. fronts, Sadat called Vance on Friday morning, September 15, to tell him he was leaving Camp David. His bags were packed, and he asked for a helicopter so the entire delegation could depart. Sadat had reached the conclusion that the conference would end in a failure. Without a solid deal to justify his remaining, any additional concessions he might make at Camp David would put him at a disadvantage in future talks.[53]

Informed of Sadat's decision, a distressed Jimmy Carter looked out the window at the Catoctin Mountains. He prayed, changed into more formal clothes, and then set out to see Sadat.[54] Alone in the cabin with the Egyptian president, Carter told Sadat that any promises temporarily made to the Israelis at Camp David would not be backed in subsequent negotiations by the United States. But he went on to state that the onus for failure would be on Sadat should he leave, that his reputation as the world's foremost peacemaker would suffer. More than that, it would end Carter's peacekeeping efforts, the special relationship between Egypt and the United States, and probably the Carter presidency. Last, but not least, Carter emphasized, it would end "Something that is very precious to me, my friendship with you."[55] If Sadat stayed, Carter believed that Egypt would not find itself in the political trap Sadat envisaged. The president later told his wife, Rosalynn, that he "had never talked with anyone else in his life the way he talked with Sadat, except maybe with his children."[56]

Sadat decided to stay. He also agreed that a provision explicitly noting the illegitimacy of the acquisitions of any territories by force might be replaced with a simple reference to UN Resolution 242, which stated that same principle.[57] When Carter, in gratitude, asked if he could do anything for Sadat, Sadat asked if he and Rosalynn would come to Egypt for a visit. Also, the Egyptian people could use a little more wheat and corn. Carter said he would be delighted to visit Egypt and would recommend more wheat and corn—a recommendation the U.S. Congress would later approve.[58]

As Sadat told the members of the Egyptian delegation after that crucial meeting:

> President Carter is a great man and extremely intelligent. He solved the problem with the greatest of ease. He told me I could make any agreement we signed dependent on the approval of the constitutional institutions of Egypt and Israel.... Were either or both of these to reject the agreement, any commitments entered into by the two sides with respect to such agreement would be canceled and not be binding on us in any future negotiations.

When Foreign Minister Kamel indicated that he still had some concerns, Sadat rejoined, "I shall sign anything proposed by President Carter without reading it."[59]

On Saturday, September 16, things began to come together. Throughout the morning and early afternoon Carter had a series of meetings with members of the Israeli and Egyptian delegations as well as his own advisors. From 4:40 to 7:00 p.m. he met with Sadat, el-Baz, and Vance. At 8:00 p.m. he began what turned out to be a marathon meeting with key members of the Israeli team—Begin, Dayan, Barak—as well as Vance and other U.S. officials. Begin finally agreed that if all other points of dispute were removed, he would ask the Knesset to remove Israeli settlements from the Sinai.[60] There was also a discussion about a letter that Begin would write agreeing that no new settlements would be established in the West Bank or Gaza for a period of time. Carter and Vance later insisted that the period of time cover the entire five-year period provided for the autonomy negotiations. Begin would later claim he had only agreed to think it over. Finally, at 1:30 a.m., the group adjourned.[61] According to Quandt's recollections, the Israeli prime minister promised only to authorize no more settlements in the West Bank for at least three months and he made a distinction that did not bar the actual onset of new construction onto old settlements.[62]

Almost predictably, on Sunday, September 17, one final dispute came close to ending the talks. Earlier, it had become evident that no agreement on the status of Jerusalem was possible. On Saturday night the parties finessed the issue by agreeing to simply write individual letters stating their national positions. But then, to win Sadat's support for unlinking the Palestine autonomy negotiations from the Sinai talks, the United States agreed to write a letter stating that they considered East Jerusalem to be "conquered territory." When one of the American negotiators showed the Israeli ambassador to the United States a draft of the letter, the ambassador quickly labeled it "unacceptable." Informed of the letter, Begin grimly noted, "We can pack our bags and go home without another word."[63]

Carter also had an unpleasant exchange with Dayan and other Israelis on the matter.[64] Carter argued that the positions expressed in the letter had been U.S. policy for a long time. "Do you want to dictate to me what to say in the name of the United States?" he asked angrily. Dayan retorted that had the Israelis known the United States intended to announce such a stand on Jerusalem, they would never have agreed to come to Camp David.[65]

Vance and Barak came to the rescue. They drafted a new letter stating that the U.S. position on Jerusalem remained as defined by the Americans in their acceptance of UN Resolution 242. The new wording did not specifically state the substance of that position—that the United States had called for international supervision of the holy places and refused to recognize Israel's annexation of East Jerusalem. The change gave Begin a face-saving exit from the situation.[66]

Before delivering the compromise draft of the U.S. letter to Begin, Carter had an inspiration. At the suggestion of his secretary, Susan Clough, Carter had obtained the names of Begin's grandchildren. Seeing a photograph of himself, Begin, and Sadat on a table in his cabin, he took up a pen and personally dedicated a photo to each of Begin's grandchildren. Then, Carter walked over to see Begin, who was sitting on the porch of his cabin. When presented with the photos, Begin turned them over one by one, and began speaking of his grandchildren. "Mr. President," he said, "This is what we're all about, isn't it? Our grandchildren." The two men then stepped inside the cabin, where Carter handed Begin the new draft of his letter. The Prime Minister did not immediately accept the new draft. Carter urged him to read it and then walked, dejectedly, back to Aspen Lodge.[67]

Worried that Israel might not budge, Carter entered into a short discussion with Powell and Jordan of what they would do. Carter's inclination, as Powell noted, was to present a frank explanation to the American people on why the summit failed.[68] Quandt, who worked on the potential "failure" speech, noted that Carter was going to place primary responsibility for the failure on the Israelis, noting their unwillingness to budge on the settlements in the Sinai and their refusal to acknowledge the relevance of UN Resolution 242 to the final negotiations on the West Bank and Gaza. It was a speech Carter did not want to give.[69]

Fortunately, Carter did not have to face that option. Begin called the president, saying he would accept the letter.[70] He then went to meet Sadat at his lodge, their first meeting since the excursion to Gettysburg. Begin shook Sadat's hand with great warmth. A little later, Sadat paid a return visit to Begin, and they drank to one another's health.[71]

At 9:34 p.m. on that Sunday, September 17, Carter, Begin, and Sadat rode to the helicopter pad at Camp David. Against the usual security precautions, the three of them, plus eight aides, took the flight together back to Washington to participate in a formal signing ceremony. The other conferees were already on their way back to Washington, either by car or helicopter.[72]

Meanwhile, more than two hundred guests, including cabinet members, leaders of Congress, and diplomats from the Egyptian and Israeli embassies, were assembling in the East Room of the White House. Rosalynn Carter, who had returned to Washington earlier in the day, made the calls. The kitchen staff had hastily assembled refreshments of cheeses, tarts, wine, and fruit juices. Powell had alerted the press, and cameras were in place so that national media could broadcast the event.[73]

Then Carter, Sadat, and Begin joined each other at a small table. The documents were signed and toasts were made. Perhaps most memorable is what Begin said about Carter. "The President took a great risk for himself and did it with great civil courage....It was a famous French field commander who said that it is much more difficult to show civil courage than military courage."[74] Few noticed, in the spirit of the moment, that the chair for Egyptian Foreign Minister Kamel was vacant. He had urged Sadat not to sign the accords, and when he was unsuccessful he had handed in his resignation.

Carter's work to secure the initial agreement on the frameworks for peace at Camp David was widely admired. Even former Secretary of State Kissinger was effusive in his praise, saying that the president deserved the "gratitude of the American people and the whole world." In the U.S. Senate, William Roth (R-DE) went so far as to sponsor a resolution that Carter should be recommended for the Nobel Peace Prize for his effort. A CBS News survey showed that popular approval of Carter's administration climbed from 38 percent in June to 51 percent the week of September 25. It rose in a Gallup Poll from 39 percent in August to 56 percent in September. When Carter took a tour of the country after Camp David, cheering crowds greeted him for his historic success.[75]

SUPPORT TEAMS AND
THE ROAD AHEAD

The "predispositions" of the three major players at Camp David, suggests Harold Saunders, then the assistant secretary of state for Near East and South Asia Affairs, were crucial to the success of the Camp David meetings: "Sadat was a visionary; Carter, the engineer; and Begin, the lawyer."[1]

Jimmy Carter was, as we have seen, at his peak at Camp David. He was tenacious, well-informed, and flexible. He also encouraged and listened to other points of view before making decisions.[2] "The presidential aides," as Israeli Foreign Minister Moshe Dayan later noted, "showed both respect and genuine affection for Carter. And his own attitude toward them—at times to members of our own delegation—was one of companionship. Neither in word nor behavior was he ever pretentious or supercilious."[3]

In Anwar el-Sadat, Carter had a genuine partner in peace. The Egyptian president was intuitive, imaginative, and committed to the big picture rather than the grinding details. Carter noted Sadat's flexibility on several occasions, telling his advisors that Sadat was always willing to accommodate him when called upon;[4] he also felt at ease with him. Sadat, in turn, was "mesmerized" by President Carter and counted on the president's personal involvement in the future to make agreements work.[5]

Menachim Begin created more problems for Carter. The Central Intelligence Agency (CIA) profile of Israeli Prime Minister Begin enabled Carter to understand some of his sensitivities in terms of his difficult history.[6] Still, Begin often tried Carter's patience. Shortly after the conference opened, Carter saw Begin as unimaginative and too preoccupied with legalisms and the exact meaning of words.[7] Indeed, on the night of their first meeting, Carter told his wife, Rosalynn, "I don't believe he has any intention of going through with a peace treaty."[8] On Sunday, September 10, Carter told Israeli Foreign Minister Dayan that he considered the prime minister to be "unreasonable and an obstacle to peace."[9] The next day, when Begin refused to accept language in the U.S. proposal that had been accepted by Israel in United Nations Resolution 242, the president exploded: "If you won't accept past agreements, then we're wasting our time here....It's time to go home. It was a mistake to have called you here in the first place."[10]

Members of the Israeli delegation came to the rescue. Moshe Dayan, Ezer Weizman, Aharon Barak, and General Avraham Tamir were much more effective in changing Begin's mind than Carter could be.[11] Dayan, according to Saunders, was the most active of the delegation at Camp David, talking to people and passing notes around the table. Barak, Israel's attorney general, was also very helpful, explaining in legal terms how an agreement could be reached. This was in contrast with Weizman, who would lean back, cross his hands, and look at the ceiling whenever a difficult point was reached.[12]

FIGURE 10.   Menachim Begin (left), Jimmy Carter (middle), and Anwar Sadat (right) at Camp David. Photograph courtesy of the Jimmy Carter Library.

FIGURE 11.   Anwar Sadat, Jimmy Carter, and Menachim Begin outside at Camp David. Photograph courtesy of the Jimmy Carter Library.

These men even gave strategic advice to the Americans. The decision on September 7 to suspend direct talks between Begin and Sadat was prompted by the suggestions of one Israeli that the tripartite talks were only making Begin more rigid. It would be better, he suggested, for the Americans to pay more attention to Dayan and Weizman.[13] The U.S. decision to put off the issue of Israeli settlements in the Sinai Peninsula until the end of the meetings was a response to a warning from Dayan and Weizman. Begin was rigid on the matter and believed it should be postponed until the other issues could be resolved.[14]

General Tamir's decision on September 12 to circumvent Begin and call General Ariel Sharon opened up the possibility that Sharon and other right-wing members of Begin's cabinet might accept a possible compromise on the Sinai settlements.[15] In securing from U.S. Defense Secretary Harold Brown the pledge that the United States would help rebuild the Israeli airfields to be dismantled in the Sinai, Weizman contributed to the resolution of another sticking point that could have ruined the talks. And Dayan's suggestion that the whole Sinai issue could be referred to a vote in the Knesset gave Begin a way to save face that several members of his delegation had come to see as a requisite for a deal.

As for the Americans, Carter was aided by a secretary of state who performed with skill and authority. Cyrus Vance undertook some concurrent talks on his own. Thus, while the president concentrated on the return of the Sinai and the status of Israel settlements, Vance spent most of his time dealing with the Palestinian part of the framework.[16] Defense Secretary Brown assisted with technical military matters, dealing with issues relating to the airfields in the Sinai.

National Security Advisor Zbigniew Brzezinski, as his Middle East advisor William Quandt has noted, was fairly active, "pushing Carter to bring the whole thing to a conclusion, and stiffening his spine to deal firmly with Begin." Widely viewed as the force behind the administration's tough policies relating to Israel, Brzezinski was ideal for confrontations with them.[17] At Camp David, his competitive streak, however, surfaced primarily in his games of chess with members of the Israeli delegation. Challenging Weizman to a game, Brzezinski tore him "to pieces." Later, he got in a tougher game with Begin. According to Brzezinski, Begin won the first game, Brzezinski the second. When Begin's military aide reported back proudly that the two men were in a game and that Begin was leading Brzezinski two to one, Hamilton Jordan pleaded with Brzezinski, "Do me a favor and make sure Begin wins…otherwise nobody will be able to get a word out of Zbig." Later, when the other Israelis informed Jordan that Begin had won the "tournament," he was relieved. Perhaps Jordan had been concerned that a "loss" would have intensified Begin's rigidity. He congratulated the prime minister.[18]

Members of the U.S. expert team provided background information on the Egyptian and Israeli delegations to Carter and Vance throughout the conference and turned broad agreements on political principles into concrete draft proposals. Often they worked late into the night. Saunders provided a draft for the U.S. proposal that Carter offered to the Israeli delegation on Sunday, September 10. Subsequently, the expert team worked on twenty-two other draft proposals, incorporating into each the changes that the politicos thought should be made to reflect Israeli and Egyptian concerns. The decision on Tuesday, September 12, to set a three-month goal for the negotiation of a peace treaty was recommended by Saunders to Carter. On Friday, Quandt prepared the draft of a speech Carter would give should the conference fail. It would spell out the progress made at Camp David, announce the concessions that Sadat had been prepared to make, and note the intransigence of Begin on the settlement in the Sinai as well as his refusal to acknowledge some "withdrawal" provisions of UN Resolution 242 as a guide in the negotiations on the status of the West Bank and the Gaza Strip.[19]

Press Secretary Jody Powell's role was to feed the media in nearby Thurmont, Maryland—informing them, for example, that Begin and Brzezinski played chess on a given night, or that on a stroll through the camp President Sadat ran into Mrs. Begin and Mrs. Carter touring the premises in a golf cart. With "real" news embargoed, Powell tried to keep them happy with these and other tidbits. Most important, he kept details of the bad blood between Sadat and Begin out of the press. When it appeared that last Sunday morning at the camp that the conference would succeed, Powell advised *Time* and *Newsweek* to hold off on their reports so that they could carry the complete story. Hodding Carter, the State Department spokesman, was brought to Camp David to assist in planning for the signing ceremony in Washington that night. Later that day, when it appeared the conference might fail, Powell met with the president to plan his report to the nation on the summit, including the explanation of its failure.[20]

Everyone on the American team was unified around a common goal. Occasionally Hermann Eilts and Samuel Lewis, the U.S. ambassadors to Egypt and Israel, respectively, saw things differently on matters in the Middle East.[21] Saunders, for example, felt that Lewis was so inundated with the Israeli view that sometimes it was difficult to make him see things from an American point of view. He and Saunders had sharp intellectual arguments, but this did not cause a rift between them. But the differences that appeared between the State Department and the National Security Council on matters such as relations to Soviet Union and others, were completely absent at Camp David.[22] Carter would later note that he could not "recall a single unpleasant difference among us."[23] For Saunders, the talks at Camp David were the best experience he had in interactions between professionals and the president. The reasons for this, he suggested, were because relations in the Middle East were not as bureaucratically complex as U.S.-Soviet relations.[24]

Other Supports

At the Camp David meetings Stansfield Turner, the director of the CIA, was a bit of an outsider. This was evident when, delivering a report to Carter in his cabin, Turner was not invited to join in the dinner for which obvious preparations were being made. Brzezinski, who observed the event, saw it as a kind of rebuff.[25] But reports from the CIA were crucial to the success of the conferences. One study provided detail on the relevance of oil production; as a result, the Americans knew more about the terrain and oil reserves of the Sinai than did either the Egyptians or the Israelis.[26] In addition, the psychological profiles of Begin and Sadat, provided by Dr. Jerry Post, enabled the president to deal which each man with some sophistication.[27]

Other members of the president's inner circle bolstered him emotionally during times of stress. First Lady Rosalynn Carter was a sounding board for the president, as he testified, she "was a partner in my thinking throughout the Camp David negotiations, and I presumed that Begin discussed all the issues freely with his wife."[28] Vance and Brzezinski kept up the president's spirits when he was discouraged. Eventually everything would turn out right, they assured him on several occasions. On Friday, the eleventh day, for example, Carter told the two that he thought the meetings would end in a failure and that the American Jewish community and much of the press would view him as the scapegoat. He saw an out when they suggested that he coordinate his initiatives with Sadat, so as to make it clear that the breakdown was the responsibility of the Israelis.[29]

Back in Washington, the vice president and various department heads covered for Carter on the domestic front. Mondale, who commuted between Camp David and Washington, handled routine domestic matters.[30] Cabinet members, who needed to consult, or to have Carter sign an official document, would drop in at Camp David. Attorney General Griffin Bell, Federal Bureau of Investigation Director William Webster, and Secretary of Defense Harold Brown all saw him about such matters. Jordan and Powell, though they were at Camp David, kept Carter posted about congressional and other political matters.[31]

Not all the action was undertaken by government officials. A back channel was facilitated by Leon Charney, an entertainment lawyer in New York, supporter of Israel, and advisor to Senator Vance Hartke (D-IN). From Israeli Defense Minister Weizman, Charney received information on the Israeli position and the political problems Begin faced. From Karl Klahanie, an Austrian Jew, corporate attorney and personal friend of Sadat, Charney was informed of the Egyptian bottom line. Prior to the opening of the Camp David conference, Charney even met with Weizman and Klahanie in Israel, where they simulated the Camp David meetings. During the Camp David talks Charney and Robert Lipshutz, legal counsel to Carter, spoke with Weizman three to four times a day. All this information was channeled through Lipshutz.[32]

The Relevance of U.S. Power

As a major head of state with ties to both the conflicting parties, Carter had advantages that less-well-placed third-party mediators would have lacked. At the opening of the Camp David meetings, he reminded Begin and Sadat that both Israel and Egypt's good relationship with the United States was at stake.[33] Later, on Thursday, September 14, when the talks seemed to reach a stalemate over the Sinai settlements, Carter told members of the Israeli delegation that failure of the conference would be "catastrophic" for relations between Israel and the United States.[34] The next day (September 15), when Sadat threatened to leave, he was reminded that his whole relationship with Carter personally, as well as the United States, was at stake. That same day, Carter and his aides began writing their analysis of the conference in ways that would place major responsibility on the Israeli delegation should it ultimately fail.[35]

Certainly the threat of a rupture did have an impact on Sadat. Like Carter, he had risked a great deal on the peace process; as Weizman pointed out, a failure would be a personal setback for the Egyptian president. Israel would be left holding the Sinai, but he, Sadat, would have to "put on sackcloth and ashes if he wanted to be taken in again by the Arab world." Weizman thought that in the event of failure Sadat would have preferred to resign.[36]

Whether or not U.S. threats were persuasive to Begin has been the subject of debate.[37] But it is clear that some members of the Israeli delegation were concerned about the broader political costs of failure in terms of Israel's relations with the United States. As Weizman remarked during a conversation with Sadat on the second day of the conference, if no concrete achievement were made at Camp David, the situation would be "very grave." Israel could not survive without American support, and when the issue of Israeli settlements became a major obstacle to agreement Weizman concluded that Israel could not forfeit peace in favor of the settlements.[38]

The resource base also provided Carter with the opportunity to provide the "sweeteners" without which a final deal would have failed. The Israelis could not have been moved to give up their air bases and oil wells in the Sinai had the United States not offered to compensate them for the losses they would suffer as a result of these withdrawals and relocations. Even Sadat, though he would gain the Sinai, could not give up on a comprehensive deal without some indication that the United States valued the political risks this concession cost him at home.

Carter, in short, could not have accomplished what he did at Camp David without the significant contributions of others. He, himself, provided the energy and the tenacity to keep things going. Sadat showed considerable courage in seeking an arrangement that benefited Egypt, but which most of the Arab world and entire delegation opposed. Dayan, Weizman, Barak, and other members of the Israeli delegation tamed a somewhat truculent Begin; they gave the Americans advice on how to deal with their own prime minister, and on one occasion they did an end-run around him. An unusually unified and dedicated American team aided Carter. Vance, and occasionally Brown, Brzezinski, or Mondale, politically engaged in the negotiations with Carter. Saunders, Quandt, and other experts provided technical advice and drafted and redrafted proposals on an hourly basis to keep up with the shifting currents in the discussion. The isolation and informal nature of the Camp David setting promoted the whole process. The Americans could choose the level at which they would communicate with the other two national groupings and deal with those most inclined toward some sort of accommodation. The extent of the United States' commitment as a nation put values at stake that might not otherwise have been present. The threat of failure hung over all the participants and provided additional incentives, which Carter would use strategically, to bring Israel and Egypt to agreeable terms.

The Rocky Road Ahead

Still, the celebrations at the close of the Camp David negotiations were premature. The road to peace was strewn with obstructions that could have aborted the actual process envisaged at the close of the Camp David talks. The two governments, it is true, quickly accepted the frameworks for peace. Enthusiastic crowds welcomed Sadat upon his return to Egypt. In Israel, the agreements won wide public approval, though Begin would have difficulties from the right wing in his own political coalition. On September 24, the Israeli Cabinet approved the Camp David Accords, including the commitment to remove settlers from the Sinai. Four days later, the Knesset approved the accords by a large majority. Though he may not have forced a strict party-line vote, Begin threatened to resign and form a new government if the agreements did not receive a majority support. A negative vote by a cabinet minister, he also stated, would be interpreted as that minister's resignation from his post.

But the agreement, viewed as a prelude to a separate peace with Egypt, was far from popular in the Arab world. Sadat's own foreign minister had even resigned before the signing of the agreement in the White House. In addition to this resignation, the Egyptian ambassador to the United States, Ashraf Ghorbal, left his post. King Hussein of Jordan, who was named as a potential participant in the negotiations for the comprehensive settlement, disassociated himself from the agreements and warned of serious consequences if Sadat signed a separate peace treaty with Israel. The more radical Arab states—Syria, Libya, and Algeria—denounced the agreements and severed all ties with Egypt. In addition, the Soviet Union and Palestine Liberation Organization leader Yasser Arafat issued a joint statement on November 1 attacking the accords.

Sadat had done little to salvage his relations with these states. On his return from Camp David, for example, he had the opportunity to meet with King Hussein in Morocco but did not do it. It was Vance who had to travel to the Middle East shortly after the talks to explain the essence of the accords to Hussein and other Arab leaders.[39]

As for Israel, Begin quickly began backpedaling on issues related to the comprehensive agreement to deal with the broader Palestinian problem. The agreement freezing settlement activity in the West Bank and Gaza began unraveling on Monday, September 18, even before the appearance of Carter before the U.S. Congress. When Harold Saunders called Israel's Simcha Dinitz to inquire about the letter from Begin in reference to the West Bank settlement freeze, he was told Begin was redrafting it. When the letter finally arrived, it did not extend the agreement through the negotiation of the comprehensive agreement as the Americans expected it would. The promise provided for a moratorium for only the three months set aside for finalizing the peace treaty between Egypt and Israel. There was a real misunderstanding about Begin's promise to send a letter with his commitment. Vance said this needed to be cleared up the next day, but "we never did [clear it up]."[40]

It would become evident by late October, before the three-month moratorium was up, that the Begin government had no real commitment to the more general autonomy talks. Begin announced plans for the expansion of West Bank settlements and revealed that he was thinking of moving his office to East Jerusalem.[41] In November 1978, the Israeli cabinet, with Begin's approval, refused to set up any timetable for the Palestinian autonomy talks. Two months later, on January 15, 1979, the Israeli government announced it had plans for three new settlements—two would be on the West bank near Jordan, the other at the southern end of the Gaza Strip.[42]

As Weizman would later note, "No sooner had the treaty been signed than Begin gave up promoting the peace process. Instead of forging ahead, leading Israel into a new era, he withdrew into pipe dreams." Increasingly dissatisfied with Begin's retreat, Weizman finally decided he could no longer serve in the government. On May 28, 1980, he resigned as minister of defense.[43]

Even the Sinai agreement presented problems. The exact timing of the Israel withdrawal from the Sinai, including the turn over of the oil fields, remained in contention for some time. Israel wanted an immediate recognition from Egypt, while Sadat wanted to delay that recognition until the Israeli withdrawal had been accomplished. Concerned about having to relocate their military airfields in the Sinai and give up oil wells, the Israelis were looking for compensation from the United States, and Carter would at first not agree to the figure they thought necessary. In addition, the Israeli settlers in the Sinai would resist any government efforts at relocation. Some of them would eventually have to be removed by force.[44]

To deal with these problems, Vance, Saunders, and Roy Atherton, special envoy to the Middle East, made several visits to the area.[45] Finally, in early March 1979, Carter decided to go to the Middle East. On March 10, nearly six months after the Camp David meetings, he flew to Israel and in an address to the Knesset chided both countries for not taking a chance for peace. His mission an apparent failure, Carter made a stopover at the Cairo airport on the way home. There Sadat accepted the final Israeli proposal. Carter called Begin to tell him the news. The final proposal provided for an exchange of ambassadors and an oil pipeline to Israel from the Sinai fields. Sadat agreed to tone down the anti-Begin rhetoric in the press, and Begin agreed to allow the Palestinians peaceful political activity, lifting some of the restraints on the inhabitants of the West Bank and Gaza.[46]

En route home on *Air Force One*, an elated president and first lady celebrated their success with a large entourage: Vance and his wife, Brown, Brzezinski, Lipshutz, Jordan, Atherton, Saunders, Rafshoon, and Quandt were on board. Carter walked through the plane, individually thanking people for their help. He singled out Secretary Vance, praising his role in contributing to the agreement.[47]

U.S. sweeteners brought a resolution to one remaining issue. The United States and Israel remained at odds over the amount of aid that the United States was to give Israel for the reconstruction of the Sinai air bases and the loss of Sinai oil fields. In a meeting at Lipshutz's house, a resolute and sometimes angry Weizman made it clear to Charney and Lipshutz that Israel would not settle for less than the $4 billion it needed. Convinced that a tight stance might scuttle all his earlier efforts, Carter finally relented on this final point. A $3 billion aid package would be provided for Israel, an amount to be added to the $1 billion Israel had already been promised. In an ancillary memo, the

United States committed itself to a fifteen-year deal guaranteeing oil supplies to Israel for any losses that it might have as a result of the return of a Sinai oil well to Egypt.[48]

To bring the Egyptians around, Carter also agreed to provide military aid to that country for the first time, promising parity with its assistance to Israel. Egypt would receive $2 billion in military assistance for aircraft, tanks, and antiaircraft weapons. This was in addition to the $750 million in economic assistance already allocated to Egypt.[49]

Finally, on March 26, Carter capped his months of effort with a triumphant signing ceremony. Sixteen hundred invited guests looked on from the White House lawn.[50] Shortly thereafter, Begin was the first Israeli prime minister to travel to Cairo. There he and Sadat agreed to establish a hotline connection, open the Israeli-Egyptian borders, and establish an air link between the two countries. El Arish in Egypt and Beer-Sheva in Israel would be alternate sites for the future Israeli-Egyptian meetings on the autonomy of the West Bank and the Gaza Strip.

At home, the final approval of the Sinai treaty provided only a small bump in Jimmy Carter's approval ratings. As for the Arab nations, a sour note was struck five days after the signing ceremony. On March 31, eighteen Arab League countries and representatives from Saudi Arabia stated that they did not see the agreements as providing a "final acceptable formula" and condemned American policy in the Middle East. In Israel there were those who believed, as Weizman puts it, that the only guarantee of their security was "to hold on to every dune in the Sinai desert" became ever more resistant to new territorial concessions.[51]

For the Palestinians, Chancellor Helmut Schmidt of West Germany suggested in his memoirs that the separate peace between Israel and Egypt left the issue of autonomy unresolved. The problems of the Middle East, he noted, were too complex for isolated solutions. Nor did the Americans, in his opinion, take measures to minimize the risk to Sadat and Egypt in terms of Egypt's isolation within the Arab League.[52] Giulio Andreotti, president of the Italian Council of Ministers, later noted the deep hostility toward Sadat for what the Arab governments called a betrayal on the part of Egypt when Sadat regained the Sinai and "weakened the common front."[53] Not anticipated by the United States at the time, the peace agreement with Egypt also enabled Israel to later undertake such risky operations as the intervention in Lebanon in 1982. Without fear of an Egyptian military response at their rear, the Israeli armed forces could move all the way up to Beirut.[54]

Yet what were the alternatives? The difficulties the parties had in coming to terms on the issues where they had the most complimentary interests—the return of the Sinai to Egypt and the establishment of diplomatic relations between the two countries—suggests that comprehensive agreements would have been impossible in any foreseeable future. The deteriorating climate in the Middle East in the summer of 1978 suggested that some action had to be taken. Relationships between Egypt and Israel were cycling downward in a series of hostile exchanges. At the bottom of the slope, renewed conflict in the Middle East and Soviet intervention was a distinct possibility. The success at Camp David halted that process and kept open the possibility that in the long run friendly relations would allow a more comprehensive agreement on the Middle East.

Still, in the woods of Maryland in the summer of 1978, Jimmy Carter had the courage and intelligence to move ahead on a better path.

As Ezer Weizman noted, the Camp David agreements even served long-term Israeli interests. "As far as I know, no American President has ever helped Israel as much as Jimmy Carter."[55]

Part 4

CRISES AND CONFRONTATIONS

CONFRONTING A REGIME CHANGE

While Jimmy Carter was at Camp David, events in Iran began to spin out of control. On September 8, 1978, Iranian troops fired on a crowd of demonstrators in Jaleh Square, killing between seven hundred and two thousand people.[1] The next day, Tehran oil refinery workers issued a call to strike to express solidarity with those massacred on the previous day and protest against the shah's imposing of martial law. The unrest spread like wildfire to Shiraz, Tabriz, Abdan, and Isfahan. In Teheran, the oil refinery workers demonstrated through October, a move that eventually resulted in an oil strike that reduced production from 5.8 to 1.9 million barrels a week. Another confrontation in early November led to groups of young men roaming around Tehran, tipping over automobiles, and setting fire to banks, movie theaters, and liquor stores. Iranian men climbed rooftops, shouting into the night air "Allah is great." Security forces fired warning shots that scattered the mobs temporarily but were unable to disperse them.[2]

The Ayatollah Ruhollah Khomeini, exiled in Paris since early October, remained the focal point of the opposition. In the last week of November he called upon his followers to take action during Muharram, the first month of the Islamic calendar and a time for Shiites to mourn the memory of the martyrdom of Husayn, the grandson of the Prophet Muhammad. "[This is] the month that blood will triumph over sword…the month the oppressors will be judged and the Satanic government abolished.…The Imam of the Muslims has taught us to overthrow tyrants. You should unite, arise and sacrifice your blood." On December 1, the eve of the holiday, thousands of Iranians, encouraged no doubt by Khomeini's words, took to the streets. The crowds on the street multiplied, and on December 10 approximately one million people gathered around the Shayad Monument, chanting "Death to the America cur."[3]

The policies of Shah Mohamed Reza Pahlavi had created enemies for him on both the religious and the democratic secular fronts. The "White Revolution" of the 1960s, a program of land reform and social and economic modernization, alienated the traditional clergy.[4] When he reduced the parliamentary process to a one-party system and unleashed the SAVAK, his secret police, on his opponents, the shah lost the support of secular democrats.[5] By the spring of 1978, crackdowns on both groups created even more opposition. For the Shias there were demonstrations mourning the victims at forty-day intervals, as their religion prescribed. This led to a self-perpetuating cycle of unrest.[6]

As the disorder spread in the fall of 1978, the shah responded with a series of half-hearted measures. First, he promised some minor reforms, which his opponents saw as a sign of weakness.[7] When these actions failed to have the desired result, he placed his chief of staff, General Gholomreza Azhari, as head of a new military government. But Azhari was a mild man with no inclinations to engage in the kind of crackdown that might have cowed the opponents of the regime.[8] When Azhari suffered a mild heart attack during the third week of December 1978, the shah's days were numbered.[9] Finally, on January 2, 1979, Shah Pahlavi told U.S. Ambassador William Sullivan that he had decided to appoint Shahpur Bakhtiar, a former leader of a reform group, the Democratic National Front, as prime minister. But the shah kept major powers for himself, undercutting the significance of the proposed reform. He even expressed his skepticism that Bakhtiar would be able to win the popular support of the Iranians.[10]

U.S. Responses

U.S. fortunes had been deeply tied to Shah Mohamed Reza Pahlavi for over two decades. He owed his throne to the United States. In the summer of 1953, the power struggle between the shah and Premier Mohammed Mossadegh (who backed a program for nationalizing oil production) was resolved by the United States in a relatively bloodless coup. General Fazlollah Zahedi was proclaimed as prime minister, and the shah, who had fled the country, returned.[11] At the time, Pahlavi was only thirty-three years old. He was handsome, fluent in English and French, an expert skier, and a skilled pilot. He had been educated in the best Swiss preparatory school, Le Institut le Rosey, and was dedicated to the Westernization of his country.[12]

The shah was also someone the Americans liked and could work with. They depended on Iran for keeping oil prices down and welcomed the listening posts Iran provided them on the southern border of the USSR. Carter, in his own words, "Continued, as other Presidents had before me, to consider the Shah a strong ally."[13] In line with these views, Carter, during the first two years of his administration, fought a bitter battle with Congress to sell the shah seven airborne warning and control system airplanes.[14] Additionally, he approved nearly all the shah's requests for advanced aircraft, tanks, and other military equipment and he agreed to sell Iran several nuclear power plants.[15]

Still, Carter was preoccupied in the fall of 1978 with following through on the Camp David talks, the China breakthrough, and the Strategic Arms Limitation Treaty talks; he paid little attention at first to the events that would eventually topple the shah's regime.

Moreover, he had received no advance warnings in the spring and summer of 1978 of the vulnerability of the shah's regime. In August, the Central Intelligence Agency (CIA) reported to Carter that "Iran is not in a revolutionary or even a pre-revolutionary situation."[16] The Defense Intelligence Agency analyses predicted that the shah's rule was stable for at least another decade.[17] Even National Security Advisor Zbigniew Brzezinski saw the shah's opposition as consisting of communists on the left and a few reactionary religious leaders on the right. In this perspective Brzezinski's deputy David Aaron, "a humorless, steely-eyed bureaucrat who had become an instant expert on the Middle East," reinforced him.[18]

FIGURE 12.   Jimmy Carter (left) and the Shah of Iran (right) flanking an unidentified man. Photograph courtesy of the Jimmy Carter Library.

Given this background, it is not surprising that Carter's response to the massacre at Jaleh Square and the continuing turmoil in September and October was to reassure the shah, both privately and publicly, that he had the United States' full backing. Neither Carter nor his closest advisors were ready to seriously confront the fragility of the shah's regime.

There were harbingers of difficulties ahead, but these did not create any mobilization of the creative forces in the White House. In late October one comprehensive Department of State memo delineating the grim alternatives in Iran was sidelined. A copy of the report was never brought to the attention of the president nor discussed at a National Security Council (NSC) meeting.[19]

In Tehran, Ambassador Sullivan was aware of the problems the shah faced. Finally in a cable to Washington on November 2, he forced a top-level meeting on the matter. The situation in Iran was deteriorating, he wrote, and the shah might abdicate or declare a military government. Sullivan requested a response within forty-eight hours.[20] At a Special Coordinating Committee meeting that evening, Brzezinski proposed sending a reply to Sullivan stating that the United States supported the shah "without reservation" and that the shah needed to take "decisive action to restore order and his own authority" in order to resolve the situation.

The president did not attend this meeting,[21] but he did authorize a message to be sent the next morning, stating, "Whatever action he [the shah] took, including setting up a military government, [we] would support him." Carter wrote in his diary, "We did not want the Shah to abdicate." But Carter gave him no specific directions. "The Shah," he later wrote, "still had a mind of his own, and had no desire for anyone in our country to give him directives. He asked for advice on occasion—from me and other foreign leaders. Sometimes he took it, and sometimes he did not."[22]

That same day Brzezinski downplayed the urgency apparent in the Sullivan cable. In his Weekly Report to the president he wrote,

> There is dissatisfaction with the Shah's tight control of the political process, but this does not at present threaten the government. Perhaps most important, the military, far from being a hotbed of conspiracies, supports the monarchy. Those who are in opposition, both the violent and the nonviolent, do not have the ability to be more than troublesome in any transition to a new regime.[23]

Unhappy with Washington's response, Ambassador Sullivan sent Washington a second cable on November 9, titled "Thinking the Unthinkable." The United States, Sullivan wrote, had to "consider alternatives should the military government fail to establish order and the Shah fall." He reminded U.S. officials that Khomeini and his supporters were "anti-Communist and anti-Soviet," that the younger officers were generally pro-Western, that "the Iranian economic ties with the West could continue, and that the Iranian military ought to be able to preserve the nation's integrity." But, he concluded, "A single misstep could produce unforeseeable consequences." Though NSC staff members tried to stop the telegram from getting to the White House, it was sent at a level whereby it automatically reached the president.[24]

The telegram infuriated Brzezinski. If Bill Sullivan felt the situation was so bad, he queried, why had he not said so before? Carter's response was to confront the CIA in a letter that he also sent to Vance and Brzezinski: Why had he not been better informed? But the ambassador received no new instructions.[25]

Displeased at the news he was receiving from Sullivan, Brzezinski in mid-November sent his own emissary to Tehran, providing him with a direct line to the shah. Sullivan granted the emissary, an unnamed businessman, full access to the embassy. But he later questioned Brzezinski about the propriety of placing a businessman in such a role. The tart response was that Washington could do as it pleased, and it was none of his business. At that point, as Sullivan saw it, he was clearly put on notice that his "views were no longer held in much regard."[26]

Later that month Carter called in former Under Secretary of State George Ball as a special consultant to take a fresh look at the situation. By this time a veritable policy chasm had opened up between Vance, Deputy Secretary of State Warren Christopher, Assistant Secretary of State for Near East and South Asia Affairs Harold Saunders, and Vice President Walter Mondale on one side and Brzezinski, with an occasional ally from the Department of Defense or the Department of Energy, on the other. Vance and his allies wanted the shah to introduce more democratic reforms and expand his political base. But Brzezinski had come to the conclusion that the shah should install a military government and be willing to use force, if necessary, to put down the resistance. And if the shah could not do that, the United States "had no choice but…to make the decision for him."[27]

Ball was horrified by what he saw as Brzezinski's bureaucratic imperialism. As he told Vance, Brzezinski was dealing directly with Tehran through Ambassador Zahedi, who had returned to Tehran without informing anyone at the State Department. In a meeting over the matter, Carter asked that he receive copies of all communications between the White House and Iran. With that, one back channel was ended.[28] As Ball later noted, Brzezinski "was operating in a free-wheeling manner, calling foreign ambassadors, telephoning or sending telegrams to foreign dignitaries outside State Department channels, and even hiring a press adviser so he could compete with the Secretary of State as enunciator of United States policy."[29]

To Brzezinski's dismay, Ball, in an eighteen-page report on December 13, recommended that the United States attempt to convince the shah to publicly announce his decision to hand over power to a council of notables and that he retain power only over the military.[30]

Rather than adopting this or any other one course of action on the shah, the president settled for a query. A cable was sent to Sullivan titled "Questions for the Shah."

The only positive impact Ball had on the policy, Ball later stated, was that he preempted Brzezinski's suggestion that he, Brzezinski, go to Iran to bolster the courage of the shah. That suggestion, Ball told the president, "[w]ith all due respect is the worst idea I have ever heard."[31]

Finally, on December 28, 1978, Vance cabled Sullivan and asked him to convey three possibilities to the shah. He should, if possible, establish a civilian government. If that were not possible, he should be encouraged to form a military government. But if he considered the costs of that alternative too great, he could opt for a regency council.[32]

The shah made no clear choice for any one of these options. He waffled and wavered between introducing basic constitutional reforms and adopting a hard-line military response, and it finally became obvious to Carter that only with his departure could order be restored.[33] Only then might Prime Minister Bakhtiar have a freer hand in constructing a credible government.

Even after the shah agreed to leave Iran, he hesitated to do so. First there was the problem of finding a spot for him in the United States. "Yes, but where will I go?" the shah implored. Sullivan called Washington and that issue was resolved via a decision that he could stay at former ambassador Walter Annenberg's Palm Springs, California, estate.[34] Then the shah thought he should wait until he could leave with dignity.[35]

Finally, as the political situation deteriorated further, the shah and his family were prodded into an immediate exile. On January 16, the shah boarded a Boeing 707 and departed for Cairo before continuing his purported "vacation" in Palm Springs.[36]

In the meantime General Robert Huyser had arrived in Tehran. Meeting with senior Iranian military officers, he assured them of the continuity of American logistical support and urged them "to maintain the integrity of their forces" on the difficult road ahead. Huyser's goal was to assure that the new Bakhtiar government, as long as it had some credibility, would have the support of the Iranian military organization. Should Bakhtiar falter, the capability of the Iranian military acting on its own should be assessed. Ambassador Sullivan's relations with Huyser were pleasant and professionally correct, but it was clear that the president was relying on the special emissary more than on his ambassador.[37]

Indeed, Sullivan's suggestion that the United States make some contact with the Khomeini forces in Paris was ignored at first. When Carter finally decided to contact Khomeini through the French rather than directly, a frustrated Sullivan sent another cable to Washington. "Our national interests," he wrote, "demand that we attempt to structure a modus vivendi between the military and religious [leaders], in order to preempt the Tudeh."[38] Carter saw Sullivan's language as insolent, and told Vance to call the ambassador back from his post in Tehran. When Vance pointed out that it would be a mistake to remove him during a crisis, Carter backed off. But from then on he almost completely ignored Sullivan, seeing Huyser as a man of more balanced views.[39]

Twelve days later the White House made one last move to counter a Khomeini takeover. On January 24, a memo was sent to Bakhtiar supporting his plans to arrest the ayatollah when his plane landed in Iran. The measure was supported by U.S. Defense Secretary Harold Brown and Brzezinski, but opposed by Vance, who saw it as a very risky option that would have unforeseeable consequences.[40] But the plan was stillborn. The airports in Tehran were closed for a short period, and Khomeini did not return at this designated time.

Finally, on February 1, after fourteen years of exile in Turkey, Iraq, and then France, Khomeini put his feet down again on Iranian soil. He was greeted by hundreds of thousands of supporters in Tehran.[41] Four days later he appointed Mehdi Bazargan as provisional prime minister, setting up a parallel government to Bakhtiar's. Several units stationed in air bases swore an oath of allegiance to Khomeini and rose up against their commanders.

On Sunday night, February 11, Ambassador Sullivan informed Christopher that the military was making its accommodation with the new Bazargan government. The U.S. defense attaché in Iran concluded his report on the events of the day, noting, "Army surrenders; Khomeini wins. Destroying all classified."[42]

Even at this late date Brzezinski was reluctant to let go of his hopes for a military coup. As the ambassador frantically sought assistance from revolutionary leaders to lift the siege of the Military Assistance Advisory Group headquarters where the top U.S. military and the Iranian general staff were hunkered down in an underground bunker, Sullivan received a call from Under Secretary of State David Newsom. Was a military coup still possible?

When this was followed up with a second call, Sullivan responded with what he later admitted was a "scurrilous suggestion." When told that his response was not very helpful, he asked whether or not he should "translate it into Polish" and then hung up the receiver.[43]

Sullivan also had to deal with his own crisis on the ground. When Iranian militants stormed the U.S. embassy on February 14, he ordered the marine guards stationed outside to not fire back, while behind a locked door embassy officials destroyed sensitive documents. Shortly thereafter, Ibrahim Yazdi, the foreign minister of Khomeini's provisional government, restored the embassy to American control. "The Provisional Government of Iran," he said, "did not want this to happen. We will try to insure your safety."[44]

Throughout these final weeks, no one in Washington was aware that the shah was suffering from lymphatic cancer. Most U.S. observers noted behavior that indicated he was going through a depressive crisis. But only his wife Farah and his French doctors knew that he was suffering from the cancer that would kill him in eighteen months.[45] Indeed, as late as November 22, 1978, the CIA reported that the shah's mood "is not inappropriate to his situation, that he is not paralyzed by indecision…and that for the most part he is in accurate touch with reality."[46]

There was also little understanding of the nature of the shah's adversaries. The Iranian ambassador to the United States, Ardeshir Zahedi, told Deputy Secretary of State Christopher on September 13, 1978, that "communists" were causing all the trouble in Iran.[47] That fall, Brzezinski sent the president and other key officials copies of Robert Moss's article "Who's Meddling in Iran," which argued that the USSR was behind the opposition to the shah, and cited it in policy meetings for weeks. A British journalist and anti-communist polemicist, Moss was not an Iranian specialist and had no hard evidence to support his claims.[48]

As late as January 12, Brzezinski warned Carter in his Weekly Report that it was the Left that had grown in influence and that we "might soon have to throw our weight behind one of the sides the Shah or the military" to protect U.S. interests. The president, obviously irritated, wrote in the margins, "Zbig—After we make joint decisions, deploring them for the record doesn't help me."[49] Even Sullivan, in his January 12 recommendations to make contact with Khomeini, fell back on the communist threat. The United States, as he saw it, should come to an understanding with military and religious leaders in Iran to check the communist party.[50]

No doubt influenced by these warnings about the communist threat in Iran, Carter told his advisors at a breakfast meeting on January 19, "[We] should tell Bakhtiar that we will not *accommodate any more to the left* [emphasis added]; we support the military in their position and in their effort to maintain stability, but we are not in favor of bringing Khomeini and his people into the government."[51] In seeing any move toward Khomeini and his coterie as a leftward thrust, Carter had misinterpreted the views expressed in Sullivan's November 9 telegram. Somehow the president had come to think that the reformers who had assembled around Khomeini were the problem, not the religious fanatics whose views he espoused.

Ultimately, the United States had to come to terms with reality. On February 16, 1979, the United States announced it would maintain normal relations with the new regime. Sullivan met with Bazargan to assure him that the United States accepted Khomeini's revolution and did not plan to intervene in the domestic affairs of the country. On February 21, the United States recognized the new government.[52]

Consequences

The fall of the shah's government created major concerns for all U.S. decision makers about a possible increase of Soviet influence in the area. Carter was aware that Iran had long been a region in which the Russians competed with the British, and later with the United States, for influence. In November 1979, he and Soviet president Leonid Brezhnev had warned each other about interference in the internal affairs of Iran. Carter had told the Soviet leader "that we would not intervene, but that we would honor our commitments to Iran and that we fully supported the Shah."[53]

Brzezinski thought that the fall of the shah could undermine the U.S. position in the Persian Gulf and its standing throughout the Arab world, as well as strengthening Soviet influence in Southeast Asia.[54] The resulting power vacuum, he later suggested, was responsible for the Soviet intervention in Afghanistan.[55] Even Vance, Huyser, and others were concerned that a civil war in Iran would provide an opportunity for the Soviets to fish in troubled waters.[56]

The immediate result of the Iranian revolution was not a Soviet intervention in that country but the loss of U.S. intelligence facilities in Northern Iran, the collapse of Iranian oil production, and the tripling of oil prices between 1979 and 1981.[57] The midterm result was that Brzezinski was able to sell Carter on his Rapid Deployment Force and the extensions of new military guarantees to the others in the Middle East.

But practically no one—hard liners or coalition pushers alike—anticipated the long-term consequences of the new forces that would be unleashed on the world. Vance understood Russian fears of Islamic fundamentalism on their southern borders in the Soviet Central Asian republics. But rather than a fundamentalist takeover, he envisaged in his memoir an improvement in U.S.-Iranian relations should a durable noncommunist regime emerge.[58]

Brzezinski assured the president that Khomeini's victory was not the "wave of the future." As he wrote the president on February 2, 1979,

> Ayatollah Khomeini's remarkable political victory over the Shah has sparked a renewed interest in the political strength of Islamic fundamentalism. Several studies are nearing completion within the government, and my staff has been consulting with leading academics and reviewing scholarly writings.
>
> One conclusion stands out: we should be careful not to over-generalize from the Iranian case. Islamic revivalist movements are not sweeping the Middle East and are not likely to be the wave of the future.[59]

Later historians, Brzezinski suggested, would evaluate whether or not the United States could have done anything differently that would have saved either the shah or a moderate successor regime.

What we do know at this point is that Carter was not aided in this whole process by a first-rate intelligence operation. Nor was he well served by an orderly and careful policy process. The president was confronted late in the game with the views of men passionately attached to diametrically opposed alternatives. But none of them provided him with detailed studies of the potential consequences of each possible move. The result was that Washington did not speak with one voice. A confusing array of messengers sent complex signals to an uncertain shah.

Still, by late 1979 there was a real limit to the U.S. ability to influence events in Iran. The shah himself was not only profoundly ill but also internally conflicted. Earlier, during the "White Revolution," he had shown himself to be a determined leader. Yet by 1978 he was torn—he did not want to give up any of his power, but as an Iranian patriot he did not want to slaughter his own people.[60] Moreover, his feeling that God favored him was crushed when he discovered he had a deadly lymphoma and the mounting opposition indicated that many of his countrymen did not seem to love him. His dependence on the United States, as his biographer Marvin Zonis has argued, only deepened as a result of his new insecurities.[61]

Vance and the others who favored democratic outreach could provide no clear indications about where and with whom the shah could find the kind of support they recommended. Indeed, by late 1978 there was no such group available. The moderates of the Iranian constitutional reform movement (which dated back to the early 1900s) failed to understand the revolutionary nature of Khomeini's movements and were unable to establish a political front that could counter him in a post-takeover showdown. By late 1978 many of them were already moving toward Khomeini, seeking to influence the government he would establish.[62]

Brzezinski's commitment to a hard-line military response was made without any serious evidence that the military men at the top could really lead. The shah had chosen all these individuals, and most were loyal to him. But they had never worked together, and it was not clear that anyone had the ability to take over the government after a military coup.[63] Brzezinski did not even have a leader in mind for the potential coup he favored. As Carter told the national security advisor on January 3, 1979, the United States should refrain from encouraging the military to stage a coup "not only because of the [historical] record but also because there is no military leader we could identify who would lead such a coup." Brzezinski simply responded that if the United States sent a clear message that it backed a coup, "A leader [would] emerge." The Huyser mission, he hoped, would be "interpreted by the Iranian military as an encouragement to take firm action when the moment of truth arrives."[64]

Sullivan's attempt to make some sort of a deal between the secular moderates and Khomeini was as futile as the other suggested alternatives. What no one in Washington seemed to realize was that Khomeini's goal was a fully theocratic state in which the mullahs would have all the final power. He had spelled out his views in his lectures at Najaf,[65] but few in the administration had read those lectures. Even Iraqi intellectuals who were acquainted with his ideas were concerned that it would be impossible for untutored men such as the clerics to establish and rule a regime to their own liking.[66] No one predicted the chaotic situation that would follow Khomeini's return to Iran. His deft and ruthless political tactics would enable him to move toward a kind of absolute rule that would make further opposition to him nearly impossible.

SCRAMBLING FOR OPTIONS

On October 20, 1979, President Jimmy Carter agreed to admit Shah Mohammad Reza Pahlavi into the United States for medical treatment in New York City. Two weeks later, on a rainy morning, several hundred militant Iranian students stormed the American embassy in Tehran. The women among them cut through the gates in front of the compound, pulling out bolt cutters hidden beneath their chadors.

Because it was a Sunday, few of the thirteen Marines charged with guarding the embassy were on duty, and none were stationed at the front gate.[1] The Iranian police around the embassy simply faded away, and by 4:00 p.m., over sixty American diplomats and aides had been taken hostage. The man who had initiated the take-over, Ibrahim Asgarzadeh, a tall and handsome engineering student at the Aryamehr University of Technology, said his original idea was to seize the U.S. embassy for "forty-eight or perhaps seventy-two hours—unless the provisional government evicted them earlier." The students' goal was to voice their complaints against America.[2]

A day after the takeover, the Ayatollah Ruhollah Khomeini, dressed in a black robe with a "perfectly wound" black turban around his head, symbolizing his descent from Muhammad, made a public statement that changed the nature of the takeover.[3] "Today," he said, "underground plots are being hatched in these embassies, mostly by the great Satan America...they must sit in their places and return the traitor [the shah] soon."[4] With this, the Provisional Revolutionary Government headed by Mehdi Bazargan resigned, yielding all governmental power to Khomeini and the secret Revolutionary Council, a body with a membership unknown to U.S. government officials.[5] Thus began the hostage crisis with which Carter would struggle until he left office almost fourteen months later on January 20, 1981.

In admitting the shah to the United States, Carter was the victim of bad advice and an intelligence failure. The shah had been a man without a country ever since his departure from Iran on January 16, 1979.[6] Beginning in the spring of 1978, former secretary of state Henry Kissinger, David Rockefeller (whose Chase Manhattan Bank represented economic interests tied to the shah's government), and National Security Advisor Zbigniew Brzezinski pressed Carter to admit him.[7] Vice President Walter Mondale joined them on July 27. Finally, at the president's October 19 foreign affairs breakfast, Secretary of State Cyrus Vance, the last holdout of Carter's advisors, came aboard. The shah, he pointed out, was suffering from a potentially fatal lymphoma, and the State Department's medical advisor concluded that he could not be properly treated in Mexico, where he currently resided.[8]

At one point in the discussion Carter raised the question, "What are you guys going to advise me to do if they overrun our embassy and take our people hostage?" When no one responded, Carter continued, "On that day, we will all sit here with long drawn, white faces and realize we've been had."[9] Carter had reason for concern. Ibrahim Yazdi, foreign minister in the Bazargan government, warned American policymakers when he was told that the shah was coming to the United States, "You're opening Pandora's Box with this."[10]

But even given the treatment ambiguities, the medical situation could have been more prudently handled. Once the shah was in the United States, the Carter administration could have assured the Iranians—suspecting as they did that his admission was just an excuse for him to reassemble and attempt a return to power in Iran—that he was indeed a very ill man. But Carter rejected the Bazargan government's request that Iranian doctors be allowed to directly review the medical findings to verify the accuracy of the diagnosis.[11] A second suggestion that the State Department agreed to—that the shah's doctors discuss the case with physicians selected by Iranian officials—fell by the wayside when the U.S. physicians refused to agree on a consultation.[12] Instead, the Iranians had to rely on an uninformative public news conference given by Morton Coleman, the shah's American cancer specialist. Coleman's suggestion that the shah might have to stay in New York for intensive chemotherapy for at least six months, and possibly up to eighteen months, reinforced Iranian fears that the shah had come to the United States not for medical treatment, but to set up counter revolutionary headquarters.[13]

The U.S. embassy in Tehran, too, could have been better protected. But the administration took at face value the assurance of the Bazargan government that, should a takeover occur, they would take care of the matter. That government had bailed out the United States in an embassy takeover the previous February, and it was assumed they would and could do it again.[14] No one in the White House seemed to have entertained the possibility that the Bazargan government itself might fall once this particular Pandora's box had been opened.[15] But in January 1980, Abolhasan Bani-Sadr and Sadegh Ghotbzadeh replaced Bazargan and Yazdi as president and foreign minister, respectively.

A Puzzling Adversary

The Carter administration lacked an understanding of the men with whom they were dealing. Certainly they failed to understand that the dour, mystical, and sometimes ruthless Ayatollah Khomeini knew how to gain and exercise power. His goal, not evident even to all of his followers at the time of his Paris stay in exile, was to establish an Islamic republic in which he retained final authority in both religious and political matters.[16] The moderate politicos who had joined him in an anti-shah operation would last only as long as they served Khomeini's political purposes.

Perhaps the ayatollah's background contributed to his hard edge. Bandits had killed his father, Ayatollah Seyyed Mostaf Musavi, when he was but a few months old, and his mother died when he was only fifteen. Educated in Islamic theory, he had specialized in jurisprudence, philosophy, and ethics.[17]

When he returned to Iran, Khomeini played out a scenario that would enhance his authority. He stationed himself for several months in the ancient religious center of Qom. Ten kings and four hundred Islamic holy men are buried there, and it is the site of the largest theological college in Iran. There his long meditations would be broken to issue political edicts exercising final authority on both religious and political matters.[18] Maintaining a maximally flexible position, he would approve some actions, passing over others that he might favor but for which he might not wish to take responsibility. He could even change his mind when that suited his political goals, keeping those around him perennially suspended in regard to what his ultimate choices might be.

Khomeini also cut down his adversaries. Leaders of the shah's regime were gathered up and killed, most of them without trials. During the first six months after Khomeini's return to Iran over six hundred leading political and military leaders identified in some way with the previous regime had been executed.[19]

The Ayatollah Khomeini also used for some time the group of well-educated men who had played roles in the anti-shah freedom movement: Prime Minister Mehdi Bazargan and Foreign Minister Ibrahim Yazdi of the provisional government were men with relatively broad experiences and vision. Bazargan, an engineer educated in Paris, had served as head of the National Iranian Oil Company that Prime Minister Mohammed Mossadegh had nationalized. The U.S. Central Intelligence Agency described him as a "devout Shi'a Muslim.... [who] is narrow-minded almost to the point of fanaticism regarding Islam and its precepts, [but] is otherwise an intelligent man.... [His] name [is] known and respected in opposition circles."[20] Yazdi had studied in the United States and served as the ayatollah's American contact. To U.S. Embassy diplomats, he "always demonstrated what a good revolutionary he was...he worked...according to diplomatic norms."[21] Both men resigned when they realized their authority was severely limited on political matters by the ayatollah.[22]

Even Bani-Sadr and Ghotbzadeh were in this mold. A former graduate student in economics at the University of Tehran and the author of more than twenty works concerning an Islamic system of government, Bani-Sadr had found Khomeini a place to live in a suburb of Paris and advised him on his public statements. Ghotbzadeh, who had a B.A. in history from the University of British Columbia, had been charged with handling Khomeini's interests in Europe and diplomatic relations with other Arab leaders. According to Iranian specialist Gary Sick, he was "clever and opportunistic, but his greatest strength was that Khomeini believed in him and treated him like a son."[23] Both Bani-Sadr and Ghotbzadeh idolized Khomeini as a religious leader, and in Paris he followed their advice, taming his political messages so they seemed less incendiary.

Yet these two individuals had not read Khomeini well. The ayatollah's speech at the Cemetery of the Martyrs on February 1, 1979, moved an astonished Bani-Sadr to observe, "It was the speech of a politician more than the speech of a religious leader."[24] And he told Khomeini directly that "he was not a political leader.... He was a religious leader. He should not forget what he'd said in Paris." Later, Bani-Sadr remarked that at the time he "wasn't sure if Khomeini had forgotten that he wasn't here to replace the shah."[25] Over time, as journalist Oriana Fallaci has suggested, Bani-Sadr came to fear the man he had once held in such high esteem.[26]

Only gradually did it become apparent to these two men that Khomeini and the conservative clerics on the Revolutionary Council would use their dealings with the external enemy, the "Great Satan," to weaken them in the battle over the nature of the emerging Islamic Republic. Their attempts, however awkward or halfhearted, to deal with Carter, the United States, or even the United Nations on the hostage crisis, would be used against them in the battle for power that followed. Bani-Sadr served only eighteen months as president before the Majlis (Iranian parliament) impeached him on June 21, 1981. Khomeini dismissed him as president and ordered his arrest on grounds of conspiracy and treason. He fled to Paris, where he continues to live today.[27] Ghotbzadeh resigned from his post as foreign minister in August 1980 after the ayatollah refused to comply with his diplomatic approach to ending the hostage situation. As a purported counterrevolutionary, he was arrested in April 1982 and executed on September 15, 1982, by the regime he had served. Sadegh Tabatabai (a relative of Khomeini and former deputy prime minister), who would undertake serious negotiations with the United States in the fall of 1980, was arrested in 1983 for attempting to smuggle opium, but his sentence was dropped. He still lives in Europe and Iran.[28]

Yet before these events, in late November 1979, Carter had to deal with the situation as he found it. Neither he nor his advisors could foresee how Khomeini would evolve in the next few months and they gave him contradictory advice on what to do. For Vance, the hostages were diplomatic colleagues, and he was prepared to accept temporary defeats and setbacks in order to protect their lives. Informed by the Department of State's Bureau of Intelligence and Research, and Iranian Task Force, which bore a major responsibility for the day-to-day management of the crisis, Vance concluded that waiting out the Khomeini government until such a time as it was willing to negotiate seemed to be the best alternative.[29] Brzezinski put national honor above the rescue of the hostages. He pressed for a variety of punitive military actions against Iran, including mining Iranian harbors, bombing the oil fields of Abadan, and a blockade of Iranian ports.[30] The Iranian government would not deal with the United States, he charged, until it was faced with punitive measures. Hostage lives might be lost, but that was the risk he was willing to take to protect national honor, even if he was the only one.[31]

The difference between these two advisors was articulated in meetings with Hamilton Jordan as early as November 9, 1979, when both men dropped by his office. Vance reminded Jordan and Jody Powell that Carter would be judged in the long run by whether or not the Americans were returned safely. But for Brzezinski this was the "first big test" of the Carter presidency—an "opportunity, a chance for the President to show the world that he is capable of handling a crisis with international implications....A chance to show American resolve."[32] As Jordan later noted, "Cy's calm approach sounded good, but Brzezinski's tough approach felt good."[33]

Feeling good, however, might get the hostages killed, and that was the dilemma that Carter faced. And he never chose between these two contradictory goals. What he brought to the situation was a profound sense of emergency and a willingness to employ a variety of probes to see what might work to resolve it.

Scrambling for Options

On November 8, 1979, Carter canceled all of his upcoming campaign trips in order to stay in Washington and take "personal responsibility for resolving the hostage crisis."[34] On Thanksgiving, the president asked Americans to engage in "a special prayer" for the hostages. A few days later, Powell sent a letter to 10,000 editors and news directors across the United States encouraging citizens to ring church bells every day at noon until the hostages were freed.[35] In his dramatic refusal to turn on the lights on the White House Christmas trees until the hostages were returned, a symbolic action that had not even been employed during World War II, Carter suggested that the whole nation had been hurt by this assault on its integrity. In his calls for a moratorium on "criticism" right after the hostages had been taken and in subsequent suggestions that his critics were unpatriotic, he reinforced the view that the United States was in a great battle, where the contribution of every American would somehow make a significant difference in the outcome.[36] Indeed, the only other twentieth-century president who had not campaigned on national security grounds was Franklin Delano Roosevelt in 1944.

Not only was the hostage crisis put on the front burner emotionally, the national security apparatus was also mobilized around the issue. Decision making for the first few months of the negotiations was centralized in the Special Coordinating Committee (SCC) of the National Security Council. It met at least once a day, sometimes seven days a week.[37] Sitting in on meetings were the vice president, the secretaries of state and the treasury, the attorney general, the press secretary, legal counsel, and the chief of staff. After the first few meetings of the SCC, a small group headed by Brzezinski that included Secretary of Defense Harold Brown, General David Jones of the Joint Chiefs of Staff, and Director of Central Intelligence Stansfield Turner met regularly in Brzezinski's office to deal with military matters. Senior departmental heads had to spend at least two hours a day on the subject, thus diverting them from other responsibilities. Congressional demands created other concerns. Vance estimated that he and his deputy, Warren Christopher, spent up to two hours a day with members of the U.S. Congress discussing that issue alone.[38] Assistant Secretary of State for Near East and South Asian Affairs Harold Saunders, who had played a major role in the Camp David and other negotiations, had practically no time for anything but the hostage crisis during its long run.[39]

Media coverage of the event and its aftermath reinforced ideas that this was a major international crisis. Each time the militants wanted to catch U.S. attention, screaming masses shouting vilifications at the "Great Satan" would appear in front of the U.S. embassy in Tehran. And, on cue, television cameras would pick up the scene for Americans, reminding them of how powerless they were to act. ABC's new television news program *America Held Hostage* suggested that the event needed its own daily update. Walter Cronkite's countdown at the end of each of his CBS newscasts reinforced the idea that somehow, by remembering the hostages each day, the American people would speed up their return.

This hyping of the crisis, unfortunately, played right into Khomeini's hands. If the ayatollah and his surrogates could personally thwart the president of the United States and paralyze the U.S. government, all the while he displayed his power on national television night after night, he clearly had something of great value. Why not hold on to this asset while he was consolidating his position in Iran?[40]

Carter's Responses

One of Carter's first moves was to pen a personal letter to the ayatollah on his special stationery suggesting that Khomeini meet with U.S. emissaries. Before receiving any kind of response, former attorney general Ramsey Clark and William Miller, a Farsi-speaking former foreign service officer, were on their way to Istanbul in hopes of meeting with the new leader.[41] Following this endeavor, Kurt Waldheim, secretary general of the United Nations, went to Iran. Finally, in early January 1980, highly secret, back-channel talks were pursued with Christian Bourguet, a left-wing French lawyer, and Hector Villalon, an Argentinean political refugee and businessman.[42] Both men had ties to Ghotbzadeh, previously one of Khomeini's representatives in Paris and now Iran's foreign minister. On January 19, 1979, Jordan and Saunders, traveling under false names, headed to London to meet these men.[43] From January 19 to April 3, in a series of highly secret negotiating sessions held in Washington, London, Paris, and Bern, a scenario was hashed out that would get the hostages released while preserving the image of both the United States and Iran. Pursuant to these discussions, Carter agreed on February 13 to send a UN International Commission to Tehran to hear their complaints about the U.S. role in that country.[44]

These efforts at diplomacy were backed up with sanctions. In November two moves were made that would provide the United States with levers that would be used to help resolve the crisis. The suspension of shipment of spare military parts to Iran for which partial payments had been made was cut off. In addition, Carter terminated all crude oil imports from Iran. The United States also took its case to the International Court of Justice, and two weeks later the court ordered Iran to immediately release all hostages to the United States.[45] By December 4, the UN Security Council had unanimously adopted its fourth appeal to Iran for release of the hostages. At the same time, the Carter Administration announced it would conduct special immigration checks on Iranian students in the United States and begin deportation proceedings against any who were here illegally or who did not report to proper officials as they had been ordered to do.[46]

The president, however, had few real military options. On November 6, the SCC informed Carter that the chances of carrying out a successful rescue operation at that time were remote. Secretary of Defense Brown, General David Jones of the Joint Chiefs of Staff, and Stansfield Turner of the CIA went on to say that each of the military actions being considered would not be successful. Charles Kirbo, the president's personal friend who was sitting in on the discussion, caught the sense of the meeting, later commenting, "Nothing…offered a course to defend U.S. honor that would not make things worse…[in] the long run."[47]

Not content with these earlier responses, Carter, at an SCC meeting at Camp David on November 23, pushed for other military options. Mining Iran's harbors, he suggested would "bring Iran to its knees." He also proposed several escalatory military actions, including the bombing of Iranian oil fields, the seizing of Kharg Island, and the expulsion of Iranian diplomats. The debate was fiery. Carter's advisors unanimously agreed that it was too soon for military action. Vance also convinced Carter not to expel the Iranian diplomats, thinking that all lines for possible diplomatic communication should be kept open.[48]

After the Soviet invasion of Afghanistan in late December, another full-scale policy review led to the conclusion that U.S. intervention could bring the Soviets into Iran, and that would have been worse for the U.S. position than even the Khomeini government.[49]

Though Carter had no responsible military card to play at the time, he did use threats and engage in a show of force. Shortly after Khomeini threatened to put the hostages on trial, Carter sent a message through Swiss diplomatic channels threatening to mine or blockade Iranian harbors should the hostages be mistreated. Publicly, the White House suggested that the United States might resort to the use of force if the remaining hostages were not freed, and Carter ordered the USS *Kitty Hawk* to join the USS *Midway* and four other ships in the Arabian Sea.

The U.S. diplomatic initiatives, it soon became apparent, would have no positive effect. Clark and Miller flew home without meeting a single Iranian official.[50] Secretary General Waldheim met with Ghotbzadeh and spoke to the Revolutionary Council, but Khomeini refused to meet with him and the students denied him access to the hostages.[51] The UN Commission originally suggested by Bourguet and Villalon spent days in Iran without seeing the hostages.[52] At one point in these negotiations, Ghotbzadeh suggested to Jordan that the United States kill the shah.[53] Even political and economic isolation exacted by the sanctions had minimal effect. Khomeini, preoccupied with the consolidation of his power at home, had little concern with the outside world at this point.

What would become apparent over time was that the only officials who wanted to deal—Bani-Sadr and Ghotbzadeh—were working at cross-purposes with Khomeini, the Revolutionary Council, the student militants holding the hostages, and sometimes each other.

In late November 1979, for example, Bani-Sadr had asked UN Secretary General Waldheim to call a special session of the UN Security Council so that he could voice Iran's grievances against the shah and demand that he be extradited. But Ghotbzadeh sabotaged his effort, running the story as U.S. "victory" in the state-run media he controlled. Two hours before Bani-Sadr's plane was scheduled to depart to New York, Khomeini called off the trip, saying the UN session was nothing but an "American trap." The next day, when Bani-Sadr and Ghotbzadeh met with Khomeini and the Revolutionary Council, the "moderates" accused Bani-Sadr of "being soft on the Americans." Shortly thereafter, Bani-Sadr decided he had had enough. On November 27, the Revolutionary Council accepted Bani-Sadr's resignation as foreign minister. Although Bani-Sadr remained in charge of the finance ministry, Ghotbzadeh became the new head of the foreign ministry.[54]

Later, as the newly elected president of the Islamic Republic, Bani-Sadr sabotaged Ghotbzadeh's attempt to deal with the hostage issue. In early March, Ghotbzadeh secured an agreement from the Muslim Students Following the Line of the Imam that control of the hostages would be transferred to the government. He thought he had Khomeini's consent to the transfer.[55] On the morning of the scheduled transfer, however, the militants told Ghotbzadeh that they would not make the transfer without Bani-Sadr's signature. For three hours, Bani-Sadr delayed, providing his signature only after Ghotbzadeh shouted at him. During this time, the students pressed for a roster of all of the American hostages—a document that did not exist. Finally, Khomeini's son, Ahmed called Ghotbzadeh and denounced him for assuming the imam's silence when he had been presented with the plan meant that he endorsed it. With that the students refused to meet Ghotbzadeh's demands. When Ghotbzadeh was able to assemble the Revolutionary Council the next day, Bani-Sadr was absent. The UN Commission of Inquiry departed Tehran shortly thereafter.[56] Furious with Bani-Sadr for an opportunity that may have been lost, Ghotbzadeh attributed "the President's fears of putting his name on paper" to his need to feel sure that "Khomeini wouldn't change his mind."[57]

The Muslim Students Following the Line of the Imam, in short, had become so intoxicated by the power they possessed to whip up crowds and perform as players on the international scene that they did not want to hand over the prisoners to the official government. For his part, Khomeini played an off-and-on-again game with the government's leaders. On March 6, he seemed to assent to a turnover of the government, but just two days later, he revoked his approval. The fate of the hostages, he said, should be in the hands of the Iranian Islamic Parliament, for which elections were not scheduled until March 14.[58]

The Canadian Caper and the Move to Panama

In the midst of these frustrations, one well-planned covert action contributed to American morale. On January 28, six State Department employees were smuggled out of Iran in a joint effort between the CIA and Canadian diplomats. Antonio J. Mendez, the CIA officer in charge of the extraction, put together a plan to rescue the six using Canadian passports to smuggle them out of the country by air. Employing the cover of a movie production group, he was able to get his own people in and out of Iran as needed. Although this cover would make everyone stand out, it would also allow them to be questioned less and perhaps even help account for any eccentricities that might be apparent. Mendez would act as the production manager and thus be in charge of the others, giving him authority to deal with problems if they arose.

Though the cover was never blown, the operation should have alerted the United States to the many snafus that can occur in even a relatively simple operation like this one. When Mendez tried to find the Canadian embassy upon his arrival in Tehran, he arrived at the Swedish embassy by mistake. He had to ask an Iranian passer-by for directions and travel across Tehran to reach the correct destination. One of the forged visa applications had an incorrect date on it. Luckily, this was caught by one of the experts in the Canadian embassy. Finally, on the day he was to depart, Mendez slept through his alarm and was awakened forty-five minutes late by a phone call from one of his collaborators. He rushed to get to the airport on time. In the end, everything went smoothly; the six Americans escaped on an Air Canada airplane after a short mechanical delay. The story broke a few days later, with much acclaim for the Canadian ambassador and his government for their role. The fake production company that was set up was so believable that it received twenty-six scripts, including one from Steven Spielberg.[59]

By late March, the United States had completed another set of moves that removed the return of the shah from the international gaming table. Throughout the early phases of the crisis, the Iranians demanded that the person of the shah and his wealth be returned to Iran. But as early as the November 8 SCC meeting, Vance suggested that the United States might encourage the shah to leave the United States, depriving the Iranians of one of their rallying points.[60] On December 2, Brzezinski called the president at Camp David to tell him that he concurred with Vance and that Averell Harriman had called him with the same advice. At first Carter was outraged. He accused Brzezinski of conspiring with Kissinger and Rockefeller to get the shah out of the country. But now "Cyrus Vance was sitting on his ass and doing nothing." Carter then hung up on Brzezinski.[61]

Carter backtracked shortly thereafter. The shah was moved from New York City to Lackland Air Force Base in Texas. When he sought to flee the scene and return to Mexico, a Mexican emissary told one of his advisors that he was no longer welcome there. When the shah entertained the possibility that he would accept Anwar Sadat's invitation to return to Egypt, the Americans convinced him that it would be dangerous for Egyptian stability. Finally, on December 15, the shah left for Panama. Hamilton Jordan had convinced his friend from the Canal negotiations, President Omar Torrijos Herrera, to provide a refuge there.

Panama, however, did not provide the shah with the kind of sanctuary he needed. There were confrontations between Panamanian and American doctors over who should remove the shah's spleen. The shah's quarters were cramped, and he was convinced the Panamanians were charging him too much for everything given him. Most important, there were some indications that the Panamanians might actually extradite him back to Iran. Carter's legal counsel, Lloyd Cutler, who had come to Panama to try to convince the shah that he should not go to Egypt, came across Christian Bourguet— Jordan's old negotiating partner—at a meeting with Torrijos on March 21. He was offering the Panamanians, it seems, $1 billion in exchange for the extradition.[62]

At this, Cutler urged an advisor to the shah to "get the hell out of here as fast as you can," and arranged a plane for the shah's immediate departure.[63] On March 23, a DC 8 charter plane provided by a CIA proprietary left for Cairo with the shah and his wife on board.[64] But not until the shah's death in Egypt on July 27, 1980, did demands for the return of his person become completely irrelevant to the Americans as well as the Iranians.[65]

The Final Round

In mid-March 1980, one last round of negotiations that the Iranians dubbed the "Second Revision" took place. On March 13, Bani-Sadr relayed a message to Jordan via Bourguet and Villalon that the American hostages still held captive at the American embassy in Tehran would be handed over to the government of Iran by the students by March 25 at the latest. After this transfer, there would be a "reactivation" of the UN Commission of Inquiry.

Impatient with the whole process, Carter met with Bourguet in Washington and handed him a note on which he had scribbled that the hostages would have to be returned by March 31. With that, the administration waited for the Revolutionary Council's response.[66]

On March 30, the Revolutionary Council again voted to assume complete control of the hostages from the militants. The United States, in return, would have to recognize the role of the Iranian parliament in the hostage crisis and refrain from taking any propaganda or military action against Iran. On April 1, at a 4:00 a.m. meeting in the White House, the package was accepted by Jimmy Carter.[67]

Three hours later, at 7:00 a.m., Carter went on national television, suggesting a deal was in hand. The announcement had been discussed with Carter's aides and may have had some impact on undecided voters in the Democratic primaries in Wisconsin and Kansas that day.[68] But before nightfall the "deal" began to fall apart. Bani-Sadr told Carter that his White House statement did not meet the conditions that had been set for transferring the hostages. With that, another hope for an end to the hostage conflict was dashed. Having heard nothing by 7:00 p.m. Tehran time, Bani-Sadr began to fear that his stance would give him troubles with Khomeini.

The proposal Jimmy Carter received on April 1 actually contained some conditions that were nonstarters. The Revolutionary Council would take over the hostages by keeping them at the embassy, with the militants becoming members of the Revolutionary Guard. Further, Carter would have to recognize the right of the new Iranian parliament to make a decision on the hostages.

At this point it was clear that Khomeini did not care about his economic and political isolation, at least in the short run. Certainly none of the American moves put him on the path of seriously addressing the issues of when and how the hostages would be returned.

Finally, on April 7, Carter expelled all Iranian diplomats from the United States, imposed a trade embargo on U.S. goods to Iran, and announced that he would ask Congress to permit Americans to settle claims against Iran by withdrawing $8 billion in assets frozen in U.S. banks.[69] Earlier, as we have seen, he had leaned toward an immediate break in diplomatic relations, but was persuaded by Vance that such action could incite Iranian fears that the United States was preparing for military action.[70]

Then, at a televised news conference on April 17, Carter said that the United States might take military action against Iran if it did not release the hostages in response to the new economic and political sanctions he had imposed. He did not set a deadline, but he did indicate that the military action would not be an invasion or a combat operation.[71]

Back in late November, Carter had considered military options. When he was assured that there were no good ones available at the time, he had relied on diplomatic probes and sanctions aimed at isolating Iran economically and politically. Military force might be threatened and even used in some extremities, but not as a first option. That potential may have kept the Americans being held hostage from being placed on trial or abused in other major ways.

In early April, Carter had another option to consider. Since November 1979, Colonel Charles Beckwith had been working on a rescue operation with a Delta Force team, an elite counterterrorism unit he had created in 1977. The force trained with a mock-up of the U.S. embassy in Tehran, the "Den of Spies" at remote Camp Smokey, North Carolina. Later, they practiced nighttime desert flying in the area near Yuma, Arizona.[72] In addition to their military training, certain Delta Force volunteers studied Farsi and traditional Iranian customs.[73] The Delta Force team was hampered because the CIA did not have operatives in Tehran to provide intelligence on the ground until late December.[74] Still, on April 15, General Jones, chairman of the Joint Chiefs of Staff, observed a command post exercise at Fort Bragg and concluded that the operatives were ready to go. All they needed was a final order from Washington.

While dealing with the fall of the shah from power and the holding of the U.S. hostages in Tehran, Carter had to face several other issues. One concern—over the Soviet brigade in Cuba—may have been a pseudo-issue brewed at home, but it did further complicate relations with the Soviet Union. The second crisis—the Soviet intervention in Afghanistan in December 1979—Carter would see as the test of his presidency. That action and his response to it led to the final renewal of the Cold War in Carter's last year in office. In addition, he would soon be facing his reelection campaign, and Senator Ted Kennedy (D-MA) was confronting him with the possibility that he might not even receive the nomination of his own Democratic Party. Without a second term he could not carry out many of the broader arms control and other foreign policy measure he had earlier championed.

THE SOVIET BRIGADE "CRISIS"

At a press conference in Boise, Idaho, on August 30, 1979, Frank Church, the new chairman of the Senate Foreign Relations Committee, put the issue of a Soviet brigade in Cuba into the political arena. "The United States cannot permit the island to become a Russian military base, 90 miles from our shores," he declared. Allowing this, he continued, would provide the Russians a base from which to intervene militarily throughout the Western Hemisphere.[1]

With this, Church unleashed a torrent of demands and critiques, with possible long-term consequences for the ratification of the Strategic Arms Limitation Treaty (SALT) that he supported. On September 6, Senator Richard Stone (D-FL), who had earlier raised questions about Soviet activities in Cuba, equated this episode to the Cuban Missile Crisis.[2] Former president Gerald Ford assailed President Jimmy Carter for implying that a Soviet combat unit had been in Cuba while he was president. "I do not believe our intelligence was so bad as to completely miss such a major development," he said.[3] Former California governor Ronald Reagan called on the United States to refuse further communications with the Soviet Union until the troops in Cuba were withdrawn.[4] Senator Henry Jackson (D-WA) joined in the fray.[5] So did *Newsweek*. In its September 10 issue, several hypotheses for the Soviet actions were offered, ranging from a possible desire to protect some as yet undetected Soviet installation, to the idea that it was a direct challenge to Jimmy Carter.[6]

The immediate impact of this whole affair was to put the SALT II discussion in the U.S. Senate on hold for over a month.[7] Ironically, it would become clear in the next few days that the "new" Soviet brigade had been in Cuba since the missile crisis of 1962. Moreover, it was an insignificant military force, no larger than the American force at the Guantanamo Bay Naval Base in Cuba. Even the Joint Chiefs of Staff, as journalists Walter Pincus and George C. Wilson reported at the time, saw the brigade as posing no direct threat to either the United States or its allies in the Caribbean. The Soviets had no ships or planes deployed in Cuba that could take their troops anywhere.[8]

Then, how did this become an issue? Partly the crisis was due to the inadequate and partial intelligence in the system and some changes in the makeup of the brigade that led to interpretation problems. The men in the brigade were at this time wearing Cuban uniforms and engaged in operations that were not clearly limited to the training of Cuban troops.[9]

More significant was the leaking of half-finished intelligence reports and the use of this information by those outside and inside the administration for their own political or foreign policy objectives.[10] The issue in particular served the short-term political interests of Senators Church and Stone. Both men were politically vulnerable, running for reelection in 1980. A tough line against the Soviets could bolster their positions with conservative voters.

President Carter and Secretary of State Cyrus Vance, this time working together, failed to quickly and decisively find a way to save face. Their mistakes were accentuated by the predispositions in the American public to accept worst-case analyses of Soviet actions. And Soviet officials, seeing this as a manufactured crisis, were not inclined to help extract an increasingly hostile administration from an embarrassing imbroglio.

Evolution of the Crisis

As early as August 1978, Zbigniew Brzezinski's aide William Odom received raw intelligence reports out of Cuba indicating that there were Soviet ground forces—including tanks and armored personnel carriers—in Cuba. Brzezinski recommended that the data be presented to the entire intelligence community.[11] When there was no immediate follow-up, Brzezinski, in April 1979, directed the Central Intelligence Agency and the National Security Agency to conduct an investigation of "the age, location, capabilities and purposes of Soviet ground forces in Cuba." Brzezinski recalled asking for this study because of other indicators of "Soviet activity promoting revolutionary activity in the Caribbean and Central America." The deals negotiated between the United States and the Soviet Union after the Cuban Missile Crisis were somewhat ambiguous, and Brzezinski thought there might be possible Soviet violations of a 1970 understanding on the Cuban city of Cienfuegos and of a 1978 understanding on Soviet MIG-23 fighter aircraft.[12] Former National Security Council staffer Odom also recalls this being a concern at the time.[13]

Early reports from the intelligence agencies were inconclusive. The CIA and NSA both found that there might be a military unit the size of a brigade in Cuba. But the NSA, in a July report, suggested that it was not necessarily an active combat brigade, and it had been present in Cuba for years.[14] Other intelligence sources, however, were concerned that the headquarters "for a Soviet brigade and some unit other than advisory groups were present" in Cuba and that their purpose remained unclear. Still, an interagency intelligence committee noted, there were no indications of "any suspicious change in recent years."[15]

In late July, Brzezinski wrote CIA director Stansfield Turner urging the agency step up its collection efforts on Cuba.[16] A month later, U.S. intelligence agencies observed a Soviet motorized rifle brigade of 2,000 to 3,000 men in a military exercise on San Pedro Beach in Cuba. They observed that the unit had been in Cuba since at least 1975 or 1976 and that that "it was at this point an independent Soviet unit doing combat-type training in Cuba."[17]

Then, on August 14, the NSA, or the CIA's National Foreign Assessment Center (depending on which source one consults), characterized the unit in Cuba, for the first time, as a "combat brigade." With that characterization the whole nature and purpose of the brigade was transformed into a possible threat to U.S. interests in the area. The

CIA, as Turner later admitted, failed to second-guess this characterization of the unit or to tie the operations observed to earlier activities. "It took a long time before we really got to the bottom of the fact that it had been agreed to back in 62–63."[18]

Throughout the late spring and early summer Brzezinski had alerted the president to what he saw as a pattern of expanding military activity in Cuba. He argued that the Soviets were "twisting agreements" and pushing the line on naval ports. On May 25, he wrote Carter that the CIA had observed some 2,000 Soviet troops in Cuba. Their activity "comes very close but does not unambiguously violate earlier assurances and promises given since 1962."[19] On July 24, 1979, he noted that the Soviet brigade could have "serious repercussions for SALT."[20] On July 27, Brzezinski wrote that the United States should make it clear by actions and words "that we hold the Soviet Union accountable for Cuba's intensified activity."[21]

At the same time Washington was afloat with rumors about an increased Soviet presence in Cuba.[22] Senator Stone expressed his concerns to the Senate Foreign Relations Committee on July 17, but was temporarily mollified by a letter from Vance indicating that the administration would keep a close watch over events in Cuba. But then on August 22, the *National Intelligence Digest*, distributed to four hundred senior officials in government, noted that a "combat" brigade had been discovered in Cuba. With this widespread a distribution, *Aviation Week and Space Technology* latched onto the story, and officials in Washington knew they had a problem.[23]

The Blowup

In mid- to late summer, Carter was dealing with political problems at home. In July, he had been engaged in his domestic Camp David conference, delivered his third proposal on the energy crisis (his famous "malaise" speech), asked for the resignation of all his cabinet members, accepting five of them, and belatedly named Hamilton Jordan as his chief of staff. In the waning days of August, the president was on the *Delta Queen*, traveling down the Mississippi River on a political "meet the people" tour, and Brzezinski was in Vermont for a much-needed vacation with his family. Robert Pastor, the NSC's Latin American specialist, was on his honeymoon. The U.S. Congress was in recess, and Senate leaders were scattered over their home political terrain. Even Soviet Ambassador Anatoly Dobrynin, with whom Vance usually met on Soviet affairs, was back in Russia attending to his critically ill mother and father.[24]

Taking charge of the issue, Vance's first moves were to short-circuit any possible political explosions. At a Special Coordinating Committee meeting on August 29, State Department representatives proposed that the United States send a diplomatic protest to the Soviets on their brigade in Cuba.[25] That same day, Under Secretary of State David Newsome contacted Vladilen Vasev, the charge d'affaires in the Soviet embassy, asking Vasev about the brigade and its possible functions. He did not respond until September 5.[26] Newsome also got on the phone to tell Senator Church and seven other congressional leaders that a combat brigade had been discovered in

Cuba and that the administration was dealing with the matter. Most of the men took the information in stride.[27] This followed a good Washington tradition dictating that senators are less likely to feel used and run with a story when they are officially kept within the loop.

But Church had other interests at stake. He was involved in a difficult campaign for reelection in Idaho, a very conservative state, and his dovish reputation was a liability. In July 1979, Church had joined Senator Jacob Javits of New York, the Republican senior member of the Senate Foreign Relations Committee, in a statement suggesting that there had been no big changes in Soviet forces in Cuba. His opponents were already running a photo of him kissing Fidel Castro on his visit to Cuba. When Church called Vance to say he would go public with the information he had been given, the secretary, according to one source, pleaded with him not to do so. According to another source, however, Vance told him "to use his own judgment on the matter."[28]

Somewhat surprisingly, the secretary of state himself fueled the crisis. At a press conference on September 5, he referred to the unit as a "combat" force, noting that the presence of such a unit in Cuba was "a matter of serious concern."[29]

Two days later, back in his hometown of Plains, Georgia, for the Labor Day weekend, Carter affirmed the existence of the brigade, noting the need for a "sense of proportion" on the matter. But he agreed with Vance that the "status quo is not acceptable." The issue, he suggested, revolved around the "stationing of Soviet combat troops here in the Western Hemisphere in a country which acts as a Soviet proxy in military adventures in other areas of the world, like Africa." He continued, in a softer tone, "this is a time for firm diplomacy, not panic and not exaggeration." The brigade was not an assault force that could threaten the United States, he added.[30] That same day, Brzezinski told a group of editors that Castro was a puppet of the Soviet Union and a "surrogate" for their foreign policy goals, but that SALT should not be linked to the issue.[31]

The straddling of the issue continued at the cabinet meeting on September 10. Vance repeated his statement that the status quo was "unacceptable." But then he noted that the brigade did not represent a threat to the security of the United States, that there was no valid comparison between this issue and the 1962 missile crisis, and that the resolution of the issue would have to await the negotiations.[32]

The president at this time had at hand recent intelligence reports indicating the Soviet insistence that the brigade had been in Cuba since the 1960s. On September 3, Admiral Bobby Inman, Director of the NSA, provided a chronology indicating that the first reference to the brigade was in mid-1968. The CIA soon corroborated this information.[33]

Correcting course, Vance was soon seeking diplomatic cover. To deal with the matter he asked Soviet Foreign Minister Andrei Gromyko to send Dobrynin back to Washington. Gromyko obliged, calling the ambassador on the phone. "Well, I do not know why they need to consult you," he said. "But if the Secretary asks, then if you do not mind, please go."[34]

On the afternoon of September 10, Dobrynin proceeded via a private elevator to the seventh floor of the State Department building and Vance's office.[35] In the meeting the following conversation ensued:

VANCE: "Anatoly, were those troops there during the Kennedy administration? During the Johnson administration? During the Nixon administration? During the Ford administration?"

DOBRYNIN: "Yes. Exactly."

VANCE: "Then what is this all about?"

DOBRYNIN (SHRUGGING): "I should ask you what it is all about."

VANCE (PLEADING): "Anatoly, can't you get them to move some ships around—to move some troops a little bit—so that we could say that it was now acceptable?"

DOBRYNIN: "You know, after the Cuban missile crisis, there is no way we are going to do that sort of thing; it would be too humiliating."[36]

Vance's instructions, drawn up after this meeting with Dobrynin, were to seek either a Soviet decision to withdraw the brigade from Cuba or assurances from them that they would change its makeup and functions in ways that would reassure the United States of its benign intent.[37] But in none of his subsequent talks with Dobrynin in Washington and Gromyko in New York did Vance persuade the Soviet Union to bail Carter out of his political difficulties.[38] As early as September 12, NSC Soviet specialist Marshall Brement wrote Brzezinski that the Soviets were not likely to back down with any sort of withdrawal or apology for the brigade.[39]

Even as the diplomats spoke, Moscow took a hard public line. *Pravda*, the Soviet's Communist Party newspaper, claimed on September 10 that the brigade had been in Cuba since 1962 for the purpose of teaching Cuba to master Soviet equipment and labeled the Carter administration's disclosures about a combat brigade as "totally groundless."[40] In a speech at the United Nations on September 25, Gromyko charged that "this propaganda is totally without force in reality," and that it was time for the United States to admit that this was a false issue.[41]

In the meantime, Brzezinski endeavored to stoke the fires. In mid-September he wrote Carter the following warning:

A cosmetic outcome will not wash. The country will see through it; SALT will be jeopardized; you will be seen as zigzagging ("the status quo is not acceptable"—except cosmetically...!) the world will see it as U.S. acquiescence....A gradual but steady toughening up in our policy is therefore the preferable alterative. It will require telling the country quite frankly that we cannot get the brigade out, short of a head-on military confrontation. Instead, there are other things that you are prepared to do in order to confront the Soviet Union with the fact that détente must be a two-way street.

The steps Brzezinski suggested included a further budget increase explicitly tied to the issue of the brigade, the deployment of additional American troops at Guantanamo Bay, the declaration of a Carter doctrine for the Caribbean, statements that the United States would oppose the organized deployment of Soviet/Cuban troops or revolutionaries across national borders, and the sale of some advanced technology to China.

The "direct political benefit" of such a course of action would be to put Senator Ted Kennedy (D-MA) on the spot: "By toughening up our posture vis-à-vis the Soviets, you will either force Kennedy to back you, or to oppose you....If he backs you, he is backing an assertive and tough President; if he opposes you, he can easily be stamped as a latter-day McGovernite."[42]

Several days later, on September 21, Brzezinski suggested that the president make public some comparisons to how President John F. Kennedy had dealt with the Soviets when they put up the Berlin Wall in 1961. "Kennedy responded to his 'unacceptable' situation, with which he had to live, by taking a number of steps designed to indicate to the public that he would assert U.S. interests, and, if necessary, be prepared to use force. He sent more troops to Berlin, and he put more emphasis on our overall defense efforts." The solution, he suggested, should be to send more troops to Guantanamo: "More defense, more intelligence, some limited steps regarding China."[43]

Though Carter resisted Brzezinski's hard-line rhetoric, certain steps taken by the administration at the height of the crisis gave the Soviet leaders reason to question U.S. intentions. On September 7, the day of Carter's first statement on Cuba, the White House had issued a press release indicating that the U.S. government would proceed with "the full scale development and deployment of a new, large, mobile ICBM [intercontinental ballistic missile], known as the MX."[44] On September 23, unnamed sources in the White House went so far as to suggest that the United States was considering retaliatory measures such as sending weapons to China and mounting a campaign of "interference" in Eastern Europe.[45] In a September 29 interview on National Public Radio, Brzezinski compared the situation to Kennedy's Berlin crisis.[46] In Beijing, Vice President Walter Mondale noted the common interests of the People's Republic of China and the United States. As the crisis peaked, Secretary of Defense Harold Brown's forthcoming visit to China was leaked to the press.[47]

Still, with no Soviet concession on the horizon, Vance began searching for another way to gracefully back down from the "crisis." On September 23, he brought Senate Democratic leader Robert Byrd (WV) onto the playing field. In a meeting with Carter at the White House, Byrd told the president that the crisis was not real. It was "inappropriate for a mighty nation to go into a delirium over about 2,300 Soviet troops that had neither airlift nor sealift capability to leave Cuba."[48] The administration, he suggested, must find some way to disengage from this issue in order to save SALT II. In the meantime, governmental leaders should cool their rhetoric. Further consultations with congressional leaders on the matter only served to hype up the issue. Indeed, Byrd had boycotted such a meeting on September 20, saying that it would only add to the appearance of a crisis situation.

The president was deeply puzzled by what Byrd told him.[49] Shortly thereafter, Vance and Legal Counsel to the President Lloyd Cutler persuaded Carter to summon a group of senior statesmen—later called the "wise men"—to look into the issue. This decision was made over Brzezinski's strong, but incorrect, insistence that such groups had never been used in the past.[50]

A tough letter from Soviet president Leonid Brezhnev on Thursday, September 27, reinforced Vance's hand. "Abandon this story," he demanded. The Soviet brigade was a military training center and had existed there for more than seventeen years. It was a training brigade that "does nothing more and can do nothing more." Brezhnev made one minimal concession to the United States, saying, "We have no intention of changing its status as such a center in the future."[51]

That same night between 8:00 and 9:00 p.m., dark limousines began rolling up to the West Wing entrance to the White House; Carter had summoned an emergency meeting of the National Security Council.

The next day, Clark Clifford strode across the lawn to the West Wing and Brzezinski's office. The fifteen "wise men" had been assembled to look into the issue of the purported combat brigade in Cuba, and he was its head.[52] Clifford had in hand a letter from former national security advisor McGeorge Bundy. It read, in part:

> [T]he present crisis over a Soviet infantry brigade in Cuba is the product of internal accident and error in the United States.... I find it unbelievable that this would have happened.... We would not have made the brigade a cause célèbre if we had known its full history; we should not make it so because we did not. The hard-line rhetoric being employed at the time was a mistake if only because we had accepted other Soviet installations all along.[53]

The "wise men" then proceeded to grill "the experts in the government on the nature of the Soviet brigade in Cuba." Clifford, in particular, was appalled to learn that the brigade had been in Cuba since 1962, that it had only become an issue, because the intelligence community had lost track of it "sometime during the previous sixteen years."[54]

On Saturday morning the group met with Brzezinski and then Carter over lunch. No overall report was made. But most participants agreed that Carter had to find a way out of the situation and some accused Brzezinski of deliberately trying to revive the Cold War with his hard-line rhetoric.[55] Photographs were taken, and the men then returned to their respective home bases.[56] After the meeting, Vance encouraged the president to treat the brigade issue "as a serious but isolated incident." It should not affect "the overall U.S.-Soviet relationship."[57]

On Saturday afternoon, after his meeting with the outside experts, Carter left for Camp David to work on the speech he was to give that coming Monday. Even at this time his advisors did not agree on what he should say. Vance and Cutler wanted to downplay the importance of the brigade.[58] Brzezinski wanted to link the brigade issue to overall Soviet adventurism and treat the Cubans simply as a Soviet proxy. The brigade, Brzezinski argued, was "the latest manifestation of Moscow's dominance of Mr. Castro" and the "increasing Soviet military support for Cuba."[59]

When Carter addressed the nation on Monday, October 1, it was clear that the Vance/Cutler team had prevailed.[60] Carter was reassuring, noting that he had received statements from the highest levels of the Soviet government that the combat brigade did not pose a threat to U.S. security or interests in Latin America. Nor did he see the brigade issue as a sufficient reason for a return to the Cold War. An offending reference to Soviet "adventurism" was cut.

Yet, given the earlier arousal of the U.S. public to the Soviet threat in Cuba, Carter could not settle for doing nothing politically. He proceeded to make some rhetorical and symbolic moves, adopting several of the recommendations Brzezinski had made to him in mid-September. The United States, he declared, could not simply trust Soviet statements that their brigade intentions were nonbelligerent. Thus, to ensure that was the case, he would increase surveillance of Cuba; establish a permanent full-time Caribbean joint task force to be headquartered in Key West, Florida; expand the U.S. capability to respond rapidly to any attempted military encroachments in the area; and increase economic assistance to other countries in the Caribbean region. A nod was made in the direction of Brzezinski with the pledge to increase the U.S. military presence in the Indian Ocean.

Carter concluded the speech with a call for the ratification of SALT II: "My fellow Americans, the greatest danger to American security tonight is certainly not the two or three thousand Soviet troops in Cuba. The greatest danger to all the nations of the world—including the United States and the Soviet Union—is the breakdown of a common effort to preserve the peace and the ultimate threat of a nuclear war."[61]

After this speech, Carter met with fifty friends and supporters to celebrate his fifty-fifth birthday. As he blew out the eight candles on his cake, the people around him shouted "eight years," referring to their hope for a second term.[62]

Brzezinski and Presidential Assistant Hedley Donovan were noticeably absent. Distressed by the president's address, both men felt that they were at a turning point in their "political fortunes within the Carter White House." Brzezinski stated, "I was particularly irritated by the fact that Cutler told some people in the White House that he succeeded in cutting from the speech the words 'Soviet adventurism,' because, as he put it, the word 'adventurism' was a foreign one."[63]

A few days later, Brzezinski confronted the president with the "most disagreeable comment" he had ever made to him. The United States, he said, "had told the Russians on several different occasions that it took great exception to their action in Vietnam, Iran, the Middle East and Africa and more recently in Cuba…but then we do nothing about it." That could be dangerous for the future, because the Russians could miscalculate U.S. responses, he argued. "The President looked quite furious," and told Brzezinski that "he had no intention of going to war over the Soviet brigade in Cuba."[64]

The fallout between Carter and Brzezinski was temporary. But the whole brigade episode left a bitter aftertaste in the mouths of several American and Soviet leaders. On September 9, Church had suspended the Senate Foreign Relations Committee hearings on SALT II, and on October 2, the Senate passed a resolution stating that there would not be a SALT II agreement until the president could give reassurance that the Soviet brigade in Cuba had no combat role.[65] The Soviet newspaper *Pravda* accused Carter of fabricating a myth of a Soviet Cuban threat so as to fuel tensions and escalate the arms race.[66] Not until October 23, when McGeorge Bundy published his letter noting the early origins of the brigade in the *New York Times*, did the issue settle down.[67]

Still, Vance continued his efforts to salvage the SALT II Treaty. Recent developments, he suggested in testimony to the Senate Foreign Relations Committee on October 16, had not changed his earlier testimony before Congress. SALT II should not be linked to Soviet activities in other realms.[68] Later, in a speech in Florida, he faced one of the questions that opponents of SALT were using as a result of the whole brigade fiasco. He was asked, "How could a U.S. satellite that had difficulties in detecting a Soviet troop buildup in Cuba monitor Soviet military activity in Russia underneath SALT?" Nuclear weapons, Vance retorted, would be easier to monitor than the activities of a group of men as manifested in the kinds of specific equipment and exercise they utilized.[69]

The Issue of Responsibility

On September 18, 1979, Tom Wicker, a columnist for the *New York Times*, wrote, "Jimmy Carter's Cuban fiasco...ranks right up there with the Dewey campaign of 1948 for snatching defeat from the jaws of victory." Only "Soviet capitulation," he countered, would have rescued Carter from an apparent acceptance of a Soviet outpost in the Western Hemisphere.[70] Certainly, the success of the Sandinistas in Nicaragua in the summer of 1979 had created a political climate in which the president and his advisors could not appear to be soft on Russian and Cuban activities in the Caribbean.[71] It did not help, as Marshall Shulman would later note, that the miniature crisis peaked over the Labor Day holiday when senators were dispersed around the country.[72]

The president, along with his advisors, however, did confront the USSR over an issue that seemed quite hollow as the facts of the case became known. Had the president or the secretary of state taken hold of the issue with early and decisive moves to dampen the rhetoric, it might have been contained. Senator Byrd and Senator Alan Cranston (D-CA), who had staked their reputations on the SALT II ratification, were particularly angry with Carter. As Byrd noted, the whole episode had been poorly handled. He declared that talk was the one thing inflation hadn't hit.[73]

Brzezinski made several contributions to the whole fray. Though he assigned responsibility for the brigade crisis to the State Department, he seeded the blowup with his pressures on the intelligence community to speed up its reporting on the Cuban situation, and he is the one who pressured the president to use the threat as a means to beef up the U.S. anti-Soviet response around the world.[74] When Carter hesitated to follow his lead, Brzezinski made public comments on his own to hype up the issue.

Senator Church stands as one of the main culprits. Although he was known as a pro-SALT senator, his tough rhetoric and calls for Soviet pullback opened the floodgates to the anti-SALT Treaty forces. It also undermined his relationship with other senators working for SALT II. One of the latter was quoted in *Time*, charging that the "the S.O.B. had sold us out for his own private purpose." Back in Idaho, Church was ridiculed by one of his supporters, the *Lewiston Idaho Times'* Bill Hall. In an editorial Hall noted, "It's not a proud moment to have the Senate Foreign Relations Committee chairman from Idaho trying to outdo every right-wing wacko in the Senate."[75] Church later told his son Forrester that it was the biggest mistake of his life.[76] The move did not even pay off for him politically. Along with six other influential Democrats, in 1980 Church lost his seat in the Senate to the Republicans for the first time since 1956.[77] (Church's loss by 4,262 votes—less than 1 percent—may be partly due to Carter's early concession speech, since Idaho is two to three hours behind Eastern Standard Time and potential voters could have been affected.[78])

The immediate result of the Soviet brigade fiasco was to stall the SALT II ratification process. Although Byrd believed the treaty ratification process was going well in July, by September it did not have the requisite two-thirds vote needed to pass in the Senate. Byrd thought it best to put off the matter until November.[79] As Brzezinski later noted, "Approximately one month of time was lost, and it became increasingly clear that the ratification of SALT would have to slip until the end of the year or perhaps into early 1980."[80] Though in the end Church led the Senate Foreign Relations Committee to recommend approval of the treaty, the episode "shook public confidence in the Administration," and created problems for the SALT II ratification process. The fiasco caused Senator Russell Long (D-LA) to shift from support to opposition of the treaty. His decision to defect could have been crucial had SALT been put to a vote.[81]

In late December the Soviet invasion of Afghanistan gave Washington a real crisis. Dobrynin later would argue that the brigade crisis had little impact on their decision. But whatever its cause, the Soviet action brought the end to an already weakened SALT support and renewed the Cold War. A process that had been evolving since Carter's first months in office would be capped as Carter embraced all of Brzezinski's efforts to curtail Soviet activities around the world.[82]

AFGHANISTAN: FORMULATING A RESPONSE

On Christmas morning in 1979, Moscow began to airlift soldiers to Kabul, Afghanistan claiming to "put down the rebellion of conservative Muslim tribesmen." In the early evening, Soviet troops seized key locations in Kabul, including the radio station. By the next day, Radio Kabul announced that the "repressive" Communist President Hafizullah Amin had been deposed. Former Deputy Prime Minister Babrak Karmal, who had been exiled and reportedly stashed away in an Eastern European capital as a strongman in reserve, was installed as head of the Afghan government. Moscow would later claim that their move into Afghanistan was at the request of the Karmal government under the terms of a twenty-year friendship treaty signed in late 1978.[1] But they made no attempt to disguise the fact that the airlift began before the coup that brought Karmal to power, thus making a mockery of their rationale. By December 29 there were an estimated 30,000 Soviet soldiers in Afghanistan.[2]

At Camp David, where Jimmy Carter and his family were spending Christmas, the president was more upset than he had been by any other event on his watch. "There goes SALT II," he exclaimed. As Rosalynn Carter later explained, "In a sense it was a negation of one of the major missions of his presidency. He had worked hard for this treaty and had been sure it was gaining support in the Senate. Now the chance for ratifying it would be gone."[3] Carter himself would later note that the failure to ratify the SALT agreements, and to secure other arms control agreements, was the greatest disappointment of his presidency.[4]

The depth of his frustration was also evident in a phone conversation with his Chief of Staff, Hamilton Jordan, who was in Atlanta at the time. As Jordan later recalled,

> I put in a call to the President and asked simply if there was anything I could do. "No," he said, "Unless you can get the Soviets out of Afghanistan."
>
> I thought for a second he was kidding, but his tone made it clear he was frustrated. I offered to go back to Washington immediately but he said no, it would take several days for the Afghanistan conflict to be clarified.
>
> "As if we didn't already have our hands full with the hostages," I said.
>
> "This is more serious, Hamilton. Capturing those Americans was an inhumane act committed by a bunch of radicals and condoned by a crazy old man. But this is deliberate aggression that calls into question détente and the way we have been doing business with the Soviets for the past decade. It raises grave questions about Soviet intentions and destroys any chance of

getting the SALT Treaty through the Senate. And that makes the prospects for nuclear war even greater."

I was chilled when I heard his analysis.[5]

A few days later, Carter told Frank Reynolds of ABC News that the Soviet action "has made a more dramatic change in my opinion of what the Soviets' ultimate goals are than anything they've done in the previous time I've been in office."[6] Distressed Senior Advisor Hedley Donovan wrote Carter that this statement opened him up to charges of political naïveté and that Carter had only become tough on foreign policy matters after December 1978.[7]

Carter should not have been that surprised by the Soviet move. The USSR had been involved in Afghanistan's politics since the end of World War II, trying to draw that country into the Soviet sphere of influence and make it a showcase for Soviet aid projects in the third world. From 1953 to 1978 noncommunist national leaders in Afghanistan cooperated with Moscow in a variety of economic and political undertakings. When one of these leaders sought to steer a course of greater independence from Moscow, the communist-oriented People's Democratic Party (PDP) took over the government in a coup. The new government, however, embraced radical policies that lost it the support of the traditional Muslim population, and the *mujahideen*, or holy warriors, began a guerilla war against the government. When the government proved incapable of restoring order, Hafizullah Amin, the leader of the pro-Soviet faction of the PDP, seized the government in yet another bloody coup. A rather unsavory character, he was unable to restore order. More than that, he had been educated at Columbia University, fanning Soviet suspicions that he had ties to the U.S. Central Intelligence Agency (CIA).[8]

The United States itself had been providing support for the *mujahideen* since the summer of 1979. In July, Carter noted in a "finding" he sent to the U.S. Congress, he was authorizing cash or military support for the insurgents either directly or via third parties. A second "finding" indicated that he had ordered the establishment of a network of agents or other contacts to be formed to "provide non-attributable propaganda" to expose "the Democratic Republic of Afghanistan and its leadership as despotic and subservient to the Soviet Union."[9] In August, CIA director Stansfield Turner urged the agency's director of operations to begin providing more assistance to the insurgents. Several options were considered, including the allocation of money and weapons to Pakistan to distribute to the insurgents.[10]

Following these measures, in September Carter ordered the Department of State to make frequent public comments about the increasing involvement of the Soviet Union in Afghanistan and to share relevant information with U.S. allies and countries in the region. He was informed that the State Department was already involved in such activities.[11] That same month, an interagency group worked on contingency planning for possible U.S. diplomatic, political, and propaganda measures should the Soviets intervene militarily in Afghanistan.[12] At a meeting on December 11, 1979, the Special Coordinating Committee (SCC) decided that the United States should expand its Voice of America broadcasts in the Muslim world.[13]

In the late fall and early winter, warnings about a more direct Soviet military involvement in Afghanistan should have reached the president's desk. National Security Advisor Zbigniew Brzezinski wrote Carter on November 3, warning of a possible Soviet military intervention.[14] Columbia University professor and State Department Soviet specialist Marshall Shulman wrote Secretary of State Cyrus Vance a memo in early December noting that the Soviet Union might undertake an open intervention in Afghanistan. Seeing a continuing "down slide" in their relations with the United States, the Soviets "may well have concluded that the advantages of more direct intervention in Afghanistan now outweigh the inevitable price the Soviets will pay in terms of regional and U.S. reactions."[15] On December 17, Turner briefed the SCC, stating, "Most of the countryside is now in rebel hands, but no major cities are expected to fall unless there are significant defections from the Army. We believe the Soviets have made a political decision to keep a pro-Soviet regime in power and to use military force to that end if necessary."[16] On December 19, the National Security Agency issued intelligence alerts, warning the president that the Soviet Union seemed to be on the verge of a substantial military engagement in Afghanistan.[17]

Initial Responses

When the actual intervention took place, Carter no doubt realized that there was little chance that the Soviets would back down on their own. But in a television speech on January 4 the president said, "The world simply cannot stand by and permit the Soviet Union to commit this act with impunity." In his diary entry for January 3, 1980, he wrote, "Unless the Soviets recognize that it has been counterproductive for them, we will face additional serious problems with invasions or subversion in the future."[18]

Only hours after the Soviet intervention, Brzezinski presented Carter with the preliminary considerations that shaped his policy responses. He wrote that it was essential "that the Afghanistan resistance continues." This would require more money and arms shipments to the rebels, a reconsideration of U.S. policy toward Pakistan, the encouragement of the Chinese to aid the rebels, the development of a program campaign in concert with Islamic countries in propaganda and covert actions, and warnings to the Soviets that their actions were placing SALT II in jeopardy and could impact Secretary of Defense Harold Brown's visit to China.[19]

Agreements on the particular actions to be taken were hammered out by Carter and his advisors in a series of meetings from December 26 to January 2. All the members of the president's team were determined to make the USSR pay for its misadventure.[20] On certain issues, the State Department even advocated stronger action than did the others. Vance even suggested that the military draft be reinstated—a measure opposed by the vice president. Carter adopted practically all of their recommendations.[21]

Carter's policies were made public in a series of speeches and interviews. In a televised address on January 4, the president characterized the Soviet actions as aggressive and a threat to world peace and order. The invasion, he said, was "a deliberate effort by a powerful atheistic government to subjugate an independent Islamic people." Measures to counter their actions included a grain embargo, a ban on the export of U.S. technology to the USSR, and U.S. economic and military aid to Pakistan.[22]

In an NBC *Meet the Press* interview on January 20, 1980, Carter announced the U.S. decision to boycott the Olympic Summer Games in Moscow if the Soviets did not withdraw from Afghanistan within the month. Carter did not want to hurt the Olympic movement, but it "seemed unconscionable to be guests of the Soviets while they were involved in a bloody suppression of the people of Afghanistan—an act condemned by an overwhelming majority of the nations of the world."[23]

Three days later, in his State of the Union address on January 23, Carter asserted, "The implications of the Soviet invasion of Afghanistan could pose the most serious threat to world peace since the Second World War." To deal with that threat, the president extended U.S. military guarantees for the first time to the Middle East and announced plans for a new regional security arrangement: "An attempt by any outside force to gain control of the Persian Gulf region will be regarded as an assault on the vital interests of the United States. It will be repelled by the use of any means necessary, including military force." To that end he envisaged the development in the Persian Gulf of "a cooperative security framework that respects different values and political beliefs, yet which enhances the independence, security and prosperity of all."[24] This new commitment, as Brzezinski later noted, was modeled on the Truman Doctrine, enunciated back in 1946 in response to the Soviet threat to Greece and Turkey.[25]

Later, in a speech before the American Society of Newspaper Editors on April 10, 1980, Carter warned that Soviet intervention in Afghanistan was a threat to the entire world political system. "To assume aggression need be met only when it occurs at one's own doorstep is to tempt new adventures and to risk new and very serious miscalculations."[26]

Decisions and Disagreements

Despite the agreed-upon need to make the Soviets pay for their intervention, there had been disagreements between Carter's foreign policy advisors on some of the sanctions Carter announced. The Olympic boycott was one of these. Mondale, who had first raised the issue, squared off against Vance, who strongly opposed it.[27] As for the grain embargo, their roles were reversed. Vance favored deep cuts in American exports while Mondale opposed cuts on domestic political grounds.[28] Carter's domestic affairs staffer, Stuart Eizenstat, had similar concerns.[29]

Secretary of Agriculture Robert Bergland even got into a "big fight" with Brzezinski about the impact of this embargo:

> We [the Agriculture Department] argued that the embargo won't have any effect on the Russians....The Russians will get grain from the Argentines and we'll get all the Argentine customers. And that's exactly what happened. Brzezinski was arguing that, "No. It won't work. We'll stop them. They can't

get this grain." ...I said, "This is bunk. Where did you get those numbers?" He said, "Well, that's the way it's going to be."[30]

Certain aspects of the new security measures for the Middle East were also a matter of controversy. In a National Security Council (NSC) meeting on December 28, 1979, the members of the inner circle tentatively decided to send Deputy Secretary of State Warren Christopher to meet with General Mohammed Zia-ul-Haq, the dictator in Pakistan who had come to power in a bloodless coup in July 1977. But how far should these new commitments go? Brzezinski had broached the idea of a regional guarantee for the area as early as 1977. But Vance and Christopher had met Brzezinski's earlier plans with skepticism. Over time, Brzezinski had been able to create bureaucratic momentum for the project. Aided by his assistant, General William Odom, and key officials in the Defense Department including Graham Clayton and Under Secretary Robert Komer, Brzezinski had won Secretary Brown over to the concept by late 1979.[31]

On January 9, 1980, Carter formally affirmed the plan. As Brzezinski noted in a letter to the president, the new security agreement would include the Egyptians, Saudis, Pakistanis, and Turks. The project would necessitate increases in U.S. defense spending, improvements in the North Atlantic Treaty Organization (NATO), and the U.S. Rapid Deployment Forces. The project, he suggested, might be called the Carter Doctrine.

"Let's do it to them," Carter wrote back on Brzezinski's memo to him. He even added a few suggestions of his own. The president demurred, however, on labeling the new policy the Carter Doctrine.[32]

Still, there was a skirmish over the issue of wording in the president's State of the Union address. In the initial draft of the message Brzezinski had included a phrase referring to a "regional security framework." Both Vance and Legal Counsel to the President Lloyd Cutler made a last-minute effort to cut out that reference. But Brzezinski caught Press Secretary Jody Powell on his way to the presidential residence with the final version of the speech. He and Powell, "standing in the semidarkness of the portico" linking the West Wing to the rest of the White House, simply penciled back in the deleted words referring to a "cooperative security framework."[33]

There were also differences over whether or not the United States should utilize diplomatic contacts with the Soviets during the crisis. The new U.S. ambassador, Thomas Watson, was never a major player. The son of the founder of IBM, he did not speak Russian, and was seen by the hard-liners at home as too soft on the USSR. Actually, he had engaged in a shouting match with Soviet Foreign Minister Andrei Gromyko shortly after the invasion took place. Watson expressed incredulity that Amin's assassination and replacement by Karmal, who arrived on a Soviet plane synchronized with the invasion, were events purely internal to Afghanistan. Gromyko leapt from his chair, moved toward Watson, and screamed that Watson and the United States were deceived. The self-righteous President Carter, with his potential sanctions, did not represent absolute justice or the judgment of God. Watson ended the conversation and left, remarking that the Cold War had resumed.[34]

Marshall Brement, the Soviet expert on the NSC staff, was one of those who saw Watson and his staff as weak. Responding to Watson's description of his January 30 meeting with Gromyko, Brement was convinced that Watson had failed to counter Gromyko's charges against the United States with a spirited point-by-point defense. The result would have been a "tough and bruising session," but it would have earned Watson Gromyko's respect. Somehow, Brement noted, no one had informed Watson that, for the Russians, "silence means consent."[35]

The next day, Brement dismissed a cable from the U.S. embassy as containing "some rather extraordinary statements, which I would hope will not be taken seriously by key policy makers." Singled out for criticism were the suggestions that the U.S. government should make it clear that it did not seek to overthrow the Soviet system and that the United States should defend its vital interest carefully, "in order to avoid having forced on us a choice between defeat on the ground and nuclear war." Brement dismissed the statement that "the Soviet leaders may actually have convinced themselves that the Carter administration is out to do them in," responding, "Is there a Soviet leader who at this stage really believes that we are attempting 'To destroy the Soviet Union?' I strongly doubt it."[36]

But Vance, unlike Brement, wanted to employ diplomatic contacts to avoid the kind of miscalculations the U.S. embassy staff in Moscow was concerned about. On February 8, he wrote Gromyko, suggesting that they meet and engage in a constructive dialogue to encourage both parties to "act with restraint." Calling for the prompt withdrawal of all Soviet military forces from Afghanistan, he also noted that while the United States was "prepared to defend its interest," a "return to a neutral, non-aligned but genuinely independent Afghanistan would be in the interest of all."[37] A week later, on February 16, Gromyko rejected Vance's suggestion for any meetings. As to where the two nations would go in the future, Gromyko suggested, "The choice lies with the United States."[38]

Vance persisted. At an Oval Office meeting on February 28, he tried to convince the president that diplomatic talks should be undertaken at the highest levels. Perhaps the United States could demand a Soviet withdrawal in return for the United States dropping its Olympic boycott. Joining the debate, Mondale pointed out that a high-level diplomatic meeting would be confusing to the allies and politically devastating domestically. Relieved at Mondale's response, Brzezinski kept quiet until the president asked for his comment. Diplomatic contacts would send the wrong message to Moscow, he suggested, and be politically disastrous at home.[39]

The next day Brzezinski spelled out his concerns in a memo to the president. The Soviet leaders were not prepared at that time to extricate themselves from Afghanistan. Indeed, for them to accept a genuinely neutral Afghanistan three conditions would have to be met: a unified allied front, an aroused Islamic world, and continued Afghani resistance. Perhaps if these three conditions could be sustained for the next six to nine months, the Soviets might seriously consider a gracious accommodation.[40]

Carter's first response was to send Soviet president Leonid Brezhnev a sharp letter on March 1, 1980. The "essential step for a fresh start is to eliminate the presence of foreign troops from Afghanistan's soil," he wrote. But he went on to assure Brezhnev that the United States would ultimately support a neutral, nonaligned Afghanistan and pursue a policy of noninterference in Afghanistan—conditional, of course, on a complete Soviet withdrawal.[41]

Yet Vance, thinking that the president had agreed to send a high-level emissary to Moscow, wrote Carter on March 2 that Marshall Shulman would be ideal for that role. Brzezinski simply attached a cover note to Vance's letter. If anyone should go, he advised the president, it should be a relative hard-liner, not someone as soft as Shulman.[42] In an earlier memo he suggested that if he decided to opt for what he considered the more risky option and send an emissary to Moscow, it should be someone like Donovan, who was more of a hard-liner.[43]

There are differing recollections as to what happened next. According to Brzezinski, Moscow never agreed to arrange for Shulman to meet with Brezhnev, and does not recall whether a special emissary was sent to Moscow at that time.[44] In his memoir, former Soviet Ambassador Anatoly Dobrynin reports that Shulman did go to Moscow, but never got to see Brezhnev.[45] But Shulman, at a conference of former U.S. and Soviet decision makers in 1995, gave the final word on the matter: he never had gone to Moscow.[46]

Could Brzezinski pull something off on his own? Back in late February he had written the president that Dobrynin came to lunch at his house. Several days later, on March 18, he invited Dobrynin to his country house. There he gave the Soviet ambassador a very complicated plan for the possible neutralization of Afghanistan. He also made other suggestions for trouble spots in what he called the "arc of crisis."[47] Though Brzezinski had suggested earlier in his Weekly Report to the president that he might meet with the Soviet representative, it is unclear whether or not Vance was aware of this move. Certainly, Dobrynin saw the whole approach as "rather queer." The Soviet ambassador was quite aware that two weeks earlier Brzezinski had told several major American CEOs that the Soviets could mount a peace offensive with a partial withdrawal, but that it would be a trap the United States must avoid. In any event, Brzezinski's ideas were rejected by Moscow. They not only distrusted Brzezinski but had also become committed to Babrak Karmal, their new man in Kabul.[48]

Vance, Watson, and Shulman were not the only ones wanting to keep the lines of communication to the Soviet leadership open. In May, French President Valéry Giscard d'Estaing met with Brezhnev in Warsaw—an unexpected and unannounced move that drew immediate criticism from British Prime Minister Margaret Thatcher and the new U.S. Secretary of State, Edmund Muskie.[49]

Even more controversial than the French efforts at diplomacy were those of Helmut Schmidt of West Germany. Concerned that any such contacts would implicitly buttress the legitimacy of the Soviet invasion of Afghanistan, an angry Carter warned the German chancellor to carefully monitor his words with the Soviets, to maintain the integrity and unified front of the NATO alliance, and not to sway from the NATO plan to place additional nuclear missiles in West Germany. Schmidt tried to assure Carter by asking for a private meeting with him later that year in Venice, while promising that Brezhnev would hear loud and clear that the NATO allies could not be divided.[50] An aide to Schmidt remembers the chancellor as a tireless but often arrogant leader: "He's convinced most of the time that he's the only real leader in the Western world. He's probably right. The problem is he's German."[51]

The whole battle over whether or not the United States should continue to talk to the Soviets during this crisis was rooted in differing assumptions about what talking with the adversary meant. For Vance, Giscard, and Schultz, the desire to talk was based on a concern that the crisis should be limited and that possible accommodations be noted if they were mutual. For Brzezinski and Brement, the concern was that the expression of a U.S. desire along these lines would indicate that the United States was irresolute and that some soft words from the Soviets might cause the United States to compromise without gaining anything in return. Talking, for Brzezinski, as for many Americans, somehow brought up images of weakness and appeasement. One could not afford that in dealing with an adversary such as the USSR.

Enemy Images

Underlying these policy conflicts between Brzezinski and Vance were two different interpretations of possible Soviet goals in Afghanistan. Brzezinski differentiated the two schools of thought as follows: there were those who thought the Afghanistan invasion was abnormal as regards Soviet foreign policy, and those who believed that the goings-on in Afghanistan were indicative of Soviet goals. The former saw possible East–West peace, the latter felt that the Soviet Union was "currently in an assertive phase of its history, with the acquisition of military power giving its foreign policy both greater scope and more frequent temptations to use its power to advance policy goals."[52]

Brzezinski embraced the second of these two theories. The Soviets were becoming "more assertive," he wrote the president on January 9, 1980, and at the same time the United States was becoming "more acquiescent." World peace and stability since World War II had depended on the United States and its allies successfully meeting aggressive Soviet probes in two central strategic zones—Europe and the Far East. With the Soviet moves in the Middle East, the United States would now have to take a stand in this third strategic arena: "We are, if you will, in the third phase of the great architectural response that the United States launched in the wake of World War II."[53]

The Soviet move into Afghanistan, Brzezinski stated in an interview with the *Wall Street Journal* on January 15, 1980, was a major strategic stretch—an attempt to win dominance in the Middle East. Once it had consolidated its position in Afghanistan, the Soviet Union would be within striking distance of the Indian Ocean and even the Persian Gulf. Moreover, Iran and Pakistan, two vulnerable countries in the region, would be likely targets of Soviet political intimidation.[54]

Vance's view of possible Soviet motivations was more nuanced. One possibility was that the incursion was primarily local and defensive, an indication of Soviet insecurity. The spread of fundamentalist Islamic movements in Afghanistan would undermine Soviet influence in the region and weaken the Soviet hold over its own Muslim population in Central Asia. Rather than risk this kind of contagion effect, the Soviet government had decided to replace Amin's regime with a more compliant and competent government and send in their own troops to provide order and stability and push the insurgents back into more remote areas. The second possibility was that the Soviet Union, seeing how badly their relations with the United States were going, simply decided that since they had nothing to lose they should try to liquidate the Afghan problem and improve their strategic position in Southwest Asia and the Persian Gulf. Control in Afghanistan would allow them to exert greater pressure on U.S. allies such as Pakistan and to counter U.S. strategic moves in the area in response to what the Kremlin perceived as a pro-China tilt by Washington.

For Vance, both of these explanations had some validity. What he did reject was the view that Moscow's policy was the result of a grand design and monolithic decisional process.[55]

The two men, in conclusion, brought to this issue the same views that had colored all their earlier dealings with the Soviet Union. Vance saw the USSR as a state that had both complementary and competing interests with the United States. In such a situation, diplomacy could be used to avoid nuclear conflict and possibly resolve other differences on the basis of recognition of a complimentary interest. Brzezinski, on the other hand, seized on the invasion as proof that his worst-case analysis of Soviet goals and behavior had now been confirmed. The only possible counter was to increase diplomatic ties with adversaries of the Soviet Union and build a greater military presence in the area.

After the Afghan intervention, Carter fully accepted the Brzezinski line that to not stand up to the USSR would simply whet the Soviets' appetite for future aggressions. Taking a tough stance against the USSR would promote peace in the world. The Soviets would have to pay for their misadventure and to that end he would facilitate no easy out for them. "We will help to make sure that Afghanistan will be their Vietnam," he told Rosalynn.[56]

EXACTING A PRICE

Jimmy Carter noted with pride that he sometimes excelled where others did not. At one of his foreign policy breakfast meetings with advisors, he said, "There is a tendency on the frazzled edges of government to drift away from the tough decisions we made. I am not going to abide that. We cannot wince now or seem unsure of ourselves."[1] Later, he would even suggest in his diary that he was cooler about these matters than others were: "I have a lot of problems on my shoulders, but, strangely enough, I feel better as they pile up. My main concern is propping up the people around me who tend to panic (and who might possibly have a better picture of the situation than I do!)."[2]

Certainly Carter saw the Afghan crisis as a test of his mettle. Some of the moves his administration embraced, he wrote later, "would require substantial sacrifice and would be very difficult to implement, but we would not flinch from any one of them." Regarding draft registration, he "listened to all the arguments some advisors marshaled against the idea, but decided to proceed."[3] As to the grain embargo, Carter was aware of some of the political risks he was running. He told White House Chief of Staff Hamilton Jordan,

> God knows…I have walked the fields of Iowa and know those farmers and realize that I promised them in the seventy-six campaign that I would never embargo grains except in the case of a national emergency! But this is an emergency and I'm going to have to impose the embargo and we'll just have to make the best of it.[4]

Still, standing up to the USSR was not difficult at first. The Soviets' intervention in Afghanistan was their first obvious crossing of international boundaries since the 1968 invasion of Czechoslovakia, and a public that had been hearing about Soviet aggression looked for an assertive response by the United States. Going to the United Nations and building up a military presence in the Middle East was widely supported. The renunciation of diplomatic, political, and cultural ties with the Soviet Union was also met with wide approbation. Even Carter's most controversial sanction, the boycott of the 1980 Summer Olympic Games, produced an immediate "rally around the flag" response from the American public.[5] The U.S. House of Representatives and Senate both passed resolutions backing Carter's Olympic stance, and the Executive Board of the U.S. Olympic Committee voted unanimously to ask the International Olympic Committee (IOC) to move, postpone, or cancel the 1980 Summer Games.[6] A few days earlier, on January 16, Ed Sanders, a special aide to Hamilton Jordan, wrote Jordan and National Security Advisor Zbigniew Brzezinski, asking to whom in the administration should a petition signed by over 50,000 people be sent. The petition requested that an alternative site for the games be found.[7]

Carter's response led a leading foreign policy hawk and founding member of the Committee on the Present Danger to welcome Carter into their fold. Eugene Rostow of the Yale Law School wrote Secretary of State Cyrus Vance that the Soviet intervention in Afghanistan was an ominous event, signaling the first open exchange in a "hot war." It was the last clear chance for the United States to stop Soviet expansionism short of a broad war. Comparing the event to the Rhineland and Czech crises of the 1930s, he urged to the president to adopt every rational means to prolong and intensify the conflict in Afghanistan. Should the president so desire, the Committee on the Present Danger could help him.[8]

That Committee's publications elaborated on the opinion enunciated in Rostow's letter that the contemporary scene was similar to that facing the West prior to World War II. Any failure to take tough stances against the Soviets was comparable to the kinds of appeasement that had whetted Adolf Hitler's appetite for aggression. Except for the recommendation that the United States employ enhanced radiation weapons in Afghanistan, Carter had embraced or would embrace almost every recommendation made by the Committee.[9]

The Domestic Battles

There was some fallout on the partisan political front. The invasion occurred at the beginning of the 1980 presidential campaign. Not unexpectedly, presidential aspirants from both parties lined up on the campaign trail to take potshots at some of Carter's policies. Senator Ted Kennedy (D-MA), who was challenging Carter for the Democratic Party's nomination, suggested in a January 28 speech at Georgetown University that Carter had overreacted by characterizing the Soviet action as "the greatest threat to peace since World War II." This action, Kennedy wryly suggested, did not overshadow the Berlin Blockade, the Cuban Missile Crisis, and the Korean War.[10]

Two sanctions in particular—the grain embargo against the USSR and the boycott of the Summer Olympics—provided the grist for the Republican Party political mills. Kansas senator and presidential contender Bob Dole commented, "Carter took a poke at the Soviet Bear and knocked out the American farmer." The candidate with the strongest anti-Soviet reputation, Ronald Reagan, quipped that "pigs, cows, and chickens" had not invaded Afghanistan. He offered the opinion that "no one segment of the economy should be asked to bear the brunt of American countermeasures" against the Soviets.[11] And though he had initially supported the Olympic boycott, Reagan would later critique that decision. "I would leave that decision to the athletes themselves," Reagan said. "I don't believe our government should be in the position of saying...you can't leave the country."[12] Except for John B. Anderson, every candidate for the Republican nomination eventually opposed the grain embargo.[13]

On these two issues Carter encountered as much resistance at home as he did abroad. Farmers were concerned about suffering economic losses and not at all sure that the USSR would suffer as a result of their sacrifice as other nations rushed to fill the grain void and meet Soviet needs. Olympic athletes saw years of intensive training going to waste, and some officials thought that the boycott would politicize an event that should be beyond politics. Even the military buildup in south Asia presented problems, as bureaucratic considerations got in the way of an expeditious resolution of the new commitments.

Once the die had been cast, all of Carter's aides rallied around the president's choices. Vice President Walter Mondale hit the campaign trail in Iowa, assuring farmers that the president would not let them suffer major economic losses as the result of his decisions.[14] Secretary of Agriculture Robert Bergland went to work with a few aides to counter any potential fall in grain prices.[15] To prevent a panic reaction to the presidential decision on the grain market, the U.S. Commodity Futures Trading Commission suspended all grain futures transactions. To maintain grain prices, the government agreed to purchase grain contracts signed with the Soviet Union before the embargo was implemented.[16] Bergland also worked to sell U.S. wheat to Mexico and China.[17]

The administration, however, faced difficulties in persuading other grain-producing countries to go along with the embargo.[18] Just as Bergland had predicted, Argentina was soon exporting grains to the Soviet Union. On January 10 the Argentine government deplored the embargo initiative as "punitive actions ... that come from decision-making centers not of our country." Four days later, Brazil joined Argentina in resistance to the grain embargo.[19] Even some friendly countries—Canada, Australia, and several members of the European community—refused to follow the U.S. lead. The prime minister of France, Raymond Barre, explained on February 7 that his country did not wish to contribute to any reawakening of the Cold War by adopting an extremist attitude. Chancellor Helmut Schmidt of West Germany was also resistant to the effort. As Carter noted in a February 25, 1980 memo to Vance and Brzezinski, "Overall I see nothing encouraging here. The FRG [Federal Republic of Germany] opposes any sanctions against Iran or the Soviets, are continuing business as usual with the Soviet Union, refuse to commit publicly to Olympic boycott, and privately are very critical of us."[20] West Germany never committed to the grain embargo, an action Carter attributed to Schmidt's concerns about critiques from the left in his approaching reelection campaign. Torn between competing political forces in Germany, Schmidt was very reluctant to take anti-Soviet stances in public.[21]

Nor did the grain embargo have its desired impact on the USSR. As Brzezinski noted in a memo to Carter on June 27, 1980, the grain exports from other countries were increasing, and the Soviet Union might "have a bumper crop" that fall. At home, the embargo was "doing serious political danger to the Administration among the farmers." But Brzezinski was concerned that the administration would face serious political problems by reversing its policies. Secretary of Agriculture Bergland and Domestic Policy Advisor Stuart Eizenstat, he reported, thought that a change in policy should be pegged to some wider accommodation with the Soviet Union. But Deputy National Security Advisor David Aaron warned that the administration should not consider dropping the grain embargo: "To do so in this context would prove more damaging politically, even with the farmers, than any conceivable political gain." Brzezinski agreed with him.[22] Carter did not move on the matter, leaving the issue to be dealt with later. The next president, Ronald Reagan, would lift the embargo in April 1982.[23]

The Olympic Boycott

Those most directly affected by the boycott of the 1980 Summer Olympic Games would also create problems for Carter. As early as January 3, Robert Kane, the president and executive director of the U.S. Olympic Committee (USOC), objected to the "use of Olympic Games as a vehicle for international politics."[24] Lord Killian, president of the International Olympic Committee (IOC), insisted in Dublin on January 16 that the IOC would be "legally bound to hold the games in Moscow, and that is where they will be held. There is no question of them being changed."[25] On February 12, the IOC announced that they had found no Soviet violation of Olympic rules and that the Summer Games would take place in Moscow as scheduled.[26]

Attempts to arrange an alternative set of games came to naught. Counsel to the President Lloyd Cutler had been put in charge of coordinating an alternative tournament to the Olympics.[27] But in March, when the USOC met with its European counterparts in Geneva to consider an alternative site or competition to the Moscow Games, only twelve nations showed up.[28]

At home, American athletes were not enthusiastic about the loss of the opportunity to show, after years of dedication and training, that in one sport or another they were the best in the world. In a meeting with 150 American athletes and coaches in the East Room of the White House on March 21, Carter insisted that they had no choice but to honor the boycott. Quoting a German political leader, Carter noted, "If only the Olympics had not been held in Berlin in 1936, the course of history could have been different. We face a similar prospect now. I am determined to keep our national interest paramount, even if people that I love and admire, like you, are required to share in disappointment, and in personal sacrifice." Then his blue eyes turned icy. "I cannot say that other nations will not go. Ours will not go." The president won only grudging applause.[29]

When polled later in the Hay-Adams Hotel, forty-four of ninety-seven athletes opposed the boycott action. Only twenty-nine were in favor of it, and there were twenty-four agonized abstentions.[30]

To bring the athletes around, Carter's main legal remedy consisted of the extreme step of invoking the Economic Emergency Controls Act.[31] He could, however, exercise other moral and financial persuasions. Threats were made to revoke the tax-exempt status of the USOC, and to block federal subsidies to the USOC. Sponsoring organizations were urged to reduce or withhold contributions to the USOC unless it backed a boycott. When the voluntary ban on exports for the Olympics created legal problems for American businesses, Carter empowered Secretary of Commerce Juanita Kreps to stop the export of goods and technology and block payments or transactions made for the Soviet Olympics. With this move NBC, which was to broadcast the games, had a legal excuse for not fulfilling their insurance policy obligations.[32]

To counter continuing resistance, Carter brought out the heavy artillery. In April he threatened to use the Economic Emergency Controls Act to prevent U.S. athletes from traveling to Moscow. Team members were told that their passports would be withheld if they attempted to go to the games.[33] Finally, on April 14, the USOC House of Delegates voted 1,604–797 in favor of the boycott. Still, one of the two Americans on the IOC called the vote "disastrous" and accused the USOC of buckling under "political pressure."[34] And nineteen U.S. would-be Olympians filed suit, challenging the legality of the USOC's decision to boycott the games. The trial court dismissed the lawsuit on a common procedural ground—failure to state a claim for which relief can be granted. The Circuit Court for the District of Columbia affirmed the lower court's decision in an unpublished opinion.[35]

Resistance to the boycott from athletes abroad compounded the president's problems. As Carter noted, most Olympic committees were independent bodies and their members did not like any government intervention in their policymaking.[36] Carter himself solicited support from Chancellor Schmidt of West Germany. In a handwritten note on January 25, 1980, he argued, "Withholding participation in the Moscow Olympic Games is the most significant and effective action we can take to convince the Soviet leaders of the seriousness of their invasion of Afghanistan." Would Schmidt, he queried, use his regional influence to pressure other Western European allies—especially President Valéry Giscard d'Estaing of France—to boycott the Moscow Games alongside the United States?[37]

That night, a somewhat ambivalent Schmidt pledged that he would do his utmost to ensure that Germany would ultimately "fall on the right side." Two weeks later, Schmidt reported that he was not optimistic about the French. The public there was against the U.S. boycott. France, he explained, was a nation that was "a little bit touchier than…the Germans.""Or any other nation," responded Carter.[38]

When the Olympic committees of sixteen European nations met in Brussels in early April, only Norway pledged to boycott the games.[39] A month later, at a follow-up on the German situation, Schmidt told Carter that the decision of the French Olympic Committee not to honor the boycott a few days earlier was making it likely that the German association might also decide to go to Moscow. When Carter expressed his dismay at this development, the German chancellor explained that there was nothing further he could do about it.

The next day, in a twist of fate, the German Committee voted 59–40 to boycott the Moscow Games. In a phone call that night, a jubilant Carter praised Schmidt's political maneuvering.[40]

At the end, eighty nations participated in the Moscow Olympics, the smallest number to do so since 1956. Sixty-five nations did not accept their invitations, with as many as fifty of those nations doing so because of the U.S. boycott. Even after pressures from their own governments, the French, British, Italians, Austrians, Belgians, Irish, Dutch, and Swedish committees stuck to their decisions to attend the games. Some governments allowed their athletes to compete in Moscow only under the condition that they march under the international Olympic flag rather than their respective national flags.[41] Japan and Germany were the only two major U.S. allies to boycott the games completely. Brzezinski noted that the boycott was "totally successful in East Asia....The four most important nations in the world...the United States, China, Germany, and Japan—are not attending."[42]

The U.S. message was particularly costly to some of its athletes. On July 30, 1980, Craig Beardsley set the world record in the 200-meter butterfly race at the U.S. Nationals—a time faster than Sergei Fesenko's gold medal effort in Moscow. But the American never won an Olympic medal nor reaped the benefit of being an American swimmer who won a big race behind the Iron Curtain. Even swimmer Tracy Caulkins, who later won four gold medals at the 1984 Los Angeles Olympic Games, was disappointed that she missed forever a chance to compete against the strong Soviet and East German swimmers. Retaliating for the snub at Moscow, both countries boycotted the Los Angeles Games. Both swimmers would demonstrate anger at the boycott some twenty years later, pointing out that the Soviet Union did not pull out of Afghanistan until 1989.[43]

Jimmy Carter himself would experience personal fallout from his decision. When an announcement was made in 1996 that Carter would carry the Olympic Torch in Georgia at the Atlanta Games, John Ruger, chair of the USOC Athletes' Advisory Council, promptly contacted Carter staff in Plains, Georgia. Shortly thereafter, the former president announced that he would not carry the Olympic Torch in Georgia, as he would be on an international trip.[44]

The Military Buildup

Several of the new military policies were simple to put into place. U.S. forces in the Persian Gulf and Indian Ocean were reinforced. The Soviets were cut off from any high-technology exports from the United States. New military equipment was sent to China, including over-the-horizon radar equipment.

However, obtaining results from the U.S. bureaucracy on some aspects of security framework was like "pulling teeth." Brzezinski wrote Carter on May 16, 1980, "[The Department of] State is fearful of military power projected into the region. Defense is unable to act expeditiously, lacks funds, especially for operations and exercises, and cannot break through service rivalries to build a command structure for the region....Nevertheless," he assured the president, "progress has been made."[45]

Difficulties existed also in dealing with Pakistan. In a National Security Council meeting on December 28, 1979, the inner circle tentatively decided to send Deputy Secretary of State Warren Christopher to meet with Pakistan's dictator, General Mohammed Zia-ul-Haq, who had come to power in a bloodless coup in July 1977. Commissioned in the British Army and trained at the U.S. Army Command and General Staff College in Kansas, he knew how to bargain. He also knew American slang: when the United States announced its $400 million package of military and economic aid, Zia called it "peanuts."

To get Zia on board with their plans, Brzezinski and Christopher made a trip to Islamabad in early February 1980. The Pakistanis were assured that the United States would back them against any intervention from the USSR, though Brzezinski demurred when it came to making guarantees relative to all of Pakistan's neighbors—including rival India, with whom Pakistan had serious disputes over Kashmir.

At the Khyber Pass, the historic gateway for battles between Britain and Russia in the nineteenth century, Brzezinski made U.S. goals explicit. "You should know that the entire world is outraged," he told a group of refugees. "That land over there is yours. You will go back to it one day, because your fight will prevail and you'll have...your mosques back again, because your cause is right and God is on your side." The U.S. objective, claimed Brzezinski (as quoted in a later CNN report), was to make the Soviets bleed as much and as long as was possible.[46]

Stopping off in Riyadh on the way back to Washington, Brzezinski also facilitated Saudi arms exports to Pakistan. U.S. arms and other support for the *mujahideen* in Afghanistan were relayed there via Pakistan's Interservices Intelligence Agency. Zia had made this assistance a part of his deal with the Americans.[47]

Eventually, the Rapid Deployment Forces, which Brzezinski had been urging Carter to develop for some time, were created. Joint military maneuvers with Egypt were undertaken. And in his adoption of Presidential Directive 59 in the summer of 1980, Carter formally embraced a nuclear war fighting strategy vis-à-vis the Soviet Union (to be detailed in chapter 21). The White House, as Brzezinski saw it, was following a consistent foreign policy line in 1980. The result, from Brzezinski's perspective, was a correction in the world's view of America having a tendency to hesitate on the international stage.[48]

On Soviet Objectives

Did the Soviet decision to invade Afghanistan justify Carter's response? Retrospective accounts of former Soviet officials suggest that the Politburo had no grand design in mind at the time of its decision. According to Anatoly Dobrynin, the Soviet ambassador to the United States, a small group in that body made the Soviet decision. In early December 1979, KGB Chief Yuri V. Andropov and Defense Minister Dimitri Ustinov, along with Foreign Minister Andrei Gromyko, convinced Soviet president Leonid Brezhnev that resolute steps had to be taken in order "not to lose Afghanistan." This small group then secured the approval of the whole Politburo at a Kremlin secret meeting on December 12.

Brezhnev bought the proposal, Dobrynin suggests, because he saw it as an easy and powerful move. But his own commitment to the Soviet occupation was apparently not total. In early 1980 at a Politburo meeting, Dobrynin raised the question of a partial withdrawal. But the troika of Andropov, Ustinov, and Gromyko convinced him that Babrak Karmal was not strong enough and would be overthrown without the support of Soviet troops. Only Ideological Chief Mikhail Andreevich Suslov and Boris

Ponomarev, secretary of the Central Committee and head of its institutional department, saw this as an "opportunity to enlarge the sphere of Marxist ideology."[49]

The plan to use troops was even opposed by the Soviet general staff and by military
officers who knew Afghanistan firsthand. Charged with preparing a plan for the invasion, Generals Nikolai Garcon, Sergey Akhromeyev, and Valentin Varennikov sent a
report to Defense Minister Ustinov warning of the dangers of inserting Soviet regular
troops into a protracted civil war in difficult and mountainous terrain inhabited by
warring tribes. Ustinov responded by reprimanding them severely: "Since when are our
military to determine foreign policy?" Ustinov commanded them to "stop reasoning"
and urgently prepare the plan for military operation.

A similar exchange occurred at one Politburo meeting, according to a former Soviet
military leader. Nikolai Ogarkov, the Soviet chief of staff, tried to express some concerns regarding the operation. He was silenced by then KGB Chief Andropov who
said, "Comrade Ogarkov, we invited you here not because we wanted to hear your opinion. You should take notes and follow orders." Viktor Kulikov, the first deputy of the
Defense Ministry and commander in chief of the Warsaw Treaty Force, and his deputy
Anatoly Gribkov, also saw the whole operation as reckless.[50]

On the diplomatic side, no one in the Soviet embassy in Washington was asked
about possible repercussions. Gromyko did not consult Dobrynin even though he was
in Moscow at the time.[51] In Kabul, the Soviet embassy opposed the invasion.[52]

In short, Dobrynin argues, "There was no grand strategic plan designed by Moscow
to seize a new footing on the way to the oil riches of the Middle East and thus gain
global superiority over the United States.... [The invasion] was a Soviet reaction to
a local situation in which the security of our southern borders was threatened by the
growing instability inside Afghanistan itself and the obvious ineptitude of the Amin
government," as well as by troubles in neighboring Iran.[53] In any case, it can be unambiguously stated that the appearance of Soviet troops in Afghanistan was not the result of a
conscious choice between expansionism and détente made by the Kremlin leadership.

The Soviet Union also misunderstood the nature of the U.S. response to its intervention in Afghanistan. Summoned back to Moscow for a consultation, Dobrynin
discovered that members of the politburo saw the U.S. "overreaction" as due either to
the emotional instability of Carter himself or to Brzezinski's domination over him.
Dobrynin tried to correct those perceptions, explaining that Carter and Brzezinski
were now as one, having convinced the American people that the Soviet Union was the
aggressor in Afghanistan and was trying to expand against U.S. interests in the Middle
East. A political dialogue with Carter at the time was beyond reach, he suggested, and
the Soviet Union should try for constructive exchanges elsewhere.[54]

As for Carter, he could not know exactly what the Soviet motivation might be.
Central Intelligence Agency reports suggesting that the move had not been part of a
grand design were supportive of Vance's perspective. Caveats in the report, however,
noted that the intervention provided the Soviets with new targets of opportunity relative to Iran and Southwest Asia.[55] A minority report by CIA Director Turner provided
additional support for hard-liners in the administration. In a cover note, Turner argued

that the Soviets, despite the doctrine of détente, had been probing the limits of U.S. tolerance.[56]

The Fallout

The Carter policies relative to Afghanistan succeeded in terms of two major objectives. Though it was unlikely that the Soviets would have used Afghanistan as a base for a drive to the Indian Ocean, the Carter administration made it clear that any decision along these lines would have resulted in a military encounter with the United States and its allies in the region. The second objective—to turn Afghanistan into the Soviet's Vietnam—did indeed bloody the USSR. Soviet troops in the mountainous terrain of Afghanistan would win their battles, only to lose control of the territories they had conquered shortly thereafter. Only after enormous costs in rubles and men and the ascension to power of Mikhail Gorbachev would the Soviets pull out of a clearly losing situation.

The United States would, however, later experience blowback from the operation. As Stephen Kinzer has pointed out, the United States "never played or sought to play a role in deciding who received the U.S. gifts." Rather, as matters evolved, the United States funneled funds and weapons via Pakistan to fundamentalist Islamists, many of whom were anti-American.

Moreover, the Saudis, who were brought in to fund the operations, had their own goals to pursue. Prince Turki bin-Faisal al-Saud, the head of the Saudi intelligence agency, sent Osama bin Laden to Afghanistan in the early 1980s where he would organize thousands of poor Muslim men, attracted by food and money, into the cause of the fundamentalist Wahabi crusade. The defeat of the Soviets only convinced him that he and other Islamic radicals could take on another superpower.[57] In an October 2001 interview, bin Laden suggested that Allah had helped Muslims drive out the Soviets after a long struggle and, he hoped, would again assist in driving out another superpower, the United States.[58]

"For God's sake," one Afghan warned Americans in the early 1980s, "You're financing your own assassins."[59]

As for Carter, in the spring of 1980 he began to look like a driven man. The Japanese ambassador told Dobrynin that Carter "was pressing for 'punitive action' against Moscow with intensity unparalleled in his diplomatic career." The ambassador noted that in his experience of anti-Soviet campaigns in the United States, he had "never encountered anything like the intensity and scale of this one." What particularly impressed him was "the president's personal obsession with Afghanistan."[60]

Vance found the whole turn of events demoralizing. In a meeting with Dobrynin in early April 1980, he rather bitterly reflected on how politically corrupt Washington had become. No longer were there any human relationships; everyone was eager to cut the ground from under others in a merciless struggle for power—or what seemed to be power. Even when speaking with Gromyko about his meeting in Vienna, taking place in May, Vance's voice was "uncharacteristically dull and he expressed no hope or wishes for the meeting." In a later encounter with Dobrynin, he noted painfully and with regret that "his personal struggle for better relations with Moscow had produced no positive results." For the first time, he frankly admitted that other forces were gaining the upper hand in Washington.[61]

Though the immediate cause of Vance's resignation on April 21, 1980, was his opposition to the U.S. rescue operations to free the hostages held in Iran, his pessimism about the future course of U.S.-Soviet relations must have played a role in his decision. At an April 29 meeting with Dobrynin, Vance confided that Carter had embraced a policy of confrontation relative to the Soviet Union that would continue into his second term if he was reelected. At a farewell dinner with Dobrynin at Vance's home, the two men spoke of their collaboration in the previous three years, and there was a mutual exchange of feelings of friendship. Dobrynin would later note in his memoir that he felt sorry that a man of such caliber had to leave during "such troubled times."[62]

A few other long-time Soviet watchers were not happy about the direction this new policy was taking. At the time of Vance's resignation, Tom Watson Jr., an arms control supporter and the U.S. ambassador to the Soviet Union, wrote the secretary of State:

> Dear Cy,
>
> Afghanistan was an unfortunate aberration and I'm sure a great disappointment to you and Marshall as it was to all. It is also proving to be a very bad decision for the Sov[iet]s. Knowing you as I do, I know that this incident will not deter you from the consistency and even-handedness you have demonstrated for a long time.
>
> We simply have to get back to the job of learning to live reasonably normally with the Soviets again even though we can never make them into friends or even understand them very well. We recommended or tracked most of the tough steps taken in early January but the contrived dribbles of new actions or threats are not constructive and you know better than I that it could be possible to goad the Soviets into serious erratic actions.
>
> From what I read and hear in Moscow, many of the greatest opponents of SALT II [the Strategic Arms Limitation Treaty] now began to wish it was in force. We are searching for ways to get arms control talks going again here and hope to have some ideas soon. Meanwhile, I wanted you to know that I believe 100% in the policies you have been following and am honored to be serving you here. Particular thanks for keeping me so well informed.
>
> Sincerely,
> Tom Watson, Jr.[63]

Henry Cabot Lodge, formerly a Republican senator from Massachusetts and President Dwight Eisenhower's ambassador to the United Nations, wrote Vance in the summer of 1980 that the "failure to ratify the SALT II treaty is a disgrace."[64] Also unhappy at the turn of U.S.-Soviet relations, Foreign Policy Task Force Chairman W. Averell Harriman, by this time eighty-nine years old, sought a meeting with Dobrynin. In their session in mid-June 1980, he suggested that the Soviets should try a dramatic gesture such as an announcement of a troop reduction. But as long as the Afghanistan war continued, he warned Dobrynin, people such as he would be helpless to remedy the situation at home. Carter, he posited, appeared to have been "hypnotized by his loquacious aide" Zbigniew Brzezinski.[65]

Even Press Secretary Jody Powell was worried. Carter was being challenged by Ted Kennedy in the Democratic primaries, and the president's ties to Brzezinski were creating a potential problem for him within his own political base. Brzezinski, Powell wrote the president on May 1, 1980, should be encouraged to confine his public pronouncements:

> To put it bluntly, Zbig needs to almost drop from public view for the next few months at least. He needs to stay away from on-the-record interviews, particularly on-camera interviews. He should pick a few columnists to cultivate privately, and we can use him during the summer to speak to constituency briefings here and to ethnic groups around the country. Unless we can get him pulled back now, he may destroy himself over the next few months and severely damage you in the process.[66]

Would a new secretary of state make a difference? Edmund Muskie, who was named to the position after Vance's resignation, had secured from the president a promise that he would be his chief foreign policymaker and spokesman. But the president, when asked about his new secretary, made a somewhat puzzling statement. He hoped Muskie would play a somewhat different role than Vance had. Muskie, he said, would be a "much stronger and more statesman-like senior citizen figure who will be a more evocative spokesman for our national policy." He would be less likely to get "'bogged down' in administrative details and protocol than his predecessor."[67] It seems Brzezinski had nothing to fear. As the administration built up its military organization and nuclear-war-fighting capabilities in the remaining months in office, Muskie would find himself sidelined, much as Vance had before him.

Part 5

RENEWAL OF THE COLD WAR

MAD AND THE PURSUIT OF PD-59

The administration of President Jimmy Carter embraced, as CIA director Stansfield Turner has noted, "a series of policies on nuclear weapons that laid the whole foundation for Reagan's expansion of nuclear weapons, and war-fighting, and war-winning capabilities."[1] Foremost among these was Presidential Directive 59, issued on July 25, 1980. A recently partially declassified portion of that doctrine reads as follows:

> Our strategic nuclear forces must be able to deter nuclear attacks on our own country but also on our forces overseas, as well as on our friends and allies, and to contribute to deterrence of non-nuclear attacks.... To this end and so as to preserve the possibility of bargaining effectively to terminate the war on acceptable terms that are as favorable as practical, if deterrence fails initially, we must be capable of fighting successfully so that the adversary would not achieve his war aims and would suffer costs that are unacceptable, or in any event greater than his gains, from having initiated an attack.[2]

In early August, when news of the policy became public, the Soviet news agency Tass exploded: "Only rabid militarists who have lost all touch with reality and are prepared to push the world into the abyss of nuclear holocaust...can conceive and sanction such plans now."[3]

Liberals within Carter's own party were almost as critical. The whole program was "apocalyptic nonsense," charged Paul Warnke, who had earlier resigned as head of the Arms Control and Disarmament Agency. Senator Edward Kennedy (D-MA) noted that it would make nuclear wars more likely, creating incentives for the parties to launch preemptive strikes. Others purported to see a "hidden agenda"—that the purpose of PD 59 was to build a case for the support of the MX missile. Kennedy and other liberals, concerned about basing mode issues and other aspects of the experimental missile, had threatened to put a plank critical of it on the Democratic platform for 1980. Carter's new presidential directive would counter these moves, making it clear that precise and mobile MX missiles would be vital to the overall nuclear strategy.[4] By signing PD 59, liberal opponents claimed, Carter was attempting to "out-Republican" the Republicans.[5]

Indeed, with this decision, the president was countering a barrage of Republican criticisms that claimed he was weak on defense. Ronald Reagan, who would become the standard bearer of the party, had argued in a speech before the Chicago Council on Foreign Relations in the spring of 1980 that the United States should embrace a counterforce strategy. What was needed, he said, was a "clear capability" to destroy missile silos and other Soviet military targets.[6] The Republican Party, in its platform, charged that Carter cut back, canceled, or delayed every strategic initiative proposed by former president Gerald Ford. He canceled production of the Minuteman missile and the B-1 bomber and delayed the production of all cruise missiles, the MX missile, and the Trident missile.[7]

Mutual Assured Destruction

PD 59 countered the whole notion of Mutual Assured Destruction (MAD), which had been U.S. policy since the sixties. At the beginning of the nuclear age, military strategist Klaus Knorr had argued that nuclear weapons were so destructive that the likely cost of their usage would always undermine their possible utility as an instrument of influence.[8] This became a major problem for the United States when the USSR in the 1960s acquired the nuclear weapons and the delivery system that would enable them to attack the U.S. mainland. The administrations of former presidents John F. Kennedy and Lyndon Johnson dealt with this problem via the policy of Mutual Assured Destruction. Defense secretary Robert McNamara argued that the United States and the Soviet Union each had an interest in maintaining the invulnerability of some of its weapons systems so each could ride out a first strike and respond. But the retaliation would be against not the weapons of the adversary or the control centers of the adversary, but rather against the cities and the economy. Each nation, assured that it could deliver an immense second strike that would result in massive destruction of the initiating country, would have no rational incentive to strike first.[9]

Ironically, the United States would continue to rely on nuclear threats to deter a Soviet assault in arenas where it might be vulnerable in terms of conventional arms. Given the fact that decision makers may in actual instances be reluctant to risk the destruction any such exchange could unleash, these deterrence threats had to be made more or less automatically. The president would make public commitments to their usage in certain situations; and the United States would place troops in Europe as a tripwire to guarantee a response should any European ally be attacked. These were all measures for burning one's bridges behind one. The "doomsday" machine in Stanley Kubrick's film *Dr. Strangelove* (1962) was the ultimate fantasy weapon along these lines. Decision making would be taken out of the hands of human beings. Unlike them, machines would not falter, preprogrammed as they were to unleash the awful weapons after a certain point of no return had been reached.

The very certainty that such a disaster would occur should the other side cross the preset fault line, it was assumed, made it less likely that such an aggression would take place.[10] Moreover, the targeting policies accompanying this doctrine provided a possible cap to the arms race. Each side needed only a sufficient number of weapons to exact massive damage on the cities and other civilian targets of the adversary should deterrence fail.

Carter himself, in some of his earlier statements, had embraced the MAD idea. In his speech at the United Nations on October 4, 1977, he had noted that nuclear war could "no longer be measured with the archaic concepts of victory and defeat."[11] He

Table 6.   Strategic Concepts

Deterrence	Strategy in which a government builds up or maintains defense and intelligence systems with the aim of discouraging others from attacking it. Usually assumes that defense lines are explicitly drawn and possible reactions communicated in advance if the deterrence lines are crossed by the adversary.
First Strike	Assumes an ability to take out most of the adversary's weapons if one strikes first with nuclear weapons and thus the adversary's ability for a massive second retaliatory strike.
Invulnerability	Nuclear weapons cannot be destroyed by another country's first strike because they are protected by hardening of cover, mobility, or hiding.
MAD	Mutual Assured Destruction: doctrine that the use of nuclear weapons by one side would result in massive retaliation against its own counter-value targets, such as cities and industrial sites. Nuclear war would automatically result in massive damages for both sides. Knowing the consequences, neither side will initiate nuclear usage.
Nuclear War Fighting	Doctrine that one can engage in and control an extended exchange of nuclear weapons. Ultimately the goal may be to decapitate the control system of the other side and thus prevail. In some scenarios the top level decision makers would be spared so they could make the necessary concessions. Capability for this kind of war is seen by some as enhancing deterrence.
Second strike	Assured ability to respond at a nuclear level to a first nuclear attack by an adversary.
Vulnerability	Weapons systems that can be destroyed in a first strike by an adversary.
Window of vulnerability	Idea proposed in the late seventies that, for a period of time, American land-based missiles were vulnerable, i.e., could be taken out by Soviet first strike.

told Soviet President and General Secretary Leonid Brezhnev and Minister of Defense Dmitriy Ustinov at the Vienna Summit in the summer of 1979 that he favored a nuclear balance in which both the United States and the Soviet Union would have invulnerabilities for some weapon systems—enabling each to ride out a first strike and retaliate. Otherwise, either party might consider it advantageous, in a crisis situation, to strike first, to use the weapons rather than run the risk of losing them.[12]

PD 59 marked a departure from this type of thinking. As Secretary of Defense Harold Brown saw it, deterrence was enhanced by the U.S. ability to target the highest values of the Soviet leaders: their lives, positions of authority, and control over regional populations that gave them their power. This attack on their highest values would provide a powerful inducement for them not to start any nuclear war.[13] As NSC Crisis Coordinator William Odom later noted, Secretary Brown considered PD

59 a "countervailing strategy," one in which the United States, if provoked, would use nuclear weapons as a legitimate response and would do so in a way that would avoid losing.[14]

PD 59, in short, provided the basis for a more assertive foreign policy. With an array of possible responses, the United States might utilize the nuclear threat to deter Soviet incursion around the world. The argument was that if the U.S. government had the ability to respond in a measured way at the nuclear level, Soviet leaders would realize that the United States would not hesitate to respond to any first move they might make. Given this recognition, the Soviet Union would be reluctant to ever initiate the process. The policy, as National Security Advisor Zbigniew Brzezinski would later explain, was based on the need to understand Soviet ways of thinking about nuclear weapons and the need to adapt U.S. policies to that way of thinking.[15] The United States, as he saw it, had managed to fashion "a new geopolitical doctrine, a revised nuclear strategy and a foreign policy in which our continued commitment to principle was reinforced by a more credible emphasis on American power."[16]

Later, at a conference of U.S. and Soviet decision makers in 1995, other Carter advisors would try differentiating the new policy goals from those embraced by president Ronald Reagan. Carter's chief of policy planning at the Department of State, Leslie Gelb, mentioned that this was not the same as Reagan's "prevailing" strategy. Carter's policy was just a variation on the themes of McNamara and Former Secretary of Defense in the Ford Administration James Schlesinger.[17] Even Carter's CIA Director Turner claimed that the United States was simply targeting Soviet silos in Eastern Europe, not Russia proper. The new technology built as a result of PD 59 would be used to address this threat; it would not be used as the "awful binary choice"—deterrence or "blowing up half the world"—but to protect interests in Europe. As proof of this, the United States was moving its targeting away from Soviet cities and industry.[18]

Paving the Way

The new secretary of state had no part in making the new policy. Edmund Muskie told reporters that he did not know about the shift in nuclear strategy until he read about it in the newspapers. As journalist Bernard Gwertzman notes, "It was taken by some observers as an admission that he had accumulated little power in the last three months."[19]

Not until the Muskie/Brown/Brzezinski meeting on August 5, ten days after PD 59 had been signed, was the secretary of state even briefed on the new policy departure.[20] Earlier, in a memo to Carter detailing the events leading up to his situation, Brzezinski implied that there had been enough public markers that Muskie should have known about the policy and that Brzezinski had planned to distribute a sanitized version of the directive shortly after its announcement. But the Defense Department had added some preplanned options, making it a more sensitive document, and Deputy Assistant for National Security Affairs David Aaron convinced Brzezinski to hold onto the memo until after the Democratic Convention in early August, during which a platform fight on the issues would probably take place. Instead, Brzezinski left instructions that Secretary Brown should orally brief the secretary of state and the director of central intelligence as soon as possible.[21]

Still, the groundwork for a new policy had been in the work for some time. Presidential Review Memorandum 10, which Carter signed on April 20, 1977, called for a complete review of U.S. foreign and strategic weapons policies. Samuel Huntington, at that time a National Security Council (NSC) staff member, oversaw the whole review process while the Department of Defense dealt with weapons and other such issues. A colleague and friend of Brzezinski's, Huntington distrusted not only the Soviet Union but also broader publics that might try to influence foreign policy. The study that he oversaw provided Carter's rationale for PD 18, issued in August 1977, which argued that the United States should build up its reserve nuclear capabilities as a means to ending a nuclear war on the best possible terms. If deterrence failed, the nation should be able to end a nuclear war on the best possible terms.[22]

In the meantime, Brzezinski's deputy William Odom met with a group of officials from the Pentagon and the White House to build support for the new doctrine and develop a draft for a policy directive along these lines. By 1978 Leon Sloss, a State Department employee, was working out of the Department of Defense, reporting to Secretary Harold Brown via Brown's aide Walter Slocombe. The project he worked on, *Nuclear Targeting Policy Review*, outlined some ways in which the United States might prevail in a strategic exchange with the Soviet Union.[23] General support for the policy appeared in Brown's posture statement to the U.S. Congress in January 1980. That spring the defense secretary formally approved of the specific positions taken in PD 59.[24]

The president, in the meantime, had been approving a series of policy directives that moved the United States incrementally toward a general nuclear war-fighting plan. In 1977 there was the aforementioned PD 18. A year later, PD 36 envisaged a shift from economic (countervalue) targets to military and political (counterforce) targets. PD 41, issued in September 1978, ordered the development of U.S. civil defense, a requisite of any endeavor to make the resort to nuclear war a viable option, and PD 53, issued in November 1979, ordered the development of plans for the maintenance of a communication system after nuclear attacks, a requisite of rational decision making in a series of controlled responses. PD 58, issued in June 1980, provided for continuity of government in case of such an attack. PD 62 and PD 63 would follow later in January 1981, further defining the U.S. commitments in the Persian Gulf.[25]

The Carter administration also sought an increase in the defense budget and the development of new weapons that would enhance capabilities for a possible U.S. first strike. In May 1977, Carter ordered the deployment of the Mark 12A warhead and NS 20 guidance systems on Minutemen III missiles, enhancing the U.S. ability to take out Soviet military forces. Later, when Carter decided not to deploy the neutron bomb—a weapon that could actually be used in the defense of Europe—he opted for another weapons system that would enhance deterrence, as he saw it, by enhancing U.S. allies' offensive abilities in Europe. As he wrote West German chancellor Helmut Schmidt, "The Alliance needs to deploy new, medium-range nuclear systems in Europe capable of reaching Soviet territory—such as Pershing II missiles, cruise missiles, or a combination of the two." These weapons, he continued, would "strengthen deterrence by providing credible escalation options, and maintain the perception in both East and West of a firm U.S. commitment to the defense of Europe. Deployments in West Germany would be a necessary part to this step."[26]

Each of these new weapons systems created problems for the nuclear stability associated with MAD doctrine. The land-based MX missile provided the accuracy needed for an effective retaliatory hard-target strike.[27] But they were vulnerable, and thus one would be tempted to use them in an uncertain situation. To deal with this problem, Carter announced on September 9, 1979, that the MX would be based on mobile launchers in Utah and Idaho. Since these missiles would be moved around on tracks, the USSR would never be certain on which car they were located at any point. As for the sea-based and land-based MIRVs and cruise missiles, they could be more easily concealed and used to retaliate after a Soviet first strike.[28] But the very concealment of these weapons made it difficult to verify whether or not their number and type remained in accord with the agreements reached at the SALT talks in 1979.

The Pershing II missiles, which the Carter administration scheduled for deployment in West Germany in early 1984, were destabilizing in other ways: they were accurate counterforce weapons, capable of reaching Soviet command and control within six minutes of being fired. But in a severe crisis, as a former CIA intelligence officer suggested at the time, the Soviets would not risk the consequences of such a strike, almost certainly opting for a policy of launch of warning. In other words, the deployment of Pershing II missiles increased the probability of a "preemptive" Soviet launch.[29]

In short, PD 59 was the result of an incremental policy and technology process. The final decision, however, may have been made without a formal meeting of the NSC. Brzezinski recalls that the president was given two options for announcing a decision: there could be either a formal NSC meeting or a briefing of the president and the vice president, to be followed by a briefing of Muskie by Brown. Carter settled for the briefing.[30]

End runs of this sort were counter to the very purposes for which the NSC had been established in 1947. Good policymaking, it had been assumed, required the assessment of military policies in terms of their relationship to the diplomatic goals of the United States, and vice versa.[31] Could the national security advisor, originally envisaged as a simple coordinator between the Departments of Defense and State and other related agencies, now properly stand in for the State Department in making such an important decision? Former national security advisor Henry Kissinger had sometimes made policy in that way. Brzezinski, too, in his final months in office moved increasingly in that direction.

Certainly, it is clear that Brzezinski did not see the State Department as an active partner in the making of decisions. He wrote Carter on May 1, 1980, shortly before Muskie would take over as the secretary of state, that the secretary should inform members of his department to look at the president's State of the Union message for guidance. These policies, the president should tell him, "must be supported by everyone." The "apparent zigs and zags" in the president's policies, Brzezinski explained, are due to a "lack of discipline in the State Department ranks." To deal with that issue, he provided Carter with a rundown on several second level persons in State, attesting to whether or not their loyalties were to the Department or to the president.[32] In a follow-up letter, Brzezinski noted favorably on Muskie's willingness to follow his lead in SCC meetings.[33]

Deterrence Revisited

Some senators had problems with the new doctrine. Their concerns were expressed in a mid-September 1980 meeting with Secretary of State Muskie and Secretary of Defense Brown.

Senator John Glenn (D-OH) queried Brown on whether or not a *limited* nuclear war was really a possibility. Brown admitted that such a war could easily escalate; but the United States, he suggested, had the ability to wage an extended nuclear conflict. At least that was what was envisaged in PD 58, which guaranteed the continuity of command over U.S. military moves during an extended nuclear war.[34]

When Senator Charles Percy (R-IL) asked if the new policies would create incentives for a first strike, Secretary Brown assured him that they probably would not have that effect. However, he looked at that possibility only from the U.S. perspective. A "launch on warning" attack, in which the United States would respond upon data that the other side was about to attack it, could be an option for the United States. But the limitations of time and the possible mechanical or computer malfunctions do not make that a credible "sole strategy."[35]

Would the Soviet leaders trust the United States not to strike first, even if this strategy provided some advantage for the United States?

> BROWN: I believe that they [the Soviet leaders] are motivated by all the same human emotions as the rest of us. They love their kids and so forth, and they don't want to see their country destroyed. What motivates them, however, is their own personal power in a way that is not easily understood by someone who has come up through the American system where, sure enough, the urge to drive for power is great all right, but not, in my view, of the same quality.
>
> SENATOR [PAUL] TSONGAS [D-MA]: You have never run for the Senate, I can see that.
>
> MUSKIE: I have, and I agree with him.
>
> SENATOR GLENN: Touché.[36]

Would the Soviets really see it that way? Secretary Muskie admitted they might have some fears about U.S. efforts at nuclear war-fighting capability. But they should know that the United States could never take out the entire Soviet ability to retaliate. The objective was just to make clear to the Soviets that they could not win in any type of nuclear war. Perhaps, Muskie mused, he should talk to Soviet foreign minister Andrei Gromyko about this.

Whatever Muskie might tell Gromyko, Soviet officials could harbor suspicions that the United States had other goals in mind. As Walter Pincus wrote in the *Washington Post* on February 11, 1979, the Department of Defense was farming out research projects exploring military possibilities that aimed at the Soviets' very demise. One envisaged eliminating the USSR as "a functioning national entity." Another project would explore the possibility of releasing "the forces of separatism" in the Soviet Union by attacks on its outlying regions. A third study would explore strategies to "paralyze, disrupt, or dismember" the Soviet government by destroying its entire governing class. If we planned to win in a nuclear exchange, one researcher said, the goal would be to take out the government with minimal damage to the people.[37]

Actually, the whole doctrine of trying to guess how the Soviets would perceive U.S. thinking, and vice versa, takes on an air of unreality, as Secretary Brown and Senator Glenn noted in the hearings:

> SENATOR GLENN: I get lost in what is credible and not credible. This whole things gets so incredible when you consider wiping out whole nations, it is difficult to establish credibility.
> BROWN: That is why we sound a little crazy when we talk about it.
> SENATOR GLENN: That is the best statement of the day....[38]

At its base, as journalist Bill Greider argued, the whole theory that the Soviets might undertake a surprise attack against the United States if the Soviets had an advantage in counterforce weapons was based on faulty assumptions about Soviet motives. Their leaders were a brutish lot, Greider agreed, but would they actually risk the lives of 100 million Russians? Would they really see any "war winning" capability as a "victory"? Going beyond Greider, one has to ask what the Soviet response might be to the U.S. development of a major counterforce, and countercommand capabilities. Would the USSR be worried about a U.S. first-strike decision?

Even the idea of a possible extended tit-for-tat nuclear exchange assumes a rationality in the decision-making teams on both sides that is highly unlikely given the suffering involved and the destruction of one side's or both sides' command and control capabilities. Speaking from the Soviet perspective, ambassador to the United States Anatoly Dobrynin suggested, at a U.S.-Soviet conference in 1995, that such rationality might not prevail.[39] Even Walter Slocombe, who had worked on the new policy, warned Carter as far back as the 1976 campaign that "substantial controversy exists over whether any such damage-limiting measures can produce any meaningful reductions in nuclear war casualties, given the measures available to the other side to offset them."[40]

The policies would also fuel an open-ended arms race without any ceilings in sight. The doctrine of sufficiency associated with MAD made extra nuclear weapons unnecessary. A relatively small number of nuclear weapons would be necessary to ride out a first strike and retaliate against the population center of an adversary, making such an option for them extremely costly. With the new counterforce doctrine each country would strive for an advantage that the other would attempt to counteract. New offensive or defensive weapons would be developed, and so it would go. As noted in earlier chapters about SALT II, the United States and the Soviet Union had engaged in such rivalry even as the talks went on. Brezhnev himself noted in his letter to Carter on September 14, 1978, a "tit-for-tat arms race is counter-productive and dangerous."[41]

More than that, the competition would actually introduce incentives to engage in a first strike. Several wars in the past have grown out of escalatory cycles, in which one side overextends itself and the other finally comes to the point that it sees a preemptive strike as the only way to avoid the worsening of its relative situation.[42] President Kennedy's handling of the Cuban Missile Crisis indicates he was also aware of the problem. Having just finished reading Barbara Tuchman's *The Guns of August*, he secretly made a trade with Soviet premier Nikita Khrushchev. The Soviets simply did not blink in an eyeball-to-eyeball encounter, as Secretary of State Dean Rusk suggested at the time (and others came to believe later). Rather, they got a deal that took account of the psychological and political problems Khrushchev would have in simply backing down from an overextended position. U.S. missiles would be removed from Turkey in exchange for the dismantling of offensive missiles in Cuba.[43]

In the spring of 1980, West German Chancellor Schmidt saw a possible parallel to earlier spirals that had spun out of control. As he noted on April 11, there was a similarity between the international situation at that time and the situation after Sarajevo that led to World War I: "Nobody wanted war. But nobody was able to avoid it."[44]

In actual practice, the nuclear policies of both sides were based on a series of bluffs. As the exchange between the secretaries and senators suggests, complicated nuclear scenarios, built on an almost infinite series of thought exchanges, make it difficult for anyone to really come to a bottom line in which the actual benefits of a resort to nuclear war could be seen as higher than the costs. Even sophisticated participants in the nuclear strategic games all seem to come, at the end of the line, to the proposition that one might fool the other side into thinking it would engage in such a war when really it would not. Most strategic thinkers, as social psychologist Steven Kull discovered in his interviews with several such individuals in the U.S. and Soviet circles, come to that point of view.[45]

Indeed, the strategic targeting practices in nuclear war exercise in both the Warsaw Pact and the North Atlantic Treaty Organization (NATO), as Soviet military leader Anatoly Gribkov pointed out in 1995, were not really based on the assumption that one might actually gain something from using them. This was all merely a game of nerves, he said, "watching how the enemy would react to your actions.... The NATO command practiced similar exercises against us."[46] The discussion in both the open and classified Soviet literature about a preemptive or retaliatory strike, Gribkov argued, was based on the Soviet desire to deter its adversary. Soviet leaders saw that any first strike, regardless of which side instigated it, would escalate into MAD.[47]

But even if the leaders on both sides actually would hesitate to initiate such an exchange, there was always the possibility of an accidental war. With both the United States and the Soviet Union opting for strategies that made striking first an advantage, computer mistakes or training exercises could have set off a hair-trigger response. There were at least two nuclear war scares on Carter's watch.

FIGURE 13.   "Obstacles and Incentives for SALT" (Glad's title). SALT II Defense Budget. Courtesy of the *Philadelphia Inquirer*.

FIGURE 14.   "Who's Ahead?" (Glad's title). The SALT Summit. Courtesy of the *Philadelphia Inquirer*.

On one occasion in the late 1970s, the National Military Command Center at the Pentagon and the North American Air Defense Command (NORAD) debated, questioning longer than they should have, if the United States had actually been under attack whether or not NORAD's tracking of a Soviet missile headed toward the Oregon coastline was real or not. Fortunately, this scare turned out to be a computer glitch.[48]

Another time, Odom called Brzezinski at 3:00 a.m. to report that 220 Soviet missiles were headed to the United States. Though the United States would have only three to seven minutes to order retaliation, Brzezinski did not immediately wake the president. Rather, he told Odom to verify a Soviet launch and confirm that the Strategic Air Command was launching its own planes in the air. One minute before Brzezinski planned to phone Carter, Odom called a third time reporting that other systems were not picking up the missiles. It turned out that someone had accidentally put a military training tape on the computer system. The entire episode had been a false alarm.[49]

Would the slow responses to these two events suggest that the decision makers around Carter did not really see the Soviet Union as being so foolhardy as to actually engage in a first strike against the United States?

Before too many questions along these lines could be raised, something happened that practically no one predicted. In the late 1980s, a new generation of reformers appeared in the Soviet Union. One of these leaders, Mikhail Gorbachev, was influenced by the very ideas that Paul Warnke had forwarded in his 1977 "Apes on the Treadmill" article in the Washington Post.[50] Using a somewhat different metaphor, Gorbachev noted shortly after coming to power in 1985 that "national security" could only be secured through "general security." The path to such agreement, he noted, had been made difficult by "super gladiators" attempting to secure a "deft blow" and "extra point" in the "bout."[51]

Seeing the futility of the nuclear arms race, as well as the economic strains that such a race placed on the Soviet economy, Gorbachev went even beyond the traditional MAD stance, initiating that same year a series of unilateral concessions of the sort that American psychologist Charles E. Osgood had been proposing with his GRIT (graduated reciprocation in tension-reduction) strategy. These led to the Intermediate-Range Nuclear Forces Agreement signed between the United States and the Soviet Union on December 8, 1987, which eliminated intermediate nuclear and conventional ground-launched ballistic and cruise missiles in Europe. Gorbachev, it turned out, was more influenced by the arguments made by Warnke than Carter had ever been. The Soviet Union turned out to be so weak internally that the attempt at domestic reform would inadvertently undermine the whole Soviet political and economic structures. But that is another story.

SHADOWING THE SOVIETS

Looking backward, one Russian observer at a conference of former U.S.-Soviet decision makers in 1995, noted that this renewal of the Cold War might be understood via the Russian concept of shadowing. Players in the game of soccer may get so fixed on following in the footsteps of a particular player that they lose sight of the larger, overall strategic purposes involved in the game.[1]

The relevance of these observations to the two major powers' territorial hopscotching around the world is quite clear: the Soviets became involved in Ethiopia, so the United States backed Somalia; the Soviets backed Vietnamese involvement in Cambodia, so the United States backed the Chinese-supported Pol Pot government as the representative of the Cambodian government in the United Nations; the Soviets intervened in Afghanistan, and the United States responded by arming a revolutionary group of warlords and peasant fighters, the *mujahideen*. Some of these forays may have reflected legitimate U.S. national interests, but others did not. Looking back at the border disputes over the Shaba Province in the Congo, several of the participants at the 1995 retrospective conference wondered about some of these interactions. How could the superpowers have become so concerned over an essentially meaningless set of border skirmishes in a part of central Africa that not one American or Russian in a thousand would have been able to find on a map?[2]

Aspects of this kind of interaction were also evident in the development of the nuclear policies of the two countries. The Soviets apparently believed in the possibility of prevailing in a nuclear war, so it was necessary that the United States adopt a similar policy. The first Strategic Arms Limitation Treaty permitted the Soviets to maintain superiority in the numbers of launchers they could possess. Critics of the treaty argued that the United States should have numerical equality with its major adversary in launchers and every other category of weapons.

The activities of the USSR contributed to this gloomy situation. The Soviet military buildup, the deployment of modern multiple independently targetable reentry vehicle–equipped (MIRVed) SS-20s, and the Backfire bomber in the European theater were three such examples. Both the State Department's advisor on Soviet affairs Marshall Shulman and Soviet military leader Anatoly Gribkov concurred at the Fort Lauderdale Conference in 1995 that the Soviet deployment of the SS-20s in Europe was a fateful decision, leading to the U.S. deployment of the Pershing missile in Europe and a deterioration of U.S.-Soviet relations.[3]

Soviet involvements in the Horn of Africa and Afghanistan as well as the support of Cuban activities in the Third World raised additional concern about their ultimate objectives.[4] Was the USSR simply aspiring to big power status so that it would be taken into account on a variety of international issues as Brezhnev claimed? Or were its leaders motivated by a grand plan to dominate the world?[5]

There were many who thought the latter was the case. As the Committee on the Present Danger commented in its January 22, 1980, newsletter,

> In the years before 1939, people watched with disbelief as the world political system disintegrated toward anarchy, and anarchy led to war. During those years, the world order, partly restored at Versailles in 1919, fell apart under the hammer blows of Adolph Hitler. Today a similar process is taking place as the Soviet Union pursues a program of expansionism even more ambitious than that of Hitler, claiming the sanction of scientific Socialism for designs in the ancient model of conquest and predation....
>
> As we Americans face the problems of foreign and defense policy, we should remind ourselves of that terrible experience. Even towering Western leaders like [Winston] Churchill and Franklin D. Roosevelt failed to prevent war. President Roosevelt, active as he later was in achieving Lend-Lease, the Destroyer-Bases Agreement, the convoys to Europe, and all the other important actions of the period after World War II had begun, did not join with Britain and France during the middle 1930s when the war might well have been prevented.[6]

The basis for these concerns, as journalist Bill Greider notes, was a "core anxiety," based on a "perception of weakness." But he saw this as a profound overreaction. The suggestion that the United States should "commit a fixed percentage of our growing national wealth to the military and argue later about how to spend it" was similar to "the primitive rite of offering sacrifices at the altar of the war god."[7]

Was this action-reaction sequence inevitable? At the 1995 Fort Lauderdalae conference, former officials of the Carter and Brezhnev decision-making teams—William Odom and George Shakhmazaro—saw the renewal of the Cold War as foreordained. The Soviets were obviously motivated by a drive for superiority and imperial extension, and the United States had no alternative but to oppose them wherever they reached out. The Soviet ambassador, Anatoly Dobrynin and U.S. Assistant Secretary of State Leslie Gelb, however, both saw their own nations as contributing to an action–reaction cycle that led to the deterioration in the relations between them.[8] In other words, Carter could have made some choices that would have muted conflicts with the Soviet Union without sacrificing the U.S. national interest.

Intelligence and Ambiguity

The president, as we have seen, had conflicting guidance about Soviet motives from his advisory staff. Secretary of State Cyrus Vance viewed the U.S.-Soviet relationship as one that should be based on the national interests of both nations—fluctuating, as it would be, between two poles of cooperation and conflict. Lending his negotiating talents to the SALT and Middle East peace talks, he generally favored diplomatic exchanges in efforts to maintain cordial relations with Soviet leaders.[9]

National Security Advisor Zbigniew Brzezinski propounded the view that the Soviets were not only seeking superiority to the United States, they had imperial designs. Many of his aides on the National Security Council—William Odom, Fritz Ermarth, and Samuel Huntington—concurred. Eventually, Secretary of Defense Harold Brown, as we have seen, came into this camp.

For the president, these differences of opinion over Soviet goals and capabilities could not simply be resolved at the time via the intelligence reports that reached his desk. A "top secret" Team B report, concluded just before Carter assumed office, provided a very alarmist perspective on Soviet motives. Appointed by George H. W. Bush, then the director of the Central Intelligence Agency (CIA), the members of the committee had been chosen for their hard-line views vis-à-vis the Soviet Union. Their report, which was leaked to the press, came to the unanimous conclusion that the Soviet Union had an undeviating "commitment to what is euphemistically called the world triumph of Socialism, but in fact connotes global Soviet hegemony." Peaceful coexistence, known as détente in the West, was a grand strategy adapted to the nuclear weapons of the moment. But the Soviets aspired to superiority in all aspects of military capabilities. At the nuclear level, their goal was a war-fighting and war-winning capability. An earlier National Intelligence Estimate (NIE) report of Soviet motives, they argued, was based on the naive view that Soviets think like Americans; the United States, by contrast, tend to view deterrence as an alternative to war fighting.[10] Team B, in short, embraced a worst-case image of the enemy.

The mainline NIE report—from Team A—that also informed the new president and his staff when they first came into office was somewhat less alarmist, noting the difficulties in estimating Soviet capabilities and intentions. But this report also concluded that in the long run the Soviet intent was military superiority in support of their expansionist goals. Indeed, the Team A report had been hardened after a November 5, 1976, meeting with Team B members. Young analysts presenting the Team A report were no match for the older and more professionally distinguished outside review team. Indeed, as Richard Pipes, the chair of Team B, recalls, a young man presenting the Team A report was even struck silent when presented with a tough question from a member of Team B. By December 2, 1976, when both teams presented their findings to the president's Intelligence Review Board, the differences between them had considerably narrowed. Team B, as Pipes suggests, in this way exerted a certain influence over the Carter presidency.[11]

An NIE report issued two years later gave a somewhat more moderate estimate of both Soviet goals and capacities than either of the earlier reports. The Soviet Union, as the authors saw it, had been assertive in engaging the West and stalwart in defending its interests in crisis situations. It would continue to fish in troubled waters on the model of Angola and the Horn of Africa. But there was no evidence that the Soviets contemplated a strategic nuclear attack before they had the military capacity to conduct one. In a real crisis, the Soviets would behave with great caution in handling their strategic weapons. Should they consider resorting to the nuclear option, this choice would arise out of U.S. efforts to resist or reverse military developments favorable to them. The USSR knew the concepts of alertness, survival, and deterrence, though these were less dominant in their thinking than they were in the thinking of the United States.

A new generation of Soviet leaders was seen as taking over in the near future. These leaders could possibly see Soviet gains as a point of departure from which to "exert more pervasive leverage on world affairs.... Alternatively, but less likely, younger leaders lacking the conditioning preoccupations of their elders ... may be inclined to give over-riding priority to the solution of internal problems which their predecessors allowed to accumulate." Soviet difficulties with their Eastern Europe satellites and hostile China were noted. Their experience at influence had been mixed at best, and they had never engaged in direct and openly avowed combat operations on a substantial scale. Their policies toward China were primarily those of containment.[12]

The pessimism manifest in the intelligence reports of 1976 gained certain credibility due to some earlier CIA miscounts. The CIA in fact had underestimated the dramatic increase in Soviet intercontinental ballistic missiles (ICBMs). Since the 1960s, the number had gone from 858 to 1,601 (the SALT I limit). When this was followed with the introduction of the new intermediate-range ballistic missiles (IRBMs) on their Western borders, the "window of vulnerability" became an issue that Carter would have to confront. If the Soviets improved the accuracy of their ICBMs, could the U.S. ground-based missiles be knocked out with a first Soviet nuclear strike? With the new IRBMs could there be any substantial retaliation from European bases?[13] Within the traditional CIA reports there were other concerns about the capability of the Backfire bomber for intercontinental war situations and the extent of the Soviet civil defense program. But there were voices on the other side, too. In the 1978 NIE report the director of the Bureau of Intelligence and Research of the State Department registered a minority view that the majority report tended to overemphasize the Soviet perception of their own military power and underestimate their underlying political and economic vulnerabilities. Rather than planning on the achievement of a war-winning or war-survival posture in the foreseeable future, the Soviet Union was guided by more proximate foreign policy goals.[14]

A few observers in policy circles, moreover, were aware of counterintelligence techniques that led even the mainline CIA analyses to exaggerate the Soviet military buildup. As three Democratic congressmen—Bob Carr (MI), Robert Leggett (CA), and Thomas Downey (NY)—wrote Brzezinski on February 1, 1977, calculating the cost of Soviet manpower by estimating what it would cost to pay for this manpower in U.S. dollars overestimated their output. Pay scales in the Soviet Union were very low, with the result that the Soviets capitalized on manpower. In the United States, technology and force planning were emphasized in an effort to hold the manpower requirements to the absolute minimum. Given these circumstances, to estimate Soviet expenditures by assuming that they paid their soldiers what the United States paid its soldiers made little sense.[15]

In addition, the CIA had overstated Soviet strength in the 1950s and early '60s in other areas. There was the bomber gap (1955–57) and then the missile gaps

(1957–61). Both sets of estimates were invalidated shortly thereafter as U.S. surveillance technology improved.[16]

Retroactive analyses of U.S. intelligence reports that Carter dealt with during the entire Cold War period show similar exaggerations regarding Soviet weapons developments, civil defense, and overall military spending. The very ambiguity of the data with which the analysts had to work, as Raymond Garthoff has noted, created incentives to make worst case analyses rather than miss some possible threat.[17] Practically all of the projections in the Team B reports were way off.[18] Even the mainline CIA reports that crossed Carter's desk were prone to exaggeration. The deployment of SS-16s and the technological upgrading of intermediate-range missiles (SS-20s) to an ICBM missile system did not occur. The accuracy of the Soviet SS-18 and SS-19 were overestimated.[19]

Moreover, the increase in Soviet national expenditures going to the military since 1976 was not 4–5 percent per year but closer to 2 percent.[20] As notes James Noren, Soviet military procurements had leveled off in the USSR after 1975. Given the slow growth—and in some years decline—of the Soviet gross domestic product, a Soviet determination to stay in the arms race rather than their creation of an actual overwhelming threat to the United States, is suggested.[21]

Assumptions about Soviet motivations were also questionable. Team B had made a valuable suggestion in its warning that Soviet objectives should not be seen as a mirror image of the U.S. goals. But there were other alternative interpretations to the enemy image embraced by Team B. The Soviet Union might be an evil regime, as the CIA's Robert Gates assumed.[22] But were Nikita Khrushchev or Leonid Brezhnev as malevolent as Joseph Stalin or Adolf Hitler? Would Soviet leaders risk the annihilation of whole populations, including their own, in a quest for world domination? Even they might hesitate to initiate a war that would kill fifteen to eighty million people, with many more casualties, given the various possible attack scenarios.[23] Were their military decisions made without regard to what they saw as external threats to their system? Their development of medium-range missiles could have been a reflection of their concern about a possible attack from a European-based adversary, and the size of their army was a reflection of the need to operate on two fronts—Europe and Asia. China was a potential adversary, with its competing ideological and territorial claims as well as past border skirmishes.[24]

The mainline CIA reports, in short, failed to consider the Soviet policy choices as a reflection of either their unique geographic position or as a reaction to U.S. policies. Implicit in the CIA's analysis of Soviet military power, according to Garthoff, was an assumption that the United States was dealing with a "given," an objective and established reality. There was essentially, and with rare exception, no recognition that the underlying reality might be contingent and dynamic or reactive; that Soviet intentions, military programs to build forces and provide capabilities, and strategies for employment of these forces and capabilities could be significantly affected by U.S. policies and actions.[25]

Nor was the Soviet Union viewed as capable of any reform from within. No one at the time anticipated that someone like Mikhail Gorbachev, with his new thinking in foreign policy, would rise to the top of the Soviet hierarchy a few years later. For Pipes, the fact that Gorbachev remained committed to communism was an indication that he had no desire to "substantially change it." Robert Gates, who would later become the director of central intelligence, saw Gorbachev's rise to power as foreshadowing no basic change in Soviet policies.[26]

For some hard-line intellectuals these views of the Soviet Union were based on some premises about the Soviet system explicitly spelled out in the works of Carl Friedrich at Harvard University and Hannah Arendt at the New School for Social Research in New York City. Writing in the early phases of the Cold War, they argued that Communist and Nazi totalitarian regimes were alike. Small elites, concerned only with the expansion of their power—able and willing to use any form of terrorist tactics to do so—were able to control every human response in their respective regimes. The very nature of the totalitarian regime made it inherently oriented toward world conquest. For those embracing this perspective, Khrushchev's critiques of Stalin at the Twentieth Party Congress in the Soviet Union, the lessened brutality of subsequent regimes, and the stresses placed on the Soviet economy were seen as having little consequence.[27] The Soviet system provided no basis for either reform from within or the possibility that it might temper its goals in response to Western diplomacy. Brzezinski, as a graduate student at Harvard, had worked with Friedrich on *Totalitarian Dictatorships*, Friedrich's seminal work in this genre.

Paul Warnke, who headed Carter's Arms Control and Disarmament Agency, had another—not altogether popular—interpretation. In his "Apes on the Treadmill" article, he wrote that the very ambiguity about who was at the top in the arms race was motivating both the United States and the Soviet Union to seek nuclear superiority. In case of doubt, one strives for an edge—the very seeking of which feeds the continuation of the competition.[28] Congressman Thomas Downey and his two colleagues came to a similar conclusion in their letter to Brzezinski on February 1, 1977. The United States, as well as the Soviet Union, they wrote, had a policy of striving for military superiority.

Actually, some Americans explicitly stated that their objective was to gain nuclear superiority over the Soviet Union. John Fisher, President of the American Security Council, made it clear that his organization did not seek mere U.S. equivalence with the Soviet Union; and the platform of the Republican Party in 1980, stated that the U.S. goal should be to achieve nuclear superiority over the Soviet Union.[29]

Even Brzezinski may have exaggerated the Soviet threat in the service of a similar objective. In the fall of 1979, he told journalist James Wooten that the Soviet Union was not the threat he often portrayed it as being. The country was in deep trouble at home, and it was "no longer as attractive an exporter of commodities as it once was in the Third World."[30] Out of office, at a Musgrove Plantation conference in 1984, Brzezinski admitted that the U.S. government had played from strength in dealing with the Soviets. The United States had been superior to in every respect, and the Soviets knew it. U.S. policies were actually a kind of imperative that came from its superior position.[31] The possibility that the United States might employ a first nuclear strike to protect its interests abroad gave its verbal threats a greater credibility.

As we now know, Soviet leaders were motivated by a variety of concerns. Mikhail Suslov, the Soviet propaganda chief, was no doubt influenced by the view that the USSR should emphasize technological developments that would enhance Soviet prestige and influence on the world scene. But Brezhnev and others, as former ambassador W. Averell Harriman tried to tell Carter, was motivated by a desire to avoid a nuclear holocaust that would overshadow even the major disaster they confronted during World War II. He and other Soviet officials, as Dobrynin has testified, regarded the United States as engaged in an anti-Soviet campaign, which they in turn had to counter. They also had somewhat diverse opinions about what specific foreign policy choices should be made and sometimes stumbled into their most provocative acts.

President Carter, in short, succumbed to pressures in the broader political climate to track the Soviet Union, blocking their moves wherever they probed; and in the nuclear arena, he sought nuclear war–winning capabilities, similar to the ones they seemed to pursue. Generally, he had a desire to be seen as tough, and National Security Advisor Brzezinski, as well as sometimes faulty intelligence reports, convinced him that the only way to stabilize relations with the Soviet Union was to threaten them. At the end of his presidency, Carter's decisions were not simply a response to the broader political setting in which he found himself, but an accommodation to the hawks in the foreign policy–making community.

THE ENEMY OF MY ENEMY IS MY FRIEND

Jimmy Carter's human rights policies, too, would be sidelined by the very anticommunism that he had warned against in his Notre Dame speech in May 1977.

One of the most jarring manifestations of this shift was his praise for one of the worst despots in Eastern Europe, Romanian President Nicolae Ceausescu. Receiving Ceausescu at the White House on April 12, 1978, Carter noted that he was "a great leader of a great country."[1] Not only that, but Romania had enjoyed most-favored-nation status in its dealings with the United States since 1975—a privilege Carter refused to extend to the Soviet Union. Later that year, Treasury Secretary Michael Blumenthal took a detour during his European tour to visit Ceausescu. Upon arriving in Bucharest on December 8, 1978, Blumenthal said, "I come to Romania at President Carter's direction to reaffirm...the importance we attach to Romanian independence and to U.S.-Romanian friendship."[2] The virtue that mattered was that Ceausescu was charting a foreign policy course somewhat independent of the Soviet Union.[3] That same spring, as the Russians sought to influence events in the Horn of Africa, the United States president embraced Mohammed Siad Barre, the erratic and ruthless dictator of Somalia.

Also ignored were potential problems regarding the Chinese dealings with their own political dissidents. On December 8, 1978, National Security Council (NSC) aide Michel Oksenberg wrote Zbigniew Brzezinski that it was too early for the president or senior officials to respond to a dissident Chinese wall poster calling on the United States to extend its human rights policies to China. In a memo he prepared for Brzezinski to send to the president, Oksenberg suggested that the administration should not yet "praise popular aspirations" in China since to do so "would jeopardize the progress" being made. On the other hand, the United States should not praise the Chinese leaders, since to do this "would legitimate an authoritarian leadership as having human rights concerns." Brzezinski did not sign the memo, remarking simply, "Need better movement."[4]

After Chinese leader Deng Xiaoping's visit to Washington, D.C., in early 1979 and the arrest of activist editor Wei Jingsheng, the administration made only one semicritical remark on Chinese human rights abuses, expressing surprise and disappointment at Wei's prison sentence.[5] A State Department report on Chinese human rights was upbeat, saying, "An encouraging trend has begun to emerge in the direction of liberalization."[6]

Carter even overlooked the crimes of one of the most genocidal regimes of human history. Ever since the Pol Pot regime came to power in Cambodia in 1975, a few

FIGURE 15.   Nicolae Ceausescu, president of Romania, at a dinner hosted by Jimmy and Rosalynn Carter. Photograph courtesy of the Jimmy Carter Library.

congressmen and journalists had been documenting its systematic elimination of the entire class of educated people and ethnic minorities. At one point, on April 1978, Carter did note that the Cambodian government was "the worst violator of human rights in the world today."[7] On October 1978, Senator William Proxmire (D-WI) persuaded seventy-nine other senators to write Secretary of State Cyrus Vance, urging him to introduce the issue to the United Nations Security Council.[8]

But it would fall to Vietnam to dislodge the Pol Pot Regime. In response to conflicts with the Khmer Rouge on its borders, Vietnam invaded Cambodia in the last weeks of December 1978. The invasion led to the discovery of massive piles of skeletons and other evidence that the Khmer Rouge had been engaged in systematic torture and mass murder. Nearly two million people had been killed.[9] A U.S. foreign service officer, Charles Twining, who had earlier become aware of the extent of the Khmer atrocities, cheered when he heard of the Vietnamese victory, but he was practically the only one in the administration to respond in that way. Preoccupied with fighting the Cold War, most U.S. foreign policy decision makers were concerned about the possible extension of Soviet influence in the region because of its recent alliance with Vietnam.[10]

After the Vietnamese invasion, the Carter administration expressed no further outrage over the Pol Pot regime. Finally on September 21, 1979, the United States supported the UN General Assembly vote (71–35, with 4 abstentions and 23 absences) to endorse the Credentials Committee recommendation that the Pol Pot regime should continue to represent Cambodia in the UN.[11] The vote was driven by Brzezinski, and reluctantly supported by Vance. Anthony Lake of the policy planning staff and Patricia

Derian, assistant secretary of state for human rights and humanitarian affairs, were opposed to it. One of the members of UN Ambassador Donald McHenry's team wrote a memo in opposition to recognition of Pol Pot that was sent up the State Department's dissent channel.[12]

At first the UN measure was openly supported by only China and North Korea.[13] Many U.S. allies, including the majority of the European community, would not have backed the Pol Pot regime as representing Democratic Kampuchea (DK), as it was called (between 1975 and 1979), without the U.S. lead. The ultimate ambivalence of the United States is evident in statements that the vote would be understood as only technical in nature. Ambassador McHenry was instructed to note in all his statements the nation's "total opposition" to seeing the DK ever return to power in Phnom Penh. Vance declined to cosponsor or lobby for the resolution.[14]

Did the United States have no other alternatives given its national interests? Before Vietnam entered Cambodia, the president and other members of the administration could have spoken out more boldly and more often about the atrocities taking place in that part of the world. They could have brought the matter before the UN General Assembly for debate. The United States might have urged some of its allies who had signed the Genocide Convention to take the crisis to the International Court of Justice.

Most important, the deposition of that bloody regime by the Vietnamese could have been accepted by the United States as an improvement over the status quo. The U.S. government could have undertaken negotiations with Vietnam (which was having its own difficulties with the local population) for a time and place for a pullout that would not let the Khmer Rouge back in. But short of that, there is no real evidence that the U.S. security relationship with the People's Republic of China (PRC) actually required the United States to back the continued seating of the Khmer Rouge regime and its allies in the UN. Why not opt for the compromise offered by Zaire to leave the UN Cambodian seat vacant?

Iran, viewed as a bastion against communist influence in Southwest Asia, was also exempt from Carter's human rights concerns.[15] When Shah Mohammad Reza Pahlavi visited Washington on November 15, 1977, confrontations between pro-shah and anti-shah factions on the south side of the White House lawn had to be broken up with the use of tear gas.[16] At the state dinner that night, Carter noted, "We look upon Iran as a very stabilizing force in the world at large. We don't fear the future when we have friends like this great country."[17] During his Eurasian tour the following month, Carter repeated that theme. In a New Year's Eve celebration in Tehran, he toasted the shah's "great leadership" in making Iran "an island of stability in one of the more troubled areas of the world."[18] In this speech, Carter also made an eloquent reference to the human rights of the Iranian people, quoting the Persian poet Saadi:

> If the misery of others leaves you indifferent
> and with no feelings of sorrow, then you
> can not be called a human being.[19]

Ironically, the Iranian resistance movement was growing at the time, and the secret police, the SAVAK, was persecuting Iranian dissidents opposed to the shah's rule. Iran was in reality neither an "island of stability" nor a champion of human rights.

As for Poland, the United States at first simply tried to loosen that nation's dependence on the Soviet Union. Carter's first state visit as president was to Poland in 1977, and in the ensuing months, the U.S. government offered Poland economic assistance by granting low-interest loans, credits for grain, and long-term debt rescheduling.[20]

The groundwork for the Polish rebellion was laid down by John Paul II on his first trip to his homeland after becoming pope. On June 2, 1979, he told a massive audience in Warsaw's Victory Square, "be not afraid...you have rights." As Polish historian Adam Zamoyski noted, the pope's words had an immediate impact. "Suddenly people stopped being afraid...and that gave the strength for Solidarity and for the destruction of the whole communist system." Adrzej Szcszypiorski, Polish author and journalist, agreed that the pope's 1979 visit "was the little stone that started the avalanche" that would eventually end communist rule across Eastern Europe.[21]

Two months later, on August 14, 1980, over 17,000 Polish workers seized the Lenin shipyard in Gdansk in protest of soaring food prices. Shortly after that, the leader of the movement, an unemployed electrician named Lech Walesa, announced the formation of the independent trade union, Solidarity, and negotiated a deal with Poland's communist deputy prime minister Mieczyslaw Jagielski that would allow the workers the right to freely organize and to strike.[22] The Solidarity movement then spread like a wildfire and the very foundation of the communist regime was being threatened.

In December 1980, the United States received word from a highly placed Central Intelligence Agency (CIA) contact in Poland that Soviet troops were conducting exercises along the borders in East Germany and Russia, and Czech and Soviet troops were training together. "The Soviets were surveying invasion routes," Carter later noted, and "had set up an elaborate communications system through Poland." They were also conducting "intensive photo reconnaissance flights out of Czechoslovakia and East Germany, and were holding their military forces in a high state of readiness."[23]

At an NSC meeting in the White House Cabinet Room on Sunday morning, December 7, 1980, Carter decided to warn Soviet president Leonid Brezhnev that the Soviets should not intervene in Poland. The United States privately shared their intelligence information with the media, key foreign powers, and opposition leaders in Poland.[24] Brzezinski was also authorized to make an unprecedented call to John Paul II. The encounter, as Brzezinski remembers it, was as follows:

> I reached him late in the evening, Vatican time, and his secretary's first response, when I identified myself and asked to speak to the Pope, was to say, 'I will see if I can find him.' The Pope came on thirty seconds later, and in a way the conversation was historically unique. Here was the Assistant for National Security Affairs to the President of the United States conferring with the Roman Pontiff in the Vatican in Polish about peace and Poland.[25]

FIGURE 16.   Zbigniew Brzezinski, Jimmy Carter, Pope John Paul II, and Rosalynn Carter. Photograph courtesy of the Jimmy Carter Library.

In short, the Vatican and the United States worked toward a common goal in Poland. The United States undertook moves to bring that country closer politically and economically to the West; the pope provided the inspiration that led the Poles to stand up for themselves. Without him, Walesa said, "There would be no end of communism, or at least [it would have come] much later and the end would have been bloody."[26] But the United States provided the backing that would make a military intervention potentially costly to the Soviet Union. As Brzezinski saw it, Carter did not want to make the same mistake that he perceived former president Lyndon Johnson had made at the time of the Prague Spring uprising in 1968. Instead, according to Brzezinski, "The President handled [the crisis] well, firmly and calmly, and there is no doubt that he had digested fully the lessons of the U.S. underreaction to the Czechoslovak crisis of 1968."[27]

The Carter administration's efforts to promote human rights via actual regime change also led to some positive results in South Africa. The administration, for example, upheld UN sanctions to maintain pressure on the South African government to dismantle the apartheid system.[28] These and other external pressures led to the release of Nelson Mandela from prison ten years later, and the subsequent negotiations with Afrikaaner President F. W. de Klerk issued in a new postapartheid regime.[29] But this was a situation in which the United States could link itself to a strong democratic movement in a country where the outgoing regime was not prepared for all-out war to maintain the status quo.

Regime Changes in Latin America

As for its own hemisphere, the administration started out with a relatively absolutist human rights policy. As early as March 24, 1977, the Policy Review Committee concluded that the United States should follow a global policy for developing nations that could be adapted to meet challenges faced in Latin America.[30] This led to Carter's policy of "benign neutrality." The United States resolved to abstain from past interpretations of the Monroe Doctrine that gave it a privileged position in Latin American polities. As Carter himself noted, the people of Latin America "if at all possible...[should] forge their own political decisions."[31] When the United States did get involved, its goal would be to find ways to persuade local dictators to soften their policies.[32] Incentives for change would be limited to the annual country reports on human rights issues, and the giving or cutting off of economic and military aid in response to these reports. These actions would be supplemented with public admonitions, selective high-level visits to states, and symbolic actions such as the public reception of political dissidents.

In line with these concerns, on February 24, 1977, Vance announced that the administration planned to reduce foreign aid to Argentina and Uruguay. First Lady Rosalynn Carter, in her tour of Latin America in June 1977, visited only countries approved by the State Department as having a positive or substantially improving human rights records. In Brazil she created a small diplomatic flurry, seeing two U.S. missionaries who had been detained for three days after expressing a desire to present her with data on certain human rights violations. That same year Patricia Derian, on her first trip as the assistant secretary of state for human rights, visited Argentina, El Salvador, Bolivia, Brazil, and Uruguay. The very announcement of the trip, as scholar Joshua Muravchik notes, was a signal that the United States had concerns about the human rights practices of these nations.

President Carter, in his visit to Brazil in March 1978, also met a dissident, this time the great human rights activist Cardinal Paulo Evaristo Arns, who provided him with a list of the Brazilian "disappeared." Three months later at an Organization of American States (OAS) meeting, Carter delivered a speech emphasizing the importance of human rights that received widespread praise.[33]

For most of the larger countries in Latin America, these actions would have minimal effect on their human rights policies. When Vance announced that the administration planned to reduce foreign aid to Argentina and Uruguay, those two countries delivered diplomatic protests, rejecting—in advance—future military aid from the United States. When on March 12 the State Department released its country report on Brazil, that country followed suit in protest.[34] Meanwhile, in Argentina, the government continued to conduct its "dirty war" against suspected opponents; thousands simply disappeared and were never heard from again.[35] Later Argentina shipped grain to the USSR, countering the Carter initiated boycott of the Soviet Union following its intervention in Afghanistan.

U.S. activities in the Caribbean, moreover, showed the Carter administration just how difficult it was for an outside force to promote democracy in even small, neighboring countries. Efforts to persuade Nicaraguan President Anastasio Somoza Debayle, a

1946 West Point graduate, to a more democratic process had little effect. At the time Carter came to office, Somoza had declared a state of siege, censored the press, imprisoned all who opposed him, and left the Nicaraguan National Guard to torture many of those whom they had imprisoned. After the 1978 assassination of Pedro Joaquin Chamorro Cardenal, a Somoza critic and publisher of the newspaper La Prensa, the conflict deepened. Following Chamorro's death, riots broke out in the capital of Managua. Business leaders called for a general strike and for Somoza's resignation. In the year of unrest that followed, the left-wing rebel Sandinistas strengthened their position and Somoza's moderate opposition was marginalized.[36]

At first Carter and his team agreed that they should use only economic aid and public statements in an effort to persuade Somoza to change his ways. In July 1978, when Somoza seemed to be responding to these early efforts, Carter wrote him a letter noting approval of certain reform steps Somoza had purportedly taken. Carter did not anticipate that Somoza would publicize the letter in an effort to bolster himself politically, and as a result the centrists the United States had also been trying to support felt abandoned. Some of them went over to the more radical Sandinista forces.[37]

In late September 1978, when it became clear that the Sandinistas were likely to emerge as major players in Nicaraguan affairs, members of the Carter team split over possible responses to the extension of left-wing governments in the area. At a meeting of the OAS, Brzezinski pushed for an OAS peacekeeping force to deal with the Nicaraguan affair. Vance, Assistant Secretary of State for Inter-American Affairs Viron Vaky, and U.S. ambassador to Nicaragua Lawrence A. Pezullo argued that Brzezinski's plan would lead to American ground troops being drawn into the conflict. The OAS settled for a call for Somoza to step down and a negotiated resolution.[38] With the rejection of his plan for an OAS peacekeeping force, Brzezinski called for direct U.S. intervention.[39]

In May 1979 the Sandinistas captured Nicaragua's major cities, including half of the capital Managua and most of the countryside.[40] At a breakfast meeting on June 22, Brzezinski argued for a U.S. intervention, warning of "major domestic and international implications of a Castroite takeover of Nicaragua. [The United States] would be considered as being incapable of dealing with problems in our own backyard and impotent in the face of Cuban intervention. This will have devastating domestic implications, including for SALT."[41] But at a meeting three days later on June 25, the Special Coordinating Committee (SCC) developed instead a compromise—the "two pillars" option, the "Somocism without Somoza" policy. The administration would attempt to keep the military that had supported Somoza in place and endeavor to broaden the base of any new government that would come. The only chip they held in the game at this time was a U.S. commitment to get Somoza to leave Nicaragua peaceably.[42]

Somoza was slow to move. As the Sandinistas were about to take over the entire capital, Warren Christopher phoned Somoza, telling him to leave the country immediately. The United States promised to send aid to the Nicaraguan National Guard and to recognize a junta that would include Sandinista members. On July 17, Somoza fled for Miami, Florida.[43] When his successor Francisco Urcuyo, the former vice president, announced that he would serve the remainder of Somoza's term, it took the efforts of both U.S. ambassador Pezullo and the now Miami-based Somoza to persuade him to step down.[44] On July 18, 1979, the Sandinistas took power and the Nicaraguan National Guard, upon which Carter had placed some hope, dissolved.

After the Sandinistas had taken over, Carter opted for a "strategy of patient accommodation" and small-scale aide packages in hopes of preventing a second Soviet-backed communist outpost in Latin America.[45] The administration supported World Bank and Inter-American Development Bank loans to Nicaragua and proposed a $75 million aid package to the U.S. Congress, which was released to the Sandinistas on September 12. The United States also provided them with over $216 million in aid, mainly paid to private organizations and not contingent on Carter's certification that the Sandinistas were not inciting violence elsewhere.[46]

Carter had also issued a formal finding providing for covert CIA operations in the Caribbean in 1980. It still is not clear what the goal of these operations might have been. Robert Gates, then director of the CIA, only states that they were "small scale, nonlethal" in nature. Robert Pastor, then the Latin American specialist on the NSC staff, states that no major U.S. action to overthrow the Sandinista government took place.[47]

Later, in the fall of 1980, the United States had to deal with a coup attempt by groups of uncertain origins.[48] At an SCC meeting on November 13, Robert Pastor warned his colleagues that several groups could be plotting coups, including Nicaraguan exiles supported by former national guardsmen.[49] In the ensuing discussion the members of the SCC considered a possible series of démarches to send to Cuba, the USSR, and other countries. Should Cuba send support troops into Nicaragua to suppress a coup, a U.S. military response might take place. General Edward Meyer noted that the U.S. Army could deploy an entire division to Nicaragua within seven to ten days and least one battalion within twenty-four hours if they were immediately put on alert. Brzezinski argued that for him the worst situation would be for the United States to give a stern warning to Cuba and then not have the military credibility or capability to follow up on it. At the end of the meeting, a final decision was reached to move the USS *Forrestal* into place at *Modlok* should a coup be attempted. As it turned out, no overt action was taken at this time. On November 16, 1980, Nicaraguan security police shot Jorge Salazar, the leader of the coup attempt in Nicaragua, in a gas station.[50] Without him, the plans for a possible coup soon fizzled.

On January 6, 1981, the CIA sent the White House an intelligence report that implicated Nicaragua in arms trafficking to rebels in El Salvador. As Pastor later noted, "That report, for the first time in my opinion, provided conclusive proof that the Nicaraguan government was providing significant amounts of aid to El Salvador." Responding to an SCC recommendation, Carter suspended all aid shipments to Nicaragua on January 16.[51]

Conflicts over Target Choices

The choices over whom to target or whom to support triggered conflicts within the administration and the broader foreign policy elites. At the State Department, Patricia

Derian pushed a relatively absolutist human rights position. As she said in March 1977, it is "important never [to] send a double message.... It will give the lie to what it is that we profess to or hope to improve."[52] The following month, she stated in testimony before a Senate subcommittee on international organizations that the inconsistency of the U.S. policy was "troublesome."[53] Her visits to various countries were often taken as a marker of which regimes presented the most troublesome records in human rights terms.[54]

Over time, Derian's activities brought her into direct conflict with officials concerned with the maintenance of good relations with allies, some of whom were less committed to human rights than the support of U.S. political positions abroad. Her critique of the human rights policies of President Ferdinand Marcos of the Philippines when she was in Manila in early 1978 led Assistant Secretary of State Richard Holbrooke to ask Vice President Walter Mondale to visit that country. Marcos had been enraged by her comments, and Holbrooke was concerned about the maintenance of U.S. bases in the Philippines.[55]

That same year, when the shah of Iran requested tear gas for use against demonstrators, Derian argued that he "could buy it somewhere else." When Under Secretary of State for Security Assistance Lucy Benson disagreed and kicked the issue upstairs, David Aaron of the NSC staff and Vance backed up Benson; the export of tear gas grenades was approved. In early December, when President Carter directed Brzezinski to telephone the shah to underscore the administration's support for him, the Bureau of Human Rights argued that the White House should not issue "blanket endorsements of the Shah and his regime."[56] On NBC's *Meet the Press* on December 25, 1978, Derian said that the increasing unrest against the shah is "an expression of the people's will. People long for liberty and certain guarantees and protections everywhere."[57]

Staff conflicts over U.S. policies toward Latin America also became quite pitched. At first the controversies were over the application of human rights policies to U.S.-friendly regimes such as those of Argentina and Brazil. When Assistant Secretary of State for Inter-American Affairs Terence Todman publicly lambasted his own colleagues on their application of human rights standards to these regimes, he was replaced by Viron Vaky, who went along with the administration's attempts to build moderate alternatives to the right-wing dictators in the Latin America.[58]

Later, conflicts developed between the top decision makers at the NSC, the Defense Department, and the diplomats and desk officers at the State Department over U.S. support of right-wing regimes in Nicaragua and El Salvador. Vaky suggested that the U.S. force Somoza out. Anthony Lake and Robert Pastor agreed that Somoza should step down, but discouraged direct American intervention. Late in the game, Brzezinski was practically the only one arguing for direct intervention to prevent a clear Sandinista victory.[59] Frustrated, he wrote Carter on July 2, 1979, that "in the wake of our own decision not to intervene in Latin American politics, there will...develop a vacuum, which would be filled by [Fidel] Castro and others."[60]

Turf issues complicated matters. Lucy Benson managed to get all her security assistance programs exempted from oversight by the Interagency Group on Human Rights and Foreign Assistance [the Christopher Group] that had been formed to consider all arms transfers and loans in terms of the recipients' human rights record. By the middle of 1978, a variety of programs including the Food for Peace Program, the Export-Import Bank, the Agency for International Development, and the International Monetary Fund were removed from the Christopher Group's purview.[61]

Others in the outer policy circle applied conflicting pressures on the administration. Congressmen concerned with human rights before Carter came to office would press the administration to take more aggressive steps than it was inclined to do. Representative Tom Harkin (D-IA) introduced legislation in 1977 that would require the administration to vote against loans to repressive nations from international financial institutions such as the World Bank and the Inter-American Development Bank. When Carter opposed the measure, the U.S. House of Representatives and Senate approved a compromise instead, and Carter reluctantly approved the bill. Senator Edward Kennedy (D-MA) proposed a rider to a measure that would have terminated all military aid to Argentina. In this case, the administration supported an alternate amendment to delay any termination of assistance until September 30, 1978. The House and Senate agreed to the amendment, and the bill was signed into law in October 1977.[62]

When the White House began to downplay the horrors of the Pol Pot regime in Cambodia in October 1978, eighty U.S. senators were sufficiently incensed to write a joint letter to Secretary Vance. Their appeal was critical of the Carter administration's decision to attempt to place the Cambodian question before the UN Human Rights Commission. Such an effort seemed to be "a rather low-key approach."[63]

As for Somoza's Nicaragua, people on both ends of the political spectrum pressured the administration. In September 1978, Representative Charles Wilson (D-TX) led seventy-eight members of Congress to push Carter to support the Somoza regime.[64] But then on October 13 eighty-six Congress members took an opposite position, urging Vance to suspend all aid to Somoza's Nicaragua.[65] Continuing the battle, five Republican senators, including Strom Thurmond (SC), Jesse Helms (NC), and Orrin Hatch (UT) sent an open letter to Carter, which appeared in a full-page ad in the June 18, 1979, edition of the *New York Times.* One hundred representatives (nearly all of them Republicans) signed an accompanying letter, holding Cuba and the Soviet Union largely responsible for Nicaragua's troubles and warning of the threat that communist influence posed in Central America. They noted that the failure of the United States to support Nicaragua had been interpreted by communist leaders as an indication of American indifference. Should the United States fail to take some action, "We will shortly find that the Soviet Union will control an area bordering on two oceans stretching from Panama to the vast oil reserves of Mexico."[66]

Similar divisions marked the broader foreign policy community. American Catholics, as we shall see, would become incensed over U.S. policies regarding the murder of Catholic reformers in El Salvador. On the right, the neoconservative coalition that would become so influential under later presidents Ronald Reagan and George H. W. Bush applauded Carter's tough moral stances against the Soviet Union. But they complained when the administration took similar stances toward "authoritarian" leaders in Brazil or Argentina. The USSR, as they saw it, was inherently evil when it came to human rights. The very makeup of the Soviet system prevented them from seeing human rights as having any legitimacy. Authoritarian regimes, on the other hand, simply departed from values held within their own system. As Jeane Kirkpatrick wrote in her November 1979 critique of Carter's policies, when authoritarian regimes abused human rights, it was socially understood to be just that—an abuse. In the USSR, however, the state was seen to be paramount to the individual, and so abuses were the accepted norm. The implication was that human rights would always be oppressed in such regimes. For Kirkpatrick and the other neoconservatives, only the USSR and its "puppet" Cuba under its dictator Fidel Castro were actively trying to export their dogma to other nations.[67]

The administration was not even exempt from criticism from U.S. allies. When German Chancellor Helmut Schmidt visited Washington on July 13, 1977, he voiced his concern that the Carter human rights campaign was overly aggressive and that it might lead to a counterproductive confrontation with the Soviet Union at the upcoming thirty-five-nation Belgrade Conference.[68]

Why the Conflicts?

Carter discovered that in the United States almost everyone supported the commitment to human rights in the abstract. But as the values were made concrete and politically relevant, political and moral differences would emerge. His problems were accentuated by the delay in having specific guidelines in place.

At a more fundamental level, however, Carter seems never to have thought through the actual limits of his human rights policies in terms of certain political realities. When one nation takes on the role of enforcer, its own values and interests get mixed into the equations. In a world where a state's national security ultimately depends on its own power and position, states will be tempted to go easy on political allies and act harshly toward adversaries. Carter was more concerned about Soviet advances in the world than he initially indicated in his Notre Dame speech, and his human rights policies came to reflect that concern.

When he pulled back on human rights issues while seeking the support of China, his assurances to the Soviet Union that his policies were not directed at them seemed hollow. Carter's warm receptions of Romania's Ceauşescu and the shah of Iran reinforced widespread perceptions that the United States had a dual standard in these matters.

After the Soviet Union intervened militarily in Afghanistan, human rights considerations gave way to a concern for attaining new strategic positions. In his last year in office, Carter provided military assistance to and sought armed bases from Iraq, Saudi Arabia, and other regimes with very little commitment to Wilsonian ideas of civil rights. Concerned about maintaining listening posts and enhancing U.S. military capabilities in the region, he no longer made human rights worries a part of the package. In Latin America, fear of Cuban-inspired revolutionary movements and the inherent difficulties in building democracy in regimes not one's own led the United States to downplay the importance of human rights principals in Nicaragua and El Salvador.

The reform of regimes from the outside is apt to be a daunting task and only possible under special conditions. Human rights proclamations, critiques of the bad behavior of other countries' governments, and the offering of moral support and possible safe havens to critics are relatively easy. But the very nature of the international order poses problems when one nation seeks to impose standards of justice and morality on another. Can one really promote from the outside the civic culture and legal frameworks that are requisite to the functioning of an order in which freedom is recognized? Even occupying powers have found that to be a difficult and expensive task.

When sanctions are applied, moreover, their efficacy will be limited when the enforcing states have to deal with either powerful or relatively isolated adversaries. The United States had little leverage relative to the Soviet Union, particularly as relations with that country deteriorated and cultural and economic ties that could be used as levers evaporated. In South America, Argentina, Brazil, Chile, and Uruguay could reach across the Atlantic for export outlets and arms support when the United States seemed to them to be overreaching. In Iran, Ayatollah Ruholla Khomeini welcomed for a time efforts to isolate Iran politically and economically. U.S. efforts could be used as evidence that the "Great Satan" was once again intervening in Iranian politics on the side of their adversaries. Only when Khomeini consolidated his power might he be ready to give up the U.S. diplomats taken hostage in November 1979 in exchange for the Iranian funds that the United States had frozen in U.S. banks. Indeed, for those regimes in Africa and the Middle East cut off from world cultural, trading, or monetary complexes no real attempts were ever made to change their human rights practices.

As Brzezinski saw it, in Carter's first two years in office the issue of human rights "tended to overshadow the pressing requirements of strategic reality. In the last two, we had to make up for lost time, giving a higher priority to more fundamental interests of national security."[69] Others were concerned that human rights commitments had evaporated during Carter's final months in office. Certainly U.S. policies relative to El Salvador, as we shall see, were a contradiction of all that Carter stood for. In April 1980, Esteban Torres, director of the White House Office of Hispanic Affairs, forwarded the president a memo he received from a prominent jurist complaining about the reduced emphasis on human rights; the jurist argued that this was a mistake. In a poignant note in the margin of Torres's letter Carter wrote, "I agree."[70]

Still, Carter's human rights policies were not without positive consequences. Pressures on the Soviet Union made diplomacy more difficult, but as long as there were some goods the USSR could expect from the United States (high-level technology, most-favored-nation status in trade), the emigration of dissidents from the Soviet Union increased.[71] U.S. policies, moreover, did have a positive impact on regimes such as those of South Africa and Poland, where the governments in power—the forces of the status quo—found it prudent to make adaptations relatively strong groups within its borders committed to human rights.

Most important, ideas have consequences for the broader political culture in which states operate. Former first lady Eleanor Roosevelt had played a central hands-on role in the formulation of the Universal Declaration of Human Rights, adopted by the UN on December 10, 1948. The revolutionary idea at the time was that there were certain absolute human values and that these values could be universally recognized. Enforcement would be left to the voluntary action of each state itself.[72]

Jimmy Carter saw himself as adding to that contribution. For him, as he noted at the thirtieth anniversary of the UN Declaration of Human Rights, human rights were "the soul of our foreign policy." Whatever the concessions and complications he embraced along the way, he put the issue on the international agenda. As Jessica Tuchman of the National Security Council noted on January 5, 1978, "the major accomplishment [of the Carter administration] ...has been to raise this issue to the forefront of world consciousness. Virtually all world leaders are now concerned with human rights. They know that now their human rights image is a significant factor in their standing in the international community—as well as in their relationships to the U.S."[73]

THE DEATH OF THE ARCHBISHOP

If human rights are the soul of U.S. foreign policy, then the Carter administration sinned in dealing with El Salvador. Jimmy Carter began his presidency by coming to the support of Andrei Sakahrov, the great Soviet human rights activist. He ended up with policies that isolated Archbishop Oscar Arnulfo Romero y Galdámez of El Salvador, a man who took even greater risks to promote human rights in his own polity.

In an open letter on February 17, 1980, Romero wrote President Carter and urged him to not support the Salvadoran government then in power. Continuing to supply military equipment and advisors to the junta would only lead to a major blood bath, Romero advised, and would "sharpen the injustice and the repression inflected on the organized people, whose struggle has often been for respect for their most basic human rights."[1]

Secretary of State Cyrus Vance, in a reply delivered by the new U.S. ambassador Robert E. White, noted that while "we understand your concerns about the dangers of providing military assistance [to the Salvadoran government, it]...offers the best prospect for peaceful change toward a more just society."[2] Behind the scenes, the administration, with Carter's full knowledge, was attempting to persuade Pope John Paul II to pressure the archbishop to drop his active role in opposing the junta.

A few days after receiving the U.S. reply, Romero was delivering Mass in the chapel of the Hospital de la Divina Providencia of San Salvador. A single bullet fired by a professional assassin from a red Volkswagen outside the chapel felled him. "May God have mercy on the assassin," were his dying words.[3]

At his funeral on Sunday, March 30, more than 50,000 people gathered at San Salvador's major cathedral. In the midst of a tribute to Romero by the Mexican cardinal Ernesto Corripto Ahumado (John Paul II's representative), a bomb exploded and was followed by several bursts of gunfire. In the end, approximately forty people were killed. Many, uninjured by the blast itself, were trampled or crushed against fences surrounding the cathedral during the ensuing panic as people tried to escape from the blast.[4]

Romero's death was due in part to his political isolation from the two forces in El Salvador—the United States and the Vatican—that might have more openly protected him from right wing elements that had penetrated the governing junta, the army and various governmental bureaus. Concerns about a left wing takeover, reinforced by the recent victories of the Sandinistas in Nicaragua, led the United States to resist Romero's open opposition to a series of juntas that at best were simply unable to bring about significant reform or control violence. The concerns of the Vatican, somewhat more complex, led to a policy that complimented that of the United States.

Saint or Politician?

At the time of his appointment as archbishop in February 1977, Romero was seen as a conservative who would correct the leftist course undertaken by his predecessor. But only three weeks after his installation, his good friend, the Jesuit priest Rutilio Grande, was murdered on his way to celebrate Mass.[5] When the then-in-place regime of General Carlos Humberto Romero (not related) failed to show any interest in actively pursuing the murderers of Grande and several other reformers, the archbishop began to move in another direction. At first he refused to appear at government events, seeing any churchly appearance as legitimizing a government that made no attempt to bring the murderers to justice. As a priest, he presided over the funerals of people killed in the pursuit of justice as he saw it.[6]

When a military junta overthrew General Romero's regime in October 1979, the archbishop shared the hopes of the Carter administration that the new government would reform the Salvadoran economic and justice systems.

But the archbishop and the Carter administration would soon come to a parting of the ways as several new governments underwent a series of resignations and failed to reduce the violence against those demanding land and political reforms. In January of 1980, the civilian members of the first junta resigned. The second junta was no more successful. On March 10, Hector Dada and five other leading Christian Democrats resigned from both the government and their party. Dada wrote in his letter of resignation that "we have not been able to stop the repression....the chances for producing reforms with the support of the people are receding beyond reach."[7] In the third junta, Dada's place was taken by Central Intelligence Agency–backed José Napoleon Duarte, leader of the now truncated Christian Democrats. He finally decided to take a direct role in the process that he had previously supported from behind the scenes.[8]

With U.S. backing, the new government enacted sweeping reforms, expropriating landholdings above 500 hectares and nationalizing commercial banks and savings and loan institutions.[9] But on March 17, shortly after the new junta announced its agricultural reform program, the minister of agriculture told Romero in a private meeting that the whole program was being sabotaged from within.[10] Violence against the recipients of the expropriated acreage by security forces went unchecked. And the "unofficial" remnants of Orden (a right wing paramilitary group), which had been disbanded on paper by the first junta, continued to roam the country, killing reformers and leftists at will.[11]

As these developments unfolded, Romero argued in a series of homilies that the juntas were just casting a veil over the same old system. When persons of goodwill have no impact on government, he said on February 17, 1980, their continued presence in it can only provide a cover for the injustices under it. "Neither the [government] Junta nor the Christian Democrats," he continued, "govern this country. Political power is in the hands of the armed forces which are unscrupulous in their use of this power. They only know how to repress the people and defend the interests of the Salvadorian oligarchy."[12]

To deal with the increasingly outspoken archbishop, Carter and his aides had turned to the Vatican. At the Special Coordinating Committee (SCC) meetings on

January 28, Zbigniew Brzezinski noted, "We are already contacting him [the pope], but perhaps we should consider more....The Pope has to get to Romero, and call him back from Salvador to talk to him."[13] The next day, January 29, Carter was informed of the SCC decision, and on January 31, Brzezinski wrote a memorandum about the conclusions from the SCC meeting. He noted that "a paper describing the status of this effort [to influence Romero]" should be forwarded to the State Department.[14]

On January 31, 1980, the State Department, responding to a request from the SCC, prepared the following letter for Brzezinski to send to the pontiff:[15]

> I am writing to you to seek your personal understanding and support and your wise counsel in dealing with a trend of events in the Central American region which is most disturbing to my government....A tide of modernization is moving through Central America that is creating irresistible pressures for rapid and profound economic, social and political reforms....Elements of the extreme left are seizing this opportunity to launch violence and terrorism designed to destroy the existing order and replace it with a Marxist one, which promises to be equally repressive and totalitarian....
>
> In El Salvador the Church under Archbishop Romero's leadership has to date played a similar role [to Nicaragua on behalf of moderation and peaceful reforms]. However, in recent weeks, the Archbishop has both publicly and privately indicated a shift away from this position. Impatient with the pace of progress of the moderate Revolutionary Governing Junta led by the Christian Democratic Party and reformist military officers, and increasingly convinced of an eventual victory by the extreme left, the Archbishop has strongly criticized the Junta and leaned toward support for the extreme left.
>
> Through our frequent and frank dialogue with Archbishop Romero and his Jesuit advisors we have warned them against such a move. We have urged them not to abandon the Junta in this critical, initial phase....
>
> Ambassador Wagner recently communicated to Secretary of State Casaroli our specific concerns regarding the situation in El Salvador and requested his assistance with the Archbishop. I am now writing to share this concern directly with you. The people of Central America urgently need the wise intervention of Your Holiness to ensure that the Church plays the responsible and constructive role on behalf of moderation and peaceful change which only it can play.[16]

It is not clear if the letter was ever sent.[17] But, earlier, on a stopover in Rome on his way to receive an honorary degree from the University of Louvain in Belgium, the pope confronted Archbishop Romero. In a meeting on Wednesday, January 30, shortly after the pope's general audience,[18] John Paul told Romero he understood the difficulties he faced and asked him to "continue to defend social justice and love for the poor." But he also cautioned Romero to be careful of ideologies that, under the pretense of defending social and human rights, could produce greater violations in the long run. Romero assured him that he always tried to present his views by "praising the spiritual,

Christian values of my people and saying that we must always defend and preserve them." Following their conversation, John Paul hugged Romero and told him that he prayed daily for peace in El Salvador.[19]

Some reports suggest that the meeting with the pope was more confrontational. One of John Paul's biographers claims that the pontiff warned the increasingly popular archbishop to be leery of a victory of the popular leftists for fear it may bring "retribution and bloodshed" to the country.[20]

The following day, Romero visited Cardinal Agostino Casaroli, the Vatican's secretary of state, who mentioned that U.S. ambassador Robert Wagner had met with him earlier and expressed U.S. concern over Romero's apparent support of "a revolutionary line of action." Casaroli agreed with Romero that he should continue to support what he saw as sound organizations in his country, both in terms of the government and popular organizations, and that the Church should not be swayed by earthly powers (i.e., the United States) but should instead "proceed in accord with its conscience and the gospel."[21]

The U.S. goal at this time, made explicit by Brzezinski at a February 15, 1980, SCC meeting, was to "split the left and neutralize the right. We have been in touch with a number of individuals, including Archbishop Romero..." and Brzezinski "had personally conveyed a message to the Pope to try to seek his support with regard to Archbishop Romero." Romero "had just gotten a message from the Pope." When diplomat and future ambassador Robert White suggested that these attempts at persuasion did not have the desired impact on Archbishop Romero, Brzezinski responded, "He would probably get another message, perhaps Monday or Tuesday." Attached to the original report, but lacking from this copy was a status report on efforts to get the Vatican to persuade Archbishop Romero.[22]

"It didn't work," Carter wrote in the margins of Brzezinski's memo describing these efforts at the February 15 SCC meeting.[23]

A few days later, on Thursday, February 21, the Carter administration sent Assistant Secretary for Inter-American Affairs William Bowdler to El Salvador to explain its policies to Romero. The U.S. goal was not to put arms in the hand of the right wing security forces but to assist "some aspect in which the army is still deficient."

Romero responded that Defense Secretary José Garcia, who was in charge of the military aide the United States sent to El Salvador, could direct it into the wrong hands. Their talks concluded with Bowdler's statement that he would suggest to the U.S. government that military aid be conditional on the actual implementation of the reforms that had been previously announced as well as "the elimination of the repressive tendencies that obviously prevail in the present government."[24]

Finally, in early March, Ambassador Robert White appeared on the scene in El Salvador.[25] White had formerly served as ambassador to Paraguay, where his human rights efforts had saved the lives of persons opposing the government and his activities led to the revelation that Josef Mengele, the Nazi war criminal, held Paraguayan citizenship. According to Latin American historian Lars Schoultz, White "stood out among all U.S. diplomatic personnel in Latin America for his effective work on behalf of human rights."[26]

Romero, in his first meeting with White on March 14, 1980, found the new ambassador "to be a man who is more than a diplomat; a man who has great respect for human rights, who has also been under fire in politics. He wants to be a true collaborator in the process or our people. He recognizes the errors that have been committed by his country and in our Latin American countries and is willing to work to create another image of the United States."[27]

Certainly White listened to Romero. A Catholic, he was actually encouraged by the formation of the Jesuit-sponsored Christian Democratic unions and political parties in Latin America. "The priests and the bishops of the Church in Latin America," the ambassador noted, "were almost always very, very well informed. They may have a particular view, but talking to them I found out what was going on. The papal nuncios usually had a very different viewpoint than the local bishops. The nuncios lived in a world where any kind of social conflict disturbed what they see as the tripartite order of the rich, the military, and the church working together."[28]

Nor did White want American troops on the scene. Shortly before coming to El Salvador, Brzezinski had asked him, "Do you want troops down there?" White responded, "I think really that's the last thing I want. I view this as a [situation] that can be solved by political means." Brzezinski shook his head. Once installed, White fired the Central Intelligence Agency station chief. When he discovered that that head of El Salvador's Treasury Police, Nicolas Caranzza, whom White considered to have "the worst record of human rights," was on the CIA payroll, he realized he would have a continuing battle with Washington, D.C. In the coming days White also had to resist the Department of Defense's efforts to send military advisors to El Salvador, even threatening to resign if they were sent.[29]

The archbishop, in the meantime, was receiving worldwide attention for his calls for justice. The Swedish Ecumenical Action honored him in a ceremony at Romero's basilica, giving him their Peace Prize. A group from the U.S. National Council of Churches was on its way to inspect conditions in El Salvador. News representatives from around the world attended his press conferences.[30]

Still, the violence at home had been building. In a February television address Major Roberto D'Aubuisson Arrieta, a former leader in the country's intelligence agency with connections to Salvadoran death squads, included the names of Archbishop Romero and Attorney General Mario Zamora (who was also a leader in the Christian Democratic Party) in his list of "subversives."[31] On February 18, the church radio transmitter and the library at Catholic University were bombed, and Romero was warned that he might be killed.[32] On February 23, Zamora was assassinated, sending a message to all the civilians associated with the junta that they should tread lightly.[33] On that same day, Romero noted in his diary that the nuncio to Costa Rica had warned him again that his life was in danger.[34] On March 10, the day after the archbishop had celebrated a Mass for Zamora, an attaché case was found near the high altar containing explosives that had failed to go off.[35]

White warned Washington that same month: "If the systematic violation of human rights in the countryside does not cease, all the agrarian and banking reforms in the world will not help."[36]

Romero was at this time rotating the places he slept; he told friends that fear often kept him awake all night anyway.[37] But the archbishop did what he had to do. As Segundo Azcue wrote, "He felt terror at it as Jesus did in the garden. But he did not leave his post and his duty, ready to drink the chalice that the Father might give him to drink."[38] Two weeks before his death he told José Calderon Salazar, a Mexican newspaper correspondent, "Martyrdom is a grace of God that I do not believe I deserve. But if God accepts the sacrifice of my life, let my blood be a seed of freedom and the sign that hope will soon be reality."[39]

Responding to these events, Romero suggested on March 23, 1980, that soldiers need not follow immoral commands:

> No soldier is obliged to obey an order in violation of the law of God. It is time you recovered your conscience, and obeyed your conscience instead of orders to commit sin. The church is the defender of God's rights, God's law, human dignity, and the worth of persons. It cannot remain silent before such an abomination. We ask the government to consider seriously the fact that reforms are of no use when they are steeped in all this blood. In the name of God, then, and in the name of this suffering people, whose screams and cries mount to heaven, and daily grow louder, I beg you, I entreat you, I order you in the name of God: Stop the repression![40]

These were the final words of his last complete sermon.

After Romero's assassination, the U.S. evacuated the dependents of the twenty-five diplomats from its embassy in San Salvador. But otherwise no major response was forthcoming.[41]

The response of the Salvadoran government to Romero's murder and the killings at his funeral suggests it had no interest in finding those responsible. El Salvador's Defense Minister Colonel Guillermo Garcia, later to be linked to the death squads, told Ambassador White that a Cuban exile had shot the archbishop. Other governmental supporters suggested that the massacre at Romero's funeral was due to an attempt by the left wing Coordinating Committee to steal Romero's body. A number of foreign visitors made a joint statement that invalidated the government's story and absolved the committee.[42]

The fates of others who reported events at the chapel where Romero was killed provided additional support that the members of the junta were complicit in the murder. These witnesses disappeared, were killed, or were at least threatened. Napoleon Martinez, who had helped carry Romero from the chapel on the day of his murder, was kidnapped in May 1981 and never seen again. On April 20, the newspaper *El Independiente* reported that the judge assigned to investigate the case declared that Major Roberto D'Aubuisson and General José Alberto Medrano had orchestrated the murder and hired an assassin. There was an attempt on the judge's life in El Salvador and he was afraid to return from exile in Venezuela.[43]

In the months that followed, Colonel Jaime Abdul Gutierrez, the leader of the conservative military faction in the junta, proceeded to weed out the reformist officers from key roles in the military, assigning them to foreign diplomatic positions and outlying areas of El Salvador. The reformist Colonel Adolfo Arnoldo Majano Remos, whose attempts to accommodate non-Marxist labor and peasant groups were undercut, survived an assassination attempt in November and was ousted from the junta on December 6 while on a visit to Panama. He returned to El Salvador in a vain effort to shore up his support among the ranks. By this time, the country was on the verge of a major civil conflict.[44] And the murder of civilians continued. On November 27, 1980, six leaders of the moderate-left Frente Democrático Revolucionario (Revolutionary Democratic Front) were mutilated and murdered.[45]

Then, on December 4, a peasant delivering milk discovered the bodies of four American churchwomen (Maryknoll Sisters Ita Ford and Maura Clark, Ursuline Sister Dorothy Kazel, and lay missioner Jean Donovan).[46] All four women had been working with the poor and the families of the "missing."

Ambassador White had dined with two of the women the night before their murders.[47] Watching the churchwomen pulled by ropes from their shallow graves, White remarked, "This time the bastards won't get away with it."[48]

There was widespread popular indignation in the United States at the murders of the women; churches around the country held memorial masses in their honor. Archbishop of the Washington, D. C., Diocese James Hickey condemned the murders in a letter to Secretary of State Edmund Muskie. The Salvadoran government, he wrote, had been granting "some of those extremists a kind of license to kill." He criticized the Carter administration for its perceived inaction and its deliverance of aid to the Salvadoran regime and called upon parishioners to speak out against the attacks. "As Christians and as Americans, we cannot stand by in silence while this senseless and deliberate violence continues."[49] A shocked Senator Edward Kennedy called President-Elect Ronald Reagan and asked him to issue a statement condemning the actions. He also called on Carter to halt the impending $5.7 million in military credit the administration had approved for the Salvadoran government until a formal investigation was launched.[50] Amnesty International lobbied the United Nations, claiming that the junta was responsible for detaining and murdering the opposition.[51]

The administration's response to these events was a temporary suspension of U.S. support and a decision to send a "fact-finding mission to El Salvador to investigate the murders." Led by William G. Bowdler and William D. Rogers, the current and former assistant secretaries of state for inter-American affairs, the commission concluded a few days later that there was no evidence linking the murders to the top officials in the junta, though low-level government officials attempted to cover them up. They recommended that U.S. aid, temporarily curtailed, be resumed. On December 12, Carter restored $20 million in aid to the country.[52] Only after the Federal Bureau of Investigation and the State Department uncovered possible military links did the Salvadoran authorities agree to cooperate. But they pointed to robbery as a motive for the murders.[53] A few days before Carter left office, the United States went further, providing $5 million in lethal aid to the Salvadorans. This aid was provided because of "State Department assurances that progress was being made in investigating the death of the four churchwomen."[54]

Throughout this process, Ambassador White had informed Washington that Salvadoran security forces were responsible for the deaths of Romero and the church-women.[55] He even sent the State Department a cable charging that expatriate Salvadoran millionaires in Miami were funding the death squads.[56]

After Reagan took office as president, White was fired as ambassador.[57] In April 1981, White told the U.S. Congress that there was "compelling, if not 100 percent conclusive evidence that D'Aubuisson ordered" Romero's murder.[58] On January 22, 1981, White publicly noted that he had "no reason to believe that the Government of El Salvador is conducting a serious investigation." He went on to suggest that the United States was concealing information, saying he was "not going to be involved in a cover-up."[59]

The Battle over Liberation Theology

One complication the Carter administration faced in El Salvador was that the opposition to right wing government was not only comprised of communists and other leftists but also Jesuit priests and other religious workers motivated by the emergence of liberation theology. Christianity for them was a force to be used for the poor, and some of them, based on their own experience, believed that a class-based privileged elite that employed violence against reformers might have to be met by countervailing force.[60] Archbishop Romero was one of these.

The Vatican, however, was concerned about the emerging liberation theology and Romero as one of its proponents. Complaints from members of the Bishops Conference of El Salvador about Romero being too political raised questions at the Vatican about his leadership. In February 1978, there was an attempt to prevent Georgetown University from giving him an honorary degree.[61] In his first visit with John Paul II, Romero had to defend his actions in El Salvador to not only the pope but also to Vatican Secretary of State Casaroli. At one point, the Vatican was considering sending an envoy to take over the actual administration of his diocese, leaving him archbishop in name only.[62] Shortly before his murder, the papal nuncio from Costa Rica pressed upon Romero the need for greater harmony in the Bishops Conference. When warned of the possible communist makeup of some of the popular organizations, Romero noted that he had been very careful to avoid such infiltration. "Anti-communism," he warned, "is many times the weapon that the economic and political powers use for their social and political injustices."[63]

But for Romero, Jesus Christ's message was that virtue must be practiced in this world.[64] The day before he was murdered, Romero claimed, "God's reign is already present on earth in our mystery. When the Lord comes, it will be brought to perfection."[65] So he condemned the "disappearances," the murders, and the forced expulsion of persons who opposed the government—all violations of widely shared norms adopted, he pointed out, in the International Declaration of Human Rights.[66] Marxist philosophy, as he saw it, was spiritually hollow at its core; but Karl Marx was onto something when he argued that institutional support for political domination and issues of social class would have to be addressed before any meaningful reforms could take place in countries such as El Salvador.[67]

Romero recalled the traditional doctrine of proportionate violence in legitimate self-defense. As he stated in his fourth pastoral letter,

> We are also aware that great numbers of campesinos, workers, slum dwell-ers, and others who have organized themselves to defend their rights and to promote legitimate changes in social structures are simply regarded as "ter-rorists" and subversives. They are arrested, tortured, they disappear, they are killed without any concern for the law of those legal institutions that are there to protect them. Confronted by this harmful and unjust situation they have frequently been forced to defend themselves, even to the point of having recourse to violence. And lately the response to this has been the arbitrary violence of the state.[68]

The words of Isaiah, as Romero's follower Jon Sobrino suggests, capture the arch-bishop's message:

> Woe to those who call evil good, and good evil,
> Who change darkness into light and light into darkness,
> Who change bitter into sweet, and sweet into bitter! [Isa. 5:20][69]

Pope John Paul II was also concerned about the poor. Three months after Romero's death the pontiff, on a visit to Brazil, told a Portuguese crowd that he was appalled at the "subhuman conditions" that existed in the country and asked the Brazilian leaders, "Do you not feel the pangs of conscience on account of your riches and affluence?"[70]

But John Paul opposed a basic tenet of liberation theology—that economic justice requires deep structural changes involving an increase in the power of the poor. He appealed to those with wealth and power to act justly to initiate reforms.[71] For him, liberation theology was too secular, too reliant on Marxist concepts of class warfare, and as a people's theology it challenged the authority of the Vatican.

In the years to come, John Paul II would uproot the very movement for which Archbishop Romero had risked his life. He appointed conservative priests to positions of responsibility and closed down or cut funds to schools and churches throughout Latin America that had become "hotbeds of liberation theology seminaries."[72] In 1989 the Vatican even divided the archdiocese of Paulo Evaristo Arns, the cardinal of Sao Paulo, Brazil. A corecipient with Carter of an honorary degree at Notre Dame in 1977, Arns had been an outspoken critic of the military junta in Brazil, an advocate for the poor, and a proponent of liberation theology.[73]

Though the pope had "no divisions," as Joseph Stalin once suggested,[74] his appoint-ment powers were used to undercut the ideas and the support for those Catholic priests who had played a significant role in the reform movement in Latin America. In this respect, he could accomplish what Jimmy Carter could not.

The Aftermath

In 1980, Carter's last year in office, the conflict in El Salvador deepened into a civil war with a death toll, over the years, of thousands. It only ended in January 1992, when the United Nations mediated the conflict between the Frente Farabundo Martí para la Liberación Nacional (the FMLN; Farabundo Martí National Liberation Front) and the government of El Salvador.[75] As a result of the Peace Accords, the radical forces under the FMLN umbrella disarmed and became a political party, while the army became subject to civilian rule. The United States had been too involved earlier to act as peacemaker. But it did pledge, with others, to buy up land to distribute to the campesinos.

The Reagan administration that followed continued to deny the junta's complicity in the murder of Archbishop Romero or the four American churchwomen. But ultimately the connections would be made. On November 19, 1987, Amado Antonio Garay gave testimony before the Commission for the Investigation of Criminal Offense suggesting that Captain Alvaria Rafael Savaria, an aide to D'Aubuisson, had played a role in the murder of Romero.[76] Savaria would never face criminal charges—he was granted amnesty by El Salvador in the 1992 Peace Accords.[77] But in a California civil trial held in 2005, Savaria was found guilty of plotting the murder and ordered to pay civil damages.[78] In 2006, Savaria asked for forgiveness from the Catholic Church. He told the Nuevo Herald newspaper that he did indeed play a role in the assassination, and he promised to identify others responsible for the crime.

Earlier, in 1984, six National Guardsmen were convicted in the murders of the American churchwomen.[79] But Judge Hard Tyler, working from papers provided him by the State Department, declared in his sentencing of Luis Antonio Colindres Aleman, who had given the order to the guards who killed the women, that Aleman had "acted at his own initiative." Several years later, in 1998, the four members of the Salvadoran National Guard who were convicted of the murders in 1984 broke their silence. One of the men confessed to reporters that Luis Aleman had told them, "Don't be worried....This is an order that comes from higher levels, and nothing is going to happen to us."[80] In 1993, a UN Truth Commission concluded that the Salvadoran National Guard, under the leadership of General Eugenio Vides Casanova and the junta's minister of defense, General José Guillermo Garcia, had organized "an official cover-up" of the murders.[81]

As for Archbishop Romero, a statue honoring him now stands above the Great West Door of Westminster Abbey. Several members of British Parliament are on record as recommending him for a Nobel Peace Prize.[82] But he remains a controversial figure for the Catholic Church. Calls to recognize Romero as a saint have stalled. San Salvador's Auxiliary Bishop Gregorio Rosa Chavez noted in March 2000 that there is "a certain degree of unease" in Rome about elevating Romero to sainthood.[83] In November 2005, the Vatican newspaper La Civiltá Cattolica concluded that Romero was murdered for his "faith-motivated actions" and not because of his politics. He "continues to be the object of deep veneration, but also of sharp criticism."[84]

Members of the Carter administration evidently want to forget this whole tragic affair. Neither Jimmy Carter nor any of his foreign policy aides even mention the archbishop in their memoirs.[85] Preoccupied at the time with a possible leftist takeover, they were blind to the excesses and failures of the right wing regimes they supported. Former ambassador White remains one exception; in October 2000, he testified against General Carlos Vides Casanova and General José Guillermo Garcia in a federal court in Florida.[86]

In early 1980 Carter had other worries, as we have seen. Iran was holding American diplomats as hostages, the Soviets had invaded Afghanistan, and Ted Kennedy was challenging Carter in the Democratic primaries. If the United States could rescue the hostages it would not only resolve Carter's personal concerns over their well-being but would free him up to campaign for a second term. Maybe then he could carry out the foreign policy reforms he had promised the American people but had not yet been able to accomplish.

Part 6
FINALE

OPERATION EAGLE CLAW

On April 11, 1980, Jimmy Carter opened a foreign policy breakfast meeting in the Cabinet Room: "Gentlemen, I want you to know that I am seriously considering an attempt to rescue the hostages." The president continued, "A team of expert paramilitary people now report that they have confidence on their ability to rescue our people."

With these statements, Hamilton Jordan's heart raced: "He's going to do it!" he said to himself, "He's had enough!"[1]

At that point the chairman of the Joint Chiefs of Staff, David Jones, spread out a big map on the table, and Secretary of Defense Harold Brown elaborated on the various stages of the mission. All present at the meeting seemed to be in agreement. Vice President Walter Mondale said he was inclined to attempt the rescue. Zbigniew Brzezinski spoke glowingly about the members of the Delta team and their previous training and backgrounds;[2] at one point, he reminded the group that the nights would be getting shorter so the operation should be undertaken as soon as possible, and he proposed that prisoners be taken as well as retaliatory steps against the Iranians at the same time as the rescue operation. Otherwise, he did not talk much, letting others carry the call. Director of Central Intelligence Stansfield Turner was positive but cautioned Jones about the conditions inside Iran.

The Secretary of Defense Harold Brown argued that that rescue was the best option for bringing the hostages home. Press Secretary Jody Powell agreed. Warren Christopher, who was sitting in for Secretary of State Cyrus Vance, said that he could not accurately represent his feelings because he had not yet discussed the mission with Vance.

By the end of the meeting, Carter was on board for the rescue mission, named Operation Eagle Claw. As Jordan observed, "The overwhelming logic of Harold's point carried the day. The other military options and sanctions wouldn't bring the hostages home, but the highly specialized Delta team probably could."[3]

The one individual who would have raised questions about the dangers and political consequences of such an operation, Secretary of State Vance, was not at the meeting. At Camp David on March 22, he had argued that the hostages would be freed only when the institutions of the Islamic Republic had solidified and Ayatollah Khomeini had no further political use for them.[4] The likelihood of physical harm to them was less than it had been, and eventually the situation inside Iran would make negotiations possible. But on this day, April 11, Vance was in Florida for a short, much-needed rest. No attempt was made to contact him before or after the rescue decision was made.[5]

Upon his return to Washington, D.C., on April 14, Vance was dismayed that such a "momentous decision" had been made in his absence. He asked for a National Security

Council meeting to hear his objections. At a meeting on April 15, Vance delineated his concerns:

1. America's allies were moving toward sanctions based on the belief that they would help the United States avoid military action. Going ahead with the mission without warning or consulting these allies would be seen as a betrayal of their trust.
2. The mission involved possible armed confrontations among hostages, crew, and Iranians. It could result in many deaths.
3. U.S. interest in the whole region could be severely damaged. The Islamic world would be outraged, causing a larger Western-Islamic conflict.
4. Even if the rescue mission were successful, the Iranians could react by taking new hostages, especially with all the American journalists in the area.[6]

When Vance had finished, the president asked if there were any reactions to his comments. An awkward silence ensued. Jordan, possibly projecting some of his own feelings, described Vance as scanning the room, "looking from Zbig to Mondale to Harold Brown, to Jody, and finally to me, his eyes begging for support. I fidgeted, feeling sorry for Cy, who sat there all alone."[7]

Carter broke the silence and personally dealt with many of Vance's objections.[8] After four months of planning, the Joint Chiefs of Staff were confident that the plan would succeed. In addition, Carter argued that (1) our allies—who were not making a great effort at supporting us—would be relieved if the rescue mission worked; (2) the mission was designed so that it could be stopped at several points if there were problems; (3) other Islamic states would be glad to see Iran put in its place; and (4) Americans in Iran, other than the diplomats, had accepted the risk of being taken hostage by traveling to Iran in the first place. Brown joined Carter in making some of these arguments.

When the president announced that he would stick to the decision he had made earlier, Brzezinski turned the group's attention to the details of the operation, including recommendations that Iranian prisoners be taken and retaliatory actions undertaken. As in the April 11 meeting, Carter showed some reluctance to accept these proposals for ancillary actions as unduly complicating the operation, though he did agree that prisoners could be taken and held until the final departure from Iran. The final decision against the concurrent retaliatory actions was not made until closer to the operation.[9]

Sensing that Carter retained some doubts, Brown arranged a secret meeting in the situation room on April 16. At the session, Carter quizzed General James Vaught, the commander of the overall operation, and Colonel Charles Beckwith, the leader of the rescue team in Iran, at length. But from the details given, it seems that the meeting was primarily a reassurance ritual for the president. The confidence, quickness, and details with which those responsible for managing the operation met his questions helped remove those doubts. One improvement—an increase of the number of helicopters from seven to eight—was made because General John Pustay, an aide to General David Jones, had whispered to a Brzezinski aide that they should look at the helicopter issue.[10]

At the meeting Carter pledged not to interfere with operational decisions. Earlier, he had discussions with Brzezinski indicating that, unlike President John F. Kennedy during the Bay of Pigs operation, he would depend on the professionals to do their job.[11] This was the opposite of the lesson Kennedy had drawn from that episode. Reacting to his reliance on Central Intelligence Agency professionals at the Bay of Pigs operation, Kennedy had retained as complete control over the military as he could during the Cuban missile crisis.[12]

Vance, who had been quiet at the meeting, was pulled aside by Jordan once it ended. To Jordan's disgust, Vance still had reservations about the operation, noting that he had learned from his earlier experience in the Pentagon that one had to be wary of such assurances from the military.[13]

Later, on the eve of the rescue operation, Carter had a meeting with U.S. Senate majority leader Robert Byrd to draw up a list of congressional leaders who should be consulted in the event of military operations. Though he intended to inform Byrd that such an operation was underway, Carter changed his mind at the last minute. He might have been concerned that Byrd would consider this failure to inform a slight. But Carter's impression at the time, he would later write, was not that he thought Byrd was untrustworthy but that he would prefer to be informed at the same time as other congressional leaders.[14]

The operation Carter had signed onto was of very high risk. There was the problem of discovery at the rendezvous site. Desert One was intersected by the only road between Mashad, a city of 500,000 people, and Yazd, a city of 100,000, and was well traveled at night due to the desert heat. When a U.S. plane landed at the site on March 31 to take soil samples and plant remote control devices to guide incoming aircraft—a procedure that probably took about an hour—six vehicles drove by.[15] The whole operation in Iran would take two days, and telltale signs of the landing left at Desert One could have blown U.S. cover, alerting Iranian authorities.[16]

But the landing on Desert One would be relatively simple compared with what would come later. American rangers would have to slip into Tehran without discovery, fly helicopters into or near the embassy compound, load the hostages into the helicopters, and then into waiting planes to fly out of a country in which the government had been aroused. American agents pre-positioned in Tehran would aid them. The earlier CIA-Canadian caper to get a few hostages out of Iran showed them how they could slip these pre-positioned agents past customs in and out of Iran.

The records of U.S. and British commando raids during World War II show a very high failure rate for such operations, and there had been no analogous large-scale raids in heavily populated areas within the past fifteen years.[17] A CIA report of March 16 suggested that the initial assault on the embassy and the process of locating the hostages was apt to result in losses of 45 percent of the total. The report, which was given to Stan Turner, went on to state the most likely outcome would result in the death of

60 percent of the hostages. Alternatively, of course, there was a likelihood that all or none of the hostages would be killed.[18] Brzezinski himself believed beforehand there would be some casualties, though he did not know how many.[19] Vance thought it would lead to the death of several hostages and possibly result in the taking of new ones.[20]

The decision to undertake the operation had been made without detailed knowledge of where each hostage was located in the compound. Khomeini, in a propaganda move, had released several women and black hostages back in November 1979, and from their debriefings the administration had some idea of where the hostages were being held at that time. But the hostages were sometimes rotated, and information on exactly where they were being held that April came into U.S. hands only a few hours before the operation was to begin. On April 23, a Pakistani cook at the embassy was allowed to leave Iran, and he boarded a plane traveling from Istanbul to Rome to visit his relatives. Next to him, by design or by accident, was a deep undercover American agent. Upon arrival in Rome, the cook told the CIA agent the location of the forty-five hostages held in the chancery and of the five held in the residence.[21]

Finally, on April 24, 1980, eight RH-53 D Sea Stallion helicopters took off from the aircraft carrier USS *Nimitz* for the flight to Desert One. At the same time, six C-130 transport planes left from Oman, transporting a total of ninety-seven Delta Force troops. At 10 p.m. April 24, the first C-130 landed at its destination at Desert One.[22] Within the hour, Colonel Beckwith called Colonel Vaught for an "abort situation."[23] Chopper 6's warning lights indicated a crack in the rotor blades, Chopper 5 had flown back to the *Nimitz* in the midst of a sandstorm, and Chopper 2 had also malfunctioned. Moreover, the choppers had landed at Desert One over an hour after their scheduled arrival time.[24] Beckwith reported that a minimum of eight functioning helicopters was a requisite for the success of the operation. If not, over twenty men would have to be left behind.[25]

That was not the end of the fiasco. A helicopter, rising for the journey back to base, ran into a C-130 fuselage. The cargo plane exploded, and eight Delta Force men aboard the plane were killed.[26] Fearing they would be discovered and fearing for their lives, the other men at the site scrambled to leave, and in the process departed without gathering up the bodies of their fallen colleagues. (Later, Khomeini would display the bodies of the eight Americans killed in a ghoulish fashion in the streets of Tehran.[27]) A plan showing the whole operation was inadvertently left behind.

At 4:57 p.m. Washington time (and 2:00 a.m. Iranian time), Secretary of Defense Brown called Carter, in the midst of a presidential campaign meeting, to tell him about the helicopter failures and of Colonel Beckwith's recommendation to call off the operation. After a brief pause, Carter consented to abort the mission.[28] Then the phone rang again. It was General Jones, who was on duty at the Pentagon and in direct contact with the Delta force. Jordan recalls the event as follows:

> "Yes, Dave..."
> The President closed his eyes. His jaw dropped and his face turned ashen. I knew right away that something terrible had happened. He swallowed

hard. "Are there any dead?" A few more seconds passed. "I understand...."
He slowly hung up. In an even voice, he informed us that during the withdrawal, a helicopter had crashed into the C-130 loaded with the Delta team members. There were some casualties and probably some dead.

No one said a word. The harsh reality of the failed mission and the tragic deaths began to sink in. Cy's voice broke the stillness. "Mr. President, I'm very, very sorry...."[29]

Jordan, who had been so enthusiastic days earlier, sought out a bathroom in which to vomit.[30] Carter asked that someone find John Kennedy's address to the nation after the failure of the Bay of Pigs incursion.[31]

At 1:00 a.m. on April 25, Press Secretary Powell delivered the first announcement of the situation.[32] At 7:00 a.m. that same day, Carter came on national television to give fuller details of the mission and to limit the political damage from it. The mission, he assured the world, was not directed against Iran or its people, nor was it a reckless undertaking. It was simply a "humanitarian mission" to rescue the hostages. "We were all convinced that if and when the rescue operations had been commenced that it had an excellent chance of success." The decision to go ahead with the plan had been motivated by his conclusion that the Iranian authorities neither could nor would resolve this crisis on their own authority. "With the steady unraveling of authority in Iran and mounting threats that were posed to the safety of the hostages themselves and [my] growing realization that their early release was highly unlikely, I made the decision to commence the rescue operations plans." Further, it did not presage other reckless action on the United States. At the end of his statement, Carter pledged, "We will see...a prompt resolution of the crisis without any loss of life and through peaceful and diplomatic means."[33]

Ironically, the failure of the mission brought a kind of relief to many Americans. As Carter noted at a later press conference, "There is a deeper failure than that of incomplete success. That is the failure to attempt a worthy effort, a failure to try."[34] The theme was picked up on talk shows and in newspapers around the country that following morning. Later, one of the men wounded in the operation said, "At least we tried...which is something we haven't been doing lately, just letting people stomp all over us."[35] The operation, as Patrick Caddell's poll suggested, had "lanced the festering boil."[36]

Later it became clear that there had been serious errors in the planning of the mission. A review of the raid by the Special Operations Review Board appointed by Carter noted, in a partially unclassified report, that additional helicopters and crew would have reduced the risk of failure. An unconstrained planner would have asked for eleven or twelve helicopters if the record of earlier comparable operations had been consulted. Further, the Desert One part of the operation had not been fully rehearsed, and there were serious problems with the rendezvous plan. There were no messengers at the site to take over in the event that nonelectronic communication had to be used. And personnel with critical functions were not known to each other; the emphasis on secrecy had kept crucial personnel from informing each other about the critical factors influencing the operation.

A table in the weather annex to the operation plan noted the frequency of low-flying dust storms in the area, but the pilots had not been permitted to see the report and had had no briefings on how to deal with such contingencies. The full scenario, to the extent that it had been reported at this time, suggested that the touchdown on Desert One was relatively simple compared to what would come later—getting the helicopter into or near the embassy compound, evacuating the hostages, and subsequently leaving the country.

The possibility of such a complex plan with so many variables was simply a matter of conjecture, the Holloway Commission reported.[37] Several observers of the operation concluded that it was fortunate the rescue option had been aborted. If the commandos had managed to reach Tehran, there would almost certainly have been massive casualties for both Americans and Iranians.[38]

Other military informants told *New York Times* reporters that the whole operation had been hampered by its interservice makeup—with personnel from the Army, Air Force, Navy, and Marines. With each service having its own mode of operation and tactical doctrine, coordination of the whole operation was made even more difficult.[39]

Consequences

Abroad, the mission's failure eroded American prestige. It was the last of many public efforts by the United States to exercise power that had failed. Joseph Luns, the secretary general of the North Atlantic Treaty Organization, thought the raid had "further complicated the already delicate situation in the Middle East."[40] More important, the apparent ineptitude with which it had been undertaken raised questions about American military prowess. Yitzhak Rabin, former Israeli prime minister and army chief of staff, expressed the reactions of many foreign observers when he queried, sarcastically, "America doesn't have enough helicopters?"[41]

Two days before the rescue operation Vance told Carter he would resign as secretary of state because he could not go out and support the raid to the public; he would not, however, implement his decision or make it public until the raid had taken place.[42] Bitter about the resignation, Carter took some indirect verbal swipes at Vance in response to a question about his new choice for secretary of state. Edmund Muskie would be a "more statesmanlike" figure.[43] Indeed, Carter was somewhat taken aback by the decision of Vance to resign: "My heart went out to Cy Vance, who was deeply troubled and heavily burdened. He was alone in his opposition to the rescue mission among all my advisors and he knew it." Carter went on to note "that there was no serious difference between us on major issues on American foreign policy."[44]

The operation did enable Carter to return to the reelection campaign he had suspended at the beginning of the crisis. On April 26, Senator Byrd told Carter he should "get out and talk" to the people of the country. "The Ayatollah Khomeini doesn't just have fifty-three hostages," he said. "He also has the President hostage."[45] Four days later, on April 30, Carter announced that he was coming out of the Oval Office. The foreign crises had become "manageable enough" to allow him to undertake a limited campaign schedule.[46] With this, Carter placed the hostage crisis on the back burner. There it would remain until political circumstances would give Khomeini a real motivation to negotiate.[47]

THE FINAL MONTHS

The Democratic Party Conventions opened at Madison Square Garden in New York City on August 11, 1980. At this point Jimmy Carter's renomination as the Democratic nominee for president was secure. By the time of the Pennsylvania primary in late April of that year, he had garnered 1,137 delegates of the 1,666 needed to win the nomination. As president and Democratic Party leader, he would be able to control the agenda and dictate the party platform.

But Ted Kennedy, who had contested Carter's nomination as the Democratic candidate for president since the previous November, was not going to give up easily. He had won the New York and other primaries in Democratic strongholds, and he now sought a change in convention rules that would allow delegates to "be free" to change their vote, deviating from prior pledges should they so desire. Though Kennedy lost on the rules change with a vote of 2,129–1,146, he upstaged Carter with an eloquent speech embracing the traditional liberal policies of his party. As Hamilton Jordan later noted, "We may have won the nomination, but Ted Kennedy won the hearts."[1] Even after that vote confirming Carter's nomination, Kennedy refused to raise Carter's hands in victory, as tradition dictated he should. Arriving late to the arena, Kennedy merely shook Carter's hand.[2]

The divisions at Madison Square Garden signaled the problems Carter would have in the fall campaign. One week before Carter accepted the Democratic ticket at the convention, an ABC News–Louis Harris survey showed the president's approval rating at 22 percent, the lowest of any president since polling began in 1939. An overwhelming 86 percent of Americans criticized Carter's management of the economy. The numbers were even worse when focusing on specific aspects of the economy, as 87 percent of Americans criticized Carter's handling of unemployment, and a full 89 percent disapproved of his anti-inflation efforts. In fact, a full two-thirds of all Democrats polled disapproved of Carter's leadership.[3]

Potentially damaging were three other matters. Carter's brother Billy had received a loan of $250,000 from Libya and refused to register as an agent of that country.[4] The economy was in bad shape. Between February and July 1980, unemployment had increased from 6.3 percent to 7.8 percent. By June 1980, corporate profits had plunged by 18 percent. Then there was the third Unity Party candidacy of John Anderson. With his record of honesty and straight talk, he provided a centrist option for voters who did not like Carter but could not accept Republican candidate Ronald Reagan. He had a following of 20 percent of the voters in the summer of 1980.[5]

But Hamilton Jordan was back on the campaign trail as deputy campaign manager. Robert Strauss, named chairman of the Carter/Mondale campaign the previous

November, remained in charge overall. It was an ideal combination—the personally loyal strategist who had engineered the 1976 campaign and the Washington, D.C., heavy hitter who was a "well informed authority" and "freely admitted to both playing the [political] game and enjoying it."[6]

The goal was to make Carter's foreign policy accomplishments a major part of the campaign.[7] As Vance wrote Carter, "In presenting our policies publicly, we should emphasize that the practical progress we have made on central issues (SALT, China, trade, the Middle East) is fundamentally strengthening both our relationships abroad and the international system."[8] The president's domestic accomplishments—the establishment of the senior civil service, the creation of the Departments of Education and Energy, the deregulation of the airline and trucking industries, and appointments of more able women and African Americans to federal judgeships than any of his predecessors— were not passion-evoking measures. But Reagan's tough talk on defense and military nuclear matters could be contrasted to Carter's relatively moderate choices. Carter had undertaken a military buildup, adopted a nuclear war fighting policy, taken a powerful stance against the USSR after its intervention in Afghanistan, and reversed his earlier commitment to a withdrawal of U.S. troops from South Korea.[9] But unlike Reagan, he was also a man of peace: he had presided over the Camp David talks, promoted the reduction of nuclear weapons, and placed human rights on the world agenda.

Matters too difficult or too controversial to handle were put on hold: the nuclear test ban treaty had been shelved for a time; plans for a Central Intelligence Agency (CIA) charter, promised by Carter in 1976 after the agency came under fire for its role in Operation Chaos and Project Resistance and other activities, were dropped. Carter had found that agency very useful and had settled for some minor reforms, including the new Foreign Intelligence Surveillance Act that would later become a point of controversy during George W. Bush's administration.[10]

Of greater importance, a resolution of the hostage crisis seemed to be in the making. On the last day of August, Secretary of State Edmund Muskie wrote a letter to Mohamed Ali Rajai, Iran's new prime minister, asking for the release of the hostages. In return, the United States would recognize the Iranian revolutionary regime and promise not to interfere in Iran's internal affairs. "With the death of the former Shah," Muskie wrote, "a chapter of Iran's history is now definitely closed. With the establishment of your government, a new chapter is opened. I believe this is the moment to take a fresh look at the problems between Iran and the United States."[11]

Twelve days later, in a speech before the Iranian parliament, Ayatollah Khomeini presented for the first time a formula that he had approved in advance, pointing toward some middle ground where the interests and values of both sides might be accommodated. In return for the release of the hostages, he said that the United States must: (1) return the late shah's property; (2) cancel claims against Iran; (3) unblock Iran's frozen assets; and (4) promise not to intervene politically or militarily in Iran's affairs. For the first time, Khomeini did not mention his previous demand for a U.S. apology.[12]

Aside from this response there were other indications that Khomeini was responding positively to Muskie's approach. On September 9, word had come to the United

States through the West German ambassador to Tehran, Gerhardt Ritzel, that Sadegh Tabatabai, a brother-in-law of the ayatollah's son Ahmed Khomeini and former deputy premier in the government of Mehdi Bazargan, was willing to act as an intermediary between the Carter administration and the new Iranian regime. His access was proven when he informed the United States of Khomeini's September 12 proposals before they were announced. Responding to the new initiatives, Deputy Secretary of State Warren Christopher met with Tabatabai in a secret West German villa outside of Bonn to discuss ways in which new proposals could be implemented.[13]

These hopes were dashed on September 22 when Iraq invaded Iran. The airport in Iran was closed, and Tabatabai was not able to get to Tehran to deliver the U.S. proposals. When Tabatabai finally managed to return, the government was too preoccupied with the war with Iraq and too suspicious of possible U.S. involvement in it to proceed with talks. Still, Harold Saunders phoned Sadegh Ghotbzadeh, who still had a tie to Khomeini, to assure him that the United States had no responsibility for the Iraqi invasion of Iran and considered Iraq the aggressor in the conflict. Muskie made a public statement to that effect on October 20.[14]

Fearing an "October surprise" in these negotiations, William Casey, who was chairing Ronald Reagan's campaign, used his contacts in the CIA, the Defense Intelligence Agency, and the National Security Council to meet with Iranian exiles to find out what was going on in that country. "By the time of the election in November," Middle East expert Gary Sick notes, "[The Republicans] had succeeded in penetrating every major agency in the national security complex of the U.S. government." To inoculate the public against a possible breakthrough, Casey used Republican sources to disseminate misleading information. One suggestion was that military hardware was being shipped to Iran. Future Reagan National Security Advisor Richard Allen headed a committee of experts who assisted in planting "the idea in the public mind that any such move [to solve the crisis] should be viewed as a cynical political gesture."[15]

Despite the Republican effort, Carter maintained his edge on foreign policy matters. A Newsweek poll conducted two weeks prior to the election showed that 55 percent of voters polled expressed "a great deal" or a "fair amount" of confidence in Carter's foreign policy, as opposed to 46 percent for Reagan.[16]

In a foreign policy debate with Reagan on October 28, however, Carter stumbled in the very area in which he was claiming superior strength. Stiff and uncertain during much of the debate, he endeavored to show a common touch and it misfired. At one point he said he had asked his fourteen-year-old daughter Amy what was the most important issue for her. She reportedly responded, "Nuclear weaponry and the control of nuclear arms." At this, Press Secretary Jody Powell "winced." Communications Director Gerald Rafshoon exclaimed, "Oh my God, not that." All of Carter's aides had advised him against using that line. As Rafshoon noted, "Cartoon artists all over the country are sharpening their pencils."[17]

Then on November 2, two days before the election, Carter thought he had the deal the Republicans feared. At 3:45 a.m. he received word in a Chicago area hotel that the Iranian parliament had adopted the conditions laid out by the Ayatollah Khomeini almost two months earlier. Hurrying back to Washington he read a copy of the full text of the parliament resolution as he strode from the helicopter across the lawn toward the Oval Office. In dismay he realized that there was no way the crisis could be resolved in the next forty-eight hours. "Until that time," Carter later recalled, "I had hoped that we could reach an agreement in principle, with details to be worked out later, that would have permitted the hostage release before November 4."[18] Whether this was realistic or not, Assistant Secretary of State Saunders was on the telephone with Ghotbzadeh for the next forty-eight hours to see if a deal on the hostages could be reached before election day morning.

Carter's real vulnerability, however, was not the stumble in the debate or the failure to secure the return of the hostages. The economy and how Carter responded to it played a key role in his electoral fate. An inflation that seemed to feed on itself was accompanied by stagnant business activity and an increasing unemployment rate. This "stagflation," which plagued Carter's last two years in office, had been building for some time.[19] Carter had backed the anti-inflationary policies of Paul Volker, chairman of the Federal Reserve Board, in the spring of 1980 and fronted some of the bad economic news himself. By the fall that year Carter was sounding more like a traditional Republican than was Ronald Reagan. Committed to a balanced budget, Carter refused to cut income taxes. By way of contrast, Reagan was proposing a 30 percent reduction in income tax rates to stimulate economic growth, and Republican economists blamed the Carter administration for deliberately producing a recession in order to ease inflationary pressures. Even the future Federal Reserve Chairman Alan Greenspan, an economic consultant who had served on President Gerald Ford's Council of Economic Advisors, summed up the situation by saying a balanced budget for fiscal year 1981 was not possible.[20]

Carter paid a political price for these stances. The mid-September Gallup Polls showed that voters believed Reagan would be better at managing the economy than Carter by a margin of 44 percent to 33 percent.[21] Less than a month before the election took place, a 54 percent majority of voters saw Reagan as the best man to manage the economy. His proposed tax cuts were credited for giving him a leg up among the voters on economic issues. A fifty-state survey conducted at this time showed Reagan as the leader in twenty-six states, with 236 electoral votes.[22]

In desperation, Carter at the last minute proposed a $27.6 billion in tax cuts for 1981. Even then, he looked more conservative than Reagan. Carter proposed directing over half of his proposed tax cuts toward businesses, while Reagan proposed directing over 90 percent of his proposed cuts to individuals over the next three years while still promising to cut corporate taxes significantly.[23] Pollsters showed Reagan leading in almost all the battleground states.[24]

On election day, Carter watched the election coverage with his family and top aides in the family quarters of the White House. The exit polls that afternoon clearly showed a Reagan lead that could not be beat. At 5:35 p.m., more than five hours before the polls closed on the West Coast, Carter decided to concede, calling Reagan on the phone to extend his congratulations. An hour and fifteen minutes before the polls closed in California and other states along the West Coast, he had already delivered his concession speech at the Washington Sheraton hotel. These early concessions were the last blow to Democrats who were already bitter toward Carter. Late-voting blue-collar workers in California faded in the long Democratic polling lines in several congressional districts.[25]

On the morning of November 5, it was clear that Reagan had won the Electoral College by 489 electoral votes to Carter's 49.[26] In the popular vote, he beat Carter by a margin of 51 to 41 percent, with John Anderson taking 7 percent.[27] Along with victory in the presidential race, Republicans gained thirty-three seats in the U.S. House of Representatives and eleven seats in the U.S. Senate—enough to win control of the Senate for the first time in twenty-six years.[28]

Anderson's independent candidacy hurt Carter but did not determine the election. According to an ABC News survey, contrary to the traditional slippage of support for third-party candidates in the final moments of a campaign, the percentage of voters who supported Anderson grew in the days prior to the election. Out of the voters who waited until the final week to make up their minds, 13 percent supported Anderson, almost twice the percentage of his presumed national base. In fifteen states Anderson's vote was greater than the difference between Carter and Reagan. Still, had Carter carried all of those fifteen states, he still would have had only 216 electoral votes, well below the 270 electoral votes needed to win.[29]

Completing the Record

Even after the Reagan victory in the November election, Carter sought to further leave his mark on both U.S. foreign and domestic policy. At home, the U.S. Congress finally approved Carter's environmental legislation for a toxic waste superfund and for protection of Alaskan lands, excluding nearly one-third of the state's land from development despite fierce opposition from various interest groups.[30]

In foreign policy, Carter rounded out the budget and military policies requisite to a major military presence of the United States in the Middle East. At a November 25, 1980, Special Coordinating Committee meeting dealing with a Defense Department paper titled *Basic Strategy Issues*, Zbigniew Brzezinski, Harold Brown, Stansfield Turner, and David Jones agreed on the burgeoning Soviet threat and the need to meet it with increased arms. The United States in the early 1980s, the paper read, faced significantly greater danger of major region or global conflict in Europe, the Persian Gulf, and possibly the Far East. In response, the United States, as Brown explained, was moving toward a three and a half to a six and a half division plan for the Persian Gulf. Three divisions would have to be taken from forces committed to the North Atlantic Treaty Organization (NATO). To deal with the situation, the NATO allies should be pressured to increase their defense budgets. There were a few disagreements on some matters, but these revolved around how fast the Japanese and Chinese could take over more of the military burden, and on whether or not the USSR would attack on two fronts at once or merely feign on one front and move on the other.[31]

Only Secretary of State Muskie raised any questions about underlying assumptions. Had the administration, with its assurances that the United States had an adequate defense, misled the public in the fall elections? Why was the administration making budgetary recommendations for fiscal years 1983–86, when Reagan would be in office? Might not the NATO powers be counted on to take the lead in some matters and fight their own battles?[32]

Bypassed earlier on the decision to recommend that the president adopt Presidential Directive (PD) 59 on nuclear weapons employment, Muskie was now informed but mainly ignored. Brzezinski, for example, made only a passing reference in his memo to Carter covering the November 25 SCC meeting that Muskie was "disturbed about not having [the paper] staffed widely in State, and was reluctant to bring it to your attention."[33]

The objective of that meeting, Brzezinski assured Carter was to help the president clarify the strategic legacy he would like to leave the Reagan administration and to aid him in deciding which "major points" he would make in his last State of the Union Address.

On January 15, 1981, five days before leaving office, President Carter put his imprimatur on the program supported by Brzezinski, Brown, and the Joint Chiefs of Staff. PD 62 warned of the increasing Soviet threat in the Middle East, Europe, East Asia, and the Caribbean. It urged increased U.S. military readiness in the Persian Gulf and recommended that NATO take on a larger role in the defense of the European continent. In Asia, it advised buttressing Japan and China as checks to Soviet influence.[34] In PD 63 the president "directed that action be taken to protect the Strait of Hormuz to strengthen our key friends in the region in the face of risks stemming from the Iran/Iraq war…and to defend our vital interests in the region." In addition, steps would be taken to diminish "radical influences in the region" while "not placing in jeopardy our relationships or the internal stability of the countries concerned by insisting on formal basing arrangements."[35] Muskie never agreed to either PD 62 or PD 63, seeing them as presumptuous.[36]

The administration was also able to secure the release of the U.S. hostages in Iran, though their actual delivery did not occur until minutes after Ronald Reagan took office. The basic formula for a deal—the return of the diplomats in return for the unfreezing of Iranian funds in U.S. banks—had been reached prior to the election. Shortly after the election, the Algerian government provided a crucial service, acting as an intermediary between Iran and the United States. To facilitate this effort, on January 7, 1981, Carter sent Warren Christopher and several State Department officials to Algiers to participate in negotiations.[37]

In the meantime, Carter had imposed a deadline for reaching a compromise. If a deal was not reached by January 16, the Iranians were told, they would have to begin the negotiations anew. Reagan's sharp denunciations during the campaign of the militants in Iran as "barbarians" and "kidnappers" made it obvious that he might not proceed with a partially negotiated deal with Iran. The president-elect gave Carter another assist in January when he said that he would honor any agreement the Carter administration would make with Iran, but reserved the right to draw up new proposals should the issue not be resolved by January 20.[38]

Although there was an agreement on a formula, a mediator, and a deadline, a settlement was still hard to come by.[39] On January 15, one day before Carter's deadline, Iran removed the last remaining major obstacle to a deal. The Iranians agreed that they would pay back all of Iran's outstanding bank loans.

The details of paying off hundreds of loans, however, presented horrendous technical problems. On Friday, January 16, officers from twelve of the largest U.S. banks worked around the clock with officials from the Departments of State and the Treasury as well as the Federal Reserve Bank of New York. Bankers and lawyers cat-napped on couches or the floors in the law offices of Shearman and Sterling in mid-Manhattan.[40] On Sunday, differences over the interest rate the Iranian Republic should pay the American and European banks for the $3.6 billion in loans they held over the last fourteen months threatened the talks. The matter was resolved with a decision to establish an escrow account at the Bank of England and arbitrate the matter after the Algerians certified that the fifty-two hostages had been transferred.

Early Monday morning, the governor of Iran's Central Bank charged that the American banks were sabotaging the deal by slipping in an appendix at the last minute that would prevent future claims by Iran on U.S. banks. Secretary of the Treasury G. William Miller got the bankers to pull out the offending appendix, and the Iranians were informed it had been dropped.

That night, instructions from Iran telling U.S. banks to move specific Iranian deposits were delayed for several hours. When the message did come at 3:00 a.m., the security code was wrong, and there were many typographical errors. Some of the bankers involved were hesitant to move on these imperfect instructions. But Treasury Secretary Miller was not prepared to have the talks fail on a technicality; he ordered the deposits moved. The Iranians then said they would not sign the section of the agreement to which the appendix had been attached. Finally, after an hour-long telephone conference with Anthony Solomon, Federal Reserve Bank President, this issue was resolved.[41]

While these final snafus were being handled, Carter placed himself in a very public theater in which the Iranians could personally insult him one last time. On Sunday morning, January 18, when he received his first phone call from Tehran that a tentative agreement had been reached, Carter flew from his presidential retreat at Camp David to Washington. That night, as the entire world watched, he camped out in the Oval Office, staying awake until midnight, when he decided to take a quick nap on the couch.[42] At 4:56 a.m., Carter announced that the United States had "reached an agreement with Iranian officials." His hope at that time was that he might meet the returning hostages in West Germany, and then return to Washington in time to attend Reagan's inauguration at noon on Tuesday, January 20. *Air Force One* was readied for the trip.[43]

But on Monday morning, as the bankers' appendix held up the final agreement, Carter reluctantly canceled what would have been his final presidential trip. That night, his last in the White House, Carter faced another sleepless ordeal in the Oval Office. At 3:16 a.m. Tuesday morning, Christopher called to say the negotiations in Algiers were complete.

Finally, at 6:41 a.m. on Inauguration Day, a supervisor in the Federal Reserve Bank of New York cable division began feeding the telex machine with instructions to the Bank of England to move funds from the special Federal Reserve holding accounts to the escrow account held by the Central Bank of Algeria; the transaction cleared at 6:43 a.m. The Bank of England then informed the Algerians that the escrow account had been opened, and by 8:06 a.m., Algeria certified to Iran that the funds were ready for the exchange with the hostages.

With the Algerian certification that the money had been moved, the hostages should have been swapped. Carter's hope was that they would clear Iranian airspace while he was still president. Gary Sick, a National Security Council aide, kept the president informed throughout the inaugural festivities. Sitting in the Situation Room in the White House, he had one telephone connected to the Algerian intermediary who would tell him when the hostages' aircraft had left Iran, and the other connected to the president. Every few minutes he called Carter—at the White House family quarters, in the limousine en route to the Capitol for the inauguration, at the Capitol building just before the inauguration.

The word did not come until 12:35 Eastern Standard Time, as Reagan was being sworn in as president. Carter received word of the hostages' freedom in his limousine en route to Andrews Air Force base for the flight home to Georgia. This was the last of several petty cruelties Carter had experienced at the hands of the Iranians.[44]

The next day, as the representative of President Reagan, Carter flew to West Germany to meet the newly freed Americans at the U.S. Air Force Base in Wiesbaden. The prisoners had the chance to share their experiences with one another aboard their twelve-hour flight out of Iran, and some were not happy. When asked about the failed rescue operation, Carter told them that "bad luck and the lack of a helicopter" led to its failure.[45] After the meeting, Carter condemned the actions of the Iranians, stating that their actions were "despicable act[s] of savagery."[46]

The final agreement, signed on January 19, reflected a decision by both sides to go back to the status quo before the takeover.[47] In that sense, it was a "victory" for the Americans. There was no provision for the establishment of an international commission to conduct hearings into Iran's grievances. The United States had not agreed to return the property of the shah of Iran. Instead, the U.S. government would freeze his property and prohibit the transfer of any of it in the United States until Iran's claims could be litigated in the U.S. courts. There was nothing even approximating an apology from the United States—though they did agree not to intervene in the domestic affairs of Iran.

As Secretary of State Muskie said in a press conference the day after it had been signed, the agreement provided for the safe return of our people on terms consistent with the national honor and interests. And it reflected what he saw as a "guiding principle in the negotiations," to return, insofar as possible, to where they stood before the hostages were seized.[48]

The Algerians had played a key role in these final negotiations, minimizing the irrationalities that could creep into the bargaining situation. They carried messages back and forth, advised the Iranians on financial matters that the latter did not understand, and explained to them the limitations the U.S. constitution and law imposed on the American government. Conversely, they explained the almost paranoid psychology of the Iranians to the Americans, helping to keep them from overreacting to the delays and negative signals from Iran. Most of all, they refused to be pulled into the Iranian game of raising and then dashing hopes. At the end, they were the neutral third-party intermediaries— guaranteeing mutual delivery of the "values" to be exchanged and relieving Iran of the need for direct dealings with the "Great Satan."[49] Carter would later recommend Algerian foreign minister Mohamed Seddik Benyahia for a Nobel Peace Prize. Vance would support a prize going to the whole negotiating team.[50]

JIMMY CARTER AND
THE AMERICAN MISSION

In the American mythos, an outsider goes to Washington, D.C., counters a corrupt establishment, and brings America around to its true and common interest. This story has inspired many politicians and countless citizens to believe in their own abilities to change the country for the better. But as Jimmy Carter found out, the most idealistic newcomer can find his dreams foundering on certain imperatives within the American political system. Moreover, as he attempts to spell out his vision of the common interest, he may well find himself in conflict with both erstwhile supporters and other political actors in the political system. Broad aspirations of choosing the good may have provided cover for him with followers embracing differing definitions of the common interest.

Certainly every new occupant of the White House will find political imperatives constraining his attempts at change. Secrecy, he will discover, may be a requisite for the success of certain diplomatic missions. "Hail to the Chief" and other trappings of office will aid him in winning the respect of the people he must lead. He will need resources and votes for policies that the U.S. Congress must support. And he will compromise on some matters he considers right in order to maintain influence and stay in power. If he is to succeed, he will also have to rely on people who have more foreign policy knowledge and understanding of the ways that Washington works.

If the outsider has neither practical experience nor education in the field of foreign policy this dependence on others will pose special problems for him. The danger is that his staff and policy choices may make him too vulnerable to the strongest voices around him. Carter originally envisaged a collegial form of foreign policymaking in which his top staff members would have equal access to him. But in the foreign policy realm, he gave Zbigniew Brzezinski a triple role as gatekeeper, policy advisor, and teacher on the nature of world politics and the practices of earlier presidents. This was the very area in which Carter lacked the broad experience or the learning that might have enabled him to provide an outside check on this most important of advisors. Instead, Carter came to rely inordinately on an advisor who had his own political agenda and extraordinary skill in creating a political milieu that would lead the president in the direction the advisor desired. Playing on Carter's desire to be seen as tough, Brzezinski also encouraged a muscular stance that led the president into policies counter to his early desires for arms limitation and the promotion of human rights around the world. With some naïveté, Carter failed to understand that even placing Brzezinski in the White House did not guarantee that he would always pursue the goals he had set as president.

Carter also embraced a morality that did not prepare him for the dilemmas and ambiguities that any head of state must confront. On the flyleaf of his campaign auto-biography *Why Not the Best?* he quoted theologian Reinhold Niebuhr to the effect that "the sad duty of politics is to establish justice in a sinful world." In the book itself Carter stated, "there is only one nation in the world which is capable of true leadership among the community of nations, and that is the United States of America." But it is a leadership, he suggested, that need not be feared. "The people of this country are inher-ently unselfish, open, honest, decent, competent, and compassionate."[1] In his January 1977 inaugural address, Carter elaborated on the theme, envisioning a nation disarmed and at peace, one in which the United States followed abroad the same principles it honored at home. "Ours was the first society openly to define itself in terms of both spirituality and of human liberty. It is that unique self-definition which has given us an exceptional appeal, but it also imposes on us a special obligation, to take on those moral duties, which, when assumed, seem invariably to be in our own best interests."[2]

In this view of the American moral mission Carter was tying into a major motif in American national life. John Winthrop, the first governor of Massachusetts, gave birth to the idea that the colony about to be established was "a city on a hill"—a city blessed by the hand of God and watched by the entire world. Later, as the new nation took on continental proportions, U.S. expansion was seen as a kind of manifest destiny. The nation's duty, as journalist John Sullivan noted in 1845, was "to overspread and to posses the whole of the continent which Providence has given us for the development of the great experiment of liberty and federated self-government entrusted to us."[3] At the end of the Spanish-American War, President William McKinley went even further, committing the United States to a colonial role. This country, he noted, had a duty to "educate the Filipinos, and uplift and civilize and Christianize them, and by God's grace do the very best we could by them, as our fellow-men for whom Christ also died." The next morning he sent for the chief engineer—the mapmaker of the War Department—and told him to "put the Philippines on the map of the United States…and there they will stay while I am president."[4]

When the United Sates began to play the role of world superpower in the twentieth century, it went beyond the role of an example for the rest of the world. Its function in this new era was to bring peace and self-determination, and new international com-mitments that would forward these values at the global level. Woodrow Wilson, with whom Carter often identified, framed the U.S. objective as a selfless endeavor, a "war to make the world safe for democracy." And he brought forth the League of Nations.[5] Even Franklin Delano Roosevelt saw this nation as one of "four policemen" who, as leaders of a new post–World War II international organization, would stop any ag-gressor in its tracks if it "started to run amok."[6]

If Carter had read Niebuhr's work more closely, he would have been aware of the dangers of equating one's national goals with a transcendent morality. The Cold War, Niebuhr posited, was not simply a mythic battle between good and evil, freedom and tyranny. The two superpowers in the Cold War, though they differed in their politi-cal aspirations, had similar imperial dimensions and power, each exercising hegemony in its respective bloc or nation. For the United States, there has long been certain innocence about its expansionistic goals, as it clothes its policies in such ideas as manifest destiny or the Wilsonian notion that it alone among nations pursues an unselfish national purpose.[7]

In moral terms, this equation can corrupt both morals and politics. Niebuhr continues:

> When the universalism of the Christian religion is corrupted into subservience to nationalism and the majesty of God is fashioned into a crown for some puny human potentate, the effect is worse than that which results from the less pretentious claims of more primitive religions. A genuinely prophetic religion speaks a word of judgment against every ruler and every nation, even against good rulers and good nations.[8]

The Moral Dimension

Moral conviction, it is true, can have some positive results. Carter's belief that he was doing the right thing gave him the tenacity and courage with which he approached the two politically risky peacemaking efforts he undertook as president. In the return of the Canal to Panama, he promoted the cause of peace in the Caribbean and Central America, while protecting legitimate U.S. interests. Republican administrations before him had moved toward that operation, but he was the one who actually took on the job of negotiating the relevant treaties and presenting them to a reluctant U.S. Senate and American public. Later, in his endeavors at Camp David, against incredible odds, Carter stepped into and reversed a downward cycle in Israeli-Arab relations. Carter's strategic vision and skills as a dedicated and astute hands-on negotiator were crucial for what turned out to be a partial resolution of the Middle Eastern conflict.

But certitude, which may at times provide the confidence requisite to the undertaking of risky project, has its downside. Carter's two most important objectives—genuine arms reduction and the promotion of human rights—were undermined by his proclivities to identify U.S. national interests with moral righteousness. Because his arms control proposals and his critiques of Soviet treatment of their human rights activists at home and their forays in the Horn of Africa were morally based, Soviet resistance to his claims was proof that they were motivated by bad intentions. When the Soviets opposed him, he was inclined to see this opposition as a personal insult. Angered, he responded with the tough talk and measures that Brzezinski encouraged him to take.

What Carter did not fully appreciate is that political competitors may have legitimate interests and concerns to which a smart leader should pay heed. Carter's inability to hear Leonid Brezhnev's warning that a departure from Vladivostok would undermine the Strategic Arms Limitation Treaty negotiations (SALT II), his rejection of Henry Kissinger's advice on how to deal with the Soviet Union, his dislike of the complex moral and political advice often given by the State Department about the Horn of Africa, his tendency to speak in hyperboles about the evil of the Soviet Union and the valor of its adversaries—all of this led him toward rhetorical and policy overshoots that contributed to deterioration in U.S. relations with the Soviet Union. The end result was series of responses and counterresponses that cycled into a renewal of the Cold War in 1979–80.

Not only did Carter's moralist approach to the world make the diplomatic task of dealing with the Soviets very difficult, it also led him into actions that could only be seen as manifestations of double standards. He pressed the Soviet Union on its human rights violations, but ignored the abuses of U.S. allies and those from whom he sought favors—Panama, China, Iran, Afghanistan, and Saudi Arabia. Foreign interventions were judged in terms of whether the intervener was friend (Somalia in the Ogaden, China in Vietnam) or foe (Vietnam in Cambodia, the Soviets in Afghanistan). Communist regimes in competition with the USSR, such as Romania or the People's Republic of China, would be spared harsh critiques. The contribution of his original SALT II proposal to the Soviet Union, the tilt toward China, and his human rights issues heightening tensions with the USSR on his watch have largely gone ignored.

In addition, as commander in chief of a major world power, Carter was confronted with what other political observers have called the "dirty hand dilemma." To serve the national security interests, a president may have to make decisions that violate some moral choices in order to serve broader and more significant goals. To prevent a left wing takeover in El Salvador, for example, Carter and his advisors undercut U.S. support for one of the great human rights workers of the twentieth century. But Carter and his top advisors fail to even mention the martyrdom of Archbishop Oscar Arnulfo Romero y Galdámez of El Salvador in their memoirs.

Attempts to deal with competing powers via a simple moral lens, in short, will tax the skills of any political leader. The nature of his political conflicts will be blurred, his energies diverted, the capacity for working out compromises weakened.

On Prudence

This is not to say that moral considerations are irrelevant in matters of state. Indeed, for the statesman, "prudence" is the most relevant virtue. The prudent leader would know "what practical goals were worth pursuing and how to pursue them, and to would do so in a way guided or informed by some sort of moral knowledge or insight as well as by factual and instrumental knowledge. Foresight, (the ability to anticipate 'opportunities and danger') and the courage to carry out difficult and sometimes risky tasks are essential ingredients of this faculty."[9] This is particularly the case in international relations where there is no common authority to apply widely respected rules against those who would disturb the peace. In the final analysis, each nation ultimately depends on its own arms, or those of its friends, to protect its legitimate interests. In short, prudence may lead one to aim high but requires one to respect limits. Pericles and Aristotle called this "practical wisdom." Those who have it "can see what is good for themselves and what is good for men in general" and "are good at managing households or states."[10]

But foresight also means that leaders will know their limits. Indeed, sometimes losses must be absorbed if there are no good answers. In many of his actions Carter respected these limits. Certainly, he resisted Brzezinski's proposal for a military coup when the shah of Iran began to falter in late 1978. In the Iran hostage crisis, he accepted the fact that a military response would be counterproductive for a time and sought a diplomatic solution. He only dropped the search for a diplomatic option and settled on a rescue operation when it became clear that Ayatollah Khomeini would use any dealings for his own domestic political purposes. Carter's decision to freeze Iranian funds in U.S. banks, as well as other sanctions, gave him the leverage that would eventually resolve the issue on the last day of his presidency.

Yet Carter's proclivity to overextend himself when speaking about situations created problems for him on the hostage issue. The decision to work full-time on the hostage crisis, the refusal to turn on the Christmas tree lights in the White House until the hostages came home, the ringing of church bells around the nation—all these choices gave Khomeini a hold over the United States that he might otherwise not have had.

Nor did Soviet entry into the Horn of Africa indicate, as Carter suggested, that the USSR was the source of trouble around the world. Even its entry into Afghanistan was not equivalent to the Berlin Blockade of 1948 or the introduction of offensive missiles into Cuba in 1962. But the "hot" rhetoric Carter employed, while emotionally satisfying, only undermined his authority in the long run. If the challenge to U.S. interests was so crucial, opponents could argue that he was weak. Why did he not take the extra measures that would have brought about a U.S. victory?

Statesmen who succeed are also aware that the advisory structures and the broader political setting in which they operate are not simple givens but settings over which they have some influence. They will also know when to delegate decision making to subordinates and when to ride the herd themselves; Franklin Delano Roosevelt, Dwight D. Eisenhower, and John F. Kennedy were three American leaders who had some skills in this manner. Carter would sometimes get embroiled in relatively unimportant policy details (as with Panama) while ignoring State Department reports that would have informed some of his dealings with the United States' most the significant adversary (e.g., the papers on Eritrea, which made it clear that the USSR was not responsible for all the conflicts in the Horn of Africa).

The prudent leader will also be aware that pursuit of power can corrupt even the best of men. As the British philosopher Edmund Burke wrote of Great Britain at the height of its power, "among precautions against ambition, it may not be amiss to take one precaution against our own. I must fairly say, I dread our own power and our own ambition; I dread our being too much dreaded. It is ridiculous to say we are not men, and that, as men, we shall never wish to aggrandize ourselves in some way or other."[11]

Fortunately, the story of American foreign policy is not only one of narrow self-interest disguised as a moral virtue legitimating all U.S. endeavors. Prudent leaders in the United States, as a matter of fact, have defined its interests in ways that served both the national interest as well as civilization as a whole. The U.S. entry into World War II, establishment of the United Nations, the Truman Plan, the Marshall Plan, the World Bank and other such institutions have contributed to world order and the economic well-being of the United States and many other nations. American containment policies limited the sphere of Soviet influence in Europe, the Eastern Mediterranean, and the Korean Peninsula without unduly provoking a nuclear-armed Soviet Union. The United States has also been at the forefront of putting human rights on the UN agenda. Eleanor Roosevelt's energetic and integral role in the formation of the Universal Declaration of Human Rights spurred a global movement to recognize both the "positive" and "negative" rights of every human being. But she realized there are real limits to what kind of morality one nation can impose on others.[12]

Indeed, since its founding, some Americans have seen the limits of the triumphalist view of the American mission. The United States acts under a broader set of moral concerns than its own laws. Even John Winthrop, the first governor of the new Massachusetts Bay Colony, noted that the colonists' action would be judged by a morality that was somehow universal. "The eyes of all people are upon us," he commented, and "[should we] deal falsely with our God in this work we have undertaken, and so cause Him to withdraw His present help from us, we shall be made a story and a byword through the world."[13] The men who signed the Declaration of Independence saw themselves as obliged to explain the moral basis for their revolution to the rest of mankind.

At other times American statesmen have been aware that the United States is subject to the same temptation of power as other nations have been. During the conflict with Mexico over the borderline of Texas in 1845, Congress passed a resolution saying the "war had been unnecessarily and unconstitutionally begun by the President of the United States."[14] In the elections of 1900, laissez faire capitalist and sociologist William Graham Sumner argued that the occupation of the Philippines imposed more burdens than benefits, while the resulting militarism inevitably and seriously threatened free government. Imperialism, Sumner posited, led to chauvinism, an aggressive outgrowth of mindless patriotism manufactured by the arrogant truculence of men and women relying on emotional sloganeering.[15] Senator Henry Cabot Lodge's opposition to the League of Nations was based on his concern that U.S. "vigor" and "moral force" would be abated "by everlasting meddling and muddling in every quarrel, great and small, which afflicts the world."[16]

The Move Away from Triumphalism

It is to Carter's credit that he never let his moralist approach morph into the triumphalist approach exemplified by the neoconservatives, who during his term in office were beginning to organize in groups such as the Committee on the Present Danger. For Carter, universal principles and rules were designed to bind the United States, as well as others. As he said in his inaugural address, "We will not behave in foreign places so as to violate our rules and standards here at home, for we know that the trust which our Nation earns is essential to our strength. The passion for freedom is on the rise."[17] In accord with these views, in 1977 alone he signed five international human rights treaties and sent them to the Senate for its advice and consent.[18]

Even his most controversial choices—covert operations in Afghanistan in 1978 and in Central America in 1980—were carried out with a respect for extant law in the United States. He did not simply act on his own but informed congressional authorities of his decision with the appropriate "findings." During the emotionally trying months of the Iran hostage crisis, Carter followed the advice of his legal advisor and recognized that Iranian students and protestors in the United States had certain rights that he would have to respect. Certainly he never engaged in the kind of dark operations that President Richard Nixon had sometimes embraced.

Nor did he show lapses in personal rectitude of the sort that would undermine the presidency of Bill Clinton later on. Whatever problems Carter had in balancing U.S. interests with his moral goals, he also undertook major efforts to promote world peace, arms limitation, and a new moral order. Indeed, his human rights country studies, as we have seen, remain a force in world politics, providing incentives for world leaders to limit their most offensive behavior while offering hope to those whose rights were violated who might be otherwise be "forgotten." Certainly they should not suffer in vain.

In 2002, the Committee bestowing upon Carter the Nobel Peace Prize noted his positive offerings to the broader world order. His "vital contribution" to the Camp David Accords between Israel and Egypt were noted in the official citation, as well as his efforts in conflict resolution on several continents and the promotion of human rights after his presidency. "In a situation currently marked by threats of the use of power, Carter has stood by the principles that conflicts must, as far as possible, be resolved through mediation and international co-operation based on international law, respect for human rights, and economic development," the citation said.[19] Notable was its omission of any reference to Carter's handling of U.S.-Soviet relations.

In his postpresidency years, Carter has even drifted toward the prophetic role that Niebuhr had originally envisaged as the proper role of a religious man. In his address accepting the Nobel Peace Prize, Carter said, "We have not assumed that super strength guarantees super wisdom, and we have consistently reached out to the international community to ensure that our own power and influence are tempered by the best common judgment."[20] Or, as he wrote in the foreword to the collection *Where We Stand*, "Instead of using [our] weapons with little restraint, even in preemptive wars, our country should be known as a champion of peace."[21]

In an interview with MSNBC's Chris Matthews, Carter noted that one cannot by "rule of arms" make a people of a different country adopt a new concept of government. The 2003 war in Iraq could have been avoided, he said, but the administration of President George W. Bush was determined that it should take place. Carter was particularly concerned that there was, at that time, no effort to bring peace in the Middle East. As for the role of religion in politics, Carter deplored the "closer intermixing of church and state" in the past twenty-five years that he saw as something greater than our forefathers had intended. Carter was particularly concerned about the tendency of some leaders to twist Christianity to bring about war, a characteristic unfounded in worshiping the "Prince of Peace."[22]

Jimmy Carter, in short, pursued a foreign policy that was in the old "city on the hill" tradition, sharing some of its virtues as well as its flaws. A moral fervor gave him the impetus to take on difficult tasks, such as the promotion of peace in the Middle East. But as his dealings with the Soviet Union suggest, a moralistic bent, accompanied by an ambitious foreign policy, can lead to overcommitment and compound difficulties when dealing with adversaries. Values stated in categorical terms can get in the way of more limited and concrete national security interests. And conflicts of interest can be too simply turned into battles between right and wrong. At the end, Carter fell subject to temptations from those in his administration who fed his frustrations with calls to be tough, to threaten, to demonstrate and prepare to use force as a means of regaining mastery over his circumstances.

Yet throughout his presidency and postpresidency years, neither Carter's "sense of mission" nor his frustrations ever led him into blind triumphal or imperialist expansionism. For him the American mission was played out within a framework of domestic and international law, and his sense of mission had several positive results. Today, as a former president playing a quasi-public role, he has moved toward a relatively modest vision of how the United States, or any other nation, can change others. Rejecting the relatively quiescent and supportive role expected of men in the "club" of ex-presidents, he is instead playing a quasi-prophetic role, calling his successors to account for what he sees as their more bellicose and overextended definitions of American national interests. To the very end Jimmy Carter remains an American original, playing in tune with the changing refrains of his own inner ear.

AMERICAN AND FOREIGN ACTORS

Specific Issues

Chapters 1, 2, 3

See tables 1–4

Chapters 4, 5, 10

Americans

GOVERNMENTAL POLICYMAKERS

Jimmy Carter, President of the United States

Cyrus Vance, Secretary of State

Zbigniew Brzezinski, National Security Advisor to the President

Paul Warnke, Director, Arms Control and Disarmament Agency

Harold Brown, Secretary of Defense

Walter Mondale, Vice President

W. Averell Harriman, Former Ambassador to the USSR, 1943–46, and Under Secretary of State for Political Affairs, 1963–65

Walter Slocombe, Deputy Under Secretary of Defense for Policy

David Jones, Chairman of the Joint Chiefs of Staff, 1978–82

Robert Gates, Special Assistant to the National Security Advisor, 1979, and Future CIA Director

Leslie Gelb, Assistant Secretary of State for Politico-Military Affairs, 1977–79

Malcolm Toon, Ambassador to the Soviet Union, 1977–79

Lloyd Cutler, Counsel to the President, NSC

Stansfield Turner, Director of the CIA

Hamilton Jordan, Assistant to the President, 1977–79, and Chief of Staff, 1979–80

Edward Rowney, Joint Chiefs of Staff Representative to the Strategic Arms Limitation Talks, 1973–79; Later Chief Negotiator for the Strategic Arms Reduction Talks (START)

POLICY IMPLEMENTATION

Frank Moore, Assistant to the President for Congressional Liaison

Robert Beckel, Special Assistant to Congressional Liaison (House)

Patrick Caddell, Pollster for the President
Anne Wexler, Assistant to the President, 1978–81
Robert C. Byrd, Senate Majority Leader (D-West Virginia)
Howard Baker, Senate Minority Leader (R-Tennessee)
Alan Cranston, Senate Majority Whip (D-California)
Edward (Ted) Kennedy, Senator (D-Massachusetts)
John Glenn, Senator (D-Ohio)
Henry "Scoop" Jackson, Senator (D-Washington) and Leading Foreign
     Policy Hawk
Richard Perle, Legislative Aide to Senator Henry Jackson
Sam Nunn, Chairman of the Senate Armed Service Committee
     (D-Georgia)
Paul Nitze, Director of Policy Planning for the State Department, 1950–53;
     Deputy Secretary of Defense Affairs, 1973–76; Co-Founder of Team B
     Report

Soviet Officials

Leonid Brezhnev, General Secretary and Chairman of the Presidium of the
     Supreme Soviet of the USSR
Anatoly Dobrynin, Ambassador to the United States
Andrei Gromyko, Foreign Minister
Andrei Grechko, Defense Minister

Chapter 6

Americans

Jimmy Carter, President of the United States
Zbigniew Brzezinski, National Security Advisor to the President
Cyrus Vance, Secretary of State
Harold Brown, Secretary of Defense
Walter Mondale, Vice President
Patricia Derian, Assistant Secretary of State for Human Rights and
     Humanitarian Affairs
Lucy Benson, Under Secretary of State for Security Assistance, 1977–80
Warren Christopher, Deputy Secretary of State
Arthur Hartman, Assistant Secretary of State for European and
     Eurasian Affairs
Anthony Lake, Director of Policy Planning, State Department
Jane Pisano, Special Assistant for National Security Affairs at NSC
Malcolm Toon, U.S. Ambassador to the Soviet Union

Frank Press, Science Advisor to the President
Juanita Kreps, Secretary of Commerce
Michael Blumenthal, Secretary of the Treasury
James Schlesinger, Secretary of Energy
Stuart Eizenstat, Chief Domestic Policy Advisor
Michel Oksenberg, Specialist on East Asia and China, NSC
Jessica Tuchman (Matthews), Director of the Office of Global Issues, NSC
William Odom, Deputy Assistant for National Security Affairs, NSC
Robert Toth, American Journalist Arrested on Espionage Charges in the
    Soviet Union

Soviet Officials and Dissidents

Leonid Brezhnev, General Secretary and Chairman of the Presidium of the
    Supreme Soviet of the USSR
Andrei Gromyko, Foreign Minister
Anatoly Dobrynin, Ambassador to the United States
Andrei Sakharov, Physicist, Dissident, and Human Rights Activist
Aleksandr Solzhenitsyn, Writer and Dissident
Anatoly Scharansky, Dissident
Alexander Ginzburg, Dissident

Chapter 7

Americans

Jimmy Carter, President of the United States
Zbigniew Brzezinski, National Security Advisor to the President
Cyrus Vance, Secretary of State
Harold Brown, Secretary of Defense
Walter Mondale, Vice President
Andrew Young, U.S. Ambassador to the United Nations, 1977–79
Stansfield Turner, Director of the CIA
Richard Moose, Assistant Secretary of State for African Affairs
Jody Powell, White House Press Secretary

Others

Anatoly Dobrynin, Soviet Ambassador to the United States
Andrei Gromyko, Foreign Minister of the USSR
Mohammed Siad Barre, Military Dictator of Somalia
Haile Mariam Mengistu, Military Dictator of Ethiopia

Chapters 8, 9

Americans

DECISION MAKERS

Jimmy Carter, President of the United States
Ellsworth Bunker, Chief Negotiator of Panama Canal Treaties
Sol Linowitz, Chief Negotiator of Panama Canal Treaties
Zbigniew Brzezinski, National Security Advisor to the President
Cyrus Vance, Secretary of State
Warren Christopher, Deputy Secretary of State
Harold Brown, Secretary of Defense
Walter Mondale, Vice President
Clifford (Cliff) Alexander, Secretary of the Army
George Brown, Chairman of Joint Chiefs of Staff, 1974–78

THE OUTER CIRCLE

Robert (Bob) Beckel, Congressional Liaison
Landon Butler, Deputy Assistant to the President
Frank Moore, Assistant to the President for Congressional Liaison
Midge Constanza, Assistant to the President for Public Liaison, 1977–78
Stuart Eizenstat, Assistant to the President for Domestic Affairs
Robert C. Byrd, Majority Leader of the U.S. Senate
Howard Baker, Minority Leader of the U.S. Senate
Dennis Deconcini, Senator (D-Arizona)
Barry Goldwater, Hawkish Senator (R-Arizona)
Henry Jackson, Hawkish Senator (D-Washington)
Frank Church, Dovish Senator (D-Idaho), Leader on SFRC
John Murphy, Chair of House Merchant Marine and Fisheries Committee
Robert Bauman, Hawkish Member of Congress (R-Maryland)
Ronald Reagan, Republican Presidential Candidate, 1976, 1980
Gerald Ford, Former President of the United States
Richard Nixon, Former President of the United States

Panamanians

Omar Torrijos Herrera, President of Panama
Rómulo Escobar Bethancourt, Chief Negotiator for Panama Canal Treaties
Jorge Illueca, Panamanian Ambassador to the United Nations
Gabriel Lewis, Panamanian Ambassador to the United States
Boyd Escobar Revilla, Foreign Minister of Panama

Other

Anatoly Dobrynin, Soviet Ambassador to the United States

Chapters 11, 12, 13

Americans

DECISION MAKERS

Jimmy Carter, President of the United States

Zbigniew Brzezinski, National Security Advisor to the President

Cyrus Vance, Secretary of State

Harold Brown, Secretary of Defense

Walter Mondale, Vice President

Leonard Woodcock, Ambassador to the People's Republic of China

Richard (Dick) Holbrooke, Assistant Secretary of State for East Asian and
    Pacific Affairs

Michel Oksenberg, Specialist for East Asia and China, NSC

Stansfield Turner, Director of the CIA

Hamilton Jordan, Assistant to the President, 1977–79, and Chief of Staff, 1979–80

Michael Blumenthal, Secretary of the Treasury

OUTER CIRCLE

David Aaron, Deputy National Security Advisor, NSC

William Odom, Military Assistant to the National Security Advisor, NSC

Jody Powell, Press Secretary to the President

Frank Press, Science Advisor to the President

James Schlesinger, Secretary of Energy

Stuart Eizenstat, Assistant to the President for Domestic Affairs and Policy

William Perry, Under Secretary of Defense for Research and Engineering

Hugh Carter, Special Assistant to the President for Administration

Karl (Rick) Inderfurth, Special Assistant to the National Security Advisor

Gerald Ford, Former President of the United States

Richard Nixon, Former President of the United States

Chinese

Hua Guofeng, Chinese Premier and Communist Party Chairman

Deng Xiaoping, Deputy Premier of China

Huang Hua, Foreign Minister of China

Chai Zemin, Head of the Liaison Mission of China in the United States

Huang Chen, Head of the Liaison Mission of China in the United States

Han Hsu, Head of the Liaison Mission of China in the United States

Soviet Officials

Leonid Brezhnev, General Secretary and Chairman of the Presidium of the
    Supreme Soviet of the USSR

Andrei Gromyko, Foreign Minister
Anatoly Dobrynin, Ambassador to the United States

Chapters 14, 15

Americans

Jimmy Carter, President of the United States
Cyrus Vance, Secretary of State
Harold Brown, Secretary of Defense
Walter Mondale, Vice President
Zbigniew Brzezinski, National Security Advisor to the President
Harold (Hal) Saunders, Assistant Secretary of State for Near Eastern and
    South Asian Affairs
William (Bill) Quandt, Specialist for the Middle East and North Africa, NSC
Rosalyn Carter, First Lady of the United States
Jody Powell, White House Press Secretary
Robert Lipshutz, Legal Counsel to the President
Gary Sick, Specialist for the Middle East and North Africa, NSC
Alfred (Roy) Atherton, Ambassador at Large for Middle East Negotiations
Hermann Eilts, Ambassador to Egypt
Samuel Lewis, Ambassador to Israel
Stansfield Turner, Director of the CIA
Jerrold Post, Professor of Psychiatry, Georgetown University, Psychological
    Profiler for CIA
Leon Charney, Lawyer in New York, Israel Supporter

Israelis

Menachem Begin, Prime Minister
Moshe Dayan, Foreign Minister
Aharon Barak, Attorney General
Ezer Weizman, Defense Minister
Simcha Dinitz, Ambassador to the United States
Dan Pattir, Press Spokesman
Avraham Tamir, Director of the Planning Branch of the Army
Ariel Sharon, Agricultural Minister

Egyptians

Anwar Sadat, President
Mohamed Kamel, Foreign Secretary of Egypt
Osama El Baz, Senior Advisor to the President of Egypt

Chapters 16, 17

Americans

Jimmy Carter, President of the United States

Zbigniew Brzezinski, National Security Advisor to the President

Cyrus Vance, Secretary of State

Harold Brown, Secretary of Defense

Walter Mondale, Vice President

George Ball, Former Under Secretary of State and Advisor to the President on Iranian Affairs

Warren Christopher, Deputy Secretary of State

Harold Saunders, Assistant Secretary of State for the Near East and South Asia Affairs

Gary Sick, Specialist for the Middle East and North Africa, NSC

William Sullivan, Ambassador to Iran

Hamilton Jordan, Assistant to the President, 1977–79, and White House Chief of Staff, 1979–81

Lloyd Cutler, Counsel to the President

Jody Powell, White House Press Secretary

Stansfield Turner, Director of the CIA

Ramsey Clark, Former Attorney General of the United States; heads delegation to deal with hostage issue

Robert Huyser, EUCOM Deputy sent to Iran in January 1979 to rally Iranian military commanders to resist the Khomeini takeover of the government

Iranians

Mohammad Reza Pahlavi, Shah of Iran, 1953–79

Shapour Bakhtiar, last Prime Minister appointed by the Shah

Ayatollah Khomeini, Iranian Leader after the 1979 revolution

Mehdi Bazargan, Prime Minister of the Iranian Provisional Revolutionary Government

Bani Sadr, Iranian Foreign Minister after Bazargan's government fell; President after January 1980

Ibrahim Yazdi, Foreign Minister of Iran's Bazargan government

Sadegh Ghotbzadeh, Foreign Minister of Iran after January 1980

Others

Kurt Waldheim, Secretary General of the United Nations

Christian Bourguet, French lawyer and unofficial representative of Iran in hostage negotiations

Hector Villalon, Argentine expatriate businessman; worked with Bourguet in hostage negotiations

Chapter 18

Americans

Jimmy Carter, President of the United States
Zbigniew Brzezinski, National Security Advisor to the President
Cyrus Vance, Secretary of State
Frank Church, Senator (D-Idaho)
David Newsom, Under Secretary of State for Political Affairs, 1978–81
Bobby Inman, Director of the National Security Agency
Stansfield Turner, Director of the CIA
Clark Clifford, Former Secretary of Defense and Truman Advisor
Hedley Donovan, Senior Advisor to the President; Former Editor of *Time*
    magazine
Richard Stone, Senator (D-Florida)
Marshall Brement, Specialist on USSR and Eastern Europe, NSC
Robert Byrd, Majority Leader of the Senate (D-West Virginia)
Ted Kennedy, Senator (D-Massachusetts)
William Odom, Military Assistant and Crisis Co-Coordinator, NSC
Robert Pastor, Specialist on Latin America and the Caribbean, NSC
Marshall Shulman, Special Advisor on Soviet Affairs to the Secretary of State
Harold Brown, Secretary of Defense
Walter Mondale, Vice President
McGeorge Bundy, Former National Security Advisor

Soviet Officials

Leonid Brezhnev, General Secretary and Chairman of the Presidium of the
    Supreme Soviet of the USSR
Anatoly Dobrynin, Ambassador to the United States
Andrei Gromyko, Foreign Minister

Chapters 19, 20

Americans

Jimmy Carter, President of the United States
Zbigniew Brzezinski, National Security Advisor to the President
Cyrus Vance, Secretary of State
Harold Brown, Secretary of Defense
Robert (Bob) Bergland, Secretary of Agriculture
Walter Mondale, Vice President
Thomas J. Watson Jr., Ambassador to the USSR
Marshall Shulman, Special Advisor on Soviet Affairs to the Secretary of State

Marshall Brement, National Security Council Staff Member

Stansfield Turner, Director of the CIA

David Aaron, Deputy Assistant for National Security Affairs

Warren Christopher, Deputy Secretary of State

Lloyd Cutler, White House Counsel to the President

Jody Powell, White House Press Secretary

W. Averell Harriman, Former Ambassador to the USSR 1943–46; Under Secretary of State for Political Affairs, 1963–65

Eugene Rostow, Yale University Professor; a Founder of the Committee on the Present Danger

Soviet Officials

Leonid Brezhnev, General Secretary and Chairman of the Presidium of the Supreme Soviet of the USSR

Andrei Gromyko, Foreign Minister

Anatoly Dobrynin, Ambassador to the United States

Yuri Andropov, KGB Chief

Dimitri Ustinov, Defense Minister

Nikolai Ogarkov, Chief of Staff

Mikhail Suslov, Ideological Chief

Viktor Kulikov, First Deputy of Defense Ministry; Commander in Chief of Warsaw Pact Forces

Anatoly Gribkov, Kulikov's Deputy

Afghans

Babrak Kamal, President of Afghanistan after the Soviet Invasion

Others

Lord Killanin (Michael Morris), President of the International Olympic Committee

Helmut Schmidt, Chancellor of West Germany

Mohammad Zia, Military Dictator of Pakistan

Chapter 21

Americans

Jimmy Carter, President of the United States

Zbigniew Brzezinski, National Security Advisor to the President

Edmund Muskie, Secretary of State, 1980–81

Harold Brown, Secretary of Defense

Walter Mondale, Vice President

Stansfield Turner, Director of the CIA

Leon Sloss, Advisor to the President on Nuclear Strategy; Assistant Director of the Arms Control and Disarmament Agency, 1976–78

Paul Warnke, Head of Arms Control and Disarmament Agency

Samuel Huntington, Co-Coordinator for National Security Planning

William Odom, Military Assistant and Crisis Co-Coordinator, NSC

Leslie Gelb, Former State Department Chief of Policy Planning

James Schlesinger, Former Secretary of Defense

David Aaron, Deputy Assistant For National Security Affairs

John Glenn, Senator (D-Ohio)

Paul Tsongas, Senator (D-Massachusetts)

Charles Percy, Senator (R-Illinois)

Edward Kennedy, Senator (D-Massachusetts)

Robert McNamara, Former Secretary of Defense

Ronald Reagan, Republican Presidential Candidate

Soviet Officials

Leonid Brezhnev, General Secretary and Chairman of the Presidium of the Supreme Soviet of the USSR

Andrei Gromyko, Foreign Minister

Anatoly Dobrynin, Ambassador to the United States

Chapter 22

Americans

Jimmy Carter, President of the United States

Zbigniew Brzezinski, National Security Advisor to the President

Cyrus Vance, Secretary of State

Harold Brown, Secretary of Defense

Walter Mondale, Vice President

Marshall Shulman, State Department Advisor on Soviet Affairs

William Odom, Military Assistant and Crisis Co-Coordinator, NSC

Leslie Gelb, U.S. Assistant Secretary of State for Politico-Military Affairs, 1977–79

Richard Pipes, Director of Team B Intelligence Report; Russian Specialist at Harvard University

Paul Warnke, Head of Arms Control and Disarmament Agency

John Fisher, President of American Security Council

W. Averell Harriman, Former Ambassador to the USSR, 1943–46; Undersecretary of State for Political Affairs, 1963–65

Helmut Schmidt, West German Chancellor

Soviet Officials

Leonid Brezhnev, General Secretary and Chairman of the Presidium of the Supreme Soviet of the USSR

Anatoly Dobrynin, Ambassador to the United States

Anatoly Gribkov, Chief of Staff of Warsaw Pact

Chapter 23

Americans

Jimmy Carter, President of the United States

Zbigniew Brzezinski, National Security Advisor to the President

Cyrus Vance, Secretary of State

Warren Christopher, Deputy Secretary of State

Rosalynn Carter, First Lady of the United States

Patricia Derian, Assistant Secretary of State for Human Rights and Humanitarian Affairs

Lucy Benson, Under Secretary of State for Security Assistance, 1977–80

Jessica Tuchman (Mathews), Director of the Office of Global Issues, NSC

Harold Brown, Secretary of Defense

Walter Mondale, Vice President

Michael Blumenthal, Secretary of the Treasury

Michel Oksenberg, Specialist on East Asia and China, NSC

Anthony Lake, Director of Policy Planning, State Department

Viron Vaky, Assistant Secretary of State for Inter-American Affairs

Donald McHenry, U.S. Ambassador to the United Nations

Robert Pastor, Specialist on Latin America and the Caribbean, NSC

Richard Holbrooke, Assistant Secretary of State for East Asian and Pacific Affairs

Lawrence A. Pezzullo, Ambassador to Nicaragua

Hedley Donovan, Senior Advisor to the President; Former Editor of *Time* magazine

THE OUTER CIRCLE

John Murphy, Member of Congress (D-New York)

Jeane Kirkpatrick, Georgetown University Political Science Professor; later U.S. Ambassador to the United Nations

Charles (Charlie) Wilson, Member of Congress (D-Texas)
Helmut Schmidt, Chancellor, West Germany

Others

Leonid Brezhnev, General Secretary and Chairman of the Presidium of the
 Supreme Soviet of the USSR
Nicolae Ceausescu, President of Romania
Deng Xiaoping, Deputy Prime Minister of the PRC
Wei Jingsheng, Chinese Dissident
Pol Pot (or Saloth Sar), Leader of the Khmer Rouge; Prime Minister of
 Democratic Kampuchea, 1976–79
Mohammad Reza Pahlavi, Shah of Iran
John Paul II, Pope
Paulo Evaristo Arns, Cardinal of Sao Paulo, Brazil; Human Rights Activist
Anastasio Somoza Debayle, Nicaraguan Military Dictator
Pedro Joaquin Chamorro Cardenal, Nicaraguan Dissident

Chapter 24

Americans

Jimmy Carter, President of the United States
Zbigniew Brzezinski, National Security Advisor to the President
Cyrus Vance, Secretary of State
Harold Brown, Secretary of Defense
Walter Mondale, Vice President
Robert E. White, Ambassador to El Salvador
Robert F. Wagner Jr., Ambassador to the Vatican
William Bowdler, Assistant Secretary for Inter-American Affairs
William D. Rogers, Former Assistant Secretary of State For Inter-American
 Affairs
Robert Pastor, Specialist on Latin America and the Caribbean, NSC
Hamilton Jordan, Assistant to the President, 1977–79; Chief of Staff, 1979–80
William D. Rogers, Former Assistant Secretary of State for Inter-American
 Affairs

Salvadorians

Oscar Arnulfo Romero, Archbishop of El Salvador
Rutilio Grande, Jesuit Priest and friend of Romero
Carlos Humberto Romero, Former Military Dictator of El Salvador

Hector Dada, Salvadoran Foreign Minister

José Napoleon Duarte, Leader of the Christian Democratic Party and Member of the Salvadoran Junta

José Guillermo Garcia, Salvadoran Secretary of Defense

Nicolas Caranzza, Salvadoran Vice Secretary of Defense and Head of the National Guard, National Police, and Treasury Police

Roberto D'Aubuisson Arrieta, Death Squad Leader and Founder of the Right-Wing Nationalist Republican Alliance (ARENA)

Mario Zamora, Salvadoran Attorney General and Leader in Christian Democratic Party

Segundo Azcue, Jesuit Priest and Romero's Confessor

José Alberto Medrano, Salvadoran General and Leader of the Right-Wing Paramilitary Organization ORDEN

Jaime Abdul Gutierrez, Right-Wing Member of Salvadoran Military Junta

Adolfo Arnoldo Majano Remos, Reformist Member of Salvadoran Military Junta

Amado Antonio Garay, Accomplice in the assassination of Archbishop Romero

Alvaria Rafael Savaria, Aide to D'Aubuisson and accomplice in the assassination of Archbishop Romero

Eugenio Vides Casanova, Leader of the Salvadoran National Guard

Others

John Paul II, Pope

Agostino Casaroli, Cardinal and Vatican Secretary of State

Paulo Evaristo Arns, Cardinal of Sao Paulo, Brazil; Human Rights Activist

Chapter 25

Americans

Jimmy Carter, President of the United States

Zbigniew Brzezinski, National Security Advisor to the President of the United States

Cyrus Vance, Secretary of State

Harold Brown, Secretary of Defense

Walter Mondale, Vice President

Hamilton Jordan, White House Chief of Staff

David Jones, Chairman of the Joint Chiefs of Staff

Stansfield Turner, Director of the CIA

Jody Powell, White House Press Secretary

Warren Christopher, Deputy Secretary of State

James Vaught, Commander of Iran Hostage Rescue Operation

Charles Beckwith, Commander of Iran Hostage Rescue Team

Patrick Caddell, Pollster and Carter Administration Public Relations Advisor
Robert Byrd, Senate Majority Leader

Others

Joseph Luns, Secretary General of NATO

Chapter 26

Americans

Jimmy Carter, President of the United States
Edmund Muskie, Secretary of State
Warren Christopher, Deputy Secretary of State
Edward Kennedy, Democratic Contender for the 1980 Democratic Presidential
    Nomination
John Anderson, 1980 Unity Party Presidential Candidate
Ronald Reagan, 1980 Republican Presidential Candidate
Paul Volker, Appointed Chairman of the Federal Reserve in August 1979;
    Reappointed in 1983 by Reagan
Billy Carter, Jimmy Carter's brother
Robert Strauss, Chairman of Carter's Election Campaign in 1976 and 1980
Hamilton Jordan, Deputy Campaign Manager; Former Chief of Staff
William Casey, Chairman of Ronald Reagan's 1980 Presidential Campaign
Richard Allen, Ronald Reagan's National Security Advisor
Harold Brown, Secretary of Defense
Stansfield Turner, Director of the CIA
David Jones, Chairman of Joint Chiefs of Staff
Gary Sick, National Security Council Staff Member and Middle East Expert
Harold Saunders, Assistant Secretary of State for the Near East and South Asia
    Affairs
G. William Miller, Treasury Secretary
Anthony Solomon, President of New York Federal Reserve Bank

Others

Mehdi Bazargan, Iranian Prime Minister
Sadegh Tabatabai, Former Iranian Deputy Prime Minister
Sadegh Ghotbzadeh, Iranian Foreign Minister
Gerhardt Ritzel, West German Ambassador to Iran
Mohamed Seddik Benyahia, Algerian Foreign Minister and Negotiator in Iran
    Hostage Crisis

Notes

Abbreviations in Endnotes

BB	Briefing Book (Found in the U.S.-USSR Conference File) at the Jimmy Carter Library
CPP	Carter Presidency Project at the Jimmy Carter Library
CR	*Congressional Record*
DSB	*U.S. Department of State Bulletin*
FF	*Facts on File*
Gallup	The Gallup Public Opinion Poll
JCL	Jimmy Carter Library
NSC	National Security Council
NYT	*New York Times*
PD	Presidential Directive
PP	*Public Papers of the Presidents*
PRC	Presidential Review Committee
PRM	Presidential Review Memorandum
SCC	Special Coordinating Committee
SFRC	Senate Foreign Relations Committee
WP	*Washington Post*
WR	Weekly Reports (of Brzezinski)
VF	Vertical files in the Manuscript Collections at the Jimmy Carter Library
YUL	Yale University Library
ZB Don	Zbigniew Brzezinski papers donated to the Jimmy Carter Library

INTRODUCTION

1. Ole Holsti and James Rosenau, "The Domestic and Foreign Policy Beliefs of American Leaders," *Journal of Conflict Resolution* 32, no. 2 (1988): 248–94.

2. Morris Janowitz, *The Professional Soldier: A Social and Political Portrait* (Glencoe, IL: Free Press, 1964).

3. Kenneth Kitts and Betty Glad, "Presidential Personality and Improvisational Decision-Making: Eisenhower and the 1956 Hungarian Crisis," in *Reexamining the Eisenhower Presidency*, ed. Shirley Anne Warshaw (Westport, CT: Greenwood Press, 1993), 182–208.

4. After Carter, even that stalwart Cold Warrior Ronald Reagan countered opposition within his own party to his decision to sign the Intermediate-Range Nuclear Forces (INF) Agreement with Mikhail Gorbachev. Richard Perle, an adamant critic of Carter's SALT II operations, even quit the Reagan administration to testify against the INF treaty in a Congressional Hearing.

5. Jimmy Carter, *Negotiation: The Alternative to Hostility* (Macon, GA: Mercer University Press, 1984).

CHAPTER 1. HIGH EXPECTATIONS

1. Television ad: Described by Witcover in Betty Glad, *Jimmy Carter*, 357.

2. Carter in polls: *Gallup* vol. 1 (1972–75): 577–78.

3. Contrasts with Nixon: Glad, *Jimmy Carter*, 314–15, 354; Jimmy Carter, *Why Not the Best?*, 155–56; Robert J. Kaiser, "Ex-Aide to Nixon Advising Carter on Executive Reorganization," *WP*, November 30, 1976.

4. No anonymous aides: Glad, *Jimmy Carter*, 411; Jimmy Carter, "Fireside Chat," *Congressional Quarterly: The Presidency*, 68A–71A, 1977.

5. No chief of staff: Glad, *Jimmy Carter*, 411; Hamilton Jordan on CBS's *Face the Nation*, November 1977.

6. Appointments based on merit: Glad, *Jimmy Carter*, 414–16.

7. Distinction from earlier inaugurals: Glad, *Jimmy Carter*, 409–10; Warren Brown, "8 Cabinet Officers, 4 Others Sworn in With Little Pomp," *WP*, January 24, 1977, A2; "Carter: I Look Forward to the Job," *Time*, January 3, 1977. Average citizens invited to the White House: *Newsweek*, March 1, 1977.

8. The wheel metaphor: Jody Powell, quoted in James Wooten, "Free Access by Staff to Carter is Planned," *NYT*, January 15, 1977. For discussion of the three possible advisory forms see: Richard Tanner Johnson, *Managing the White House: An Intimate Study of the Presidency*, 1–8, 234, 238.

9. Carter couldn't live up to promises: Gary Trudeau, *Doonesbury*, in *Newsweek*, March 1, 1977.

10. Talent Bank 77 questionnaires: Dom Bonafede, "Carter Sounds Retreat from 'Cabinet Government,'" *National Journal*, November 18, 1978, 1852–57. Glad, *Jimmy Carter*, 416.

11. Washington insiders: Hugh Sidey, "Grafting Job: Old Body, New Head," *Time*, January 17, 1977, 13. For an overview of the cabinet government, see Shirley Anne Warshaw, *Powersharing*.

12. New Attorney General Griffin Bell was a member of the Atlanta law firm to which Carter's advisor Charles Kirbo also belonged. Philip Klutznick, a prominent Atlanta attorney, would join the cabinet as secretary of commerce in 1979. Bert Lance, president of the Georgia Bank of Commerce, had been a financial supporter of Carter since his first campaign for governor in 1966. James McIntyre, who would replace Lance as head of the Office of Management and Budget when he resigned in September 1977, had served Carter as director of the Georgia Office of Planning and Budget. Glad, *Jimmy Carter*, 102, 414.

13. White House politicos: Glad, *Jimmy Carter*, 102, 414. Carter appointments: "Carter Uses New Screening Procedures," *Congressional Quarterly: The Presidency*, 1977, 39–52.

14. Youth and inexperience: Jordan had been Governor Carter's chief of staff and presidential campaign manager. Press Secretary Powell had been his campaign press secretary and congressional liaison. Moore had served as Carter's chief of staff when he was governor and as his congressional liaison during the campaign. Robert Lipshutz, an established Atlanta attorney who had been Carter's financial campaign manager in 1976, was named legal counsel to the president. Eizenstat, a Harvard graduate, had been a speechwriter and researcher for former president Lyndon Johnson and had performed as issue director in the Carter gubernatorial campaign in 1970 and presidential campaign in 1976. Gerald Rafshoon, appointed White House communications director in 1978, had his own Atlanta advertising agency and had been a Carter supporter since 1966. For Carter's staff, see Glad, *Jimmy Carter*, 414; "Carter Uses New Screening Procedures," *Congressional Quarterly: The Presidency*, 1977, 39–52; *National Journal*, December 30, 1977, 2085. On Eizenstat: see Edward Walsh, "Rising Status, Mild Criticism for Eizenstat Policy Staff," *WP*, December 27,

1977. Ironically, it was the Washington outsiders who would create political problems for Carter during his first few months in office. Powell, Jordan, and Moore's down-home style and obvious lack of experience in Washington would soon be the object of critical press attention. Bert Lance, head of the OMB, would be embroiled throughout the last half of 1977 in conflict-of-interest problems that would undercut the Carter administration's claim to ethical superiority.

15. Staff growth: Stephen Hess, *Organizing the Presidency*, 23; James Pfiffner, *The Modern Presidency*, 52, 93.

16. Demands on the president's time: Alexander George, *Presidential Decision Making in Foreign Policy*, 209–16. For an overview of staff relationships, see Karen Hult and Charles Walcott, *Empowering the White House*.

17. Jordan not wanting the job: Jimmy Carter, interview, 1982, CPP, 7–8, JCL.

18. Carter wanting control: Bert Lance and Bill Gilbert, *The Truth of the Matter*, 97.

19. Carter's inner circle: Michael Link, "The Presidential Kaleidoscope" (Ph.D. diss.), 285–87. For other analyses of relationships among the Carter White House staff, see John H. Kessel, *The Domestic Presidency*; and Robert J. Thompson, "The Spokes of the Wheel in Operation: The Carter Example," paper presented at the Eighth Presidential Conference, Hofstra University, Hempstead, New York, November 15–17, 1990.

20. The group with the least access included Secretary of the Treasury Michael Blumenthal; Chairman of the Council of Economic Advisors Charles Schultz; and the OMB directors—first Bert Lance and later James McIntyre.

21. Rosalynn Carter's role: Lloyd Cutler, interview, 1982, CPP, 27, JCL.

22. Rosalyn Carter in Latin America: Roberta Cohen, "Human Rights Diplomacy: The Carter Administration and the Southern Cone," *Human Rights Quarterly* 4 (1982): 222; "First Lady Biography: Rosalynn Smith Carter," retrieved January 5, 2008, from http://www.first ladies.org/biographies/firstladies.aspx?biography=40.

23. The roles of Kirbo and Bell: Charles Kirbo, interview, 1983, CPP, 4, JCL.

24. Strauss's role: Robert Bergland, interview, 1986, CPP, 110, JCL; Jack Watson, interview, 1981, CPP, 25–26, JCL.

25. Caddell's role: Michael W. Link and Betty Glad, "Exploring the Psycho-Political Dynamics of Advisory Relations: The Carter Administration's 'Crisis of Confidence,'" *Political Psychology* 15 (1994): 470–71. Persons with apparently equally official responsibilities, it should be noted, did not have equal access to the president. Bert Lance had a much closer relationship with Carter than did his successor at OMB, James McIntyre. Though both Hamilton Jordan and Jack Watson held important formal posts in the White House, Jordan clearly had greater access than did Watson.

26. Schuman's role in airline deregulation: David B. Cohen and Chris J. Dolan, "Debunking the Myth: Carter, Congress, and the Politics of Airline Deregulation," paper presented at the Annual Meeting of the Southern Political Science Association, Atlanta, October 2000, 41; see also Bert Carp and David Rubenstein, interview, 1982, CPP, 40–41, JCL.

27. For the discussion of types of services, see Betty Glad with Michael W. Link, "President Nixon's Inner Circle of Advisors," *Presidential Studies Quarterly* 26 (Winter 1996): 12–40.

28. On Comprehensive Test Ban treaty: Hamilton Jordan to Jimmy Carter, "Relationship of SALT II to CTB," n.d., Jordan Collection, Box 34, Comprehensive Test Ban Treaty, SALT, 1978, JCL. See also Frank Moore to Jimmy Carter, July 7, 1978, Jordan Collection, Box 34, Comprehensive Test Ban Treaty, SALT, 1978, JCL.

29. SALT II: Gerald Rafshoon to Jimmy Carter, February 1977, Rafshoon Collection, Box 27, Greg Schneiders files, JCL.

30. Advice on malaise speech: Link and Glad, "Exploring the Psycho-Political Dynamics," 470–71.

31. In the Nixon Administration, Chief of Staff John Halderman ignored some of the more impulsive orders of the president and mediated White House territorial fights and reprimanded

or fired aides, something Nixon was reluctant to do. See Glad and Link, "President Nixon's Inner Circle," 21–22, 26–27.

32. Lance's role: Lance and Gilbert, *Truth of the Matter*, 85, 111.

33. The need for political work: Hamilton Jordan to Jimmy Carter, "Early Months Performance," n.d., 1977, Jordan Collection, Box 34, Memos to President, JCL.

34. Chuck Colson's "dark work" for Nixon and John Dean's enemy's list: Glad and Link, "President Nixon's Inner Circle," 21–22, 26–27.

35. Carter's bad cop: Hamilton Jordan to Joseph Califano, January 19, 1977, Jordan Collection, Box 33, Handwritten Notes, JCL.

36. Staff hurdles endemic: Hess, *Organizing the Presidency*, 231. During the Reagan Administration, Secretary of State Alexander Haig had to wait over the weekend for White House approval to discuss instructions to send to his chief Middle East negotiator at a crucial point in Israel's advance toward Beirut during its incursion into Lebanon in 1982. See Haig, *Caveat*, 310–11.

37. Jordan restricting access: Robert Bergland, interview, 1986, CPP, 25, JCL.

38. Brzezinski restricting access: Bell, interview, 1988, CPP, 22–23, JCL.

39. Brzezinski maneuvers: Lance and Gilbert, *Truth of the Matter*, 107.

40. For court politics: Elizabeth W. Marvick, "Comments on Lewis A. Dexter's 'Court Politics,'" *Administration and Society* 9 (1977): 285–92; Lewis A. Dexter, "Court Politics: Presidential Staff Relations as a Special Case of a General Phenomenon," *Administration and Society* 9 (1977): 268.

41. Staff competitions: Lance and Gilbert, *Truth of the Matter*, 104.

42. Presidency creates awe: Jordan to Carter, "Early Months Performance," March 1988, Jordan Collection, Box 34, JCL.

43. Cabinet members not speaking out: Greg Schneiders to Jody Powell, May 18, 1977, Powell Collection, Box 36, Memoranda: Jody Powell 1/21/77–7/18/77, JCL.

44. Staff pecking order: George Reedy, *The Twilight of the Presidency*, 204.

45. For how lack of candor can contribute to premature accord on a matter, Janis, *Groupthink*, 245.

46. Alienating department heads: Lance and Gilbert, *Truth of the Matter*, 113.

47. Cutting off discussion: Betty Glad, "Personality, Political and Group Process Variables in Foreign Policy Decision-Making: Jimmy Carter's Handling of the Iranian Hostage Crisis," *International Political Science Review* 10 (1989): 35–61.

48. Scolding the governor: Lance and Gilbert, *Truth of the Matter*, 38–39.

49. Greater coordination needed: Powell to Jimmy Carter, January 16, 1978, Powell Collection, Box 36, Memoranda: Jody Powell 1/9/78–2/28/78, JCL.

50. Tone of energy remarks memo: Stuart Eizenstat to Jimmy Carter, 25 April 1979, Powell Collection, Box 37, F: Memoranda 4/2/79–5/31/79, JCL.

51. Gerald Rafshoon to Jimmy Carter, n.d., Susan Clough File, Box 34, F: Campaign Strategies 1980, JCL. For further admonitions, see Jody Powell to Jimmy Carter, Box 36, July 7, 1978, JCL; Rafshoon to Jimmy Carter, July 7, 1978, Jordan Collection, Box 34, JCL.

52. Making final decisions: Angus Deming et al., "Show of Strength," *Newsweek*, July 3, 1978, 20.

53. Views of Sorensen: "Presidential Advisors," in Thomas Cronin and Sanford Greenberg, eds., *The Presidential Advisory System*, 3.

54. No Svengalis: Hess, *Organizing the Presidency*, 174.

55. "Motivated tactician" in the management world: Fiske and Taylor, *Social Cognition*. For the relationship of Woodrow Wilson and Colonel Edward House along these lines, see Alexander George and Juliette George, *Woodrow Wilson and Colonel House*, 267–68.

56. The need for balanced information processing: George, *Presidential Decision Making*, 139–43.

57. On strategic wisdom, see Paul Quirk, "Presidential Competence," in Nelson, ed., *The Presidency and the Political System*, 171–97.

58. For a somewhat different formulation of the skills relevant to presidential successes, see Fred Greenstein, *The Presidential Difference*, 5–6, 22–25.

CHAPTER 2. THE FOREIGN POLICY TEAM

1. "The Resolute": Tom Mathews et al., "A New Spirit," *Newsweek*, January 31, 1977, 14; see also "*Resolute* Partner's Desk," retrieved January 5, 2008, from http://www.whitehousehistory.org/04/subs_pph/PresidentDetail.aspx?ID=19&imageID=797.

2. Being tough: *Robert Gates, From the Shadows*, 178–79.

3. Loading up, backbiting, attention to detail: Jimmy Carter, interview, 1982, CPP, 54, JCL. Academic requirements: Jimmy Carter to Harold Brown, December 21, 1977, Plains File, Box 32 F: President's Comments on Memos 1977, JCL.

4. Role models: Betty Glad, *Jimmy Carter*, 63. Rickover's style: Jimmy Carter, "Speech to National Wildlife Federation," March 15, 1975, *Campaign 1976*, I, 1, 65. Details on Rickover's management style, promotion: Blair, *The Atomic Submarine and Admiral Rickover*, 119–20, 173–269. See also Jimmy Carter, *Why Not the Best?*, 53–55.

5. Making decisions easily: Jimmy Carter, interview, 1982, CPP, 54, JCL.

6. On the view that on domestic matters Carter saw himself as trustee of the people, see Charles Jones, *The Trusteeship Presidency*.

7. Ambitious agenda: Clark Clifford and Richard Holbrooke, *Counsel to the President*, 656.

8. For time studies, see Jimmy Carter, Presidential Diaries, Box 102, JCL.

9. After a year at Georgia Southwestern University, Carter enrolled in the Navy ROTC program at Georgia Tech. There he took courses in seamanship, navigation, and other military sciences; For standard course offerings see *Catalog of Course Instruction at the US Naval Academy Annapolis, MD: 1941–46*, Author's files. See also Glad, *Jimmy Carter*, 48–53.

10. On details: Gates, *From the Shadows*, 572.

11. Mini-seminars: Zbigniew Brzezinski, *Power and Principle*, 22.

12. Classes and entertainments: Jimmy Carter, Plains Files, Box 6, F: President's Daily Diaries, JCL.

13. Carter's religion, campaign: Glad, *Jimmy Carter*, 333–40.

14. Use of religion: Jody Powell to Jimmy Carter, Handwritten note, n.d., Powell Collection, Box 6 F: Staff Meetings—JLP Notes, 9–10/76, JCL.

15. Soup and sandwiches: Peter Goldman, "Picking the New Team," *Newsweek*, December 13, 1976, 21.

16. Foreign policy discussion: Cyrus Vance, *Hard Choices*, 31–34.

17. Offer: Brzezinski, *Power and Principle*, 12.

18. Model for cooperation: Brzezinski, *Power and Principle*, 10–11.

19. George Ball: Brzezinski, *Power and Principle*, 10–11. Cooperation envisaged: Bernard Gwertzman, "Brzezinski Revamps Security Unit Staff," *NYT*, January 16, 1977.

20. Vance background: John M. Goshko, "Cyrus Vance, Carter's Secretary of State, Dies." *WP*, January 13, 2001; McLellan, *Cyrus Vance*, 6–9, 10–19.

21. Vance's approach to problems: Melchiore J. Laucella, "A Cognitive-Psychodynamic Perspective to Understanding Secretary of State Cyrus Vance's Worldview," *Presidential Studies Quarterly* 34 (2004): 227–71. For an updated version see Laucella, "Secretary of State Cyrus Vance's Worldview," *Institute for Political Psychology and the Study of Foreign Policy*, May 15, 2007, 3.

22. Vance as survivor: Tom Mathews et al., "The Crisis Manager," *Newsweek*, December 13, 1976, 29.

23. Popular choice: Jimmy Carter, *Keeping Faith*, 51.

24. Brzezinski: Steven Campbell, "Brzezinski's Image of the USSR" (Ph.D. diss.).

25. Brzezinski's books: Zbigniew Brzezinski, exit interview, 1981, 3–4, JCL.

26. Brzezinski with Rockefeller: James Wooten, "Here Comes Zbig!" *Esquire*, November 1979, 117–24. See also Bourne, *Jimmy Carter*, 380.

27. Brown: Meg Greenfield, "Arms and the Man," *Newsweek*, March 18, 1977, 88.

28. Brown's discipline: Carter, *Keeping Faith*, 55.

29. Mondale: See Jack Lechelt, "The Semi-Institutionalized Vice Presidency" (Ph.D. diss.), chaps. 2, 3. Mondale's early life and political career, and his relationship with Carter: Steven Gillon, *The Democrats' Dilemma*, 80–122, 163–85, 215–49; Finlay Lewis, *Mondale*.

30. Mondale's experience: Jimmy Carter, interview, 1982, CPP, 9, JCL.

31. "Mr. Dooley," quoted in Dom Bonafede, "Vice President Mondale—Carter's Partner with Portfolio," *National Journal* 11 (1978): 376.

32. Mondale's role: Jimmy Carter, interview, 1982, CPP, 5, JCL.

33. The time study done by Hamilton Jordan's staff excluded large group meetings and time spent outside of Washington. "Six Week Allocation of President's Time," Plains Files, Box 104, Presidential Diary, JCL. See also Lechelt, "The Semi-Institutionalized Vice Presidency," 55–56.

34. Mondale's role: Bonafede, "Vice President Mondale," 378, 379, and 384. See also Bert Carp and Dave Rubinstein, interview, 1982, CPP, 12, JCL; Jimmy Carter, interview, 1982 CPP, 9, JCL; Robert Bergland, interview, 1986, CPP, 87, JCL; Aldo Beckman, "Carter Sending Mondale on World Tour," *Chicago Tribune*, January 9, 1977; and "A Veep with Clout," *U.S. News and World Report*, January 31, 1977, 30. Mondale's role can be contrasted to Nixon's vice president Spiro Agnew, who lacked virtually any White House access and often made public statements that ran counter to Nixon's policies.

35. Turner graduated with the Annapolis class of 1947, receiving a Rhodes Scholarship a year later. Carter later stated he had been in competition for a Rhodes Scholarship against an "Elizabethan scholar." There is no evidence that Carter was ever a finalist. See Glad, *Jimmy Carter*, 53, 59.

36. Young: Tom Mathews with Vern E. Smith, "Young Takes a Risk," *Newsweek*, December 27, 1976, 21.

37. On Warnke nomination: SFRC *Hearings*, "Warnke Nominations," February 8–9, 1977, 185–192, passim. One of the contenders for the secretary of defense position, James Schlesinger, was given a slot as the president's energy advisor and later moved to the cabinet as the newly created Energy Department's first secretary. He had earlier served as chair of the Atomic Energy Commission, as CIA director, and as secretary of defense in the administrations of Richard Nixon and Gerald Ford. A brilliant man, Schlesinger was also viewed by others as arrogant. As defense secretary under Ford, he was fired for being too critical of the administration. See *U.S. News and World Report*, October 16, 1978; Jack Anderson, *WP*, October 6, 1978.

Paul Nitze, an anti-Soviet hard-liner who had advised almost every president since Harry S. Truman, was offered no position. Though he had advised Carter on foreign issues in the summer of 1976, Carter felt uncomfortable with him. On their meeting, see Nitze, *From Hiroshima to Glasnost*, 348–50.

38. See Vance, *Hard Choices*, 42–43. For Lucy Benson, see Vance, *Hard Choices*, 43. On Patricia Derian, see "Patricia Derian," retrieved January 5, 2008, from http://www.thenation.com/directory/bios/bio.mhtml?id=1713.

39. Carter on Vietnam, Calley: Glad, *Jimmy Carter*, 205–10. Carter did not declare a William Calley Day, as several Georgians were urging him to do, proclaiming instead an American Fighting Men's Day; he asked Georgians to fly the flag and drive with their headlights on.

40. Others burned by the experience: Brzezinski, *Power and Principle*, 73.

41. According to Greenfield, "Arms and the Man," 88, the "hard-liners" in Washington saw Brown as "the closest thing they have to a soul mate in the upper reaches of the administration."

42. Vietnam and Vance: McLellan, *Cyrus Vance*, 8–9.

43. Mondale's changing views on Vietnam: Lewis, *Mondale*, 175–76, 181–85.

44. Lake: "Nine Ex-Kissinger Aides Denounce U.S. Moves," *NYT,* May 12, 1972.

45. The wounds of Vietnam: Richard Melanson, *American Foreign Policy since the Vietnam War,* 98.

46. Counterbalance to doves: Brzezinski, *Power and Principle,* 11, 13, 36.

47. Concerns: Eugene V. Rostow to Zbigniew Brzezinski, February 21, 1977, WHCF-Subject File, Federal Government—Organizations, Box FG 6-1-1/Brzezinski, Zbigniew 2/16/77–3/7/77, Box FG-25, JCL. Quoted in Caldwell, *The Dynamics of Domestic Politics and Arms Control,* 29–30.

48. Vance on diplomacy: Melchiore J. Laucella, "Secretary of State Cyrus Vance's Worldview," paper presented at the Conference on the Carter Presidency: Policy Choices in the Post–New Deal Era, Atlanta, February 20–22, 1997.

49. Brzezinski on the Soviets: Campbell, "Brzezinski's Image," 126–28.

50. Vance's family: McLellan, *Cyrus Vance,* 3.

51. Brzezinski's heritage: *Chicago Sun Times,* December 23, 1979.

52. "We never had to struggle": Vance, quoted in Tom Mathews, "The Crisis Manager," *Newsweek,* December 13, 1976, 29.

53. Kissinger on Vance: "Vance: Man on the Move," *Time,* April 24, 1978, 13.

54. Brzezinski history: Campbell, "Brzezinski's Image of the USSR," 38.

55. Brzezinski relishing dueling: Gates, *From the Shadows,* 70.

56. Overwhelming Vance: Peter Goldman, "Picking the New Team," *Newsweek,* December 13, 1976, 21.

57. Clifford's advice: Clifford, *Counsel to the President,* 621.

58. Vance as builder: William Neikirk, "Carter's Global Strategist," *Chicago Tribune,* October 23, 1977.

59. Good relationship: Brzezinski/Aides interviews, 1982, CPP, 71–72, JCL.

60. Brown as mediator: Brzezinski, *Power and Principle,* 44–45.

61. Friends with Vance: Carter, *Keeping Faith,* 51.

62. Handwritten note on Zbigniew Brzezinski to Jimmy Carter, WR #34, 28 October 1977, ZB Don, Box 41, JCL.

63. Breakfast meetings: Vance, *Hard Choices,* 38–39. Later the group would expand to include Jordan, Powell, special advisors Hedley Donovan and Lloyd Cutler, and Deputy Secretary of State Warren Christopher.

64. VBB luncheon meetings: Vance, *Hard Choices,* 39. Vance also sent a nightly report to the president, usually two to five pages in length. He gave Carter little advice.

65. Competition develops: Brzezinski/aides interviews, 1982, CPP, 72, JCL.

66. Brzezinski as chief of staff: Brzezinski/aides interviews, 1982, CPP, 86–87, JCL.

67. Press reports on conflicts: Sally Quinn, "If Brzezinski reminds you of Kissinger...," *Chicago Sun Times,* December 23, 1979.

68. Jordan on relationship: Associated Press, "Brzezinski: An Aide with Plenty of Ideas, Clout," *Chicago Sun Times,* July 17, 1978.

CHAPTER 3. THE BRZEZINSKI ADVANTAGE

1. Meetings with Carter: Plains Files, Box 6, F: President's Daily Diaries, JCL. "Amphibious" operations: term from Colin Campbell, *Managing the Presidency,* 199–203.

2. Trip to Korea: Brzezinski/aides interviews, 1982, CPP, 79, JCL.

3. Role as national security advisor: Brzezinski/aides interviews, 1982, CPP, 62, JCL.

4. NSC central role: Zbigniew Brzezinski, *Power and Principle,* 57.

5. Needing someone like Brzezinski: Brzezinski/aides interviews, 1982, CPP, 74, JCL.

6. With Vance's first foreign policy appointments, Brzezinski began to fear that the president would not receive the kind of hard-nosed advice that should balance his more idealist

views. He addressed the issue by emphasizing the need for greater diversity by pulling from the defense/arms control cluster. Brzezinski, *Power and Principle*, 58–59. Sea Island Proposals reworked: Brzezinski/aides interviews, 1982, CPP, 63, JCL.

7. Procedures codified: "PD/NSC-2: The National Security Council System." January 20, 1977, VF, JCL.

8. Brzezinski's control over NSC reports: Cyrus Vance, *Hard Choices*, 37.

9. Protests from Vance: Vance, *Hard Choices*, 37. See also Brzezinski, *Power and Principle*, 62.

10. Reviewing summaries at White House: Vance, *Hard Choices*, 37.

11. Brzezinski's rationales: Brzezinski/aides interviews, 1982, CPP, 62–63, JCL.

12. Retrospective on the summaries: Vance, *Hard Choices*, 37.

13. Turner, Annapolis, Rhodes scholarships: Betty Glad, *Jimmy Carter*, 52–53, 59.

14. Turner sidelined: Brzezinski, *Power and Principle*, 64, 68. According to Gates, Turner delayed his departure from the CIA for three weeks time due to his concerns that Gates might assist Brzezinski in circumventing the DCI's proper role. Robert Gates, *From the Shadows*, 69.

15. Morning briefings: Brzezinski/aides interviews, 1982, CPP, 78, JCL.

16. At the president's side: Brzezinski/aides interviews, 1982, CPP, 78–79, JCL. Eventually, Brzezinski noted, the president had no other source of foreign policy advice in the White House. "A couple [Turner and Mondale] tried" but failed. See Brzezinski/ aides interviews, 1982, CPP, 84, JCL.

17. Meeting: W. Averell Harriman and Jimmy Carter conversation, March 8, 1978, VF, Box 117, USSR-US Conf. 5/94, BB II, JCL.

18. On control over paper flow: Brzezinski/aides interviews, 1982, CPP, 79–80, JCL. For Denend, see 6.

19. Papers going directly to Carter: Brzezinski/aides interviews, 1982, CPP, 80, JCL.

20. Finding reports valuable: Zbigniew Brzezinski to Jimmy Carter, handwritten note, October 21, 1977, WR 34, ZB Don, Box 41, JCL.

21. Vance's meetings required eighteen index cards to note his meetings with Carter in 1977. Presidential Diaries, Plains File, Boxes 108–110, JCL.

22. Nightly reports: Vance, *Hard Choices*, 38–39. See also Plains Files, Box 39, State Department Evening Reports, JCL.

23. Brown's visits in 1977 required only eleven index cards. Presidential Diaries, Plains File, Boxes 108–110, JCL.

24. Not bothering the president: Brzezinski/aides interviews, 1982 CPP, 87, JCL.

25. Spokesman role: Vance, *Hard Choices*, 35.

26. Brzezinski as spokesman: Brzezinski/aides interviews, 1982, CPP, 65–66, JCL.

27. On Schecter role: Brzezinski, *Power and Principle*, 77–78. In 1979, Schecter moved into the private sector and Albert Friendly, a "highly sophisticated journalist and Soviet expert," took over the job of press secretary.

28. Brzezinski's role the result of default: Jimmy Carter, interview, 1982, CPP, 40, JCL. Brzezinski/aides interviews, 1982, CPP, 65–66, JCL. Problems with arrangement: Vance, *Hard Choices*, 35–36.

29. Nuances: Brzezinski/aides interviews, 1982, CPP, 65–66, JCL.

30. Vance not a "shrinking violet": Jimmy Carter, interview, 1982 CPP, 40, JCL.

31. Denend's role on NSC: Brzezinski/aides interviews, 1982 CPP, 45.

32. Brzezinski pushes Owen: I.M. Destler, *Making Foreign Economic Policy*, 226.

33. Others welcome appointment: Zbigniew Brzezinski to Jimmy Carter, March 7, 1978, JCL.

34. Eizenstat objects: Stuart Eizenstat to Jimmy Carter, March 9, 1978, JCL.

35. Owen appointed: Zbigniew Brzezinski to senior cabinet members and White House staff, 3-78, JCL.

36. Owen's role expands: Destler, *Making Foreign Economic Policy*, 226–27; Brzezinski, *Power and Principle*, 60–61.

37. On the use of cover notes: Brzezinski/aides interviews, 1982, CPP, 74, JCL.

38. Other secretaries were less successful, according to Odom: "With Harold Brown in the chair, you get a moderately disciplined result. You put Vance in the chair; he'd drift about, and provide much less focus." Brzezinski/aides interviews, 1982, CPP, 53, JCL.

39. Thinner briefing books: Brzezinski/aides interviews, 1982, CPP, 53, JCL.

40. Free hand: Brzezinski/aides interviews, 1982, CPP, 64, JCL. His aides included Colonel William Odom, a former student of Brzezinski and a defense attaché in Moscow; his major Soviet expert, Samuel Huntington, the director of the Center of International Affairs at Harvard University and once a fellow graduate student with Brzeznski; Michel Oksenberg, a professor at the University of Michigan, who was assigned to Chinese affairs; and David Aaron, a former Foreign Service officer, who had served as Walter Mondale's foreign affairs adviser and would assist Brzezinski in revamping the NSC organization and staff. All these men shared Brzezinski's views in their relevant policy arenas. For other key aides, see table 4, Foreign Policy Department Heads and Staff.

41. Staff advice not political: Brzezinski/aides interviews, 1982, CPP, 24–25, JCL.

42. Little direct access to Carter: Brzezinski/aides interviews, 1982, CPP, 48, JCL.

43. Brzezinski more pointed: Denend, in Brzezinski/aides interviews, 1982, CPP, 24–25, JCL.

44. Resisting review: Zbigniew Brzezinski to Jimmy Carter, June 12, 1978, Plains File, Box 29, F6-12/1978, JCL.

45. Carter's response: Zbigniew Brzezinski to Jimmy Carter, June 12, 1978, Plains File, Box 29, F6-12/1978, JCL.

46. Brzezinski's turf: Jimmy Carter, interview, 1982, CPP, 39–40, JCL.

47. Brzezinski to Powell and Jordan: Brzezinski/aides interviews, 1982, CPP, 81, JCL.

48. Dismisses critiques of Brzezinski: Jimmy Carter, *Keeping Faith*, 53.

49. Brzezinski on normalization: Brzezinski, *Power and Principle*, 41.

50. Brzezinski explains: Brzezinski, *Power and Principle*, 41.

51. Lightning rod: Jimmy Carter, quoted in Brzezinski, *Power and Principle*, 41.

52. Brzezinski's reaction: Bob Carr and Tom Downey to Jimmy Carter, August 9, 1978, Plains File, Box 55, Subject File, SALT 11/77-8/78, JCL.

53. Carter's response: Jimmy Carter to Bob Carr and Tom Downey, August 15, 1978, Plains File, Box 55, Subject File, SALT 11/77-8/78, JCL. Brzezinski reinforced this view. For example, he wrote Carter that he believed that Arms Control and Disarmament Agency officials were leaking information in an effort to force the president to take a given course. Zbigniew Brzezinski to Jimmy Carter, WR 71, 1 September 1978, ZB Don, Box 41, JCL. The apparent "zig-zags" in Carter's policy were even attributed to the failure of Vance and the State Department to back the president's policies, and Brzezinski evaluated specific departmental leaders in terms of their skills and loyalty to Carter. Zbigniew Brzezinski to Jimmy Carter, May 1, 1980, ZB Don, Box 23, Meetings—Muskie/Brown/Brzezinski: 5/80–6/80, JCL. The next day, September 2, Carter wrote Vance that "if there are spokesmen in your dept. who cannot support me and my policies, they should resign." Jimmy Carter to Cyrus Vance, note on Evening Reports, Plain Files, Box 32, F: President's Comments on Memos, 1978.

54. Awarding Medal of Freedom: Carter, quoted in Brzezinski, *Power and Principle*, 31.

55. Echoing Brzezinski's words: Brzezinski/aides interviews, 1982, CPP, 75, JCL.

56. Albright on their relationship: Brzezinski/aides interviews, 1982, CPP, 56, JCL.

57. Brzezinski in office: Carter, *Keeping Faith*, 51–52.

58. Weekly Reports: Brzezinski, *Power and Principle*, 19.

59. Mini-seminars: Brzezinski, *Power and Principle*, 350.

60. Carter an eager student: Carter, *Keeping Faith*, 51.

61. Brzezinski's interests: Carter, *Keeping Faith*, 51.

62. Only when he returned home, three weeks later, did Carter agree to reverse his policies in light of the new intelligence estimates. Perhaps Brzezinski knew that others would do all the heavy lifting on this issue. Korea: Vance, *Hard Choices*, 128–30.

63. Quote and detail on South Korea: Vance, *Hard Choices*, 128–30. Neither Carter nor Brzezinski deals with this issue in their memoirs.

64. Similarities between Carter and Brzezinski: "Brzezinski: An Aide With Plenty of Ideas, Clout," *Chicago Sun Times*, July 17, 1978.

65. Carter and Brzezinski as outsiders: Brzezinski/aides interviews, 1982, CPP, 80, JCL.

66. Bert Lance, Georgia Department of Transportation manager under Governor Carter, doled out roads and other perks, based in part on how the legislators voted. During his presidential campaign, the private plane belonging to the Bank of Georgia (Lance chaired the board) was at times placed at his disposal. Hamilton Jordan and Jody Powell were very political, fashioning the strategies and rhetoric that enabled Carter to outmaneuver other Democrats in 1976. One of Carter's earliest associates would later engage in clear fraud: Erwin David Rabhan, an operator of a nursing home chain in Georgia, who had provided Carter with a plane for his gubernatorial run in 1966, was given an office in the governor's mansion for a short period of time, and eventually fled Georgia, with federal investigators just behind him. As president, Carter showed an interest in getting his former friend out of an Iranian jail. "Swainsboro Man Sentenced to Five Years," *Savannah News*, February 7, 2003.

67. On being feared: Zbigniew Brzezinski to Jimmy Carter, February 24, 1978, WR 48, ZB Don, Box 41, JCL.

68. On being tough: See WR 54 (April 14, 1978); 24 (August 19, 1977); 33 (October 21, 1977); 53 (April 7, 1978); 38 (December 2, 1977); 37 (November 18, 1977); 55 (April 21, 1978); all ZB Don, Box 41, JCL.

69. A historical accomplishment: "Brzezinski: The Advocate," *WP*, June 6, 1978.

70. Normalization would be Carter's accomplishment: Zbigniew Brzezinski to Jimmy Carter, WR 66, July 7, 1978, ZB Don, Box 41, JCL.

71. Explaining policies to Carter: Zbigniew Brzezinski to Jimmy Carter, WR 83, December 28, 1978, Plains File, Box 29, JCL.

72. Congenial communication style: Brzezinski/aides interviews, 1982, CPP, 61, JCL.

73. Simplifying Soviet expansionist goals: Zbigniew Brzezinski to Jimmy Carter, "A Long-term Strategy for Coping with the Consequences of Soviet Action in Afghanistan," January 9, 1980, VF, USSR-US Conf. 5/6-9/94, F: USSR-1980–1993, JCL.

74. Quick mind: Richard Burt, "Zbigniew Brzezinski: A New Lone Ranger?" *Atlanta Constitution*, August 28, 1978.

75. On Brzezinski staff: Carter, *Keeping Faith*, 53.

76. On State Department restrains: Jimmy Carter, interview, 1982, CPP, 40–41, JCL.

77. Brzezinski's appeal: Gary Sick, quoted in Rose McDermott, *Risk-Taking in International Politics*, 60.

78. Gelb's explanation: James Blight to Jimmy Carter, April 17, 1995, VF, Box 117, USSR-US Conf. 3/95, BB1, JCL.

CHAPTER 4. EARLY FUMBLES

1. Vance's schedule in Moscow: March 27–29, 1977, Vance Mss, Box 12, F: 41, YUL. Background details: Murrey Marder, "Vance Arrives in Moscow to Push 'Deep Cuts' in Arms," *WP*, March 27, 1977, A1; "Vance in Moscow: A Frank Discussion" *Time*, April 4, 1977, 23; "The SALT Standoff," *Time*, April 11, 1977, 11.

2. U.S. proposals: Jimmy Carter, *Keeping Faith*, 219; Zbigniew Brzezinski, *Power and Principle*, 159–60, 163;Cyrus Vance, *Hard Choices*, 48–56. Brzezinski claimed there were three proposals, but Carter and Vance claimed only two.

3. Elimination of nuclear weapons: "Inaugural Address," January 20, 1977, *PP*, 1–4; Jimmy Carter, *Keeping Faith*, 215; Jimmy Carter, *Why Not the Best?*, 155–56.

4. On avoiding an arms race: Jimmy Carter to Leonid Brezhnev, January 26, 1977, Plains File, Box 17, F: Brezhnev-Carter Corr. 1977, JCL.

5. Brezhnev and Gromyko responses: Richard Steele et al., "Testing Carter," *Newsweek*, April 11 1977, 26–30.

6. Proposal rejected, meeting breaks up: "The SALT Standoff," *Time*, April 11, 1977, 11; Steele et al., "Testing Carter," 26–30.

7. Tass response: Warren Brown, "Top-Level Arms Talks Broached," *WP*, April 11, 1977; James T. Wooten, "Head of Pentagon Doubts Soviet Pact before Freeze Ends," *NYT*, April 2, 1977.

8. Cyrus Vance, "News Conference, Moscow," March 30, 1977, *DSB*, 400–404. See also "The SALT Standoff," 11.

9. Gromyko press conference: David K. Shipler, "Gromyko Charges U.S. Seeks Own Gain in Arms Proposals," *NYT*, April 1, 1977.

10. Gromyko on U.S. "fast as a snake": Paul Warnke, interview, 1989, in Alexander Moens, *Foreign Policy under Carter*, 75.

11. Pall over the White House: Steele et al., "Testing Carter," 26.

12. Setting for JC press conference: Steele et al., "Testing Carter," 26.

13. Press conference: Jimmy Carter, "SALT Negotiations with the Soviet Union," March 30, 1977, *PP*, 538–44. See also Carter, *Keeping Faith*, 219.

14. Brzezinski adding fuel to fire: "Presidential Assistant Brzezinski's News Conference," April 1, 1977, *DSB*, 414–21.

15. Warnke refusing press conference: Paul Warnke, interview, 1989, in Moens, *Foreign Policy under Carter*, 75. Earlier Warnke had told Dobrynin that he was opposed to the Carter deep cuts proposals and had put forward a step-by-step approach. Anatoly Dobrynin, *In Confidence*, 389.

16. Negative press: Steele et al., "Testing Carter," 26–30.

17. Critiques: Hedrick Smith, "In Washington, Challenge," *NYT*, April 1, 1977.

18. Kissinger response: Dobrynin, *In Confidence*, 397.

19. Dobrynin on SALT: Transcript of the proceedings of the conference "Global Competition and the Deterioration of U.S.-Soviet Relations, 1977–1980," March 23–26, 1995, Ft. Lauderdale, Florida, 174, VF USSR-US Conf., Box 117, JCL.

20. Memo of conversation, Jimmy Carter, Walter Mondale, Henry Kissinger, Lawrence Eagleburger, and David Aaron, November 20, 1976, Vance Mss, Box 8, F: 6, YUL. (See also appendix on weapons.)

21. Memo of conversation, Carter, Kissinger, et al.

22. Ibid.

23. Ibid.

24. Carter announcement: Glad, *Jimmy Carter*, 287.

25. Versus détente: "The Television and Radio Campaign Commercials of Carter in 1970 Campaign for Governor and 1976 Campaign for President," on deposit, University of Georgia. For a summary see Glad, *Jimmy Carter*, 393.

26. Debate with Ford: Jimmy Carter, quoted in Raymond Garthoff, *Detente and Confrontation*, 564. Originally in "Transcript of Foreign Affairs Debate between Ford and Carter," *NYT*, October 7, 1976.

27. Critique of Ford: Garthoff, *Détente and Confrontation*, 564. For similar comments, see "Head-to-Head on the Issues," *U.S. News and World Report*, September 13, 1976, 19; Robert Scheer, "The Playboy Interview," *Playboy*, November 1976, 74; Jonathan Moore and Janet Fraser, *Campaign for President*, 143–44.

28. Confidential back channel: Dobrynin, *In Confidence*, 380, 396.

29. Neglect of ambassadors: David Mayers, *The Ambassadors and America's Soviet Policy*, 225–32, 236–38.

30. Astonished Joint Chiefs: Brzezinski, *Power and Principle*, 157. See also Dobrynin, *In Confidence*, 385.

31. Jimmy Carter to Leonid Brezhnev, January 26, 1977, Plains File, Box 17, F: Brezhnev-Carter Corr. 1977, JCL. "The President's News Conference," February 8, 1977, *PP*, 92–100; Jimmy Carter, "The President's News Conference," March 9, 1977, *PP*, 340–48.

32. One step or two: "Excerpts from the White House Transcript of Carter's First Interview as President," *NYT*, January 25, 1977.

33. Brzezinski on SALT: Brzezinski, *Power and Principle*, 50, 146.

34. Soviet rejection as propaganda victory: Brzezinski, *Power and Principle*, 162. See also Brzezinski, interview, 1989, in Moens, *Foreign Policy under Carter*, 78.

35. On cuts: Harold Brown, "Position Paper on SALT," May 16, 1976, Vance Mss, Box 8, F: 8, YUL.

36. Recollections: Moens, *Foreign Policy under Carter*, 78. Brzezinski told Moens he made no attempt to influence the SALT considerations during this period of time.

37. Carter legitimating Brzezinski's position: SCC Meeting, February 3, 1977, ZB Don, Box 26, Meetings-SCC2: 2/3/77, JCL; Brzezinski, *Power and Principle*, 157.

38. Placing deep cuts on the table: Zbigniew Brzezinski to Jimmy Carter, Summary of Conclusions of SCC Meeting, February 3, 1977, VF, Box 116, F: USSR 1980–95, JCL.

39. On deferral option: Zbigniew Brzezinski to Jimmy Carter, February 3, 1977, VF, Box 116, F: USSR 1980–95, JCL. See also Brzezinski, *Power and Principle*, 157. Brzezinski was doubtful that the Soviets would find any deep cuts proposal to be acceptable.

40. For deep cuts: Minutes of SCC Meeting, February 25, 1977, VF, Box 116, F: USSR 1980–95, JCL. Compare Moens, *Foreign Policy under Carter*, 67. Options: Strobe Talbott, *Endgame*, 46–47; Robert G. Kaiser and Murrey Marder, "In Pursuit of a SALT II Agreement," *WP*, April 11, 1977. Secretary Brown noted that he favored strict limits on the Backfire bomber, though he saw this as a bargaining chip. The discussion of the ground-launched cruise missile raised the issue of U.S.-based versus theater(i.e., European)-based capability for a deep strike against the Soviet Union. Difficulties in resolving the distinctions between nuclear-tipped versus conventionally tipped cruise missiles, it was noted, would present clear verification problems.

41. On SCC meeting, March 10: Zbigniew Brzezinski to Jimmy Carter, March 11, 1977, ZB Don, Box 26, Meetings SCC 9 [Empty], JCL. In early meetings, the State Department and the ACDA favored an accommodation in which strict limits would be imposed on cruise missiles (on which the United States held the advantage at that moment); the Backfire bomber would remain outside the deal. The Defense Department and the Joint Chiefs came in with "diametrically opposing" perspectives. Brzezinski, *Power and Principle*, 158.

42. Carter principals meeting on March 12: Talbott, *Endgame*, 58–59.

43. Proposal as long shot: Cyrus Vance and Paul Warnke to Jimmy Carter, March 17, 1978, quoted in Vance, *Hard Choices*, 49; Brzezinski, *Power and Principle*, 159. Brzezinski claims the letter was sent on March 18.

44. Rationales: Vance, *Hard Choices*, 49–52. Vance had secured in return a third fallback proposal should the other two fail. However, in Moscow, the president, backed by Brzezinski and Mondale, rejected using that alternative. Brzezinski, *Power and Principle*, 162.

45. On deep cuts: Walter Slocombe, quoted in Alexander Moens, *Foreign Policy under Carter*, 71.

46. Proposal made public: Jimmy Carter, "United Nations," March 17, 1977, *PP*, 444–51. Other moves: Betty Glad, *Jimmy Carter*, 428.

47. Seeking Kissinger's advice: Jimmy Carter, *Keeping Faith*, 219.

48. Talbott not recalling the exchange: Strobe Talbott, *Endgame*, 65.

49. On further cuts: SCC Meeting, March 19, 1977, ZB Don, Box 26, Meetings SCC 9 [Empty], JCL. Brzezinski lists it as a "top-level meeting." See also Cyrus Vance, *Hard Choices*, 51–52; and Talbott, *Endgame*, 61. Brown's suggestion that the cruise missile range be changed

to 2,500 km was adopted at this meeting. A March 22 NSC meeting was held to get the Joint Chiefs on board. See Brzezinski, *Power and Principle*, 159–60.

50. Efforts capped: Presidential Directive/NSC-7, "SALT Negotiations," VF, JCL.

51. "A hungry trout's nose": Talbott, *Endgame*, 59.

52. Deep cuts not vetted: Talbott, *Endgame*, 59–65.

53. Kissinger: Dobrynin, *In Confidence*, 380–81.

54. State Department on Sakharov: Glad, *Jimmy Carter*, 427.

55. Warning the administration: Dobrynin, *In Confidence*, 385.

56. Vance's concern: Dobrynin, *In Confidence*, 380–81.

57. Toon distances: Mayers, *The Ambassadors and America's Soviet Policies*, 230.

58. Attempt to delegitimate: Dobrynin, *In Confidence*, 388.

59. Covert operations: Robert Gates, *From the Shadows*, 90–95.

60. The quote comes from Powell's recollection. Jody Powell, e-mail correspondence with the author, October 31, 2008. Prior to Harriman's visit, Powell talked with a tall, personable, English-speaking "journalist" who claimed to be doing a personality profile of Carter but who probably worked for the KGB. After checking with security, Powell talked with the man for some time. Near the end of their conversation, the journalist asked for some advice on how his government might deal with Carter. After thinking for a moment, Powell suggested that it might be a bad idea to test Carter, that they would not be happy with the response. It was after this exchange and Harriman's visit to Moscow that Harriman told Carter the Soviets would avoid testing him. From Glad-Powell conversation at "Jimmy Carter Conference: Lessons for the 21st Century, University of Georgia, 19 January 2006." See also Garthoff, *Détente and Confrontation*, 585; Dobrynin, *In Confidence*, 378–80.

61. Substantial Soviet reductions: Talbott, *Endgame*, 61.

62. Tula speech: Leonid Brezhnev, quoted in *Pravda*, in Garthoff, *Détente and Confrontation*, 585–86, 771; Dobrynin, *In Confidence*, 379–80.

63. Deliberations equitable: Leonid Brezhnev to Jimmy Carter, February 4, 1977, Plains File, Box 17, Brezhnev-Carter Corr. 1977, JCL.

64. Dobrynin, *In Confidence*, 381, 385, 390, 392.

65. Dobrynin recalls Grechko protest: in "Global Competition" conference transcript, 172, JCL.

66. Tough letter: Leonid Brezhnev to Jimmy Carter, February 25, 1977, Plains File, Box 17, Brezhnev-Carter Corr. 1977, JCL; Dobrynin, *In Confidence*, 390–92.

67. Brutal letter: Brzezinski, *Power and Principle*, 154–55.

68. Brezhnev response as foretaste: Zbigniew Brzezinski to Jimmy Carter, WR 3, March 5, 1977, ZB Don, Box 41, JCL.

69. Vance response: Dobrynin, *In Confidence*, 391.

70. Reply: Jimmy Carter to Brezhnev, March 4, 1977, Plains File, Box 17, Brezhnev-Carter Corr. 1977, JCL.

71. Initiative toward China: Brzezinski, *Power and Principle*, 155.

72. Politburo showing strength to Americans: in "Global Competition" conference transcript, 173, JCL.

73. Pressures on the Soviets: Brzezinski, *Power and Principle*, 162.

74. Success: Zbigniew Brzezinski to Jimmy Carter, WR 7, April 1, 1977, ZB Don, Box 41, JCL. These newspapers included the London *Times*, *Le Figaro* in Paris, *Die Welt* in Bonn, *Corriere della Sera* in Milan, and *La Nazione* in Florence.

75. Soviet concerns: Vance, *Hard Choices*, 54–55.

76. Paul Warnke, interview, September 8, 1989, in Moens, *Foreign Policy under Carter*, 74.

77. Harold Brown, interview, September 8, 1989, in Moens, *Foreign Policy under Carter*, 75.

78. Walter Slocombe, interview, September 11, 1989, in Moens, *Foreign Policy under Carter*, 77.

79. Jimmy Carter, interview, 1982, CPP, 58, JCL.

CHAPTER 5. RECOVERY

1. Seeking better relations with the Soviets: Anatoly Dobrynin, *In Confidence*, 395.

2. Shakhnazarov on goals: Transcript of the proceedings of the conference "Global Competition and the Deterioration of U.S.-Soviet Relations, 1977–1980," March 23–26, 1995, Ft. Lauderdale, Florida, VF, USSR-US Conf. 5/6–9/94(2). Box 117, 191, JCL.

3. Gribkov on parity: in "Global Competition" conference transcript, 213.

4. Turner on outrunning SALT: in "Global Competition" conference transcript, 223.

5. Odom on equality: in "Global Competition" conference transcript, 223.

6. Soviets hostile: Zbigniew Brzezinski, *Power and Principle*, 165.

7. Wanting agreement: Brzezinski, *Power and Principle*, 167.

8. Soliciting Jordan: Brzezinski, *Power and Principle*, 167. See also William Odom, in "Global Competition" conference transcript, 161.

9. On hot and cold: Odom, in "Global Competition" conference transcript, 161–62, JCL.

10. New three-tiered approach: Carter, *Keeping Faith*, 220.

11. Earlier Kissinger advice: Memo of conversation, Jimmy Carter, Walter Mondale, Henry Kissinger, Lawrence Eagleburger, and David Aaron, November 20, 1976, Vance Mss., Box 8, F: 6, YUL.

12. Seeking meeting: Jimmy Carter to Leonid Brezhnev, January 26, 1977, Plains File, Box 17, F: Brezhnev-Carter Corr. 1977, JCL.

13. Harriman's proposal: Brzezinski, *Power and Principle*, 175–76.

14. Signals for meeting: Dobrynin, *In Confidence*, 397–98.

15. Ungracious response: Leonid Brezhnev to Jimmy Carter, June 30, 1977, Plains File, Box 17, F: Brezhnev-Carter Corr. 1977, JCL.

16. Open to possible meetings: Leonid Brezhnev to Jimmy Carter, February 4, 1977, Plains File, Box 17, F: Brezhnev-Carter Corr. 1977, JCL.

17. Next move: Zbigniew Brzezinski to Jimmy Carter, June 7, 1977, VF, Box 116, F: USSR 1980–95, JCL. How PRM 10 was used to bring the president around: Brzezinski/aides interviews, 1982, CPP, 30–37, JCL. See also Garthoff, *Detente and Confrontation*, 787–88; Brzezinski, *Power and Principle*, 177–78. Meetings on PRM 10: "Summary of Conclusions of SCC Meeting," July 7, 1977, VF, Box 116, F: USSR 1980–95, JCL.

18. PD/NSC 18, "U.S. National Strategy," August 24, 1977, VF, JCL.

19. Activist policy: Brzezinski, *Power and Principle*, 177.

20. Thaw in relations: Garthoff, *Détente and Confrontation*, 615. Regarding NATO, the United States agreed to fulfill its commitment to its allies by raising defense levels by 3 percent per year. NATO would also continue to rely on a combination of strategic nuclear, theater nuclear, and conventional forces for deterrence. In a nod toward Vance and his State Department colleagues, initiatives were discouraged in areas under the USSR's control.

21. Gift to Gromyko: Carter, *Keeping Faith*, 222.

22. Response to gift: Andrei A. Gromyko, *Memoirs*, 289–90. Gromyko said that when Carter tried to pronounce Russian place names "all that came out was a sequence of incomprehensible noises," and that he "had difficulty in grasping even the most elementary basic features of the Soviet-U.S. relationship."

23. Souvenir in apartment: Dobrynin, *In Confidence*, 400.

24. On SALT framework: Carter, *Keeping Faith*, 221; Dobrynin, *In Confidence*, 399.

25. In the interim, Vance and Gromyko met several times. See Strobe Talbott, *Endgame*, 148, 151.

26. Soviet protests U.S. "hostility": Dobrynin Journal, VF, Box 16, USSR-US Conf 6/94, BB III, JCL. Gromyko warned Vance on May 31, 1978, that the "explosion of propaganda

hostile to the Soviet Union in the United States" could be an impediment to progress in the talks.

27. Harriman enters process: Ruby Abramson, *Spanning the Century*, 688–91.

28. On SALT committee: W. Averell Harriman and Jimmy Carter, conversation, March 8, 1978, VF, Box 117, USSR-US Conf. 5/94, BB II, JCL.

29. Jordan on meeting: Harriman and Carter conversation, March 8, 1978. Later that fall, Harriman was "horrified" when Brzezinski told him that he had asked the German ambassador to get a message to Alexandrox (unidentified) that Brzezinski would be willing to have a conversation with him. Shulman knew nothing about the contact, and Harriman vowed to tell Vance about it at their next meeting. W. Averell Harriman and Zbigniew Brzezinski, conversation, November 21, 1978, VF, Box 117, USSR-US Conf. 5/94, BB II, JCL.

30. Harriman's meetings were as follows: March 3, 1978, with Dobrynin; March 8 with Carter; March 14 with Dobrynin; August 17 with Vance; September 14 with Dobrynin; September 19, with Warnke; November 11 with Vance; November 21 with Brzezinski; March 26, 1979, with Dobrynin; April 12 with Dobrynin; June 6 with Carter. All in VF, Box 117, USSR-US Conf. 5/94, BB II, JCL.

31. Need for unanimity: SCC Meeting, September 1, 1978, ZB Don, Box 26, JCL. See also Brzezinski, *Power and Principle*, 326–27.

32. On the backfire bomber: NSC Meeting, September 2, 1978, ZB Don, Box 24, Meetings NSC Staff (1/78-6/80), JCL. See also Brzezinski, *Power and Principle*, 328–29.

33. Meeting with Gromyko: Jimmy Carter, *Keeping Faith*, 231–32.

34. On Moscow trip: penciled notes on Cyrus Vance to Jimmy Carter, October 19, 1978, Plains File, Box 39, State Dept. Evening Report, 10/78. Carter wrote, "Unless the main purpose of trip is to arrange a summit, I see no reason for you to go." See also Zbigniew Brzezinski to Jimmy Carter, WR 79, November 9, 1978, ZB Don, Box 42, JCL.

35. Remaining issues: Jimmy Carter, interview, 1982, CPP, 58, JCL. See also Carter, *Keeping Faith*, 232.

36. Carter confronts Vance on Backfire bombers: Brzezinski, *Power and Principle*, 328–29.

37. Downplay on progress: Brzezinski, *Power and Principle*, 326.

38. Ability to aggravate the Soviet dilemma: Zbigniew Brzezinski to Jimmy Carter, WR 18, June 24, 1977, ZB Don, Box 41, JCL.

39. On U.S. buckling: Zbigniew Brzezinski to Jimmy Carter, WR 20, July 8, 1977, ZB Don, Box 41, JCL.

40. On incentives: Zbigniew Brzezinski to Jimmy Carter, WR 33, October 21, 1977, ZB Don, Box 41, JCL.

41. Soviet motives: Zbigniew Brzezinski to Jimmy Carter, WR 53, 7 April 1978, ZB Don, Box 41, JCL.

42. Soviet Assertiveness: Zbigniew Brzezinski to Jimmy Carter, WR 57, May 5, 1978, ZB Don, Box 41, JCL.

43. "Sitting tight": Memo, Zbigniew Brzezinski to Jimmy Carter, WR 15, June 3, 1977, ZB Don, Box 41, JCL.

44. On negotiating process: Zbigniew Brzezinski to Jimmy Carter, WR 81, December 2, 1978, ZB Don, Box 42, JCL.

45. In October 1999, Patrick Tyler charged that Brzezinski had almost total control over the final negotiations with China, a charge that Carter and Brzezinski both denied. See Patrick Tyler, "The (Ab)normalization of U.S.-Chinese Relations," *Foreign Affairs* 78, no. 5: 93–122. Carter's reply: "Being There: Letters to the Editor," *Foreign Affairs* 78, no. 6: 164–65.

46. Soviets stiffening their positions: Cyrus Vance, *Hard Choices*, 112–13.

47. Encryption issue: Vance, *Hard Choices*, 111–12. Being prepared to sign: Anatoly Dobrynin, in "Global Competition" conference transcript, 147; Brzezinski, *Power and Principle*, 329–30.

48. Bottles of scotch: Marshall Shulman, in "Global Competition" conference transcript, 149.

49. White House on encryption issue: Vance, *Hard Choices*, 111–12; Strobe Talbott, *Endgame*, 240–42; Brzezinski, *Power and Principle*, 329–30. Dobrynin (in "Global Competition" conference transcript, 147) argued that with a deal between the leaders at the top, the remaining technical problems could have easily been worked out.

50. Arms to China: Carter, *Keeping Faith*, 234.

51. Too many deadlines: Zbigniew Brzezinski to Jimmy Carter, WR 83, December 28, 1978, Plains File, Box 29, F: 6-12/78, JCL.

52. Explaining Carter's distinctive policy: Brzezinski to Carter, WR 83, December 28, 1978, Plains File, Box 29, F: 6-12/78, JCL.

53. Soviet nightmares: Talbott, *Endgame*, 252.

54. Despair at the State Department: Talbott, *Endgame*, 252.

55. Switch in roles suggested: Zbigniew Brzezinski to Jimmy Carter, WR 89, February 24, 1979, ZB Don, Box 42, JCL.

56. Carter wanting SALT: February 7, 1979 meeting with Dobrynin; Dobrynin, *In Confidence*, 417–20.

57. United States creating problems: Leonid Brezhnev to Jimmy Carter, n.d. [after April 19, 1979], Plains File, Box 17, F: Brezhnev-Carter Corr. 1979, JCL.

58. Responses: Jimmy Carter to Leonid Brezhnev, March 7; March 27; April 11; and April 20, 1979, Plains File, Box 17, F: Brezhnev-Carter Corr. 1979, JCL.

59. Vance-Dobrynin meetings: Raymond Garthoff, *Détente and Confrontation*, 821.

60. Encryption deal: Carter, *Keeping Faith*, 251, 259.

61. Other issues resolved: Vance, *Hard Choices*, 133–35.

62. War exercises: Leonid Brezhnev to Jimmy Carter, April 13, 1979, ZB Don, Box 18, F: USSR-Carter-Brezhnev Corr. 1/79–6/79, JCL.

63. White House leaks: Dobrynin, *In Confidence*, 409.

64. Impact of CIA: Robert M. Gates, *From the Shadows*, 115–16.

65. On Soviet double dealing: Zbigniew Brzezinski to Jimmy Carter, WR 96, May 12, 1979, Plains File, Box 29, JCL.

66. Choice of summit: Dobrynin, *In Confidence*, 420.

67. The agenda: Marshall Shulman and Robert L. Barry, memo on Vienna Summit Preparations, June 5, 1979, VF, USSR-US Conf 6/94, BB III, JCL. For the Soviet role, see Dobrynin, *In Confidence*, 421–22.

68. Annoyance at agenda: Carter, *Keeping Faith*, 240.

69. Size of team: Jimmy Carter to Zbigniew Brzezinski, June 13, 1979, ZB Don, Box 19, USSR-Vienna Summit 10/78–6/79.

70. On Soviet leadership: W. Averell Harriman and Jimmy Carter, conversation, June 6, 1979, VF, Box 117, USSR-US Conf. 5/94, BBII, JCL. Harriman memo: Zbigniew Brzezinski to Jimmy Carter, June 12, 1979, Plains File, Box 5, USSR, 9/77-12/80, JCL. Carter also had in hand a background paper on Brezhnev and the Politburo, with a copy of Harriman's conversation with Brezhnev in 1976 attached.

71. Addendum to Harriman-Carter conversation, June 6, 1979, VF, Box 117, USSR-US Conf. 5/94, BB II, JCL.

72. Advice: Vance to Jimmy Carter, June 8, 1979, VF, Box 117, USSR-US Conference, BBII, JCL.

73. Deal on Backfire bombers: Carter, *Keeping Faith*, 250–52.

74. Ideological sparring: Carter, *Keeping Faith*, 254–57.

75. Dinner table rivalry: Ibid., 257.

76. Signing ceremony: Gromyko, *Memoirs*, 290–91.

77. Meeting again: "Fifth and Last Plenary Meeting between President Carter and President Brezhnev," VF, Box 116, F: USSR Rel. Docs (II), JCL. Carter, in an aside, noted one advantage of such meeting was that they could "correct the mistakes that would inevitably be made by their Foreign Ministers." Gromyko objected "vigorously."

78. Jimmy Carter to Leonid Brezhnev, June 18, 1979, Plains File, Box 17, F: Brezhnev-Carter Corr. 1979, JCL.

79. In an attached document, the Soviets stated that the Backfire bomber was a medium-range bomber, that it would not be given a long-range capability, and that annual production would not exceed thirty such missiles.

80. Compromise on weapon types, development of MX missile: Moens, *Foreign Policy under Carter*, 82.

81. Reliance on offensive strategies: Odom, in "Global Competition" conference transcript, 223.

82. Politburo approval: Dobrynin, *In Confidence*, 428.

83. Being warned of the domestic hurdles: Memo of conversation, Jimmy Carter, Walter Mondale, Henry Kissinger, Lawrence Eagleburger, and David Aaron, November 20, 1976, Vance Mss., Box 8, F: 6, YUL.

CHAPTER 6. HUMAN RIGHTS AND THE SOVIET TARGET

1. First meeting: Anatoly Dobrynin, *In Confidence*, 384–86. Carter had sent a telegram of support to Soviet dissident Vladimir Slepak even before taking office, and secretary of state designate Cyrus Vance had met with exiled Soviet dissident Andrei Amalrik. On February 7, 1977, the State Department expressed concern over the arrest of Soviet dissident Aleksandr Ginzburg for currency violations. Raymond Garthoff, *Detente and Confrontation*, 568–69.

2. Sakharov posed for photographers with Carter's letter in front of the U.S. embassy; Robert A. Strong, *Working in the World*, 71, 80–81.

3. Carter and Bukovsky: Garthoff, *Détente and Confrontation*, 569.

4. Legal commitments: "Helsinki Accords," retrieved February 2, 2008, from http://www.historycentral.com/Today/HelsinkiAccords.html. In exchange for the recognition of the legitimacy of the Baltic governments in Eastern Europe, the Soviets agreed to "respect fully human rights and fundamental freedom, including the freedom of thought, conscience, religion, or belief...and to promote and encourage the effective exercise of civil, political, economic, and social, cultural, and other rights...which derive from the inherent dignity of the human person." Gideon Gottlieb argues that these provisions, though not really legally binding, "engage States politically and morally, in the sense that they are not free to act as if they did not exist." See Gottlieb, "Relationism: Legal Theory for a Relational Society," *University of Chicago Law Review* (1983): 567, 582. For the proposition that the Helsinki Final Act created new legal obligations, see Anthony D'Amato and Leo Gross, "Human Rights, European Politics, and the Helsinki Accord: The Documentary Evolution of the Conference on Security and Co-operation in Europe 1973–1975," *American Journal of International Law* (1984): 960. In 1975, Carter had critiqued the Helsinki agreements on the grounds that they facilitated the "Russian takeover of Eastern Europe."

5. Dissidents and the Charter 77 movement: Human Rights Watch, "Who We Are" (2006), retrieved February 8, 2008, from http://www.hrw.org/about/whoweare.html; "All Nobel Prize Laureates," retrieved February 8, 2008, from http://nobelprize.org/search/all_laureates_y.html. On Amnesty International, see: Amnesty International, "Who We Are," retrieved February 8, 2008, from http://www.amnesty.org/en/who-we-are.

6. "Grown like topsy": Robert G. Kaiser, "Rights Improvisation Strains Détente," *WP*, February 27, 1977.

7. Absence of country studies: Jane Pisano to David Aaron re Interagency Group on Human Rights, Brzezinski Material Subject File, Box 10-32, Human Rights, 5/77–11/78, JCL.

8. Jimmy Carter, "Commencement Address, University of Notre Dame," May 22, 1977, *PP*, 959, 962.

9. Responses: "Plain Talk about America's Global Role," *Time*, June 6, 1977.

10. Carter as missionary: Hugh Sidey, "Hazardous Course for Carter," *Time*, June 27, 1977. Sidey noted that, weeks after the speech, Carter called ten Southern Baptist leaders together to plan a global strategy.

11. As one administration official admitted earlier in the year, the United States had actually supported some of the world's worst regimes, such as those of Spain's Francisco Franco, Portugal's Antonio de Oliveira Salazar, and Greece under the junta: "Human Rights: Other Violators," *Time*, March 7, 1977.

12. PD/NSC 30: "Human Rights," February 17, 1978, VF, JCL.

13. Compromises in plan: "Human Rights," February 17, 1978.

14. Brzezinski, Talbott, and Tuchman on policy: "A Crusade That Isn't Going to Die: Controversial Campaign for Human Rights Is Gaining Ground," *Time*, February 27, 1978.

15. Institutional framework: Victor S. Kaufman, "The Bureau of Human Rights during the Carter Administration," *Historian* 61, no. 1 (1998): 51–67; Zbigniew Brzezinski, *Power and Principle*, 75.

16. Country studies: Joshua Muravchik, *The Uncertain Crusade*, 230–33. The State Department's human rights reports from 1999 to the present are available from its website: http://www.state.gov/g/drl/rls/hrrpt/.

17. Strong, *Working in the World*, 82; "Human Rights Treaties," February 23, 1978, *PP*, 395–96. The Senate consented to none of these treaties on Carter's watch. In the following years, only three of them (the International Covenant on Civil and Political Rights, the Convention on Elimination of all Forms of Racial Discrimination, and the International Genocide Convention) gained Senate approval.

18. Purists versus pragmatists: Hauke Hartmann, "U.S. Human Rights Policy under Carter and Reagan, 1977–1981," *Human Rights Quarterly* 23, no. 2 (2001): 402–30.

19. Odom on human rights as propaganda: Brzezinski/aides interviews, 1982, CPP, 49, JCL

20. On Vance's Georgia Law speech: Hauke Hartmann, "U.S. Human Rights Policy," 406, 411.

21. On human rights as party unifier: John Dumbrell, *The Carter Presidency*, 117–18.

22. Staying politically neutral: Betty Glad, *Jimmy Carter*, 81. Forty miles south of Plains, Georgia, the Albany Movement took hold in 1961 when two Student Nonviolent Coordinating Committee members made a Freedom Ride from Atlanta. Martin Luther King Jr. and others were sent to the Americus, Georgia, jail for parading without a permit.

23. Carter as school board chairman: Glad, *Jimmy Carter*, 78.

24. On Maddox: Glad, *Jimmy Carter*, 106. Those who took up the civil rights struggle too early could never have run successfully for political office. Even the modest efforts of Carter's personal friend and lawyer Warren Fortson made him so controversial that he had to leave town for some time, losing all contact with Carter for several years.

25. Campaign for governorship: Glad, *Jimmy Carter*, 133–40.

26. Calley issue: Glad, *Jimmy Carter*, 205.

27. *Time* cover: Glad, *Jimmy Carter*, 204–5.

28. Carter and Gromyko on Shcharansky: Andrei A. Gromyko, *Memoirs*, 292–93; FBIS (Foreign Broadcast Information Service), *USSR National Affairs*, July 10, 1978; "U.S. Government Denounces Moscow Sentence as 'Gross Distortion,'" *NYT*, May 19, 1978, A3.

29. Carter on Gromyko: Carter, *Keeping Faith*, 221. See also Brzezinski, *Power and Principle*, 169–70.

30. Dobrynin on Gromyko: Dobrynin, *In Confidence*, 399–400.

31. Carter to Gromyko on repercussions of trials: "Memorandum of Conversation," May 27, 1978, USSR-US Conf. 5/94, BBIII, VF, Box 116, JCL. Gromyko saw these matters as internal affairs of the Soviet Union.

32. Toon, and cancellation of press visit: Dobrynin, *In Confidence*, 413.

33. Shcharansky sentencing: Foreign Broadcast Information Service (FBIS), *USSR National Affairs*, July 14, 1978; David K. Shipler, "Ginzburg Given 8-Year Sentence by Soviet Court," *NYT*, July 14, 1978, A1, A8; David K. Shipler, "Scharansky Given 13 Years in Prison and Labor Camps," *NYT*, July 15, 1978.

34. Tuchman warns Brzezinski: Brzezinski Material Subject File, Box 10-32, Human Rights, 5/77–11/78.

35. New licensing requirements: Richard Burt, "Carter, Reacting to Trials in Soviet Union, Will Control Oil-Technology Sales," *NYT*, July 19, 1978; Garthoff, *Détente and Confrontation*, 611.

36. Approval of oil drilling equipment: Garthoff, *Détente and Confrontation*, 615; Dobrynin, *In Confidence*, 418.

37. Carter and Brezhnev: Jimmy Carter, *Keeping Faith*, 260. See also David S. McLellan, *Cyrus Vance*, 124; Garthoff, *Détente and Confrontation*, 732–40; Brzezinski, *Power and Principle*, 340–44.

38. MFN, breakfast meeting: Brzezinski, *Power and Principle*, 418. Jewish emigration: Garthoff, *Détente and Confrontation*, 615.

39. Bolshoi dancers: Eric Pace, "Gudonov, Bolshoi Dancer, Defects to U.S.," *NYT*, August 24, 1979; Eric Pace, "Bolshoi Couple Say They Defected for Personal and Artistic Freedom," *NYT*, September 19, 1979; Kevin Klose, "Bolshoi Ballerina Hailed in Moscow, Denounces U.S.," *WP*, August 28, 1979, A1. See also Garthoff, *Détente and Confrontation*, 744; John M. Goshko, "US Still Holding Ballerina's Plane as Soviets Protest Angrily," *WP*, August 26, 1979, A1.

40. Dissidents: Vance, *Hard Choices*, 102–3.

41. Brezhnev objects: Garthoff, *Détente and Confrontation*, 572–73.

42. Pseudo-humanitarian slogans: Brzezinski, *Power and Principle*, 155.

43. Hartman response: Dobrynin, *In Confidence*, 389–90.

44. Carter on mistaken beliefs: "The President's News Conference," July 12, 1977, *PP*, 1235.

45. Impervious to warnings: "The President's News Conference," June 30, 1977, *PP*, 1197–1206.

46. Impact on dissidents: Garthoff, *Détente and Confrontation*, 571.

47. Correspondents excluded from trial: Politburo CC/CPSU, June 22, 1978, VF, Box 117, USSR-US Conf. 6/94, BB III, 14, JCL.

48. Andropov on sentence: Politburo CC/CPSU, June 22, 1978. On trial: Garthoff, *Détente and Confrontation*, 571–72.

49. Toth's expulsion: Garthoff, *Détente and Confrontation*, 571.

50. Journalists convicted of libel: "SALT II and the Growth of Mistrust: A Chronology of Events; Prepared by the National Security Archive," USSR-US Conf. 5/94, BBI, I-33, VF, Box 117, JCL.

51. Soviet response: Resolution of the CC/CPSU, January 5, 1979, from Andrey Kozyrev to comrade A. A. Gromyko, re: the UN Commission on Human Rights, VF, USSR-US Conf. 6/94, BB III, JCL. On January 12, 1979 the Thirty-Fifth session of the UN Commission on Human Rights opened in Geneva.

CHAPTER 7. COMPETITION IN THE HORN OF AFRICA

1. On compatibility of advisors: Jimmy Carter, "Fort Worth, Texas," 23 June 1978, *PP*, 1159–60; Edward Walsh, "President Tough on Soviets," *WP*, June 24, 1978, A1, 4. See also "Soft Words—and a Big Stick," *Time*, July 3, 1978, 12–14.

2. Singling out Brzezinski: Jimmy Carter, "The President's News Conference," June 26, 1978, *PP*, 1180–85, passim.

3. Query of House members: "Carter Stresses Unified Foreign Policy," *FF*, June 30, 1978, 490. See also Dobrynin, *In Confidence*, 410–11.

4. On Soviets in the Horn: Anatoly Dobrynin, *In Confidence*, 402. See also Ambrose and Brinkley, *Rise to Globalism*, 277. On Soviet aid to Ethiopia: JC to Valery Giscard d'Estaing, January 27, 1978, ZB Don, Box 28, Meetings SCC 56 2/10/78, JCL. On American aid to

Somalia: "Moscow: Carter Distorts Facts on Somali-Ethiopian Conflict," January 13, 1978, ZB Don, Box 18, JC-Brezhnev Corr. 1/78-12/78, JCL.

5. On low-key approach: Zbigniew Brzezinski to Jimmy Carter, "PRC Meeting on Ethiopia and Horn of Africa," April 11, 1977, VF, Box 117, USSR-US Conf., BBI, JCL.

6. Later that summer: Zbigniew Brzezinski to Jimmy Carter, "PRC Review of Horn," August 26, 1977, VF, Box 117, USSR-US Conf., BBI, JCL.

7. Young at UN: Zbigniew Brzezinski, *Power and Principle*, 179–80.

8. Media on military threat: Hedrick Smith, "US Says Castro Has Transferred 60's Policy of Intervention to Africa," *NYT*, November 17, 1977, A1, A11.

9. Protest to Dobrynin: Brzezinski, *Power and Principle*, 179–80.

10. On oil cut off: Dobrynin, *In Confidence*, 406–7. Dobrynin asked Brzezinski how he thought the Soviet Union could actually cut the oil routes. "Would it attack and sink American tankers? That would constitute a direct act of war. Did the White House really have such absurd ideas?" Brzezinski conceded that the "White House did not give much credence to such a scenario, but such oversimplified concepts were widespread in the Congress and the American media.

11. Carter not to be trifled with: Cyrus Vance, quoted in Dobrynin, *In Confidence*, 406.

12. Views on the Horn conflict: Vance, *Hard Choices*, 84–85.

13. Views on the conflict: Brzezinski, *Power and Principle*, 181–86, passim.

14. On sending a message: Ibid., 182.

15. SCC Meeting on Feb. 10: Ibid., 180–83.

16. On task force: Cyrus Vance, *Hard Choices*, 87.

17. Debate on task force: SCC Meeting, February 22, 1978, ZB Don, Box 28, SCC meeting 59, JCL.

18. SCC Meeting, February 22, 1978, ZB Don, Box 28, SCC meeting 59, JCL.

19. Ibid.

20. On meeting: Brzezinski, *Power and Principle*, 183–84.

21. Approval less likely: Ibid., 184–85.

22. On negotiating provisions: SCC Meeting, March 1, 1978, ZB Don, Box 28, Meetings-SCC 61: 3/2/78, JCL.

23. At National Press Club: JC, "The President's News Conference," March 2, 1978, *PP*, 440–42.

24. Heated exchange: SCC Meeting, March 2, 1978, Box 28, ZB Don, Meetings SCC 61, F: 3-61 to 3-2-78, JCL. In this memo Brzezinski suggests a "discussion of steps…to [show] our displeasure.…The Secretary of State was strongly opposed to any linkage with SALT." Details on heated exchange from Brzezinski, *Power and Principle*, 85–86. Carter wrote to French President Giscard about his worries that Soviet and Cuban involvement in the Horn would complicate détente as well as the SALT ratification process. JC to Giscard, January 27, 1978, ZB Don, Box 28, Meetings SCC 56, 2/10/78, JCL.

25. Other Issues: SCC Meeting, March 2, 1978, ZB Don, Box 28, Meetings SCC 61, JCL.

26. A note of realism: Ibid. For U.S. support of Barre: Vance, *Hard Choices*, 86–88.

27. Horn and Chinese: SCC Meeting, March 2, 1978, ZB Don, Box 28, Meetings SCC 61, JCL.

28. Shoring up Carter: Zbigniew Brzezinski to Jimmy Carter, March 3, 1978: quoted in Brzezinski, *Power and Principle*, 186.

29. On Soviet access to Horn: Zbigniew Brzezinski to Jimmy Carter, WR #53, April 7, 1978, ZB Don, Box 41, JCL.

30. Carter's address at Wake Forest: JC, "Winston-Salem, North Carolina," March 17, 1978, *PP*, 529–38. Quote on 532.

31. On innate racism: JC, "Spokane, Washington," May 5, 1978, *PP*, 875.

32. On Cuban involvement: Jimmy Carter, "Remarks of the President at the Opening Ceremonies of the North Atlantic Treaty," May 10, 1978, Organization Summit, White House Central Collection, Box CO-59, Countries CO 165 [7/1/78-7/31/78], JCL.

33. Behavior in Horn: Jimmy Carter, "The President's News Conference," May 25, 1978, *PP*, 972, 974–79. At one point in 1978 Carter asked Paul Austin, of Coca-Cola to meet Castro and inform him that their activities in Africa were impeding the normalization of relations between Havana and Washington. Castro retorted that not a single Cuban soldier would cross the Somalia border. But he affirmed his policies of supporting "revolutions and national liberation movements everywhere." See Dobrynin, *In Confidence*, 407, 411.

34. Soviets behind world conflicts: Jimmy Carter, *Keeping Faith*, 256.

35. On surrogates: Jimmy Carter, "The President's News Conference," 25 May 1978, *PP*, 978.

36. Ratchets up rhetoric: Brzezinski, "Interview on 'Meet the Press,'" May 28, 1978, *DSB* 78: 2016 (July 1978) 27. That same day newspapers reported that NSC Soviet specialist Sam Huntington had briefed the Chinese in Beijing on two U.S. top-secret memos, PRM 10 and PSD 18, delineating U.S. policies toward the Soviet Union and others.

37. *Pravda* on Brzezinski: "East-West Relations: China Briefed on US Global Views," *FF*, June 2, 1978, 399; Craig R. Whitney, "Pravda Denounces Brzezinski on Zaire," *NYT*, May 31, 1978, A13.

38. Verbal exchanges reported: From *Facts on File Yearbook*, 1979.

39. Dispel misperceptions: Vance to Jimmy Carter, May 1978, quoted in Vance, *Hard Choices*, 101–2.

40. Urges consistency: Vance, *Hard Choices*, 101–2.

41. On setting of address: Edward Walsh and Don Oberdorfer, "Carter Challenges Soviet Leaders" *WP*, June 8, 1978, A1, A20. Murray Marder, "President Challenges Soviet Leaders," *WP*, June 8, 1978, A1, 20.

42. Jimmy Carter commencement address: "United States Naval Academy," June 7, 1978, *PP*, 1052–57.

43. Ibid. For Brzezinski's concept of détente: Brzezinski, *Power and Principle*, 147–50.

44. On speech: Greg Schneider to Gerald Rafshoon, June 5, 1978, Rafshoon Files, Box 8, Annapolis Speech, 6/7/78/[2], JCL.

45. Two different speeches: Marder, "President Challenges Soviet Leaders," A1, 20.

46. Church, *Tass* responses to speech: "Talking Tough to Moscow," *Time*, June 19, 1978, 32–33.

47. Dobrynin's response to speech: Dobrynin, *In Confidence*, 411.

48. Vance on speech: Ibid., 411–12. Ironically, the day after Carter's Annapolis speech the Russian novelist Solzhenitsyn excoriated the West for its superficiality and moral mediocrity in his commencement address at Harvard. "Solzhenitsyn: Decline of the West," *Time*, June 19, 1978, 33.

49. Speech a pastiche: Vance, *Hard Choices*, 102.

50. On contributions to speech: Brzezinski, *Power and Principle*, 320–21.

51. As early as April 4, 1977, Carter had written Sadat that the threats to the Egyptians included Soviet involvement in Africa. At Camp David on September 12, 1978, he told Sadat that a success at Camp David would free Egypt to face its own adversaries, including Soviet Union's possible encroachments in South Yemen, Afghanistan, Ethiopia, Libya, Iraq, Syria, and Sudan. Carter to Sadat, September 12, 1978, quoted in Carter, *Keeping Faith*, 282; Camp David proceedings, Carter, *Keeping Faith*, 384.

52. Minimizes disagreements: Zbigniew Brzezinski to Jimmy Carter, "The Soviet Union and Ethiopia: Implications for US-Soviet Relations," March 3, 1978, ZB Don, Box 28, F: Meeting SCC 61, JCL. See also Bz to JC, "SCC Meeting on the Horn of Africa," March 3, 1978, ZB Don, Box 28, F: Meetings SCC 6, JCL.

53. On March 2 meeting: "The Soviet Union and Ethiopia," March 3, 1978, ZB Don, Box 28, F: Meeting SCC 61, JCL.

54. More complex papers: Zbigniew Brzezinski to Jimmy Carter, "PRC Meeting on Ethiopia and Horn of Africa," April 11, 1977, VF, Box 117, USSR-US Conf., BBI, JCL.

55. "INR," March 15, 1978, VF, Box 117, F: US/USSR Conf. 3/95, BBI, JCL.

56. Background on Eritrea: Department of State, "SCC Meeting, Horn of Africa," March 23, 1978, VF, Box 117, USSR-US Conf., BBI, JCL.

57. On pumping up the issue: Bz to JC, "SCC Meeting on the Horn of Africa, March 2, 1978, Summary of Conclusions," March 3, 1978, ZB Don, Box 28, Meetings SCC 61, JCL. Paul Henze, NSC expert on Soviet operations in the Middle East, critiqued on several occasions the U.S. tilt toward the Somalis and the rush into a complex area that could not be easily managed. See Henze to Brzezinski, March 9, 1978, March 10, 1978, March 16, 1978, March 27, 1978, April 7, 1978, June 2, 1978. All in ZB Don, Meetings SCC: Box 28, 3/10/78–5/5/78, JCL.

58. On costs of hyping up the conflict: Vance, *Hard Choices*, 88.

59. Better to have stood tough: Brzezinski, *Power and Principle*, 186.

60. On cycles and move toward China: Brzezinski, *Power and Principle*, 189.

61. Soviet motives: Dobrynin, *In Confidence*, 404–5. The Soviet press agency Tass claimed the US was ignoring the aggression against Ethiopia and was sending arms to Somalia, even though Carter denied these accusations. "Carter Distorts Facts on Somali-Ethiopian Conflict," January 13, 1978, ZB Don, Box 18, Jimmy Carter-Brezhnev Corr. 1/78–12/78, JCL.

62. On diverse Soviet motives: Dobrynin, *In Confidence*, 404–5.

63. Gebru Tareke, "The Ethiopia-Somalia War of 1977 Revisited," in Board of Trustees, Boston University, The International Journal of African Historical Studies. Boston University African Studies Center, 2000, 630–42.

64. More on Ogaden conflict: Peter Woodward, *The Horn of Africa*, 55–61.

65. The strategic issue, according to Gelb, was control over Berbera, which earlier had provided for the "Soviets' strategic entrée into that part of the world." Gelb, in transcript of the proceedings of the conference "Global Competition and the Deterioration of U.S.-Soviet Relations, 1977–1980," March 23–26, 1995, Ft. Lauderdale, Florida, 75, VF, USSR-U.S. Conf., Box 117, JCL.

66. On Bush and Clinton: Stephen Zunes, "The Long and Hidden History of the U.S. in Somalia," *Znet*, January 21, 2002, http://www.zmag.org/content/ForeignPolicy/zunes0117.cfm (February 22, 2008).

67. Brutents: in "Global Competition" conference transcript, 24.

68. Comparison to chess: Dobrynin, *In Confidence*, 376.

CHAPTER 8. NEGOTIATIONS WITH PANAMA

1. Torrijos' remarks: "Carter, Torrijos Sign Canal Pacts in the Presence of Latin Leaders," *NYT*, September 8, 1977, A1, A11.

2. Coverage of event: Hamilton Jordan to Jimmy Carter, August 24, 1977, Box 36, Jordan Collection, Panama Canal Treaty 8/77 [1], JCL.

3. Guest list: "State Dinner Honoring Panama Canal Signing Ceremony Participants," Plains File, Box 7, F: 9/5/1977–9/18/1977, JCL. The Queen's Bedroom in the White House had been reserved that night for Lady Bird Johnson and the Lincoln Bedroom for former president Gerald Ford; "Torrijos, Here for Treaty Signing, Praises U.S. for Ending 'Injustice,'" *NYT*, September 6, 1977. Dinner description: Linowitz, *The Making of a Public Man*, 189.

4. Top of list: PRM/NSC 1, "Panama," Presidential Proclamations, January 21, 1977, VF, Box 1, JCL; PRM/NSC 17, "Review of U.S. Policy toward Latin America," Presidential Proclamations, January 26, 1977, VF, Box 1, JCL. PRM 17 set up an exploration of possible U.S. foreign policy goals for Latin America more generally. At Sea Island these items were placed at the top of the presidential agenda; see Zbigniew Brzezinski, *Power and Principle*,

134–35. The Linowitz Commission's influence appears to have extended to the vast majority of the administration's subsequent policies toward Latin America. Of the Commission's twenty-eight recommendations, twenty-seven became administration policy. Robert A. Pastor, *Whirlpool*, 45.

5. Transcript of meeting with Henry Kissinger: Memo of conversation, Jimmy Carter, Walter Mondale, Henry Kissinger, Lawrence Eagleburger, and David Aaron, November 20, 1976, Vance Mss, Box 8, F: 6, YUL.

6. Yielding to nationalist pressures: Cyrus Vance, *Hard Choices*, 157.

7. Using the honeymoon: Brzezinski/aides interviews, 1982, CPP, 9, JCL.

8. Hamilton Jordan, interview, 1981, CPP, 54, JCL.

9. Appointments: Jimmy Carter, *Keeping Faith: Memoirs of a President*, 156; Linowitz, *The Making of a Public Man*, 151–53. Joe Holley, "Sol Linowitz Dies; Carter-Era Envoy Helped Found Xerox," *WP*, March 19, 2005; Howard B. Shaffer, "Ellsworth Bunker: Global Troubleshooter, Vietnam Hawk," *Foreign Service Journal*, November 2003.

10. A 1968 law permitted special ambassadorial assignments under presidential appointment without Senate confirmation for up to 180 days; Linowitz, *The Making of a Public Man*, 151.

11. Given a wide berth: Linowitz, *The Making of a Public Man*, 152; Vance, *Hard Choices*, 143–44. Their aides Morey Bell, Tom Dolvin, and Dick Wyrough worked together with harmony and effectiveness; William J. Jorden, *Panama Odyssey*, 357.

12. Torrijos' goals: Sol M. Linowitz, *The Making of a Public Man*, 155.

13. Opening at Contadora: Ibid., 155–58.

14. Move to Washington: Ibid., 158–63; William J. Jorden, *Panama Odyssey*, 358.

15. Secret meetings: Jorden, *Panama Odyssey*, 357–58.

16. Lewis/Jorden meetings: Ibid., 386–87.

17. Proposal for two treaties: Jimmy Carter, *Keeping Faith*, 157.

18. A brilliant stroke: Cyrus Vance, *Hard Choices*, 146.

19. Early proposals: Jorden, *Panama Odyssey*, 371–77.

20. Breaks impasse: Ibid., 373, 378–79.

21. Serious offers: Ibid., 380–81.

22. Note for Torrijos: Ibid., 382–84.

23. Terms of neutrality agreement: Carter, *Keeping Faith*, 157.

24. Panamanian payment claims: Linowitz, *The Making of a Public Man*, 164–65; Carter, *Keeping Faith*, 158.

25. A ridiculous request: Carter, *Keeping Faith*, 158.

26. Last offer: Carter, *Keeping Faith*, 158; Jorden, *Panama Odyssey*, 425. Jorden notes that Carter's letter had a "considerable impact" on Torrijos, who "believed the president when he said that any larger payments would pose a serious political danger to the fate of the treaty." Advice on letter: Zbigniew Brzezinski to Jimmy Carter, June 7, 1977, Jordan Collection, Box 36, F: Panama Canal Treaty 6/-/77, JCL.

27. Wrap-up meeting: Linowitz, *The Making of a Public Man*, 169–71.

28. "As a present to Sol": Linowitz, *The Making of a Public Man*, 173.

29. Panama's lifeblood at stake: Ibid., 173.

30. Panama Canal Agreements in Principle, enclosed in Richard Hutcheson to Stuart Eizenstat et al., August 11, 1977, Eizenstat Collection, Box 252, Panama Canal (O/A 6242), JCL.

31. Carter congratulating Linowitz and Bunker: Linowitz, *The Making of a Public Man*, 175–76.

32. On reading line by line: "Selling the Treaty," *Atlanta Journal*, August 12, 1977; Compare the statement that Carter relied on the diplomats, in Linowitz, *The Making of a Public Man*, 176.

33. Briefing by Bunker and Linowitz in White House: Transcript released by Office of White House Press Secretary, August 12, 1977, Eizenstat Collection, Box 252, Panama Canal

(O/A 6242), JCL. Carter's introduction of the ambassadors: President's Statement, August 12, 1977, Lipshutz Collection, Box 41, Panama Canal Zone, 3/77–4/78 (CF, O/A 121), JCL.

34. Carter's commitment: Linowitz, *The Making of a Public Man*, 163–64.

35. Carter's foibles: Ibid.

36. Carter in Yazoo City: Ibid., 168.

37. Recommending sea-level canal: Ibid.

38. National interest and history of sea level canal: Ibid.

39. On feasibility studies: Stuart Eizenstat to Jimmy Carter, October 11, 1977, Eizenstat Collection, Box 252, Panama Canal O/A 6242, JCL; Eleanor Randolph, "Talk of Another Canal," *Chicago Tribune*, August 14, 1977.

40. U.S. veto over construction: Linowitz, *The Making of a Public Man*, 168.

CHAPTER 9. DEALING WITH CONGRESS

1. Burned in effigy: Sol M. Linowitz, *The Making of a Public Man*, 178.

2. Torrijos bio: "Omar Torrijos," *The Columbia Encyclopedia*, 6th ed. (New York: Columbia University Press, 2007).

3. VFW: "Carter Not Invited," *NYT*, August 25, 1977, 29.

4. Reagan quoted: "Ford Gives Support to New Agreement on Panama Canal," *NYT*, August 17, 1977.

5. Goldwater: Linowitz, *The Making of a Public Man*, 189–90; William J. Jorden, *Panama Odyssey*, 532.

6. Bauman: "Ford Gives Support."

7. Hate mail to Wayne: Jorden, *Panama Odyssey*, 502.

8. Ford's approval: "Ford Gives Support."

9. Kissinger: Marjorie Hunter, "White House Is Lobbying Unusually Hard on Canal Pacts," *NYT*, September 1, 1977.

10. Buckley: Linowitz, *The Making of a Public Man*, 185–88.

11. Paul H. Nitze to Jimmy Carter, August 25, 1977, and Jimmy Carter to Paul H. Nitze, August 29, 1977, Jordan Collection, Box 36, Panama Canal Treaties, JCL.

12. Wayne's views: Linowitz, *The Making of a Public Man*, 185–88.

13. Joint Chiefs endorsement: James T. Wooten, "Joint Chiefs Pledge to Help Carter in Bid for Approval of Canal Treaty," *NYT*, August 12, 1977. Note that it was inappropriate to send Joint Chiefs on speaking mission: Landon Butler to Laurie Lucey, August 24, 1977, Butler Collection, Box 121, Panama Canal support 7/12/77–12/22/77, JCL.

14. Lemnitzer and Taylor: Jorden, *Panama Odyssey*, 187–88.

15. Sol M. Linowitz to Landon Butler, July 7, 1977, Butler Collection, Box 118, Panama Canal, JCL. See also Jorden, *Panama Odyssey*, 442.

16. For Citizens Committee Members: Sol M. Linowitz to Landon Butler, July 7, 1977, Butler Collection, Box 118, Panama Canal, JCL. Key names to be funneled via Mondale: Angier Biddle Duke to Walter Mondale, October 25, 1977, Box 19, Panama Canal Correspondences O/A 5153, JCL.

17. For overall outreach plan: Hamilton Jordan to Jimmy Carter, August 30, 1977, Jordan Collection, Box 36, Panama Canal Treaty, 9/77, JCL; "Status Report on Panama Canal Treaty," Hamilton Jordan to Jimmy Carter, n.d., Jordan Collection, Box 36, Panama Canal Treaty 8/77 [1]; "Panama Canal Treaty Support," Steve Selig and Richie Reiman to Landon Butler and Joe Aragon, September 30, 1977, Schlesinger Collection, Panama Canal 8/77–11/7 [O/A 5003], JCL; Hamilton Jordan to Zbigniew Brzezinski, October 18, 1977, Jordan Collection, Box 56, Panama Canal Treaties [CF, O/A 413] [2], JCL. Interest group outreach: Joe Aragon to Hamilton Jordan, August 23, 1977, Jordan Collection, Box 36, Panama Canal Treaties 8/77 [2], JCL. Corporate endorsements: Landon Butler to Jimmy Carter, August 26, 1977, Jordan Collection, Box 36, Panama Canal Treaties 8/77 [2], JCL. Women leaders: "Interest Group Briefing on

Panama Canal Treaties," Margaret Costanza, November 8, 1977, Staff Offices Schlesinger, Box 23, Panama Canal 8/77–11/77 [O/A 5003], JCL.

18. Briefing sessions: See Jorden, *Panama Odyssey*, 517.

19. State campaigns: Rosalynn Carter, *First Lady from Plains*, 216. See also Linowitz, *The Making of a Public Man*, 188, 192.

20. Carter on state campaigns, congressmen to Panama: Jimmy Carter, interview by Vision Associates, November 1, 1984, 34, JCL.

21. Speaking campaign: "Administration Panama Travel," Aragon Collection, Box 19, Panama Admin. Travel, 12/77–1/78, O/A 6247, JCL. His effectiveness: Vance, *Hard Choices*, 144–45.

22. Panamanian leaders and ratification efforts: Jorden, *Panama Odyssey*, 365, 521–23.

23. Vance and Brzezinski preoccupied: Robert Beckel, interview, 1981, CPP, 6, JCL.

24. Brown and Brown: Jorden, *Panama Odyssey*, 472–73.

25. Linowitz assists negotiations: Ibid., 477–79.

26. Arranging visits of congressmen: Ibid., 491, 496–500.

27. Rogers: Ibid., 491, 577–79.

28. Work of Christopher, "Gang of Four": Vance, *Hard Choices*, 155–56; Jorden, *Panama Odyssey*, 504, 517, 525–26; Hamilton Jordan, interview, 1981, CPP, 52, JCL.

29. Announcement checklist and public relations scenario: Hamilton Jordan to Jimmy Carter, August 9, 1977, Butler Collection, Box 118, Panama Canal, O/A 740, JCL. Advice on speech: Hamilton Jordan to Jimmy Carter, January 1978, Jordan Collection, Box 50, Panama Canal Treaty O/A 413, JCL.

30. Congressional liaison: Bob Thomson and Bob Beckel via Frank Moore to Hamilton Jordan, October 24, 1977, Jordan Collection, Box 50, Panama Canal Treaty O/A 413, JCL. See also Jimmy Carter, interview, 1982, CPP, 50–51, JCL. Lists, counts of senators and their leanings: Bob Thomson and Bob Beckel to Frank Moore, October 24, 1977, Jordan Collection, Box 50, Panama Canal Treaties, 1977 [CF, O/A 413] [2], JCL. Frank Moore to Jimmy Carter and Senior Staff, December 12, 1977, Lipshutz Collection, Box 40, Panama 9/77–1/78 [CF O/A 714], JCL. Frank Moore, Bob Beckel, and Bob Thomson to Jimmy Carter, February 6, 1978, Box 81, Panama Canal—Status Briefing 4/19/78, JCL. Senators opposing treaty: Clifford L. Alexander Jr. to Landon Butler, April 18, 1977, Butler Collection, Box 118, Panama Canal (binder) [CF, O/A 740], JCL.

31. Mondale's assignments: Laurie Lucey to Landon Butler, July 13, 1977, Butler Collection, Box 119, Panama Canal Background Information 7/13/77–11/23/77 [CF, O/A 86], JCL. Mondale strategy: Hamilton Jordan to Jimmy Carter, August 1977, Jordan Collection, Box 36, Panama Canal Treaties 8/77[2], JCL. Overall plans: Robert G. Beckel to Robert Thompson, August 11, 1977, Jordan Collection, Box 36, Panama Canal Treaties 8/77[2], JCL; Steve Selig and Richie Reiman to Landon Butler, August 26, 1977, Butler Collection, Box 119. Calling corporate influentials: Steve Selig and Richie Reiman to Landon Butler, August 26, 1977, Butler Collection, Box 119, Panama Canal Background 7/15/77–11/27/77, JCL.

32. Ford telephone calls: Handwritten note, Jimmy Carter to Hamilton Jordan, February 2, 1978, Jordan Collection, Box 50, Panama Canal Calls (CF, O/A 413), JCL.

33. Brown and Brown: Jorden, *Panama Odyssey*, 472–73.

34. Vance at SFRC: Cyrus Vance, *Hard Choices*, 147; Linowitz, *The Making of a Public Man*, 191–92.

35. Others stressing the importance of the treaties: Linowitz, *The Making of a Public Man*, 195.

36. Carter and Torrijos resolving differences: Jimmy Carter, *Keeping Faith*, 162–63.

37. Expedited passage: Vance, *Hard Choices*, 149–50.

38. Arranging visits of congressmen: Jorden, *Panama Odyssey*, 491, 496–500.

39. Dealing with alleged violations: Steve Selig and Richie Reiman to Landon Butler and Joe Aragon, "Panama Canal Treaty Support," September 30, 1977, Schlesinger Collection, Panama Canal 8/77–11/7 [O/A 5003), JCL.

40. Human rights: Zbigniew Brzezinski to Jimmy Carter, November 14, 1977, Jordan Collection, Box 36, Panama Canal Treaty 10, 11, 12/77, JCL.

41. Jordan as special emissary to Torrijos: Hamilton Jordan, interview, 1981, CPP, 52, JCL. See also Hamilton Jordan, *Crisis*, 75. Buddy relationship: Brzezinski/aides interviews, 1982, CPP, 89, JCL.

42. Byrd and Baker rewrite: Jorden, *Panama Odyssey*, 500, 504–9.

43. Armed Services Forum: Carter, *Keeping Faith*, 163.

44. Scathing critiques: Jorden, *Panama Odyssey*, 521, 511–14, 527–28; Carter, *Keeping Faith*, 167–68.

45. Others pilloried: Linowitz, *The Making of a Public Man*, 197–98.

46. McIntyre on opponents: Jorden, *Panama Odyssey*, 527–28. An irritated Torrijos held his tongue. Ambassador Jorden had warned Torrijos that treaty opponents would engage in such tactics. Tactics and warning Torrijos: Jorden, *Panama Odyssey*, 522–23.

47. DeConcini amendment: Jorden, *Panama Odyssey*, 520.

48. DeConcini demands revisions: Jorden, *Panama Odyssey*, 533.

49. Christopher and administration concede: Jorden, *Panama Odyssey*, 535–51. Content of amendment: Linowitz, *The Making of a Public Man*, 199.

50. Torrijos induced to remain silent: Zbigniew Brzezinski, *Power and Principle*, 138.

51. Warnings: Jorden, *Panama Odyssey*, 536–37, 548–51. At the White House, Christopher and Jordan would later claim that they had never received this warning.

52. Torrijos pens letters: Jorden, *Panama Odyssey*, 568–69.

53. Negative press reaction: Ibid., 573–74.

54. DeConcini determines fate: Handwritten note, Hamilton Jordan to Zbigniew Brzezinski (on Rick Inderfurth to Hamilton Jordan), April 10, 1978, Jordan Collection, Box 50, Panama Canal Treaties 1977 (CR, O/A 413) (4), JCL.

55. Meeting canceled: Jorden, *Panama Odyssey*, 587–89.

56. DeConcini goes public: DeConcini, quoted in Jorden, *Panama Odyssey*, 587–88.

57. Backlash against DeConcini: Jorden, *Panama Odyssey*, 590.

58. On DeConcini: Frank Moore, Robert Beckel, and Bob Thomson to Jimmy Carter, March 20, 1978, Jordan Collection, Box 50, Panama Canal Treaties 1977 (CF, O/A 413), JCL.

59. Carter considers TV appearance: Jorden, *Panama Odyssey*, 591.

60. Moore et al: Attachment on note, Rick Hutcheson to Frank Moore, April 18, 1978, Box 81, BB Panama Canal 4/18/78, JCL.

61. Leadership reservations: Jorden, *Panama Odyssey*, 592–94.

62. Senate leaders, Panamanians compromise: Ibid., 603–9.

63. DeConcini confronted: Ibid., 613–14; Linowitz, *The Making of a Public Man*, 203.

64. Hour before vote: Robert G. Kaiser, with Richard L. Lyons and Edwards Walsh, "Senate Approves Final Canal Treaty," *WP*, April 19, 1978.

65. Uncertainty for final vote: Jorden, *Panama Odyssey*, 619–20; Linowitz, *The Making of a Public Man*, 203.

66. Thanks to Byrd: Jorden, *Panama Odyssey*, 620.

67. Announcing Torrijos's acceptance: Kaiser, "Senate Approves."

68. Ceremony in Panama: Jorden, *Panama Odyssey*, 638–40, 645.

69. Photographs of dignitaries, others: Martin Tolchin, "Carter and Torrijos Conclude Treaties on Canal's Transfer: President Hailed in Panama," *NYT*, June 17, 1978.

70. Leading backers absent, sidelined: Jorden, *Panama Odyssey*, 645.

71. Carter speaking in Spanish: Tolchin, "Carter and Torrijos Conclude."

72. Sour note: Jorden, *Panama Odyssey*, 622–23. Controversies continue: Carter, *Keeping Faith*, 180.

73. On horrible experience: Jimmy Carter, interview, 1982, CPP, 51, JCL.

74. Attempted House revisions: Jorden, *Panama Odyssey*, 663–67. See also Carter, *Keeping Faith*, 180–81.

75. On Bauman's tactics: Jorden, *Panama Odyssey*, 678–80.

76. On rising to challenge: Carter, *Keeping Faith*, 183.

77. A great democracy: Ibid., 184.

78. Averting problems in Caribbean: Vance, *Hard Choices*, 156. Linowitz gave a more guarded evaluation of their joint project: "[T]he world saw us ultimately do the right thing against very heavy odds," but because the president did not pursue Latin American affairs, "the opportunity to create a new era of inter-American relations was lost." Linowitz, *The Making of a Public Man*, 204–5.

79. Crisis avoided: Brzezinski, exit interview, 1981, 10, JCL. See also Brzezinski, *Power and Principle*, 145, 521, 527.

80. Payoff in the long run: Jordan, *Crisis*, 84.

81. Albright on treaties: Brzezinski/aides interviews, 1982, CPP, 23–24, JCL.

82. Difficulties encountered: Carter, *Keeping Faith*, 184.

83. High price paid: Zbigniew Brzezinski, exit interview, 1981, 9, JCL.

84. Public opinion: Jill A. Schuker to Joseph Aragon, "Working Paper on Panama/Public and Press Outreach Strategy," June 17, 1977, Jordan Collection, Box 36, Panama Canal Treaty 6–7/77, JCL. Reaction on incoming calls to White House comments offices: Hugh Carter to Jimmy Carter, November 23, 1977, Jordan Collection, Box 36, Panama Canal Treaty, 10, 11, 12/77[3], JCL. The callers were increasingly in favor of the treaty in late October and early November 1977.

85. Bauman's influence: Jorden, *Panama Odyssey*, 677.

86. Failure to acknowledge others: Jorden, *Panama Odyssey*, 645.

87. Relying too much on staff, Murphy: Jorden, *Panama Odyssey*, 659.

88. No political momentum: Jordan interview, 1981, CPP, 7, JCL. Jordan was "at the cross-roads of both the politics of the ratification fight and also the substance of the issue." At one point, Carter wrote Vance, Brzezinski, Jordan, and Moore that they "should consult and agree on clear answers to questions about canal maintenance and operations costs." Jimmy Carter to Vance, Brown, Brzezinski, Jordan, Moore, February 7, 1978, Jordan Collection, Box 36, Panama Canal Treaty 1978, JCL.

89. Looking weak: William Safire, *Safire's Washington*, 368.

CHAPTER 10. SALT AND THE SENATE

1. "Vienna Summit Meeting," June 18, 1979, *PP*, 1087–92.

2. Looking tired: "Nation: Signed and Sealed…," *Time*, July 2, 1979, 28–32.

3. Outlook: Bernard Gwertzman, "President, Warning of Arms Race, Sets Theme for Debate on the Pact," *NYT*, June 19, 1979; "Down from the Summit Clouds," *NYT*, June 19, 1979; Joseph Charles Mohr, "Arms Pact Faces Senate Challenge in the Fall and an Uncertain Fate," *NYT*, June 19, 1979.

4. *Gallup*, 1979, 195, 198. Anti-Soviet feeling: Joseph S. Nye Jr., "Can America Manage Its Soviet Policy?" in Joseph S. Nye, ed., *The Making of America's Soviet Policy*, 329; Dan Caldwell, *The Dynamics of Domestic Politics and Arms Control*, 91.

5. Both decisions were based on prudential considerations. The B-1 bomber, as Byrd wrote Carter, was very expensive and there were other, cheaper alternatives. Compared to ICBMs, he continued, the bomber had less flexibility, less evasive maneuverability, and a much higher fuel-consumption rate. Cruise missiles, too, could be placed on bombers that would not have to penetrate Soviet borders. Instead they could launch missiles from outside the USSR. Robert Byrd to Jimmy Carter, June 23, 1977, Plains File, Box 17, F: B-1 Bomber 6–7/77, JCL. As for the neutron bomb, there were other weapons systems—the Pershing II and cruise missiles—that could be used to better the NATO and Warsaw Pact balances in Europe. However, at the SCC meeting of November 16, 1977 (ZB Don, Box 27, F: SCC, JCL), there was a consensus that the United States should produce the enhanced radiation warhead. But concerns that the United States could not use it as a bargaining chip and a lack of a firm commitment from Chancellor Schmidt

for their deployment in Germany caused Carter on April 1, 1978, to defer production of the weapons. In August, Schmidt told Carter that neither he nor his successor would deploy ERW in Germany unless one other European nation went along (which was quite unlikely). Jimmy Carter to Zbigniew Brzezinski, August 2, 1978, ZB Don, Box 22, F: Defense ERW 3/78–8/78, JCL. See also Zbigniew Brzezinski to Jimmy Carter, Plains File, Box 21, F: NSC WR 6–12/78, JCL. Carter's mistake was that his decision making was too public, making him look erratic.

6. Church on anti-Soviet rhetoric: Anatoly Dobrynin, *In Confidence*, 412.

7. Anatoly Dobrynin to Andrei Gromyko, July 11, 1978, "Soviet-American Relations in the Contemporary Era," VF, Box 117, USSR-US Conf, BBII, JCL.

8. Henry M. Jackson to Carter, "Memorandum for the President on SALT," February 15, 1977, VF, Box 117, USSR-US Conf 5/94, BB II, JCL. Jackson also tried to insert himself in the negotiation process. Henry M. Jackson to Jimmy Carter, April 22, 1977, and August 22, 1977; and Henry M. Jackson to Zbigniew Brzezinski, April 27, 1977. Brzezinski did transmit material to Jackson in October 1977, suggesting to Carter that they would "provide him with ammunition." But Carter wrote Jackson on October 10, 1977, that it was "not appropriate for me to give to you my negotiating instructions to our U.S. delegation, although you have been informed about our basic position which has not changed." All in ZB Don, Box 40 F: SALT, 20 October 1977, JCL.

9. Not meeting with Jackson: Zbigniew Brzezinski to Jimmy Carter, WR 36, November 11, 1977, ZB Don, Box 41, JCL.

10. Proposals for advisory committee: Landon Butler to Hamilton Jordan, Hamilton April 25, 1977, Jordan Collection, Box 53, SALT Notebook [CF, O/A 648], JCL. Suggested members: Frank Press to Landon Butler, May 25, 1977, Jordan Collection, Box 53, SALT Notebook [CF, O/A 648], JCL.

11. Need to follow through: Paul Warnke to Landon Butler, December 20, 1977, Jordan Collection, JCL.

12. State Department working group: Matt Nimetz to Landon Butler on the Administration Plan for SALT II Ratification, December 14, 1978. Activities of the State Department: Butler Collection, Box 130, SALT II 1/2/79–1/19/79, JCL.

13. Communications plan: Gerald Rafshoon to Jimmy Carter, December 6, 1978, Staff Offices Collection, Box 2, SALT Notebook [CF, O/A 648], JCL.

14. Anticipating problems in the Senate: Frank Moore and Robert Beckel to the SALT Working Group on Congressional Planning, October 12, 1978, Jordan Collection, Box 54, SALT II (CF, O/A 414), JCL. Jackson, they argued, was too far out on a limb to come around, but there was hope they could win over Sam Nunn. The Senate Intelligence Committee, they noted, would play a key role in the verification aspect of SALT: "[Senator Birch] Bayh, as chairman and a SALT supporter will be helpful." Byrd was particularly helpful, playing a key role in the resolution of the Soviet brigade in the Cuba episode.

15. Work of White House staff: Frank Moore to Jimmy Carter, May 8, 1979, Plains File, Box 35, SALT II Senate Update, 5/8/79, JCL.

16. SALT outreach: Anne Wexler to Landon Butler, October 12, 1979, Jordan Collection, Box 54, F: SALT, 1979 [CF, O/A 647], JCL.

17. Appointment of Cutler: Dan Caldwell, *Dynamics*, 71–72.

18. Need to woo hawks: Landon Butler to Hamilton Jordan, May 8, 1978, Gerald Rafshoon Files, Box 6, SALT [3], JCL.

19. Endeavoring to win support of senators: Frank Moore and Robert Beckel to the SALT Working Group on Congressional Planning, October 12, 1978, Jordan Collection, Box 54, SALT II (CF, O/A 414), JCL.

20. Military buildup: George McGovern, Mark Hatfeld, and William Proxmire to Jimmy Carter, March 2, 1979, reprinted in the *CR*, March 5, 1979, S 204.

21. Nuclear stability with USSR: Alan Raymond to Gerald Rafshoon, Landon Butler, and Robert Beckel, August 20, 1979, and Schneider to Gerald Rafshoon, June 5, 1978, both in Rafshoon Collection, Box 8, JCL.

22. Mondale's speech on February 22: "Arms Control: Preserving Freedom and Peace in a Nuclear Age," *DSB* 79, no. 2025 (April 1979): 14.

23. U.S. power: Jimmy Carter, "Foreign Policy Conference for Editors and Broadcasters," February 22, 1979, *PP,* 311.

24. Jimmy Carter, "US Airpower Compared to Soviets at Annual Convention of American Newspaper Publishers Association: New York City, New York," April 25, 1979, *PP,* 693–69. Later, Carter concluded a press conference in Bardstown, Kentucky, with a vow "to make sure our Nation is always as strong as or stronger than the Soviet Union no matter what happens." "Bardstown, Kentucky," July 31, 1979, *PP,* 1351.

25. No end to East–West competition: Zbigniew Brzezinski to Chicago Committee of the Council on Foreign Relations, "Arms Control: SALT II and the National Defense," *DSB* 79, no. 2026 (May 1979): 48–51.

26. Brown, "Arms Control: SALT II and the National Defense," *DSB* 79, no. 2026 (May 1979): 51–54. On September 7, 1979, Carter announced a $33 billion dollar plan to base the new MX missiles in a "track" system in the Western U.S. desert and to increase defense spending by a real growth rate of 3 percent per year. Senator Byrd would later claim that the commitment to the MX program was a requisite for his approval of the treaty. See "Defense: Carter Seeks 3% Budget Hike," *FF,* September 14, 1979, 678. To strengthen its hand in dealing with the Senate, the administration also won the support of the foreign and defense ministers of its NATO allies. See "Atlantic Alliance: NATO Foreign Ministers Back SALT," *FF,* June 8, 1979, 415. While Senator Nunn never declared himself as for or against SALT, he did vote against the release of an Armed Service Committee's negative report.

27. Pro-SALT senators and military buildup: *CR,* 96th Congress, Part 3, March 5, 1979, 3835–39.

28. Hatfield's concerns about MX: "Defense: Carter Approves MX Missile," *FF,* June 15, 1979, 438.

29. Twelve senators write Carter: "Disarmament: Carter Opposes Arms Tie to SALT," *FF,* August 10, 1979, 591.

30. The administration responds: Caldwell, *Dynamics,* 134–35.

31. Cranston and nineteen other pro-SALT senators met regularly with administration officials to anticipate the arguments that would be made against the treaty and plan their response; Caldwell, *Dynamics,* 150. Their Senate staff members came to formalize a common rhetoric. Rather than emphasize the importance of détente with Russia, they would argue that the treaty would enable the United States to assess the Soviet threat and actually increase the national security of the United States. Lloyd Cutler to Jimmy Carter, October 12, 1979, Chief of Staff Jordan, Box 53, File: SALT, 1979 [CF, O/A, 647], JCL.

32. Baker and Nunn on SALT: Landon Butler, Frank Moore, and Zbigniew Brzezinski to Jimmy Carter, January 23, 1979, White House Central File, Foreign Affairs, Box 6, F: FO-6-1, 11/21/78–2/10/79, JCL.

33. Ratification requiring budget increases: "Disarmament: Carter Opposes Arms Tie to SALT," *FF,* August 10, 1979, 590–91.

34. Jackson charges of appeasement: Strobe Talbott, *Endgame,* 5. In May and June, the White House Office of Congressional Relations sent each senator lengthy briefing books on SALT II. High-level White House officials contacted everyone interested. Caldwell, *Dynamics,* 67.

35. Frank Church, quoted in *Senate Foreign Relations Committee Hearings The SALT II Treaty, October and November 1979,* part 1, 84. Hereafter cited as *SFRC Hearings, SALT II,* with part number added.

36. *SFRC Hearings, SALT II,* part 6, "Markup," 2.

37. Endorsement of treaty: Cyrus Vance, in *SFRC Hearings, SALT II,* part 1, 88–96, 123; "Arms Control: Secretary Vance's Testimony on SALT II," *DSB* 79, no. 2029 (August 1979): 30–37.

38. Brown and Jones remarks: *SFRC Hearings, SALT II,* part 1, 111–19, 396; "Disarmament: U.S. Senate Begins SALT Debate" and "Disarmament: Joint Chiefs Support Treaty," *FF,* July 13,

1979, 510. Under its terms the United States could move forward with the rapid development of an alternative basing mode for ICBMs, procure a high-quality strategic bomber and cruise missile tanker system with a high prelaunch survivability, reexamine U.S. civil defense programs, and reinvigorate ABM research and development programs.

39. Nitze testimony against SALT: *SFRC Hearings, SALT II*, part 1, 433–51.

40. Rowney on minimal standards: *SFRC Hearings, SALT II*, part 1, 536–98. Bargaining table: *SFRC Hearings, SALT II*, part 1, 553. Lugar confrontation: *SFRC Hearings, SALT II*, part 1, 554.

41. Church on extensive hearings: *SFRC Hearings, SALT II*, part 6, 1.

42. Final committee vote on treaty: *SFRC Hearings, SALT II*, part 6, 543–44. The SFRC's path had been facilitated by a unanimous vote of the Senate Intelligence Committee on October 5, which concluded that the treaty would actually enhance the ability of the United States to "monitor those components of Soviet strategic weapons forces which are subject to the limitations of the Treaty." *SFRC Hearings, SALT II*, part 6, 532–52.

43. Explanations of Democratic supporter votes: *SFRC Hearings, SALT II*, part 6: Church 541–43; Muskie, 532–34; Pell, 539–40; Zorinsky: 534–36; McGovern 514–15; Sarbanes 528–30.

44. Javits and Percy explanations: *SFRC Hearings, SALT II*, part 6, 515–20, 537–39.

45. Glenn on vote: *SFRC Hearings, SALT II*, part 6, 520–23. But he indicated that he might be persuaded to change his mind for the final vote in the Senate should he be satisfied on the verification issue. *FF*, November 16, 1979, 864.

46. Other opponents: *SFRC Hearings, SALT II*, part 6: Stone, 526; Baker, 523–25; Lugar, 530–32; Helms, 526–28; Hayakawa, 525–26.

47. Gromyko warnings: "Disarmament: Gromyko Warns U.S. on SALT II," *FF*, July 6, 1979, 496.

48. Proposals: *SFRC Hearings, SALT II*, part 6, 551–68.

49. Rowney as staff member: *SFRC Hearings, SALT II*, part 6, 344–49, 434. Rowney's support for crippling amendments: *SFRC Hearings, SALT II*, part 6, 468–71.

50. Definition of categories: *SFRC Hearings, SALT II*, part 6, 2–3, 575–78.

51. Glenn killer amendment: *SFRC Hearings, SALT II*, part 6, 420–29.

52. Church finesse: *SFRC Hearings, SALT II*, part 6, 399–413.

53. Two conditions: *SFRC Hearings, SALT II*, part 6, 548–49.

54. Sam Nunn et al. to Jimmy Carter, December 17, 1979, Butler Collection, Box 128, SALT 12/6/79–4/14/80, JCL.

55. Armed Service vote, jurisdictional issues: "Disarmament: Senate Committee Opposes SALT II," *FF*, December 31, 1979, 979.

56. Richard Perle, quoted in Caldwell, *Dynamics*, 145.

57. Administration sees setback: Anne Wexler, quoted in Caldwell, *Dynamics*, 145.

58. Moore and Beckel: Caldwell, *Dynamics*, 60–62.

59. Not making a difference: Alan Raymond to Gerald Rafshoon, Landon Butler, and Robert Beckel, August 20, 1979, Box 8, JCL.

60. Exhausted political capital: George Moffett III, *The Limits of Victory*, 207, cited in Caldwell, *Dynamics*, 58.

61. Declining support for SALT: Roper Survey, figure 4.3 in Caldwell, *Dynamics*, 86; NBC and Harris Polls, figure 4.2 in Caldwell, *Dynamics*, 84.

CHAPTER 11. THE TILT TOWARD CHINA

1. Informing Dobrynin: Brzezinski, *Power and Principle*, 232. Brzezinski had assured Dobrynin in their meeting that the new relationship with the PRC was not directed against anyone. But as Brzezinski later noted, that statement was "formally, a correct observation; but substantively, a touch of irony."

2. Dobrynin meeting reporters: "Carter Stuns the World," *Time*, December 25, 1978, 18.

3. Carter's announcements: "Diplomatic Relations between the United States and the People's Republic of China," December 15, 1978, *PP*, 2264–66. See also Joint Statement, December 15, 1978, ZB Don, Box 9, JCL. Press commentary: David Broder and Bill Peterson, "U.S. to Normalize Ties with Peking," *WP*, December 16, 1978; Edward Walsh, "U.S. to Normalize Ties with Peking, End Its Defense Treaty with Taiwan; Credibility of U.S. Hurt, Critics Say," *WP*, December 16, 1978; Russell Watson et al., "China Breakthrough," *Newsweek*, December 25, 1978, 14.

4. "Carter Stuns the World," *Time*, December 25, 1978, 18.

5. Responses to normalization agreement: Jay Mathews, "Sudden Shift Stuns Taiwan; Leaders Embittered," *WP*, December 16, 1978; Don Oberdorfer, "Balancing Relations with Two Rival Giants of Communism," *WP*, December 16, 1978; John M. Goshko, "Taiwan Spurns Peking Unification Hints," *WP*, December 21, 1978; Andrew Nagorski, "Anger on Taiwan," *Newsweek*, December 25, 1978, 16.

6. Opposition to normalization: Angus Deming et al., "A Chinese New Year," *Newsweek*, January 15, 1979, 24.

7. Vance's concern: Cyrus Vance, *Hard Choices*, 109–10, 118. See also Brzezinski, *Power and Principle*, 230–31.

8. Vance putting on the best face: "Carter Stuns the World," *Time*, December 25, 1978, 19.

9. Brzezinski on China: Strobe Talbott, "What Brzezinski Sees," *Time*, December 25, 1978, 19.

10. "Deng Xiaoping," *China Daily*, June 25, 2004, retrieved February 11, 2008, from http://www.chinadaily.com.cn/english/doc/2004-06/25/content_342508.htm. Fox Butterfield, "China's Road to Progress Is Mostly Uphill," *NYT*, February 4, 1977.

11. On Vietnamese normalization: Brzezinski, *Power and Principle*, 228.

12. Vietnam invading Cambodia: Fox Butterfield, "Sihanouk in Peking on Way to the UN," *NYT*, January 7, 1979; David Shipler, "Soviets Terse in Invasion Report, Implying No Decision on Action," *NYT*, February 18, 1979; Christopher Jones, "In the Land of the Khmer Rouge," *NYT*, December 20, 1981.

13. On normalization: Zbigniew Brzezinski to Jimmy Carter, February 7, 1977, ZB Don, Box 8, China (PRC) 3–6/77, JCL.

14. Soviet activities in the Horn: Brzezinski, *Power and Principle*, 404.

15. Seen as pro-Soviet, anti-Chinese: Brzezinski, *Power and Principle*, 228.

16. Proxies for USSR: Bernard Gwertzman, "Indochina Conflict Seen as 'Proxy War,'" *NYT*, January 9, 1978.

17. Maintaining equilibrium: Cyrus Vance, *Hard Choices*, 76.

18. Cyrus Vance, quoted in Brzezinski, *Power and Principle*, 423. By January 1, 1979, when the normalization of the relationship between the United States and the PRC actually took place, it was clear that Carter and Brzezinski had finally determined to go beyond full diplomatic recognition. China would not only be recognized as one entity but all military and official diplomatic personnel would be removed from Taiwan within four months. Nor did the Chinese give any assurance that any attempts to change the political status quo would be made only via peaceful means. Final Joint Communiqué between United States and China, January 1, 1979, Plains File, Box 18, Cabinet Minutes 9/78–12/79, JCL. See also James Mann, *About Face*, 91. Brzezinski, in short, "pulled off" the China normalization policies of the president, as he would later say. Brzezinski/aides interviews, 1982, CPP, 73, JCL.

The goal of the earlier Nixon endeavors had been to use China as a means for inducing the Soviet Union to cooperate with the United States. But Brzezinski was committed to policies that would bait the Soviet bear rather than tempt it. In the process, he would employ the strategies typified in management literature as those of the motivated tactician. Advisors who are motivated tacticians may push their own agendas on a CEO. They control access to the decision-making group; use salami-slicing tactics (securing incremental commitments from the CEO); set the agenda (choosing the order in which options are introduced); change the decisional rules; frame decisions (i.e., placing a situation or event in a context so that others will see or interpret it in a certain way); and engage in leaking stories to influence public responses. At the interpersonal level, the motivated tactician can directly bolster or legitimate the desired option, secure extra support of the CEO via coalition building, make personal appeals, or warn of negative consequences. See Jean A. Garrison, *Games Advisers Play*, 27–28.

19. Advice on meetings with Hua: Zbigniew Brzezinski to Jimmy Carter, February 7, 1977, ZB Don, Box 8, China (PRC) 3–6/1977, JCL.

20. PRM/NSC 24, "Peoples Republic of China," April 5, 1977, ZB Don, Box 8, China (PRC) 7–9/77, JCL.

21. Jimmy Carter, speech at University of Notre Dame, May 22, 1977, *PP*, 961. See also Brzezinski, *Power and Principle*, 199.

22. Deferred normalization: Jimmy Carter, *Keeping Faith*, 192.

23. Pleased but worried: Brzezinski, *Power and Principle*, 201.

24. Directive to Vance, August 18, 1977, ZB Don, Box 36, F 8/77–8/78, JCL. See also Carter, *Keeping Faith*, 191.

25. Reception: Vance, *Hard Choices*, 79–81. For Hang Hua's toasts of August 22 and August 25 and schedules, see Vance Mss, Box 9/14, YUL.

26. Issues discussed: Dennis Chapman to Rick Inderfuth re Secretary Vance PRC trip, "Memorandum for Rick Inderfurth," August 29, 1977, Staff: Jordan, Box 34, JCL. Formally correct: Vance, *Hard Choices*, 81–83. See also Richard Holbrooke and Michel Oksenberg to Leonard Woodcock, October 23, 1978, and October 27, 1978, ZB Don, Box 9, JCL.

27. On NSC leak: Michel Oksenberg to Zbigniew Brzezinski and David Aaron, on Deng interview, September 6, 1977, ZB Don, Box 8, China, JCL. See also Vance, *Hard Choices*, 82–83; and Brzezinski, *Power and Principle*, 202.

28. PRC response: David J. Rothkopf, *Running the World*, 19.

29. Vance as "WASP elite": Brzezinski, *Power and Principle*, 43.

30. Brzezinski in control: Brzezinski/aides interviews, 1982, CPP, 6–20, 59–64, 78–80, JCL.

31. Queries for Woodcock: Zbigniew Brzezinski to Jimmy Carter, July 17, 1977, ZB Don, Box 8, China-PRC 3-6/77, JCL.

32. White House control: Brzezinski to Carter, July 17, 1977.

33. Monitoring cables: Brzezinski, *Power and Principle*, 225–26.

34. Closer relations with Chinese: Zbigniew Brzezinski to Jimmy Carter, September 21, 1977, ZB Don, Box 8, China (PRC) 7/77–9/77, JCL. In November, following a proposal made by Secretary Brown, Brzezinski suggested that Brown brief the Chinese on U.S. NATO policies in a "routine fashion." The goal, Brzezinski argued, was to produce a "low-level consultative relationship" between the Chinese military attaché in Brussels and NATO.

35. Senior officials in the White House: Brzezinski, *Power and Principle*, 198, 202.

36. Soliciting invitation: Michel Oksenberg to Zbigniew Brzezinski, October 22, 1977, ZB Don, Box 8, China (PRC) 10/77–1/78, JCL.

37. Receiving invitation: Michel Oksenberg to Zbigniew Brzezinski, November 2, 1977, ZB Don, Box 8, China (PRC) 10/77–1/78, JCL.

38. Accepting invitation: Brzezinski, *Power and Principle*, 202–3.

39. Soliciting the president: Zbigniew Brzezinski to Jimmy Carter, November 22, 1977, ZB Don, Box 9, PRC Brzezinski Trip: 11/19/77–5/14/78, JCL.

40. Zbigniew Brzezinski to Jimmy Carter, February 16, 1978, ZB Don, Box 9, PRC Brzezinski Trip: 11/19/77–5/14/78, JCL; Brzezinski wrote, "During a period in which no other high-level contacts with China are planned, a trip to Beijing would permit authoritative exchanges on broad global and strategic issues (e.g. SALT, Middle East, Africa). A trip to China

would also signal to the USSR the potential costs of pressing for unilateral advantages in the Horn. I would not expect to be drawn into negotiations on the terms of normalization." See also Zbigniew Brzezinski to Jimmy Carter, February 27, 1978, ZB Don, Box 9, PRC Brzezinski Trip, 11/19/77–5/14/78, JCL.

41. Trip to be consultative: Zbigniew Brzezinski to Jimmy Carter, February 16, 1978, ZB Don, Box 9, PRC-Brzezinski Trip 11/19/77–5/14/78, JCL; Zbigniew Brzezinski to Jimmy Carter, February 27, 1978, ZB Don, Box 9, PRC-Brzezinski Trip 11/19/77–5/14/78. See also Brzezinski, *Power and Principle*, 204. Aides pushed Brzezinski to obtain a commitment: "Vance cannot go to China unless we're prepared to discuss normalization, which we're not." Michael Armacost and Michel Oksenberg to Zbigniew Brzezinski, February 1, 1978, ZB Don, Box 9, China PRC-Brzezinski Trip, JCL.

42. Brzezinski less visible than Mondale: Brzezinski, *Power and Principle*, 205.

43. On turf protection: Brzezinski, *Power and Principle*, 204–5.

44. "Best for Zbig to go": Jimmy Carter to Walter Mondale and Cyrus Vance, March 16, 1978, ZB Don, Box 9, China-PRC Brzezinski Trip, JCL.

45. On Vance's mistake: Oksenberg to Brzezinski, March 3, 1978, ZB Don, Box 8, China-PRC 2–5/78, JCL.

46. Seeking "authoritative consultation": Zbigniew Brzezinski to Jimmy Carter, March 21, 1978, ZB Don, Box 8, China(PRC): 2–5/78, JCL.

47. More sustained initiatives: Zbigniew Brzezinski to Jimmy Carter, ZB Don, Box 41, 9 April 1977, JCL.

48. Brzezinski's expectation of consultations: Michel Oksenberg to Zbigniew Brzezinski, April 25, 1978, ZB Don, Box 9, China-Alpha Channel 11/19/77–5/14/78, JCL: "You have stressed to Han Hsu that you will be speaking for the President, that the President approved the trip on recommendation of the Secretary of State, and that we seek authoritative consultations at the highest levels."

49. Jackson and normalization: Zbigniew Brzezinski to Jimmy Carter, May 4, 1979, ZB Don, Box 9, China-PRC Brzezinski Trip, JCL.

50. On Kennedy and normalization: Zbigniew Brzezinski to Jimmy Carter, May 5, 1978, ZB Don, Box 9, China-PRC Brzezinski Trip, JCL. In the meantime, Beijing was sending subtle signals—issuing family reunification exit visas, increasing social contacts between Chinese military attaches and others aboard—indicating an increased interest in broadening their relations with the United States. The administration responded with a decision to accommodate some of the PRC's concerns regarding Taiwan. Michel Oksenberg to Zbigniew Brzezinski, March 16, 1978, Brzezinski/NSA Box 8, China, JCL; Zbigniew Brzezinski and Cyrus Vance to Leonard Woodcock, September 5, 1978, ZB Don, Box 9, Alpha Channel-China, JCL.

51. Broad instructions: Jimmy Carter to Zbigniew Brzezinski, May 17, 1978: VF, Box 117, USSR-US Conf., BB1, JCL.

52. Broad mandate: Brzezinski, *Power and Principle*, 206–8.

53. Red carpet: Ibid., 209–10. The Chinese may have been particularly warm as Soviet troops had made an incursion into China on May 8, later claiming that it was an accidental landing on Chinese territory.

54. Holbrooke in Beijing: Brzezinski, *Power and Principle*, 209, 213. Samuel Huntington shared information on PD 18 with the Chinese. Zbigniew Brzezinski to Jimmy Carter, WR 60, May 26, 1978, ZB Don, Box 41, JCL.

55. On Taiwan: Brzezinski, *Power and Principle*, 213–14, 218.

56. Anti-Soviet speech: Huang Hua's toast at Brzezinski banquet, May 20, 1978, ZB Don, Box 9, PRC Brzezinski Trip 5/15/78–5/22/78, JCL.

57. Anti-Soviet challenges at Great Wall: Fox Butterfield, "Brzezinski, in China, Calls Goal Full Ties," *NYT*, May 21, 1978; Jay Mathews, "Brzezinski Trip Brings No Signs of Chinese Shift," *WP*, May 24, 1978; Fox Butterfield, "Brzezinski in China," *NYT*, May 24, 1978; Holger

Jensen with Sydney Liu, "Polar Bear Tamer," *Newsweek*, June 5, 1978, 61. Statements at farewell banquet: *FF*, May 26, 1978, 384; Richard C. Thornton, *The Carter Years*, 117–19.

58. Holbrooke excluded: Rothkopf, *Running the World*, 190; Brzezinski, *Power and Principle*, 213.

59. Scathing attacks: "Interview on 'Meet the Press,'" May 28, 1978, *DSB* 78, no. 2016 (July 1978): 26–28.

60. Carter castigates Brzezinski: Jimmy Carter, quoted in Brzezinski, *Power and Principle*, 220–21.

61. Amicable relations: "U.S., in Gesture to Peking, Drops Jet Sale to Taiwan," *NYT*, July 1, 1978, 2. See also Brzezinski, *Power and Principle*, 226–27.

62. Woodcock as ally, strong on normalization: Lee Byrd/Associated Press, "Woodcock Sees U.S. Establishing Full Peking Ties," Box 8, ZB Don, Country file China 2–5/78.

63. Carter's terms to Chai: Brzezinski, *Power and Principle*, 229.

64. Vietnamese normalization: Vance, *Hard Choices*, 122–23; Brzezinski, *Power and Principle*, 228–29.

65. Impeding progress: Brzezinski, *Power and Principle*, 228–29. President Nixon, in a private letter to Carter, warned that a rapprochement with the Vietnamese would impede any possible deal. From a real politik perspective, the U.S. decision may have impacted on the formation of their alliance with the Soviet Union, though Carter did not think so. But Brzezinski saw the Vietnamese as simply puppets of the USSR. Richard Nixon to Jimmy Carter, December 20, 1978, Plains File, Box 39, State Department Evening Reports, JCL. See also Brzezinski, *Power and Principle*, 228–29; Vance, *Hard Choices*, 125; and Carter, *Keeping Faith*, 195.

66. Post–Vietnam War guilt: Zbigniew Brzezinski to Jimmy Carter, WR 75 (and Carter's response: handwritten note on memo), October 13, 1978, ZB Don, Box 42, JCL.

67. Draft proposals, discussions in Beijing: Brzezinski, *Power and Principle*, 228–30; Rothkopf, *Running the World*, 191. For shorter account of negotiations, see Carter, *Keeping Faith*, 198–99.

68. Inviting leaders: Brzezinski, *Power and Principle*, 230.

69. On the verge of unraveling: Rothkopf, *Running the World*, 192; Brzezinski, *Power and Principle*, 231–32.

70. Handling arms issues later: David Rothkopf, *Running the World*, 192–93.

71. Rationale for going public: Vance, *Hard Choices*, 110; Carter, *Keeping Faith*, 199.

72. The need to keep the circle tight: Zbigniew Brzezinski to Jimmy Carter, WR 8, October 6, 1978, ZB Don, Box 42, JCL. As evidence he pointed out that there had been a leak, only attributable to the State Department, that Strobe Talbott of *Time* magazine had been consulting Herbert Brownell on the best way to terminate the Mutual Defense Treaty with Taiwan.

73. Frozen out of meetings: Vance, *Hard Choices*, 119; Rothkopf, *Running the World*, 191–93.

74. Carter directing moves: Carter, *Keeping Faith*, 197, 199.

75. Discovering ambiguity: Rothkopf, *Running the World*, 192.

76. One State Department official, for example, suggested that in the summer of 1977, Brzezinski himself was behind the damaging leak stating that the Chinese had shown considerable flexibility in their talks with Vance. See Rothkopf, *Running the World*, 190.

77. Brzezinski "proud": quoted in Rothkopf, *Running the World*, 193.

CHAPTER 12. BUILDING THE SECURITY RELATIONSHIP

1. Dinner: Zbgniew Brzezinski, *Power and Principle*, 405.

2. Jackson, details on Deng visit to the United States: Michael Evans, "Bearbaiting," *Newsweek*, February 12, 1979, 22–27; Angus Deming et al., "A Chinese New Year," *Newsweek*, January 15, 1979, 24. See also Jimmy Carter, *Keeping Faith*, 202–11; and Brzezinski, *Power and Principle*, 405–7.

3. Transcript of Deng's press conferences and interview with Cronkite and other TV networks: "Interview of His Excellency Deng Xiaoping, Vice Premier of the State Council of the People's Republic of China, by Walter Cronkite, CBS, James Lehrer, PBS, Frank Reynolds, ABC, and David Brinkley, NBC," January 31, 1979, in Lipshutz Collection, Box 7, China: Miscellaneous Closed, 4/77–6/79, [CF, O/A 710,]JCL.

4. Most historic visit: Michel Oksenberg, quoted in Evans "Bearbaiting," 22–27.

5. On goodwill: Evans, "Bearbaiting," 22–27; Deming et al., "A Chinese New Year," 24.

6. Deng's political mission: Evans, "Bearbaiting," 22–27.

7. Other political goals: James Mann, *About Face*, 97–99, 113.

8. On hegemony: Joint Communiqué, December 15, 1978, ZB Don, Box 9, China (PRC)-Normalization: 12/18/78–12/31/78, JCL.

9. Another apology: Brzezinski, *Power and Principle*, 402–8.

10. Deng on invasion of Vietnam: Carter, *Keeping Faith*, 206; Brzezinski, *Power and Principle*, 408–10.

11. Carter response: Brzezinski, *Power and Principle*, 410; Jimmy Carter, *Keeping Faith*, 206.

12. The result, Brzezinski suggested, was that the United States was not locked into a position that would require it to later condemn China for its actions: Brzezinski, *Power and Principle*, 409–11.

13. Contingency response: Zbigniew Brzezinski to Cyrus Vance, February 16, 1979, ZB Don, Box 10, Sino-Vietnamese Conflict, JCL. Brzezinski, *Power and Principle*, 411–12.

14. Meetings on intervention: NSC Meeting, February 16, 1979, NSA Staff Material–Far East, Oksenberg File, Box 46, F: Mtgs. 2/1–18/79, JCL.

15. That same day: Jimmy Carter to Leonid Brezhnev, February 17, 1979, Plains File, Box 17, F: Brezhnev-JC Corr. 1979, JCL.

16. Soviet response: Brezhnev to Carter, February 18, 1979, Plains File, Box 17. F: B2, Brezhnev-JC Corr. 1979, JCL.

17. Moscow Radio, February 19, 1979, Box 29, Brzezinski Subject File Meetings-SCC 141, JCL.

18. Dobrynin on Moscow beliefs: Cyrus Vance, *Hard Choices*, 121–22.

19. Gromyko's Minsk address: Craig R. Whitney, "Gromyko Says China Obstructs Improved U.S.-Soviet Relations," *NYT*, February 27, 1979.

20. *Pravda* warning: Edward Cowan, "Blumenthal Delivers Warning," *NYT*, February 28, 1979.

21. Blumenthal's warning: Cowan, "Blumenthal Delivers Warning."

22. Harsh resistance: China estimated that approximately 20,000 soldiers and civilians on both sides died in the seventeen-day war. Terry McCarthy, "A Nervous China Invades Vietnam," September 27, 1999, retrieved February 16, 2008, from http://www.time.com/time/asia/magazine/99/0927/pingxiang.html.

23. Denial of Soviet buildup: Vance, *Hard Choices*, 121–22.

24. Trip diplomacy: Brzezinski, *Power and Principle*, 417.

25. Mondale support: Brzezinski, *Power and Principle*, 417–18. By late 1978, Brown and Brzezinski had concluded that the United States should not oppose European shipments of arms to the PRC, and Carter so informed the presidents of Britain, France, and Germany at Guadalupe in January 1979. Brzezinski, *Power and Principle*, 420.

26. Future run: Brzezinski, *Power and Principle*, 205–6.

27. Aaron's briefing: Brzezinski, *Power and Principle*, 418.

28. MFN status: Jimmy Carter, *Keeping Faith*, 201–2, 209. Decoupling MFN, informing the Chinese, and reluctant Vance support: Brzezinski, *Power and Principle*, 418.

29. MFN reversal: Brzezinski, *Power and Principle*, 418–20. Back in December 31, 1978, the president wrote in his diary that he wanted to move toward MFN treatment of the Soviet Union and China at the same time.

30. Mondale's visit: "Mondale Begins Week-Long China Visit," *WP*, August 26, 1979; Jay Mathews, "Mondale: U.S. Backs Strong China," *WP*, August 28, 1979; Jay Mathews, "Mondale Given Huge Welcome in Xian," *WP*, August 30, 1979; Jay Mathews, "Mondale the Whirlwind," *WP*, August 31, 1979.

31. August 27 speech in Beijing: "Vice President: Visit to East Asia," *DSB* 79, no. 2031 (October 1979): 10–12.

32. Initiative on Nixon: Hamilton Jordan to Jimmy Carter, "Proposed Call to Nixon on Normalization," December 17, 1978, Jordan Collection, Box 34, Chinese Normalization, JCL.

33. Insists on trip: Rick Inderfurth to Zbigniew Brzezinski, February 8, 1979, ZB Don, Box 9, China-PRC 1–3/79, JCL.

34. No need to bother president: Brzezinski response to Oksenberg memorandum, "Former President Nixon's Trip to China," Michel Oksenberg to Zbigniew Brzezinski, August 6, 1979, ZB Don, Box 9, China-PRC 8-9/79, JCL.

35. Nixon's visit to China: Stephen E. Ambrose, *Nixon: Ruin and Recovery*, 568.

36. Move against canceling Brown's visit: Zbigniew Brzezinski to Jimmy Carter, September 18, 1979, ZB Don, Box 9, China-PRC Geographic File, JCL. See also Brzezinski, *Power and Principle*, 422.

37. Other trips to China: Mann, *About Face*, 110–14.

38. Mondale's motivations: Brzezinski, *Power and Principle*, 205–6.

39. George Brown wrote Harold Brown, "We are working on the U.S.-Soviet problem to keep the U.S.-PRC-USSR triangle somewhat more equilateral." "Memorandum for the Secretary of Defense, Subject: US-Chinese (PRC) Military Contacts," February 7, 1977. Then, Brown wrote a memorandum to the president in response: "Parallel approaches to the PRC could mitigate that problem [i.e., "adverse effects on our relations with the Soviets"]. Harold Brown to Jimmy Carter, "Memorandum for the President, Subject: US-PRC Military Contacts," February 8, 1977, ZB Don, Box 8, Country F: China, JCL.

40. Holbrook on Blumenthal trip: Michel Oksenberg and William Odom to Zbigniew Brzezinski, February 19, 1979, ZB Don, Box 10, China (PRC)-Sino-Vietnamese Conflict 2/17–2/21/79, JCL. Pol Pot in UN: Vance, *Hard Choices*, 124–26.

41. Fight with Muskie: Brzezinski/aides interviews, 1982, CPP, 74–76, JCL.

42. On Blumenthal trip: Michel Oksenberg and William Odom to Zbigniew Brzezinski, February 19, 1979, ZB Don, Box 10, China (PRC)-Sino-Vietnamese Conflict 2/17–2/21/79, JCL.

43. Handwritten note: David Aaron to Zbigniew Brzezinski, n.d., ZB Don, China country file, 4-5/79, JCL.

CHAPTER 13. THE IMPACT OF A MOTIVATED TACTICIAN

1. Definition of framing: Jean A. Garrison, *Games Advisers Play*, 26–27.

2. For an earlier study reviewing the management literature and applying it to aspects of Carter's decision making, see Garrison, *Games Advisers Play*, 27–28.

3. Framing confrontation: Zbigniew Brzezinski to Jimmy Carter, "The Soviet Union and Ethiopia: Implications for US-Soviet Relations," March 3, 1978, ZB Don, Box 28, 61: 3/2/78. JCL. Brzezinski wrote, "I think we should consider suspending a number of bilateral programs, starting with space."

4. Frightening the Chinese: Zbigniew Brzezinski to Jimmy Carter, WR 111, October 5, 1979, ZB Don, Box 42, JCL.

5. "Evenhanded or balanced" wording: Michel Oksenberg to Zbigniew Brzezinski, January 26, 1979, ZB Don, Box 9, China-PRC 1/3/1979, JCL. Shortly after the Chinese invasion of Vietnam (February 1979), Odom and Oksenberg in a memo to Brzezinski recalled the President's injunction at the NSC meeting of Friday, February 16, that "the Soviet-backed Vietnamese invasion of Cambodia gave the Chinese little choice but to invade Vietnam." The

policy of "evenhandedness" or "balance" they recommend should be used to support this stance. William Odom and Michel Oksenberg to Zbigniew Brzezinski, February 19, 1979, ZB Don, Box 9, China-PRC 1/3/1979, JCL.

6. Two interventions: Zbigniew Brzezinski to Jimmy Carter, WR 84, January 12, 1979, ZB Don, Box 42, JCL.

7. Shared responsibility: Zbigniew Brzezinski, draft of letter to Leonid Brezhnev, February 17, 1979, ZB Don, Box 46, NSC Meetings 2/1979, JCL.

8. Complimenting Carter: Zbigniew Brzezinski to Jimmy Carter, "Meeting with Leonard Woodcock," July 7, 1977, ZB Don, Box 8, China (PRC), JCL. In December 1978, Brzezinski circulated to senior cabinet officials an article in which his accomplishments were mentioned favorably compared with Vance. See "East Meets West," December 23, 1978, *Economist*, 7–9.

9. On post–Vietnam War guilt: Zbigniew Brzezinski to Jimmy Carter (and Carter's response, handwritten note on memo), WR 75, October 13, 1978, ZB Don, Box 42, JCL.

10. State Department leak: Zbigniew Brzezinski to Jimmy Carter, WR 74, October 6, 1978, ZB Don, Box 42, JCL.

11. Discretion for Brzezinski: Brzezinski/aides interviews, 1982, CPP, 85–87, JCL. Critique of USSR by Brzezinski: "Interview on 'Meet the Press,'" May 28, 1978, *DSB* 78, no. 2016 (July 1978): 27.

12. Cutting Gordian knots: Zbigniew Brzezinski, *Power and Principle*, 43.

13. Agents for change: Brzezinski, *Power and Principle*, 42.

14. Carter viewed as tough: Hamilton Jordan, interview, see 1981 CPP, 30, JCL.

15. Using Deng's words: Brzezinski, *Power and Principle*, 406–7.

16. "It got done": Brzezinski/aides interviews, 1982, CPP, 73, JCL.

17. Seduced by Chinese: Jimmy Carter, *Keeping Faith*, 196.

18. Enthusing on Deng lesson: Brzezinski, *Power and Principle*, 410.

19. Zemin's dress: James Mann, *About Face*, 90–91.

20. The Chinese as patient negotiators: Ibid. See also memo of conversation, Jimmy Carter, Walter Mondale, Henry Kissinger, Lawrence Eagleburger, and David Aaron, November 20, 1976, Vance Mss, Box 8, F: 6, YUL.

21. The Chinese as members of the Middle Kingdom: Carter, *Keeping Faith*, 189.

22. China and Soviet visits contrasted: Carter, *Keeping Faith*, 236.

23. Impression of Deng: Ibid., 202.

24. Chinese sensitivity: Ibid., 211.

25. Chinese slights: Thomas P. Thornton to Zbigniew Brzezinski, "The Hua Non-Meeting and Sino-US Relations: A Polemic," September 27, 1977, ZB Don, Box 8, China (PRC), 7–9/77.

26. "What's his name?": Brzezinski, *Power and Principle*, 418.

27. Taiwan issue: Fox Butterfield, "Peking Says Taiwan Can Keep Autonomy under Unification," *NYT*, January 10, 1979; Bernard Gwertzman, "Teng, on Capitol Hill, Says Peking Must Keep Taiwan Options Open," *NYT*, January 31, 1979. Retrieved on March 28, 2009, http://www.time.com/time/magazine/article/0,9171,947305-2,00.html.

28. Taiwan arms sales: "Absorbing the Painful Blow," *Time*, May 28, 1979. Retrieved on April 7, 2009, http://www.time.com/time/magazine/article/0,9171,947305,00.html.

29. Stunned at announcement: Stuart Eizenstat, interview, 1982 CPP, 67, JCL.

CHAPTER 14. MAESTRO OF THE CAMP DAVID TALKS

1. "Blessed are the peacemakers": Betty Glad, *Jimmy Carter*, 433.

2. Texts of agreements: Framework for Egypt-Israel Peace Treaty Conclusion, Plains File, Box 28, F: Mid-East, CDS, PWP, undated, JCL. See also William Quandt, *Camp David*, 376–87.

3. Transcript of the proceedings of the conference "Global Competition and the Deterioration of U.S.-Soviet Relations, 1977–1980," March 23–26, 1995, Ft. Lauderdale, Florida, 91–100, VF, Box 117, JCL.

4. Issues explored at Leeds Castle: Moshe Dayan, *Breakthrough*, 138–48; Cyrus Vance, *Hard Choices*, 216.

5. Sadat and the Arab bloc: Quandt, *Camp David*, 142, 154. See also the remarks on Camp David by Harold Saunders, Hermann Eilts, and William Quandt in Herbert Rosenbaum and Alexej Ugrinsky, eds., *Jimmy Carter*, 176, 178, 183.

6. Contributions of the president: Quandt, *Camp David*, 258.

7. Admiration of Carter: Ezer Weizman, *The Battle for Peace*, 362–63.

8. Admiration of Carter: Edward Sanders to Jimmy Carter, "Transcript of the Press Conference of Foreign Minister Moshe Dayan and Defense Minister Ezer Weizman," September 21, 1978, Executive File, F06-7, C074, F05-3, JCL.

9. Standing in the polls: Betty Glad, *Jimmy Carter*, 443.

10. Harsh press coverage: Jody Powell, *The Other Side of the Story*, 71.

11. Though Brzezinski seemed to favor a push for a settlement at Camp David, he relayed the message that Mondale suggested a "less assertive strategy, playing for time and limiting the damage to our relations with Israel and the Jewish community." If the United States decided to confront, he suggested, "We need to make certain the rejection of our suggestions is too risky for any of the parties." Zbigniew Brzezinski to Jimmy Carter, WR 66, July 7, 1978, ZB Don, Box 41, JCL. Pessimistic aides: Charles Kirbo, Clark Clifford, Sol Linowitz, and businessman Irving Shapiro tried, in early June, to talk Carter out of a deeper personal involvement in the Middle East negotiations. See Rosalynn Carter, *First Lady from Plains*, 239.

12. Considering a summit: Quandt, *Camp David*, 201.

13. Work at Harriman estate: Cyrus Vance, *Hard Choices*, 218–19; Quandt, *Camp David*, 209–14. Earlier work: Harold Saunders, interview by the author, July 2, 1996, Vancouver, BC.

14. Saunders interview, July 2, 1996.

15. Carter studies: Carter, *Keeping Faith*, 321–22.

16. "Not aiming high enough": Jimmy Carter, quoted in Rosenbaum and Ugrinsky, eds., *Jimmy Carter*, 161–62.

17. Motives of participants: Zbigniew Brzezinski to Jimmy Carter, August 31, 1978, quoted in Brzezinski, *Power and Principle*, 253–54.

18. Plans for Camp David, Carter quote, Quandt response: in Rosenbaum and Ugrinsky, eds., *Jimmy Carter*, 162; See also Quandt, *Camp David*, 206; Carter, *Keeping Faith*, 321.

19. The choice of Camp David was made while Carter walked through the woods with his wife, Rosalynn. He could not see how "anybody could stay in this place, close to nature … and still carry a grudge." Rosalynn Carter, *First Lady*, 238. For other advantages, see Angus Deming et al., "Hideaway Summit," *Newsweek*, September 18, 1978, 22–26. Israeli Defense Minister Ezer Weizman discovered that he could not call up one of his Egyptian friends at the camp without going through the Americans; Weizman, *The Battle for Peace*, 343. Though eavesdropping devices were not installed in the cabins, the Egyptians and Israelis thought they had been, so they conducted their private conversations outdoors; Quandt, *Camp David*, 186. See also Powell, *The Other Side of the Story*, 60–69.

20. Carter has noted that due to the size of Camp David, the number of advisors present from all three countries was limited; Carter, *Keeping Faith*, 324. When Menachem Begin invited two senior Israel officials in Washington to join him at the camp, the White House "disinvited" them. See Glad, *Jimmy Carter*, 324, 432.

21. Amenities at Camp David: Rosalynn Carter, *First Lady*, 235–37; Carter, *Keeping Faith*, 323–24. Sadat was assigned to Dogwood and the Begins to Birch Lodge, with the Carters in Aspen Lodge, in between. Other members of the delegations doubled up in the smaller cabins at the site.

22. Dealing with Sadat, other Israelis: Samuel Lewis in Rosenbaum and Ugrinsky, eds., *Jimmy Carter*, 158.

23. U.S. negotiating teams: Carter, *Keeping Faith*, 326. According to Saunders, Vance headed the core group, which included Quandt, Atherton, Saunders, and Jerrold Post (of the CIA). Brzezinski, Powell, and Jordan made up the other group. Saunders interview, July 2, 1996.

24. Israeli and Egyptian teams: Carter, *Keeping Faith*, 326.

25. Agreeing on a prayer: Weizman, *The Battle for Peace*, 345.

26. "Primed for bear": Hermann Eilts, quoted in Rosenbaum and Ugrinsky, eds., *Jimmy Carter*, 152. See also Weizman, *The Battle for Peace*, 351–52.

27. Begin response and jokes: Carter, *Keeping Faith*, 345. See also Quandt, in Rosenbaum and Ugrinsky, eds., *Jimmy Carter*, 162.

28. Taking a stroll: Carter, *Keeping Faith*, 345–46. When Begin did not seem upset at the Egyptian proposal, Carter concluded that he realized it could not serve as a basis for agreement. See also Weizman, *The Battle for Peace*, 353–55.

29. Assuring Weizman: Weizman, *The Battle for Peace*, 356.

30. Assurances from Sadat: William Quandt, in Rosenbaum and Ugrinsky, eds., *Jimmy Carter*, 162–63.

31. Israeli response: Weizman, *The Battle for Peace*, 355–56. The Israeli delegation countermanded the next day with claims for war damages from the Arab states.

32. A mean exchange: Rosalynn Carter, *First Lady*, 247.

33. Another round: Carter, *Keeping Faith*, 357–59.

34. Threats to leave: Ibid., 355.

35. More animosity: Quandt, *Camp David*, 224.

36. Wildfire rumors: Carter, *Keeping Faith*, 360.

37. Sadat forlorn: Rosalynn Carter, *First Lady*, 248.

38. Linkage: Saunders interview, July 2, 1996.

39. Carter wrote the first draft of the Egypt-Israel agreement: Quandt to author, 31 August 2004. On removing linkage: Saunders interview with author, 2 July 1996. Quandt surmises that Carter's commitment to a comprehensive agreement may have changed after spending time with Sadat at Camp David in February, 1978. William Quandt to author, August 31, 2004.

40. Sinai agreement: in Rosenbaum and Ugrinsky, eds., *Jimmy Carter*, 159–62.

41. U.S. proposals: Weizman, *The Battle for Peace*, 363–65; Dayan, *Breakthrough*, 164. For text of the first draft, see Quandt, *Camp David*, 361–68.

42. Begin distressed: Weizman, *The Battle for Peace*, 363–65.

43. Separation of Begin and Sadat: Quandt, *Camp David*, 224–25.

44. Jordan: Saunders interview, July 2, 1996.

45. Sticking points: Weizman, *The Battle for Peace*, 369.

46. Talks on Monday: Carter, *Keeping Faith*, 379–83.

47. Israeli divisions on Tuesday: Weizman, *The Battle for Peace*, 370.

48. Sharon consulted: Weizman, *The Battle for Peace*, 370–72.

49. Apprehensions about Sadat: Brzezinski, *Power and Principle*, 265; Carter, *Keeping Faith*, 388–89.

50. Dayan shift on Sinai settlements: Weizman, *Battle for Peace*, 371.

51. Vance being tough with the Israelis: Brzezinski, *Power and Principle*, 266–67.

52. Proposal on airfields: Weizman, *The Battle for Peace*, 371; Brzezinksi, *Power and Principle*, 267.

53. Sadat threatens to leave: Carter, *Keeping Faith*, 391–93; Quandt, *Camp David*, 238–39; Brzezinksi, *Power and Principle*, 271–72; Rosalynn Carter, *First Lady*, 163–64.

54. President prays: Carter, *Keeping Faith*, 392.

55. Meeting Sadat: Brzezinksi, *Power and Principle*, 271–72; Carter, *Keeping Faith*, 392–93.

56. Tough talk with Sadat: Rosalynn Carter, *First Lady*, 263.

57. Sadat stays: Weizman, *The Battle for Peace*, 372.

58. In gratitude: Rosalynn Carter, *First Lady*, 263.

59. Sadat on Jimmy Carter: Kamel, *The Camp David Accords*, 356–57.

60. Begin concession, Sinai settlements: Weizman, *The Battle for Peace*, 372.

61. Side letter: Carter, *Keeping Faith*, 394–97. Overview of dispute: Quandt, *Camp David*, 252–53.

62. Begin's promises: William Quandt to author, August 31, 2004.

63. Final disputes: Weizman, *The Battle for Peace*, 373; Dayan, *Breakthrough*, 178–79; Carter, *Keeping Faith*, 398–99.

64. Unpleasant exchange with Dayan et al.: Carter, *Keeping Faith,* 398–99.

65. Carter's angry retort: Dayan, *Breakthrough*, 158–59. Dayan wrote, "It would take a lot more than Camp David, to prevent us from preserving Jerusalem as the capital of Israel. Whoever wished to do so would have to rewrite the Bible…wipe out three thousand years of history."

66. To the rescue: Quandt, *Camp David*, 252; Weizman, *The Battle for Peace*, 373–74; Carter, *Keeping Faith*, 399.

67. Meeting with Begin, photos: Carter, *Keeping Faith*, 399.

68. Possible failure: Carter, *Keeping Faith*, 390–91; Brzezinksi, *Power and Principle*, 267. On Thursday, Carter warned the Israelis that a failure in the talks would be "catastrophic" for relations between the United States and Israel and that he would be "obliged to report to Congress" that Israel bore a responsibility for that failure. Dayan, *Breakthrough*, 173.

69. Responsibility on Israelis: Quandt, *Camp David*, 240–41.

70. Begin accepts letter: Carter, *Keeping Faith*, 399.

71. Sadat, Begin meet: Weizman, *The Battle for Peace*, 377; Carter, *Keeping Faith*, 400–401.

72. Back to DC: Jimmy Carter, President's Daily Diaries, Plains Files, Box 11, F: 9/4-24/78, JCL. Ironically, the camp setting may have contributed to the success of the talks in ways Carter had never anticipated. Several members of the Israeli and Egyptian delegations thought Camp David had a claustrophobic feeling about it: Weizman, *The Battle for Peace*, 342. Dayan preferred the sun and desert; Dayan, *Breakthrough*, 155. Begin, half in jest, referred to it as a "concentration camp": Vance, *Hard Choices*, 223. Sadat would only admit that it was "better than Cell 20 in which he had been imprisoned for four years in Egypt." See Hermann Eilts, in Rosenbaum and Ugrinsky, eds., *Jimmy Carter*, 185; Kamel, *The Camp David Accords*, 321.

73. On press arrangements: Powell, *The Other Side of the Story*, 83–87.

74. East Room ceremony and Begin quote: Rosalynn Carter, *First Lady*, 267–69.

75. Domestic response to Carter's success, August 21: Glad, *Jimmy Carter*, 433.

CHAPTER 15. SUPPORT TEAMS AND THE ROAD AHEAD

1. Harold Saunders, interview by the author, July 2, 1996, Vancouver, BC. Ambassador Samuel Lewis also thought that "personality interactions played an enormous role in the outcome of President Carter's greatest diplomatic triumph." Quoted in Herbert Rosenbaum and Alexej Ugrinsky, eds., *Jimmy Carter*, 159.

2. Carter "open": Hermann Eilts to the author, November 14, 2003.

3. Attitude of aides toward Carter: Moshe Dayan, *Breakthrough*, 166.

4. Comfortable with Sadat: Zbigniew Brzezinski, *Power and Principle*, 259.

5. Sadat mesmerized: Hermann Eilts in Rosenbaum and Ugrinsky, eds., *Jimmy Carter*, 181.

6. CIA profiles: Gerald Post, interview by the author, November 13, 2004, Washington, DC. See also Jimmy Carter, *Keeping Faith*. 319–20.

7. Relationship to Begin: Brzezinski, *Power and Principle*, 255; Carter, *Keeping Faith*, 332–38; Rosalynn Carter, *First Lady from Plains*, 244.

8. Begin's goals: Rosalynn Carter, *First Lady*, 244; Carter, *Keeping Faith*, 337.

9. Begin being unreasonable: Carter, *Keeping Faith*, 378.

10. Being angry with Begin: Rosalynn Carter, *First Lady*, 254–55.

11. Other Israelis facilitate talks: Carter, *Keeping Faith*, 356; Samuel Lewis in Rosenbaum and Ugrinsky, eds., *Jimmy Carter*, 158.

12. The Israeli team: Saunders interview, July 2, 1996. Barak contributions: Moshe Dayan, *Breakthrough*, 156. See also Cyrus Vance, *Hard Choices*, 223.

13. Advice on cutting around Begin: William Quandt, *Camp David*, 224.

14. Rigid on Sinai settlements: William Quandt, letter to author, August 31, 2004.

15. Tamir, Sharon, and Begin: Ezer Weizman, *The Battle for Peace*, 369–71.

16. Dual track in negotiations: Quandt, *Camp David*, 257.

17. William Quandt to the author, August 31, 2004. Brzezinski's secondary role: Saunders interview, July 2, 1996. See also Weizman, *The Battle for Peace*, 259, 363; and Dayan, *Breakthrough*, 166.

18. Competition in chess: Weizman, *Battle for Peace*, 347; Brzezinski, *Power and Principle*, 259.

19. Expert team: Cyrus Vance, *Hard Choices*, 219; Jimmmy Carter, *Keeping Faith*, 326. The group included Harold Saunders, the Assistant Secretary of State for Near East Affairs; Ambassador at large Alfred (Roy) Atherton; William Quandt from the NSC; U.S. Ambassador to Israel Samuel Lewis; and the U.S. Ambassador to Egypt, Hermann Eilts. Even before the meetings began, Ambassadors Lewis and Eilts both warned Carter, with some perspicacity, that he should not try to get Sadat and Begin together at the beginning of the meetings. Lewis and Eilts in Rosenbaum and Ugrinsky, eds., *Jimmy Carter*, 151–59.

20. Handling the press: Jody Powell, *The Other Side of the Story*, 60–69, 81–87.

21. Differences between ambassadors: Hermann Eilts to author, November 14, 2003.

22. Saunders interview, July 2, 1996.

23. No unpleasant differences: Carter, *Keeping Faith*, 332.

24. Best experience: Saunders interview, July 2, 1996.

25. Turner and dinner: Brzezinski, *Power and Principle*, 260. Certainly it was a role reversal. At Annapolis, Turner had been the big man on campus, the athlete, the company commander, and the one everyone expected to succeed, and had won a Rhodes Scholarship. Carter claimed only to have been a finalist in that competition. Betty Glad, *Jimmy Carter*, 53, 59.

26. CIA reports: Saunders interview, July 2, 1996.

27. Jerrold Post, "The Role of Political Personality Profiles in the Camp David Summit," drawn from the article "Personality Profiles in Support of the Camp David Summit," *Studies in Intelligence*.

28. Rosalynn as sounding board: Carter, *Keeping Faith*, 326.

29. Keeping spirits up: Vance, *Hard Choices*, 222–23; Brzezinski, *Power and Principle*, 266.

30. Mondale at Camp David: Carter, *Keeping Faith*, 370.

31. Cabinet members' visits: Jimmy Carter, Daily Diary, Plains Files, Box 11, F: President's Daily Diaries, JCL. See also Carter, *Keeping Faith*, 370, 383.

32. During this simulation Kahane informed Charney and Weizman that Sadat (whom he had just seen in Egypt) was willing to accept an agreement with Israel based on the return of the Sinai and leaving the Palestinian issue to be resolved later. Charney sent the information to Lipshutz, who in turn sent Carter this information. Charney, Weizman, and Lipshutz had been friends prior to the Camp David Talks. Lipshutz memo, March 13, 1979, sent to the author with attachments, 2004. See also Leon H. Charney, *Special Counsel*.

33. Dependence on U.S. goodwill: Carter, *Keeping Faith*, 335.

34. Breakdown catastrophic for Israel: Moshe Dayan, *Breakthrough*, 173.

35. Responsibility for breakdown: Carter, *Keeping Faith*, 390–93; Brzezinski, *Power and Principle*, 266–67. U.S. credibility at stake: Quandt, *Camp David*, 335.

36. Consequence for Sadat: Weizman, *The Battle for Peace*, 362.

37. On Begin's tactics: Quandt, *Camp David*, 255–57. Quandt argues that Begin was a skilled negotiator, making sure Israel had a relatively free hand in dealing with the West Bank and Gaza. The problem with this view is how close the conference was to breaking down at several points. Nadav Safran of Harvard University wrote his friend Brzezinski prior to the conference that the Israelis and Egyptians would probably come to Camp David with no real expectations of a deal. Indeed, the day the conference opened, Brzezinski wrote the president that Israel might find a deadlock—a weakened status quo—to its advantage. Safran to Brzezinski, August 10, 1978, JCL. See also Brzezinski, *Power and Principle*, 253.

38. Israeli need for U.S. support: Weizman, *The Battle for Peace*, 357–58.

39. Sadat's return: Saunders interview, July 2, 1996.

40. Debate over freeze agreement: Vance, *Hard Choices*, 228. "We never did": Quandt also recalls that Begin made a distinction between a decision to authorize new settlements and the actual onset of construction. William Quandt to the author, August 31, 2004.

41. Moratorium not observed: Carter, *Keeping Faith*, 408. See also Vance, *Hard Choices*, 235; and Powell, *The Other Side of the Story*, 83, 88.

42. Israeli plans: *FF*, April 27, 1979, 296.

43. Resignation: Weizman, *The Battle for Peace*, 384–87.

44. Israelis resisting government efforts: Lester Sobel, *Peacemaking in the Middle East*, 223–24.

45. Others to Middle East: *FF*, February 2, 1979, 69.

46. Carter to Middle East: Carter, *Keeping Faith*, 424–25; Vance, *Hard Choices*, 245–52.

47. *Air Force One*: Robert Lipshutz, memo, March 13, 1979, dictated on *Air Force One*, sent to author.

48. U.S. aid to Israel: Leon H. Charney, *Special Counsel*, 147–55.

49. U.S. "sweeteners": See "Israeli Cabinet, Parliament Approve Egyptian Peace Treaty: Egyptian-Israeli Military Talks," *FF*, March 23, 1979, 198. Quandt notes that Egypt later claimed the United States promised "parity" in aid levels. The disparity in aide, on a per capita basis, was "largely a function of domestic politics. In a rational world, Israel would no longer be getting economic aid." William Quandt to author, August 31, 2004.

50. On signing ceremony: Glad, *Jimmy Carter*, 426–29; *FF*, March 30, 1979, 221–22. For transcripts of speeches, see Israel Ministry of Foreign Affairs, "Treaty of Peace between Israel and Egypt: Protocols, Annexes, Letters, Memorandum of Agreement between Israel and the United States, Addresses of Presidents Carter and Sadat, and Prime Minister Begin," March 26, 1979, retrieved February 11, 2008, from http://www.mfa.gov.il/MFA/Foreign%20Relations/Israels%20Foreign%20Relations%20since%201947/1977-1979/251%20Treaty%20of%20Peace%20between%20Israel%20and%20Egypt%20Memor.

51. Need to hold sand dunes: Weizman, *The Battle for Peace*, 387.

52. Unresolved issues: Helmut Schmidt, *Men and Power*, 193–94, 199–200.

53. Hostility to Sadat: Giulio Andreotti, *The USA Up Close*, 102–3; Mohamed Abdel Chani El-Gamasy, *The October War*, 396.

54. Subsequent intervention in Lebanon: Betty Glad, "The United States' Ronald Reagan," in Barbara Kellerman and Jeffery Rubin, eds., *Leadership and Negotiation in the Middle East*, 200.

55. Helping Israel: Weizman, *The Battle for Peace*, 382. Carter's perspectives on Israel: Jimmy Carter, *The Blood of Abraham*, 41–59.

CHAPTER 16. CONFRONTING A REGIME CHANGE

1. Jaleh Square massacre: David Farber, *Taken Hostage*, 92.

2. Riots in Tehran: David Harris, *The Crisis*, 99–101; William Sullivan, *Mission to Iran*, 169.

3. Khomeini's call for action, riots: Harris, *The Crisis*, 117–20.

4. White revolution: James Bill, *The Eagle and the Lion*, 148.

5. One party system: Marvin Zonis, *Majestic Failure*, 75.

6. Opposition to the shah: Gary Sick, *All Fall Down*, 34–37; Alexander Moens, "President Carter's Advisers and the Fall of the Shah," *Political Science Quarterly* 106, no. 2 (1991): 217; Cyrus Vance, *Hard Choices*, 324–27.

7. Shah's reforms: Vance, *Hard Choices*, 327.

8. Azhari conciliates: Vance, *Hard Choices*, 329; Sick, *All Fall Down*, 79.

9. Days numbered: Zbigniew Brzezinski, *Power and Principle*, 371.

10. Bakhtiar's powers limited: Vance, *Hard Choices*, 334–35.

11. Overthrow of Mossadegh: Bill, *The Eagle and the Lion*, 98. The British played a secondary role in the coup. Zahedi's son, Ardeshir, would go on to serve as the shah's ambassador to the United States during Carter's presidency. Marvin Zonis, *Majestic Failure*, 144.

12. Background on shah: Alexander Moens, "President Carter's Advisers," 215–16; Bill, *The Eagle and the Lion*, 192–97.

13. Common interests with shah: Brzezinski, *Power and Principle*, 357; Vance, *Hard Choices*, 315–16.

14. AWACS sale: Jimmy Carter, *Keeping Faith*, 435; Vance, *Hard Choices*, 319–23.

15. Other sales: Sick, *All Fall Down*, 44–45. See also Roger Labrie et al., *U.S. Arms Sales Policy*.

16. CIA on Iran: U.S. Congress, House of Representatives, Permanent Select Committee on Intelligence, January, 1979, *Iran: Evaluation of U.S. Intelligence Performance Prior to November 1978*; Carter, *Keeping Faith*, 438. Reasons for intelligence failures: Sick, *All Fall Down*, 164–65.

17. The DIA on stability: Brzezinski, *Power and Principle*, 359.

18. For elaboration of the roles of the major players, see Bill, *The Eagle and the Lion*, 243–80.

19. State Department memo: Sick, *All Fall Down*, 58–60. Sidelining of Henrt Precht, the country desk officer for Iran: Sick, *All Fall Down*, 69–71. For the president's views at the time, see Carter, *Keeping Faith*, 439–40.

20. November 2 cable: Moens, "President Carter's Advisers," 219.

21. Response to cable: Brzezinski, *Power and Principle*, 364–65. See also William Sullivan, *Mission to Iran*, 171–72.

22. Carter's response: *Keeping Faith*, 439; Cyrus Vance, *Hard Choices*, 328–29; Sullivan, *Mission to Iran*, 172. See also Moens, "President Carter's Advisers," 220.

23. Opponents no threat: Zbigniew Brzezinski to Jimmy Carter, WR 78, November 3, 1978, Plains File, Box 29, F: 6–12/78, JCL.

24. November 9 cable: Sullivan, *Mission to Iran*, 173, 201–3. See also Sick, *All Fall Down*, 81–87.

25. White House response: Brzezinski, *Power and Principle*, 367–68; Vance, *Hard Choices*, 329; Sullivan, *Mission to Iran*, 203.

26. Businessman: Harris, *The Crisis*, 114–15; Brzezinski, *Power and Principle*, 367–68.

27. Making the decision for the shah: Brzezinski, *Power and Principle*, 397.

28. Back channel: Vance, *Hard Choices*, 328.

29. Ball on Brzezinski maneuvers: Bill, *The Eagle and the Lion*, 249–53. See also George Ball, *The Past Has Another Pattern*, 457–58.

30. Ball's advice: Brzezinski, *Power and Principle*, 372–73; Vance *Hard Choices*, 330.

31. Preempting Brzezinski trip: Bill, *The Eagle and the Lion*, 253; Brzezinski, *Power and Principle*, 373.

32. Vance on options: Brzezinski, *Power and Principle*, 375.

33. Shah needs to leave: Carter, *Keeping Faith*, 443–46.

34. Vacillating: Sullivan, *Mission to Iran*, 230–31.

35. Conditions for departure: Carter, *Keeping Faith*, 443.

36. Shah's departure: Harris, *The Crisis*, 143–45; Farber, *Taken Hostage*, 100–101. See also Carter, *Keeping Faith*, 448.

37. Huyser's mission: Sullivan, *Mission to Iran.* 228–29.
38. To preempt Tudeh: Ibid., 233; Farber, *Taken Hostage*, 99–100.
39. Carter on Sullivan: Carter, *Keeping Faith*, 446; Moens, "President Carter's Advisers," 224.
40. Supporting arrest: Brzezinski, *Power and Principle*, 388.
41. Attracting crowds: Carter, *Keeping Faith*, 448; Farber, *Taken Hostage*, 104.
42. Military collapse: Sick, *All Fall Down*, 154–56.
43. Scurrilous suggestion: Sullivan, *Mission to Iran*, 252–53.
44. Embassy seized: David Farber, *Taken Hostage*, 113–14.
45. Shah's secret illness: Harris, *The Crisis*, 110.
46. CIA on shah: Brzezinski, *Power and Principle*, 368.
47. Zahedi on Communists: Vance, *Hard Choices*, 326. Bill, *The Eagle and the Lion*, 433. Bill notes, "American friends of Pahlavi such as…Walt Rosentow, Henry Kissinger, and Zbigniew Brzezinski, were repeatedly warned by the shah of the serious communist menace in his country." Concern of Brzezinski and Sick that Soviets would become "protectors" of the new Muslim regime: Sick, *All Fall Down*, 95–96.
48. Robert Moss, "Who's Meddling in Iran? The Telltale Signs of Soviet Handiwork," *New Republic*, December 2, 1978, 15–18. See also Vance, *Hard Choices*, 315–16; Bill, *The Eagle and the Lion*, 277.
49. Brzezinski on the left: Brzezinski, *Power and Principle*, 381–82. See also Moens, "President Carter's Advisers," 229–30.
50. Preempting Tudeh: Sullivan, *Mission to Iran*, 233. Suggestion of talking with Khomeini: Farber, *Taken Hostage*, 99–100.
51. Carter versus left in coalition: Brzezinski, *Power and Principle*, 387; Carter, *Keeping Faith*, 442–43.
52. Recognition of new government: Vance, *Hard Choices*, 343.
53. Exchanges with Brezhnev: Brzezinski, *Power and Principle*, 369.
54. Consequences of fall: Brzezinski, *Power and Principle*, 385–86.
55. Possible Soviet intervention in Afghanistan: Brzezinski, *Power and Principle*, 354, 356.
56. Huyser on civil war: Vance, *Hard Choices*, 348.
57. Tripling of oil prices: Vance, *Hard Choices*, 346–48.
58. On stable noncommunist regime: Vance, *Hard Choices*, 346–48.
59. Fundamentalism and future: Zbigniew Brzezinski to Jimmy Carter, WR 87, February 2, 1979, Plains File, Box 29, F: 6–12/78, JCL.
60. Shah torn: Zonis, *Majestic Failure*, 248–50.
61. New insecurities: Zonis, *Majestic Failure*, 240. For other analyses of his character, see Sick, *All Fall Down*, 163; and Brzezinski, *Power and Principle*, 361.
62. Moderates unable to oppose Khomeini: Sick, *All Fall Down*, 85.
63. Military and possible coup: Bill, *The Eagle and the Lion*, 98, 99, 249. See also Sick, *All Fall Down*, 170–71.
64. Leaders will appear: Brzezinski, *Power and Principle*, 378.
65. Lectures at Najaf: Sick, *All Fall Down*, 85; Sullivan, *Mission to Iran*, 140–41, 219–20. For more on the lectures see Rhuhollah Khomeini, *Islam and Revolution*, and Shaul Bakhash, *The Reign of the Ayatollahs*.
66. Iraqi intellectuals: Sullivan, *Mission to Iran*, 140–41. Underestimation of mullahs: Sick, *All Fall Down*, 165.

CHAPTER 17. SCRAMBLING FOR OPTIONS

1. No marines at the gate: David Farber, *Taken Hostage*, 31.
2. Takeover goals: David Harris, *The Crisis*, 199–200.
3. Khomeini on takeover: Ibid., 29.

4. Return the traitor: Farber, *Taken Hostage*, 41–42.

5. Secret Revolutionary Council: Harold Saunders, "The Crisis Begins," in Warren Christopher et al., eds., *American Hostage in Iran*, 74–77. Khomeini had established the Provisional Government the day after his return to Iran in February. Throughout 1979, the government focused on the management of the "social machinery" while Khomeini's Revolutionary Council created the policies for the country: Harris, *The Crisis*, 155.

6. A man without a country: Harris, *The Crisis*, 143. Carter's invitation to the shah to come to the United States where he could stay at the estate of publisher Walter H. Annenberg in California was never reversed even after American intelligence reports indicated that if the shah were admitted into the United States the American embassy would be attacked. Zbigniew Brzezinski, *Power and Principle*, 377.

7. Pushing admission: Terrence Smith, "Why Carter Admitted the Shah," *NYT Magazine*, May 17, 1981, 42, 44, 48; Brzezinski, *Power and Principle*, 472–74; Jimmy Carter, *Keeping Faith*, 452.

8. Lack of treatment facilities in Mexico: Lawrence Altman, "The Shah's Health: A Political Gamble," *NYT Magazine*, May 17, 1981, 44, 50. Uninformed of possible medical options in Mexico, Carter still had only the one viable political alternative. As Gary Sick points out, if Carter had refused the shah access to medical treatment in the United States "he would have been soundly criticized by David Rockefeller, Henry Kissinger and virtually all Americans who would have seen his refusal as an abject rejection of humanitarian traditions." Gary Sick, *All Fall Down*, 186.

9. Long faces: Harris, *The Crisis*, 193.

10. Opening Pandora's box: Terence Smith, "Why Carter Admitted the Shah," *NYT*, May 17, 1981; Brzezinski, *Power and Principle*, 472–75; Cyrus Vance, *Hard Choices*, 372–73.

11. Rejecting Barzagan request: Carter, *Keeping Faith*, 455.

12. Physicians on consultation: Ibid., 455.

13. Concern about shah's counterrevolutionary goals: Altman, "The Shah's Health," 48, 50–63.

14. The previous February: Harris, *The Crisis*, 158–60.

15. Fall of Bazargan government: Smith, "Why Carter Admitted," 46.

16. In Paris, Khomeini employed Bani-Sadr and other Paris lawyers to draft a constitution for a new republic; Harris, *The Crisis*, 169.

17. Khomeini's education: Harris, *The Crisis*, 33–36.

18. Meditations: Ibid., 168–72.

19. Executions: Ibid., 170.

20. Bazargan: Ibid., 154–55.

21. Yazdi: Ibid., 155.

22. Bazargan later headed the Freedom Movement of Iran. Yazdi later ran a publishing company for the ayatollah but moved to Texas after several disagreements with the clerical faction. After Bazargan's death in 1995 at age eighty-eight, Yazdi was named president of the Freedom Movement of Iran and moved back to Iran to take an active role in the opposition. As of 2009, he lived in Tehran and continued to lead the Freedom Movement. Harris, *The Crisis*, 433–34.

23. Bani-Sadr "like a son": Sick, *All Fall Down*, 263.

24. Response to speech at the cemetery: "1979: Exiled Ayatollah Khomeini returns to Iran," February 1, 1979, retrieved February 14, 2008, from http://news.bbc.co.uk/onthisday/hi/dates/stories/february/1/newsid_2521000/2521003.stm.

25. Not here to replace shah; Harris, *The Crisis*, 153.

26. Fears Khomeini: Oriana Fallaci, "Iranians Are Our Brothers," *NYT*, December 16, 1979.

27. Bani-Sadr leaves: Harris, *The Crisis*, 431.

28. Tabatabai's future: Ibid., 435.

29. Vance alternative: Sick, *All Fall Down*, 295.

30. Brzezinski on punitive military actions: Brzezinski, *Power and Principle*, 480–83.

31. Risks considered: After an SCC meeting in late November Brzezinski worried that "the one to speak up for American honor was a naturalized American. I wondered what this indicated about the current American elite." Brzezinski, *Power and Principle*, 480–83.

32. A chance to show resolve: Sick, *All Fall Down*, 304.

33. Brzezinski's approach "felt good": Hamilton Jordan, *Crisis*, 53.

34. President takes responsibility: Farber, *Taken Hostage*, 148.

35. Church bells rung: Denise Bostdorff, *The Presidency and the Rhetoric of Foreign Crisis*, 147.

36. United States in a great battle: Betty Glad, *Jimmy Carter*, 462.

37. SCC meetings: Sick, *All Fall Down*, 211; Brzezinski, *Power and Principle*, 477–78.

38. Vance and Christopher's time devoted to crisis: Vance, *Hard Choices*, 14.

39. Saunders' time spent on crisis: Saunders, "The Crisis Begins," 67.

40. The importance of television in hyping the crisis was manifested after Western reporters had to leave Iran. Thousands of people gathered around the American embassy on July 4, shouting angry slogans. Yet Americans could not be "hurt" by this event because it was not on their evening television news. Carter had stopped most critiques of his handling of the hostage affair for six months after the takeover with his suggestions that the hostages would somehow have been hurt by any show of disunity. A similar call to the colors might well have shamed the television newscasters into giving it less prominence. At least Jeff Gralnick, the executive producer of ABC's *World News Tonight* thought so. See Vance, *Hard Choices*, 380; Sick, *All Fall Down*, 173.

41. Clark/Miller mission: Vance, *Hard Choices*, 376; Saunders, "The Crisis Begins," 74–77. Three days after the hostages were taken, in another endeavor Leon Charney tried to act as intermediary between the United States, Chancellor Bruno Kreisky of Austria, and the Palestine Liberation Organization. Yasir Arafat would purportedly contact Khomeini. It went nowhere. See Robert Lipshutz, "The Hostages—The Austrian Connection," n.d., Plains File, Box 23, F: Iran, undated, JCL.

42. Bourguet and Villalon had been brought to the attention of Carter by General Omar Torrijos, of Panama who had dealt with them in extradition talks concerning the shah of Iran. Smith, "Why Carter Admitted," 86.

43. Jordan and Saunders trip: Hamilton Jordan, *The Crisis*, 112–13.

44. A script the *New York Times* obtained read as follows: The commission would hear the testimony of the alleged crimes, visit the hostages, prepare a report and meet with the Revolutionary Council. Once the hostages had been transferred, the commission would return to New York and submit its findings to UN Secretary General Kurt Waldheim. Three days later, the hostages would leave Iran, and one hour after their departure Waldheim would release the report. The Americans would express their regrets at the "widespread perception of U.S. intervention in Iran's internal affairs." Iran, for its part, would "admit the moral wrong of holding hostages, and promise to respect international law." Smith, "Why Carter Admitted the Shah," 91.

45. On March 19, 1980, the International Court of Justice in the Hague held hearings on U.S. appeals for the release of the hostages based on the information obtained from the thirteen hostages released on November 20, 1979. "US Appeals to World Court," *FF*, March 21, 1980, 203.

46. On student deportation: Brzezinski, *Power and Principle*, 480. See also "Iranian Students in the United States," November 10, 1979, *PP*, 2107; David Aaron to Jimmy Carter, "Deportation of Iranian Students," December 1, 1979, Jordan Collection, Box 34, F: Iran 11/79, JCL.

47. SCC meeting on November 6: Harris, *The Crisis*, 211.

48. SCC meeting on November 23 dealing with military options: Harris, *The Crisis*, 243–44.

49. Intervention could bring Soviets in: Sick, *All Fall Down*, 247, 282.

50. Clark and Miller mission failure: David E. Rosenbaum, "Images of Events that Shocked a Suddenly Vulnerable Nation," *NYT*, January 19, 1981.

51. Waldheim mission failure: Sick, *All Fall Down*, 248.

52. Commission departs Iran: "Khomeini Backs Iranians Holding U.S. Hostages," *FF*, March 14, 1980, 177.

53. Ghotbzadeh suggests killing the shah: Jordan, *Crisis*, 165; Harris, *The Crisis*, 304.

54. Ghotbzadeh to foreign ministry: Harris, *The Crisis*, 249–53.

55. Muslim students on transfer: Ibid., 313.

56. UN Commission of Inquiry: John Kifner, "How a Sit-In Turned into a Siege," *NYT*, May 17, 1981.

57. Bani-Sadr's fears: Harris, *The Crisis*, 313–17.

58. Determining outcome in elections: Tom Mathews, "And Still the Hostages Wait," *Newsweek*, March 3, 1980, 22–24.

59. Rescue: Jean Pelletier, *Canadian Caper;* "Canada to the Rescue," *Time*, February 11, 1980, 20–21. See also Vance, *Hard Choices*, 374–75.

60. Brzezinski was distressed by this effort, feeling that the national honor of the United States was at stake. Brzezinski, *Power and Principle*, 480–81.

61. Carter hanging up: Ibid., 482.

62. Bourguet in Panama: Harris, *The Crisis*, 323.

63. Cutler urges shah to leave: Ibid., 326.

64. Plane departs: Ibid., 326, 328.

65. Shah's death: Sick, *All Fall Down*, 308.

66. Carter's meeting with Bourguet: Harris, *The Crisis*, 333–35. On March 27, Khomeini's office published what was purported to be an apology from Carter. Powell denied that any such apology had been offered, though the published text did include whole or part of previously secret messages to Iran, and Carter had earlier suggested that he might express some sort of concern over events in Iran. Jody Powell, interview, 1981, CPP, 60–63, JCL.

67. Package accepted by United States: ABC Television News (transcript), 43.

68. Announcement: Jimmy Carter, "American Hostages in Iran," April 1, 1980, *PP*, 576–77. Primary results: Glad, *Jimmy Carter*, 470.

69. New sanctions: "Carter's New Take on Iran," *Newsweek*, April 21, 1980, 32.

70. No diplomatic break: Vance, *Hard Choices*, 378.

71. Military threat: "U.S. Warns that Military Move Remains Only Option if Iran Fails to Release American Hostages in Tehran," *FF*, April 18, 1980, 281.

72. Yuma training: Charles Beckwith and Donald Knox, *Delta Force*, 177, 201–2.

73. Training in language and customs: Jason Manning, "The Desert One Disaster" (2000), retrieved March 20, 2009, from http://eightiesclub.tripod.com/id297.htm.

74. CIA operatives on ground in December: Charlie A. Beckwith and Donald Knox, *Delta Force*, 178, 196.

CHAPTER 18. THE SOVIET BRIGADE "CRISIS"

1. Church press conference: "2,300-Man Soviet Unit Now in Cuba," *WP*, August 31, 1979. See also Jimmy Carter, *Keeping Faith*, 262; Cyrus Vance, *Hard Choices*, 361.

2. Stone: Raymond Garthoff, *Detente and Confrontation*, 830.

3. "Ford Angered at Implication He Failed to Spot Troops," *WP*, September 9, 1979.

4. Reagan quoted: *FF*, September 14, 1979, 674.

5. "Jackson Insists Soviet Withdraw Planes in Cuba," *NYT*, September 12, 1979.

6. Soviet motives: David Butler et al., "Russia's Cuban Brigade," *Newsweek*, September 10, 1979, 18–19.

7. SALT Hearing postponed: *FF*, September 7, 1979, 657.

8. On Joint Chiefs: Walter Pincus and George C. Wilson, "Dilemma: Saving SALT II," *WP*, September 9, 1979.

9. Interpretation problems: Anatoly Gribkov, in transcript of the proceedings of the conference, "Global Competition and the Deterioration of U.S.-Soviet Relations, 1977–1980," March 23–26, 1995, Ft. Lauderdale, Florida, 289, VF, USSR-US Conf., Box 117, JCL.

10. Leaks, political goals: William Odom, in "Global Competition" conference transcript, 294.

11. Early intelligence: Ibid., 293.

12. On roles of Odom and Brzezinski in intelligence searches: Zbigniew Brzezinski, *Power and Principle*, 346–47; Jean Garrison, *Games Advisers Play*, 102.

13. Concerns: Odom, in "Global Competition" conference transcript, 296–97, JCL.

14. For NSA Report: Don Oberdorfer, "Cuban Crisis Mishandled, Insiders and Outsiders Agree," *WP*, October 16, 1979; Robert M. Gates, *From the Shadows*, 155, 158–60.

15. No suspicious changes: Gates, *From the Shadows*, 155.

16. Stepping up: Zbigniew Brzezinski to Stansfield Turner: Zbigniew Brzezinski, *Power and Principle*, 346–47.

17. Interpretations of the brigade: Cyrus Vance, *Hard Choices*, 360; Raymond Garthoff, *Détente and Confrontation*, 832–37.

18. Turner, quoted in David D. Newsom, "Foreword," *The Soviet Brigade in Cuba*, viii–x. "Got to the bottom": Stansfield Turner in "Global Competition," conference transcript, 228–30, 302. Use of the word "combat": Garthoff, *Détente and Confrontation*, 835. Turner later recalled that the term had first been used by the National Security Agency (see also Turner in "Global Competition" conference transcript, 300–301). See also Oberdorfer, "Cuban Crisis Mishandled."

19. On Soviet activity: Zbigniew Brzezinski to Jimmy Carter, WR 98, May 25, 1979, Plains File, Box 21, 4/79–9/79, JCL.

20. Warning the president: Brzezinski, *Power and Principle*, 346–47.

21. Holding the Soviet Union accountable: Zbigniew Brzezinski to Jimmy Carter, WR 104, July 27, 1979, ZB Don, Box 42, JCL.

22. Afloat with rumors, dealing with Stone: Newsom, *The Soviet Brigade in Cuba*, 14–15, 20–21. See also Gates, *From the Shadows*, 156; and Garthoff, *Détente and Confrontation*, 835.

23. *Aviation Week* story: Newsom, *The Soviet Brigade in Cuba*, 22; Garthoff, *Détente and Confrontation*, 835–36; Gates, *From the Shadows*, 157. Speculation that anti-SALT participants in the policy process made the leaks: Gloria Duffy, "Crisis Mangling and the Cuba Brigade," *International Security* 8, no. 1 (1983): 67–87.

24. On ill parents: Anatoly Dobrynin, *In Confidence*, 428–29.

25. Report of SCC meeting: August 29, 1979, ZB Don, Box 10, Cuba 9/78–9/79, JCL; there is no mention of Vance attending this meeting. Compare Brzezinski, *Power and Principle*, 347.

26. Communications with Vasev: Garthoff, *Détente and Confrontation*, 837–38.

27. Informing senators: David D. Newsom, *The Soviet Brigade in Cuba*, 20, 34–35.

28. Church's political vulnerabilities: Garthoff, *Détente and Confrontation*, 828, 836–37. Kissing Castro: Marshall Shulman, in "Global Competition" conference transcript, 312–13.

29. Vance press conference: "Soviet Combat Troops in Cuba," September 5, 1979, *PP*, 1602–3.

30. Carter in Plains: Butler et al., "Russia's Cuban Brigade," *Newsweek*, September 10, 1979, 18–19.

31. Brzezinski interview in Garthoff, *Détente and Confrontation*, 831. Robert Pastor, the Latin American expert on the NSC staff, wrote Brzezinski on September 21, 1979, saying that it would be most accurate to describe the Cubans not as "puppets" but as a "Soviet satellite, collaborator, ally or partner"; Robert Pastor to Zbigniew Brzezinski, September 21, 1979, Countries, Executive Files, Box C021, WHCF, CO38 7/1/79–1/20/81, JCL. Pastor realized that the Cubans were dependent on the Soviet Union. But Cuba, he noted, "saw itself as an independent actor and of course there was no way the Soviets could have ordered the Cubans to play a roll internationally if they chose not to do so" (Pastor, telephone interview with the author, August 30, 2004).

32. Straddling of the issue: Cabinet Meeting Minutes, September 10, 1979, Plains File, Box 18, Cabinet Minutes 9/78–12/79, JCL.

33. Inman chronology and CIA corroboration: Robert Gates, *From the Shadows*, 158. Conclusions that the Soviet troops had been in Cuba since the 1960s and did not represent a threat to the United States: "Updated Report on Soviet ground Forces Brigade in Cuba," interagency memo, September 18, 1979, White House Central Files, Box 34, Jordan Confidential File, Cuba–USSR Brigade, JCL.

34. Gromyko calls: Dobrynin, in "Global Competition" conference transcript, 287.

35. Dobrynin at State Department: "Cooling the Cuba Crisis," *Time*, September 24, 1979, 19; Anatoly Dobrynin, *In Confidence*, 428–29.

36. Vance queries: Dobrynin, in "Global Competition" conference transcript, 313.

37. Instructions to Vance: Zbigniew Brzezinski to Jimmy Carter, "Soviet Brigade in Cuba," September 19, 1979, Geographic File, Box 10, Cuba 9/78–9/79, JCL.

38. Negotiating sessions: Gates, *From the Shadows*, 158–59; "Vance Sees Dobrynin, Gromyko," FF, October 5, 1979, 738; James Hershberg, in "Global Competition" conference transcript, 305.

39. Soviets not backing down: Marshall Brement to Zbigniew Brzezinski, September 12, 1979, Brzezinski Subject File, Box 33, F: VBB Meetings 8/79–9/79, JCL.

40. *Pravda* quoted: Kevin Klose and Don Oberdorfer, "Kremlin Defends Troops in Cuba as Training Unit," WP, September 11, 1979. See also "Global Competition" conference transcript, 287–90, 304; Garthoff, *Détente and Confrontation*, 838–39.

41. Gromyko's UN Speech: Tom Morganthau et al., "Has Carter Saved SALT?" *Newsweek*, October 15, 1979, 63–67. Dobrynin assisting on wording of communiqué: "Global Competition" conference transcript, 304. See also Dan Caldwell, *The Dynamics of Domestic Policies and Arms Control*, 165.

42. Cosmetic outcome, suggested steps, political benefits: Zbigniew Brzezinski to Jimmy Carter, memo, September n.d., Geographic File, Box 10, Cuba 9/78–9/79, JCL.

43. Comparison to Berlin Wall: Zbigniew Brzezinski to Jimmy Carter, September 21, 1979, Geographic File, Box 10, Cuba 9/78–9/79, JCL.

44. Jimmy Carter, press announcement on MX basing, Speechwriters File, Box 52, F: 9/7/79, JCL.

45. Unnamed sources: Caldwell, *Dynamics*, 165.

46. Brzezinski comparison to Berlin crisis: Oswald Johnson and Don Irwin, "Carter Plans Actions on Cuba Troop Issue," *Los Angeles Times*, September 29, 1979, quoted in Caldwell, *Dynamics*, 165, n. 53.

47. Brown's visit to the PRC: Newsom, *The Soviet Brigade in Cuba*, 49.

48. Byrd meeting with the president: Brzezinski, *Power and Principle*, 350; Carter, *Keeping Faith*, 263; Robert G. Kaiser, "To Save SALT, Sen. Byrd Huddled in Secret with Soviet," WP, October 18, 1979.

49. Deeply puzzled: Kaiser, "To Save SALT." See also Joanne Omang, "Byrd Urges Colleagues Not to Link SALT to Cuban Situation," WP, September 9, 1979; Brzezinski, *Power and Principle*, 350.

50. Opposing "wise men": Brzezinski, *Power and Principle*, 350; Vance, *Hard Choices*, 363–64.

51. Response: Leonid Brezhnev to Jimmy Carter, September 27, 1979, ZB Don, Box 18, F: Carter–Brezhnev Corr., 9/79–2/80, JCL.

52. The wise men were a bipartisan group of formerly high-level Republican and Democratic policymakers. Included were three former secretaries of state—Dean Rusk, William Rogers, and Henry Kissinger, plus George W. Ball, McGeorge Bundy, Clark Clifford, Roswell L. Gilpatric, W. Averell Harriman, Nicholas de Katzenbach, Sol Linowitz, John J. McCloy, John A. McCone, David Packard, James Schlesinger, Brent Scowcroft, and William Scranton. "The Alumni Committee," Plains File, Box 21, Cuba: Soviet troops, 9–10/79, JCL. Other details: "Carter

Defuses a Crisis," *Time*, October 15, 1979, 44; Don Oberdorfer, "Vance, Dobrynin Confer Again on Troops in Cuba," *WP*, October 1, 1979. Former secretary of defense Clark Clifford, who headed the new group, had assembled many of the same men to advise Lyndon Johnson to seek an exit from Vietnam in 1968. John Donovan, *Cold Warriors*, 248–50. See also Clark Clifford, *Counsel to the President*, 637–39.

53. Folly on brigade: McGeorge Bundy to Clark Clifford, September 26, 1979, White House Central File, Chief of Staff: Butler, Box 130, SALT Memoranda and Correspondence 9/1/79–1/3/80, [CF, O/A 563], JCL.

54. Losing track of brigade: Clifford, *Counsel to the President*, 637; McGeorge Bundy, "The Brigade Is My Fault," *NYT*, September 12, 1979.

55. "Wise men" meet with Brzezinski: "Carter Defuses a Crisis," 44; Vance, *Hard Choices*, 363–64.

56. Photographs: William Scranton to Jimmy Carter, October 15, 1979, Plains File, Box 21, Cuba: Soviet Troops, 9–10/79, JCL.

57. Isolating issues: Cyrus Vance, *Hard Choices*, 363–64; Brzezinski, *Power and Principle*, 348–49.

58. Battle over speech: Jean Garrison, *Games Advisers Play*, 116, n. 172. Participants: Harold Brown, Zbigniew Brzezinski, Stansfield Turner, Lloyd Cutler, Warren Christopher, and David Aaron; Don Oberdorfer, "Vance, Dobrynin Confer Again on Troops in Cuba," *WP*, October 1, 1979.

59. The brigade: Brzezinski, *Power and Principle*, 350. Allied with Brzezinski were economic consultants Henry Owen and Robert Strauss, both of whom wanted the speech to end with an emphasis on a military buildup. Hamilton Jordan sent the president a memo suggesting that he should say "I am not going to play politics with the security of the United States." Hamilton Jordan to Jimmy Carter, "Cuba Speech," September 29, 1979, Speechwriters File, Box 55, JCL.

60. Addressing the nation: "Carter Defuses a Crisis," 43–44.

61. Jimmy Carter, "Carter's Speech on U.S. Intentions Toward Cuba," *FF*, October 5, 1979, 738–39. See also draft of speech, Rick Hertzberg to Susan Clough, September 30, 1979, Speechwriters File, Box 55, JCL. A background briefing downplayed the potential threat: "We have available for use the forces to defend ourselves, forces which to this are as a giant to an ant." "Background on the Question of Soviet Troops in Cuba," *DSB* 79, no. 2032 (November 1979): 9–11. The follow-up was a military demonstration. On October 5, SR-71 reconnaissance flights resumed over Cuba. Twelve days later 1,800 Marines, under the new Caribbean Joint Task force, landed in Guantanamo Bay for a military exercise.

62. Birthday party: "Carter Defuses a Crisis," 43.

63. Advisors absent: Brzezinski, *Power and Principle*, 351.

64. Confrontation with Carter: Ibid., 351–52.

65. Senate resolution: Angus Deming et al., "Carter's Cuban Dilemma," *Newsweek*, October 8, 1979, 24–25.

66. *Pravda* editorial: Klose and Oberdorfer, "Kremlin Defends Troops."

67. Bundy takes blame: Bundy, "The Brigade Is My Fault," *NYT*, October 23, 1979.

68. Vance on SALT, October 10: "Arms Control: SALT II—A Summation," *DSB* 70, no. 2032 (November 1979): 24.

69. Explanation of monitoring: "The Secretary: Where We Stand with SALT II," October 26, 1979, *DSB* 79, no. 2033 (December 1979): 21, 23.

70. Snatching defeat from victory: Tom Wicker, "Out of the Closet," *NYT*, September 18, 1979.

71. Broader concerns about Cuban activities in the Caribbean: Zbigniew Brzezinski to Jimmy Carter, WR 111, October 5, 1979, ZB Don, Box 42, JCL. For the Cutler paper on the topic, see Gates, *From the Shadows*, 160.

72. Labor Day: Shulman, in "Global Competition" conference transcript, 312.

73. Byrd on mishandling crisis: "Search for a Way Out," *Time*, October 8, 1979, 26.

74. Assigning responsibility: Zbigniew Brzezinski to Jimmy Carter, WR 112, October 12, 1979, ZB Don, Box 42, JCL.

75. Hall quoted: "Search for a Way Out," 26.

76. Biggest mistake: Forrester Church, *Father and Son*, Church himself would tell his son Forrester that it was the biggest mistake of his life.

77. Vote in 1980: Arthur Schlesinger, *History of American Presidential Elections, 1789–1984*, supplemental vol., 221. Stone also lost.

78. Church's loss: R. Gwenn Stearn, "Frank Church Chronology," March 17, 2006, Frank Church Papers, Boise State University Library, retrieved February 14, 2008, from http://library.boisestate.edu/special/church/church1.htm. The exit polls' influence on voters is discussed in Seymour Sudman, "Do Exit Polls Influence Voting Behavior?" *Public Opinion Quarterly* 50, no. 3 (1986): 331–39.

79. Byrd on SALT: Brzezinski, *Power and Principle*, 350.

80. Result of fiasco: Ibid., 352–53.

81. Long and the loss of a crucial vote: Raymond Garthoff, *Détente and Confrontation*, 847, n. 57.

82. Soviet suspicions: Garthoff, *Détente and Confrontation*, 840–41; Dobrynin, in "Global Competition" conference transcript, 287. Though Ambassador Dobrynin saw the U.S. actions regarding the brigade as rooted in faulty intelligence and political mistakes, other Soviet officials saw purposive action—an endeavor by the administration to sink SALT II. They did not understand, as Dobrynin noted, the decentralized nature of much foreign policymaking in the United States.

CHAPTER 19. AFGHANISTAN: FORMULATING A RESPONSE

1. On friendship treaty: Leonid Brezhnev to Jimmy Carter, December 29, 1979, ZB Don, Box 17, Geographic File: Southwest Asia/Persian Gulf/Afghanistan, 12/26/79–1/4/80, JCL.

2. Entry into Kabul: "Steel Fist in Kabul," *Time*, January 7, 1980, 72–73, 76. See also "How the Soviet Army Crushed Afghanistan," *Time*, January 14, 1980, 20–24.

3. Carter upset: Rosalynn Carter, *First Lady from Plains*, 314–15.

4. Disappointment: Jimmy Carter, *Keeping Faith*, 265.

5. Depth of frustration: Hamilton Jordan, *Crisis*, 99.

6. For the text of the interview, see Jimmy Carter, "The White House Interview with the President," interview by Frank Reynolds, ABC News, December 31, 1979, Geographic File: Box 17, Southwest Asia/Persian Gulf/Afghanistan, 12/26/79–1/4/80, JCL. Carter response: "My Opinion of the Russians has Changed Most Drastically," *Time*, January 14, 1980, 10–17. See also Anatoly Dobrynin, *In Confidence*, 445.

7. Hedley Donovan to Jimmy Carter, January 2, 1980, Donovan Collection, Box 2, Memos to the President 8/21/79–8/14/80, JCL.

8. Soviet distrust of Amin: Anatoly Dobrynin, *In Confidence*, 436. Counterproductive measures: Zbigniew Brzezinski, *Power and Principle*, 427.

9. Presidential findings: Staff Offices, Counsel Cutler, Box 60, CIA Charter 2/9–25/80, JCL. CIA alerts in the fall: Robert M. Gates, *From the Shadows*, 132–33.

10. CIA, weapons to Pakistan: Gates, *From the Shadows*, 146–47.

11. Orders to State Department: Brzezinski, *Power and Principle*, 428. See also Peter Tarnoff to Zbigniew Brzezinski, October 11, 1979, VF, USSR 7/77–12/79, JCL. See also Gates, *From the Shadows*, 132–33.

12. Interagency contingency plans: Gates, *From the Shadows*, 133; Brzezinski, *Power and Principle*, 427–28.

13. On broadcasts to Muslims: Brzezinski, *Power and Principle*, 428.

14. On possible Soviet intervention: Zbigniew Brzezinski to Jimmy Carter, WR 78, November 3, 1978, ZB Don, Box 42, JCL. As Brzezinski recalls, the day that the Soviets officially

crossed the border, he wrote to Carter: "Indeed, for almost ten years, Moscow had to carry on a war unsupportable by the government, a conflict that brought about the demoralization and finally the breakup of the Soviet empire." Brzezinski, "Oui, la CIA est entrée en Afghanistan avant les Russes…," interview by Vincent Jauvert, *Le Nouvel Observateur*, January 15, 1998, translated by Bill Blum; retrieved February 14, 2008, from_http://www.counterpunch.org/brzezinski. html. Still, at the time Brzezinski was not "too sanguine about Afghanistan becoming a Soviet Vietnam." As he pointed out, the guerillas were poorly organized, had no sanctuaries, no central government, and limited foreign support. Zbigniew Brzezinski to Jimmy Carter, December 26, 1979, "Reflections on Soviet Intervention in Afghanistan," ZB Don, Box 17, Geographic File: Southwest Asia/Persian Gulf/Afghanistan, 12/26/79–1/4/80, JCL.

15. "Down slide" in Afghanistan: Marshall Shulman to Cyrus Vance, December 14, 1979, VF, USSR-US Conf., BBII, 2–3, JCL.

16. Pro-Soviet regime: SCC Meeting, December 17, 1979, ZB Don, Box 31: F Meetings-SCC: 11/14/1979–01/14/1980, JCL.

17. NSA Alerts: Gates, *From the Shadows*, 133.

18. Serious problems in future: Jimmy Carter, quoted in Jordan, *Crisis*, 100; Rosalynn Carter, *First Lady from Plains*, 315.

19. Preliminary considerations: Zbigniew Brzezinski to Jimmy Carter, December 26, 1979, Box 17, Geographic file: Southwest Asia/Persian Gulf/Afghanistan 12/26/79–1/4/80, JCL.

20. Making Soviets pay: Carter, *Keeping Faith*, 472.

21. Standing tough: Robert Bergland, interview, 1986, CPP, 102, JCL; Carter, *Keeping Faith*, 476.

22. Atheistic government, measures: "Soviet Invasion of Afghanistan," January 4, 1980, *PP*, 21–24; Jordan, *Crisis*, 100; Carter, *Keeping Faith*, 483; Brzezinski, *Power and Principle*, 427–32, 456.

23. Declaring U.S. boycott of the Olympics: *Meet the Press*, January 20, 1980, *PP*, 107–8. See also Carter, *Keeping Faith*, 481–82. Cutler and Wexler to Carter, "Briefing with Athletes," n.d., ZB Don, Box 34-68, Subject File, Olympics, 3/80, JCL.

24. Most serious threat to security framework: Jimmy Carter, "State of the Union Address," January 21, 1980, *PP*, 163–79. Extending military guarantees to Middle East: Brzezinski, *Power and Principle*, 444–45; Carter, *Keeping Faith*, 473, 476. Final policy: PD/NSC-63, "Persian Gulf Security Framework," January 15, 1981, ZB Don, Box 24, Meetings: Muskie/Brown/Brzezinski, 10/80–1/81, JCL.

25. Modeled on Truman doctrine: Brzezinski, *Power and Principle*, 445–46.

26. Threat to world political system: Jimmy Carter, "American Society of Newspaper Editors," April 10, 1980, *PP*, 636, 642.

27. Olympic boycott, NSC meeting: Carter, *Keeping Faith*, 481.

28. Mondale versus grain embargo: Ibid., 476, 482–83; Jordan, *Crisis*, 100.

29. Opposing grain embargo: Stuart Eizenstat to Jimmy Carter, January 3, 1980, Cutler Box, Staff Offices, JCL.

30. Embargo not hurting Russians: Robert Bergland, interview, 1986, CPP, 102, JCL. See also Blaine Harden, "Bergland Taken Out as Farmers Storm Agriculture," *WP*, March 12, 1978.

31. Building support for security relationship: Brzezinski/aides interviews, 1982, CPP, 31–32, JCL; Brzezinski, *Power and Principle*, 444–45.

32. Members of security group: Zbigniew Brzezinski to Jimmy Carter, memo, January 9, 1980, VF, USSR-US Conf. 5/6–9/94, F: USSR 1980–1993, JCL.

33. Controversy over address: Brzezinski, *Power and Principle*, 444, 450.

34. Screaming match: David Mayers, *The Ambassadors and America's Soviet Policy*, 233–37.

35. Embassy report: Marshall Brement to Zbigniew Brzezinski, February 7, 1980, ZB Don, Box 34, F: VBB: 1/80–3/80, JCL. For original cable, American Embassy–Moscow to Secretary of State, January 30, 1980, ZB Don, Box 34, F: VBB 1/80–2/80, JCL.

36. Dismissing cable: Marshall Brement to Zbigniew Brzezinski, February 7, 1980, ZB Don, Box 34: F: VBB 1/80–3/80, JCL.

37. The interest of all: Cyrus Vance to Andrei Gromyko, February 8, 1980, Plains File, Box 17, F: Brezhnev–Carter Corr. 1980, JCL. See also Cyrus Vance, *Hard Choices*, 394–95; and Dobrynin, *In Confidence*, 446–49.

38. Gromyko rejects meeting: Dobrynin, *In Confidence*, 449.

39. Oval Office meeting: Brzezinski, *Power and Principle*, 435–36.

40. Conditions for the Soviets: Zbigniew Brzezinski to Jimmy Carter, WR 131, February 29, 1980, ZB Don, Box 42, JCL.

41. Sharp letter: Jimmy Carter to Leonid Brezhnev, draft, February 29, 1980, ZB Don, Box 18, F: Carter-Brezhnev Corr. 9/79–2/80, JCL.

42. Cover letter: Brzezinski, *Power and Principle*, 435–36.

43. Jimmy Carter to Zbigniew Brzezinski, February 29, 1980, ZB Don, Box 18, F: Barter-Brezhnev Corr., 9/79–2/81. He also noted that he had Dobrynin out to his house for lunch to "reiterate that this is a serious approach, on which we can deliver from our end."

44. Brzezinski on Shulman: Zbigniew Brzezinski to the author, March 1, 2005.

45. Shulman to Moscow: Dobrynin, *In Confidence*, 450; Vance, *Hard Choices*, 395.

46. Shulman's answer: Transcript of the proceedings of the conference "Global Competition and the Deterioration of U.S.-Soviet Relations, 1977–1980," March 23–26, 1995, Ft. Lauderdale, Florida, 282, VF, USSR-U.S. Conf., Box 117, JCL.

47. Meeting with Dobrynin: Zbigniew Brzezinski to Jimmy Carter, WR 131, February 29, 1980, ZB Don, Box 42, JCL.

48. "Rather queer": Dobrynin, *In Confidence*, 450–51.

49. Criticism of French meeting: "Paris Affirms Right to Meet with Soviet," Paul Lewis, *NYT*, May 22, 1980.

50. "Schmidt, in a Letter to Carter, Asks Private Meeting at Venice Talks," *NYT*, June 19, 1980; "Schmidt Plans to Tell Brezhnev Moscow Cannot Divide Allies," *NYT*, June 24, 1980.

51. John Vincour, "The Schmidt Factor," *NYT*, September 21, 1980.

52. Schools of thought: Zbigniew Brzezinski to Jimmy Carter, WR 134, March 28, 1980, ZB Don, Box 42, JCL.

53. Soviets more assertive: Zbigniew Brzezinski to Jimmy Carter, "A Long-term Strategy for Coping with the Consequences of Soviet Action in Afghanistan," January 9, 1980, VF, USSR-US Conf. 5/6–9/94, F: USSR-1980–1993, JCL. See also Jerel Rosati, *The Carter Administration's Quest for Global Community*, 87.

54. Soviet moves in Middle East: Brzezinski, "Interview," *Wall Street Journal*, January 15, 1980.

55. Soviet motives: Cyrus Vance, *Hard Choices*, 367–88.

56. R. Carter, *First Lady from Plains*, 315.

CHAPTER 20. EXACTING A PRICE

1. Pride at breakfast meeting: Hamilton Jordan, *Crisis*, 112.

2. Cooler than others: Jimmy Carter, *Keeping Faith*, 524.

3. Draft registration, sacrifice: Ibid., 482–85.

4. Carter on the grain embargo: Jordan, *Crisis*, 100.

5. Public support: Of Americans surveyed, 57 percent said they approved of the way Carter was handling the Afghanistan situation; 76 percent approved of Carter's decision to halt grain sales to the Soviet Union; and 72 percent favored moving the 1980 Olympics to another nation as a protest against Soviet intervention in Afghanistan. *Gallup*, The Gallup Poll: Public Opinion 1980, 17–18.

6. Other supporters: "Carter Olympic Stand Gains Support," *FF*, February 1, 1980, 67.

7. Petition: Ed Sanders to Hamilton Jordan and Zbigniew Brzezinski, January 16, 1980, ZB Don, Box 34-68, NSA-Olympics 6/79–2/80, JCL.

8. Prolonging battle: Eugene Rostow to Cyrus Vance, January 9, 1980, Vance Mss., Cutler Box, Staff Office, YUL.

9. Committee on the Present Danger: Charles Tyroler III, *Alerting America*, 175, 177. The committee's January 22, 1980, newsletter noted, "The tides are once again rushing the world toward general war." Even after Reagan had come to office, in its March 1982 newsletter the committee warned that the "failure to close the window of vulnerability could tempt the Soviet Union to exploit its vast military power." See Tyroler, ed., *Alerting America*, 196–97.

10. Critique: "Transcript of Kennedy's Speech at Georgetown University on Campaign Issues," January 29, 1980, *NYT*. See also Anthony Lewis, "Abroad at Home," *NYT*, January 31, 1980; "Kennedy Winds Up Debating Rosalynn Carter from Afar," *WP*, February 2, 1980, A4.

11. Republican critiques: Jordan, *Crisis*, 101.

12. Reagan critiques: Lou Cannon, "Reagan: Let Athletes Make Olympic Games Decision," April 1, 1980, *WP*.

13. Anderson: Robert Mackay, "Two Who Also Run: Anderson and Crane," *Illinois Issues*, March 6, 1980; Carter, *Keeping Faith*, 477. After not doing well in the Republican primaries, Anderson would later run on the National Union Party ticket.

14. Mondale in Iowa: Carter, *Keeping Faith*, 476; Zbigniew Brzezinski, *Power and Principle*, 430.

15. Works to implement: Robert Bergland to the author, January 14, 2005.

16. Grain embargo at home: "US Grain Trading Suspended," *FF*, January 7, 1980, 2; "U.S. to Buy Soviet Grain contracts," *FF*, January 11, 1980, 9.

17. Carter on embargo: Carter, *Keeping Faith*, 476.

18. Persuading others: Ibid., 474–78.

19. Argentine response: "Argentina Rejects Grain Ban," *FF*, January 18, 1980, 28.

20. Problems with West Germany: Brzezinski, *Power and Principle*, 462.

21. Germany's decisions: Carter, *Keeping Faith*, 537.

22. Problems, grain embargo: Zbigniew Brzezinski to Jimmy Carter, WR 146, June 26, 1980, ZB Don, Box 142, JCL.

23. Reagan lifts embargo: "Back in Business Again," *Time*, June 22, 1981, 16.

24. Kane's Opposition: F. Don Miller to Jimmy Carter, January 3, 1980, ZB Don, Box 34-68, Olympics 6/79–2/80, JCL.

25. Responses of Kane, Killian, IOC: Barry Lorge, "Olympics Pullout Eyed," *WP*, January 17, 1980.

26. IOC on Olympic violations: Lloyd Cutler to Zbigniew Brzezinski and Jimmy Carter, February 12, 1980, ZB Don, Box 34-68, Olympics 6/79–2/80, JCL.

27. Cutler's alternative to Olympics: Brzezinski, *Power and Principle*, 434.

28. In Geneva: Diane K. Shah, "The Carter Games Plan," *Newsweek*, March 31, 1980, 68.

29. Jimmy Carter, remarks to U.S. Summer Olympic representatives, March 21, 1980, Plains File, Box 18, Staff Office: Speechwriters, Olympics 1980, 1/1/1980–8/31/19 JCL. Plans regarding this meeting: Lloyd Cutler and Anne Wexler to Jimmy Carter, "Briefing with Athletes," n.d., ZB Don, Box 34-68, Olympics, 3/80, JCL.

30. Responses of U.S. athletes: Kenny Moore, "Stating Iron Realities," *Sports Illustrated*, March 31, 1980, 16–17.

31. Limited legal authority: Lloyd Cutler and Joe Onek to Carter, January 17, 1980, ZB Don, Box 34-68, Olympics, 6/79–2/80, JCL.

32. Other pressure: Clyde Farnsworth, March 29, 1980, Plains File, Box 19, Staff Office: Speechwriters, Olympics 1980, 1/1/1980–8/31/1980, JCL.

33. Heavy artillery: Shah, "The Carter Games Plan," 68. On passports: Andy Walton, "CNN Cold War Spotlight: Olympic Boycotts," retrieved February 14, 2008, from http://www.cnn.com/SPECIALS/cold.war/episodes/20/spotlight.

34. USOC vote: Shah, "The Carter Games Plan," 68.

35. Legal challenge: *De Frantz v. United States Olympic Committee*, 492 F. Supp. 1181 (D.D.C. 1980): United States Olympic Committee, *Olympic Related Court Cases Index*, 2008,

retrieved October 29, 2008, from http://teamusa.org/content/index/1576. See also Warren Christopher to Jimmy Carter, May 13, 1980, Plains File, Box 40, State Department Evening Reports, 5/1980, JCL.

36. Independent bodies: Carter, *Keeping Faith*, 526.

37. Jimmy Carter to Helmut Schmidt, January 25, 1980, Plains File, Box 1, Presidential Correspondence, F: Federal Republic of Germany, 9/77–8/80, JCL.

38. Conversation with Schmidt two weeks later: Transcript, Plains File, Box 1, F: Federal Republic of Germany, 9/77–11/80, JCL.

39. Other responses: "European Olympic Panels Rebuff U.S." *FF,* April 11, 1980, 259. Norway: Shah, "The Carter Games Plan," 68.

40. Conversation with Schmidt: Transcript, May 15, 1980, Plains File, Box 1, F: Federal Republic of Germany, 9/77–11/80, JCL.

41. Attendance at Olympics: "The Saddest Olympics," *NYT,* July 19, 1980; Walton, "CNN Cold War Spotlight: Olympic Boycotts"; "France Says 'Oui' to the Moscow Olympics," Paul Lewis, *NYT,* May 18, 1980. The House of Commons of Great Britain voted overwhelmingly for the boycott, and British officials exerted great pressure to stop their own athletes from going. But "the public sided with them [the athletes] rather than with Mrs. Thatcher and the Commons." R. W. Apple Jr., *NYT,* March 26, 1980, Plains File, Box 18, Staff Officers Speechwriters-Olympics 1980 1/1/1980–8/31/1980, JCL.

42. Success: Zbigniew Brzezinski to Jimmy Carter, WR 144, June 6, 1978, ZB Don, Box 41, JCL.

43. Cost to athletes: Christine Brennan, "25 Years Later, Olympic Boycott Gnaws at Athletes," *USA Today,* April 13, 2005, retrieved February 14, 2008, from http://www.usatoday.com/sports/columnist/brennan/2005-04-13-brennan_x.htm.

44. On carrying the torch: Mike Moran, "Almost Armageddon," October 15, 2002, from http://www.usolympicteam.com/moran/story3.html.

45. Pulling teeth: Zbigniew Brzezinski to Jimmy Carter, WR 141, May 16, 1980, ZB Don, Box 41, JCL.

46. Brzezinski at Khyber Pass: CNN Report, "Episode 20: Soldiers of God," n.d., retrieved October 29, 2008, from http://www.cnn.com/SPECIALS/cold.war/episodes/20/script.html.

47. Saudi arms, Zia aide: Zbigniew Brzezinski, *Power and Principle*, 448–49.

48. Corrections of impressions: Zbigniew Brzezinski to Jimmy Carter, June 3, 1980, cited in Brzezinski, *Power and Principle*, 460.

49. Mixed motives in Politburo: Anatoly Dobrynin, *In Confidence*, 437–42.

50. Military opposition: Anatoly Gribkov, in transcript of the proceedings of the conference "Global Competition and the Deterioration of U.S.-Soviet Relations, 1977–1980," March 23–26, 1995, Ft. Lauderdale, Florida, 291, VF, USSR-U.S. Conf., Box 117, JCL. A week before the troops were deployed, Gribkov suggested to Ogarkov and Kulikov that the attack would be reckless. Nobody, especially Ustinov, wanted to listen.

51. Diplomats not consulted: Dobrynin, *In Confidence*, 439.

52. Embassy in Kabul opposed: Ibid., 436.

53. Invasion as Soviet reaction: Ibid., 441.

54. Soviets on U.S. response: Ibid., 452.

55. The CIA "eyes only" report to the president, "Soviet Options in Southwest Asia After the Invasion of Afghanistan," argued that the Soviet move was not the first setup in a highly articulated "grand design for control over all of Southwest Asia" that had long been probing the limits of U.S. tolerance. Robert M. Gates, *From the Shadows*, 147–48.

56. Intelligence reports: Ibid.

57. Blowback: Stephen Kinzer, *Overthrow* (New York: Times Books, 2006), 263–71.

58. Bin Laden on Soviets and the United States: "Transcript of Bin Laden's October Interview" [conducted by Al-Jazeera correspondent Tayseer Alouni], February 5, 2002, retrieved

February 14, 2008, from http://archives.cnn.com/2002/WORLD/asiapcf/south/02/05/binladen.transcript/.

59. Quote on financing own assassins: Kinzer, *Overthrow*, 269.

60. Japanese ambassador on Carter: Dobrynin, *In Confidence*, 453–54.

61. Demoralization of Vance: Ibid., 446.

62. Vance's resignation: Ibid., 453–54.

63. Vance's resignation: Thomas J. Watson to Cyrus Vance, February 20, 1980, Vance Mss, Box 54/78, YUL.

64. SALT nonratification: Henry Cabot Lodge to Cyrus Vance, June 9, 1980, Vance Mss, Box 12/38, YUL.

65. Harriman's response: Dobrynin, *In Confidence*, 457.

66. Need to drop from public view: Jody Powell to Jimmy Carter, May 1, 1980, Powell, Box 38, 5/1/80–5/30/80, JCL.

67. Muskie: Jimmy Carter, "Department of State," *PP*, April 29, 1980, 791–92. See also Jimmy Carter, "Philadelphia, Pennsylvania," *PP*, May 9, 1980, 881.

CHAPTER 21. MAD AND THE PURSUIT OF PD-59

1. Anticipating Reagan: Turner, in transcript of the proceedings of the conference "Global Competition and the Deterioration of U.S.-Soviet Relations, 1977–1980," March 23–26, 1995, Ft. Lauderdale, Florida, 224, VF, USSR-US Conf., Box 117, JCL.

2. "PD/NSC-59, Nuclear Weapons Employment Policy," July 25, 1980, VF, JCL.

3. Tass, quoted in Dusk Doder, "Soviets Assail Carter Nuclear Plan as 'Insanity,'" *WP*, August 12, 1980.

4. Warnke, Kennedy, and others on PD 59: Richard Burt, "Pentagon Chief Reassures Allies on War Strategy," *NYT*, August 11, 1980, A1.

5. Being more Republican than the Republicans: Burt, "Pentagon Chief Reassures Allies"; Richard Burt, "The World: A New Order of Debate on Atomic War," *NYT*, August 17, 1980.

6. Reagan critique: Steven V. Roberts, "Reagan, in Chicago Speech, Urges Big Increases in Military Spending," *NYT*, March 18, 1980. See also Don Oberdorfer, "Carter's Foreign, Defense Policies Denounced by GOP," *WP*, March 2, 1979.

7. Republican Party platform: Donald B. Johnson, *National Party Platforms of 1980*, 205–6.

8. On nuclear weapons: Klaus Knorr, *On the Uses of Military Power in the Nuclear Age*, 1–16, 173–76.

9. MAD: Burt, "The World."

10. Theory of commitments: Thomas C. Schelling, *The Strategy of Conflict*, 119–61.

11. Address to General Assembly: Jimmy Carter, "United Nations," October 4, 1977, *PP*, 1716. See also Zbigniew Brzezinski, *Power and Principle*, 49–50.

12. Invulnerability concept, Ustinov and Brezhnev: Jimmy Carter, *Keeping Faith*, 251–52.

13. Harold Brown, e-mail to the author, October 18, 2008.

14. Odom on strategy: "Global Competition" conference transcript, 225–33.

15. Understanding Soviet thinking: Brzezinski, *Power and Principle*, 455–59. For Harold Brown's discussion of this topic, see Harold Brown, *Thinking about National Security*, 80–83.

16. Emphasis on U.S. power: Brzezinski, *Power and Principle*, 469.

17. Gelb on Schlesinger: "Global Competition" conference transcript, 225–33.

18. Turner on silos in Eastern Europe: "Global Competition" conference transcript, 225–33, JCL.

19. Slighting of Muskie: Bernard Gwertzman, "It's a Tough Company for On the Job Training," *NYT*, August 17, 1980; Bernard Gwertzman, "Muskie Wasn't Told of New War Policy before It Was Set," *NYT*, August 10, 1980.

20. Secretary of State told at breakfast: Zbigniew Brzezinski to Jimmy Carter, WR 150, August 22, 1980, ZB Don, Box 42, JCL. Odom told Brzezinski that Brown might raise the PD 59 issues at lunch that day, and "the sooner you let Muskie know the better." Zbigniew Brzezinski to Jimmy Carter, WR 150, August 22, 1980, ZB Don, Box 42, JCL.

21. Recounting PD 59 history, informing Muskie: Zbigniew Brzezinski to Jimmy Carter, WR 150, August 22, 1980, ZB Don, Box 42, JCL.

22. On PD 18, U.S. National Strategy, August 24, 1977: Brzezinski, *Power and Principle*, 456.

23. Sloss developed many of the key concepts that would find their way into the presidential directive—e.g., the need for a reserve nuclear force and targeting military and political centers. There were provisions, he claims, for the withholding of "attacks on targets in Moscow area...precisely to permit them to retain control over their nuclear forces. There was also the Moscow–Washington hotline...that would have permitted us to send messages signaling restraint. Whether there were specific plans to do this once a war began, I do not know." Leon Sloss to the author, February 21, 2005 and November 2, 2004. Sloss claims that NSDM 242 made more significant changes to traditional policy than PD 59, though the latter "gave the President more options." For more on Sloss, see Richard Burt, "The New Strategy for Nuclear War," *NYT*, August 13, 1980, A3.

24. Odom, discussions in Pentagon: Brzezinski, *Power and Principle*, 456–57. Brown, as a campaign advisor to Carter in 1976, spoke of two goals regarding nuclear weapons: improving or stabilizing deterrence, and improving likely outcome for the United States in case of thermonuclear exchange, Brown memo, May 16, Box 8/page 8, Vance MSS, YUL.

25. All of these directives are available in the Presidential Directives File of the Vertical File at JCL. See also Brzezinski, *Power and Principle*, 456–59.

26. Jimmy Carter to Helmut Schmidt, June 1, 1979, Box 1, Plains File, Afghanistan 3/77–2/80, JCL.

27. Even Brzezinski noted that "Putting the M-X missile in Minutemen silos...would increase crisis instability." Trident II, a "survivable hard target-weapon," he suggested, was an answer to this problem; Zbigniew Brzezinski to Jimmy Carter, WR 50, March 10, 1978, ZB Don, Box 41, JCL. In a memo to Carter on May 26 Brzezinski noted that the MX missile as a land-based weapon was vulnerable to a first strike by the increasingly accurate Soviet ICBMs, making it a missile one would have to use first or lose: Zbigniew Brzezinski to Jimmy Carter, WR 60, May 26, 1978, ZB Don, Box 41, JCL.

28. MIRVs and concealment: David Aaron to Jimmy Carter, WR 59, May 19, 1978, ZB Don, Box 41, JCL.

29. Launch on warning incentive: Arthur M. Cox, *The Dynamics of Détente*, 25–26, 84.

30. No formal meeting: Brzezinski, *Power and Principle*, 458.

31. Good policy and the NSC: David J. Rothkopf, *Running the World*, 51–60.

32. Rundown on State: Zbigniew Brzezinski to Jimmy Carter, May 1, 1980, ZB Don, Box 23, F: Meetings Brown/Brzezinski, JCL.

33. Muskie following up: Zbigniew Brzezinski to Jimmy Carter, WR 144, June 6, 1980, ZB Don, Box 42, JCL.

34. Brown on limited nuclear war possibility: U.S. Congress, Senate, *Nuclear War Strategy: Hearing before the Committee on Foreign Relations*, September 16, 1980, 25–26.

35. Percy queries: U.S. Congress, *Nuclear War Strategy: Hearing before the Committee on Foreign Relations*, September 16, 1980, 25–26.

36. Brown on asymmetry of motivations: Ibid.

37. Farmed out projects: Walter Pincus, "Thinking the Unthinkable: Studying New Approaches to a Nuclear War," *WP*, February 4, 1979.

38. Air of unreality: U.S. Congress, *Nuclear War Strategy: Hearing before the Committee on Foreign Relations*, September 16, 1980, 22.

39. Unlikely to remain rational: Dobrynin agrees with Turner, in "Global Competition" conference transcript, 215–33.

40. The deterrence dilemma remains: Walter Slocombe to Stuart Eizenstat and Richard Holbrooke, August 6, 1976, Vance Mss., Box 8, F: 7, YUL. Slocombe argued that mutual deterrence was based on both sides having secure second-strike capabilities. He also suggested there were substantial controversies over whether damage limiting measures could produce any meaningful reduction in nuclear war casualties.

41. "Tit-for-tat arms race": Jimmy Carter to Leonid Brezhnev, September 14, 1978, Plains File, Box 17. F: Brezhnev-Carter Corr. 1978, JCL.

42. Eisenhower's decision to not even face the USSR by sending U.S. troops into Hungary to support the uprising there was based on his concern that it could lead to a very destructive war. See Kenneth Kitts and Betty Glad, "Presidential Personality and Improvisational Decision-Making: Eisenhower and the 1956 Hungarian Crisis," in Shirley Anne Warshaw, ed., *Reexamining the Eisenhower Presidency*, 183–208.

43. Kennedy and missile crisis: Holsti, "Crisis Management," in Betty Glad, ed., *The Psychological Dimensions of War*, 116–42.

44. Helmut Schmidt, quoted in Jimmy Carter, "Interview with the President," *PP*, April 12, 1980, 673.

45. Fooling the other: Steven Kull, *Minds at War*, 115.

46. Game of nerves: Anatoly Gribkov, in "Global Competition" conference transcript, 186. CIA studies, as Brzezinski noted on December 2, 1977 (WR 38, ZB Don, Box 41, JCL), suggested that the Soviet command authority to release nuclear weapons was "not in military hands."

47. Escalating to MAD: Gribkov, in "Global Competition" conference transcript, 186.

48. On computer glitch: Robert M. Gates, *From the Shadows*, 114–15.

49. War scares: Gates, *From the Shadows*, 114–15. The Soviets, too, may have experienced a war scare in 1983, alerting KGB officials around the world (Operation Ryon) to collect any plans for an American first strike. See Anatoly Dobrynin, *In Confidence*, 523–24.

50. Paul C. Warnke, "Apes on the Treadmill," *WP*, February 6, 1977.

51. On Gorbachev: Betty Glad and Eric Shiraev, "The Reformer in Office," in Betty Glad and Eric Shiraev, eds., *The Russian Transformation*, 6. See also Robert D. English, *Russia and the Idea of the West*, 2, 205–15. Ironically, one of the chief negotiators of the Intermediate Nuclear Forces arms limitation treaty was Paul Nitze, who had earlier questioned Warnke's ideas on the need for stability in the strategic balance. See Betty Glad and Jean Garrison, "Ronald Reagan and the Intermediate Nuclear Forces Treaty," in Eric J. Schmertz, Natalie Datlof, and Alexej Ugrinsky, eds., *President Reagan and the World*, 91.

CHAPTER 22. SHADOWING THE SOVIETS

The retroactive intelligence analyses in this chapter are from U.S. Central Intelligence Agency, Center for the Study of Intelligence, Gerald K. Haines and Robert E. Leggett, eds., *Watching the Bear: Essays on CIA's Analysis of the Soviet Union*, available online at https://www.cia.gov/library/center-for-the-study-of-intelligence/csi-publications/books-and-monographs/watching-the-bear-essays-on-cias-analysis-of-the-soviet-union/index.html. Princeton University's Center of International Studies; the Center for the Study of Intelligence; and former and current CIA analysts, academics, and media representatives were joined by former U.S. policymakers to make these assessments. Cited hereafter as *WB*. Pagination is separate for each article. The actual intelligence reports in this chapter are in the National Archives.

1. Soccer metaphor: quoted by James Blight in letter to Jimmy Carter, April 17, 1995, VF, Box 117, USSR-US Conf. 3/95, BB1, 2, JCL.

2. On territorial hopscotch: Ibid.

3. Shulman and Gribkov: Transcript of the proceedings of the conference "Global Competition and the Deterioration of U.S.-Soviet Relations, 1977–1980," March 23–26, 1995, Ft. Lauderdale, Florida, 231, VF, Box 117, USSR-US Conf, JCL.

4. Vance, diagnosis: "NATO Ministers Meet," December 12, 1979, *DSB* 80, no. 2035 (February 1980): 16.

5. Foreign policy analysts Karen Brutent's and Marshall Shulman's speculations on motivations: "Global Competition" conference transcript, 23, 181.

6. Soviet threat: Charles Tyroler III, ed., *Alerting America*, 176–77. Eugene Rostow, Paul Nitze, Richard Perle, and Donald Rumsfeld were all members of the Committee on the Present Danger. Nitze was also a member of the Team B Committee.

7. William Greider, "Hysteria Is Coming! Hysteria Is Coming!" *WP*, September 28, 1980.

8. Interpretations of Cold War: James Blight to Jimmy Carter, April 17, 1995, JCL.

9. On the eve of the Camp David talks, Vance wrote Gromyko explaining Carter's invitation of Begin and Sadat to meet with him at Camp David; Cyrus Vance to Andrei Gromyko, n.d., from Archives of the Russian Foreign Ministry, VF, Box 117, USSR-US Conf., BBII, JCL. It was an apparent attempt to smooth over Soviet perturbations that they had been cut out of the Middle East negotiations. At a difficult phase in the SALT negotiations, Vance publicly noted that Gromyko, in the diplomatic trade, had "few peers in the modern world." Vance, "Visit to Africa, the United Kingdom, and the U.S.S.R.," *DSB* 78, no. 2015 (June 1978): 26. Compare Kissinger's appreciation of Gromyko in the introduction to Gromyko *Memoirs*, vi–xi.

10. U.S. Central Intelligence Agency, *Intelligence Community Experiment in Competitive Analysis: Some Soviet Strategic Objectives—An Alternative View, Report of Team B* (Washington, DC: National Archives, 1976; hereafter, cited as CIA Team B Report). The Team B committee was established in response to charges by strategist Albert Wohlstetter that the mainline CIA intelligence reports had underestimated Soviet capabilities. Pipes selected Paul Nitze (a major contributor to NSC 68, of 1950, and the Gaither Report of 1957), Lt. General Daniel Graham (a director of the Defense Intelligence Agency and later on Reagan's Strategic Defense Initiative team), William van Cleave (professor at the University of Southern California; senior research fellow on national security affairs at the Hoover Institute of War, Revolution, and Peace, Stanford University; and later senior defense advisor and defense policy coordinator for Reagan's 1979–80 presidential campaign), and other hard-liners to be members of his team. See Pipes, "Team B: The Reality behind the Myth," *Commentary*, October 1986, 32–35. For Pipes's background as a Polish refugee and his critiques of George Kennan and Henry Kissinger and their views of the Soviet Union, see Richard Pipes, *Vixi*. For critics of the Team B Report, see Anne H. Cahn, *Killing Détente*, 163–76; John Prados, *The Soviet Estimate*, 252, 255; and Lisl Marburg Goodman, *Omnicide*, 130, 132.

11. Less alarmist: U.S. Central Intelligence Agency, *National Intelligence Estimate: Soviet Forces for the Intercontinental Conflict Through the Mid-1980s*, vol. 1, *Key Judgments and Summary. Report of Team A*, NIE 11-3/8-76, December 1976. The State Department's Bureau of Intelligence Research disagreed, saying that there were no such Soviet goals for the foreseeable future.

12. Moderate analyses and policies toward China: U.S. Central Intelligence Agency, *National Intelligence Estimate: Soviet Goals and Expectations in the Global Power Arena. Approved for Release, CIA Historical-Review Program*, NIE 11-4-78, February 21, 1978, 11–12, 55–58.

13. NIE underestimating ICBMs: Raymond L. Garthoff, "Estimating Soviet Military Intentions and Capabilities," *WB*, 13.

14. Minority view: CIA, *Soviet Goals and Expectations in the Global Power Arena*, 21–22. Backfire bomber capabilities: Clarence Smith, "CIA's Analysis of Soviet Science and Technology," *WB*, 15, 21.

15. Bob Carr, Thomas Downey, and Robert Leggett to Zbigniew Brzezinski, February 1, 1977, WHCF, Subject File, Countries Box CO-57, CO-165, 1/20/77–2/28/77, JCL. Under McNamara, the militarily relevant Soviet manpower was costed out in terms of what it would

cost in U.S. dollars. Then, U.S. expenditures would be costed out in terms of rubles, as they would be if produced in the USSR. The parallel sets of figures were thought to give a direct picture of Soviet military costs as compared with those of the United States. John Prados, *The Soviet Estimate*, 245–46. In one study, the CIA concluded that the Soviets devoted 11 to 13 percent of their gross domestic product to defense, compared with the United States' 6 percent. While this comparison does not take into account the different sizes and efficiencies of the two economies it does say something about the relative willingness of each to accept the defense burden. Victor Utgoff to Zbigniew Brzezinski, February 10, 1977, WHCF, Subject File, Countries, Box CO-57, CO-165, 1/20/77–2/28/77, JCL.

16. Mainline CIA on bomber and missile gaps: Raymond Garthoff, "Estimating Soviet Military Intentions and Capabilities," *WB*, 5–6, 13. Whereas the CIA analysis estimated 700–800 heavy bombers, the USSR never fielded more than 150 (an additional 50 were configured as tankers). Missile gap: Various intelligence sources and satellite photography in 1961 proved that the Soviet leaders had waited for a more suitable second generation ICBM before deploying just over a handful of bulky SS-6s.

17. Ambiguity and worst-case analysis: Douglas F. Garthoff, "Analyzing Soviet Politics and Foreign Policy," *WB*, 2.

18. Team B projections off: R. Garthoff, "Estimating Soviet Military Intentions and Capabilities," *WB*, 17–20.

19. Threat overblown: Ibid., 10–11, 16–17.

20. Spending: Ibid., 12.

21. Expenditures leveling off: James Noreen, "CIA's Analysis of the Soviet Economy," *WB*, 12–13.

22. Assumptions of static regime and policy: Donald P. Steury, "Origins of CIA's Analysis of the Soviet Union," *WB*, 24; R. Garthoff, "Estimating Soviet Military Intentions and Capabilities," *WB*, 2.

23. Costs of nuclear war: A CIA report estimated Soviet casualties at about 120 million (with 85 million fatalities). With little to no preparation there would be 100 million fatalities. If both sheltering and evacuation were successful there would be 40 million casualties (and 15 million fatalities). Ibid., 23.

24. Comparing Soviets to others: Ibid., 25.

25. Soviet external situation: Ibid., 16; Raymond Garthoff, *The Great Transition*, 20–26.

26. Pipes, *Vixi*, 226. Robert Gates, the CIA liaison to the NSC, predicted that Gorbachev would initiate no radically different policies for the USSR. See his *From the Shadows*, 329–37; compare R. Garthoff, "Estimating Soviet Military Intentions and Capabilities," *WB*, 23.

27. Soviet system: Hannah Arendt, *The Origins of Totalitarianism*; Carl J. Friedrich and Zbigniew Brzezinski, *Totalitarian Dictatorship and Autocracy*.

28. Striving for an edge: Paul Warnke, "Apes on the Treadmill," *WP*, February 6, 1977.

29. Fisher on superiority: "Defense Group formed," *FF*, August 11, 1978, 604. Republican platform: Donald B. Johnson, *National Party Platforms of 1980*, 205–6.

30. Brzezinski, quoted in James Wooten, "Can Rafshooning Save Jimmy Carter?" *Esquire*, March 13, 1979, 20. When confronted on the impact of his Polish origins on his view toward the Soviet Union, Brzezinski pointed out that his view was shared by many non-Polish leaders and public. "Damn sumbitch got me," Wooten exclaimed.

31. Brzezinski on actual U.S. superiority as goal: James Blight to Jimmy Carter, April 17, 1995, VF, USSR-US Conf., 3/95, BB1, JCL.

CHAPTER 23. THE ENEMY OF MY ENEMY IS MY FRIEND

1. Praise for Ceausescu: Helmut Sonnenfeldt, "Information Bank Abstracts," *NYT*, April 12, 1978.

2. Blumenthal to Romania: Steven Strasser, "Conflicting Signals," *Newsweek*, December 18, 1978.

3. Ceausescu moving away from USSR: John M. Goskho, "Romanian President Warns of Need for Mideast Settlement," *WP*, April 13, 1978.

4. Ignoring Chinese dissidents: Michel Oksenberg to Zbigniew Brzezinski, December 8, 1978, ZB Don, Box 9, China-PRC 12/78, JCL. When Derian testified before Congress on Chinese violations of the rights of some of their own dissidents, Holbrooke countered by sending his aide to testify that there was "an encouraging trend" toward liberalization in the PRC. See James Mann, *About Face*, 102–3.

5. On Wei's arrest: Mann, *About Face*, 102–103; *Newsweek*, October 29, 1979, 53.

6. State Department on China: Mann, *About Face*, 103.

7. Carter on Cambodia: *FF*, April 28, 1978, 301. For more on genocide, written by the U.S. ambassador to Cambodia, see Joseph Mussomeli, "The Worst Genocide Ever (No, Not the Holocaust)," *Wall Street Journal*, August 1, 2006.

8. Pol Pot atrocities: Samantha Power, "*A Problem From Hell*", 13–34. In the U.S. House of Representatives, Stephen Solarz (D-NY) and others entered press reports of these atrocities in the *Congressional Record*. In the Senate, Claiborne Pell (D-RI) and William Proxmire (D-WI) pushed for U.S. adherence to the International Genocide Convention, noting the events in Cambodia as evidence that this was needed. Journalists Jack Anderson, Les Whitten, and William Safire likened the actions to those of Adolf Hitler's Holocaust. Senator George McGovern (D-SD) called for the United States to take the lead in both political and military action against the regime. The Khmer Rouge was not like other communist regimes, he argued, and would have such a flimsy hold over its people that it could be toppled with relative ease.

9. Vietnamese invasion, evidence of mass murder: Power, "*A Problem from Hell*," 141–43.

10. U.S. reaction: Ibid., 146–47.

11. UN vote: Ibid., 152.

12. Donald McHenry, interview by the author at "Jimmy Carter Conference: Lessons for the 21st Century," University of Georgia, January 19, 2006.

13. Cited in 1980 World Year Book: "Events of 1979," 230.

14. Controversy within administration: Cyrus Vance, *Hard Choices*, 126; Power, "*A Problem From Hell*," 146–48.

15. Shah exempt from criticism: Alexander Moens, *Foreign Policy under Carter*, 140; Coral Bell, *President Carter and Foreign Policy*, 52; Anthony Parsons, *The Pride and the Fall*, 47.

16. Tear gas at the White House: Cyrus Vance, *Hard Choices*, 321–22.

17. Toast at state dinner: "Visit of Mohammed Reza Pahlavi, Shahanshah of Iran," *PP*, November 15, 1977, 2026–27.

18. New Year's celebration: "Tehran," *PP*, December 31, 1977, 2220–22.

19. Saadi, quoted in Gary Sick, *All Fall Down*, 30.

20. Carter's interest in Poland: Zbigniew Brzezinski, *Power and Principle*, 297–300.

21. Pope's role in Poland: Helen Whitney and Jane Barnes, "John Paul II: The Millennial Pope," PBS *Frontline*, April 2, 2005, retrieved January 5, 2008, from http://www.pbs.org/wgbh/pages/frontline/shows/pope/etc/script.html.

22. By sticking to their tenet of nonviolent change, the leaders of Solidarity were able to enlist the support of trade unions in America and from Pope John Paul II. Jeffrey Donovan, "Poland: Solidarity—The Trade Union that Changed the World," Radio Free Europe/Radio Liberty, August 25, 2005. The union swelled from one million to nine million members by December 1981. Alarmed, Polish Prime Minister General Wojciech Jaruzelski outlawed the organization and declared martial law in December 1981. The pope publicly denounced the declaration of martial law and encouraged Polish priests to make public stances against the Communist leadership. See "Pope John Paul II CIA Files," retrieved February 11, 2008, from http://www.paperlessarchives.com/pope.html.

23. Possible Soviet invasion: Zbigniew Brezezinski, *Power and Principle*, 466; Jimmy Carter, *Keeping Faith*, 584; SCC meeting on Poland, September 23, 1980, VF: Box 117, USSR-Related documents opened (11), JCL.

24. Warning to Soviets, foreign leaders notified: Carter, *Keeping Faith*, 584.

25. Brzezinski calls pope: Brezezinski, *Power and Principle*, 466–67.

26. Walesa on the pope: "World mourns Pope John Paul II," April 3, 2005, retrieved February 11, 2008, from http://www.cnn.com/2005/WORLD/europe/04/02/world.reax/index.html.

27. Brzezinski, *Power and Principle*, 469.

28. South Africa: Ibid., 55.

29. Later negotiations: Betty Glad and James Blanton, "F. W. De Klerk and Nelson Mandela: A Study in Cooperative Transformational Leadership," *Presidential Studies Quarterly* 27 (1997): 565–90.

30. PRC meeting: Robert A. Pastor, *Whirlpool*, 46–47.

31. Neutrality: John Dumbrell, *The Carter Presidency*, 150–51; Walter LeFeber, *Inevitable Revolutions*, 230–31; Brzezinski, *Power and Principle*, 49.

32. Problems in Latin America: Brzezinski, *Power and Principle*, 49.

33. Derian and Jimmy Carter visits: Joshua Muravchik, *The Uncertain Crusade*, 43. First lady's visits: Rosalynn Carter, *First Lady from Plains*, 207, 210–11. Details on Arns: Francis McDonagh, "Brazil's Arns Embodies Vatican II Church," *National Catholic Reporter*, July 26, 1996, 5. Reaction to speech at OAS: Brzezinski Collection, Box 41, F: Weekly Reports 61–71: 6/78–9/78–6/23/1978, JCL.

34. Muravchik, *The Uncertain Crusade*, 28–29.

35. "Argentina Dirty War 1976–1983," April 27, 2005, retrieved August 5, 2008, from http://www.globalsecurity.org/military/world/war/argentina.htm.

36. Unrest and strengthening of the Sandinistas: William M. LeoGrande, *Our Own Backyard: The United States in Central America*, 18.

37. Carter's letter: Ibid., 20.

38. OAS meeting: Robert A. Pastor, *Condemned to Repetition*, 148; Dario Moreno, *U.S. Policy in Central America: The Endless Debate*, 58–59.

39. Brzezinski's reaction: Dario Moreno, *U.S. Policy in Central America*, 59.

40. Final Sandinista offensive: LeoGrande, *Our Own Backyard*, 23.

41. Breakfast meeting: Pastor, *Condemned*, 147–48.

42. "Somocismo sin Somoza": Moreno, *U.S. Policy in Central America*, 57–58. Two pillars: Pastor, *Condemned*, 151–52.

43. John J. Tierney Jr., *Somozas and Sandinistas*, 65; LeoGrande, *Our Own Backyard*, 27.

44. Urcuyo: Pastor, *Condemned*, 183–87.

45. Patient accommodation: John Dumbrell, *The Carter Presidency*, 159–60.

46. Aid to Sandinistas: "U.S. Finally Releases $75 Million Aid," *FF*, September 19, 1980, E2, 709. Still, the Carter administration hedged its bet, supplying anti-Sandinista forces almost $1 million. Dumbrell, *The Carter Presidency*, 161.

47. Covert findings: Robert M. Gates, *From the Shadows*, 126–28, 242.

48. Pastor, *Condemned*, 221–22.

49. SCC Meeting, November 13, 1980, ZB Don, Box 33, Meetings SCC 349A, JCL.

50. Salazar assassinated: Pastor, *Condemned*, 223.

51. Nicaraguan shipments: LeoGrande, *Our Own Backyard*, 69.

52. Patricia Derian, quoted in Victor S. Kaufman, "Bureau of Human Rights during the Carter Administration," *Historian* 61, no. 1 (1998), 60.

53. Ibid.

54. Visits as markers: Joshua Muravchik, *The Uncertain Crusade*, 43.

55. Conflict over Philippines: Kaufman, "Bureau of Human Rights," 57.

56. No blanket endorsements, Derrin quote: Terrence Smith, "Rights Policy: Uneven Stress," *NYT*, December 12, 1978."

57. Derian on *Meet the Press:* "State Official Sees Heartening Signs on Chinese Rights," quoted in *WP,* December 25, 1978.

58. Todman and Vaky: LeoGrande, *Our Own Backyard,* 19–21.

59. Other staff conflicts over Nicaragua: Ibid., 20–23; Moreno, *U.S. Policy in Central America,* 56.

60. Brzezinski frustrated: Pastor, *Condemned,* 162.

61. Turf issues: Kaufman, "Bureau of Human Rights," 58.

62. Congressional inputs: Ibid., 60.

63. Senators on Cambodia: Robert G. Kaiser, "Press U.N. on Cambodia, 80 Senators Urge Vance," *WP,* October 13, 1978.

64. Wilson on Nicaragua: Pastor, *Condemned,* 98.

65. Senators want to cut aid: Ibid., 98–99.

66. Full-page ad, *NYT,* June 18, 1979.

67. Jeane Kirkpatrick, "Dictatorships and Double Standards," *Commentary* 68 (1979): 34–45.

68. Critiques of foreign leaders: Murrey Marder, "Carter, Schmidt Mute Differences on Rights," *WP,* July 14, 1977.

69. Strategic realities: Brezezinski, *Power and Principle,* 145.

70. Torres, and Carter's response: Graham Hovey, "US Says It Remains Concerned over Human Rights in Argentina," *NYT,* June 3, 1980.

71. During the first two years of Carter's administration, the number of Jewish emigrants totaled 45,700, compared to 27,000 during the Ford administration. In 1979, Jewish emigration was triple the annual total during Ford's years in office. See graph, "Jewish Emigration from the USSR," Soviet Jewry Research Bureau/National Conference on Soviet Jewry, 1985, AC Moses, Box 10, "Jews, Carter 1980," JCL.

72. Roosevelt and the Declaration of Human Rights: see Elizabeth Borgwardt, *A New Deal for the World.*

73. Carter at anniversary: "Universal Declaration of Human Rights," December 6, 1978, *PP,* 2164. Barbara Tuchman, quoted in David F. Schmitz and Vanessa Walker, "Jimmy Carter and the Foreign Policy of Human Rights," *Diplomatic History* 28, no. 1 (2004): 133.

CHAPTER 24. THE DEATH OF THE ARCHBISHOP

1. Archbishop Oscar Romero to Jimmy Carter, February 17, 1980, quoted in James Brockman, *The Word Remains: A Life of Oscar Romero,* 227.

2. Secretary of State Cyrus Vance to Archbishop Oscar Romero, quoted in James Brockman, *The Word Remains,* 228. See also Oscar A. Romero, *A Shepherd's Diary,* 525.

3. Assassination and dying words: Jonathan Kwitny, *Man of the Century,* 353. United Nations Commission on the Truth, *From Madness to Hope:* chap. 4, retrieved January 4, 2008, from http://www.usip.org/library/tc/doc/reports/el_salvador/tc_es_03151993_casesD1_2. html#D1. The Commission on the Truth was created on April 27, 1991, as part of the UN's El Salvador peace agreements negotiated between 1989 and 1992 between the FMLN and the government of El Salvador.

4. Funeral: Christopher Dickey, "40 Killed in San Salvador," *WP,* December 5, 1980.

5. On Grande's murder: Brockman, *The Word Remains,* 9–11.

6. Romero's change after murder of Grande: Ibid., 4–5, 9.

7. Dada, quoted in Tommie Sue Montgomery, *Revolution in El Salvador: from Civil Strife to Civil Peace,* 135.

8. Background on the juntas: *El Salvador Civil War,* April 27, 2005, retrieved October 29, 2008, from http://www.globalsecurity.org/military/world/war/elsalvador2.htm. Resignations: Jon Sobrino, *Archbishop Romero,* 121; Brockman, *Romero,* 216–17, 237.

9. Reforms: *El Salvador Civil War.* See also Oscar A. Romero, *A Shepherd's Diary,* 511.

10. Sabotage: Romero, *A Shepherd's Diary*, 508, 528, 531.

11. On Orden: *El Salvador Civil War.*

12. February 17 homily: James Brockman, *The Word Remains*, 231.

13. Need to contact John Paul: SCC Meeting, January 28, 1980; ZB Don, Box 32, Meetings SCC 174.

14. Zbigniew Brzezinski to Jimmy Carter, January 29, 1980; ZB Don, Box 32, SCC Meetings 261: 1/28/1980; Zbigniew Brzezinski memo, January 31, 1980; ZB Don, Box 32, F: SCC 1/80–4/80. Earlier, the White House, in an effort at some kind of accommodation, had engineered a plot to get General Carlos Humberto Romero and Archbishop Romero together in the United States. See Brockman, *The Word Remains*, 107.

15. Brzezinski had met Cardinal Karol Wojtyla in Boston before he became the pope and invited him to tea and conversation. Later Brzezinski wrote him about some of their common concerns. Zbigniew Brzezinski to author, March 1, 2005. In October 1979, when the Pope John Paul II toured the United States, Carter met privately with him in the Oval Office for an hour. The two men discussed their religious commitments and world affairs. They agreed, according to a White House statement that same day, that "efforts to advance human rights constitute the compelling idea of our times."

16. Draft letter: Zbigniew Brzezinski to Pope John Paul II (under cover letter from Peter Tarnoff), January 31, 1980; ZB Don, Box 32, SCC 1/80–4/80.

17. Not recalling the letter being sent: Zbigniew Brzezinski to author, March 1, 2005.

18. The January 30, 1980, visit was apparently more cordial than his first meeting with the pope in 1979. At a general conference, the pope requested to see Romero privately, but then kept him waiting for days before granting an audience. Oscar A. Romero, *A Shepherd's Diary*, 214–15. Rome also intervened when Romero was to be awarded an honorary degree from Georgetown University. Archbishop Jean Jadot, the apostolic delegate, and Cardinal Gabriel Garrone, prefect of the Congregation for Catholic Education, tried to delay or stop the degree. Officials decided it was too late to change plans; Brockman, *The Word Remains*, 106–7, 166–67.

19. Second visit with the pope: Romero, *A Shepherd's Diary*, 465–67; Brockman, *The Word Remains*, 224–25.

20. Meeting with pope more confrontational: Kwitny, *Man of the Century*, 352.

21. Visit with Casaroli: Brockman, *The Word Remains*, 225.

22. Brzezinski on messages to the pope: SCC Meeting, February 15, 1980, ZB Don, Box 32, Meetings SCC 274.

23. It didn't work. Carter note on memo: Zbigniew Brzezinski to Jimmy Carter, SCC meeting on El Salvador and Honduras, February 15, 1980, ZB Don, Box 32, F: Meetings SCC 1/80–4/80.

24. Bowdler visit: Romero, *A Shepherd's Diary*, 496–97; Sobrino, *Archbishop Romero*, 122.

25. The very conservative Senator Jesse Helms (R-NC) had held up White's appointment for four months. Margaret O'Brien Steinfels, "Death and Lies in El Salvador: The Ambassador's Tale," *Commonweal* 128, no. 18 (2001): 14.

26. Paraguay: Steinfels, "Death and Lies in El Salvador." Standing out: Schoultz, *Human Rights and United States Policy toward Latin America*, 360.

27. White: Romero, *A Shepherd's Diary*, 524–25.

28. White on bishops, nuncios: Steinfels, "Death and Lies," 17.

29. White's resistance to pressures: Ibid., 14; William M. LeoGrande, *Our Own Backyard*, 44–45.

30. Peace Prize, National Council of Churches, press conferences: Romero, *A Shepherd's Diary*, 506, 512–16, 533.

31. D'Aubuisson warnings: Brockman, *The Word Remains*, 251.

32. Radio station and church bombings: Jonathan Kwitny, *Man of the Century*, 352–53; Brockman, *The Word Remains*, 231.

33. Murder of Zamora: Brockman, *The Word Remains*, 251; "Attorney General Slain" *FF,* February 29, 1980, 149. United Nations, *From Madness to Hope.*

34. Warnings: Brockman, *The Word Remains*, 233.

35. Attaché case: Ibid., 238; United Nations, *From Madness to Hope.*

36. White's warning: Steinfels, "Death and Lies," 14–15.

37. Rotating places of sleep: Jonathan Kwitny, *Man of the Century*, 353.

38. Expressing fear: Brockman, *The Word Remains*, 233.

39. Possible martyrdom: Ibid., 247–48.

40. "Stop the repression": Jon Sobrino, *Archbishop Romero*, 116.

41. Embassy evacuation: "Archbishop Romero Assassinated," *FF,* March 28, 1980, 220.

42. Attempts to shift blame: Brockman, *The Word Remains*, 247, 249.

43. Witnesses, Martinez disappear: *El Independiente* as cited in Brockman, *The Word Remains*, 249–51. In May, D'Aubuisson and several of his associates were arrested for plotting to overthrow the junta. One of the men, Captain Alvaria Rafael Savaria, had a notebook filled with entries noting payment for items such as a telescopic sight, a car, and a driver that had been used in the Romero assassination. The State Department received a copy of the Savaria book and Ambassador White, who had this document analyzed, informed the State Department that D'Aubuisson had ordered Romero's death. Brockman, *The Word Remains*, 251.

44. Conflict in El Salvador: *El Salvador Civil War.*

45. Murder and mutilation: Steinfels, "Death and Lies," 18–19.

46. Murders of churchwomen: "Bodies of 4 American Women are Found in El Salvador," *NYT,* December 5, 1980; Christopher Dickey, "4 U.S. Catholics Killed in El Salvador," *WP,* December 5, 1980.

47. White and the churchwomen: Steinfels, "Death and Lies," 18.

48. Churchwomen's exhumation: William M. LeoGrande, *Our Own Backyard*, 62.

49. Archbishop James Hickey to Edmund Muskie, January 10, 1981, Plains File, Box 41, F: State Dept. Evening Reports, 11/80, JCL. See also Marjorie Hyer, "Four Murders Trigger U.S. Catholic Priests," *WP,* December 10, 1980.

50. Kennedy's response: "Bodies of 4 American Women are Found in El Salvador."

51. Amnesty International: Dickey, "4 US Catholics Killed."

52. Fact-finding mission, aid restored: Juan de Onis, "Carter Reported Undecided on Salvador Military Aid," *NYT,* December 24, 1980; John Goshko, "Salvadoran Junta Seen Not Linked to Nuns' Killing," *WP,* December 12, 1980.

53. Salvadoran authorities cover-up: Juan de Onis, "Envoy Disputes U.S. on Salvador Deaths," *NYT,* January 22, 1981.

54. New aid: Steinfels, "Death and Lies," 19.

55. White's refusal to cover-up: Ibid.

56. Cable to state: LeoGrande, *Our Own Backyard*, 50.

57. White fired: Steinfels, "Death and Lies," 18–19.

58. White on D'Aubuisson: LeoGrande, *Our Own Backyard*, 49.

59. White on responsibility of security forces, cover up: De Onis, "Envoy Disputes U.S. on Salvador Deaths."

60. Liberation theology: Brockman, *The Word Remains*, 191–92.

61. Georgetown doctorate: Ibid., 106–7.

62. Attempts to discipline Romero: Ibid., 127–33, 167–70.

63. Nuncio's visit: Romero, *A Shepherd's Diary*, 520–21.

64. Christ's message: Sobrino, *Archbishop Romero*, 105, 131, 147–49.

65. "Perfection": Oscar A. Romero, *The Violence of Love*, 206.

66. Romero citing Universal Declaration of Human Rights: Brockman, *The Word Remains*, 121–25.

67. Marxist philosophy: Ibid., 75–76, 191–92.

68. Legitimate resort to violence: Sobrino, *Archbishop Romero*, 94–95, 141. See also Brockman, *The Word Remains*, 191–192.

69. Quote from Isaiah: Sobrino, *Archbishop Romero*, 107.

70. John Paul II on poor in Brazil (June 30, 1980): Kwitny, *Man of the Century*, 365–66.

71. John Paul II's views on liberation theology: Ibid., 315–16.

72. John Paul II's critiques of political priests in Nicaragua: *WP*'s Robert Suro and ABC's Bill Blakemore, quoted in Helen Whitney and Jane Barnes, "John Paul II: The Millennial Pope," *Frontline*, April 2, 2005; transcript retrieved January 5, 2008, from http://www.pbs.org/wgbh/pages/frontline/shows/pope/etc/script.html. See also Carl Bernstein and Marco Politi, *His Holiness*, 366; Kwitny, *Man of the Century*, 466–67. Seminaries as hotbeds: David Stoll, *Is Latin America Turning Protestant? The Politics of Evangelical Growth*, 170.

73. Cardinal Arns: Chris Kraul and Henry Chu, "Part of the Flock Felt Abandoned by the Pope," *Los Angeles Times*, April 10, 2005; Laura Greenhalgh, "Cardinal Arns of Brazil on Pope John Paul II, the Vatican and the Poor," April 4, 2005, retrieved January 5, 2008, from http://www.opendemocracy.net/faith-catholicchurch/article_2406.jsp.

74. "The Pope?! How many divisions has he got?" Joseph Stalin to Pierre Laval, May 13, 1935, quoted in Winston Churchill, *The Gathering Storm*, 8.

75. Costs and end of civil war: United Nations, *From Madness to Hope*. See also Carol Luebering, "Afterword," in Romero, *A Shepherd's Diary*, 537.

76. Savaria had made Garay drive "a young bearded man" to the Divine Providence Hospital, from which Garay could see Romero delivering mass. When Garay was ordered to "pretend to be working on the car's gearshift," he heard a shot from the back of the car. Later, when he dropped the man off at the house from which he had picked him up, he heard him tell Savaria, "Mission accomplished." See Brockman, *The Word Remains*, 253–54. The United Nations Report, *From Madness to Hope*, notes that "in very closed circles" D'Aubuisson took credit for the planning of Romero's assassination.

77. Savaria asking forgiveness: Gerardo Reyes, "End of Silence in 1980 Death of Archbishop," *Miami Herald*, March 24, 2006.

78. Savaria ordered to pay damages: Richard Higgins, "The Martyr of El Salvador," *International Herald Tribune*, March 25, 2006; retrieved January 5, 2008, from http://www.iht.com/articles/2005/03/25/opinion/edhiggins.php.

79. Conviction: Steinfels, "Death and Lies," 12.

80. Higher orders: Larry Rohter, "Salvadorans Who Slew American Nuns Now Say They Had Orders," *NYT*, April 3, 1998.

81. Cover-up of churchwomen's murders: United Nations, *From Madness to Hope*.

82. Romero statue: "The Nave," n.d., retrieved January 5, 2008, from http://www.westminster-abbey.org/visitor/plan-of-the-abbey/13610.

83. Sainthood stalled: Heidi Schlumpf, "A Martyr Remembered," *U.S. Catholic* 65, no. 6 (2000): 11.

84. On veneration and criticism: Gianpaolo Salvini, S.I., "Il 25° Anniversario Della Morte Di Mons. Romero" [The 25th anniversary of the death of Mons. Romero], *La Civiltá Cattolica*, November 5, 2005, retrieved January 5, 2008, from http://www.laciviltacattolica.it/Quaderni/2005/3729/Articolo%20Salvini.html.

85. Only Robert Gates, the CIA representative to the National Security Council during the Carter administration, touches on the whole episode. In 1984, when Gates was deputy director of intelligence for the Reagan administration, the CIA's Directorate of Intelligence attempted to follow up on newspaper stories raising questions about whether or not the United States had actually collaborated with the Salvadoran death squads. When Gates attempted to report to Congress on the matter, the directorate of operations tried to restrict his access to all available information. By mid-April, the CIA inspector general reported that, to date, there was "no basis for concern" that the CIA had any sort of relationship with the death squads. Even so, as Gates also notes, this announcement did little to rectify the situation, and rumors of alleged connections

continued to circulate. See Robert Gates, *From the Shadows: The Ultimate Insider's Story of Five Presidents and How They Won the Cold War*, 304–5.

86. In the 1980s official State Department documents reiterated the conventional line that "the chaotic and permissive atmosphere at the time, not high-level military involvement, was behind the crime." Rohter, "Salvadorans Who Slew American Nuns." In October 2000, former ambassador White testified against General Carlos Vides Casanova and General José Guillermo Garcia in a federal court in Florida. The two former Salvadoran officers, given permanent residency status in Florida, were charged with responsibility for the murders of the four American churchwomen. Though Casanova and Garcia were not convicted in this trial, they were eventually ordered to pay $54 million in damages to three civilians in another civil suit filed under the Torture Victim Protection act. Bill Ford, brother of Sister Ita Ford, said of the verdict, "It may be fitting that the winning plaintiffs were Salvadoran....The churchwomen would approve of that fact." On the churchwomen's case, see Steinfels, "Death and Lies," 12; David Gonzalez, "2 Salvador Generals Cleared by U.S. Jury in Nuns' Deaths," *NYT*, November 4, 2000. On the 2002 case, see David Gonzalez, "Torture Victims in El Salvador Are Awarded $54 Million," *NYT*, July 24, 2002.

CHAPTER 25. OPERATION EAGLE CLAW

1. The president's opening statement: Hamilton Jordan, *Crisis*, 250–51; also contains details of other comments at the meeting.

2. Brzezinski and others at meeting: Zbigniew Brzezinski, *Power and Principle*, 492–93; Jordan, *Crisis*, 250–51. Mission name: David Farber, *Taken Hostage*, 171.

3. Jordan's observations: Jordan, *Crisis*, 251.

4. Vance at Camp David: Cyrus Vance, *Hard Choices*, 408. Likelihood of harm: David McClellan, *Cyrus Vance*, 20, 159.

5. Vance out of town: Vance, *Hard Choices*, 409; Zbigniew Brzezinski, *Power and Principle*, 493–94.

6. Vance's objections: Vance, *Hard Choices*, 410; Gary Sick, *All Fall Down*, 293.

7. Vance at April 15 meeting: Jordan, *Crisis*, 252–54.

8. President breaking silence: Ibid.

9. Final decision: Brzezinski, *Power and Principle*, 494–95.

10. Secret meeting in situation room: Ibid., 495; Jimmy Carter, *Keeping Faith*, 507; Jordan, *Crisis*, 254–64.

11. Pledge not to control military: Brzezinski, *Power and Principle*, 495.

12. Kennedy and Bay of Pigs: Ole R. Holsti, in "Crisis Management," in Betty Glad, ed., *Psychological Dimensions of War*, 129; compare Sick, *All Fall Down*, 302.

13. Vance pulled aside: Jordan, *Crisis*, 264.

14. Meeting with Byrd: Carter, *Keeping Faith*, 73, 514. Carter was well aware that Byrd was sensitive to slights and he should have anticipated that his already bad relations with party leaders in the Senate would be further impaired by this failure to take them into his confidence.

15. U.S. plane at Desert One: Paul B. Ryan, *The Iranian Mission*, 48.

16. Problems with Desert One site: Ibid., 48–49; U.S. Department of Defense, *Rescue Mission Report*, 49.

17. World War II history: Stephen F. Hayward in *Congressional Record*, May 6, 1980: 229–30.

18. Likelihood of deaths: Pierre Salinger, *America Held Hostage*, 237–38.

19. Casualties: Brzezinski, *Power and Principle*, 490.

20. Vance on hostages being killed: Vance, *Hard Choices*, 410. One can compare Carter's handling of this situation with the handling of the eighty-three crewmembers aboard the intelligence ship USS *Pueblo*, which was seized by North Korea in 1968. Even though the crew members were tortured, the administration of President Lyndon Johnson handled the affair quietly and the crew was returned a year later.

21. Meeting with Pakistani on plane: David Harris, *The Crisis*, 353; Ryan, *The Iranian Mission*, 35.

22. Initial launch: Harris, *The Crisis*, 354.

23. "Abort situation": Ibid., 357.

24. Chopper problems: Ibid., 356–57.

25. Bodies left behind: David Farber, *Taken Hostage*, 174.

26. Cargo explosion: Harris, *The Crisis*, 359; Farber, *Taken Hostage*, 175.

27. Display of bodies: "Secretary of State Cyrus Vance Resigns," *FF*, May 2, 1980, 321.

28. Carter informed of helicopter failures agrees to abort mission: Jordan, *Crisis*, 271–72; Harris, *The Crisis*, 357–58.

29. "Very sorry": Jordan, *Crisis*, 272–73.

30. Jordan vomits: Ibid., 273.

31. Kennedy's speech: Ibid., 272–74.

32. Jody Powell announcement: Harris, *The Crisis*, 361.

33. Television address: Jimmy Carter, "Rescue Attempt for American Hostages in Iran," April 25, 1980, *PP*, 772–73.

34. "A failure to try": Jimmy Carter, "The President's News Conference," April 29, 1980, *PP*, 793.

35. "At least we tried": Joseph Beyers III, quoted in Drew Middleton, "Going the Military Route," *New York Times Magazine*, May 17, 1981, 111.

36. "Lanced the festering boil": Rosalynn Carter, *First Lady from Plains*, 328.

37. Holloway report: Ryan, *The Iranian Mission*, 26; Middleton, "Going the Military Route," 108–9. See also Sick, *All Fall Down*, 277–81.

38. Fortunate that the operation was aborted: James A. Bill, *The Eagle and the Lion*, 301.

39. Lack of coordination: Middleton, "Going the Military Route," 108.

40. Joseph Luns, *FF*, 1981, 321.

41. Yitzhak Rabin, quoted in Middleton, "Going the Military Route," 108.

42. Carter without Vance: "Secretary of State Cyrus Vance Resigns," *FF*, May 2, 1980, 321.

43. "More statesmanlike": Betty Glad, "Personality, Political and Group Process Variables in Foreign Policy Decision-Making," *International Political Science Review* 10, no. 1 (1989), 56.

44. Vance: Carter, *Keeping Faith*, 513.

45. Robert Byrd, quoted in A. O. Sulzberger Jr., "Byrd Was Briefed before Iran Action," *NYT*, April 27, 1980, 17. Compare Carter, *Keeping Faith*, 514.

46. Campaign manageable: Glad, *Jimmy Carter*, 471.

47. It is not clear that the hostages were in any greater danger in April than they had been earlier. The United States had warned the Iranians the previous November that any harm to the hostages would lead to an American military response. Moreover, the International Red Cross had visited the hostages on April 15 and found all the hostages accounted for. Carter would be aided in his endeavors to put the issue on the back track by the expulsion of American journalists on April 23 as a reaction to the U.S. diplomatic break with Iran. When Iranians gathered around the U.S. embassy later that summer, there would be no live reports of it on U.S. evening television.

CHAPTER 26. THE FINAL MONTHS

1. Quote and convention details: Hamilton Jordan, *Crisis*, 327–34.

2. Other convention details: Alvin Sanoff, "Democrat's Turn in the Spotlight," *US News and World Report*, August 18, 1980, 23–25; Gerald M. and Marlene Michels Pomper, *The Election of 1980*, 23, 27, 32; Arthur M. Schlesinger Jr., *History of American Presidential Elections*, 215–16. The party platform contained little about foreign policy. The Carter people had a majority of the major committees drawing up the platform and had won almost every vote.

3. In August 1980 a *Time* poll showed that 42 percent of potential voters favored Carter, compared to 44 percent who favored Reagan. Ed Magnuson, "Carter Battles a Revolt," *Time*, August 11, 1980.

4. Billy Carter and Libya: Lloyd Cutler to Jimmy Carter, Staff Offices, Box 60, JC—Personal, June 26, 1980, JCL. Billy finally registered on July 14, 1980, during the Republican National Convention. Robert Pear, "Billy Carter Settles Charges by U.S. and Registers as Agent of Libya," *NYT*, July 15, 1980.

5. Anderson's candidacy: "John Anderson Breaks Away," *Time*, May 5, 1980. Retrieved from http://www.time.com/time/magazine/article/0,9171,948844-1,00.html.

6. The campaign: Jordan, *Crisis*, 59, 295–97, 300–301; Robert Ajemian, "A New Job for Ham Jordan," *Time*, June 23, 1980.

7. Foreign policy in campaign: Betty Glad, *Jimmy Carter*, 452.

8. Foreign policy assessment: Cyrus Vance to Jimmy Carter, n.d., Plains File, Box 39, State Department Evening Reports 1/79, JCL. But William Odom later wrote Brzezinski that the United States should make clear that it would "*engage* the USSR *competitively*." Odom, "East-West Relations: A Formula for U.S. Policy in 1981 and Beyond," September 3, 1980, JCL.

9. New CIA assessments in July 1979 of North Korea's military capability had provided a rationale for this withdrawal. Three months later, after the assassination of South Korean President Park Chung Hee, an aircraft carrier had been sent to the area to show U.S. support for the government. See Cyrus Vance, *Hard Choices*, 130.

10. Carter and the CIA: Robert M. Gates, *From the Shadows*, 142–43. CIA charter: Zbigniew Brzezinski to Jimmy Carter, "Intelligence Charter," April 22, 1980, Staff Office, Box 61, F: Cutler, JCL.

11. Negotiations reopened: Edmund Muskie to Mohammad Ali Rajai, August 20, 1980, *DSB*, November 1980, 54–55.

12. Khomeini response: Gary Sick, *All Fall Down*, 363–68.

13. Meeting with Tabatabai in Germany: David Harris, *The Crisis*, 384–89.

14. Muskie statement on support of Iran: Bernard Gwertzman, "Muskie Assures Iran on U.S. Role; Expectations Not Raised," *NYT*, October 20, 1980.

15. Republican infiltration and the "October surprise": David Harris, *The Crisis*, 382–83, 399–400; Jody Powell, *The Other Side of the Story*, 252–74.

16. Carter's edge in foreign policy: David Alpern, "Poll Shows Carter Moving Up," *Newsweek*, November 3, 1980, 28.

17. Carter in debate: Jordan, *The Crisis*, 355–56.

18. Carter's hopes: Gaddis Smith, *Morality, Reason and Power*, 98.

19. On stagflation: American consumers began to expect continuous increases in the price of goods, so they bought more. This increased demand pushed up prices, leading to demands for higher wages, which pushed prices higher still. The government pegged some payments, such as those for Social Security, to the Consumer Price Index, swelling the budget deficit and causing an increase in government borrowing. These responses, in turn, pushed up interest rates as business investment languished and unemployment rose to uncomfortable levels. See "Jimmy Carter vs. Inflation," *Time*, March 24, 1980, 8–13; Harry Anderson et al., "Carter's Attack on Inflation," *Newsweek*, March 24, 1980, 24–30.

20. Carter and Reagan on balancing the budget: "The Bad News Gets Worse," *Time*, June 16, 1980, http://timeinc8-sd11.websys.aol.com/time/magazine/article/0,9171,924220,00.html.

21. Voters on Reagan: Steven Rattner, "The Economy of the Ballot," *NYT*, November 2, 1980.

22. Reagan better on economy: Alpern, "Poll Shows Carter Moving Up," 28.

23. On tax cuts: Rattner, "The Economy of the Ballot."

24. Reagan leading in battleground states: "The Winner?" *U.S. News and World Report*, November 3, 1980, 26–28.

25. Carter concedes: George Church, "Reagan Coast-to-Coast," *Time*, November 17, 1980, 22–24.

26. Electoral College vote: Church, "Reagan Coast-to-Coast."

27. Popular vote: Hedrick Smith, "Reagan Easily Beats Carter," *NYT*, November 5, 1980.

28. Republicans control Senate and House: "The GOP's Senate Surprise," and "Reagan's House Coattails," *Newsweek*, November 17, 1980, 40.

29. Anderson's impact: David Broder, "Carter Yields Early in Night," *WP*, November 5, 1980; Church, "Reagan Coast-to-Coast."

30. On environmental legislation: Burton Kaufman and Scott Kaufman, *The Presidency of James Earl Carter*, 247–48.

31. War plans, SCC Meeting, November 25, 1980, ZB Don, Box 27, F: Memos 3/78–11/80.

32. Muskie questions: SCC Meeting, November 25, 1980, ZB Don, Box 27, F: Memos 3/78–11/80. See also Zbigniew Brzezinski, *Power and Principle, 1977–1981*, 468–69.

33. Report on SCC meeting: Zbigniew Brzezinski to Jimmy Carter, November 25, 1980, Box 23, F: Memos 3/78–11/80, JCL.

34. PD 62: PD/NSC-62, VF, JCL.

35. PD 63: PD/NSC-63, VF, JCL.

36. Muskie finds new plans presumptuous: Brzezinski, *Power and Principle*, 469.

37. Algerian assistance: Gary Sick, *All Fall Down*, 371–98; Don Oberdorfer, "Christopher Flies to Algiers in Last-Ditch Bid."

38. Reagan assists: Bernard Gwertzman, "Carter Says Possibility that Hostages Will Be Freed Now 'Looks Better,'" *NYT*, January 13, 1981.

39. The Iranians made some impossible last-minute demands—first, that all property and land owned by the late shah and his family should be returned to Iran; and second, that $24 billion be given them in guarantees for the recovery of the frozen assets and the late shah's wealth.

40. Bankers and lawyers catnap: Smith, *Morality, Reason and Power*, 100; transcript of ABC News broadcast "America Held Hostage," 60–67; "How U.S. Negotiations Saved Hostage Deal at the Eleventh Hour," *Wall Street Journal*, January 23, 1981.

41. The transfer: Harris, *The Crisis*, 418–19. As a first step, Iranian assets would be transferred from private banks to an escrow account with the Bank of England—in the name of the Algerian Central Bank. When word came that the fifty-two hostages had left Iran, the Algerian Central Bank would release part of those assets to Iran. Thus, both sides were protected. If the hostages were released, the United States would lose further control over these funds. If they were not, they would be returned at no extra expense to the United States.

42. Carter waits: Terrence Smith, "Carter, Aides and Reporters Share a Vigil and Concern," *NYT*, January 19, 1980, A3.

43. Carter on agreement: "Hostages Haunt Carter to the End," *U.S. News and World Report*, February 2, 1981, 7.

44. Final word: Jimmy Carter, *Keeping Faith*, 4–14. See also Harris, *The Crisis*, 420–21; Gary Sick, *All Fall Down*, 397–98.

45. Wiesbaden: Jordan, *Crisis*, 413. In his memoirs, Carter argues that the riskiest phase of the operation was getting the American men into Iran. But even here he underestimates the problems of discovery at the landing site. He notes that the road intersecting the landing site was unpaved and mostly unused; and in the map in his memoir, it is hard to find even that road. See Carter, *Keeping Faith*, 508–9. See also Betty Glad, "Personality, Political and Group Process Variables in Foreign Policy Decision-Making: Jimmy Carter's Handling of the Iranian Hostage Crisis," *International Political Science Review* 10, no. 1 (1989), 56.

46. Carter denouncing Iranians: "Twice the Fun," *Economist*, January 24, 1981, 24. Bradley Graham and Edward Walsh, "Carter Charges U.S. Hostages Suffered 'Acts of Barbarism' in Iran," *WP*, January 22, 1981.

47. Back to status quo: "Agreement on the Release of the American Hostages," *DSB* 81, no. 2047 (February 1981): 1–13; "Unfinished Business of Iran," *Business Week*, February 2, 1980,

14–15; Herman Nickel, "The Iran Deal Doesn't Look Bad," *Fortune*, February 23, 1981. In the final agreement, the United States agreed to terminate all litigation against Iran in the U.S. courts by domestic claimants against Iran. Economic groups could still present their claims to an international tribunal, to be established. The hostages were blocked from taking any direct action against Iran for damages suffered.

48. Muskie's interpretation: "Agreement on the Release of the Hostages: Special Briefing, Jan. 20 1981," *DSB* 81, no. 2047 (February 1981): 16.

49. Algeria as intermediaries: Sick, *All Fall Down*, 377–98; "The Europeans Must Leave," *Time*, February 3, 1981, http://www.time.com/time/magazine/article/0,9171,872042,00. html; "At Last the Smile Said Yes," *MacLean's*, February 2, 1981.

50. Nobel recommendation supported by Vance: "Nobel Peace Prize Award," November 9, 1981, Vance Mss, Box 31, F: 207, YUL.

CHAPTER 27. JIMMY CARTER AND THE AMERICAN MISSION

1. The moral role of the United States: Jimmy Carter, *Why Not the Best?*, 123–24.

2. Jimmy Carter, "Inaugural Address," *Inaugural Addresses of the Presidents of the United States*, 350.

3. John L. O'Sullivan, "Annexation," *United States Magazine and Democratic Review*, July–August 1845, 426–30.

4. William McKinley, "Interview with President McKinley" by General James Rusling, *Christian Advocate*, January 22, 1903; reprinted in Daniel B. Schirmer and Stephen Rosskamm Shalom, eds., *The Philippines Reader*, 1987.

5. Wilson and League of Nations: Reinhold Niebuhr, *Faith and Politics*, 230–31.

6. "Four policemen": Stanley Meisler, *United Nations*, 3.

7. Dangers of moralizing: Niebuhr, *Faith and Politics*, 100, 225, 232–33; Robert Kagan, *Dangerous Nation*, 357–416.

8. Corrupting morals and politics: Niebuhr, *Faith and Politics*, 100.

9. Definition of prudence: Dan Sabia, "Character and Judgment in Machiavelli and More," paper prepared for the annual meeting of the Society for Utopian Studies, Buffalo, NY, October 4–7, 2001, 2, 19, 21.

10. Aristotle on practical wisdom: *Nicomachean Ethics* 6.5; retrieved February 9, 2008, from http://www.constitution.org/ari/ethic_06.htm.

11. Edmund Burke, *Reflections on the Revolution in France*, 65.

12. For Eleanor Roosevelt's work as head of the UN Commission on Human Rights, see Joseph Lash, *Eleanor*, 55–81. See also "Eleanor Roosevelt," retrieved February 9, 2008, from http://www.udhr.org/history/Biographies/bioer.htm.

13. Winthrop, quoted in Reagan, "City upon a Hill."

14. Congressional resolution: Thomas A. Bailey, *A Diplomatic History of the American People*, 263.

15. On colonialism: William Graham Sumner, *War and Other Essays*, retrieved February 9, 2008, from http://oll.libertyfund.org/files/345/0255_Bk.pdf.

16. "Henry Cabot Lodge Speaks Out against the League of Nations, Washington, D.C., August 12, 1919," *CR*, 66th Cong., 1st sess., 1919, 3784. Retrieved February 9, 2008, from http://www.firstworldwar.com/source/lodge_leagueofnations.htm.

17. Jimmy Carter, "Inaugural Address," *Inaugural Addresses of the Presidents of the United States*, 351.

18. To date, only one of the treaties—the Covenant on Civil and Political Rights—has been ratified. The other four have languished in the Senate for lack of interest on the part of subsequent administrations. On June 14, 1993, however, President Clinton's Secretary of State, Warren Christopher, announced that the Clinton administration would pursue ratification of the remaining four treaties (see "International Human Rights Treaties: Their Origins, Purposes,

and Significance to the United States," retrieved February 9, 2008, from http://worldpolicy.org/projects/globalrights/treaties/1993-0721-congressionalseminar.html).

19. "The Noble Peace Prize 2002," retrieved February 9, 2008, from http://nobelprize.org/nobel_prizes/peace/laureates/2002/press.html.

20. Jimmy Carter, "The Nobel Lecture," retrieved February 6, 2009, from http://nobelpeaceprize.org/en_GB/laureates/laureates-2002/carter-lecture/.

21. Jimmy Carter, "Foreword," in Anthony Dunbar, ed., *Where We Stand*, 9.

22. Carter's worries about church and state: *Hardball with Chris Matthews*, October 18, 2004, transcript retrieved February 9, 2008, from http://www.msnbc.msn.com/id/6281085/.

Bibliography

Interviews Consulted

CPP: All interviews cited below are from the Carter Presidency Project conducted by the White Burkett Miller Center of Public Affairs at the University of Virginia. The documents now reside at the Jimmy Carter Library and are cited in the endnotes with interviewee's name and year, followed by the designation "CPP, JCL."

Albright, Madeleine. See entry for Zbigniew Brzezinski below. Cited in endnotes as Brzezinski/aides interviews.

Beckel, Robert. November 13, 1981.

Bell, Griffin. March 23, 1988.

Bergland, Bob. November 21, 1986.

Brzezinski, Zbigniew, Madeleine Albright, Leslie Denend, and William Odom, February 18, 1982. Cited in endnotes as Brzezinski/aides interviews.

Cable, William. See entry for Frank Moore below.

Carp, Bert, and David Rubinstein. March 6, 1982.

Carter, Jimmy. November 29, 1982.

Denend, Leslie. See entry for Zbigniew Brzezinski above. Cited in endnotes as Brzezinski/aides interviews.

Eizenstat, Stuart. January 29–30, 1982.

Hertzberg, Hendrick, and Achsah Nesmith. December 3–4, 1981.

Jordan, Hamilton, and Landon Butler. November 6, 1981.

Kahn, Alfred E., Ron Lewis, and Dennis Rapp. December 10, 1981.

Kirbo, Charles. January 5, 1983.

Klutznick, Philip. October 2, 1986.

Lance, Bert. May 12, 1982.

Marshall, Ray. May 4, 1988.

McDonald, Al, and Michael Rowny. March 13–14, 1981.

McIntyre, James, Hubert Harris, and Van Ooms. October 28–29, 1981.

Moore, Frank, William Cable, Dan Tate, and Robert Thomson. September 18–19, 1981.

Odom, William. See entry for Zbigniew Brzezinski above. Cited in endnotes as Brzezinski/aides interviews.

Powell, Jody, Patricia Bario, Al Friendly, Rex Granum, Ray Jenkins, Dale Leibach, and Claudia Townsend. December 17–18, 1981.

Rafshoon, Gerald. April 8, 1983.

Watson, Jack, Berry Crawford, Jane Hansen, and Bruce Kirschenbaum. April 17, 1983.

Weddington, Sarah. January 2, 1981.

Wexler, Anne, Michael Chanin, Richard Neustadt, and John Ryor. February 12, 1981.

Exit Interviews: The National Archives' Office of Presidential Libraries conducted exit interviews with members of Jimmy Carter's White House staff. Those exit interviews consulted for this book are listed below. The documents reside at the Jimmy Carter Library and are cited in the endnotes with interviewee's name and year, followed by the designation "exit interview, JCL."

Abramowitz, Beth. August 23, 1979.
Brzezinski, Zbigniew. February 20, 1981.
Cable, William H. February 2, 1981.
Cutler, Lloyd. March 2, 1981.
Donovan, Hedley. August 14, 1980.
Edwards, Anne. September 5, 1980.
Eizenstat, Stuart. January 10, 1981.
Free, James. December 16, 1980.
Lipshutz, Robert J. September 29, 1979.
Moffett, George. December 5, 1980.
Powell, Jody. December 2, 1980.
Rafshoon, Gerald. September 12, 1979.

Jimmy Carter was also interviewed by Vision Associates for use in exhibits at the Jimmy Carter Library. This interview is cited in the text as "Jimmy Carter, Vision Associates interview, November 1, 1984, JCL."

Oral Histories

The National Archives and Records Administration (NARA) conducted interviews with some members of the Carter and Smith families for the Carter Library Oral History Project. The oral histories of those persons consulted are cited below with the interviewer and the date of the interview.

Carter, Jack, with interviewer Martin I. Elzy, June 25, 2003.
Elzy, Martin I., with interviewer Albert Nason, April 20, 2004.

Interviews, Responses to Author's Inquiries, Responses to Questionnaires

Bergland, Robert. Letter. January 14, 2005.
Brown, Harold. Letter. October 18, 2008.
Brzezinski, Zbigniew. Telephone conversation with author. January 13, 2005.
———. Letter. March 1, 2005.
Christopher, Warren. Letter. November 7, 2003.
Eilts, Hermann. Questionnaire response. November 14, 2003.
———. Questionnaire response. September 16, 2004 and August 18, 2007.
Eizenstat, Stuart E. Letters. September 16, 2004 and October 18, 2007.
Ermarth, Fritz W. Letter. October 16, 2004.
Gelb, Leslie. Questionnaire response. October 14, 2008.
Glenn, John. Questionnaire response. September 2004.
Holbrooke, Richard. Questionnaire response. November 2008.
———. Telephone conversation with author. November 2008.
Inman, B. R. Letter. October 6, 2004.
Kissinger, Henry. October 21, 2008. Permission granted to quote and cite his comments
    in conversation in Plains, Georgia, November 20, 1976, Cyrus Vance Papers,
    Manuscripts and Archives, Box 8, F: 6, Yale University and Library.
Lipshutz, Robert J. Memorandum to File, March 13, 1979. Dictated aboard *Air Force One*
    on Carter's return trip to Washington, D.C., from Israel and Egypt. This and other
    materials were included in Robert J. Lipshutz' letters to author. November 5, 25, 2003.

McHenry, Donald. Interview. January 19, 2006. At "Jimmy Carter Conference: Lessons for the 21st Century," University of Georgia.

Newsom, David D. Letter. November 8, 2003.

———. Questionnaire and letter. November 13, 2003.

Odom, William E. Questionnaire. November 13, 2003.

Pastor, Robert. Telephone interview. August 30, 2004.

———. Letter and Questionnaire.

Pipes, Richard. Letter. October 8, 2004.

Post, Jerrold M. E-mail correspondence. September 2, 2004.

Powell, Jody. Conversation. January 19, 2006. At "Jimmy Carter Conference: Lessons for the 21st Century," University of Georgia.

———. E-mail correspondence. October 31, 2008.

———. Letter. October 31, 2008.

Quandt, William B. Letters. August 31, 2004 and October 11, 2008.

Saunders, Harold. Interview. Vancouver, Canada, July 2, 1996.

Sloss, Leon. Letter.

———. Letters in response to questionnaire, November 25, 2004, February 21, 2005.

Vance, Cyrus. Cyrus Vance Papers, Manuscripts and Archives, Yale University Library.

Watson, Tom Jr. Letter to Cyrus Vance, February 20, 1980, Cyrus Vance Papers, Manuscripts and Archives, Box 54/78, Yale University Library. Permission to cite letter granted by International Business Machines Corporation.

Public Documents and Reports

Carter, Jimmy. Presidential Directives. Atlanta, GA: Jimmy Carter Library. Available online at http://www.jimmycarterlibrary.org/documents/pres_directive.phtml.

United Nations Commission on the Truth. *From Madness to Hope: The Twelve-Year War in El Salvador: Report of the Commission on the Truth for El Salvador.* New York: United Nations, 1993. Retrieved January 4, 2008, from http://www.usip.org/library/tc/doc/reports/el_salvador/tc_es_03151993_casesD1_2.html#D1.

U.S. Central Intelligence Agency. *Intelligence Community Experiment in Competitive Analysis: Some Soviet Strategic Objectives—An Alternative View, Report of Team B.* Washington, DC: National Archives, 1976.

U.S. Central Intelligence Agency. *National Intelligence Estimate: Soviet Capabilities for Strategic Nuclear Conflict through the Late 1980s.* Vol. 1, *Summary. Approved for Release, CIA Historical Review Program.* NIE 11-3/8-79. March 17, 1980. Reprint, Washington, DC: National Archives, 2003.

U.S. Central Intelligence Agency. *National Intelligence Estimate: Soviet Forces for the Intercontinental Conflict Through the mid-1980s.* Vol. 2, *The Annexes: Intelligence Community Experiment in Competitive Analysis. Soviet Strategic Objectives, an Alternative View. Report of Team B.* December 1976. Reprint, Washington, DC: National Archives, 2003.

U.S. Central Intelligence Agency. *National Intelligence Estimate: Soviet Forces for the Intercontinental Conflict Through the mid-1980s. Key Judgments and Summary. Report of Team A.* NIE 11-3/8-76. December 1976. Reprint, Washington, DC: National Archives, 2003.

U.S. Central Intelligence Agency. *National Intelligence Estimate: Soviet Goals and Expectations in the Global Power Arena. Approved for Release, CIA Historical Review Program.* NIE 11-4-78. February 21, 1978. Reprint, Washington, DC: National Archives, 2003.

U.S. Central Intelligence Agency, Center for the Study of Intelligence. *Watching the Bear: Essays on CIA's Analysis of the Soviet Union.* Edited by Gerald K. Haines and Robert E. Leggett. 2003. Available online at https://www.cia.gov/library/center-for-the-study-of-intelligence/csi-publications/books-and-monographs/watching-the-bear-essays-on-cias-analysis-of-the-soviet-union/index.html.

U.S. Congress, House of Representatives, Committee on Armed Services, Subcommittee on Intelligence and Military Application of Nuclear Energy. *SALT II: An Interim Assessment. Report on the Strategic Arms Limitation Talks and the Comprehensive Test Ban Treaty. 95th Congress, 2nd Session.* Washington, DC: GPO, 1978.

U.S. Congress, House of Representatives, Committee on House Administration. *The Presidential Campaign, 1976.* Washington, DC: GPO, 1978–79.

U.S. Congress, House of Representatives, Committee on Intelligence, Subcommittee on Oversight. *CIA Estimates of Soviet Defense Spending: Hearing before the Committee on Intelligence, Subcommittee on Oversight. 96th Congress, 2nd Session.* Washington, DC: GPO, 1980.

U.S. Congress, House of Representatives, Permanent Select Committee on Intelligence. *Iran: Evaluation of U.S. Intelligence Performance prior to November 1978.* Washington, DC: GPO, 1980.

U.S. Congress, Senate. *Executive Sessions of the Committee on Foreign Relations Together with Joint Sessions with the Senate Armed Services Committee, 87th Congress, 2nd Session.* Washington, DC: GPO, 1986.

U.S. Congress, Senate. *Nuclear War Strategy: Hearing before the Committee on Foreign Relations, 96th Congress, 2nd Session, on Presidential Directive 59, September 16, 1980.* Washington, DC: GPO, 1981.

U.S. Congress, Senate. *The SALT II Treaty: Hearing before the Committee on Foreign Relations, 96th Congress, 1st Session.* Washington, DC: GPO, 1979.

U.S. Congress, Senate. *Warnke Nomination: Hearings before the Committee on Foreign Relations, 94th Congress, 1st Session, on Nomination of Paul C. Warnke to be Director of the United States Arms Control and Disarmament Agency, with the Rank of Ambassador during his Tenure of Service as Director, February 8 and 9, 1977.* Washington, DC: GPO, 1977.

U.S. Department of Defense. *Rescue Mission Report.* Washington, DC: GPO, 1980. Includes Statement of Admiral J. L. Holloway III, USN Chairman (Ret.), Special Operations Review Group; also referred to as the *Holloway Report.*

U.S. Department of State. *Country Reports on Human Rights Practices: Report Submitted to the Committee on Foreign Relations, U.S. Senate and Committee on Foreign Affairs, U.S. House of Representatives, by the Department of State in Accordance with Sections 116(d) and 502B(b) of the Foreign Assistance Act of 1961, as Amended.* Washington, DC: GPO.

U.S. Department of State. *United States Department of State Bulletin.* Washington, DC: Office of Public Communication, Bureau of Public Affairs, 1977–81. Issued periodically, weekly through 1977, monthly 1978 and later. Cited in endnotes by article title, the designation "*DSB*", and date.

U.S. Government, Office of the Federal Register. *United States Government Manual 1977/78, 1979/80.* Washington, DC: National Archives and Records Service. Published annually.

U.S. President. *Public Papers of the Presidents of the United States.* Washington, DC: Federal Register Division, National Archives and Records Service, General Services Administration, 1977–81. Issued annually in 1–2 vols. Cited in the endnotes by title of presentation, the designation "*PP*", and year.

Books and Dissertations

Abramson, Rudy. *Spanning the Century: The Life of W. Averell Harriman, 1891–1986*. New York: William Morrow, 1992.

Allison, Graham. *Essence of Decision: Explaining the Cuban Missile Crisis*. Boston: Little, Brown, 1971.

Ambrose, Stephen E. *Nixon: Ruin and Recovery 1973–1990*. New York: Simon and Schuster, 1991.

Ambrose, Stephen, and Douglas Brinkley. *Rise to Globalism: American Foreign Policy Since 1938*. New York: Penguin Books, 1997.

Andreotti, Giulio. *The USA Up Close: From the Atlantic Pact to Bush*. New York: New York University Press, 1992.

Andrew, Christopher M. *For the President's Eyes Only: Secret Intelligence and the American Presidency from Washington to Bush*. New York: HarperCollins, 1995.

Arendt, Hannah. *The Origins of Totalitarianism*. Fort Washington, PA: Harvest Books, 1973.

Bailey, Thomas A. *A Diplomatic History of the American People*. New York: F. S. Crofts, 1940.

Bakhash, Shaul. *The Reign of the Ayatollahs: Iran and the Islamic Revolution*. New York: Basic Books, 1984.

Ball, George W. *The Past Has Another Pattern: Memoirs*. New York: W. W. Norton, 1983.

Beckwith, Charlie A., and Donald Knox. *Delta Force*. San Diego: Harcourt Brace Jovanovich, 1983.

Bell, Coral. *President Carter and Foreign Policy: The Costs of Virtue?* Canberra, Australia: Department of International Relations, Research School of Pacific Studies, Australian National University, 1980.

Berkowitz, Bruce D., and Allan E. Goodman. *Strategic Intelligence for American National Security*. Princeton, NJ: Princeton University Press, 1989.

Bernstein, Carl, and Marco Politi. *His Holiness: John Paul II and the History of Our Time*. New York: Doubleday, 1996.

Bergen, Peter L. *Holy War, Inc.: Inside the Secret World of Osama Bin Laden*. New York: Free Press, 2001.

Bill, James A. *The Eagle and the Lion: The Tragedy of American-Iranian Relations*. New Haven, CT: Yale University Press, 1989.

Biven, Carl W. *Jimmy Carter's Economy: Policy in an Age of Limits*. Chapel Hill: University of North Carolina Press, 2002.

Blair, Clay. *The Atomic Submarine and Admiral Rickover*. New York: Henry Holt, 1954.

Bonner, Raymond. *Waltzing with a Dictator: The Marcoses and the Making of American Foreign Policy*. New York: Times Books, 1987.

Borgwardt, Elizabeth. *A New Deal for the World: America's Vision for Human Rights*. Cambridge, MA: Harvard University Press, 2005.

Bostdorff, Denise M. *The Presidency and the Rhetoric of Foreign Crisis*. Columbia: University of South Carolina Press, 1994.

Botchway, Benjamin O. *The Impact of Image and Perception on Foreign Policy: An Inquiry into the American Soviet Policy during the Carter and Reagan Administrations*. Munich, Germany: Tuduv Verlag, 1989.

Bourne, Peter G. *Jimmy Carter: A Comprehensive Biography from Plains to Post-Presidency*. New York: Simon and Schuster, 1997.

Breckinridge, Scott D. *The CIA and the U.S. Intelligence System*. Boulder, CO: Westview Press, 1986.

Brinkley, Douglas, *The Unfinished Presidency: Jimmy Carter's Journey beyond the White House*. New York: Penguin Books, 1999.

Brockman, James. *The Word Remains: A Life of Oscar Romero.* Maryknoll, NY: Orbis Books, 1982.

——. *Romero: A Life.* Maryknoll, NY: Orbis Books, 1990.

Broer, Michael, Frederick Donovan, and James Goodbye. *The Neutron Bomb and the Premises of Power: President Carter's Neutron Bomb Decision.* Washington, DC: Brookings Institution Press, 1994.

Brown, Harold. *Thinking about National Security: Defense and Foreign Policy in a Dangerous World.* Boulder, CO: Westview Press, 1983.

Brzezinski, Zbigniew. *Power and Principle: Memoirs of the National Security Advisor, 1977–1981.* New York: Farrar, Straus and Giroux, 1983.

Burke, Edmund. *Reflections on the Revolution in France.* New York: Penguin Books, 1982.

Burke, John. *The Institutional Presidency.* Baltimore: Johns Hopkins University Press, 1992.

Cahn, Anne H. *Killing Detente: The Right Attacks the CIA.* University Park, PA: Pennsylvania State University Press, 1998.

Caldwell, Dan. *The Dynamics of Domestic Politics and Arms Control: The SALT II Treaty Ratification Debate.* Columbia: University of South Carolina Press, 1991.

Campbell, Colin. *Managing the Presidency: Carter, Reagan and the Search for Executive Harmony.* Pittsburgh: University of Pittsburgh Press, 1986.

Campbell, Steven. "Brzezinski's Image of the USSR." PhD diss., University of South Carolina, 2003.

Carter, Jimmy. *The Blood of Abraham: Insights into the Middle East.* Fayetteville: University of Arkansas Press, 1993.

——. *Keeping Faith: Memoirs of a President.* New York: Bantam Books, 1982.

——. *Negotiation: The Alternative to Hostility.* Macon, GA: Mercer University Press, 1984.

——. *Talking Peace: A Vision for the Next Generation.* New York: Penguin Books, 1993.

——. *Why Not the Best? The First Fifty Years.* New York: Bantam Books, 1976.

Carter, Rosalynn. *First Lady from Plains.* Boston: Houghton Mifflin, 1984.

Charney, Leon H. *Special Counsel.* New York: Philosophical Library, 1984.

Christopher, Warren, Harold H. Saunders, Gary Sick, Robert Carswell, Richard J. Davis, John E. Hoffman Jr., Roberts B. Owen, Oscar Schachter, and Abraham A. Ribicoff, eds. *American Hostages in Iran: The Conduct of a Crisis.* New Haven, CT: Yale University Press, 1986.

Church, F. Forrester. *Father and Son: A Personal Biography of Frank Church of Idaho.* New York: HarperCollins, 1985.

Churchill, Winston. *The Second World War.* Vol. 1, *The Gathering Storm.* Boston: Mariner Books, 1986.

Clifford, Clark, with Richard Holbrooke. *Counsel to the President: A Memoir.* New York: Random House, 1991.

Cox, Arthur M. *The Dynamics of Detente: How to End the Arms Race.* New York: W. W. Norton, 1976.

Cronin, Thomas E., and Sanford D. Greenberg. *The Presidential Advisory System.* New York: Harper and Row, 1969.

Dayan, Moshe. *Breakthrough: A Personal Account of the Egypt-Israel Peace Negotiations.* New York: Alfred A. Knopf, 1981.

Destler, I. M. *Making Foreign Economic Policy.* Washington, DC: Brookings Institution Press, 1980.

Dobrynin, Anatoly. *In Confidence: Moscow's Ambassador to America's Six Cold War Presidents.* New York: Crown, 1995.

Donovan, John C. *The Cold Warriors: A Policy-Making Elite.* Lexington, MA: DC Heath, 1974.

Dumbrell, John. *The Carter Presidency: A Re-evaluation.* New York: St. Martin's Press, 1993.

Dunbar, Anthony, ed. *Where We Stand: Voices of Southern Dissent*. Montgomery, AL: New South Books, 2004.

Eilts, Hermann F., and Robert B. Satloff, eds. *Approaching Peace: American Interests in Israeli-Palestinian Final Status Talks*. Washington, DC: Washington Institute for Near East Policy, 1994.

El-Gamasy, Mohamed Abdel Ghani. *The October War*. Cairo: American University in Cairo Press, 1993.

English, Robert D. *Russia and the Idea of the West*. New York: Columbia University Press, 2000.

The Europa World Year Book, 1980. New York: Routledge, 1980.

Farber, David. *Taken Hostage: The Iran Hostage Crisis and America's First Encounter with Radical Islam*. Princeton, NJ: Princeton University Press, 2006.

Fiske, Susan T., and Shelley E. Taylor. *Social Cognition*. New York: McGraw Hill, 1991.

Follet, Ken. *On Wings of Eagles*. London: Collins, 1983.

Freedman, Lawrence. *U.S. Intelligence and the Soviet Strategic Threat*. 2nd ed. Princeton, NJ: Princeton University Press, 1986.

Friedrich, Carl J., and Zbigniew Brzezinski. *Totalitarian Dictatorship and Autocracy*. Cambridge, MA: Harvard University Press, 1956.

Gallup, George. *The Gallup Poll: Public Opinion*. Wilmington, DE: Scholarly Resources, 1972–77 (vols. 1 and 2), 1978, 1979, 1980.

Garrison, Jean A. "Games Advisers Play." PhD diss., University of South Carolina, 1996. Later published as the book *Games Advisors Play: Foreign Policy in the Nixon and Carter Administrations*. College Station: Texas A and M University Press, 1999.

Garthoff, Raymond. *Detente and Confrontation: American-Soviet Relations from Nixon to Reagan*. Washington, DC: Brookings Institution Press, 1985.

——. *The Great Transition: American-Soviet Relations and the End of the Cold War*. Washington, DC: Brookings Institution Press, 1994.

Gates, Robert M. *From the Shadows: The Ultimate Insider's Story of Five Presidents and How They Won the Cold War*. New York: Simon and Schuster, 1996.

George, Alexander L. *Presidential Decision Making in Foreign Policy: The Effective Use of Information and Advice*. Boulder, CO: Westview Press, 1980.

George, Alexander L., and Juliette L. George. *Woodrow Wilson and Colonel House: A Personality Study*. New York: John Day, 1956.

Gill, Stephen. *American Hegemony and the Trilateral Commission*. Cambridge: Cambridge University Press, 1990.

Gillon, Steven M. *The Democrats' Dilemma: Walter F. Mondale and the Liberal Legacy*. New York: Columbia University Press, 1992.

Glad, Betty. *Jimmy Carter: In Search of the Great White House*. New York: W. W. Norton, 1980.

Glad, Betty, ed. *The Psychological Dimensions of War*. Newbury Park, CA: Sage Publications, 1990.

Glad, Betty, and Eric Shiraev, eds. *The Russian Transformation: Political, Sociological, and Psychological Aspects*. New York: St. Martin's Press, 1999.

Gleysteen, William H. *Massive Entanglement, Marginal Influence: Carter and Korea in Crisis*. Washington, DC: Brookings Institution Press, 1999.

Goldhamer, Herbert. *The Advisor*. New York: Elsevier, 1978.

Goodman, Lisl Marburg. *Omnicide: The Nuclear Dilemma*. New York: Praeger, 1990.

Grant, Stan. *Jimmy Carter's Odyssey to Black Africa*. Miami, FL: Courier Press, 1980.

Greenstein, Fred I., ed. *Leadership in the Modern Presidency*. Cambridge, MA: Harvard University Press, 1988.

——. *The Presidential Difference: Leadership Style from FDR to Clinton*. New York: Martin Kessler Books/Free Press, 2000.

Gromyko, Andrei A. *Memoirs*. Translated by Harold Shukman. New York: Doubleday, 1989.

Haas, Garland A. *Jimmy Carter and the Politics of Frustration*. Jefferson, NC: McFarland, 1992.

Haig, Alexander M., Jr. *Caveat: Realism, Reagan and Foreign Policy*. New York: Scribner's, 1984.

Halliday, Fred. *The Making of the Second Cold War*. London: Verso, 1983.

Halperin, Morton. *Bureaucratic Politics and Foreign Policy*. Washington, DC: Brookings Institution Press, 1974.

Hammond, Thomas T. *Red Flag over Afghanistan*. Boulder, CO: Westview Press, 1984.

Hargrove, Erwin C. *Jimmy Carter as President: Leadership and the Practice of the Public Good*. Baton Rouge: Louisiana State University Press, 1988.

Harris, David. *The Crisis: The President, the Prophet, and the Shah—1979 and the Coming of Militant Islam*. Boston: Little, Brown, 2004.

Hart, Paul T. *Groupthink in Government: A Study of Small Groups and Political Failure*. Baltimore: Johns Hopkins University Press, 1990.

Hauner, Milan. *The Soviet War in Afghanistan*. Philadelphia: University Press of America, 1991.

Hess, Stephen. *Organizing the Presidency*. 2nd ed. Washington, DC: Brookings Institution Press, 1988.

Hurst, Steven. *The Carter Administration and Vietnam*. New York: St. Martin's Press, 1996.

Hult, Karen M., and Charles E. Walcott. *Empowering the White House: Governance under Nixon, Ford, and Carter*. Lawrence: University Press of Kansas, 2004.

Inaugural Addresses of the Presidents of the United States from George Washington to Bill Clinton. Charleston, SC: BiblioBazaar, 2007.

Janis, Irving L. *Groupthink: Psychological Studies of Policy Decisions and Fiascoes*. 2nd ed. Boston: Houghton Mifflin, 1982.

Janowitz, Morris. *The Professional Soldier: A Social and Political Portrait*. Glencoe, IL: Free Press, 1964.

Johnson, Donald B. *National Party Platforms of 1980: Supplement to National Party Platforms, 1840–1976*. Urbana: University of Illinois Press, 1982.

Johnson, Loch K. *America's Secret Power*. New York: Oxford University Press, 1989.

Johnson, Richard Tanner. *Managing the White House: An Intimate Study of the Presidency*. New York: Harper and Row, 1974.

Jones, Charles O. *The Trusteeship Presidency: Jimmy Carter and the United States Congress*. Baton Rouge: Louisiana State University Press, 1988.

Jordan, Hamilton. *Crisis: The Last Year of the Carter Presidency*. New York: G. P. Putnam's Sons, 1982.

Jorden, William J. *Panama Odyssey*. Austin: University of Texas Press, 1984.

Kagan, Robert. *Dangerous Nation: America's Place in the World, from Its Earliest Days to the Dawn of the Twentieth Century*. New York: Alfred A. Knopf, 2007.

Kamel, Mohamed Ibrahim. *The Camp David Accords: A Testimony by Sadat's Foreign Minister*. New York: Kegan Paul International, 1986.

Kaufman, Burton I., and Scott Kaufman. *The Presidency of James Earl Carter, Jr.*, 2nd rev. ed. Lawrence: University Press of Kansas, 2006.

Kaufman, Scott. *Plans Unraveled: The Foreign Policy of the Carter Administration*. DeKalb: Northern Illinois University Press, 2008.

Kellerman, Barbara, and Jeffrey Rubin, eds. *Leadership and Negotiation in the Middle East*. New York: Praeger, 1988.

Kessel, John H. *The Domestic Presidency: Decision-Making in the White House*. North Scituate, MA: Duxbury Press, 1975.

Khomeini, Ruhollah. *Islam and Revolution: Writings and Declarations of Imam Khomeini*. Translated by Hamid Algar. Berkeley, CA: Mizan Press, 1981.

Kiernan, Ben. *The Pol Pot Regime: Race, Power, and Genocide in Cambodia under the Khmer Rouge (1975–79)*. New Haven, CT: Yale University Press, 1996.

Kinzer, Stephen. *Overthrow: America's Century of Regime Change from Hawaii to Iraq*. New York: Times Books, 2006.

Knorr, Klaus. *On the Uses of Military Power in the Nuclear Age*. Princeton, NJ: Princeton University Press, 1966.

Kull, Steven. *Minds at War: Nuclear Reality and the Inner Conflicts of Defense Policymakers*. New York: Basic Books, 1988.

Kwitny, Jonathan. *Man of the Century: The Life and Times of John Paul II*. New York: Henry Holt, 1997.

Laber, Jeri, and Barnett R. Rubin. *A Nation Is Dying: Afghanistan under the Soviets*. Evanston, IL: Northwestern University Press, 1988.

Labrie, Roger P., John G. Hutchins, Edwin W.A. Peura, and Diana H. Richman, eds. *U.S. Arms Sales Policy: Background and Issues*. Washington, DC: American Enterprise Institute for Public Policy, 1982.

Lake, Anthony. *Third World Radical Regimes: U.S. Policy under Carter and Reagan*. New York: Foreign Policy Association, 1985.

Lance, Bert, with Bill Gilbert. *The Truth of the Matter: My Life In and Out of Politics*. New York: Summit Books, 1991.

Lash, Joseph. *Eleanor: The Years Alone*. New York: W. W. Norton, 1972.

Lechelt, Jack. "The Semi-Institutionalized Vice Presidency." PhD diss., University of South Carolina, 2005.

Lee, William T. *Understanding the Soviet Military Threat: How CIA Estimates Went Astray*. New York: National Strategy Information Center, 1977.

Leeden, Michael, and William Lewis. *Debacle: The American Failure in Iran*. New York: Alfred A. Knopf, 1981.

LeFeber, Walter. *Inevitable Revolutions: The United States in Central America*. New York: W. W. Norton, 1983.

LeoGrande, William M. *Our Own Backyard: The United States in Central America*. Chapel Hill, NC: University of North Carolina Press, 1998.

Lewis, Finlay. *Mondale: Portrait of an American Politician*. Rev. ed. New York: Perennial Library, 1984.

Light, Paul C. *The President's Agenda*. Baltimore: Johns Hopkins University Press, 1991.

Link, Michael William. "The Presidential Kaleidoscope." PhD diss., University of South Carolina, 1996.

Linowitz, Sol M. *The Making of a Public Man: A Memoir*. New York: Little, Brown, 1985.

Maga, Timothy, and Thomas Katsaros, eds. *The World of Jimmy Carter: U.S. Foreign Policy, 1977–1981*. New Haven, CT: Yale University Press, 1994.

Mann, James. *About Face: A History of America's Curious Relationship with China, from Nixon to Clinton*. New York: Alfred A. Knopf, 1999.

Mayers, David. *The Ambassadors and America's Soviet Policy*. New York: Oxford University Press, 1995.

McDermott, Rose. *Risk-Taking in International Politics*. Ann Arbor: University of Michigan Press, 1998.

McFadden, Robert D. *No Hiding Place*. New York: Times Books, 1981.

McLellan, David S. *Cyrus Vance*. American Secretaries of State and Their Diplomacy, vol. 20. Totowa, NJ: Rowman and Allanheld, 1985.

McPherson, Alan, ed. *Anti-Americanism in Latin America and the Caribbean: Past and Present*. New York: Berghahn Books, 2006.

Meisler, Stanley. *United Nations: The First Fifty Years*. Boston: Atlantic Monthly Press, 1997.

Melanson, Richard A. *American Foreign Policy since the Vietnam War: The Search for Consensus from Richard Nixon to George W. Bush*. 4th ed. Armonk, NY: M. E. Sharpe, 2005.

Miller, Linda. *Shadow and Substance: Jimmy Carter and the Camp David Accords.* Washington, DC: Georgetown University Institute for the Study of Diplomacy, 1992.

Moens, Alexander. *Foreign Policy under Carter: Testing Multiple Advocacy Decision-Making.* Boulder, CO: Westview Press, 1990.

Montgomery, Tommie Sue. *Revolution in El Salvador: from Civil Strife to Civil Peace.* 2nd ed. Boulder, CO: Westview Press, 1995.

Moore, Jonathan, and Janet Fraser, eds. *Campaign for President: The Managers Look at '76.* Cambridge, MA: Ballinger, 1977.

Moreno, Dario. *U.S. Policy in Central America: The Endless Debate.* Miami: Florida International University Press, 1990.

Morgenthau, Hans J. *Politics among Nations.* New York: McGraw Hill, 2005.

Morris, Kenneth Earl. *Jimmy Carter: American Moralist.* Athens: University of Georgia Press, 1996.

Moses, Russell Leigh. *Freeing the Hostages: The Carter Administration, the Soviet Union, and Revolutionary Iran.* Pittsburgh: University of Pittsburgh Press, 1995.

Muravchik, Joshua. *The Uncertain Crusade: Jimmy Carter and the Dilemmas of Human Rights Policy.* Lanham, MD: Hamilton, 1986.

Nelson, Michael, ed. *The Presidency and the Political System.* 8th ed. Washington, DC: Congressional Quarterly, 2005.

Neuringer, Sheldon. *The Carter Administration, Human Rights and the Agony of Cambodia.* Lewiston, NY: Edwin Mellen Press, 1993.

Neustadt, Richard E. *Presidential Power: The Politics of Leadership.* New York: John Wiley and Sons, 1962.

Newsom, David D. *The Soviet Brigade in Cuba: A Study in Political Diplomacy.* Bloomington: Indiana University Press, 1987.

Niebuhr, Reinhold. *Faith and Politics: A Commentary on Religious, Social and Political Thought in a Technological Age.* New York: George Braziller, 1968.

Nitze, Paul H., with Ann M. Smith and Steven L. Rearden. *From Hiroshima to Glasnost: A Memoir of Five Perilous Decades.* New York: Weidenfeld and Nicolson, 1989.

Nye, Joseph S. *The Making of America's Soviet Policy.* New Haven, CT: Yale University Press, 1984.

Orman, John. *Comparing Presidential Behavior: Carter, Reagan and the Macho Presidential Style.* Westport, CT: Greenwood Press, 1987.

Packer, George. *The Assassin's Gate: America in Iraq.* New York: Farrar, Straus and Giroux, 2005.

Parsons, Anthony. *The Pride and Fall: Iran, 1974–1979.* London: Butler and Tanner, 1984.

Pastor, Robert A. *Condemned to Repetition: The United States and Nicaragua.* Princeton, NJ: Princeton University Press, 1988.

——. *Whirlpool: U.S. Foreign Policy toward Latin America and the Caribbean.* Princeton, NJ: Princeton University Press, 1992.

Pelletier, Jean, and Claude Adams. *The Canadian Caper.* New York: William Morrow, 1981.

Pfiffner, James P. *The Modern Presidency.* New York: St. Martin's Press, 1994.

Pious, Richard M. *The American Presidency.* New York: Ballentine, 1988.

Pipes, Richard. *Vixi: Memoirs of a Non-belonger.* New Haven, CT: Yale University Press, 2003.

Pomper, Gerald M., and Marlene Michels Pomper. *The Election of 1980: Reports and Interpretations.* Chatham, NJ: Chatham House, 1981.

Porter, Roger B. *Presidential Decision Making.* New York: Cambridge University Press, 1980.

Powell, Jody. *The Other Side of the Story.* New York: William Morrow, 1984.

Power, Samantha. *"A Problem From Hell": America and the Age of Genocide.* New York: Basic Books, 2002.

Prados, John. *The Soviet Estimate: U.S. Intelligence Analysis and Russian Military Strength.* New York: Dial Press, 1982.

The Presidency, 1977. Washington, DC: Congressional Quarterly, 1979.

Quandt, William. *Camp David: Peacemaking and Politics.* Washington, DC: Brookings Institution Press, 1986.

Queen, Richard. *Inside and Out: Hostage to Iran, Hostage to Myself.* New York: G. P. Putnam's Sons, 1981.

Ramazani, Rouhallah K. *The United States and Iran.* New York: Praeger, 1982.

Reedy, George. *The Twilight of the Presidency.* New York: New American Library, 1970.

Romero, Oscar. *A Shepherd's Diary.* Translated by Irene B. Hodgson. Cincinnati: St. Anthony Messenger Press, 1986.

Romero, Oscar A. *The Violence of Love.* Translated by James R. Brockman. Maryknoll, NY: Orbis Books, 2004.

Rosati, Jerel. *The Carter Administration's Quest for Global Community: The Impact of Beliefs on Behavior.* Columbia: University of South Carolina Press, 1987.

Rosen, Barbara, George Feifer, and Barry Rosen. *The Destined Hour: The Hostage Crisis and One Family's Ordeal.* Garden City, NY: Doubleday, 1982.

Rosenbaum, Herbert D., and Alexei Ugrinsky, eds. *The Presidency and Domestic Policies of Jimmy Carter.* Westport, CT: Greenwood Press, 1993.

——. *Jimmy Carter: Foreign Policy and Post-Presidential Years.* Westport, CT: Greenwood Press, 1994.

Rothkopf, David J. *Running the World: The Inside Story of the National Security Council and the Architects of American Power.* New York: Public Affairs Books, 2005.

Rowe, David N. *The Carter China Policy: Results and Prospects.* Branford, CT: Rowe, 1980.

Rozell, Mark J. *The Press and the Carter Presidency.* Boulder, CO: Westview Press, 1989.

Rubin, Barry M. *Paved with Good Intentions: The American Experience and Iran.* New York: Oxford University Press, 1980.

Ryan, Paul B. *The Iranian Mission: Why It Failed.* Annapolis, MD: Naval Institute Press, 1985.

Sabato, Larry J. *The Rise of Political Consultants.* New York: Basic Books, 1981.

Safire, William. *Safire's Washington.* New York: Times Books, 1980.

Salinger, Pierre. *America Held Hostage: The Secret Negotiations.* Garden City, NY: Doubleday, 1981.

Sanders, Jerry W. *Peddlers of Crisis: The Committee on the Present Danger and the Politics of Containment.* Boston: South End Press, 1983.

Saunders, Harold H. *The Other Walls: The Arab-Israeli Peace Process in a Global Perspective.* Princeton, NJ: Princeton University Press, 1991.

Schelling, Thomas C. *The Strategy of Conflict.* Cambridge, MA: Harvard University Press, 1960.

Schirmer, Daniel B., and Stephen Rosskamm Shalom. *The Philippines Reader: A History of Colonialism, Neocolonialism, Dictatorship, and Resistance.* Boston: South End Press, 1987.

Schlesinger, Arthur M., Jr. *History of American Presidential Elections, 1972–1984.* Supplemental volume. New York: Chelsea House, 1986.

Schmertz, Eric J., Natalie Datlof, and Alexei Ugrinsky, eds. *President Reagan and the World.* Westport, CT: Greenwood Press, 1997.

Schmidt, Helmut. *Men and Power: A Political Retrospective.* New York: Random House, 1989.

Schoultz, Lars. *Human Rights and the United States Policy toward Latin America.* Princeton, NJ: Princeton University Press, 1981.

Sick, Gary. *All Fall Down: America's Tragic Encounter with Iran.* New York: Random House, 1985.

Skidmore, David. *Reversing Course: Carter's Foreign Policy, Domestic Politics, and the Failure of Reform.* Nashville, TN: Vanderbilt University Press, 1996.

Slavin, Ed. *Jimmy Carter.* New York: Chelsea House, 1989.

Smith, Gaddis. *Morality, Reason and Power: American Diplomacy in the Carter Years.* New York: Hill and Wang, 1986.

Smith, Hedrick. *The Power Game: How Washington Really Works.* New York: Ballantine Books, 1987.

Sneh, Itai N. *The Future Almost Arrived: How Jimmy Carter Failed to Change U.S. Foreign Policy.* New York: Peter Lang, 2008.

Sobel, Lester. *Peacemaking in the Middle East.* New York: Facts on File, 1980.

Sobrino, Jon. *Archbishop Romero: Memories and Reflections.* Eugene, OR: Orbis, 1990.

Spencer, Donald S. *The Carter Implosion: Jimmy Carter and the Amateur Style of Diplomacy.* New York: Praeger, 1988.

Stoll, David. *Is Latin America Turning Protestant? The Politics of Evangelical Growth.* New York: University of California Press, 1991.

Strong, Robert A. *Working in the World: Jimmy Carter and the Making of American Foreign Policy.* Baton Rouge: Louisiana State University Press, 2000.

Sullivan, William H. *Mission to Iran.* New York: W. W. Norton, 1981.

Talbott, Strobe. *Endgame: The Inside Story of SALT II.* New York: Harper and Row, 1980.

Thompson, Kenneth W., ed. *The Virginia Papers on the Presidency.* Washington, DC: University Press of America, 1981.

Thornton, Richard C. *The Carter Years: Toward a New Global Order.* New York: Paragon House, 1991.

Tierney, John J. *Somozas and Sandinistas: The U.S. and Nicaragua in the Twentieth Century.* Washington, DC: Council for Inter-American Security Educational Institute, 1982.

Twiggs-Lanham, Joan. *The Tokyo Trade Negotiations: A Case Study in Building Domestic Support for Diplomacy.* Lanham, MD: University Press of America, 1987.

Tyroler, Charles, III, ed. *Alerting America: The Papers of the Committee on the Present Danger.* Washington, DC: Pergamon Brassey, 1984.

Van Meter Crabb, Cecil, and Kevin V. Mulcahy. *Presidents and Foreign Policy Making: From FDR to Reagan.* Baton Rouge: Louisiana State University Press, 1986.

Vance, Cyrus. *Hard Choices: Critical Years in America's Foreign Policy.* New York: Simon and Schuster, 1983.

Walcott, Charles E., and Karen M. Hult. *Governing the White House: From Hoover through LBJ.* Lawrence, KS: University Press of Kansas, 1995.

Warshaw, Shirley Anne. *Powersharing: White House–Cabinet Relations in the Modern Presidency.* Albany: State University of New York Press, 1996.

Warshaw, Shirley Anne, ed. *Reexamining the Eisenhower Presidency.* Westport, CT: Greenwood Press, 1993.

Weizman, Ezer. *The Battle for Peace.* New York: Bantam Books, 1981.

Williams, Walter. *The Carter Policy Staff: Research in Public Policy Analysis and Management.* Greenwich, CT: JAI Press, 1986.

Wolfe, Thomas W. *The SALT Experience.* Cambridge, MA: Ballinger, 1979.

Woodward, Peter. *The Horn of Africa: State Politics and International Relations.* New York: St. Martin's Press, 1996.

Zogby, James J., ed. *The Carter Administration and Palestinian Rights.* Detroit: Association of Arab-American University Graduates, 1977.

Zonis, Marvin. *Majestic Failure: The Fall of the Shah.* Chicago: University of Chicago Press, 1998.

Permissions for Citation and Extensive Quotation of Books

Brockman, James. *The Word Remains: A Life of Oscar Romero.* Maryknoll, NY: Orbis Books, 1982. Permission to quote or cite granted from Orbis Books.

Brzezinski, Zbigniew. *Power and Principle: Memoirs of the National Security Advisor, 1977–1981.* New York: Farrar, Straus and Giroux, 1983. Permission to quote and cite granted by author.

Carter, Jimmy. *Keeping Faith: Memoirs of a President.* New York: Bantam Books, 1982. Permission to quote or cite granted from F. T. Courtright, the Permissions Company.

Clifford, Clark, with Richard Holbrooke. *Counsel to the President: A Memoir.* New York: Random House, 1991. Quotation and citation permissible under fair use.

Dayan, Moshe. *Breakthrough: A Personal Account of the Egypt-Israel Peace Negotiations.* New York: Alfred A. Knopf, 1981. Quotation and citation permissible under fair use.

Facts on File material: permission to quote or cite granted from Facts On File Yearbook. Copyright 1997 by Facts on File, Inc., an imprint of Infobase Publishing. Reproduced with permission of the publisher.

Harris, David. *The Crisis: The President, the Prophet, and the Shah—1979 and the Coming of Militant Islam.* Boston: Little, Brown, 2004. Permission to quote or cite granted by the author.

Moens, Alexander. "President Carter's Advisors and the Fall of the Shah," Political Science Quarterly, Vol.106 (November 1991). Permission to quote or cite granted by the Academy of Political Science.

Moens, Alexander. *Foreign Policy under Carter: Testing Multiple Advocacy Decision-Making.* Boulder, CO: Westview Press, 1990. Permission to quote or cite granted by the author.

New York Times papers: Permission granted to quote or cite granted from the *New York Times.*

Niebuhr, Reinhold. *Faith and Politics: A Commentary on Religious, Social and Political Thought in a Technological Age.* New York: George Braziller, 1968. Quotation or citation permitted by fair use.

Quandt, William. *Camp David: Peacemaking and Politics.* Washington, DC: Brookings Institution Press, 1986. Permission to quote or cite granted by the Brookings Institution Press.

Rosenbaum, Herbert D., and Alexei Ugrinsky, eds. *The Presidency and Domestic Policies of Jimmy Carter.* Westport, CT: Greenwood Press, 1993. Quotation or citation permissible under fair use.

Schirmer, Daniel B., and Stephen Rosskamm Shalom. *The Philippines Reader: A History of Colonialism, Neocolonialism, Dictatorship, and Resistance.* Boston: South End Press, 1987. Permission to quote or cite granted from South End Press.

Sobrino, Jon. *Archbishop Romero: Memories and Reflections.* Eugene, OR: Orbis, 1990. Permission to quote or cite granted from Orbis Books.

Sullivan, William H. *Mission to Iran.* New York: W. W. Norton, 1981. Permission to quote or cite granted from W. W. Norton & Company, Inc.

Talbott, Strobe. *Endgame: The Inside Story of SALT II.* New York: Harper and Row, 1980. Permission to quote or cite granted from Brookings Institution.

Vance, Cyrus. *Hard Choices: Critical Years in America's Foreign Policy.* New York: Simon and Schuster, 1983. Permission to quote or cite granted from Simon and Schuster.

Index